MAN
of the
CENTURY

Books by Jonathan Kwitny

Acceptable Risks

The Crimes of Patriots: A True Story of
Dope, Dirty Money, and the C.I.A.

Endless Enemies: The Making of an
Unfriendly World

Vicious Circles: The Mafia in the Marketplace

Shakedown (a novel)

The Mullendore Murder Case

The Fountain Pen Conspiracy

MAN

of the

CENTURY

THE LIFE AND TIMES OF
POPE JOHN PAUL II

JONATHAN KWITNY

A *Little, Brown* Book

First published in the United States in 1997
by Henry Holt and Company, Inc.
115 West 18th Street
New York, New York 10011
First published in Great Britain in 1997
by Little, Brown and Company

A CIP catalogue record for this book
is available from the British Library.

ISBN 0 316 64086 7

Printed and bound in Great Britain by Clays Ltd, St Ives plc

Photographs appearing on pages i; vi; 2 (Wotyla with Pope Paul VI, Cardinal
Jozef Glemp, Wyszynski with John Paul II); 22 ("As pope"); 106 ("A blessing,"
Wanda Poltawska, "On the road"); 298 (Adam Michnik); and 596 (General
Wojciech Jaruzelski, the Pope, Cardinal Joseph Ratzinger) are by Grzegor
Galazka, courtesy of Robert Moynihan and *Inside the Vatican*. Those on pages 2
(Father Mieczyslaw Malinski); 106 (Archbishop Paul Marcinkus and Bohdan
Cywinski); and 298 (Anna-Teresa Tymieniecka) were provided by the subjects.
All other photographs are from the Polish Information Agency (PAI Expo).

Little, Brown and Company (UK)
Brettenham House
Lancaster Place
London WC2E 7EN

FOR WENDY

...But there was only one.
A century in which everything was part
Of that Century and of its aspect, a personage,
A man who was the axis of his time.

—Wallace Stevens

The Pope? And how many divisions has the Pope?

—Joseph Stalin

It began with Peter. At the moment of Christ's arrest at Gethsemane, Peter had drawn his sword. It had been a natural reaction. Whoever is attacked unjustly has the right to defend himself. And he has also the right to defend another innocent person. However, Christ said to Peter: "Put your sword back into its place; for all who take the sword will perish by the sword." And Peter understood. He understood up to his last breath that neither he nor his brothers could fight with the sword; because the kingdom to which he had been called had to be won with the power of love, and with the power of truth, and only in this way. . . . I think, dear Brothers and Sisters, that precisely at this moment we are on this very path.

—Pope John Paul II
February 23, 1980

CONTENTS

PREFACE

I undertook this book because years of reporting—for the *Wall Street Journal*, previous books, and *Kwitny Report* documentaries in Poland—persuaded me that the story of the Cold War is widely misperceived. On the evidence, the Cold War was won not by Washington, but by a nonviolent mass movement, like those of Mahatma Gandhi and Martin Luther King, Jr., led by a man whose religious office has precluded him from talking about it openly.

Karol Wojtyla, as bishop of Krakow, forged the Solidarity revolution—in his philosophy classes, his community synods, his secret ordination of covert priests, his clandestine communications seminars, the smuggling network he oversaw throughout the Eastern Bloc, and above all by his example. Even in its name, Solidarity was not just a shipyard union, but an idea rooted in Catholic tradition and formulated afresh by Wojtyla starting with a 1953 book daringly published underground and made public here for the first time, with excerpts. In interviews, colleagues reveal how Wojtyla guided them into a major hunger strike that was the Boston Tea Party of the Solidarity revolution and handed out envelopes of cash to sustain their work. Time and again, as pope, he single-handedly rescued the revolution he begat, often in dramatic private confrontations.

Fabrications, widely repeated in the press, led people to misjudge his alliances and adversaries. Not only did the White House deny aid to a desperate Solidarity, by evidence it tried to help John Paul's opponents destroy Solidarity. The Vatican has been at odds with Washington over fundamental issues throughout John Paul's reign—even down to the capture of General Manuel Noriega in Panama. What defeated communism was not any incapacity to build weapons, but an incapacity to accommodate the human spirit.

One obstacle to understanding John Paul is summarized by his friend and former student, Halina Bortnowska: "Most people are interested just in his teaching on sex. And since they don't like what he says about sex, they miss what is important." Contrary to popular belief, his clearest changes in Catholic doctrine as pope have been toward pacifism, respect for other religions, and willingness to admit error. His blunders have been big—abetting major financial and sex crimes, wounding friends, fueling lethal conflict with Orthodox Christians—but born of good intent.

In all, he is truly a man of this century. It would be hard to find another who had touched and been touched by so many of its great events, even to the happenstance of nearly dying from the opening shots of its most cataclysmic war.

Finally, please don't let the occasional Polish names in this book trouble you. A pronunciation guide appears at the end, but if you find it easier to go through the story thinking of the city of Wroclaw as "Rock-law" instead of "Vroht-swahv," go ahead. If purists scold you, blame me.

MAN
of the
CENTURY

ABOVE: *Wojtyla with Pope Paul VI*

BELOW: *Father Mieczyslaw Malinski*

Cardinal Jozef Glemp

Wyszynski with John Paul II

BOOK ONE

REVELATIONS

1

The morning was the kind Monsignor Tony Bevilacqua had grown used to at the busy office of the Brooklyn Archdiocese of the Catholic Church. Bevilacqua had become a priest thirty years before for love of a spiritual world that lay beyond the physical things most people ever saw, or heard, or touched. But an archdiocese such as Brooklyn was so visible, audible, and touchable that its spirituality was sometimes in danger of getting lost.

The office where Bevilacqua worked, and dozens like it across the country, administered hundreds of churches and schools, some universities and hospitals, dozens of foster-care agencies and other charities, publishing and broadcast concerns, and gathering places for people of all ages. It employed more than ten thousand priests, nuns, lay teachers, nurses, social workers, janitors, and lawyers and supervised many volunteers. It lobbied hard at City Hall and in Washington. Just the real estate it owned was worth a fortune you couldn't calculate because nothing like it was for sale.

To manage this empire, some priests were diverted from assisting individual Church members and assigned instead to the administration, or "curia," at diocesan headquarters. These administrative priests peered up a chain of command rising from monsignors such as Bevilacqua, the lieutenants of the Church, to bishops and an overall archbishop.

What disrupted office routine October 16 was that everyone got a new boss. One hundred twelve archbishops from around the world had gathered in Rome to choose a pope. These were select archbishops who had been honored by a previous pope with the title cardinal. Aside from some ceremonial dignities and a red hat and sash, all that distinguished a cardinal from other archbishops was a vote on the new pope when the reigning one died. Pope John Paul I had stunned everyone by dying two weeks before, after a mere thirty-three days in office.

Much as Tony Bevilacqua cared about his Church, the Vatican seemed far away. He had been born in Brooklyn, and now, at age fifty-five, he figured to finish his career there. Although Italian by lineage, Bevilacqua could not be confused with the native Italian churchmen who had selected one of their own for the papacy in each election over the past 455 years—and for most of the Church's nineteen-hundred-year history.

The Italians who ruled Church headquarters in the Vatican often used coldness and inscrutability as tools of power. Bevilacqua is an amiable American, his talk animated—especially when he tells of his surprise that the new pope plucked him out of obscurity for a secret mission: to block a wayward nun who threatened the Church's abortion policy. He seems amazed that after he succeeded, the pope rocketed him into the job of cardinal/archbishop of Philadelphia, ranking him among the few most powerful men in the American Church. Today he stands ready to go to Rome himself the next time a pope needs electing.

Bevilacqua's face turns quizzical, however, when he thinks back to October 16, 1978. Just past noon, someone in the office reported that after two days of deliberating, the cardinals had finally settled on a pope—the latest heir to Saint Peter, the first pope, who they believed was appointed almost two thousand years earlier by God. Everyone gathered around the radio to hear who the Church's new leader was. The broadcast was live from St. Peter's Square, at the Vatican. Bevilacqua remembers the voice of Cardinal Pericle Felici saying the traditional words: "*Annuntio vobis gaudium magnum*. . . . I announce to you a great joy . . . *habemus papam* . . . we have a pope . . . His Eminence the Most Reverend . . . ," and then a name.

Who?

After so long in the game, Bevilacqua assumed he had learned the major players. But everyone in the office was glancing around blankly. "Nobody knew who he was," Bevilacqua recalls. "Someone thought he was an Oriental. It sounded like a Chinese name."

Father Andrew Greeley was among hundreds of thousands of people who jammed St. Peter's Square to hear the announcement live. Floodlights illuminated the surrounding stone columns erected by the great baroque sculptor Giovanni Bernini, and the majestic face of St. Peter's Basilica, which closed the columns at one end. Opposite the basilica, a full moon hung low in the darkness over the Tiber River. (Though lunchtime in Brooklyn, it was 6:45 P.M. in Rome.)

Father Greeley hadn't been and probably never would be promoted to monsignor. But he was much better known than Tony Bevilacqua or most bishops and cardinals. Greeley wrote popular articles and best-selling books, even suspense novels set in the Church milieu.

One reason Greeley's writings were so popular was that he often spoke for most Catholics born in the United States. Their beliefs, and those of many Western Europeans, differed from the pronouncements of the Church hierarchy on some issues they thought important, especially contraception and women in the priesthood. When the Church decided to celebrate the tenth anniversary of its 1968 statement banning modern birth-control methods, Father Greeley wrote that such an observance "seems to me to make as much sense as celebrating the sinking of the *Titanic*." Many American Catholics, who saw disputes as part of their democratic heritage, cheered him. Vatican officials, who saw themselves as transmitting the commands of God, frowned.

A trained sociologist, Greeley taught at the Universities of Chicago and Arizona, where his classes were oversubscribed by students who sat mesmerized through his inspirational lectures.[1] Greeley also helped run the National Opinion Research Center in Chicago, which had just completed a computer analysis of each cardinal's opinions in an effort to identify the likely next pope. The analysis had produced a dozen possibilities: eight Italians, an Argentine, an Austrian, a Dutchman, and an Englishman.

Also, however, Father Greeley had been engaged in a secret enterprise that, had it been known, might have kindled doubts even in his most ardent admirers. He and some lay friends had undertaken what he called a "conspiracy" to "rig" the vote of the cardinals so that the papacy would go to a man receptive to Western views similar to his. Part of this "conspiracy" entailed toppling his own cardinal/archbishop, John Cody of Chicago, whose authoritarianism was widely disliked, and whom Greeley suspected of financial impropriety.

As he stood in St. Peter's Square that October day, Greeley knew that any plot to fix the papal election (the mere imagining of which was a sign of naïveté) had come to naught. He would recoup by writing a best-selling book, *The Making of the Popes 1978*.[2] The eventual discovery of his "conspiracy" would embarrass Greeley, an otherwise kind and genial priest. It would also embarrass his unwittingly conscripted hero, Archbishop Joseph Bernardin, who was in line to replace Cody as cardinal/archbishop of Chicago. Bernardin, who died in 1996, was probably the most effective spokesman for the American position Greeley believed in; he was also—for the moment, at least—a growing friend of the man who was about to become pope.

Cardinal Felici's appearance on the balcony of St. Peter's Basilica drew a roar from the throng. At his statement *"Habemus papam"* rose a louder roar and wild applause. The crowd held its breath for the next words: the identity of the new pope. In everyone's memory, this announcement had always been followed by a culminating explosion of shared joy.

In response to the name Karol Wojtyla ("Voy-TIH-wa"), however, came a stunned silence, with just a smattering of hand-claps.[3]

"Most people in the piazza don't seem to know who he is," Greeley wrote in his book. Greeley described the crowd as "angry, confused, sullen." As for himself, even if his computer list of twelve top candidates had missed Wojtyla, he was hardly alone in his oversight. The Vatican curia itself had just issued a guide for the press containing biographies of three dozen likely candidates—a third of the whole college of cardinals—and Wojtyla wasn't on that list, either.

A stranger asked Greeley if the new pope was black.

"No," Greeley answered with a laugh, "*un Polacco* [a Pole]."

"*Un Polacco?*" The man gasped and then, Greeley says, "pounded his head in astonishment," fairly capturing the mood of most in the crowd.

Not only in the crowd. Cardinal Franz König of Vienna recalls that he and his colleagues were unsteady as they filed out of the Vatican's Sistine Chapel, where they had just cast their ballots amid Michelangelo's wall and ceiling frescoes. A cardinal from Australia, looking totally at sea, wandered up to König. "This is such a big surprise," the Australian stammered. "Now what do we do?"

In an old but tidy neighborhood of Chicago, Bishop Alfred Abramowicz noticed that lunchtime was approaching and popped into the kitchen at his parish, the Church of the Five Holy Martyrs. The cook had the radio on, and suddenly they heard a news bulletin that diverted attention from the meatloaf.

When Bishop Abramowicz heard the name Karol Wojtyla, he says, he "shouted with joy" and dashed out to the roomful of senior citizens who were waiting to have lunch at the church.

"We have a Polish pope!" Abramowicz proclaimed, and the response, he says, "was joy, joy, joy."

Karol Wojtyla had visited the Church of the Five Holy Martyrs on trips to the United States in 1969 and 1976. In Wojtyla's home diocese of Krakow, he had often been visited by Bishop Abramowicz, who for many years ran a church organization that collected aid for Poland. As for the parishioners gathered at the church in Chicago that day, Abramowicz says, "seventy-five percent came from Krakow. Many of those people [or their children] were baptized by him, confirmed, or married."

Father Konrad Hejmo was standing on an outdoor train platform in Poznan, Poland, where he traveled every weekend to the office of *Inroads*, a magazine for Polish Catholic youth. *Inroads* needed Hejmo's editing help to get past the government censors. It also needed his finagling to find enough paper to print on. That Monday, as every Monday, Hejmo was headed back to Gdansk, 150 miles north. There, as far as the government was concerned, he had his real job, at a monastery.

Suddenly, looking out from the train platform, Hejmo saw a strange sight: nuns dancing in the street. He called out to them: what was going on? When they said that the archbishop of Krakow had just been elected pope, Hejmo decided that his work at the monastery could wait. Wojtyla had lectured to Hejmo's university classes and now contributed regularly to his magazine. The priest dashed back to the church residence he used in Poznan and joined the group that had gathered in front of the TV.

Later Hejmo would recall what Wojtyla's election had meant for his own life. In a few months he was yanked out of his routine and assigned to help organize a politically charged trip by the pope to Poland. Within a year, he was in Rome helping to run a secret news service that evaded the communist censors. And in five years, Hejmo was summoned to rescue the Solidarity rebellion's vital lifeline from Rome after links surfaced between the money flow to Poland and an embarrassing bank scandal. Envelopes of cash had come from big-time crooks, and Hejmo's orders were to clean it up, then hush it up.

Miroslaw Chojecki heard the announcement on the radio of his Polish-built Fiat, bouncing along the streets of Warsaw. He used the Fiat to transport paper stolen from government storerooms to scattered, clandestine printing plants he had established. He knew that he, and the secret group behind him, operated under the hidden patronage of the archbishop of Krakow.

Wojtyla was also the secret force behind the new "flying university" that was spreading an intellectual revolt unprecedented in Poland under communism. Chojecki understood the importance of the network that looked to Wojtyla for moral leadership and physical protection. The news that Wojtyla was now pope was more than merely gratifying to Chojecki: as the spearhead of Poland's underground press, Chojecki foresaw that under a more powerful Wojtyla, he would have the chance to expand his illegal network. Soon his hundred underground book titles would become fifty-thousand underground newspapers a week. Ahead lay the realization of his dream of covert broadcasting.

"There is a very big difference between a bishop and a pope," Chojecki thought. "The pope can talk to the superpowers."

"Communism," he decided, "was about to collapse."

Before it did, Chojecki would, by his count, be arrested forty-four times.

Kazimierz Kakol, the minister of religious affairs of the Polish government, and Jozef Czyrek, vice foreign minister (and later foreign minister), were holding a press conference for foreign reporters in Warsaw. The topic was, of all things, church-state relations. An office worker heard the news on a radio, scribbled a note, and rushed into the briefing room to hand it to the communist officials.

"It seemed so unrealistic that I left the room to check it out," Kakol recalls. He came back and nervously made the announcement to the surprised reporters.

"Their first reaction to the name Wojtyla was, '*Who?*'" says Czyrek. He and Kakol provided from memory some basic facts about the archbishop of Krakow. Then Czyrek tried to put the best possible face on it. "We are proud the Polish Church has given birth to such a man," he said. When a reporter asked what the new pope was likely to do, Czyrek replied, "I am satisfied that Wojtyla is so familiar with the Polish historical experience, he will be a pope of peace and international agreement. He will favor the principles of social justice."

As Czyrek talked, Kakol's mind was churning. "I knew he was going to come to Poland. We were scared."

Stefan Bratkowski, a Warsaw journalist, had rejected Catholicism as many communists had. Priests dotted his family tree, but as far as he was concerned they had been partners with the Polish military in a "cruel and aggressive" system left over from the Middle Ages to protect large landholdings.

Bratkowski had been editor of the "Modern Life" supplement to a major Warsaw newspaper. But because of his penchant to sneak the truth into his stories occasionally, the government fired him and blacklisted him from the news industry. Since the government laid claim to all the paper, ink, and presses in Poland, its blacklist was potent. Bratkowski subsequently made a living grinding out "how-to" manuals. Like most Poles and citizens of other communist countries, he had abandoned his creativity, lowered his sights and adapted.

When the radio brought news of Wojtyla's election, Bratkowski recalls, "It was a shock, like, literally, an unexpected jolt of electricity." What happened to the Catholic Church didn't matter to him. But Bratkowski had studied philosophy under Wojtyla in the 1950s. The new Pope didn't come from nobility, but from a simple and tragedy-plagued family. He was an intellectual—a fellow believer in ideas, as well as in the goodness and worth of individual people. He tried—as Bratkowski had tried at the newspaper—to tell the truth while living within the letter of communist law. "The election of the new pope was the election of a new national leader of Poland," Bratkowski says.

It also meant a new life for Bratkowski. He was tired of cynicism and despair. He would cast his lot with the underground. The system was vulnerable. Given the new situation, an alliance with the Church might even be possible. Wojtyla would understand that.

Eventually, fate would actually bring the men together.

Father Jean-Marie Lustiger, a French parish priest, had dedicated the day to prayer, at a convent outside Paris. There was no radio, and he was reluctant to interrupt his meditations even when someone said that Karol Wojtyla, a scholar and philosopher like Lustiger himself, was the new pope.

But Lustiger was delighted "that it was somebody not Italian, from an Eastern country. They are people who suffered. We rarely heard information from the Eastern countries. That the cardinals dared elect somebody from there, it seemed an important decision for freedom."

Then Lustiger returned to his meditations. It was beyond his imagining that papal politics had any personal implications for him. To think that he would soon be promoted from parish priest to cardinal/archbishop of Paris, and in the mid-1990s even be mentioned as a candidate for the papal succession, would have struck anyone as ludicrous—anyone but Karol Wojtyla. Lustiger was, after all, Jewish. His family had been slaughtered at Auschwitz.

Lustiger openly asserted what other French churchmen denied: that their institution suffered from anti-Semitism. Among the few others who publicly acknowledged this was the new pope.

Bishop Francis Arinze of Enugu, Nigeria, was in Belfast, Ireland, delivering a series of lectures at the behest of the Irish Missionary Union. He was a valuable fund-raiser—learned, articulate, and African; he filled auditoriums. Arinze was in midlecture at a secondary school when a priest interrupted him with the news. He paused, reflecting on his encounters with Wojtyla at the international Synod of Bishops, a new papal advisory body to which both men had been elected by their peers.

"We are going to have order in the Church," Arinze told his audience.

It was a quick and accurate insight. Of course, Arinze had no idea that he would soon be whisked from Nigeria to Rome to help create that order; or that the African Church was about to be rendered independent, a marked change from its status as a colony to European missionary societies; or that in the 1990s, thanks to the initiatives of Karol Wojtyla, knowledgeable people would be speaking of Arinze, too, as the possible next pope.

While other Catholics felt bewilderment or exuberance at the news, it was panic that struck Annibale Gammarelli, the fifth-generation Gammarelli tailor to outfit the pope. The family faced major embarrassment because it claims to be the number-one handicapper of prospective popes, way ahead of the Vatican press office or Father Greeley's computer.

The Gammarellis' secret is that they also outfit most of the cardinal-electors. The tailors always take time while measuring to conduct discreet interviews, so they can assess the odds on who will be elected. Each papal election, the family is assigned to be ready with three white papal cassocks, sized to fit the largest and smallest likely candidates and someone midway between. The Gammarellis contend they are always prepared when a pope dies. Yet Wojtyla's name had eluded the Gammarelli list, as it had the others.

Embarrassment had already struck, in 1958. Cardinal Roncalli, the patriarch of Venice, was elected and chose the papal name John XXIII. Roncalli had a reputation for modesty, but not at the dinner table: he was of extraordinary girth. As he appeared on the balcony after his election, straining the buttons of his desperately undersized cassock, the jokes of the world's press rained down on the Gammarellis. The family insists that Annibale had handicapped the race perfectly and made a Roncalli-sized cassock; they say an excited Vatican valet simply gave the new pope the wrong box.

With Wojtyla, though, there had been a genuine oversight. He rarely bought a new cassock, generally preferring secondhand ones, so nobody knew what size he was.

But one look brought a sigh of relief. In physical measurement—though, it would turn out, in nothing else at all—Karol Wojtyla was precisely average: five feet eleven inches, one hundred seventy pounds, normal proportions. The medium size fit him perfectly.

Kazimierz Barcikowski was working late, as usual, at his desk in Party headquarters in Krakow.* In the communist system, the Party ran the government,

* Officially, there was no communist party in Poland. The Polish United Workers' Party, however, was clearly the "party" in the Marxist-Leninist sense.

and in Krakow, First Secretary Barcikowski ran the party. Its headquarters was about the only gray, blocky, communist-style building in the charming Old Town area of Krakow; party members seemed not to notice the building's drabness, and the rest of Krakow thought it appropriate.

As Barcikowski prepared to go home, the phone rang. He instantly recognized the voice on the other end of the line as that of Ryszard Frelek, an official from the Party's Central Committee in Warsaw. Frelek said Wojtyla had just been elected pope.

"My first reaction was that he was joking," Barcikowski recalls. "He said to turn on the radio. I did. The news was an absolute bomb."

Even now, Barcikowski is grim as he describes the scene.

A false story still circulates in Krakow that the first thing Barcikowski did after hearing the news was call the chief of the secret police, Gotzbiowski, and demand the file on Wojtyla. Actually, Barcikowski was already so familiar with Wojtyla's file that he could have recited much of it from memory. He even knew Wojtyla's university grades—two classes higher than his own.

Among the parts of the file Barcikowski knew best was the improbable story of how Wojtyla had become archbishop of Krakow in 1964, enabling his climb to cardinal and eventually pope. Wojtyla was promoted in 1964 only because the Polish minister of religious affairs at the time, Zenon Kliszko, had decided that of all the candidates, Wojtyla would be best for the communists.

Kliszko had figured the situation this way: Wojtyla was the most modern and informal of the prominent churchmen and the least political. Being the most different from Cardinal Stefan Wyszynski, head of the Polish Church, who came from noble stock, Wojtyla was most likely to embarrass the Church by breaking with Wyszynski. And Wojtyla, a philosophy professor, was also the least likely candidate to get into political fights with the Party: prominently noted in Wojtyla's file was his voluntary, friendly approach to the Party's first secretary in 1959, to negotiate a common-sense compromise in a silly dispute over dormitory space. Such cooperation was unprecedented in a high churchman.

Kliszko further knew that Wyszynski had never liked Wojtyla. In both lineage and style, they were opposites. For a year and a half, Wyszynski had thrown name after name at Kliszko for the Krakow job, and Kliszko had rejected them all. Finally, Wyszynski succumbed and gave the Party the name Kliszko had specifically demanded—Karol Wojtyla's.

Barcikowski's immediate problem was how to keep the popular excitement from erupting into antigovernment demonstrations, which might have to be met with force. Figuring the Church wouldn't want a night of rioting any more than he did, Barcikowski dialed the Krakow diocese, Cardinal Wojtyla's old office.

Would the local curia order churches open, so people would assemble there peacefully instead of crowding the streets? It turned out the curia was already arranging services, with the same thought in mind. So Barcikowski called Police Chief Jablonski to inform him that the jubilation was being successfully channeled into prayer. With luck, the night would not be disruptive.

That settled, Barcikowski faced the long-range problem of how to keep the new papacy from sparking a rebellion in Poland. It would require years of vigilance, and he had to start fast. "One thing was certain," he says today, describing his thoughts at the time. "Within a few days Krakow was going to be penetrated by Western reporters. All documents concerning Wojtyla would become objects of desire."

So, at what should have been the end of a long day, Barcikowski began to make a series of phone calls ordering every scrap of paper about Wojtyla to be retrieved and brought to the Central Committee office. He told Secret Police Chief Gotzbiowski to assign every available man to the task and to make sure the reporters, when they came, found nothing that cast Wojtyla as a critic of the government. This meant gathering "all his files from the university, all the letters he sent to the city council," Barcikowski recalls. And the secret-police dossiers? "Them, too."

A few blocks away, in his third-floor Krakow apartment, Father Andrzej Bardecki's mind worked as fast as Barcikowski's. Father Bardecki was religious editor of *Tygodnik Powszechny*, a semi-independent weekly Catholic newspaper that had been in and out of publication since 1945, as communist censors allowed.

The newspaper had stayed alive because it genuinely supported some of the communists' economic and social ideas. To be sure, the editors were anticommunist, as was almost everyone in Poland. But *Tygodnik Powszechny* tended to share that part of the socialist dream supported by the democratic socialist parties popular in Western Europe. It believed in government action to channel a large portion of the nation's wealth to the workers and farmers—though the paper's editors, like the Western socialists, believed this could be accomplished without smothering personal freedom in a police state.

Back in 1949, *Tygodnik Powszechny* had featured on its front page the work of Karol Wojtyla. Over time, the paper had continued to publish his work, often under a pseudonym. Father Bardecki had frequently been his editor.

In recent years, as Wojtyla had become the newspaper's patron and protector, Bardecki had evolved into the cardinal's personal scribe, transcribing and editing tape recordings of Wojtyla's weekly sermons and other talks. It was a body of work on human rights that Bardecki felt was important to maintain for posterity.

When Father Bardecki heard the stunning news that Wojtyla had been elected pope, his first thought was to preserve this record. The Party's men, Barcikowski and Gotzbiowski, would be after it. Ten months earlier, their thugs had jumped Bardecki as he left a late-night meeting with Wojtyla at the cardinal's office, beating him so savagely that only a chance interruption had saved his life. Another Wojtyla ally had been murdered in a similar attack not long before.

Wojtyla had rushed to Bardecki's side right after the medical team finished with him. "You got that for me," Wojtyla told him.

Now Bardecki had to do something else for Wojtyla—secure the six thousand pages of the new pope's transcribed words. They were stored with a secretary who lived alone in a ground-floor apartment near the newspaper office. The best burglars in communist Poland were the police. Bardecki had to find a better hiding place, then smuggle the papers to a Western publisher. He hurried out the door.

2

"Americans of certain ages remember where they were when Pearl Harbor was attacked, when President Roosevelt died, when President Kennedy was assassinated," author George Weigel has observed. "Poles remember where they were when John Paul II was elected."

The new pope's first words, however, were directed not at Poles but at the mostly Italian crowd, still stunned and even hostile, in St. Peter's Square. It was not obligatory that a new pope speak more than a quick blessing; John Paul I, for example, had not. But Italy needed reassuring. By tradition, the pope is also the bishop of the local archdiocese of Rome. So, after blessing the crowd, John Paul II spoke to them in Italian, as their pastor.

> Dearest brothers and sisters, we are still all grieved after the death
> of the most beloved Pope John Paul I. And now the most reverend
> cardinals have called a new bishop of Rome. They have called him
> from a faraway country, distant but always so close to the community of Christian faith. . . .
>
> Even if I cannot express myself well in your—in *our*—language,
> if I make mistakes, please correct me.

It became a famous slip of the tongue—some thought intentional. If not, it was providential, for at last it stirred the cheers that people were accustomed to giving at papal elections. Father Greeley, who had been studying Church leaders for years, said it was the first time he had ever seen the dour Cardinal Jean Villot, head of the Vatican bureaucracy, laugh.

As John Paul continued to break the ice, Monsignor Virgilio Noe, the papal "master of ceremonies," or schedule keeper, motioned for him to stop. No more was required, and any further extemporaneous talk risked the pope's saying the wrong thing.

But this pope had already outshouted Nazi loudspeakers and an artillery salute to communist military officials. Monsignor Noe couldn't silence him.

As John Paul II bantered on in Rome, the streets of Poland filled. Church bells rang. Within hours, Masses were in progress before packed congregations.

Wanda Gawronska, by blood a Polish aristocrat, was a member of Rome's high society. Her father, a diplomat, had married into a prominent Italian publishing family (of the newspaper *La Stampa*) and stayed in Rome after World War II.

In the early 1970s, she had noticed an influx of Polish intellectuals who came to Rome to be exposed to Western ideas, largely thanks to Cardinal Wojtyla's initiatives. When these thinkers returned to Poland, Gawronska knew, they injected important fresh air into her homeland. So she decided to expand Wojtyla's project. She rented some rooms for additional intellectual travelers and started a foundation[1] to solicit financial support for them. Some visitors "said we were the Polish embassy in Rome," she laughs.[2]

"It was very difficult to raise money" for the communist-occupied countries of Eastern Europe, she says. "Nobody believed in helping." She scraped together donations from individuals and grants from the Ford Foundation and a few smaller private groups. But it was hard even to find publishers for books written by Poles.

Wojtyla's election changed the landscape, Gawronska decided. Her first undertaking must be to assist Poles to come to Rome in great numbers for his inauguration. She phoned Antonio Bisaglia, the minister for state enterprises, who was also a social friend. Instantly, he offered free use of Italian government aircraft to ferry Polish Catholics for the big ceremony.

But when Gawronska notified Archbishop Bronislaw Dabrowski, secretary of the Polish Church administration in Warsaw, he told her that planes weren't the major problem. He needed television transmission. The Polish government had said the inauguration couldn't be televised because there wasn't enough money in the budget.

She called Bisaglia back. He agreed to have RAI, the Italian state television network, provide free transmission to Poland. It would be the first Catholic Mass ever on Polish TV.

Certain aspects of being elected pope were like being taken prisoner. Wojtyla and his secretary, Monsignor Stanislaw Dziwisz, could not again live in their homeland while the pope reigned. They were immediately ushered into the papal quarters, which John Paul knew well from visits to his mentor, Pope Paul VI.

It was not in the new pope's character to surrender to the traditional routine his handlers tried to impose on him, however. His first morning on the job, he left the Vatican to go where he felt he belonged: at the bedside of a friend, a Polish bishop assigned to the Vatican who had just been felled by a stroke. TV cameras were at the hospital to greet John Paul. When he stopped to speak with reporters, Monsignor Noe again tried to interrupt.

Pointing offscreen, the pope said, "There are people here telling me it's time to leave now. I'm the pope. I'll leave when I want to leave."

Meanwhile, he sent word back to Archbishop Dabrowski in Warsaw to round up some books. Dabrowski found them, heavily underlined, and Bishop Tadeusz Pieronek, a former student aide to Wojtyla, brought them to Rome two days later. "His only request was for books, no other belongings," Pieronek says. "He had no attachment to things. I brought him Polish sausage, but that was mostly for the nuns" who came from Poland to cook and clean house for the new pope.

As they walked in the rooftop garden outside the papal apartment, John Paul asked how Poles felt about their new pontiff. Pieronek tried to tell him, then did as John Paul himself liked to do, and answered a question with a question: What did the pope think?

"I think," John Paul said, "that God raised me to be pope"—implying, from childhood—"to do something for the world. I have to do something for the good of the world, and for Poland."

Recalls Pieronek now, "That sounded a little pompous. But looking back, it sounds not pompous at all."

October 21, at a press conference for two thousand journalists, John Paul openly revolted against Monsignor Noe and the Vatican staff. For five days he had succumbed, as John Paul I had before him, to seeing his *I*'s and *my*'s turned into *we*'s and *our*'s by people out to maintain the Vatican's ancient monarchical style. No more, he declared.

He spoke defiantly in the first person, in French, then plunged into the crowd to meet individual reporters. A monsignor assigned to stop such things tried to, but John Paul waved him off, took a microphone extended to him by a reporter, and talked into it.

"Would you like to visit your native Poland?" he was asked.

"If they'll let me," he replied. Quoted in print, he seemed to mean, "If the communists let me." But people at the scene say he clearly was pointing to his Vatican handlers and saying, "If *they'll* let me." And he gave the same answer to other questions, including whether he would continue to ski. He answered questions for forty minutes, speaking in Polish, English, German, French, Italian, and Lithuanian.

Experienced Vatican hands detected a real blow-up between John Paul and his handlers afterward. One shaken monsignor told a reporter,[3] "I dread ever crossing this man. If you get in his way he will run a bulldozer over you. Then he will back it up and run over you again."

As John Paul left the press conference, the handlers reminded him that he hadn't blessed the reporters. John Paul turned to the crowd, cupped his hands around his mouth, and shouted an apology, then a blessing. If that had happened before at the Vatican, it had been a while.

At a reception for bishops, John Paul encountered Bishop Theodore Mc-Kerrick of New York (now archbishop of Newark, New Jersey). In 1976 McKerrick, then a monsignor and secretary to New York's Cardinal Terence Cooke, had been called back from a Caribbean vacation to translate during a visit by Cardinal Wojtyla to New York. That apparently had embarrassed Wojtyla, who had repeatedly asked McKerrick whether he could get compensating vacation time. (McKerrick said he probably couldn't.) Two years later, in the aftermath of the papal election, McKerrick didn't expect John Paul to remember him at all. But the pope walked right up, concerned: "Did you ever get your vacation?" (He hadn't.)

Poles streamed in for the inauguration. Communist authorities, wanting to make the best of it, accelerated visa applications.

Life suddenly changed for Father Hieronim Fokcinski, who ran a once-sleepy Polish library and cultural center in Rome, where Cardinal Wojtyla had often given quiet talks or studied. Now Fokcinski's small building and staff were overrun by journalists and touring Poles. Obviously, his center would have to be expanded and reorganized. Reporters, filmmakers, scholars, and authors, attracted by the new pope, sought information. All this would help focus the world's attention on Poland and challenge prevailing Western attitudes about communism. Despite the happiness of the inauguration, for Fokcinski the weekend was pandemonium.

On Sunday, for the ceremony, the sky was gray, but the mood was sunny. Princess Grace and Prince Ranier of Monaco (for whom John Paul would later have to rethink his principles in an annulment matter) were there. Zbigniew Brzezinski, America's Polish-born national security adviser, who had met Wojtyla for tea in 1976, represented his country along with Speaker of the House Thomas P. ("Tip") O'Neill. King Juan Carlos of Spain and the Archbishop of Canterbury were on hand in their finery. Polish communist officials showed up smiling—even some who had been badgering the Church for decades.

In Poland, streets were deserted. Public activities stopped. Thanks to Wanda Gawronska, everyone was watching the ceremony on TV.

The greetings of the cardinals alone took an hour, highlighted by a dramatic, prolonged exchange of hugs and kissing of rings with Primate Wyszynski, head of the Polish Church.[4] When a small boy broke through the barriers and rushed up with flowers, a monsignor tried to hustle him away, but the new pope grabbed the boy and hugged him. The decision of Pope John Paul I, an Italian, to omit the papal tiara and some other pomp made it easier for John Paul II, a foreigner, to do the same. "This is not the time to return to" regal symbols, the new pope said.

John Paul opened his sermon with the words Peter, the first pope, had said as he began his own mission: "You are the Christ, the son of the living God." He cited a Polish novel that he said gave "magnificent literary expression" to Peter's story. He talked a bit about Jesus, and about the Second Vatican Council, then came to the words that history remembers:

> Do not be afraid! Open wide the doors for Christ. To his saving power open the boundaries of states, economic and political systems, the vast fields of culture, civilization and development. Do not be afraid!

It was an electrifying moment. In Poland, "there was often a cat-and-mouse game using religious language" for political purposes, says a Krakow friend.[5] "When he said, 'Don't be afraid to open the doors wide to Christ,' the language was explicitly religious but unmistakably political."

Bishop Frantisek Lobkowicz of Czechoslovakia, then a thirty-year-old priest, recalled, "The communists wanted us to be afraid. After that we weren't afraid anymore."[6]

It was the defining message of the next decade—the same tool Franklin Roosevelt had used to fight the Great Depression when he said, "The only thing we have to fear is fear itself."

Wojtyla had been teaching individual Poles this lesson throughout his adult life. Now, proving his point, he proclaimed his message of freedom from fear before the witness of the world. Knowing that explicit language would only rouse opposition and censorship, he used reminiscences, questions, and even silence to drive the message home. As if the rest of the world weren't even listening, he spoke directly "to you, my dear fellow countrymen"—to the thousands of Poles in St. Peter's Square, many waving red and white national flags, and to the TV cameras carrying his message to every Polish family. He slipped in the name of an ancient Polish hero, Saint Stanislaw, who had stood up to a tyrannical king—an image that Poles understood and communists hated. Then the pope asked:

> What shall I say? Everything that I could say would fade into insignificance compared with what my heart feels, and your hearts feel, at this moment. So let us leave aside words. Let there remain just great silence before God, the silence that becomes prayer. I ask you: be with me at Jasna Gora [the national shrine at Czestochowa, Poland] and everywhere. Do not cease to be with the Pope who prays today with the words of the poet. . . .

And then he came up with a closing message from the Polish epic *Pan Tadeusz,* by national poet Adam Mickiewicz. Wojtyla, as an actor, had performed these lines both in school and professionally, throughout World War II. Now the words fell as a gauntlet at the communists' feet:

> *. . . my country, thou*
> *Art like good health; I never knew till now*
> *How precious, till I lost thee. Now I see*
> *Thy beauty whole, because I yearn for thee.*
>
> *O Holy Maid, who Czestochowa's shrine*
> *Dost guard and on the Pointed Gateway shine*
> *And watchest Nowogrodek's pinnacle,*
> *As thou didst heal me by a miracle . . .*
> *So by a miracle thou wilt bring us home!*

Back in the papal apartment after the ceremony in the square below, the pope came to the window to greet the crowd again. Most had stayed, especially the Poles with their banners. Three times they called him out for more, until he jokingly begged to eat his lunch.

Over the next few days, Poles were herded into the apartment for lunches, dinners, and afternoon audiences. The new pope sent a special message home with Cardinal Wyszynski, to be read from all pulpits in Poland, saying "the will of Christ" had made the Polish Church "a Church of special witness toward which the eyes of all the world are turned." He noted the "prison and suffering" Wyszynski had endured, a symbol of the long communist persecution of the Polish Church. As a former seminary mate of John Paul's puts it, "This was no more than the truth, but a momentous thing for the pope to say."[7]

Talks began immediately about a papal visit home. Kakol, the Polish minister for religious affairs, told reporters that "if the pope comes to Poland it is certain that he will be warmly welcomed by the state authorities as well as by the people." Soviet leaders were furious at Kakol for saying this.[8] Wyszynski urged reporters to keep asking about a trip. Public pressure would speed the day.

Karol with his mother and father

Karol as a young worker

As sportsman

As administrator

As pope

BOOK TWO
GENESIS

1

Karol Wojtyla was born May 18, 1920, about the same time as modern Poland.

During the middle centuries of the millennium, Poland had been a great power in Europe, with an empire that included what is now Ukraine, Belorus, and Lithuania. Supported by aristocratic landholding families and the slave labor of their serfs, the kingdom of Poland produced memorable literature and military victories.

The tide turned when the Turkish (Ottoman) Empire conquered the Balkans and invaded central Europe. Poles beat back the Turks at Vienna in 1683, a critical moment for Christendom. But the effort weakened Poland before its emerging neighbors, Germany, Austria-Hungary, and Russia. By the 1700s, Poland, once the champ at the center of the European ring, had withered into a continental punching bag. In a shuffle of alliances between 1772 and 1795, the surrounding powers each incorporated about a third of Poland's territory. Poland was not just defeated but erased. Such humiliation doesn't merely affect a people; it *defines* them.

"You've got to know the history," says Bishop Abramowicz of Chicago, whose father left for America in 1915, as many others already had. "There was no Poland on the map for 125 years, back to my great-great-grandfather. My father came here saying he was hurt that when he was in Poland, his ship card was stamped in Russian."

During this long foreign occupation, the Church was the only institution that gave shape and leadership to Polish nationhood. It protected and sustained Polish literature, language, and culture, which the occupiers periodically tried to eradicate by law. In empire days, the Polish Catholic primate had served as an "interrex," or temporary head of state during political transitions; from 1772 to 1918, the Church was effectively interrex for nearly a century and a half.

It's significant that Poles were sustained strictly by their own Catholic Church, not by the Church in Rome. The best-known English-language history of Poland says the Vatican was "negligent, if not openly hostile, to Polish aspirations."[1]

The democratic wave begun by the French Revolution of 1789 had cost the Vatican the support of Catholic monarchs. It also introduced radical social change, including universal rights. The estates of the Church's wealthy supporters became less profitable when the owners could no longer also own the people who did the tilling and harvesting.

Moreover, republican government seemed to go hand in hand with Protestant, Enlightenment attitudes that reduced the influence of the Church in daily life. With the success of the United States as an example, and republican rebellion spreading across Europe, the Vatican wasn't about to help Poles overthrow the good Christian monarchs who occupied Poland. It was during this time—not just under communism, as is often thought—that the Polish Church developed a unique degree of independence from the Vatican.

After one anti-Russian insurrection, in 1832, Pope Gregory XVI condemned Poles in an encyclical. After another, in 1863–64, bishops were jailed and Church jobs taken over by Russians and Germans. Teaching or even using the Polish language was banned.

Partly, though, the 1863–64 violence marked not just an independence drive, but a civil war among Poles. The Russian tsar had just freed the serfs, including in his part of Poland. It was the time of the American Civil War. Like Confederate plantation owners, Polish aristocrats wanted to maintain a way of life that relied on widespread slavery. Many Poles, not just serfs, opposed this, and the Church was divided with the rest of Polish society.

An inherent split-personality over economic advantage burdens the Catholic Church right down to our own day. On the one hand, the Church prospered through the centuries—it may have survived at all—because of its comfortable arrangements with political leaders in the countries where it operates. These leaders usually represented a country's wealthiest plutocrats; only recently have they also, sometimes, represented the will of the majority.

On the other hand, the Church is run by men who have accepted the admonition of Jesus, which many take very seriously, to champion the poor, supplant avarice with generosity, and generally subordinate worldly wealth to spiritual values.

During Karol Wojtyla's priesthood, there was still talk in Poland of a Church of the aristocracy and a Church of the people.

cℐ℘

Poland became a country again because of World War I. The thirteenth of U.S. President Woodrow Wilson's famous "Fourteen Points" for a just peace called for an independent Polish state. Idealism aside, a lasting peace required a Poland, if only to separate Russia from Germany. For economic viability, the new Poland was granted use of a Baltic seaport—Gdansk in Polish, Danzig in German.

Scarcely had World War I ended, however, than another war began, a war mostly ignored in American texts and misrepresented in Polish ones. Most Poles will tell you their country was invaded by the Red Army of newly communist Russia in 1920. What they don't say is that Poland started the war. Here's what happened:

In early spring 1917, as World War I raged, democratic socialists overthrew the Russian monarchy. The German war command decided to encourage further havoc in Russia to distract it from pursuing the war. But the Germans made a mind-boggling miscalculation.

Wanting to throw the new Russian government off balance, Germany sent to the Russian border a sealed railway car carrying V. I. Ulyanov, a radical firebrand who had adopted the nom-de-révolution Lenin. Until then, the Germans had kept Lenin safely in Switzerland, the Russians having exiled him. Loose in St. Petersburg, Lenin and a small band of communists seized power and began installing their dictatorship of workers' committees, or "soviets," around the country. Their communist state claimed all property, even people's homes, in the name of "the workers."

It also instituted militant atheism. The communists said progress required complete trust in the social and physical sciences. They also despised the Russian Church, which had persistently allied itself with the wealthy. Communism, however, proved to be a replacement religion, not an elimination of religion. Busts of Lenin went up where crucifixes came down, and after Lenin died, his preserved body was displayed as a national shrine.

At the World War I peace conference, the new Russian government was allowed to keep lands accumulated by the tsar. Britain, France, and the United States decided that Poles should be happy just to have a country at all, and over Polish objections awarded the eastern provinces of old Poland to Russia.

Various Polish exile groups claimed rights to govern the new Poland, while American President Wilson dreamed of free elections. Ironically, though, it was the defeated Germans who charted the course of the new Polish republic. A day before the armistice took effect, they released Marshal Jozef Pilsudski from a prison in Germany, transported him to Warsaw, and left him in charge of the administration as German troops pulled out.

Although Pilsudski ruled Poland as a military dictator, he had credentials as a popular hero. His earlier protests against foreign occupation had landed him in Russian and German jails. The Germans probably chose to elevate him to power on the assumption that at least he would never ally with Russia. In that, as in their estimation of Lenin's potential for causing turmoil, the German plotters were more right than they had imagined.

By 1920, Pilsudski decided to go to war with Russia to reclaim the formerly Polish territories that the Versailles peacemakers had given away. He guessed that the Red Army was exhausted, having just fought a two-year civil war against Western-backed anti-communists for control of Russia. Pilsudski's attacking troops captured the Ukrainian capital of Kiev with deceptive ease.

Although Lenin intended someday to assist communist revolutions outside Russia, he was, for now, wholly occupied with reconstruction at home. He had repeatedly endorsed Polish independence and even expressed sympathy over Poland's mistreatment under the tsars.[2] But Pilsudski's aggression enraged Lenin. He found the Ukrainian population eager to repel the Poles, afraid that Polish aristocrats would again force Ukrainians to be serfs in their own country, as in centuries past.[3] So with local support, the communist Red Army regrouped and recaptured Kiev in mid-May.

When Karol Wojtyla was born, Lenin, Stalin, and Soviet Defense Minister Leon Trotsky were debating the future of Poland. Wojtyla's father, a lieutenant in the Polish army, certainly had a stake in their decision—which was to pursue and defeat Pilsudski's fleeing forces. Russian troops poured into Poland, seeking to wipe it out again and reestablish Russia's prewar border with Germany.

Democracy and civil liberties were not big issues. The communists were at least honest about renouncing such virtues. In "free" Poland, there was no parliament, and the press was tightly censored by the dictatorship. Even in the United States in 1920, federal agents rounded up thousands of political dissidents; when President Wilson's Attorney General, A. Mitchell Palmer, was foiled by the U.S. Constitution in his stated desire to put peaceful socialists in "concentration camps" (his words), he forcibly deported many.

Karol Wojtyla was baptized June 20, 1920, in a little church on the town square of Wadowice. Within days, Trotsky's army was driving toward the Vistula River on the edge of Warsaw, 180 miles northeast. The world expected a rout of the Poles. Pilsudski begged in vain for help from the victorious allies of World War I. "Defense Crumbles as Foe Nears Warsaw; Soviet Rule Set Up in Occupied Poland," said the banner headlines of the *The New York Times* on August 4.

Proclaimed Trotsky, "In a year, all Europe will be Bolshevist [communist]." He asked Polish workers and peasants to form committees to replace the Pilsudski government.

But the Russian army was also described as "ragged and starved" and without ammunition. Trotsky, Stalin, and a top general bickered over the attack plan. And after 125 years of occupation, Polish nationalism was primed to erupt. A Church message, read at every pulpit, called young men "to your battle stations." Volunteers flocked to Warsaw with a polyglot of leftover World War I uniforms and weaponry. Citizens hiked across the Vistula bridges to dig trenches and string barbed wire in the fields east of the city.

Pilsudski, in a purportedly brilliant military maneuver, cut off the advancing Russian columns. By mid-August, the Russians were routed and fleeing scattershot. Tens of thousands were captured. Within a week, Pilsudski had advanced to the Polish-Russian border again.

Polish tradition credits the victory neither to the energy of the citizens nor to the bravery of the army, but to the Virgin Mary. It is known as "The Miracle of the Vistula."

Pilsudski, however, hadn't learned his lesson and plunged his troops back into Ukraine, still aiming to conquer it. This time, defenders were organized and ready. After long weeks of stalemated killing, negotiations ended the war along much the same boundary that had existed when the bloodletting began, a year earlier.

Many proud Poles say their country's miracle victory at the Vistula saved Western Europe from communism. Lenin clearly hoped to help German communists win control of Germany, where the heart and brains of communism had long resided and where popular support was much greater than in Russia. Socialist parties (most of them democratic) accounted for more than half the vote in Germany, the rest being largely monarchist. Communists took power in Munich in 1919, and nearly did in Berlin, hoping to proclaim Germany a Soviet republic.

The ambitious young Adolf Hitler, with relatively little support, asserted a radical anticapitalist program. He called for abolition of incomes not earned by work, state control of big companies, a ban on land speculation, subsidies for small traders, and the death penalty for usurers and profiteers. (He slyly changed his program as needed to attract industrialists' money to his cause.)[4]

A mostly democratic, mostly free-market government clung tenuously to authority in Germany, backed by the World War I victors. But Hitler brushed it aside in 1933, while Karol Wojtyla was still playing schoolyard soccer. If Lenin's army had defeated Poland in 1920 and reached the German border, it would have strengthened Hitler's fiercest opponents; instead, Lenin's defeat gave Stalin and Hitler years of isolation in which to consolidate their regimes. Given what happened, it's hard to say who benefited most in the long run from the Miracle of the Vistula. But it gave Wojtyla a relatively free, safe environment for his youth.[5]

2

Wojtyla's father, also named Karol Wojtyla, stayed with his wife and two sons in Wadowice during the great battle. Some recall him as an army postal clerk. Later, he issued draft notices. Surviving military records indicate he spoke fluent Polish and German, typed neatly and fast, and was modest, kind, hardworking, dutiful, and serious. He was a private, family man, if anything, to a fault.

The Wojtyla family traces back to the tiny village of Czaniec, just west of Wadowice. When Austria swallowed the area up in the dismemberment of Poland in the late 1700s, John Paul's great-great-grandfather Bartlomiey was a farmer there. (The pope's genealogy is listed in *Kalendarium*, a Vatican-authorized record of his early life.[1])

The pope knew none of his grandparents, all of whom died in middle age. He knew little family at all. His aunt Stefania lived in Krakow until 1962 and sometimes visited Wadowice. A photograph shows the pope-to-be walking with her in a Krakow park as a young man, but she seems to have been peripheral in his life.[2] He had great-uncles named John and Paul, but he knew them little, if at all. Paul's son, Franciszek Wojtyla, a singer, is the only known link besides Stefania between those earlier generations and the pope; Franciszek's funeral in 1968 was conducted by then-Cardinal Wojtyla, though there isn't evidence of much contact between them when he lived.

Karol Wojtyla senior worked briefly as a tailor, then either was drafted by or volunteered for the Austrian army in 1900, at age twenty-one. After service in the east, he was posted back to Wadowice in 1904 and soon married twenty-year-old Emilia Kaczorowska, the pope's mother.

Emilia was born in Biata, a mountain parish now in the city of Bielsko-Biata, less than ten miles (all uphill) from the Wojtyla home village of Czaniec and just a dozen miles from what would become the Czechoslovakian border. Her father, Feliks, a saddler, and her mother, Maria, were town-dwellers, a cut wealthier and better educated than farmers. In 1885, with infant Emilia, they moved to Krakow. They had nine children in all, who suffered mostly calamitous health. Two lived less than a year; only three lived a full life. By 1908, both Maria and Feliks themselves were dead.

Emilia's family disdained Karol senior for being poor and beneath their station, according to Maria Kydrynska Michalowska, a close friend of the Wojtylas' in the 1930s. "They thought Emilia made a bad choice. They were wealthy bourgeois and didn't like him," she says. Her account is corroborated by the obvious distance that separated the two families later.

In 1906, two years after Karol senior and Emilia were married, a son, Edmund, was born. In 1914,[3] Emilia bore a daughter who died at birth or soon after; the family grieved her loss to the end of their days. A decade after the baby died, Emilia told a neighbor that she "always felt sorrow because of the loss of her daughter."[4] In 1979, the pope himself, briefly recounting his family history for a writer, mentioned the "big sister who died."[5] That had been sixty-five years earlier, and six years before his own birth.

Karol senior sought a transfer to the civil service in 1914, but the outbreak of World War I kept him in the army. Other than that, the war affected the Wojtylas surprisingly little. Austria was defeated along with its ally Germany, but Karol senior apparently stayed at his desk, emerging as a lieutenant in the new Polish army. In 1920, Emilia, then thirty-six, bore a second son, Karol. The name is the Polish equivalent of "Charles." He was called Lolek, or Lolus, standard nicknames like "Chuck" or "Charlie" in English.

It's not certain when the slightly built Emilia developed her chronic heart and kidney problems. But Lolek's friends say she was sickly as far back as they remember and that Lolek was often kept away from her.[6] As pope, John Paul once commented that he'd felt deprived whenever his mother left for Krakow in her constant search for medical treatment.[7]

Given the early deaths of so many siblings, Emilia's illness could have come as no surprise. Because Polish culture includes a near fetish for politeness, privacy, and formality, even close friends didn't know or ask precisely what illness she suffered from.[8] Since children were kept away, some doctors speculate that her condition may have resulted from an infectious disease; friends, though, were told she had to be secluded from children to avoid exertion.[9]

Descriptions of Emilia are universally flattering. She was caring and thoughtful of others, friendly without the reserve of her husband, and cheerful as could be, given the circumstances. But the circumstances were onerous.

Wadowice, the Wojtylas' town, was a center of crafts in the 1700s and of industry in the 1800s. Under Austrian rule, it became a district capital and the home of an infantry regiment. By the 1920s, its nine thousand civilian residents were mostly solid burghers and farmers. Still, most households had more people than rooms, and the rooms were small.

The four Wojtylas crowded into a rear second-floor apartment in a two-story building fronting the town square. Their door, in back, opened onto a pretty walled courtyard. Up a circular metal staircase, the Wojtylas' three rooms were arranged railroad-style: living room in front, then a kitchen/bedroom and another bedroom.

The most remarkable feature of the apartment was its location across a narrow lane from Wadowice's main church. Although the church was rebuilt in the 1700s, parts date back to 1400. It was so close to the Wojtyla apartment that a priest with an average nose would have smelled the family dinner. Unlike the stone basilicas that soar over some Polish villages, the Wadowice church is masonry, and only a few stories high. Nevertheless, it cast a physical shadow over the Wojtyla home, and doubtless a spiritual one, too, considering that both parents were very religious to begin with.

The pope at Lolek's birth, Benedict XV (1914–1922), stands out for his social conscience, virtue, and frustration. Described as "a frail, stoop-shouldered little man"[10] from a patrician family in Genoa, Benedict had been elected by cardinals seeking to end a rancorous dispute within the Church. Ever since the naturalist Charles Darwin published *Origin of Species* in 1859, traditional Church teachings had been challenged by "modernists"—Catholics impressed by the rapid new developments in science.

When modernists, with their laboratory tests, began questioning the traditional story of how the Bible itself was written, Benedict's predecessor, Pius X (1903–1914), decided he would stamp out modernism for good. He began throwing modernists out of Church jobs, university chairs, and even the priesthood. Committees were organized to hunt down heretics wherever they existed. Some people even drew comparisons with the Spanish Inquisition, although— significantly—no one was burned, crushed, or drowned.

Many Catholics, even some who found the modernists' position excessive, were offended by Pius X's reaction. He seemed to be leading a pontifical war on thought. When Pius X died, Benedict—though conceding no issues to the modernists—called off the witch-hunt. With the crisis abated, the issues remained to be faced at a more peaceful time.[11]

Benedict's success ended, however, when he emerged from internal Church disputes to try to save the world from itself during World War I. But it was his noblest hour. He consistently and unreservedly denounced the war as a "useless slaughter" and the "darkest tragedy of human hatred and human madness." He urged the participants to stop killing each other, while being mindful himself to stay neutral on the points of contention between them.

Thus Benedict antagonized Catholics everywhere. Most believed God was on their side in the conflict, whichever side that happened to be. They wanted no part of a Vatican neutralist.

Some historians believe that Benedict's proposals for the Versailles conference, which included creating an international system for arbitrating disputes, would have held up better than the schemes the conference actually enacted, which were easily shrugged off. But Benedict so lacked support that he wasn't even allowed to attend the conference. He died in 1922, uncompromised and, for a pope, remarkably unloved.

In Italian matters, too, Benedict was ahead of his time. Ever since the Church's vast landholdings, including Rome, had been seized in the unification of Italy in 1870, a succession of popes had boycotted Italian politics. Benedict finally acknowledged that Italian unification was permanent, thereby enabling Catholic voters to build the Popular party into a powerful mainstream force. The party Benedict fostered was a forerunner of the Christian Democratic parties that stabilized Western Europe after World War II. It blocked both the ruling Socialists and the black-shirted Fascists from taking full control.

But Benedict's successor, Pius XI (1922–1939), lacked Benedict's foresight. Fearing that socialism would become communism, he withdrew support from the Popular Party and wittingly helped the rise of Fascist Benito Mussolini, later Hitler's strongest ally.

Democracy, torpedoed in Italy, fared no better in Poland. Marshal Pilsudski, the dictator, called a constitutional convention in 1921. When it refused to give him the unilateral power he wanted, he quit. By 1926, when a profusion of splinter parties couldn't build a governing majority, Pilsudski sensed that Poles had grown impatient with squabbling and indecision. He staged a coup. Nearly four hundred soldiers defending the constitutional government were slain. After that, Pilsudski ruled, essentially by decree.

3

Through Lolek's school years, his brother, Edmund, was away at university and then medical college. Despite her illness, Emilia took in sewing to earn money, according to Boguslaw Banas, a schoolmate of Lolek's.[1] Banas's mother was among the women Emilia liked to talk to, sometimes at a neighborhood well, while Banas and Lolek kicked a soccer ball nearby.

Banas's parents ran a small whiskey and snack bar in Wadowice and a dairy outside town. "Karol's father used to let down a milk-can from their window on a string, and I would fill it with milk so as not to have to climb the stairs," Banas remembered. Asked who Karol senior's personal friends were, people cite Banas's father and no one else.[2]

A favorite indoor game of the boys in town was playing priest before makeshift altars erected in living rooms. Lolek, too, liked the game, Banas said. He dressed in a cape Emilia made him, topped with a piece of white cloth to imitate a priest's garb.

Another school friend Lolek played with regularly was Jerzy Kluger, son of a wealthy Jewish family. Jews composed a quarter of Wadowice's population. Jerzy's father, a lawyer, had an office on the square, in sight of the church and the Wojtyla family home. In occupation days, Polish Jews congregated in Poland's southwest, the Austrian sector, where Wadowice was, because the German and Russian sectors had strict anti-Semitic laws. Throughout Lolek's youth, the Wadowice town priest, Father Leonard Prochownik, preached Catholic-Jewish partnership. To this day, Jerzy Kluger credits Father Prochownik with the lack of anti-Semitism in Wadowice then.[3]

In summer the boys would splash in the cold, shallow waters of the Skawa River, just east of town. Winters, they skated or played hockey on a frozen-over tennis court. Before they were even ten years old, they would hike two miles to ski, despite the wolves that still roamed the countryside. At Jerzy's grandmother's nearby farm, they sampled fruit from the cherry and apple orchards.

Sometimes they visited Jerzy's aunt and uncle, who owned the primary industry—other than the army barracks—in the slightly larger town of Oswiecim, just seventeen miles up the main road north from Wadowice. The Kluger relatives had taken over a distillery established there in 1806. Oswiecim, though, wouldn't achieve world renown until 1940, when a German officer named Richard Gluecks selected it as the site for a "quarantine camp," with facilities for slave labor and mass murder. By then the town was called by its German name, Auschwitz. Karol senior's friend Banas, among others, died there.

Emilia Kaczorowska Wojtyla died April 13, 1929, after what *Kalendarium* says was a short illness, from her related heart and kidney ailments. Neighbors recalled that toward the end, she suffered increasing paralysis in her legs.[4] Sources differ over whether Emilia died at home or away at treatment.[5]*

Karol senior went to Lolek's school, reported his wife's death, and left after asking a teacher to pass the news to his son.[7] The teacher, Zofia Bernhardt, called Lolek out of class to tell him, and when she tried to console him, she was stunned by his terse, too-old-for-his-age reply: "It was God's will."[8] Lolek's friend Janina Mrozowa says he later told her that he cried on Emilia's grave and wrote a poem about her.

Father Prochownik gave the service. Afterward, Karol senior, Edmund, and Lolek went immediately to a place of rare beauty: Kalwaria Zebrzydowska, a monastery and woodland retreat about ten miles east of Wadowice, on the road to Krakow. It stayed sacred to Lolek throughout his life, and he returned to it often. Kalwaria was inspired when the wife of a nobleman named Zebrzydowski reported in 1595 that she had seen a vision of Jesus on the cross there. Her husband honored the spot by reconstructing the historical places in Jerusalem where Jesus is said to have gone in his last twenty-four hours. By tradition, Catholics went to Jerusalem to retrace this route, the so-called Stations of the Cross. Poles unable to make that physical trip could now make a spiritual one, at Kalwaria.

Although the Stations of the Cross are today commemorated at many sites, including one outside the Colosseum in Rome that the pope walks each Good Friday, Kalwaria stands apart. Instead of fourteen stations ranged about fifty paces apart along a paved path, which is the format elsewhere, Kalwaria has several dozen stops strung out over nearly five miles of gorgeous wooded trail, dotted with vistas of the surrounding countryside. Many of the stations are stone replicas of classical temples.[9] Even without Christian references, a visitor's thoughts turn spiritual as the clatter of modern commerce vanishes in favor of birdsong and rustling leaves.

---

* At least four major reputable published or televised accounts have repeated the widespread belief that Emilia, though forty-five, died in childbirth, the baby stillborn.[6] But witnesses provide no evidence at all to support these stories, which probably result from confusion over the family's lingering grief for the daughter who had died fifteen years before. As detailed in an endnote, one of the four reports that Emilia died in childbirth appeared in a book officially authorized by the Vatican (which contained other, documentable, factual errors); two others were recommended to me by cardinals. This highlights the difficulty of dealing with the Vatican on matters of fact: The Vatican seems surprisingly uninterested in detailed accuracy. Its press office, while gracious and competent, is swamped with daily work. Even cardinals contradict one another, and a biographer has no official source to consult to resolve questions.

With Wadowice situated midway between Kalwaria and Auschwitz, Lolek grew up literally a few hours' walk from either heaven or hell—at least as close as one could come to them on Earth.

4

According to *Kalendarium*, Karol senior retired in 1927. But Lolek's friends say he continued to work at his army office at least part-time well past Emilia's death. He usually fixed breakfast and supper for his son and lunched with him at Banas's restaurant. When Lolek had to fend for himself, neighbors often helped. Kluger remembers Karol senior's reading to the boys in the evening— usually Polish history, a subject in which he was self-educated—to augment their school lessons. The elder Wojtyla's head, once thick with dark hair, grew bald, and his large mustache was trimmed to a small triangle. "He was severe in appearance, but very gentlemanly," Kluger says. "He used a low voice always— not dynamic as Karol turned out to be."

A bowl of holy water (blessed by a priest) was kept in the hall just as in a church. In the back bedroom, which father and son shared, the lieutenant's saber hung on a wall, across from a small altar Emilia had made, where Lolek would pray in a white robe she had also made for him.[1] In the evenings, father and son often went walking together or played one-on-one soccer matches in the living room with a rag ball and a makeshift goal.[2]

Lolek's elementary school was crowded onto the second floor of a municipal building, with up to sixty students in a class. His grades were consistently "very good"—apparently the highest mark given—in all subjects. After school, he was always first choice in his age group for the position of goaltender in pickup soccer games. He now ventured as far as ten miles from town to find choice ski locations with his friend and classmate Zbigniew Silkowski, whose mother regularly fed the boys milk and bread smeared with pork grease.[3] On rainy days, young Banas's Ping-Pong set provided indoor exercise, and when things got dull they went to the Silkowski house, near the train station, and watched the railroad workers.

Besides the pieties one expects to hear about a local boy who became pope ("honest," "intelligent," "reverent," etc.), one unusual trait is cited by almost everyone who knew Lolek: he never got into arguments with peers or teachers. He seemed to harbor no animosities and to have a knack for dodging the interpersonal disputes that pop up in most people's everyday lives. Although this unflappable composure was uniformly admired, some people wondered whether an emotional fountain might be welling up inside him.

In 1930, Karol senior and junior went together to Edmund's graduation from the medical school at Jagiellonian University in Krakow. It was, at last, a joyous turn, not the least part of which was that Edmund would now live closer to Wadowice. He accepted work as head of a ward at the Bielsko-Biala hospital, in his mother's old hometown. A constant visitor home, Edmund became Lolek's "model," showing him "how to use time to achieve as much as possible in life," Silkowski said.[4] They were regulars at soccer matches, Karol perched on Edmund's shoulders to see better.[5]

Lolek left the grammar school in January 1931 to attend a public junior-senior high school, which was free for boys. From this age, girls who wanted formal education had to pay a high tuition at a private academic school or a teachers' training school; many simply dropped out.

The workload increased. Though most boys played games and ran around after school, Silkowski recalls that "Karol was different. After half an hour, he would go home to study. When I came back from the playground, I went to him to copy the Latin homework he had already done." Teachers and parents held up Lolek's work as an example—the Greek teacher particularly called on him when other students were stymied—but he never seemed embarrassed.

In the summer of 1932, Lolek traveled with a group organized by the Wadowice church to the town of Czestochowa. At the end of the town's main street is a hill topped by a 650-year-old walled monastery that houses the Polish national treasure, a painting known as the Black Madonna. Seeing it is almost a rite of citizenship.

Many religious miracles are ascribed to the painting, including military victories centuries ago against invading Hussites, Swedes, and others. Legend says it was painted by Luke, the gospel author, on a piece of wood that had served as the table at Jesus' family home in Nazareth. Few art historians agree, and Luke lived half a century after Jesus, but folklore needn't be true to be powerful.

The painting was carried out of Venice in 1381 by King Louis I of Hungary and Poland, whose warriors sacked the city. Later the same ruler gave it to some Hungarian monks he had installed at Czestochowa, both for safekeeping and to help draw crowds. Raiders slashed the painting in 1430, but rather than repair it, the monks let it stand defaced, over the centuries, the slash marks appearing as symbolic tear-streaks down the mournful-looking Madonna's right cheek.

By the time of Lolek's visit, summertime pilgrimages were a tradition. Except for the exposed faces and hands of Mary and Jesus, the painting was covered with jewels and trinkets brought by centuries of visiting worshipers. Their mementos also bedecked the walls of the room where the Madonna is displayed. The monastery itself—built and rebuilt over the centuries—has fortresslike battlements, a moat, a tower for children to climb, parapets to walk, and history to absorb, with cannonballs from ancient wars still embedded in its walls.

All this must have impressed young Lolek, even without knowing how often he would return—or that one day, more than fifty years later, he would at this very spot stumble onto a meeting planned behind his back between high communist authorities and members of his own curia to try to thwart the revolution he had sparked.

In his early high-school years, Lolek encountered two men who would change his life. Kazimierz Figlewicz, a young priest who taught religious classes in the high school, became his personal confessor. Figlewicz's influence, however, was slow to form and took a decade to bear fruit. The immediate change in Lolek's life came through the Kotlarczyks, Wadowice's first family of theater.

Poland has a tradition of locally produced live theater that doesn't exist in the United States. Residents who are doctors, clerks, or laborers by day can, in the evening, earn applause and perhaps even a few zlotys [the Polish currency] performing. Wadowice had an exceptionally strong theater tradition even for Poland. The largest resident theater, dating from the nineteenth century, had been run for many years by Stefan Kotlarczyk; on his death, in 1931, leadership fell to his son and disciple, Mieczyslaw.

By 1932, Lolek had been drawn into the Kotlarczyk family orbit. Their apartment was opposite his school, and from church, he knew the family's nineteen-year-old neighbor and helper, Janina Opidowicz, who eventually married Mieczyslaw Kotlarczyk. Lolek quickly took to pitching in on set construction and soaking up the atmosphere at rehearsals. He so enjoyed acting that when he visited Edmund at the Bielsko-Biala hospital, he entertained the patients with one-man routines he had learned.

In December 1932, Lolek, just twelve years old, saw the Kotlarczyk production of *Achilles*, by Stanislaw Wyspianski (1869–1907), one of a half-dozen classic Polish poet/playwrights of occupation days. The production proceeded despite an outbreak of scarlet fever in the area and was followed by a lecture by Emil Zegadlowicz, a nationally known poet born and raised in Wadowice. Lolek was left dazzled by the evening and by the world of the theater.

The thrill faded, though, with the news a few days later: Dr. Edmund Wojtyla, Lolek's brother and hero, had contracted scarlet fever from one of his patients and died, just about that fast. To Lolek, the death was an even bigger shock than his mother's.[6]

"Today, antibiotics would have saved him," John Paul would recall as pope.

> My mother's death made a deep impression ... and my brother's
> perhaps a still deeper one because of the dramatic circumstances in
> which it occurred and because I was more mature. Thus quite soon
> I became a motherless only child.[7]

A neighbor, Helena Szczepanska, said she saw Lolek, glum, on the street soon afterward and went up to console him. "My poor Lolus, you lost your brother," she said. She was astonished (as a teacher, she thought she knew children) to get the same stoic answer that had stunned Zofia Bernhardt after Emilia died. "Such was God's will," Lolek said again.[8]

As jolting as Edmund's death must have been for Lolek, one can imagine its impact on his father, after the loss of a daughter and a wife. Over the years Lolek told many people about the powerful impact of his father's frequent prayer as these calamities mounted. In his most revealing public interview as pope, he told French journalist André Frossard,

> Almost all my memories of childhood and adolescence are con-
> nected with my father. The violence of the blows that struck him
> opened up immense spiritual depths in him; his grief found its out-
> let in prayer. The mere fact of seeing him on his knees had a deci-
> sive influence on my early years. He was so hard on himself that he
> had no need to be hard on his son; his example alone was sufficient
> to inculcate discipline and a sense of duty.[9]

Within a few months of his brother's death, Lolek went to a teacher in the high school, Mr. Jelonek, and obtained his sponsorship for founding a chapter of a religious youth group, the Marian Sodality, named for Jesus' mother.[10] There is little memory of how many joined, but according to Jerzy Kluger, Lolek did recruit his deskmate, the son of the local stationmaster and previously a professed agnostic, into the fold.

More impressive and persistent was Lolek's private dedication to prayer. Catholic children were supposed to stop in church on the way to school to pray before class, but most merely knelt quickly at the altar and dashed off—often observing as they did so, that Lolek was a fixture, lost in prayer, until he had to run to get to class just in time, his shock of thick hair perpetually mussed.

He served as altar boy for multiple services in a day, going beyond the normal turn-taking most Catholic boys did. Friends noted that when their families arrived for services, Lolek would already be there, on his knees, praying.[11] One student, Antoni Bohdanowicz, who occasionally did his homework at the Wojtyla apartment, wondered why after each subject Lolek would go into another room for a few minutes; finally, through an open door, he saw that Lolek was praying.[12]

From childhood, Lolek developed a practice that throughout his career was remarked on by other Catholics, even other priests. Instead of praying at the main altar, as most did, he would find a side chapel in the church and make that his consistent place of prayer.

Synagogues and Protestant churches tend to be constructed around an assembly hall, much as a theater, designed for a community of worship focusing on a central event. But the traditional Roman Catholic church is a maze of nook-and-cranny altars and chapels designed for private prayer. Individuals or small groups may focus on a memorial for a relative or on personal trials. The vitality of these mini-churches is ironic, considering that one reason Protestants broke away from Rome in the first place was that they wanted a more direct relationship with God than Catholicism was thought to afford.

All his life, Lolek was to make exceptional use of this personal religion. At each change of address, he quickly located not just a church but a particular chapel or altar *within* that church—sometimes even an isolated spot within the chapel. In Wadowice, it was not in the main sanctuary that Lolek was so often seen praying while others knelt and ran; it was in a chapel off to the side, before a statue of Mary.

5

Lolek's high-school class of forty included the son of a rich family that owned one of Wadowice's six motor cars, the sons of coal miners, and even a young socialist firebrand. All had to wear blue uniforms displaying the school emblem, even out of school. According to Jerzy Kluger, there was some cheating on tests, passing of notes in class, and smoking of cigarettes swiped from teachers, but Lolek steered clear of these transgressions. He did sometimes go with friends to Wadowice's lone movie house, where the fare was almost exclusively American.

The Polish language teacher, Mr. Babinski, sometimes took classes to Krakow to attend the theater. Many boys scorned such "sissy" activity and played hooky on theater days. Lolek, Kluger remembers, not only always went with the class, but sometimes asked friends to go to Krakow with him on weekends to an opera or play.

The history teacher, Mr. Gebhardt, was a socialist who wore a red tie on May Day, the traditional workers' holiday. Ironically, he was also the school prude who voluntarily policed the so-called Avenue of Love in the evenings with his dog, though Kluger says "just an innocent hug or kiss" was the most that ever occurred there anyway; the students' greatest fun lay in evading Mr. Gebhardt. Curfews of eight o'clock in winter and nine o'clock in summer, a holdover from the Austrian occupation, were theoretically still enforced.

After-school soccer games were often contests between Catholics and Jews, with visitors from other schools joining the Jews to help even the numbers. Lolek was so regularly the Catholics' goalkeeper that he was sometimes called "Martyna," after a national star at that position. Poldek Goldberger, the dentist's son, protected the Jewish goal, with jackets and book bags standing in for nets on both sides. Kluger says the games sometimes deteriorated into roughhousing, and he remembers shouts of "Get the Jew!" But he insists that anti-Semitism was only hinted at before the late 1930s.[1]

Though the school was all-boys, it was there that Lolek met the girl most often linked to him when the press tries to answer the inevitable question of whether he had a girlfriend. Halina Krolikiewicz was the daughter of the headmaster, whose family lived at the school; so Halina and Lolek saw each other daily from age thirteen.

When you ask men about Halina today, even if they knew her only casually in youth, they almost always interrupt other thoughts to volunteer that she was heart-stoppingly attractive in face and figure. (When I met her, in 1993, she was still a handsome woman with a striking elegance, even as to her apartment furnishings.) She recalls watching the afternoon soccer games from her kitchen window and noticing that the goaltender was "tall, strong, good-looking."

Although she lived on the grounds of the only public high school in town, Halina nonetheless had to walk a mile or so to the private girls' school. Like others, as she scurried in and out of church for a kneel at the altar just before eight A.M., she noticed Lolek stationary, lost in prayer.

What brought Lolek and Halina close was their love of theater. Even in high school, both must have sensed that for them it was more than an avocation; it was a profession. Both joined the School Drama Circle, directed by the boys' Polish language teacher.[2] By 1933, Polish language was already recorded by the school as Lolek's "special-interest" subject.

In June 1933, he had a nonspeaking part in a traditional outdoor pageant celebrating the coming of summer. Performers in costumes rode through town on wagons to a park where the spectacle was performed amid bonfires.[3] Lolek appeared in two student productions over the next two years, while also accepting invitations from the Kotlarczyks that made him practically a family member in their professional theater. "A lot of artistic people were attracted to Wadowice because of my grandfather's house," says Mieczyslaw Kotlarczyk's daughter Anna. "Being an orphan in his early life, Lolek was trying to find friends and close family. He felt really lonely after his brother died. And he was growing in theatrical circles."

Mieczyslaw's younger sister Janina, then eighteen, says that the Wojtylas "were short on money. There was talk they were poor. But [Lolek] told me often his father was taking good care of him." Once, she says, Karol senior sewed Lolek a coat from what had been a green military coat of his own, after which people would tease Lolek with the name "Karol of the Green Coat."

While the Kotlarczyks' house was relatively modern, it seems amazing now that the two rooms, though large, housed Janina, Mieczyslaw, two other brothers and a sister, and their mother (and their father, too, until his death) even while serving as auxiliary headquarters for the theater troupe. Mrs. Kotlarczyk began mothering Lolek and told him to go directly there from school. She would cook dinner for all: vegetable soup, then Polish crepes with bits of minced meat, rice, and apples—or Polish sausage or pierogi (dumplings) or macaroni.

After dinner, Lolek and Mieczyslaw would talk about theater or poetry—basically it was a tutorial for Lolek on performing. But by three P.M., Lolek would begin casting glances out the window for his father, who would arrive about then from his work at the army draft office. As soon as Lolek spotted Karol senior coming, he would declare that he had to leave, then dash out the door to meet him on the street. Then they would be off to Banas's restaurant for what would be Lolek's second dinner in little more than an hour, his father apparently unaware that he had already consumed a first.

Banas's was hardly a wild place but did have its moments. A policeman used to stop by after duty and occasionally left his gun with the Banases for safekeeping when he felt he'd downed a few too many whiskeys. Once, Boguslaw, the son, picked up the pistol and accidentally discharged it in Lolek's direction. Except for the grace of a few inches, he later recalled, he would have ended the career of the future pope right there.[4] It was the first of many narrow escapes from death that distinguished Lolek throughout life.

There never seemed any question that Karol senior would remain a bachelor, devoted to the memory of his late wife and care of his surviving son. He hiked with Lolek in the Tatra Mountains between Wadowice and Czechoslovakia. Once he became separated from Lolek and a neighbor in dense fog; after searching and shouting for hours, they returned to the hotel, where Karol senior was waiting, safe.[5]

For all his virtues, Karol senior seems strange and distant in many ways. Day after day, for years, he came to collect his son at the Kotlarczyks', who were feeding Lolek, teaching him their trade, and otherwise extending themselves graciously for him. Yet never once, according to Janina, did the elder Wojtyla stop in to talk to them. They would watch out the window as Lolek and his father met and walked away, with never a glance back. I asked Janina if she knew why. "Maybe he was in a hurry," she offered.

Karol senior, who had sent a teacher to tell Lolek of his mother's death, showed no interest in his son's demanding career in the theater. No one recalls that he attended a single performance by his son, either at school or in the Kotlarczyks' professional acting group—or even attended his son's graduation from high school, where Lolek spoke. If Lolek minded, however, he never let on.[6]

6

During his boyhood, Lolek saw constant clashes between the righteous, traditional wing of the Church and a changing civil society—clashes whose reappearance would confound Pope John Paul II after communism ended. Poland was glued together in the 1930s by Dictator Pilsudski's odd authoritarian mix. Political dissidents and labor agitators were thrown into concentration camps, but in other ways Pilsudski nurtured civility and tolerance.

He kept a firm lid on anti-Semitism, which Primate Augustin Hlond all but promoted.[1] He infuriated Church leaders by trying to put marriage under civil law and legalize divorce (which the Church forbids); only Cardinal Hlond's threat to call a general strike stopped him. Pilsudski even quit the Church and was baptized a Lutheran in order to divorce his first wife and marry a Jewish woman. Yet under him, the Church flourished. The size of the clergy doubled. Hundreds of Church newspapers and magazines dominated the press, while government censorship of political news kept down competition.

Lolek saw one confrontation firsthand when scandal hit Emil Zegadlowicz, the poet from Wadowice who Lolek had heard lecture. Memorizing Zegadlowicz's poetry was required in the high school. When the poet came home to be honored with an evening of theater in 1935, Lolek and fellow students took part. Soon afterward, however, Zegadlowicz published what one scholar has described as an "anti-clerical and provocatively sexual" novel about a boy growing up in a Wadowice-like town. Teachers were "sadistically cruel." The heroes were an agnostic and a socialist. Wadowice's town fathers, outraged, stripped Zegadlowicz of his honorary citizenship and made him persona non grata.[2]

Yet Lolek wasn't intimidated by witnessing this retribution against dissent. Years later, when he and Kotlarczyk founded an underground theater in Krakow, they revived Zegadlowicz's work, specifically including excerpts from the controversial novel about Wadowice.[3]

By the fall of 1935, when they starred opposite each other in a school production of the Greek tragedy *Antigone*, it was apparent that Karol Wojtyla and Halina Krolikiewicz were the most talented and devoted teenage thespians in Wadowice. (Halina would go on to a celebrated national stage and television career.) Each took naturally to the stage and the spoken word and enjoyed the thrill actors get before an audience. Surviving programs say performances were introduced by Halina's father, the headmaster, and concluded with "a recitation by our colleague Wojtyla."

When a nationally acclaimed actress, Kazimiera Rychterowna, gave a one-night poetry reading in Wadowice, Lolek and Halina summoned the courage to go up afterward and ask her to return to Wadowice to judge the annual high-school poetry-reading competition. "Everybody knew there were two favored competitors, me and Karol," Halina says. They wanted a definitive judge. The actress agreed.

Came the big day, the favorites chose radically different poems. Lolek, Halina says, picked "a long, difficult philosophical poem" based on the Greek legend of Prometheus, written by the Pole Cyprian Norwid (1821–1883), "the most difficult poet I know." Lolek lulled the audience with a style that she says "was quite different from what we see in movies—very quiet and intellectual."

In contrast, Halina went for a crowd-pleaser, a dramatic poem about rain, full of alliterative flourishes: "It was easy to get effect. I got first prize. But it wasn't fair." Saying so today, she rises from the sofa, pulls down a volume, and dramatically reads lines from Lolek's recitation: "Beauty is not to stay hidden/ Neither is salt of the earth to be used only in the kitchen/ But beauty is to make you eager to work/ And work is for a man to gain his resurrection. . . ."

As she read, I recognized a similarity between this passage and one I had read in a library a few weeks before. The lines from the poet Norwid, which Lolek selected for a poetry competition at age fifteen, argue that toil is not a curse but rather is the creative spark that defines and enriches each person. Forty-six years later, this same thought became the centerpiece of *Laborem Exercens*, his first major economic encyclical as pope:

> Work . . . whether manual or intellectual . . . is [a] characteristic that distinguishes man from the rest of creatures, whose activity for sus-

taining their lives cannot be called work.... A human being expresses and fulfills himself by work.

Laborem Exercens went on to say, as did Norwid's poem, that something of the individuality of each person's work remained uniquely his own, not the property of an employer. Norwid's poem formed the basis of the pope's later philosophy, which opposed both communism and pure capitalism.

Lolek wasn't just doing his homework back in 1935. He was *learning* from it.

In February 1936, a high-school production starring Lolek and Halina traveled to nearby towns and was reviewed by a general-circulation youth magazine, which said, "The comedy was a complete success. Gustaw (Wojtyla) and Aniela (Krolikiewicz) played their roles like two young people truly in love"; the audience responded with "roars of laughter." With that, Kotlarczyk offered the sixteen-year-old Lolek his first professional, adult acting job, which also drew acclaim. From being a semi-orphan taken in at the family dinner table, Lolek had become a star pupil—a personal project—of Mieczyslaw Kotlarczyk's.

Kotlarczyk's sister Janina recalls him, pacing the two-room apartment with Lolek a step behind. Kotlarczyk would read a passage of nineteenth-century poetry as he thought it should be read; Lolek would repeat it, somehow getting it wrong, at least to Kotlarczyk's thinking. Once or twice Lolek turned back to Janina with a look of frustration and gestured as if tearing out his hair.

Kotlarczyk also brought Halina into the professional theater to play opposite Lolek. "We always played the major romantic male-female parts," Halina says. "That's why it was common thinking [that] we were a couple. He would see me off after rehearsals" and carry her book bag around for her. The two danced together at their graduation dance. "But I never dated him—never."

Ever since Lolek became pope, tabloid journalists, searching for some love interest in his background, have written of a torrid affair between him and Halina, even that she had children with him. Only German State Television, she says, included her denial along with the story. Her tone suggests she found Lolek a bit too pious for her taste: "Everyone knew he was very religious. Other students watched their language around him—no vulgar words."

Even if there had been some affection between them, couples were rarely allowed alone together in those days. Says Jerzy Kluger, "If I met a girl, before I got home my grandmother already knew." Virginity was normal even among university graduates, and, says a classmate, "living in the same apartment [before marriage] was unthinkable."[4]

But the most persuasive evidence that Lolek and Halina weren't the romantics they appeared comes from Kotlarczyk's sister Janina (now Mrs. Janina Mrozowa), who says that Halina was more interested in her brother Stefan. "They went for walks, and there was talk [that] Stefan was in love with Halina," she says. (Halina denies having any serious romances before she eventually married.)

Further, Janina says, Lolek had his eyes on another girl. His romantic crisis, she says, came during his best-known Wadowice performance, in the 1937 production of *Balladyna*, a major play by renowned national poet Juliusz Slowacki (1809–1849). Lolek's character falls in love with a woman who was played by a student at the teachers' training school, Kasia Zak. Kasia had "a sunburnt complexion, beautiful long blond hair, and very blue eyes," Janina says, features that helped her play the heroine to the dark-haired, sophisticated-looking Halina's jealous villain.

One day Lolek came to Janina looking dejected. He said that he and Kasia had been rehearsing their love scenes alone, and that when they had finished, he had confronted Kasia with a confession: "I wish it were so in reality!"

As Lolek waited for her response, Kasia merely laughed, threw up her hands in a gesture of refusal, and cried the Polish phrase *Potrzebuje tego*, which literally means, "I need it," but whose colloquial meaning was exactly the opposite—a sarcastic "I don't want it." In other words, the future pope had been curtly rejected and was, Janina says, crushed.[5]

Balladyna had a run of ten performances at a local cultural center, with 150 to 200 people in each audience. In one performance, the youth assigned to a major role had been suspended over a school prank, and Lolek volunteered to play both parts. Kotlarczyk, Halina, and the rest of the group were astonished that anyone could memorize so much difficult poetry in less than a day—but Lolek did it with no mistakes.

What had begun as high-school and civic-theater performances had clearly risen above that level. Rarely would a town like Wadowice be graced at one time with three talents—Lolek, Halina, and Mieczyslaw Kotlarczyk—of a quality usually found in national professional theaters. Besides being fortunate for the audience, this unusual situation must have inspired the three principals.

7

Ginka Beer, a budding actress and medical student who lived in Lolek's building, was a family friend of Jerzy Kluger's. As Lolek's interest in theater grew,

Ginka coached and encouraged him. One day, Lolek told Kluger that Ginka was greatly upset, and suggested they visit her. They found her crying and packing. She had been sent home from medical school in Krakow on the accusation that she had a friend whose fiancé was a communist. What it clearly boiled down to was anti-Semitism.

She was going to Palestine, she told them. "Have you seen what's happening against the Jews in Germany?" she asked. Well, it was spreading to Poland.

They accompanied her to the train station, cautioning that her flight was rash. In fact, the escape saved her life; bypassing Auschwitz, she enjoyed a successful career as an actress in Israel.[1] She later recalled that as she left Wadowice, Lolek's father told her, "Not all Poles are anti-Semitic. You know I am not!"[2]

After Pilsudski died, in 1935, he was replaced by colonels who copied his authoritarianism but lacked his substance. A figurehead parliament was dominated by Polish-chauvinist parties, the largest of which supported an economic boycott, called *Owszem*, against Jews. Racist newspapers sprang up.

Even Lolek was lured into doing an antidemocratic, anti-Semitic play. The priest who ran the local Catholic theater had persuaded him to star in some religious productions, one of which cast Lolek as the defender of a feudal Christian monarchy against a plot by evil Jewish socialists posing as Christians. Although the play's political overtones seem in retrospect a dangerous sign of the times, they may have gone over Lolek's head; in real life, he behaved differently.[3]

Early in 1938, Jewish lawyers—including Jerzy Kluger's father—were forced to add a Hebrew name to their office nameplates. Some students and teachers joined the growing ranks of the anti-Semitic National Democratic Party, and fights sometimes broke out in the streets. According to Kluger, Lolek tried to do the right thing in his nonconfrontational way, quoting Father Prochownik's sermons to the effect that anti-Semitism was anti-Christian.

Occasionally, rowdy gangs, mostly from out of town, would picket Jewish stores and offices, urging Poles to stop patronizing them, and ridicule all Jews. Many townspeople, not just Jews, protested the intruders. One night a mob came through town and broke windows in buildings owned by Jews; the next day teachers and townspeople spoke out against the vandalism. Mr. Gebhardt, the socialist history teacher who tried to stamp out teen necking, taught a lesson on Adam Mickiewicz (1798–1855), the revered national poet who had spoken out for equal rights and esteem for Jews.

It was a losing battle. The recurrent paradox was again believed: Jews constituted a single conspiracy that included both the wealthy financiers who controlled society and the socialist revolutionaries who hoped to overthrow it. Throughout Europe, fascism was ascending and democracy fading.

Hungary had long been run by its military. Czechoslovakia, in contrast, was a functioning democracy until the Munich Conference of 1938, at which Britain and France agreed to let Hitler take over the heart of that country. At Hitler's request, no Czechs were even allowed at the conference table. British Prime Minister Neville Chamberlain told the world—and two flabbergasted Czechoslovakian diplomats—that his betrayal of Czechoslovakia would prevent another big war.

In Rome, Pope Pius XI signed what became known as the Lateran Treaty with dictator Mussolini. In exchange for title to the lands the Church had lost in 1870 and wouldn't get back anyway, the Church received title to the walled city of the Vatican—109 acres around St. Peter's—and an endowment in lire worth $85 million, which put the papacy on sound financial footing for many decades. Mussolini made Catholicism the state religion, put crucifixes in schools and public buildings, and bestowed special legal status on the Catholic clergy.

All Pius XI had to surrender in exchange for this bounty was the Church's blessing on a man whom Italians would later string up by his heels, though only after more than twenty-five million deaths and the destruction of much of Europe.[4]

July 20, 1933, Pius XI concluded a concordat, or church-state agreement, with Hitler. The concordat was said to have "lent the Hitler government much badly needed prestige."[5] It was signed by Pius XI's secretary of state (the top appointed official), Cardinal Eugenio Pacelli, who would succeed him in 1939 as Pope Pius XII.

Italy invaded and conquered backward Ethiopia in 1935, causing the future Pope John XXIII, then papal nuncio (or diplomatic representative) in Istanbul, to write to his sister that Mussolini's victory "makes it seem that a hidden force is guiding him and protecting Italy." Even a man who would one day be known for supporting peace and democracy could believe in 1936 that fascism was acceptable because "in countries where liberty triumphs," the result was "socialism and communism!"[6]

As the world darkened, Lolek studied the lives of two eighteenth-century Polish generals, Kosciuszko and Pulaski, who had crossed the Atlantic to fight with George Washington in the American Revolution. He learned that Mickiewicz, the Polish poet he probably memorized most, had gone to Italy to fight with General Giuseppi Garibaldi *against the pope* for national unification and the ideal of a constitutional state. He further discovered that Cyprian Norwid, whose poem had won Lolek second prize in the high-school recitation contest, had traveled to New York in the 1850s to join the campaign to abolish slavery.

By 1938, Lolek knew that the world could be unjust and that people could change this and ought to try.

cℐ

Lolek graduated with mostly the equivalent of As, though he had occasionally stumbled in chemistry, physics, and history. Language—any language—was his gift. June 6, 1938, Archbishop Adam Sapieha of Krakow came to the high school for the graduation celebration. Though his Church title automatically made him a prince, Sapieha was a prince by lineage also. His grandfather and father had joined rebellions against Russia, and his father had served in the Austrian House of Lords.

So important was the family that when it came time for Adam Sapieha to be ordained a bishop, in 1911, Pope Pius X did the job himself, in the Sistine Chapel. After World War I, however, Sapieha's relations with Rome soured. He led the Polish bishops in seeking more local power for the Polish Church, and even turned away a papal representative to Poland in a confrontation.

Pope Pius XI pointedly denied Sapieha the title of Cardinal, which normally came with a large archdiocese like Krakow. Pius also forced Sapieha to resign his seat in the Polish parliament, where he had represented the National Democratic Party, the chauvinistic group that favored discrimination against Jews and others who weren't ethnic Poles.

Now, at seventy-one, Sapieha seemed to have his most important years behind him. But he didn't. It was how he spent the rest of his life, under fascism and communism, that distinguished him.

Lolek, who finished first in his class, was chosen to give a welcoming address to Archbishop Sapieha. (A week earlier, Lolek had given the class speech at the actual graduation ceremony.) Sapieha was so impressed with the young man that he turned to Father Zacher, the town pastor, and in a voice loud enough for everyone to hear, said, "Does that boy intend to become a priest? We could do with someone like that in the Church." Zacher replied that to his regret, Lolek was smitten with the theater and intended to study Polish language at the university in the fall.

"That's a pity," Sapieha replied.[7]

"I was quite sure that I would remain a layman," Lolek later recalled. "Committed, to be sure . . . to participate in the life of the Church; but a priest, certainly not."[8]

8

In August, after a few weeks' compulsory military training, which he spent doing kitchen work for a road-repair crew, Lolek moved with his father to

Krakow. Lolek had inherited his mother's share of a gray, three-story masonry house there, owned by her family. Her brother Robert and her two maiden sisters—Lolek's aunts—lived on the top two floors; they were all that remained of Emilia's family. The Wojtylas got the bottom floor, which is partly underground.

The building is enviably situated on the south bank of the Vistula, only a stone's toss from the water, with a pretty promenade and a view of Krakow on the north bank. It is a brief walk from the charming Debnicki market square and a bridge that leads to the old town, near the archbishop's palace and the university. But a contemporary account says the "basement flat" the Wojtylas got "was a sad place indeed. Hardly any daylight filtered through its narrow windows, the rooms were small and cramped, while the lack of sunshine made the place cold and inhospitable. Locals called it the Debnicki 'catacomb.' "[1]

For the tragedy-tossed Wojtylas to be dumped into the dungeon of such a potentially nice house suggests that there was indeed an estrangement between the two sides of Lolek's family. Even stronger evidence is provided by the apparent noncommunication between Emilia's relatives and the Wojtylas while they shared one house during six of the most dramatic years in Polish history. The many accounts of those years by Lolek and his friends don't mention his uncle and aunts. Lolek referred to his father as his last surviving family member, while continuing his search for a larger family to be part of, as if the blood relatives upstairs didn't even exist.

Yet his institutional roots ran deep. Attending the Jagiellonian University—founded in 1386—was not just going to college; it was sharing a cultural cornerstone of his people. Copernicus had gone there, and Poles ever since. Marcin Wadowite, the sixteenth-century theologian for whose family Wadowice was named, had been rector. Some fundamental differences in outlook are explained—and perpetuated—by the different yardsticks Poles and Americans use to measure time; history gives Europeans a better sense of their roots and Americans a better facility for change. Human prosperity requires a harmony of roots and change, but conflict between them challenged Lolek later in life.

Among the first people he met in Krakow was Wojciech Zukrowski, another incoming student, who lived with his parents a few houses down the Vistula from the Wojtylas. Zukrowski had aimed for the Jagiellonian law school but was rejected by a dean and sent to major in Polish language instead. Polish language was thought of as a teacher-preparatory course and "was not considered a real department for a man to study," Zukrowski says. He and Lolek found themselves in a class with "seven men and three dozen women."

The other five men all aimed to be professional writers. Ironically, the two men who entered the class *not* intending to write (Lolek wrote poems, but his real aim was acting) would have the most success at it: Lolek, whose words as pope are disseminated in the millions of copies, and Zukrowski, who became the best-selling novelist of postwar Poland.

One of the three dozen women in class had a familiar face: Halina had left her family at the high school in Wadowice, rented a room in Krakow, and enrolled in language at the university, too.

That September, 1938, before classes started, Lolek met a friend from his summer roadwork, Jerzy Bober, who was also entering the university with acting ambitions. Bober proposed an evening of theater and poetry reading and invited some acting students to his parents' apartment to plan it. Lolek brought Halina along.

"Karol's bearing was full of dignity," Bober later remembered.[2] "A new brown hat with a wide band. Instead of regular pants he wore fashionable knickerbockers, and brown shoes of above-ankle cut." A classmate remarked that Lolek's hair was uncommonly long, "falling on his neck." Bober had already spread the word that Lolek's poetry "was not very understandable."

Lolek had raved so about Halina and her talent for recitation that everyone assumed she was his girlfriend. The boys noted her beauty jealously. But their suspicions proved unfounded. As the group consumed soft drinks and cookies on a balcony that summer's day, they didn't just schedule a theater evening; they all, including Halina, formed romantic interests that were pursued in the coming months—all except Lolek.

The evening of the performance, dozens of ticket buyers packed the room, and though some were rowdy, the applause was hearty. One aspiring actress[3] remembered Lolek as "the most distinctive personality there. It was not fashionable to be so different. He talked with grand hand gestures. He had an open collar—all the other men wore neckties." She also noticed his long hair.

Afterward, the performers were exuberant. With eighteen zlotys in each one's pocket, a substantial sum in those days, they decided to finish the evening at a popular tavern. But on the way, according to Bober, "Karol—who had already sobered from the euphoric mood—stopped us with a theatrical gesture. With a vexed look on his face, he explained that he didn't feel well and that he was not going to drink or celebrate the event. Hearing this, I handed him two zlotys and said, 'Have it, Lolek, and buy yourself some candies.' " Lolek, Bober reports, took the money and left, while the others, "astonished . . . resumed our walk to the tavern."

The university's Gothic stone-and-brick buildings and tree-lined walkways sit aside the old city. Lolek signed up for Eighteenth-century Polish Drama, Analysis of Drama Theory, Fourteenth- and Fifteenth-century Polish Literature, Ancient Polish Language, and Russian Language. Other students later recalled that he usually came to and left class alone and said little while there.

Irena Orlewiczowa, who shared a two-seat desk with Lolek, said that he listened in class "as if wanting to soak up every word." To Maria Bobrownicka, he avoided a limelight that could have been his. Zofia Zarnecka remembered his paying special attention to a Jewish girl in class, "as if he were protecting her from pan-Polish chauvinism. His opinion of pan-Polishness was negative, and he didn't try to hide that." Mostly, though, his classmates judged Lolek to be quiet—less sophisticated and less self-confident than the average student.[4]

No one seems able to account for the difference between the dashing Lolek who impressed his actor friends with his garb in September and the more tattered Lolek his classmates remember later; his father may have splurged on a new outfit to begin school. As time passed, friends noticed that the once-flashy boots wore down, until one day Lolek showed up with new, extra-thick soles that were obviously homemade by his father.

In the further poetry evenings, while a dozen others recited the poems of friends, Lolek alone read his own work. He continued to recite in a different style and to duck out on the tavern parties afterward, saying, "I have no time to waste on such things."[5] Individuality is not always admired among youth. Halina concedes that a little more conformity would have made Lolek more popular. But she says his intelligence ensured that everyone respected him.

"He was an actor surrounded by women," Zukrowski recalls. "But he was not especially interested in girls."

During Easter Week 1939, Lolek attended Archbishop Sapieha's services at the cathedral in the Wawel, Krakow's ancient walled seat of government. After the services, he was seen deep in prayer before the tomb of the university founder, Jagiello. That May he went on a student pilgrimage to Czestochowa, to revisit the Black Madonna. These acts showed above-average religious dedication but were hardly extraordinary, especially given the deaths in his family.

February 2, 1939, Sapieha mailed his resignation to Pius XI. At seventy-two, "and with increasing decline of health, I feel myself incapable of carrying the weight of a diocese," Sapieha wrote.

He never got an answer; Pius died February 10. Because of their feud, Sapieha wasn't a cardinal, and thus didn't attend the conclave (meeting of cardinals) in Rome to pick a successor.[6]

The new pope, Pius XII, like so many before him, seemed raised from birth to join a select class tracking toward the papacy. He was privately educated near the Vatican, where his grandfather served as a senior lay official. His father, head of the Bank of Rome, counseled the Vatican on finances, while his brother Francesco was lead negotiator for Pope Pius XI on the Lateran Treaty with Mussolini. The new pope's own priesthood was political, not pastoral; he began it in Vatican diplomatic posts and eventually became Pius XI's secretary of state.

In April 1939, Sapieha went to Rome to greet the new pope and hand him his resignation. But a political crisis was building: Poland had rejected Hitler's demand that it return the port of Gdansk, which Germany had lost in World War I. The Vatican nuncio in Warsaw advised that Sapieha's health was good, so Pius refused his resignation.

At the university, a few blocks from Sapieha's office, Lolek passed his exams; afterward, he danced and drank wine with everyone else at a celebration at the home of a classmate.[7] Since early in the year, he had been participating in Studio 39, a theater group started by an older student. On June 7, after some sixty rehearsals, the group premiered its big show in a courtyard off the university quadrangle. Called *Moon Cavalier*, it was a musical about a comically evil woman who tormented the devil through her management of the zodiac. Lolek played Taurus, the bull.

More important than the show itself were the friendships it established. During rehearsals, the student who played Aquarius, Juliusz Kydrynski, began inviting Lolek to his parents' apartment nearby. Soon he became Lolek's best friend. The Kydrynski family provided the future pope with food and affection, as had the Kotlarczyks in Wadowice. Lolek took a particular liking to Jadwiga Lewaj, a retired French teacher who lived with the Kydrynskis; she began giving him lessons, and in the months that followed, he was frequently seen studying a French book between other activities.

In the audience at *Moon Cavalier* was Juliusz Osterwa, the most famous actor in Poland. He was so enthused by the performance that he invited the cast to his apartment afterward. This was a big thrill for the young actors, especially when Osterwa told Lolek and his friend Kydrynski to stay in touch about possible future projects.

By fall, two student participants in *Moon Cavalier* had lost their lives. May 22, 1939, Mussolini had signed a "Pact of Steel" allying Italy with Germany; the very next day, Hitler had summoned his top generals and told them that war was inevitable. But "war" may be too sporting a term for what Germany did to Poland that year.

That summer, Germany's relentless demands for more territory exposed the shameful miscalculation the British and French had made in sacrificing Czechoslovakia at the Munich Conference the year before. Hitler had not even broken any promises; none had been extracted from him. His generals still said privately that a war would be unwinnable, but his last meaningful political opponents—some high-ranking colleagues planning a coup against him—were silenced by his success.

In early summer 1939, Britain and France discussed an anti-German alliance with Stalin, hoping to discourage Hitler by surrounding him. But Poland's refusal to allow Russian troops on its soil stalled the deal. August 23, 1939, the world was stunned by the announcement instead of a treaty between Stalin and Hitler. The two tyrants had betrayed everyone who still believed in their idealistic pretenses. The shooting gallery was open, and as usual, Poland was the middle duck in the front row; the new treaty called for Germany and the USSR each to get half of the hapless land that lay between them.

Two days later, August 25, England signed a mutual-defense treaty with Poland, evidently not suspecting how quickly events would expose the British government's intent not to honor the treaty.

9

Father Kazimierz Figlewicz—the high-school religion teacher who had heard Lolek's confessions in Wadowice—had been transferred to Krakow in the mid-1930s. "He was the first person I came to see when we moved here," Lolek later told a friend.[1]

September 1, 1939, was the first Friday of the month, Lolek's day to confess to Figlewicz at the Wawel cathedral. Just as they met, they heard the first sounds of German aircraft, the harbinger of seventy-five German divisions, with twenty-four hundred tanks, that were pouring into Poland. Some two thousand German planes bombed Polish cities that day.

"This was . . . the world's first experience of the blitzkrieg: the sudden surprise attack," the American correspondent William L. Shirer later wrote. "The fighter planes and bombers roaring overhead . . . self-propelled, rapid-firing heavy guns rolling forty miles an hour down even the rutty Polish roads . . . the whole vast army of a million and a half men on motorized wheels, directed and coordinated through a maze of electronic communications."[2]

If not for surviving photographs, the Polish army's resistance would be hard to believe: cavalry, on horseback, went out to meet the tanks with sabers and lances! They were slaughtered.

"There was general panic in the staff, and no one to assist in the Mass," Father Figlewicz later recalled. "Karol came. I remember our Mass in the scream of sirens and noise of explosions."[3]

As soon as the Mass was over, Lolek and Figlewicz rushed to a vantage point on the Wawel walls and saw planes bombing communities south of the Vistula, buildings afire and smoke rising. With a hurried good-bye to his confessor, Lolek ran off to find his father.[4]

Juliusz Kydrynski later recalled[5] being on the street with Lolek right after the attack started, moving household goods on handcarts to the homes of friends who lived farther from the town center. They were caught in an air raid on a nearby radio station: "Karol remained calm. Even during the worst explosions we did not exchange a word. Eventually his calmness spread to me."

Word came that German tank divisions were rolling toward Krakow. Lolek and his father decided to leave their home on the Vistula and head east, away from the front. They found the roads jammed with thousands of people carrying what they could on carts or trucks or their backs. The elderly struggled under loads. Peasants led cows. Women pushed prams.

Because Karol senior was weak, Lolek begged a lift partway on a military truck. They survived an attack by low-flying German aircraft that fired machine guns into the ribbon of refugees.[6] Eventually the Wojtylas made it to the San River, more than a hundred miles east, along mostly main roads. There they ran into some ragged Russian soldiers who told them they would probably be safer and certainly more comfortable returning home. So "we returned to Krakow," Lolek later wrote. "My father could not stand such heavy walking. It was a very tiring experience for him."[7]

Jerzy Kluger, Lolek's Jewish friend from Wadowice, also went east with his father that day, seeking their Polish military reserve units, never expecting that the Germans would summarily execute the women they left behind.

Poles often blame Britain and France for not rescuing their country in 1939. "The war could have ended quickly," asserts Wojciech Roszkowski, a leading Polish historian. "Hitler had three-fourths of his forces in Poland. The French outnumbered him on the Rhine four to one. The British had the aircraft. The Russians wouldn't have entered."[8] True or false, Poles were brought up believing this, and it fueled a distrust of the West.

Most Western histories dismiss the possibility of a counterattack then. Winston Churchill's acclaimed account of the war says that by the time troops could have been mustered, German forces would have returned from Poland to repel them. Yet during the Nuremberg war-crimes trials, in 1948, three top German generals testified that Germany had indeed been vulnerable: "If we did not collapse in 1939, that was due only to" British-French inaction, said General Alfred Jodl.[9] Hitler had gambled, in defiance of his generals—and he had won.

September 6, Krakow fell, and the government in Warsaw fled to London. To the shock of many, the primate, Cardinal Hlond, fled with them. "Poland was in a hell of a fix and the leader was outside the country," charges Church historian Father Robert Graham, in Rome. The Vatican ordered Hlond to return, but Germany wouldn't allow it; instead he went to France, where he was arrested and kept in German prisons until American troops freed him in 1945.

September 17, 1939, Stalin saw that Polish resistance had melted and that Hitler's troops were nearing what was to be the Russian half of Poland. He sent the Red Army in to claim his share.

"Now life is waiting in line for bread, scavenging for sugar, and dreaming of coal and books," Lolek wrote Kotlarczyk in a letter someone brought to Wadowice in late September. He said some friends had returned to Krakow after fleeing, but others were still missing. The Germans had allowed a theater to open, and Lolek's group was preparing a play. He had met with a professor he hoped to study with that term.

"We students were so naïve we thought we would be able to complete our studies," Halina says. She arrived from Wadowice on a horsecart with bushels of cabbage and potatoes to pay her room rent, as paper currency was worthless. "On the first day, all the students came to the university, but the Gestapo surrounded it," she recalls. Students were identified and released.

With the university shut, Halina returned to Wadowice, only to find that it was now part of Germany, as was all western Poland up to the Skawa River— the river just east of Wadowice, where Lolek used to swim. The area from there east to the Soviet zone was declared the "General Government," an occupied territory that included Krakow.

October 13, the territory's governor, Hans Frank, a Nazi since 1927, wrote in his journal, "The Poles shall be the slaves of the German Reich." He told a German journalist that he would not replicate the German scare tactic used in Czechoslovakia, where pictures of those who had been shot were publicly posted; he intended, rather, to shoot so many Poles that "there would not be enough forests in Poland with which to make paper for these posters."[10]

Within a year, 1.2 million ethnic Poles and 300,000 Jews had been forcibly relocated from the new German territories to the General Government zone, so as to exterminate them more easily. In the Russian zone, by 1941, another million and a half people had been shipped to camps in Siberia, from which many never returned.[11]

Unable to attend regular classes, students began arranging informal, underground meetings with professors. Lolek planned to start a clandestine linguistics course November 6. When that day came, however, the students received instead what must be among the most ghastly political-science lessons ever taught. A notice had been posted for all professors to meet in the university auditorium. Once they were inside, the Gestapo surrounded the building. The hundreds of professors were herded into waiting vehicles and taken to the Oranienburg and Sachsenhausen concentration camps near Berlin, where half or more died. "Many of them [were] elderly and eminent," Lolek noted later.[12]

"One of the first things the Nazis did in Poland was close humanistic studies," a Vatican spokesman says. "They wanted to destroy the culture."[13] In his next letter to Kotlarczyk, Lolek proposed that after liberation they build "a theater that will be a church where the national spirit will burn." He pledged to be Kotlarczyk's lieutenant, as the apostle John had been Saint Peter's.[14]

As during the occupation of the previous century, the Church elsewhere now seemed to cut Poland adrift in its struggle to survive. German Catholic bishops agreed not merely to support Hitler but to counsel German youths vigorously to overcome their scruples about butchering humanity. All soldiers were ordered to "swear by God this oath: to obey the Führer unconditionally." When some objected, the bishops ruled that the oath was acceptable because Hitler was the constitutional head of state and wasn't ordering anyone to do anything "against the will of God."[15] In Austria, Cardinal Innitzer welcomed the Nazis into his country and urged churchgoers to support them.

The crisis turned Lolek, now nineteen, toward ever more serious, even extravagant, ideas. November 14, 1939, he smuggled, with someone going to

Wadowice, a letter to Kotlarczyk that included pages from a book he was writing—and apparently never finished—about Slavic culture. Good Polish theater
was better than Shakespeare, Lolek wrote, because it was more uplifting and
more spiritual. But he declared that no good Polish plays had been written
since the turn of the century. Restoring great theater would be his life's mission: "I am not a cavalier of the sword, but rather an artist!"

The Germans, though, had other plans. They decreed compulsory work for
all men fourteen through sixty, and most women. Anyone not in an approved
job would be sent to a concentration camp (if the arresting officer was in a
good mood) or shot dead (if he was in a bad one). Lolek took a job as a messenger for a restaurant run by a distant relative of his mother's.

One evening before curfew there was a knock on the Wojtylas' door: Halina.
She had flirted with some German border guards outside Wadowice and persuaded them to let her cross into the General Government zone. Carrying news
and letters, she had hopped a train for Krakow (also illegally) and headed back
to her old room, where she found that her potato-and-cabbage rent was still
valid. She had the required employment certificate, as a seamstress.

Within hours, the old theater gang was reunited, deciding to stage theatrical
performances in defiance of the German ban, using the Kydrynskis' relatively
spacious and sunny corner apartment. Everyone wanted to participate, despite
knowing that a slave camp or even instant death awaited them if they were discovered.

Throughout 1940, Halina regularly made the daring, illegal trip transport-
ing messages from Wadowice to Krakow and back. "It was easier for a girl," she
explains now. She read the letters she carried and began to sense that just as
Lolek had proposed, Kotlarczyk intended to make Lolek his protégé and collaborator in an ambitious plan to restore the Polish theater to greatness once
the Germans were gone.

Although many people had idle time because of the work restrictions and curfews, Lolek had never been busier, he wrote to Kotlarczyk on December 28,
1939. "I surrounded myself with books, fortified myself with Art and Science," he said. He had written a long dramatic poem, "David," the first of a
series he was contemplating based on biblical stories—but recasting the Jewish
king as a Slav for dramatic purposes. It was dedicated to his mother.

"Sometimes I feel terrible pressure, sadness, depression and harm," he
wrote. "But sometimes I see daybreak and great light."

One night that month, the Germans burst into the apartment of Kotlarczyk's brother Tadeusz, pulled him from his terrified wife, and shipped him to

the Mauthausen concentration camp in Austria. His crime: being an intellectual. His arrest should have warned the whole Kotlarczyk family, but they didn't leave. "My parents told me they believed the war would finish in a few weeks," Mieczyslaw's daughter Anna recalls. "Everyone did. The young people never believed the Germans would be there many years."

In February 1940, Archbishop Sapieha informed the Vatican that twenty-six of his priests had been jailed. "An appeal to the Gestapo is impossible. My cathedral has been closed for three months and only twice a week can two priests go in to celebrate holy Mass. The seminary is occupied by the police." Such letters, penned in a tiny hand and carrying no signature, were smuggled to the papal nuncio in Berlin, who was still allowed communications with the Vatican. Sapieha's most frequent courier was his chaplain, who, even when he was once caught and tortured, did not reveal the source of the note he carried.[16] Sapieha himself stayed free because he was related to Italian nobility; Hitler was still patronizing Mussolini.[17]

10

With the end of school, and thus of his affiliation with the ancient Wawel cathedral, Lolek began attending his local parish church of St. Stanislaw Kostka, a modern masonry building just a few blocks from his home. He and some other youths so enjoyed a prayer retreat there that they asked for more meetings. The young priest, though, was overwhelmed filling in for other parish priests who had been sent to concentration camps. Unable to find time for Lolek and his friends (soon he, too, would lose his life to the occupiers), he asked a uniquely spiritual layman from the parish to lead a weekly youth group.

And that is how Lolek met Jan Tyranowski. At forty, Tyranowski looked like a Nordic Christ with his fair hair, boyish radiance, and piercing eyes. A lifelong bachelor, trained as an accountant but now working as a tailor, Tyranowski lived with his mother, countless books, and three sewing machines in an apartment just across a market square from the Wojtylas. A photograph shows him propped in bed, dressed in white between perfectly pressed lace sheets, his hair long and wavy, his face impassive, as if in a coffin. But his eyes burn right off the paper and into the memory.

Beginning February 20, 1940, Tyranowski met weekly at the church with Lolek and two dozen other youths. He called the group the Living Rosary, invited them to his home, and tried to apply his teaching to every moment of their lives. It wasn't the theological facts of religion that he talked about but

rather the mystical experience of it. He meditated for four hours every morning and occasionally during the day. Sometimes he appeared lost in a spiritual
state while present at worldly activities (something that would later be said of
the grown-up Lolek). He stressed the power of will and feeling over intellect.[1]
At first, Lolek resisted him.

"What he tried to teach us was new," Lolek later recalled.

> He wanted to pull new listeners to this new life. Young people
> think they know everything. . . . They ask themselves, "What does
> this man want from me?" At the beginning, they just couldn't
> understand him—the truth about a . . . wholly internal life that was
> part of Jan, and for them, completely unknown.

Eventually, Lolek went with Tyranowski to his apartment and there received
his first book of writings by Saint John of the Cross (1542–1591), a Spanish
priest, poet, and essayist. For Lolek, it was literary love at first sight. The writing of Saint John not only illuminated the enigmatic Tyranowski, it also told
Lolek much about his own hidden feelings, which had often separated him from
others.

Saint John, born Juan de Yepes, gave up normal ministry work in a diocese
in order to join the Carmelite order of priests and nuns. The religious orders
(we will meet many in our story) date from near the beginning of this millennium; originally, they were groups of priests and nuns who received papal
approval to remove themselves from normal life and to search, hermitlike, for a
better understanding of the universe. Each order had its own administrative
structure, which overlapped the Church's regular geographical command lines.
The leader still reported to the pope (now through a special department at the
Vatican), but priests in the orders weren't (and aren't) subject to the bishop and
archbishop in their geographic area.

By the early Renaissance, new orders had sprung up to specialize in some
particular human problem (education, the poor, etc.). Most prominent were
the Franciscans, the Dominicans, the Augustinians (all named for various
saints), the Carmelites (named for a mountain in Israel), and, from 1534, the
Jesuits. Each originated with a distinguishing mission, but today membership
in the orders comes largely through personal networking, and their pursuits
overlap so much that the original distinctions can be misleading.

By age twenty-five, Juan (John) de Yepes was fixated on philosophy and
planning to leave the Carmelites for an older, more strictly contemplative order.
Then he met a Spanish Carmelite nun, Teresa of Avila (now Saint Teresa), who

was establishing a new branch of Carmelite nuns that would combine contemplation with human service. She needed priests to perform Mass, confession, and so on. De Yepes fit right into her band of ascetics. Since shoes were among the earthly goods they had pledged to surrender, they became known as the shoeless (or, in a biblical word, "discalced") Carmelites.

Then, as now, local bishops often resented the independence of the religious orders. Spanish bishops persuaded Pope Pius V that de Yepes's Carmelites had abused their autonomy and should be repressed. Much of Saint John's writing was done in jail, under the lash.

Probably his most definitive work, which Lolek surely read early, is *The Ascent of Mount Carmel*, with Mount Carmel defined as "the perfect spirit." To attain the perfect spirit, Saint John said, you must give up two things: everything you know and everything you want. "Only those who set aside their own knowledge and walk in God's service like unlearned children receive wisdom from God," he wrote. "To reach union with the wisdom of God, a person must advance by unknowing rather than by knowing."[2] (There is a definite overlap between Saint John's spiritualism and Zen Buddhism.)

He said, "They are indeed ignorant who think it is possible to reach this high state of union with God without first emptying their appetite of all . . . things that can be a hindrance to them." He listed some particular hindrances: "possessions, joy, knowledge, consolation, [and] rest. . . . Until the appetites are eliminated, one will not arrive, no matter how much virtue one practices. For one will fail to acquire perfect virtue, which lies in keeping the soul empty, naked, and purified of every appetite." He quoted the Gospel of Luke: "The one who does not renounce all possessions cannot be my disciple."[3]

Saint John of the Cross repeatedly stressed that one must not just leave one's physical possessions temporarily but must genuinely forsake them permanently. While the description would be incomplete, you could accurately say that Saint John urged the rejection of everything that capitalism needs in order to function. And more than just writing this, Juan de Yepes lived it.

So, too, in the context of 1940 Krakow, did Jan Tyranowski. When Lolek finally came around to accepting this new mentor, he decided that Tyranowski was

> one of those unknown saints, hidden amid the others like a marvelous light at the bottom of life, at a depth where night usually reigns. He disclosed to me the riches of his inner life, of his mystical life. In his words, in his spirituality, and in the example of a life

given to God alone, he represented a new world that I did not yet know. I saw the beauty of the soul opened up by grace.

Still, he added, "I was not yet thinking of the priesthood."[4]

One day Lolek walked into Tyranowski's apartment and met a neighbor he did not know: Mieczyslaw Malinski.

Just seventeen, Malinski had resisted Tyranowski at first. He figured the long-haired stranger in the black coat who approached him outside the church was either a recruiter for underground commandos or a spy from the Gestapo; either way, he wasn't interested. Speaking in a "characteristically high-pitched voice, almost a falsetto," the stranger "asked me to accompany him home," Malinski says. "I kept asking what he wanted. He said, 'I have been watching you for some time. I would like to invite you to join the Living Rosary.'"

Malinski finally accepted Tyranowski's offer to lend him some books from his apartment. Scarcely had Malinski entered than in popped Lolek—a "somewhat stooped" figure, Malinski recalls, describing the characteristic posture that has often been blamed on a truck accident, which in fact happened later (thus suggesting that Lolek came by the stoop naturally).

What struck Malinski most, however, was Lolek's clear voice and enunciation. When they were back on the street, he asked about it. Immediately, he says, Lolek began explaining a theory of theater that he was promoting in readings at the Kydrynski apartment. "The main idea," Lolek said, "is to pronounce every vowel and every word with the greatest possible precision, not slurring or swallowing anything, but at the same time not exaggerating, so that the effect is attractive and natural . . . giving full weight to the punctuation . . . so as to convey everything that the text contains."

Where had Lolek got all this? Malinski inquired politely. "From Mieczyslaw Kotlarczyk," Lolek said, "the Master of the Word."

To Malinski, it sounded a bit pompous. Still, he began joining Lolek for early-morning prayer at the unheated Stanislaw Kostka church, even when temperatures outside dropped as low as thirty-three below zero (Fahrenheit). Malinski also attended Tyranowski's "Living Rosary" meetings, though maintaining his reserve. It was a world "of thorough discipline and self-control," he says today. "Every moment of the day was organized for activity or relaxation." Notebooks were to be kept as a record of each day's prayers, homework, and thoughts.

As Tyranowski moved into theology, "I came to enjoy our meetings less and less," Malinski says. "There was something bossy about his manner, and I kept wondering what he really wanted of me." Finally, Malinski confessed his misgivings to Lolek and also mentioned rumors that Tyranowski had been mentally ill.

Lolek replied that Tyranowski had "undergone a major conversion. He doesn't like talking about it or about himself. Look at what is inside him, not his outward appearance. Yes, his language is formal and old-fashioned, but you mustn't mind that. He really is a person who lives close to God."[5]

So Malinski agreed to read Saint John of the Cross, listen more to Tyranowski, and think. Today, Malinski—*Father* Malinski—is more comfortable with Tyranowski's teaching: "It followed a coherent plan. He took us through each stage calmly and methodically until we reached the essential core of his teaching—what he called the plenitude of inner life. What I call fellowship with God. His influence with Lolek was gigantic. I can safely say that if it wasn't for him, neither Wojtyla nor I would have become priests."

11

March 5, 1940, Joseph Stalin delivered orders to the Soviet top leadership assembled in Moscow that shook the souls of war-seasoned generals and communist revolutionaries.

In their invasion and occupation of eastern Poland, the Soviets had rounded up 25,700 Polish military officers, landowners, officials, factory owners, clergymen, and policemen. Now Stalin wanted them all removed from jails and camps and brought to Katyn, a forest area outside Smolensk, Russia, near the Belorus border. There they were all to be "executed by firing squad."

There are convincing reports that many in the room gagged at Stalin's orders. But no one wanted to join the execution list by objecting. The Katyn massacre was completed within weeks. Almost an entire generation of Polish leaders was wiped out. After the war, Stalin blamed it on the Germans.

Lolek and Kydrynski finally got invited back to the apartment of Juliusz Osterwa, the great actor.[1] With the theaters closed, Osterwa had free time and soon the young men were visiting him almost weekly. Lolek gave him a play of Kotlarczyk's to read, and he praised it—prompting an immediate letter from Lolek to Kotlarczyk, expressing abject awe for both him and Osterwa. Lolek compared Kotlarczyk's letters to "Holy Scripture" and "Greek tragedy." He followed his own retelling of the David story from the Bible with a longer poem-play expressly equating the tale of Job to the German occupation of Poland.

Although this work was never produced (his friends didn't like it, he wrote), the comparison it drew was all too true. With the Gestapo tightening its checks for German-approved work certificates, Lolek was going to have to do more than merely run messages for his relative's restaurant. His friends needed approved jobs, too. A solution came from Wojciech Zukrowski, the disappointed law student and neighbor of Lolek's. Zukrowski's grandfather, a physician, cared for the staff at a large sodium quarry south of Krakow. When Zukrowski learned that German-approved work was available there, he signed up and got similar jobs for Lolek, Kydrynski, and Tadeusz Kwiatkowski (a fellow member of their theater group from its beginning).[2]

A three-mile walk from the Wojtyla apartment, the quarry is perhaps a mile across, with cliffs dropping hundreds of feet to the quarry floor (which is now flooded). Standing on its lip feels almost like being on the edge of the Grand Canyon. Just getting to the work floor must have consumed immense time and energy. Lolek's job was loading heavy stones—chunks of huge rock broken up by others—onto rail cars and helping to maintain the cars.

Zukrowski worked with dynamite, which blasted the rocks free. Apparently no one thought to ask why young Zukrowski was so interested in explosives: in fact, in December 1939, he had joined the so-called Home Army, a secret guerrilla force that harassed the Germans throughout the war and helped speed their defeat. Acquaintances from his prewar army training had recruited him and now taught him how to smuggle dynamite to them.

Blithely unaware, Lolek helped Zukrowski carry dynamite boxes.[3] When Zukrowski had drilled holes in the rock, Lolek would leave his other work to help pack the dynamite into the holes with a long rod.

"Every week I was able to sneak out a stick of dynamite in such a way as Karol didn't know about it," Zukrowski says. He would cull out one stick, bite off the fuse, and suck the butterlike explosive mixture into his mouth. Within minutes, he says, he would spit it into the wrappings from his breakfast and put it in his pack or his shoe. Without a detonator, he says, there was no danger the dynamite would explode (though the practice probably would not be recommended by the American Dental Association).

Why didn't he bring Lolek into the plot? "In a conspiracy it's better not to inform anyone," Zukrowski says. "And I enjoyed risky situations. Lolek wasn't that way. It was enough [for him] being in the underground theater. It would have been a shame if anything happened to him." Instead, Zukrowski says, he spent his time with Lolek introducing him to some French novelists (Malraux and Mauriac) and also Paul Claudel, a Catholic mystical poet whose work Zukrowski says Lolek dug into and, in his own writing, imitated.

In early May 1940, Governor Frank called in his police commanders to relay orders he had just received from Hitler: "The men capable of leadership in Poland must be liquidated. Those following them . . . must be eliminated in their turn. There is no need to burden the Reich with this." Everyone understood this to mean that the targets were to be murdered in Poland. In his diary (produced at the Nuremberg war trials, along with the orders), Frank boasted that thousands of Polish intellectuals, men and women, had already been murdered under his leadership.

May 10, 1940, Hitler unleashed his forces on France, Belgium, and the Netherlands. Five days later, Churchill, whose British troops were on the Continent to help defend it, was shocked to learn that the tide of battle was overwhelmingly German, though the two sides were roughly equal in troops and equipment. Even after Poland was conquered—and by then, Norway and Denmark as well—the West still didn't comprehend the effectiveness of the blitzkrieg.

June 10, 1940, Mussolini, hearing how easy the Germans were having it, joined them in declaring war on France. The papal envoy to Turkey—who would later become Pope John XXIII—wrote to his sister, "Look at the war from Italy's point of view. It was the work of providence, and we really must thank Mussolini as its instrument. . . . Would to God that England would understand that peace now would be to its advantage."[4]

Four days later, June 14, Danuta Michalowska, a high-school student and aspiring actress, wandered the streets of Krakow with a girlfriend,[5] weeping openly. "German loudspeakers were booming all over town," she says. "Paris had fallen. Everyone had believed a French offensive would end the war. The fall of France was, like, to shatter all hopes." A friend suggested that she join the underground theater. She had met Kydrynski before and at his home recognized Lolek from a poetry reading she had attended.

Within weeks, Lolek, Danuta, and Kydrynski were rehearsing a drama that Juliusz Osterwa had starred in before the war—and what was more, Osterwa was directing them! The excitement of working with a popular star ("All young girls were in love with Osterwa," Danuta says) electrified everyone. Two hours of rehearsal were sandwiched nightly between work and curfew. Upon learning that Osterwa was retranslating such classics as *Antigone* and *Hamlet* because the existing translations "put you to sleep," Lolek himself began translating *Oedipus Rex* into Polish.[6] (Osterwa ultimately rejected his rendition as untheatrical.)

For the Osterwa play and others that followed, audiences had to come and go in ones and twos over a staggered period to avoid drawing attention. Only about thirty people could squeeze in for each performance. Once when the chairs were set up a few hours ahead of time, the Gestapo stormed into the building, terrifying Kydrynski's mother while the boys were at the quarry. The Gestapo carted off a neighbor they had come for, then noticed the suspicious arrangement and began questioning Mrs. Kydrynska, who managed to persuade them that the furniture had been moved for housecleaning.[7]

Osterwa seemed to lose interest in the group after it performed his play, but Lolek wrote to Kotlarczyk that he didn't much care:

> His [artistic] influence on us is not as big as it used to be. Basically, I am more attached to people with a secret, great interior. It doesn't mean that the director [Osterwa] is not such a man, but I have had a bit enough of celebrities, maybe because we cannot talk on the same level.

Lolek's growing love for Mrs. Lewaj, the French teacher, seemed to fulfill a need in him. "In her, I can feel maternity," he wrote. As for the quarry job, "When you work, the time runs very fast. A man becomes more a man."

Then word came from Wadowice that Tadeusz Kotlarczyk would be coming home from the concentration camp where he had been interned; he had lost his leg in a rockslide while working at a quarry. His wife met the assigned train with a horsecart, only to learn that he had died en route. Janina and another brother fled to a mountain village. Halina once more risked her life to bring the news to Lolek and others in Krakow. Lolek wrote back to Kotlarczyk,

> Can the pain that is inside you create a new word? Can it be the foundation for a new building? Can you build a new life on it? I believe yes. I believe a tidal wave hits the shore to leave its mark. A tidal wave is a creative power.

Exactly when Lolek wrote his poem "The Quarry" is not certain. The thoughts behind it surely took shape at this time, even though its style seems more mature than his other 1940 work. It was first published in 1957, during a brief thaw in communist censorship. The poem reveals much about not only his life at age twenty but his continued thoughts concerning human labor. Parts of the poem also capture the feeling of secrets shared by a subjugated community—feelings Lolek would still be dealing with long after the Germans had been replaced by Russians.

> Listen: the even knocking of hammers,
> so much their own
> I project onto the people
> to test the strength of each blow.
> Listen now: electric current
> cuts through a river of rock.
> And a thought grows in me day after day:
> the greatness of work is inside man.
>
> Hard and cracked
> his hand is differently charged
> by the hammer
> and thought differently unravels in stone
> as human energy splits from the strength of stone
> cutting the bloodstream, an artery
> in the right place.
>
> Look, how love feeds
> on this well-grounded anger
> which flows into people's breath
> as a river bent by the wind,
> and which is never spoken, but just breaks high vocal cords.
>
> Passersby scuttle off into doorways,
> someone whispers: "Yet here is a great force."
>
> . . . Bound are the blocks of stone, the low-voltage wire
> cuts deep in their flesh, an invisible whip—
> stones know this violence.
> When an elusive blast rips their ripe compactness
> and tears them from their eternal simplicity,
> the stones know this violence.
> Yet can the current unbind their full strength?
> It is he who carries that strength in his hands:
> the worker.

Hands are the heart's landscape. They split sometimes
like ravines into which an undefined force rolls.
The very same hands which man only opens
when his palms have had their fill of toil.
Now he sees: because of him alone others can walk in peace.

Hands are a landscape. When they split, the pain of their
     sores
surges free as a stream.
But no thought of pain—
no grandeur in pain alone.
For his own grandeur he does not know how to name.

No, not just hands drooping with the hammer's weight,
not the taut torso, muscles shaping their own style,
but thought informing his work,
deep, knotted in wrinkles on his brow,
and over his head, joined in a sharp arc, shoulders and veins
     vaulted.

So for a moment he is a Gothic building
cut by a vertical thought born in the eyes.
No, not a profile alone,
not a mere figure between God and the stone,
sentenced to grandeur and error.

Work starts within . . .
. . . With work then it begins: the growing in the heart and
     mind,
great events, a multitude of men are drawn in.
Listen to love that ripens in hammers, in even sounds.
Children will carry them into the future, singing. . . .

This inspiration will not end with hands.
. . . In man grows the equilibrium
which love learns through anger.

Neither is ever exhausted in man,
ever ceases in the shoulders' tension

in the heart's hidden gesture.
They partake of each other, fulfilling each other,
raised by a lever which joins movement and thought
in an unbreakable circle.

If from afar you want to enter and stay in man
you must merge these two forces into a language
simple beyond words
your speech must not break at the lever's tension:
the fulcrum of anger and love. . . .[8]

12

The Wojtylas spent Christmas Eve 1940 at the Kydrynskis'.

"The father didn't feel well or hear well," Maria Kydrynska[1] recalls. At sixty-one, Karol senior no longer cooked, so on Lolek's work days, Maria would bring him a pot of her mother's afternoon meal, walking more than a mile in any weather and reheating the food at the Wojtyla apartment. It was a miserable winter. Juliusz Kydrynski and Lolek walked to the quarry at seven in the morning, their faces smeared "with a thick layer of Vaseline" to protect them from the thirty-below-zero cold.[2]

The underground university persisted, though few professors remained free. Halina moved to Krakow for good and enrolled in a secret *"complet"* of seven students. Lolek and Kydrynski were in another *complet*. Classes and discussion groups moved among apartments, security tight. The price of knowledge could at any moment be death. Halina took double risks, teaching in an underground high school to earn her room and board from the families of her students. "I lived very cheap and very cold," she remembers—as did they all.

Various romantic liaisons struck up as the circle of friends sought refuge from the oppression. Here again, Lolek seems to have been the odd man out. In one letter to Kotlarczyk he complained that he wanted to read his poetry to Halina, "but I don't think I can because she is in a hurry all the time."

"When I was having love problems," Danuta recalls, "I thought if [Lolek were] a priest I would go and confess to him. People looked at him in a more spiritual way. Even when we discussed a play, he would focus on the spiritual aspect. What he was feeling inside, who knows. But he didn't show anything."

❧

Karol senior was mostly bedridden that harsh winter. February 18, 1941, Lolek ran out to a public health center for his father's medicine, then stopped at the Kydrynskis' to pick up dinner for the two of them. The family persuaded him to stay and eat with them. Afterward, he and Maria walked back over the Vistula bridge to the Wojtylas' basement apartment, carrying a soup of dried fruit and ground-meat patties for his father.

They found him sprawled on the bed, dead, his legs over the edge, as if he had been trying to get up when a stroke or heart attack felled him.

Maria says Lolek embraced her and, in full composure, said, "I was not at the deathbed of my mother, my brother, or my father."

"Just run to get the priest," Maria replied.

She waited outside. When Lolek came with the priest from St. Stanislaw Kostka, she dashed home to get her brother. Juliusz Kydrynski stayed through the day and night with Lolek. "They prayed together and stayed up all night talking about life and death," Maria recalls, but she says her brother never shared the substance of that conversation with her.[3]

The next day, Mieczyslaw Malinski, the young fellow student of Tyranowski's, ran into Lolek on the street. Still shaken over being gone when his father died, Lolek told him, "I had just gone shopping. . . . He was quite all right. When I got back, it was all over."

That same day, Mrs. Kydrynska—whom Lolek addressed as "Mother"—persuaded Lolek to move in with her family. "The fact that he was left alone, without parents, was as if his destiny," Maria Kydrynska says. "He was without obligations, without a family." The uncle and aunts living on the floors above him were apparently little more than strangers to him.

"At twenty, I had already lost all the people I loved," he later said.[4] "God was in a way preparing me for what would happen. My father was the person who explained to me the mystery of God and made me understand. Even now, when I awake at night, I remember seeing my father kneeling, praying."[5]

As soon as he moved in with the Kydrynskis, Lolek found a church across the street. Each morning he would run across to pray, then return for Juliusz, to go to the quarry together.[6] Juliusz also brought Lolek to see his former schoolteacher Irena Szkocka, an elderly widow with a bright apartment along the Vistula, who turned out to be devoted to the theater. Soon Lolek brought Malinski to see her, saying that he looked upon Mrs. Szkocka "practically as my grandmother." Kydrynski didn't realize how much he was giving away when he gave Lolek a new maternal figure.

∽

In June 1941, Hitler turned on Stalin. German troops swept across the Soviet zone of Poland, swallowed it into the General Government, then headed into the Soviet homeland.

Kotlarczyk and his wife finally moved to Krakow, as Lolek had been urging for months. Besides the danger of being among the last Polish intellectuals in Wadowice, they were caring for an infant niece, one of whose parents was in a concentration camp, the other in the underground. With Lolek at the Kydrynskis', the Kotlarczyks moved with the baby into the vacant Vistula apartment.

"From the moment Wojtyla and Kotlarczyk were together," Halina says, "the birth of the Rhapsody Theater"—their company—"was inevitable." Lolek's friends, however, did not share his joy at Kotlarczyk's passionate and dogmatic view of the theater.

"When Kotlarczyk came, everything became political," Danuta recalls. "Kydrynski and Kotlarczyk couldn't be in the same room together. Kotlarczyk had very defined politics"—tied to 1930s nationalists who favored a big Church role in government. Kydrynski, on the other hand, was a liberal who opposed civil power for the clergy. More ominous, Kotlarczyk had arrived to seize charge of a group of actors that Kydrynski had helped assemble—yet Kotlarczyk rejected the human dramas (like the Osterwa play) that most appealed to Kydrynski. Kotlarczyk wanted to stage exclusively highbrow, intellectual work. "For Lolek it didn't matter. He could be close to both," Danuta says. But he was the only one.

This crisis revealed a lifelong trait of the man who would be pope: he focused on universal themes that could carry mankind from one century to the next, while sometimes overlooking practical problems that stopped individuals from getting from Monday to Tuesday. Sometimes this enabled him to build bridges, but at other times it rendered him blind to chasms. Both Kotlarczyk and Kydrynski were smart, creative, idealistic, and brave. Both wanted to expel the Germans, nurture Polish culture, and pack audiences into theaters. And Lolek *liked* them both. So whatever divided them seemed unimportant—to him.

Kydrynski attended one session with Kotlarczyk, then dropped out of the Rhapsody Theater. For many, the conflict was bitter. Danuta says she and Kydrynski didn't speak for twenty years. Lolek moved back to the Vistula with the Kotlarczyks, but he, Halina, and one or two others continued to dine weekly at the Kydrynskis' in an effort to maintain their friendship. The theatrical split, however, was irreparable.

With the loss of Kydrynski, the group also lost its theater—his apartment. But it was soon replaced by the big apartment of Irena Szkocka, the widow Kydrynski had introduced Lolek to. Now that he was no longer living with Mrs. Lewaj, the French teacher who boarded at the Kydrynskis', Lolek had latched on to Mrs. Szkocka, and even called her Grandma. He had been adopted again: the Szkocka family quickly slipped into the personal and professional place in Lolek's life formerly held by the Kydrynski family, and before it the Kotlarczyks.

Mrs. Szkocka made tea and cakes for Rhapsody Theater audiences; her son-in-law, a musician, supplied music where appropriate. As the players rehearsed and performed, loudspeakers outside announced the names of those who had just been executed for offenses less serious than the one the theater troupe was committing.

For their premier production, November 1, 1941, Kotlarczyk chose a classic play[7] about the martyrdom of Saint Stanislaw, an eleventh-century archbishop of Krakow (not to be confused with Saint Stanislaw Kostka). Under the Germans, and then the Soviets, Stanislaw seemed to symbolize the moral power of the Polish Church against tyranny; Lolek would evoke Stanislaw's image during his papal inaugural address.

Onstage, Lolek played the tyrannical King Boleslaw, who kills Stanislaw for opposing him. Yet Lolek changed the style of the role: instead of playing it with the usual villainous flair, he made the king quietly introspective. When his colleagues—except Kotlarczyk—protested, he told them, "I wanted to perform it as if he were in front of his priest after many years, confessing his sin."[8]

As much as Lolek's poetry idealized quarry work, another winter of it was an awful thought. After Kwiatkowski and Kydrynski found indoor jobs, Mrs. Lewaj, the French teacher, used a personal connection to get Lolek transferred to the factory that processed the sodium from the quarry. The chance to work indoors was well worth the extra two miles' walk each way.

The factory was known as the Solvay Works, after Ernest Solvay, a Belgian chemist (1838–1922) who invented ways to process sodium. Lolek's job was to soften the mineral content of the plant's incoming water. Balancing two buckets at a time on a stick across his shoulders, he carried chemicals from storage bins a hundred yards away into the building and up a flight of stairs to the boiler.

Recollections by his fellow workers were compiled for a tribute to him in 1966.[9] They had been puzzled that "a student like him" was there at all. "Wojtyla did his job well," one man recalled, "but whenever he had any free time in the afternoon he would stick his nose in a book. He always carried books around. I once said to Krauze, the foreman, 'I wonder what it's all for.' Krauze said, 'Well, let him go on studying if he's got time.' "

Wladyslaw Cieluch, who shared the night shift, saw Lolek kneel every midnight on the factory floor "and say his prayers. Not all the other workers took kindly to this. Some used to tease him by throwing things, bits of tow and so on." When the noon church bells rang, daytime workers saw the future pope drop the buckets he was carrying, cross himself, and pray. "Then he went on with his work, not embarrassed in the least," one said.

"He wore coarse, shabby clothes," said a stoker, "a waterproof jacket, short drill trousers, and wooden clogs over his bare feet." A kitchen worker felt so sorry for him that she consulted a female manager, who said he was an orphan; together they decided to secretly increase his four-ounce ration of bread during the daily food break—"his only meal," the worker explained.

Once, some colleagues "tried to introduce him to a girl," but, one recalled, "he wasn't having any. He didn't make a fuss, just ignored the subject. I asked him if he meant to be a priest, but he wouldn't admit to that, either." He talked little about anything.

In the fall of 1941, Halina says Lolek dropped out of the underground university, where she and Danuta were still students. Time was tight, and Tyranowski had given him what he thought was an adequate reading list. He kept his life compartmentalized: his theater friends never met Tyranowski and only rarely saw Malinski.

The Tyranowski group had expanded. Each of fifteen original members now headed another group of fifteen, and the strongest leaders from these secondary groups were chosen to lead still other groups. The Home Army tried to recruit them and called them cowards for not joining. But Tyranowski taught action through prayer and self-discipline, and admonished his followers against using violence.[10]

"When I left for school in the morning and my brothers and sisters went off to work, we never knew whether we would see one another at supper," Malinski says. "Police roundups, deportation, death by shooting in the street—all these were part of daily life. Any night, the Gestapo might batter down the door and drag one off. Shots were frequently heard. The whole town was in a state of constant terror. Hatred toward the German enemy became more and more intense. Members of the resistance movement would come by at night and execute death sentences on informers and traitors."

December 7, 1941, Japan bombed Pearl Harbor, bringing the United States into the war.

Soon afterward, the Gestapo swooped down on a Krakow café favored by intellectuals, arrested two hundred people, and sped them to Auschwitz. One of those interned was Juliusz Kydrynski. A distant relative in the Austrian officer corps somehow got him out; two months later, those arrested with him were shot, their only crime having been conversation over coffee. Kydrynski wrote about the experience in an underground magazine that Zukrowski and Kwiatkowski put out.

"Lolek could have been scooped up similarly," Zukrowski says. "He was just lucky."

The opening lines of the Gospel of Saint John say, "In the beginning was the Word, and the Word was with God, and the Word was God." Mieczyslaw Kotlarczyk called his new theater style the Theater of the Word. One objective was to keep alive the work of the great Polish patriotic poets of partition times, like Norwid and Mickiewicz. Further to stress the importance of "The Word," the sets were spare, sometimes just a piano and a candelabra. For costumes, the cast wore black. Performances were reduced almost to readings.

At first, during postperformance discussions, some in the audience objected to the Kotlarczyk style. They were put in their place in September 1942, however, when the famous actor Juliusz Osterwa showed up for a Norwid drama and vigorously defended Kotlarczyk's approach. Only one other underground theater operated steadily in Krakow during the war; the two groups enjoyed roughly equal attendance and esteem.

Through the war, Lolek's troupe prepared ten plays (though three were canceled after security threats) and some readings. All were Kotlarczyk's choices, but at Lolek's suggestion Saint John of the Cross entered the repertoire. Jerzy Turowicz, who would later edit the weekly newspaper *Tygodnik Powszechny*, attended the Rhapsodic Theater as a youth in wartime and says, "I think it was the general opinion that Wojtyla was the best actor in the small group."

During a memorable performance of Mickiewicz's epic "Pan Tadeusz," probably Poland's best-known poem, German loudspeakers interrupted from the street to announce a victory in the Soviet campaign. Just as they passed, it came Lolek's turn to speak the words of Mickiewicz's dying hero. Witnesses say he carried it off without losing a word.

One work the group presented, written in 1849 by Juliusz Slowacki, was prophetic, to say the least:

> *The harbinger of Slavic hopes fulfilled—*
> *The Papal Throne!*
> *This Pope will not—Italian-like—take fright*
> *At saber-thrust*

But brave as God himself, stand and give fight. . . .
Now he approaches, he whose hand constrains
Globe-spanning forces:
He whose word turns back along our veins
The blood that courses. . . .

Our Slavic Pope, brother to all mankind,
Is there to lead![11]

13

The first week of November 1942, Lolek asked Malinski to accompany him to the priests' residence opposite the Wawel cathedral for his monthly confession to Father Figlewicz. The priest poured Malinski tea, then disappeared with Lolek—still in his blue factory overalls—as was their usual practice. But on this occasion they did not soon return. Malinski grew nervous.

When they finally came out, they parted wordlessly. Lolek and Malinski walked across the bridge toward the Debnicki section where they lived, still in silence. At last, Lolek said, "I've decided to become a priest. That's what I was talking to him about." Figlewicz had taken him immediately to see Archbishop Sapieha, who interviewed Lolek and accepted him.

Malinski knew he and Lolek could say no more, either to each other or to anyone else. No seminary was authorized, and attendees faced execution if discovered. Lolek had wanted to let Malinski in on his secret, but apparently no one else knew, except the churchmen involved in the underground training.

As pope, Lolek recalled:

> I felt that I cannot be other, cannot realize myself and my mission in life, only as being [a] priest. . . . It was the time of the war, the great suffering of the whole people. It may be that influenced [my decision]. . . . The direct examples of priests I met—I'm very grateful to all of them. . . . But the acting person in this process is the Holy Spirit.[1]

In a 1979 interview, he said,

> After my father's death, I gradually became aware of my true path. I was working at the factory and devoting myself, as far as the ter-

rors of the occupation allowed, to my taste for literature and drama. My priestly vocation took shape in the midst of all that, like an inner fact of . . . absolute clarity. . . . In the autumn [of 1942], I knew that I was called. I could see clearly what I had to give up, and the goal that I had to attain, without a backward glance.[2]

Bishop W. Thomas Larkin of St. Petersburg, Florida, a housemate. of Lolek's at graduate school in Rome, recalls his saying that "he was very happy in the university [in Krakow], and was going to study seriously for a diploma in drama. When Hitler attacked, things changed. His vocation was born during that time of occupation."

No one thing can account for such a momentous decision, but it is safe to say—as the pope himself almost acknowledges—that if Germany hadn't tyrannized Poland, he probably would never have become a priest, let alone pope. He had committed great emotional and physical resources to an acting career. But that career was being suffocated. His listeners, after playing hide-and-seek with the Gestapo, were hardly more than visited most priests on a weekday.

He could pretend he was continuing his university studies by taking underground courses—ducking through alleyways to somebody's apartment to meet a teacher who wasn't important enough to be arrested—but to what end? He learned more from Jan Tyranowski and his library of mystical Christian writers than he did from make-believe academic classes.

And civil life showed no promise of improving. The autumn of 1942 was the pit of pessimism: France was comatose, England lay exposed before Hitler's hungry glare, the United States was preparing for a possible Japanese invasion of its Pacific coast, and the German war machine was engulfing the Soviet Union and its vast resources.

In a few months the defenders of Stalingrad would turn the tide by punching the surprised Führer's first round-trip ticket. But when Wojtyla went to see Sapieha, there seemed no reason to believe that Poland could be freed in the foreseeable future.

Ironically, Wojtyla may be the most spiritual and holy man to occupy the papacy in modern times. But it was politicians who thrust him into the priesthood, politicians who pushed him into high church office, and, most of all, it would be politicians who would reel from the impact of his papacy.

Not letting on that anything had changed, Lolek starred in a flurry of Rhapsody Theater productions that winter of 1942–43. Privately, though, his thoughts were elsewhere. During a four-hundredth-anniversary observance of the birth of John of the Cross, Lolek had a talk with Father Jozef Prus, a Carmelite who visited the archbishop's palace. Confiding his love for John's writing, Lolek said he hoped to enter a Carmelite convent after his seminary work, and there to live a holy, contemplative life.[3]

Kotlarczyk's wife remarked on Lolek's strange behavior at the Vistula apartment. "He used to pray a tremendous lot," she told Malinski. "I used to find him sleeping on bare floors. Every week he would go to visit his father's grave at Rakowicki cemetery. He always kept aloof from girls. There was a [female] relative of ours who stayed in the house for some time. He once said, 'She keeps eyeing me. I wish you'd say something to her, it makes me feel awkward.' "

The most outward sign of Lolek's new dedication was the reading matter he took with him to work at the Solvay factory. Gone—for now—was the mysticism of Tyranowski; instead, his seminary teachers had assigned him metaphysics. It was, he later said, "an intellectual conversion."[4] The toughest hurdle was *Ontology or Metaphysics*, a 1926 text by Father Kazimierz Wais (1865–1934).

"It's hard going," he complained to Malinski that winter. "I sit by the boiler and try to understand it." Many years later, he would confess:

> For a long time I couldn't cope with the book, and I actually wept over it. My literary training centered around the humanities [and] had not prepared me at all for the scholastic theses and formulas. I had to cut a path through a thick undergrowth of concepts, without even being able to identify the ground over which I was moving. It was not until two months later, in December and January [1942–43], that I began to make something of it. After hacking through this vegetation, I came to a clearing, to the discovery of the deep reasons for what until then I had only lived and felt. But in the end it opened a whole new world to me. It showed me a new approach to reality, and made me aware of questions that I had only dimly perceived. This discovery has remained the basis of my intellectual structure. So it all really began with the book of Wais.[5]

Six other secret seminarians were undergoing this agony along with him. Most lived in the countryside and served as aides to parish priests. Only Lolek had a civilian job.

After the run of a Slowacki play that spring,[6] he finally told Kotlarczyk, "Please don't cast me anymore. I'm going to be a priest."

"It was some kind of shock for the group, even though he obviously was very religious and didn't hide it," Halina says.

The director was most shocked of all. "Kotlarczyk tried for days to dissuade him," Danuta remembers. "Kotlarczyk was a theater fanatic. He believed that the theater was the most important thing in the world. He said one's duty to God and country could best be fulfilled through the theater."

The argument didn't work. The group finally decided that Juliusz Kudlinski, the founder of the acting troupe at the university, whom Lolek respected, would stay through curfew for an all-night talk—a last-ditch effort to preserve Lolek's theatrical career. Kotlarczyk no doubt hovered by the door that they shut behind them.

Stories were long told about that night. "God gives talents to people, and if you have talent you should also use it," Kudlinski argued. "In the Bible there is a story of two people with equal talents. One couldn't multiply his talent. The other did, and was praised by God. The message is, you must multiply the talent given by God." The Bible story failed to convince Lolek, so Kudlinski quoted Norwid: "Light does not exist to be kept under a bushel."

Nothing worked. Lolek was determined "to become a monk in an order of very strict rules," as Halina heard it. Finally, Kudlinski, "seeing that Karol's resolution was unshakable, persuaded him to become just a regular priest" rather than a Carmelite.[7]

Later, the actors claimed they had at least been responsible for a compromise that kept Lolek from living his life as a recluse. In fact, though, this may just have been Lolek's way of getting them to give up their struggle. He hadn't abandoned the idea of a contemplative life at all.

14

With human rights desperately needing a champion, the Catholic Church did not distinguish itself in World War II.[1] Relations between the Polish Church and the Vatican, sour for a century, got worse, and for good reason.

No high German Catholic churchman confronted Hitler. Of more than 20,000 German priests, only 418 were arrested; 169 died, 59 by formal execution.[2] By contrast, 3,647 Polish priests—about one in four—were sent to concentration camps, along with 1,117 nuns and 730 other ecclesiastics. Of these, 1,996 priests, 238 nuns, and 113 others died. Many laymen were also put to death for their faith.[3] In regions near Germany, U.S. intelligence reported, "practically the whole Catholic clergy of Polish descent has been eliminated by death, imprisonment and exile."

Not only did Pope Pius XII keep a papal nuncio in Berlin[4] throughout this slaughter, he made the same nuncio his representative to German-occupied Poland, effectively condoning the German takeover.[5] As conquering Germans replaced Polish bishops with their own, Pius approved. Polish dioceses were put under the authority of German Cardinal Bertram, whom U.S. intelligence described as "one of the most collaborationist bishops in Germany."[6] Bertram trumpeted German patriotism and called the war "a crusade for the defense of Western civilization."

Bishop Kaczinski, the ranking churchman with the Polish exile government in London, publicly accused Pius of violating the Vatican concordat with Poland—a stunning outburst by a bishop against the head of his Church. An American military intelligence report May 24, 1943,[7] asserted, "Moderate underground Polish papers are taking a stand against the pope because he remained silent in the face of the Nazi atrocities in Poland.... Among the lower clergy there is a trend in the direction of severing ties with the Vatican."

Some Polish priests, risking their own lives, distributed phony baptismal certificates to Jews in hiding, to help them escape. (Published stories have claimed that Lolek aided this work; while he would doubtless have approved it, there is no evidence that he was even aware of it.)

By 1943, even the formerly pro-Fascist Monsignor Angelo Roncalli, papal nuncio to Turkey and the future Pope John XXIII, had seen the light. The German ambassador to Turkey, gambling with his life, came to Roncalli on behalf of a group offering to try to overthrow Hitler if the allies would negotiate a settlement. Roncalli urged Rome to seize this chance to broker a peace, but he was dismissed as naïve.[8] Unlike Pope Benedict at the end of World War I, Pius wouldn't get involved.

February 29, 1944, Lolek worked a double shift, day and night, at the factory. As he trudged the five miles home in the dark, a speeding German army truck struck him from behind, knocked him off the road, and vanished into the night.

Jozefa Florek, who lived nearby, found a young man lying motionless by the road, covered with blood. She flagged down a car. A German officer got out, took a look, and told Ms. Florek to fetch some water. With the blood cleaned away, the officer decided the comatose youth was still alive and ordered a passing truck to take him for treatment. Lolek had dodged death once again.

He awoke in a hospital bed, his head bandaged, a cast on his arm. He ached from a severe concussion, bad cuts, and a shoulder injury. Three weeks he lay there, until the bed was needed for a new patient. During that time, the Kotlarczyks' daughter Anna was born, meaning they now had two small children at home. So Irena Szkocka and her family invited Lolek to recuperate in their apartment, where he had once participated in so much theater. He moved in for a few weeks.

He later called this time off work "a spiritual retreat sent from God." He prayed, read, meditated, and became fully at peace with his decision to enter the priesthood.

About this time, Mieczyslaw Malinski made the same decision. As soon as Lolek was on his feet again, he brought Malinski through the big gate and into the stone courtyard of the archbishop's palace to seek a spot in the seminary. They walked, as Lolek had with Father Figlewicz, down corridors lined with painted portraits of past archbishops of Krakow going back to at least 1423,[9] and up the stone stairs to see Sapieha. The archbishop gave Malinski a catch-up reading regimen, and the two friends left.

The Germans were already fortifying Krakow against the Soviet army, which had been advancing slowly ever since the stunning turnaround at Stalingrad the year before. Street patrols and checks of civilians for papers increased, and shots were often heard, coming from Polish partisans as well as Germans. "We felt close to death at all times," Malinski says. "I remember the shock I experienced when in retaliation for the shooting of a soldier, a group of hostages were brought near the railway station and shot." Sapieha regularly predicted that as soon as the Germans had killed all the Jews, they would begin exterminating all Poles the same way.[10]

June 6, 1944—D-day—Allied forces stormed ashore in northern France, and suddenly Germany had more than the Russians to worry about.

Lolek had quit the Rhapsody Theater, but not his playwriting. The summer of 1944, he showed priests a draft of a new work full of political sentiments and revealing autobiographical undercurrents.[11] This new play told the story of Adam Chmielowski, best known to Poles as Brother Albert; Lolek remained fascinated by Albert for years and, as pope, started him toward sainthood.

After losing a leg as a teenage rebel in the anti-Russian uprising of 1863, Chmielowski had become a well-known painter. But he was pulled—like the actor Lolek—by spiritual yearning. In 1887, deciding that art would never be able to alleviate the pain of his countrymen, he renounced his career and his belongings and founded an order of Albertine monks and nuns to care for the poor.

Albert became renowned in Poland as a sort of Mother Teresa with political leanings. He avoided imprisonment, though few missed the partisanship of his charity. He even helped Lenin, an active revolutionary writer, when Lenin lived in Krakow, from 1912 to 1914. Albert died in 1916; Sapieha, then a bishop, attended his funeral.

A longtime colleague[12] says that Lolek considered Brother Albert's association with Lenin to be a model for the proper relationship between the Church and political change, and that as pope he remembered Albert when making important decisions about priests who wanted to participate in revolutions. While Albert's words and deeds encouraged the overthrow of the tsarist system, he carefully confined himself to philosophical and moral fundamentals, never political specifics. He gave Lenin only humanitarian assistance.

Lolek's play about Albert, *Our God's Brother*, failed like his other plays—stuck in a gap between true theater and the kind of dialogues Plato used as a philosophical exercise. But it strongly suggests the thought process that led young Lolek to the priesthood.

It begins in a gallery, as Albert confronts a dilemma between pursuing his art and addressing human ills. "We cannot permit a whole mass of people to swarm through the poorhouses, leading almost animal lives . . . no, no!" he shouts. In succeeding scenes, he discusses this with other artists, with the poor themselves, and with a revolutionary. Finally, a wise priest leads him to conclude, "I cannot love two different things, for I cannot love by halves."

In a scene years later, at his monastery, Albert is surrounded by monks he has recruited, all of whom once struggled with poverty. He tells them that they became free when they "pledged to be beggars. . . . The vows changed it all. You have come to love poverty . . . and to be wed to it." The words are pure John of the Cross, though alone, they could be taken as antirevolutionary advice, a plea to be content with one's lot.

Just before the curtain drops, however, news arrives that the revolution has come. Workers are on general strike, shops and offices are closed, and the streets are filled with workers and police. Albert calmly counsels, "I have known about this for a long time. It had to come. . . . Anger has to erupt, especially if it is great. And it will last, because it is just."

The play's conclusion takes pains to show that personal virtue and social revolution are compatible—in fact, it says, both are necessary. Lolek's main point was not about revolution, however: the curtain falls on Albert's line, "I know for certain . . . that I have chosen a greater freedom."[13]

By the summer of 1944, the advancing Soviet army had "liberated" much of eastern Poland, including the university city of Lublin. July 22, some Polish communists there announced that they had been recognized by Stalin as the new Polish national government. The Polish government-in-exile in London had not been consulted.

The aristocratic and socialist politicians who combined to make up the London group had been at each other's throats throughout the 1930s but, surprisingly, had agreed on a democratic, social-welfare direction for Poland after the war. The government would redistribute land, and "every peasant will own the land he tills. . . . Manual and clerical workers will have a voice in the control of industrial production, and a share in its fruits. . . . Workers will be protected from exploitation and assured a decent standard of living."

This wasn't communism (in which the state, not the farmer, owns the land). Nor did it trust economic decisions to pure capitalism. But it comported well with the ideals of labor declared by Norwid and picked up by the young Karol Wojtyla. According to U.S. intelligence,[14] the London group's policies had strong support both from Washington and from most of the Polish underground.

A new Russian-Polish border was agreed to by Churchill, Stalin, and Roosevelt at a "Big Three" meeting in Teheran in 1943. Originally proposed by Britain in 1920, the new border gave Russia much of ancient Poland, but this land was occupied mostly by Ukrainians and other non-Poles, who would be minorities wherever they wound up. To compensate, Poland got former German land. The London exiles mostly agreed—though Stalin probably already knew he would take all of Poland anyway.

That summer of 1944, as Russian troops advanced toward Krakow, Halina married Tadeusz Kwiatkowski, an original member of their acting group. Wojciech Zukrowski, the writer and dynamite expert who collaborated with Kwiatkowski on an underground publication, recalls that the marriage was "a big surprise." In fact, Zukrowski says, he got two surprises. When he learned that Halina was marrying, he went to Lolek in case his friend needed a morale boost.

"How about a fiancée—find some girl," Zukrowski said cheerfully, offering to make a match for Lolek. That was when Lolek told Zukrowski he was going to be a priest.[15] Zukrowski believes that Lolek went into the priesthood, as he has almost certainly remained since then, a virgin. The evidence supports that.

In late July 1944, Soviet tanks reached the Vistula River on the edge of Warsaw and broke through the German lines. Radio Moscow called on Polish resisters to speed the victory by rebelling. The London exile government endorsed this, thinking that hastening the German departure might prevent a systematic destruction of the city.

So at precisely five P.M. July 31, 1944, the Warsaw Uprising began, with a four-day supply of ammunition. Poles opened fire on Germans wherever they were seen, and the Germans retreated to strategic positions. Days passed. The Poles ran out of ammunition. The Germans began to round them up and kill them, while the Russians stood at the Vistula.

Churchill personally cabled Stalin to move into Warsaw and rescue the Polish resisters before the Germans wiped them out. Stalin, of course, *wanted* them wiped out, and Warsaw in ruins. Weeks later, satisfied, he marched into the city.

On Warsaw's outskirts, a forty-three-year-old priest with a reputation for writing scholarly papers on the rights of workers distinguished himself as a war hero. Without planning it, he also transformed a quiet forest retreat for intellectuals into a fortress of freedom that would later help topple the Soviet Union. He was Stefan Wyszynski, and he would be the most important person within the Polish Church in the twentieth century and a towering figure in Karol Wojtyla's life.

Wyszynski was born in 1901 in a village northeast of Warsaw. His lineage was aristocratic, but Russian occupiers had long ago seized the family lands. His mother died when he was nine, after he had quit school in anger at a teacher, a Russian, who had ridiculed her chronic illness. Wyszynski and his father were caught and persecuted by Germans during World War I.

He grew into a homely man, with narrow eyes, not much chin, and a prominent mole under one eye. He went into a seminary believing it was his late mother's wish, but he almost lost his priesthood because of persistent tuberculosis. Only the intercession of an admiring housekeeper persuaded the bishop to ordain him.[16]

He dedicated himself to Mary, and particularly to her image at Czestochowa, "so that I could have a mother, a mother who is forever and does not die," he told his biographer.[17] He was on the same maternal search as Karol Wojtyla. The two also shared a fascination with human labor and a visceral distaste for capitalist values.

Once past his tuberculosis, Wyszynski studied sociology and in 1931 wrote that the Great Depression was "not a temporary interruption of the economic boom, but in large part a necessary consequence of the world capitalist economy.... The privileged ... enjoy ... all pomp and modern luxury.... Endlessly created artificial needs impair the capacity for charity.... One can easily end up on the side of lawlessness! ... They talk about the decline of morality among the working class in order to prepare an adequate number of prison cells.... They talk about the increase in communism, and yet they do not want to believe that the reason ... is the lack of work, of bread, and of a roof over one's head."[18]

Assigned to the industrial parish of Wloclawek, he promoted the Christian labor movement. Under the less tolerant dictatorship that followed Marshal Pilsudski's death, Wyszynski found it necessary to write under a pseudonym (as would Lolek under the communists). His views were well known enough that the invading Germans put a price on his head. Although his bishop and the entire staff of his seminary were arrested, Wyszynski, warned by neighbors, escaped.

He became a chaplain for the underground Home Army. Among the places he hid out was a lovely forest compound near Warsaw called Laski, which was later to play a critical role in the Solidarity revolution. Laski's buildings and paths had been constructed in 1926 by a Polish countess as a place to train the blind to work and live on their own. Over the years, it also became a retreat for Catholic intellectuals.

During the Warsaw Uprising, Wyszynski converted Laski into a secret hospital for the wounded. He helped transport and care for injured men, sometimes carrying them a mile on his back. He and colleagues at Laski "worried that any moment the Germans would come and kill the wounded and those taking care of them," says Zofia Morowska, the woman who ran it then—and still did in 1994, at age ninety. Amid the chaos and terror, Wyszynski worked around the clock, preaching hope to everyone.

After the war he returned regularly to his beloved Laski, a retreat from invaders new and old.

15

August 6, 1944—later known as Black Sunday—dawned a beautiful day for an outing. Malinski led a group of schoolboys to the limestone-laced hills outside Krakow, where they played soccer. When Lolek failed to show up as planned, Malinski figured his friend had just found something else to do.

Descending to town at dusk, Malinski and the boys spotted caravans of Germans searching house to house, down each block. Taking to the bushes, Malinski's group met fleeing men and boys who described an unprecedented dragnet in which even work certificates had not saved healthy-looking males from abduction. After the Warsaw Uprising, Governor Frank had determined to avoid any such episode in Krakow by eliminating potential participants in advance.

Malinski left his young charges shivering but temporarily safe in the mountain night, while he sneaked back to town through fields and backyards, past barking dogs, in pitch blackness. The city was in terror, but Malinski persuaded a friend with a shed to let him bring the boys there to hide. In the morning they hoped to be able to blend in with the rush-hour crowds and go home. When morning came, however, the streets were nearly deserted: Krakow was eerily different.

And Lolek had stared down another barrel of doom. The Germans had searched houses down the Vistula road and reached the home of his aunts and uncle. Soldiers tramped through the top two floors but assumed that no one lived in the basement. They left as Lolek waited behind the door, his "heart pounding."[1] Zukrowski, the resistance member, says Lolek was still trembling when they met hours later. "Lolek said he survived by some miracle. He was lying facedown in his house in a cross shape," Zukrowski says.

Through the long night, Lolek kept waiting. With first light came a soft knock on the door—too soft for Germans. It was a priest sent by Sapieha. Lolek was to gather essential belongings and get to the archbishop's palace. Irena Szkocka, his adopted grandmother, also appeared and offered to guide him there, walking one block ahead of him, looking for soldiers. Down the street and over the Vistula, Lolek followed her. Soldiers guarded the bridge, as always, but paid them no mind. Up one long street and through the green park that rings the old city of Krakow they made their way. Across from the palace, Germans guarded a supply depot on the grounds of a church. (It was German practice to store weapons at churches.)

Still a block ahead of Lolek, Mrs. Szkocka turned in to the palace gate. He followed. Up the stairwells and down the portrait-lined corridors he went, to Sapieha's quarters. Metal beds, desks, and chairs had been arranged in a room near the archbishop's chapel. Lolek was immediately given a priest's cassock to disguise him if the Germans came. As he put it on, he learned that during the sweep, a friend had been shot dead for harboring Jews.

Three hours later, Malinski arrived, escorted from his home by a woman the Church had sent. He heaved a sigh to see Lolek safe. Later in the day, the few remaining seminarians straggled in from their rural parishes. All got cassocks and false identity cards.

Sapieha looked down from the window at the sentries guarding the arms depot across the street. "I prefer not to think what would happen if they ever decided to come in here," he said.

And so the door closed on Lolek's civilian life.

At first glance, the archbishop's palace in Krakow appears to be a fortresslike stone quadrangle, several stories high, with a gateway and windows giving on to the street and a spacious interior courtyard. Less obvious is that the palace connects, mazelike, to Church-owned buildings on other streets. The Church owns considerable property in downtown Krakow.

Day at the seminary began at six. Plumbing conditions were "primitive," to use Malinski's word. Everyone prayed for half an hour, then Sapieha said Mass. The archbishop took personal charge of everything, from studies to recreation in the courtyard. Wojtyla's nose was generally in a book whenever it was not directed to be elsewhere. Sometimes he hid in the chapel to read undisturbed, holding his head in one hand as he does to this day. His colleagues marveled at his unflagging self-discipline.

Everyone knew what was going on outside: the Warsaw resistance was crumbling. All had friends at Auschwitz, which had already become the world's biggest cemetery. Krakow was flooding with refugees. All the seminarians were frustrated they couldn't leave the compound to help with relief work or check on their loved ones.

The night's sleep was constantly interrupted by bombs, aircraft sirens, and distant artillery fire. Germans were seen mining bridges and monuments and carting off valuables, determined to leave a wasteland behind them. "Somehow we did not mind this, provided it meant that the Germans were going," Malinski says. "But as yet, it did not seem certain that they were."

One seminarian who came in from the countryside August 7, 1944, was Kazimierz Suder, who would become Wadowice's parish priest during John Paul II's papacy. He says Wojtyla asked few questions and "never mentioned his family." Lolek seemed confident, yet, as at the university, he concealed his potential. "But as the result of tests, and questions asked, I soon became convinced he was the most intelligent" of the group, Suder says.

"Even if someone else was chosen to lead some discussion, it was always Wojtyla who ended up being the leader," Malinski says. "He was the soul of our little circle."[2]

Wojtyla's lone self-indulgence was maintaining contact with what Suder calls "all these acting people. He was in love with acting. He recited whole poems from memory." He even persuaded Juliusz Osterwa, the famous actor, to coach the seminary class on elocution.

But Wojtyla was still starkly ascetic. His classmate Franciszek Konieczny remarked at the way he would study textbooks on his knees, as if in prayer. Shortly after entering the seminary, he asked for and got permission from Sapieha to have his head shaved; gone for good was the idiosyncratically long hair that had distinguished him as an actor. He dressed shabbily, even to the eyes of other seminarians, hardly fashion plates themselves. He wore old denim pants and wooden clogs, still going without socks even in winter. Once Kotlarczyk brought him a pullover sweater, but his classmate Konieczny saw him give it away the next day to a poor man.[3]

Mostly, though, Suder says, "We all had one dream, one wish: for Poland to regain its independence."

In December 1944, American officials became alarmed over reports from eastern Poland, where Soviet troops had gradually gained control.[4] The "Polish liberation government" announced in Lublin in July claimed to represent the Home Army, but its members were prewar socialist militants. Many had been studying in the USSR and had come back to Poland with the Soviet army. Although elections had been promised, the governing bodies were all appointed.

At first, in the joy over the Germans' departure, few people objected. Many if not most Poles welcomed a socialist-oriented government in place of the old dictatorship bent on protecting the rights of the aristocracy. Soon, though, the new leadership began to rotate at the whim of the Soviets. "People suspected of taking a more independent line are immediately removed from office," a U.S. intelligence report said.

Dissenters were labeled Enemies of the State and ordered to register. There was no relief from the starvation and disease of war; the Red Army commandeered what meager food the villagers had.

Meanwhile, the seminary students in Krakow looked out their windows each night to watch German trucks carting valuables westward as the Russians approached. January 17, 1945, truck traffic quickened, and during seminary classes, gunfire outside increased. Everyone looked out. The Germans were gone. Suddenly a thunderous explosion rattled the students' bones. Smoke billowed around the railroad bridge across the Vistula.

The seminarians gathered in the chapel, a room about ten by twenty-five feet. As Sapieha intoned the evening Mass, a new blast rocked the building and knocked the prayerful from their knees. Every remaining window shattered, and as winter winds whipped in, Sapieha stopped the service and ordered everyone to a designated shelter downstairs. Long into the night, they sang hymns and prayed amid the sounds of battle outside. When Soviet soldiers arrived, the seminarians offered them the finest they had—hot tea and dry bread.

The welcome given to the Soviets in those early days was genuine.

On the first morning, as the Soviet commander and two generals paid a polite visit to Sapieha, Wojtyla chatted with a Soviet soldier who said he might like to enter a seminary himself someday.[5]

The students were already at work that day replacing window panes with new glass Sapieha had managed to procure from somewhere. During a midday break, Wojtyla and Malinski walked back to Debnicki. The streets were jammed with Russian soldiers and their trucks, as well as civilians with pushcarts and pony carts. The Debnicki bridge was gone except for the girders, but little matter: the Vistula was frozen solid enough to hold not just pedestrians but tanks, a few of which now sat stalled there. The ice was also littered with the bodies of soldiers.[6]

For the rest of January, Malinski recalls, "we worked busily to reglaze the windows and retile the roof. Day after day hundreds of the most varied people filed through the palace to submit problems or vent their joys and sorrows. Everyone wanted help in some form."

Seeking aid, Sapieha went to Rome, where he met Father (now Bishop) Aloysius Wycislo of Catholic Relief Services in New York. They arranged a flow of American relief, beginning with supplies that Sapieha smuggled home at the end of that same trip, "circumventing customs, hiding what he was taking in the roof of his sleeping car," Wycislo says.[7]

The seminarians, having restored the palace, now turned to the seminary, which sat roofless and windowless across a park. The Germans had used it as a prison, where the inmates kept warm "by lighting open fires in the rooms," Malinski says. "The state of the lavatories was appalling, with piles of frozen excrement which had to be chopped up and carted away. Karol and I and a few other students volunteered to do this. The stench was dreadful, and we found the only way to keep from vomiting was to breathe through the mouth. It was quite a long job as there were three lavatories on each floor. After that, we had the easier task of carrying tiles up to the roof, where they were fitted by a small team of experts."

The Germans had even rifled the library, stealing the most valuable books. What remained was cleaned and put right. The peaceful courtyard garden and pretty chapel were restored.

Wojtyla had once again found his prayerful spot, and it was not in the palace or seminary. To the left of the main sanctuary in the church across the street from the palace—the one the Germans had converted into a munitions dump—is a chapel lined with an unusual series of pictures of Jesus dragging his cross. Most such pictures elsewhere depict a visibly divine Jesus who seems to be suffering only symbolically; these pictures, in contrast, show Jesus looking as a man might while being tortured to death. Whenever Wojtyla could steal a moment, he came here to pray.

Three weeks after the Russians reached Krakow, Churchill, Roosevelt, and Stalin met for a second and final time, at Yalta, a Russian resort on the Black Sea. Like

Munich in 1938, Yalta became a political symbol as much as it was a city. The agreement signed there authorized Western and Soviet forces to occupy the ground they had taken, hold elections, and install democracies. Many people blame the Yalta accord for Soviet rule in Eastern Europe after 1945.

For Karol Wojtyla, as for many Eastern Europeans, Yalta could be neither forgotten nor forgiven. "He spoke of Yalta at various occasions," says Professor Stanislaw Grygiel, a longtime friend. "He thought it was a great political mistake and morally unacceptable."

Many American Republicans later accused Roosevelt of selling out. Unlike Munich, however, which is excused by almost no one, Yalta has been vigorously defended as the best agreement the West could have obtained at the time. The United States had just suffered heavy casualties in a German offensive (the Battle of the Bulge) while the Soviets were rolling into Germany from the east. In the Pacific theater, Japan was fighting tenaciously, and Stalin promised at Yalta to supply forces to help there.

Russia had paid dearly for its triumphs. To deny it the same rights in the East that the United States and Britain claimed in the West would have dashed the alliance—and with it, all hopes for a United Nations. It might also have required a new and not necessarily winnable war, since the only territory Yalta ceded to Stalin to administer was that already held by his troops.

Moreover, Stalin pledged to dismantle his communist Lublin government and hold free elections. "I trusted his declarations about the sovereignty, independence and freedom of Poland," Churchill wrote later.[8] As the conference closed, the *New York Times* reported "a tendency here to regard the decision [on Poland] as in part a victory for the United States and Britain."[9]

Yet when the Yalta agreement was signed, in 1945, Stalin had already been lying and killing remorselessly for a quarter of a century. The bloody betrayal of the Warsaw Uprising alone should have proved to Roosevelt and Churchill that Stalin wanted no part of their democratic principles. "Every single peasant in Poland and Czechoslovakia knew this was nothing but an empty word," says John Paul's friend and adviser Professor Grygiel. "It is amazing that men like Roosevelt and Churchill believed it." Polish historians are nearly unanimous on this point.

At the home of Irena Szkocka, where Wojtyla again still visited his adopted grandmother, there were discussions about Yalta. "We were angry," says Szkocka's granddaughter Barbara Pozniak. "People didn't feel we won the war. Our government came from Russia."

Still, could the Western allies realistically have turned on Stalin at Yalta? Even Professor Grygiel doesn't think so. But the pope's close friend offers another option—one seldom mentioned in debates over Yalta. "You didn't have to go to war again," he says. "Just do not sign it. That is all. If Yalta had not been signed, the situation would have been the same, but morally more clear."

Today, with politicians boasting that they defeated communism by winning an arms race and forty-five years of military showdowns, talk of moral clarity without military action may seem almost a joke. But Grygiel is serious. He and Wojtyla really believe playwright Edward Bulwer-Lytton's famous evaluation of pens and swords (that the pen is mightier). How this belief worked out shapes the rest of our story.

16

In late March 1945, the Jagiellonian University, including the seminary, resumed operation. Students and lectures moved out of the palace, and those professors who were still alive came out of hiding.

"Events followed so quickly" that there was no time for social chatter, says Wojtyla's classmate Kazimierz Suder. Students worried about continuing Soviet occupation, but mainly "there was a double load of lectures. We were absorbed in our studies." Their diet improved slightly thanks to American-supplied canned fish, cheese, and margarine.

Many students were "dressed in rags, half-starved, and lived in cellars or hovels," Malinski says. "Many were [really] ill, especially those who had come from POW or labor camps, not to speak of escapees from extermination camps. But they kept on studying." Wojtyla was elected vice chairman of a university student government that distributed used clothing and other aid from the West.

His course titles included General Sacraments, The Eucharist, Introduction to the Gospels, Liturgics, Introduction to the Old Testament, Church Art and Monument Preservation, Hebrew Language, Logic, Metaphysics, Cosmology, Moral Theology, Church History, History of Philosophy, and Greek. During breaks, he studied Spanish.

Outside of class, he withdrew into the quiet contemplation he had long sought. He saw few people. Once, though, walking to class, he was approached by a poorly dressed woman who reminded him that he had once worked double shifts at the Solvay plant so that her husband, a coworker, could stay home with her during an illness. In thanks, she had brought Wojtyla a pair of new shoes. Wojtyla accepted them, then gave them away without ever wearing them.[1]

Malinski observed from the next seat that Wojtyla headed every page of class notes with a small prayer in the corner, either "J + M," for Jesus and

Mary, or "OAMDG" for *omnia ad majorem dei gloriam*—"all for the greater glory of God."

As Polish boundaries shifted again, old religious and ethnic rivalries were reignited. Polish Catholics took over predominantly Protestant areas in what had been eastern Germany, while as eastern Poland was swallowed up by the Soviet Union, areas that were once Catholic fell under the rule of atheists and Eastern Orthodox (a Christian group that broke from Catholicism in 1054 A.D.).

Complicating things further were the Ukrainian Catholics, who had left the Church along with the Orthodox in 1054 but later returned to Roman rule, with the proviso that they be allowed to retain their distinctive religious rites. The two thirds of Poland's population who were ancestrally Polish treated the Ukrainian Catholics as outcasts and often referred to them, to their chagrin, as Uniates rather than Catholics.

Illustrating the confusion and animosity this caused, American intelligence agents in February 1945 reported the story of one youth who had just been freed from a German concentration camp and sought to join the Polish army. Despite his Polish citizenship, he was turned down at one enlistment center because of his Ukrainian ancestry and at a second because of his Orthodox religion. He finally learned some Catholic gestures (for example, a distinctive way of crossing himself) and went to a third center, where he was accepted after lying about his nationality and religion.

Although the skin colors of the two groups were alike, racial prejudice plagued Poland as certainly as it did the American South during the same era. Polish bishops and even Pope Pius himself scorned aid requests from desperately poor Uniate churches, on occasion even insulting them.[2] Those Uniates who fell into Stalin's grasp fared even worse: the Uniate leadership in former eastern Poland, some eight hundred clerics, were rounded up and imprisoned in Siberia.

Having already invited Karol Wojtyla into an underground seminary, Archbishop Sapieha now struck yet another blow whose ultimate effect on totalitarianism he could not have imagined. Seeing a hiatus in censorship after the Germans left and a continuing lack of reliable information, he started a newspaper. He called it *Tygodnik Powszechny*—the "Universal Weekly"—to emphasize that it was independent and covered general topics, not just religion.

The Church was among the few institutions that could provide a stable base for such an enterprise. Sapieha arranged for the paper to have an office in the palace and a staff, including an experienced newspaper editor known for his socialist-inclined politics, Father Jan Piwowarczyk.

Tygodnik Powszechny first appeared March 3, 1945. Wojtyla almost certainly read it, including a prophetic article by Father Piwowarczyk entitled "Toward a Catholic Poland." Piwowarczyk endorsed the fundamental social and economic change the communists sought, but he argued that Catholics must make sure the new socialist society recognized "the primacy of the spirit" and "individual ethical responsibility," without "the tyranny of materialism."[3]

Materialism was Marx's stock in trade, but Poland had plenty of what might be called "cafeteria Marxists"—people who supported a reallocation of wealth and privilege away from the aristocracy, but who at the same time rejected the rigid Soviet regimen. Quickly, however, it became clear to even the most hopeful that Moscow didn't permit exceptions.

By March 1945, the government in Lublin had confiscated all radios and typewriters. Several thousand landlords had been arrested and deported. "Land reform" turned out to mean that crops were collected from farmers by Soviet soldiers on behalf of the state. Heroes who had fought against Germany with the Home Army were sent to concentration camps, and some even executed. Old Polish money—whatever people had saved—was declared worthless. To get a ration card, one had to be on a government labor register.

Refugees reported "deportations, shootings, imprisonments without regard to legal procedure, on an ever-growing scale." U.S. intelligence noted that a "definite effort is being made to clear the country of all elements unfriendly to Russia."[4]

A leader had emerged in Lublin: Boleslaw Krasnodebski, who, like Lenin and Stalin before him, had taken a nom de révolution: Bierut. He had been among five thousand Polish socialists who fled to the USSR in the 1930s to escape repression by Poland's military dictators. Most had been murdered by Stalin; those who survived were, like Bierut, devoted to Stalin. When the Soviets followed Hitler into Poland in 1939, Bierut was sent with the troops to identify "enemies of the people," thus fingering his own countrymen for death or a slave camp.

Gradually, a group around Bierut, appointed by the Kremlin, became the government of Poland, headquartered in Warsaw.

By July 1945, *Tygodnik Powszechny* expanded to larger quarters on the second floor of a Church-owned commercial building around the corner from the archbishop's palace. The government confiscated many Church buildings but for some reason never seized that one. Editor Piwowarczyk hired as his assistant the thirty-two-year-old Jerzy Turowicz, who had risked his life to attend the Rhapsody Theater during the war. In 1997, the newspaper remains in the same office, and Turowicz is its editor in chief.

All through the communist period, the paper covered culture, society, and religion, while carefully skirting the line of politics that could, at any time, have brought its demise. When Wojtyla was elected pope, the international press described Turowicz as his best friend.

That summer of 1945, the United States tested the first atomic bomb, then dropped two more on cities. The world gasped. Japan surrendered. Stalin turned enviously to his scientists and ordered them to produce such weapons.

Right after the war, a new split developed between the Polish Church and the Vatican. Poles—both communist and Catholic—wanted to cement Poland's grip on the new territories it had received from Germany by installing Polish bishops atop the dioceses. The Vatican, however, had a long-standing policy of not recognizing boundaries changed in war until a peace treaty was signed, a policy intended to protect popes from territorial disputes.

Germany could not sign a peace treaty because it was divided. (The Western allies ceded their occupation zones to a democratic state, West Germany, while the USSR created a communist puppet state in East Germany.) So Vatican policy left the newly Polish dioceses in the hands of German churchmen who had supported Hitler.

Considering this situation intolerable, Primate Hlond, on his own, put Polish bishops in temporary command of the new dioceses, infuriating Pius XII. Pius had a well-known pro-German bias. A German nun, Sister Pasqualina Lehnert, was his most trusted adviser, though she was officially only a housekeeper. He defended Germany's rights to the territory it had forfeited, and let Catholic clergy across Europe help German war criminals escape to the West.

The new Polish government was so pleased by Hlond's action that for a while it went easier on its local Church than did other communist regimes in neighboring countries.[5]

But the Soviet grip on half of Europe became ever clearer. March 5, 1946, Churchill declared, "From Stettin [Szczecin] in the Baltic to Trieste in the Adriatic, an iron curtain has descended across the continent." The words were controversial then, but they defined the next era of history.

Despite the promise his theater friends thought they had extracted from him, Wojtyla still visited Father Jozef Prus, the discalced Carmelite he had met at the palace, and pursued other Carmelites about joining. Sometime around December 1945, he asked to move to the Carmelite convent to complete his theological studies there and live a life detached from the mundane world. Sapieha refused him permission. "You are to finish what you have started," Sapieha told him.

Still, Wojtyla maintained his contacts. In 1946 the Carmelites published his first printed collection of poems, under the title *Song of the Hidden God.* It brought more trouble. Publication by seminarians was forbidden, and the Carmelite editor put Wojtyla's real name on the book instead of a pseudonym. The archbishop made him reprint the book as Anonymous.[6]

When professors suggested that he do an honors thesis, Wojtyla wrote on the Carmelite Saint John of the Cross, and his view that only faith could unite the soul with God. Jan Tyranowski visited the seminary regularly to discuss the thesis[7] while the faculty picked it apart at weekly seminars throughout the spring of 1946.

Outside the seminary, Jewish suffering continued despite the defeat of Germany. More than a thousand Polish Jews who had somehow survived the extermination camps to be liberated were then murdered on their return home by Poles who blamed them for the communist occupation. Primate Hlond fueled the anti-Semitism. After anti-Semitic riots in 1945 and 1946, he publicly declared, "The fact that conditions for Polish-Jewish coexistence are worsening is to a great extent due to Jews' . . . trying to impose a system of government that a majority of society does not want."[8]

For several reasons, Jews did constitute a disproportionately large minority among socialist revolutionaries. Shut out by race from the power structure, they were less attached than Christians to the status quo; thus, in the 1970s and '80s, Jews also played an outsized role in leading the *anti*-communist revolution in Poland. Because of the priority they placed on universal education, Jews also constituted more than their share of the intellectual class, which was disproportionately inclined toward socialism. Moreover, since Polish Jews had been largely exterminated, most Jews in Poland after the war came from the USSR; for many European Jews, service in the Red Army had been the only alternative to execution by the Germans, and they appreciated that.

Jews who came to Poland from the USSR as part of the communist establishment, however, were generally protected. Most Jews who were murdered on their return home weren't political activists of any kind, but hapless victims trying to pick up the remnants of their lives. Betrayed Poles sought revenge against the only handy target.

In part, Poles suffered from what has been called the Nagasaki Syndrome, which once induced the mayor of Nagasaki to announce that the only thing worse than being the first city to be A-bombed was being the second city to be A-bombed. Hiroshima's martyrdom was universally recognized, while Nagasaki was simply leveled. So with Poland: history has recorded the Jewish Holocaust as the worst crime ever committed, all but forgetting, except within Poland, that if the Holocaust hadn't happened, the German murder of the Poles would take its place as the worst crime ever.[9]

Tadeusz Mazowiecki, a longtime Catholic colleague of Wojtyla's, and Poland's first prime minister after the fall of communism in 1989, says that when Westerners learn he was a prisoner at Auschwitz, they usually exclaim in surprise, "I didn't know you were Jewish!" (He isn't, and didn't have to be.)[10] In real numbers (though not proportionally), Poles suffered almost as many non-combat murders as Jews did.

Resentment over this lingered for decades and was exploited by the communists. Wojtyla's emotional reaction to continuing anti-Semitism—not just to the Holocaust—helps account for John Paul II's passion for improving the Church's relations with Jews.

Just as events not of his doing made Wojtyla a priest, so they would give him a topflight Church education in Rome. Sapieha went there in the summer of 1946 to receive the cardinal's hat that had been denied him by the previous pope, Pius XI. The trip convinced him that he must procure a Roman education for a prized new seminary student, Stanislaw Starowieyski, a baron of high intellect who seemed sure one day to become a bishop. Only as an afterthought, Malinski says, did Sapieha decide that Starowieyski should have a companion.

That opened the door for Wojtyla. When the school year ended, he received the highest grade in all but one subject, barely missing in that. With his intellect, Sapieha guessed he would be a career academic. Yet even for a diligent student, the wartime Krakow seminary had been "grossly inadequate" (in the words of one Catholic educator).[11] And the outlook was not improving. Communist police were harassing bishops. Leaders of three Catholic lay organizations had been murdered, apparently by police.

So Wojtyla would go to Rome with Starowieyski. Sapieha ordained the future pope alone, ahead of his classmates, in the second-floor chapel where the students had gathered on the night the Russians arrived. Figlewicz was the only witness. (Starowieyski was to be ordained when he completed his Roman studies.)

It was November 1, 1946—All Souls' Day,[12] an amazing sight in Poland. Unlike the United States, which has reduced the celebration to Halloween, a comic children's spectacle the night before, in Poland, most of the population leaves work or school to jam cemeteries and nearby roadways. They carry candles, flowers, and religious mementos to decorate the graves of relatives or other loved ones. By midafternoon in any cemetery, graves are blanketed with mums, and the surrounding ground is a blazing sea of melting candle wax. Priests work overtime in cemetery chapels, repeating Masses chain-style, much the way a movie is repeated throughout the day, while assistants outside distribute communion wafers and wine to the overflow crowds.

After his ordination, Wojtyla said Mass for his parents and brother in quite a different setting—among the sarcophagi of ancient kings and other Polish national heroes at the Wawel. In succeeding days he said additional "first" Masses at the churches in Wadowice and Debnicki. Mrs. Szkocka hosted a celebratory lunch for old friends in her apartment, where many of them had once performed as the Rhapsody Theater. Within days, Halina's new daughter, Monika Kwiatkowska, became Wojtyla's first baptism. Wojciech Zukrowski, the dynamite man, was godfather; Wojtyla would soon be handing out copies of Zukrowski's first novel as Christmas gifts.[13]*

17

Two weeks later, November 15, 1946, Wojtyla and Starowieyski boarded a train for Rome, stopping five days in Paris on the way. Wojtyla's letters seem surprisingly unenthusiastic about the remarkable sights suddenly on display to a young man from Wadowice. In page after page that he penned to Mrs. Szkocka and her family, all he mentions of Paris is that he delivered a letter from Mrs. Lewaj, his old French teacher, to friends there.

Across the Italian border, he stopped in Turin, a city rich in European history. But here he noted only a visit to the tomb of a nineteenth-century priest.[1] Rome, too, seemed to hold amazingly little nonreligious interest for Wojtyla. He wrote only of visits to "the catacombs—Rome of early Christians, Rome

---

* A widely published story claims that before Wojtyla left for Rome, he declined the request of a Polish couple to baptize a six-year-old Jewish boy they had accepted as a baby from parents who were on their way to die. The story—which surfaced only after Wojtyla became pope—says he instead had the boy sent to Jewish relatives. Although the boy did go to relatives in North America, I have concluded, based on interviews with the principals, that Wojtyla's role in all of this was a fabrication, along with other published yarns that he rescued Jews from concentration camps, or sent them there, or stole German rocket secrets.

of Apostles, Rome of martyrs, Rome that is the foundation of the Church, and also of that great culture that we inherit."[2]

In all these travels, he seemed oblivious to living on the cusp of history, at the end of the great war of his century. He was on a mission, for a doctorate in theology. Throughout his years abroad, his many letters home were mostly long expressions of affection, frustratingly devoid of observations about what he saw or did.

Since the old Polish College had been destroyed in the war, Sapieha and Hlond arranged for their charges to live in the Belgian College. Not a teaching institution, the college rather serves the purpose of the American fraternity house it resembles: to provide a home-away-from-home for students. It is half a block down a quiet, tree-shaded street from the Quirinale, the presidential palace (formerly the papal summer home) atop one of Rome's seven hills. Its direct view of St. Peter's, across the city below, is spectacular.

Down the street the other way is the church of Santa Andrea al Quirinale, where Wojtyla quickly found a favored spot for daily prayer. By coincidence, the church is the burial place of Saint Stanislaw Kostka (1550–1568), the patron saint of Polish youth, who gained fame by walking from Poland to Rome, and whose name had been taken by Wojtyla's parish church in Debnicki.

November 27, 1946, Wojtyla enrolled at the Angelicum, the Dominican order's university, founded in 1577. Sapieha sent him there because his nemesis, Pope Pius XI, as papal nuncio to Poland, had directed an earlier generation of young churchmen to his own Roman alma mater, the Jesuit-run Gregorian University. Now Sapieha disparaged the Gregorian.[3] Admiring the Dominican scholars who were active near Krakow, he settled on their Angelicum as the place for his protégés in Rome.

The star of the Angelicum faculty in those years was Professor Reginald Garrigou-Lagrange, known as "Reginald the Rigid."[4] Aged seventy, a professor at the Angelicum since 1909, he had just published *La Synthèse Thomiste* (which one scholar translates as "Thomas in a Nutshell"),[5] a distillation of the ideas of the Church's current philosophical guiding light, Saint Thomas Aquinas (1225–1274).

During Thomas's own lifetime, the leading Catholic theologian had been Saint Augustine (354–430). Thomas had set out to blend Augustine's ideas with the rediscovered work of the ancient Greek philosopher Aristotle. But the two sets of ideas were so different that many scholars—especially non-Catholics—argue that Thomas departed from Augustine and followed Aristotle instead. Augustine is now usually more closely associated with Plato, on the opposite end from Aristotle and Thomas of a basic spectrum of human thought that transcends religion.*

In an extreme nutshell, Aristotle and Thomas represent a more objective, coldly rational, fact-based view of the world. Each tried to set down an orderly framework in which all laws governing human behavior could fit—and they tried, as well, to fill in specific details of those laws. Plato and Augustine, on the other hand, had a more emotional, poetic view of existence that stressed the complexities of the mind—a personal world beyond the one we see around us.

Of course, all four thinkers understood that life requires a combination of the rational and the emotional, the brain and the heart. The issue is emphasis and balance. Aristotle and Thomas Aquinas tended to write impersonally and exactly, often numbering their statements. Plato and Augustine mostly let arguments percolate out of stories they told. (Augustine wrote first-person experiences, while Plato recounted the deeds of Socrates, his partly real, partly fictional hero.)

One question these two viewpoints have presented to Catholicism is whether there is natural law, a set of confirmable, orderly rules that precede human thought. Aristotle and Aquinas believed there was such law, and that it could be precisely described. Plato and Augustine left things more to personal interpretation. Augustine certainly believed in God, but like Plato, he found divine order hard to discern on earth.

Philosophy historian Bertrand Russell once wrote, "In the Aristotelian theory, forms are immutable and eternal . . . more important than matter. . . . In Plato, logical points arise here and there . . . as the mood of the moment dictates."[6] Says another scholar, "Aristotle studies politics by collecting constitutions. Plato asks, 'What is justice?' "[7]

Wojtyla's early heroes—Jan Tyranowski, John of the Cross, and even Brother Albert—tended toward Platonism. But institutions with temporal authority, like the Vatican, have strong incentives toward Thomism (pronounced Tome-ism), which sees a more hierarchically ordered world, and thus

---

* To understand Wojtyla, a philosophy scholar, it is necessary to understand a few fundamentals of the major philosophers he studied. Summarizing their ideas, however, is tricky. This is a book of journalism, a profession built on the faith that anything true and important can be simply explained. Philosophy, in contrast, is built on the faith that anything simply explained must be either untrue or trivial. (I joke only slightly.) I have shown the section that follows and a later passage on phenomenology to half a dozen philosophy scholars, none of whom will agree on the same words to explain even those basic concepts that they seem to share. I have tried to make the passages conform both to the gist of what they said as the words are used in everyday English, and also to my own reading of some of the works involved and to common basic reference works.

encourages the acceptance of authority. Plato, John of the Cross, and Tyra-nowski downplayed institutions and encouraged individual searching and questioning, which pose problems for authority.

Augustine's adherents held their own for a few centuries after Thomas wrote. But eventually Thomism came to dominate the Church. Both Protestantism and the rise of nation-states drained the papacy of political power and left it more an authority on religious dogma; Thomism played into that. The First Vatican Council, in 1869–70, declared that the pope could speak infallibly in certain circumstances. Later, Pope Leo XIII (1878–1903) urged adherence to "the golden wisdom of Thomas." By 1923, Pius XI declared in an encyclical that "the Church has adopted [Thomas's] philosophy for her very own."

As Thomism became dominant, however, it diverged at times from what its founder actually wrote. For example, Thomas held that God did not infuse a fetus with a human soul until the skull developed, more than a month into pregnancy. Recently, in condemning abortion, the Church has taught that a human being is created when a sperm cell enters an egg. (Asked about this apparent contradiction in 1986, Pope John Paul II replied that Thomas's word on fetuses "never was accepted by the magisterium [official teaching] of the Church. It was a theory based on ideas of Aristotle. Modern biology makes it absolutely clear that a human life exists at the moment of conception.")[8]

When Wojtyla attended the Angelicum, though, Thomism was at the threshold of a more fundamental revision. Some scholars—Jacques Maritain of France being the most famous—proclaimed that Thomas had been a more adventurous thinker than was sometimes suggested by stodgy rulebooks issued in his name. By the 1960s, traditional Thomist rules were giving way to the study of what Thomas actually said. Wojtyla thus went to school at what may turn out to have been the high-water mark of the influence of traditional Thomism.

The Angelicum and its Professor Garrigou-Lagrange, despite important nuances,[9] pulled Wojtyla mostly in an old-Thomist direction. Soon after Wojtyla met him, Garrigou-Lagrange became the principal drafter of Pope Pius XII's most famous encyclical, *Humani Generis,* issued in 1950. *Humani Generis* assailed those who would "weaken … concepts … long held by the Church, and return instead to the language of the Bible."[10] This seemed to warn *against* searching for truth, even in scripture, if it went against dogma.

Wojtyla knew from the start that he wanted to write his doctoral dissertation on Saint John of the Cross. But his adviser, Father Mario A. Ciappi (now a cardinal), suggested that he should first ground himself in basics by writing a preliminary paper on the theology of Thomas. Wojtyla wrote it in Latin, Thomas's language.

"In class, he spoke only to answer questions, and not frequently," Ciappi remembers. Wojtyla "did not seem remarkable until the oral exam for his thesis," in the spring of 1947. Professors Ciappi, Garrigou-Lagrange, and Pierre-Paul Philippe (a Frenchman who also later became a cardinal) each awarded Wojtyla a rare 10 points out of 10—"a perfect 30!" Ciappi exclaims.[11]

In January 1947, the gates of tyranny clanged shut on Poland. A rigged parliamentary election was said by the Soviets to fulfill Stalin's promise at Yalta. Two priests were sentenced to death for communicating with secret anti-communist organizations.

18

Wojtyla's heart belonged to mysticism. He'd heard of a Padre Pio, a monk whose stories of personal contact with God and the devil drew thousands of visitors to a monastery in east-central Italy. Pio claimed supernatural powers that he would display on occasion, though only to carefully selected witnesses. He claimed to be an exorcist, capable of purging the devil from distressed people. Believers would depart saying that through his services, their cancer or paralysis had been cured.

Shortly after Easter 1947, Wojtyla and his fellow seminarian Starowieyski traveled to see Pio. Wojtyla did not test or investigate Pio's claims any more than anyone else did. Although a million and a half visitors a year eventually attended Pio's Masses—including a coterie of female faithful—Pio refused to see reporters, photographers, or almost anyone else likely to question his genuineness. Still, believers waited in line for days to confess to him. Wojtyla was such a believer.

His devotion began with that 1947 visit and would ultimately grow to affect Church policy. It was the strangest relationship of Wojtyla's life and his greatest act of pure faith—for while many Catholics accepted Pio's claims, others thought him a fraud. Still others—including several popes and other Vatican officials—thought he was, to put it politely, a few beads short on his rosary.

Born Francesco Forgione, May 25, 1887, Pio joined the Capucin order in 1903 after an "intimate conversation with the Lord." He spent almost his entire adult life at the monastery at San Giovanni Rotondo, near the city of Foggia. From his seminary days, colleagues were accustomed to finding his room a shambles, bruises on his body, and other signs that, in the words of biographer C. Bernard Ruffin, "his flat must be the scene of drunken brawls."[1]

But Pio explained that during the night, demons "in the most abominable form . . . hurled themselves upon me . . . struck me violently, and threw pillows, books, and chairs." Adjoining rooms were kept vacant. Pio said in letters that the demons stripped him naked in order to beat him more effectively and that "those evil creatures would have thrown themselves all over me if sweet Jesus hadn't helped me."

In 1918, when he was thirty-one, Pio appeared before colleagues with wounds on each hand and foot and one on his body—the wounds Jesus suffered when nailed to his cross. Since first reported by Saint Francis of Assisi (1182–1226), more than a hundred cases of "stigmata" have been reported, generally by females; some say Pio was the first man since Francis to display these wounds.

Although some local doctors said they examined Pio in the first few years after the wounds appeared, impartial scientists apparently never did. Throughout his decades of celebrity, he wore fingerless gloves to cover his hand wounds whenever he was with outsiders, but would doff the gloves to reveal the wounds from afar at his widely attended 5:00 A.M. daily Mass. The stigmata were attested to by colleagues at the monastery, which became the center of a multimillion-dollar tourist industry, complete with guesthouses and trinket shops.

In 1926 and again in 1931, the Vatican Holy Office—which polices strict adherence to the faith—ordered Catholics to stop visiting Pio. In 1933, the Vatican lifted the ban but pointedly distanced itself from Pio's claims. The Church kept Pio under wraps for decades, and Pope John XXIII tried to close down his operation altogether.

Yet in 1947, Wojtyla joined the crowd confessing to Pio. For decades afterward, Wojtyla "spoke about him with the greatest esteem—he believed that Padre Pio would [one day be made] a saint," says Father Bardecki, Wojtyla's colleague at *Tygodnik Powszechny*. Cardinal Alfons Stickler of Austria says that Wojtyla once confided to him that "Padre Pio told him he would gain the highest post in the Church. Wojtyla believed when he was created a cardinal, the prophecy was realized."

Until his death, in 1968, Pio continued to assert that he regularly wrestled with the devil, emerging barely able to stand. There is evidence that, at least late in life, he took Valium and other mind-altering drugs.[2]

As Wojtyla was visiting Padre Pio, his mentor Jan Tyranowski, in Krakow, was dying a slow death from a spreading infection, refusing painkillers despite having to undergo at least one amputation. He died July 15, 1947. Wojtyla wanted to return home to be with him, but Sapieha ordered Wojtyla and Starowieyski to travel through Europe that summer instead. He told them to see the sights but also "to study pastoral methods," as Wojtyla put it, and to pay particular attention to how the Church worked.[3]

Three American priests who were staying at the Belgian College while the North American College was being repaired donated several hundred dollars of their own money to pay for Wojtyla's trip.[4] They understood that his purpose was to do relief work in Belgium and Holland. "He took the money and went up to the Lowlands to minister to Polish refugees," says Bishop W. Thomas Larkin of St. Petersburg, Florida, then a graduate student. "I was kind of impressed that he spent the money that way. He was poor as a churchmouse."

The trip opened Wojtyla's eyes. In Marseilles, Lourdes, and Paris, he was shocked to see that only a third of France attended weekly Mass. "There are saints all over Paris," he wrote Maria Kydrynska Michalowska, referring to France's long Catholic tradition, "but the people are not so religious."

At Garrigou-Lagrange's suggestion, he observed the so-called worker-priest movement begun by the cardinal/archbishop of Paris, through which priests were sent to docks and factories to share the workers' lives and recruit parishioners. In Paris, he stayed at a seminary for emigré Poles. His companion, Starowieyski, was bothered by the rudeness and overcrowding on the subways, but Wojtyla found that riding them afforded "an excellent opportunity to practice the internal life"—to meditate.[5]

Belgium, he wrote to "Grandma" Szkocka and her family, "is extremely well developed, full of railway lines, trams, etc., generally very rich. The standard of living is much above ours from before the war. . . . The Flemish are farmers and burghers . . . strongly religious in a traditional way, as we are. Walloons are more or less like the French . . . a Christianized society . . . [but] their Catholic religion . . . lacks the sincere feelings and spontaneity . . . of our religion."

Thanks to the Belgian College, Wojtyla and Starowieyski were under the care of a prominent Belgian bishop, later a cardinal.[6] In September, Wojtyla did pastor to Polish workers near the town of Charleroi. He wrote home for help in finding the father, back in Poland, of a mine worker he met who had been deported during the war; a Szkocka relative was able to track the man down. But Wojtyla reported no other information about the Polish refugees, nor whether he stayed with them for a few weeks or a few hours.

He wrote in a neat hand but already had a somewhat stilted style, and he rarely disclosed what he was thinking.[7]

Monsignor Joseph Dawson of Florida, who arrived at the Belgian College in October 1947 to do graduate work, immediately noticed Wojtyla, constantly with his prayer book, "knees on the chapel floor, not on a kneeler. I didn't ever see any other priest do that."

Wojtyla loved hearing confessions every other Sunday at a parish in suburban Rome: "Italian is probably one of the most beautiful languages in the world, especially when the simple people speak it," he wrote Mrs. Szkocka. "These Sundays are like a living stream of grace that flows through our human, truly priestly, life."

"He always carried a book, and if you were at the train station it would come out. He never seemed to waste a minute," says Bishop Larkin, then a young priest from America, who drew the spot next to Wojtyla at the dining table. "He was very curious about America, how the Church makes out in a country that has separation of Church and state. A lot of Europeans didn't buy into religious freedom. We told him it worked out very well. The whole idea was new to him."

Wojtyla joined pickup volleyball games at the college and sometimes skied in the nearby mountains. He talked only sketchily of his family, or of the Nazis or communists. Friends gleaned mainly that life in Poland required great secrecy. "I think he felt very much at home in Rome," says Monsignor Dawson. "Every inch of soil is drenched with the blood of martyrs. Poland went through martyrdom."

Still, Wojtyla wrote to Mrs. Szkocka, "I think about my country all the time." To Kotlarczyk, he wrote that he read the Gospels aloud in Polish every day, changing his inflection and style each time. He performed as Brother Albert at a talent show.

Thanking Grandma Szkocka and Mrs. Lewaj, the French teacher, for their help, he noted that to owe others was "only to owe everything to God more easily and continuously." He said God created debts among people "to help [them] find Him more easily."

Wojtyla's dissertation, "The Essence of Faith in John of the Cross,"[8] confronted the prevailing Thomist view that intellect was more important than will because it enabled one to understand the given truth. Both Saint John and Jan Tyranowski had emphasized the importance of will, to help *find* the truth (which Thomists believed was already found). But Wojtyla wrote tactfully and open-mindedly enough not to endanger his future Thomist credentials. He also wrote strictly of Christian theology, in terms that wouldn't apply to other forms of meditation.[9]

Probably most impressive is that at age twenty-seven, Wojtyla had already read John of the Cross in Spanish, discussed him in Italian with his teachers, written about him in Latin, and chatted about the whole process in French over dinner at the Belgian College. He seemed not even to notice such linguistic transitions, even though none of these was his primary language or even his second one (German).

A list reproduced in *Kalendarium* of library books he checked out shows a narrow focus on Catholicism. Seven times he borrowed a book on moral theology by Sapieha's former mentor at the University of Innsbruck, whom Sapieha must have spoken of.[10] At least three times he checked out *The Interior Life* by Cardinal Desire Mercier, who sought to apply Thomism to modern science and to reunify the Anglican Church with Rome. Notably absent from the list are works by Immanuel Kant and other thinkers not patronized by the Church.

While *Kalendarium* asserts that Wojtyla received another perfect score on his doctoral dissertation, Cardinal Ciappi insists he got only 29 of a possible 30, and graduated magna cum laude (with high honors), not summa cum laude (highest honors). "I still never thought I saw a sign of a cardinal or pope," Ciappi adds. "Many students get summa."

Whatever his score, Wojtyla didn't receive his doctorate for another thirty years because he could not afford to pay for the publication of his dissertation, as the Angelicum requires. When he was elected pope, the Angelicum finally waived the requirement and gave him his sheepskin.

Baron Starowieyski, the scholar who Sapieha expected would become a powerful bishop and whose need for a good education had allowed Wojtyla to tag along to Rome, was barred by the communists from returning to his homeland. He went instead to Brazil, where he was a priest until his death, in 1988.

World War II was fading fast from Western memories. New battle lines had been drawn. The Knights of Malta, a Vatican-sponsored international honorary organization, gave its highest award, the Grand Cross of Merit, to General Reinhard Gehlen, Hitler's anti-Soviet spy chief. Gehlen, who might otherwise have been hanged for war crimes, was now secretly recruiting former Nazis to serve the newly established U.S. Central Intelligence Agency, and became the first director of West Germany's new spy agency, which received CIA money.

Italian clergy were ordered to deny absolution from sin to communists or Marxist socialists. In 1948, the U.S. government intervened illegally in Italian elections, using money raised covertly from American corporations doing business in Europe, as well as Church funds provided by Cardinal Francis Spellman of New York. The money was deposited in the Vatican bank and paid for campaigns to defeat the Communist Party, which was supported by millions of financially strapped Italians.

After the war, Pius XII had returned to Benedict XV's dream of a Christian Democratic party, one that would fundamentally support business while also spreading benefits compassionately throughout society. Pius XI had let the idea die in favor of fascism. Now, with U.S. help, the Vatican again promoted the Christian Democratic Party, but this time clandestinely rather than openly.

A long-standing procedure was inaugurated. From 1948 until the end of the Cold War, the State Department and CIA secretly recruited U.S. businessmen to divert corporate funds to aid covert American military and propaganda activities overseas. This secret funding shielded the operations from public or congressional scrutiny.[11]

In the end, the Christian Democrats won, probably due less to any secret manipulation than to the value that most of Pius's Italian countrymen placed on their freedom. The Italian Communist Party remained strong, however, and eventually became a defiant counterforce to the Soviets. (Wojtyla, as pope, would befriend and praise the Party's leaders.) The organization of so much secret American aid had its greatest effect in the cultivation of a continuing, hidden national-security state within the United States.

The Cold War was on. The two sides were defined and engaged.

As Wojtyla prepared to return to Poland in June 1948, Stalin tried to force the Western allies out of Berlin by blockading road and rail traffic into the city. U.S. President Truman responded with an airlift. Hundreds of thousands of flights, sometimes at three-minute intervals, ferried food, fuel, and other sustenance into Berlin until the Soviets gave up, a year later.

Meanwhile, the communist government of Poland rounded up and detained some seven hundred priests. Larkin, Wojtyla's housemate, asked if he was afraid to go back: "He said yes, he was, but people needed him. He could easily have gotten some kind of appointment in Rome. Cardinal Furstenburg [director of the Belgian College] said he was the [most] outstanding student who ever resided there. But [Wojtyla] said he felt he was ordained for his people. He owed it to them to go back and help them in any way he could."

June 25, 1948, Karol Wojtyla boarded a train for Poland to begin his service.

Archbishop Paul Marcinkus

A blessing

Wanda Poltawska

Bohdan Cywinski

On the road

BOOK THREE

LAMENTATIONS

1

"He was skin and bones when he came back from Italy," says Kazimierz Suder, Wojtyla's seminary classmate.

Straightaway, Wojtyla asked how things were at the university.

"The philosophy department is now mainly Marxist. God doesn't exist," Suder told him. Distress crossed Wojtyla's face.

Within two weeks of Wojtyla's return, Sapieha appointed him assistant pastor, or "curate," in the hilltown of Niegowic, about a dozen miles southeast of Krakow. "Cardinal Sapieha sent him to a country parish to fatten him up," Suder says, only half joking. Malinski maintains that "the parish priest [in Niegowic] was one of the finest in the diocese," and that Sapieha chose him "to give Karol the best possible start in his pastoral career."

When Niegowic's residents first saw their new curate, July 28, 1948,[1] he was approaching on foot from the market town of Gdow. "He wore shabby trousers, a waistcoat, worn-out shoes, and carried a briefcase that I would be ashamed to take with me to market," according to Stanislaw Substelny, a parishioner. Wojtyla asked Substelny for directions, then turned away and "knelt before a wayside shrine. He prayed for a long time and then he got up and went the way I told him."[2]

Niegowic's church and the priests' quarters had neither running water nor electricity. Wojtyla lived among cows, chickens, and lime trees. His job was traveling by horsecart among nearby villages to teach in the schools. He told Malinski he was most concerned with confession—what he called the "personal ministry." A penitent would kneel and whisper through a grille to the priest, barely visible in a wooden booth. "Confession is the height of our activity as priests," Wojtyla believed. "You can't settle matters with a smooth word. You have to have a really serious, heartfelt talk with them."

While Wojtyla was in Niegowic, professors at the Jagiellonian read his dissertation from the Angelicum, approved it, and gave him the doctorate in Krakow that he had been denied in Rome because he couldn't pay the printing bill.

October 22, 1948, Primate Hlond died.[3] As was customary, he had written to Pope Pius from his deathbed to recommend a replacement. His choice was Stefan Wyszynski, the sociologist and wartime fugitive who had created a makeshift forest hospital at Laski during the Warsaw Uprising and who was now the bishop of Lublin.

Wyszynski's new book, *The Spirit of Human Work*, expanded on his positions of the 1930s—friendly to labor, wary of capitalism. His views, however, were only marginally more pro-labor than those expressed in Pope Leo XIII's landmark 1891 encyclical, *Rerum Novarum* ("Of Revolutions"), and in most subsequent papal pronouncements on economics, all of which represented a big change in Vatican policy.

In centuries past, popes had been associated with great riches. They seized or extorted vast estates from believers.[4] Some priests objected, arguing that if Jesus and his disciples hadn't owned property, neither should the Church; for this, they were burned at the stake (and excommunicated). Popes had begun to reverse such excesses even before Garibaldi's army confiscated Church property in 1870.

Communists ignored this evolution, however, and still depicted the Church in its ancient pose, as among Christendom's richest landlords—an institution that would predictably support property rights over labor rights. Communism would have been more welcome if the Church had maintained its extreme capitalist position. In fact, communism found its road easiest in Eastern Europe and Latin America, where the Church was slower to change its attitude toward labor.

Soviet-styled communism, however, was more extreme than the Church had ever been, even at its most rapacious. A five-year plan had just been introduced to collectivize agriculture and throw the wealth and energy of Poland into state-owned heavy industry. The economy would be directed by appointed officials, without regard to market demand.

While all this was done by Stalin's decree, it would be misleading not to note that many Poles supported communist economic policy (though few favored the police state that came with it). Lucjan Motyka, who would later rise to become head of the Party in Krakow and a pivotal figure in Wojtyla's life, exemplified the kind of Pole who made a peaceful communist administration possible.

Back in the 1940s, Motyka was a neighbor and acquaintance of Wojtyla's friends Halina and Tadeusz Kwiatkowski, though his support of the communists would divide them. "From the very beginning," Motyka says, "I was shaped as a man of the Left." In 1937, as a twenty-three-year-old labor-union secretary, Motyka had been thrown into a concentration camp for socialists by the Polish dictatorship. "Then the Nazis put me in Auschwitz."

After the war, he saw "Warsaw in ruins. Forty percent of our civilization was destroyed. Seven million people in the countryside [about one fourth of the population] had no land. There were millions of illiterates. Many people who disagreed with the Soviet model nevertheless saw communism as bringing some form of social justice. Common access to free education. To get rid of feudal elements in the social order."

Mieczyslaw Rakowski, the last communist prime minister of Poland, still argued in 1994 that "for millions of peasants, the new system was better than the prewar system. Poland was an undeveloped country between the wars. Between 1945 and 1980, seventeen million people went from farm to town. They found a better world."

Bishop Stefan Wyszynski believed that the Church itself should stand for such a better world. A CIA report called him an "enlightened and liberal thinker . . . often considered a radical," who "therefore seemed ideally suited to guide the Church" through these times.[5]

When Wyszynski was formally installed as primate in Poland, for many Poles he was also installed as interrex, a provisional national leader until an acceptable civil authority was restored. Yet even as he faced constant communist harassment on the one side, Wyszynski also had to cope with what the CIA called "the hidebound hierarchy" of the Church on the other. Many Polish clerics, often from aristocratic families that sent sons off to be bishops, thought the Laski intellectual circle that Wyszynski was associated with was too liberal and internationalist, a breeding ground for dangerous Western ideas that sought to transfer inherited wealth to working folk.

Wyszynski understood from the beginning that to succeed against the communists, he would have to bring the Church into accord with the resentment that many Poles still felt toward the old system. He "set out to change the Polish Church, to make it a Church of the peasants, the common people," says the historian Zygmunt Kubiak, a surviving member of the Laski group. "He slept little. He worked hard. He visited seminaries and tried to promote priests from peasant circles. He tried to work for social change. And he achieved it. Without this Church of the common people, there could never have been a Solidarity or a Walesa."

Most American and other Western anti-communists, however, favored a very different approach, despite the CIA report's praise for Wyszynski. In the West, the most famous Eastern European Church leader was Primate/Cardinal Jozsef Mindszenty of Hungary, Wyszynski's opposite. Mindszenty publicly defied his country's communist government and appealed to the United States and United Nations to undermine it. He issued a pastoral letter denouncing the government's redistribution of farmland and told farmers to refuse to accept land that had been seized from the Church. He rejected the government's offer to retain religious education in the schools in exchange for the Church's cooperation in making them public.

On a trip to the United States in 1947, Mindszenty, at a dinner, sat next to Monsignor John Krol of Cleveland, later the cardinal/archbishop of Philadelphia. Curious about Mindszenty's outspoken denunciation of "communist liars," Krol asked, "Don't you think there's a danger to you?" Replied Mindszenty, "Don't you think a dead cardinal might be much more serviceable to the Church in Hungary than a live one?" Krol, a man not easily silenced, was stopped in his tracks.[6]

In contrast, Wyszynski prepared for a militant battle that would remain peaceful. These very different attitudes—and the fact that Wojtyla would follow Wyszynski's model while the United States extolled Mindszenty—had a lot to do with how communism actually ended.

December 26, 1948, Mindszenty was arrested in Budapest, setting the stage for the era's most celebrated communist show trial. A propaganda display rather than a trial in the Western sense, it began in Budapest February 3, 1949. The world read in literal disbelief Mindszenty's confessions about conspiring with Americans and others to return the royal Hapsburg family to the Hungarian throne. Western observers speculated that he had been drugged, though visitors who had seen him said the cardinal had seemed all right the week before. Canceled checks drawn on a New York bank showed that Mindszenty had received large sums of money from Cardinal Spellman. The Hungarian government said he was using this money to overthrow it, though evidence suggested that he had spent at least some of it on limousines to ride in.

Mindszenty was sentenced to life in prison.

As Moscow consolidated power, it swept away nationalist window dressing from the governments of Eastern Europe. At the December 1948 Party Congress in Warsaw, the communists seized all authority. Even longtime Polish revolutionaries were purged from office if they had defended Polish sovereignty against Stalin or opposed the forced collectivization of small farms. Many were jailed, including Wladyslaw Gomulka, the closest thing to a genuine popular figure that the Polish communists ever put forward. He and his lieutenants were replaced in office by Stalinists. Bierut, who was widely perceived as an alien agent, became the undisputed Polish Party boss.

"The Soviets accused Gomulka of being a right-wing nationalist," says Motyka, Halina's neighbor, who attended the congress as a Gomulka supporter. So it is fair to ask why people like Motyka, if they truly cared for Poland, remained communist after the puppet nature of the regime became clear in 1948.

"I was once asked [this] by a Polish emigré [in the West], who reproached me for collaborating," Motyka replies. "I said, 'It is easy for you to say so. Here [in Poland], it was quite difficult to suggest to seven hundred people who were part of the Socialist Party that they should resist [the communist takeover]. Even in World War II, the real freedom fighters were [only] a tiny part of the nation. The rest just wanted to live.' "

2

Visiting Wojtyla in Niegowic in March 1949, Malinski noticed the way children approached and kissed Wojtyla's hand as they strolled. "He stroked their heads, and sometimes kissed their foreheads, which they raised expectantly." Wojtyla said young people often interrupted his reading through the day, but he seemed to welcome it.

At that moment in their careers, most future papal candidates would be manning a desk at the Vatican in preparation for a diplomatic posting overseas. Wojtyla had spent the winter making the rounds of neighboring villages. He told Malinski, "The snow sticks to the hem of your cassock and melts when you're indoors. Then in the open air it freezes so that the cassock is stiff and heavy and interferes with walking. By evening, you feel you can hardly go a step further, but you have to because you know people have been waiting for this visit all year. You go in and say, 'Blessed be Jesus Christ,' you greet the whole family, you pray with them and sprinkle the cottage with holy water, and the stables, too, so that the cattle will prosper during the coming year. Then you go back into the house and you can't escape sitting and talking to everyone for a bit."

Whenever he visited a village, he said, he would plan to sit in the confessional all day, believing that the Church had to extend itself to workers. Many villagers hadn't seen a priest in a year. He worried that priests were often becoming "bureaucrats," as he had seen happening in France, where many youths no longer knew who Jesus was, he said.

Even in Niegowic, however, Wojtyla's style of Christianity wasn't universally understood. Seeing him sleep on bare boards, sympathetic parishioners chipped in to buy him a featherbed; for Christmas, girls in the youth association sewed him a quilt. But when a woman in town was robbed, he gave her the featherbed, and after accepting the quilt gratefully, he gave it to three girls whose mother had recently died. Some parishioners were vocally upset that he had, to their minds, misappropriated their generosity.[1]

On the other hand, Wojtyla started a "Living Rosary" like Tyranowski's, and coached a drama group that performed a play. He married thirteen couples and baptized forty-eight children. When parishioners volunteered to paint the church for the pastor's birthday, Wojtyla suggested building a new church instead and organized a committee that, after his departure, built it.

That March, after a mere eight months in Niegowic, Wojtyla got a plum new assignment from Sapieha: St. Florian's Church in Krakow. Although technically just another parish, St. Florian's is right outside the old town, a haunt of students and professors at the Jagiellonian, and five minutes' walk from the market square.

As in Niegowic, Wojtyla's arrival, this time on a rickety country horsecart with a small valise and a few books, impressed parishioners as a demonstration of poverty. Some older parishioners complained that his sermons were both too long and too concerned with "asceticism and renunciation" in a society starved for goods.[2] But with youth, Wojtyla was an immediate hit. He visited the Jagiellonian campus often. He started another "Living Rosary" chapter and a singing group that specialized in Gregorian chants. He held seminars and weekend retreats for students and ran three-hour Thursday-night meetings for male students. Still in close touch with the Carmelites, he organized separate retreats for its priests and nuns.

He inaugurated courses for couples contemplating marriage and invited successfully married Catholics and other "experts" to lecture. All this amounted to an unusual whirlwind of activity for a new priest. As if that were not enough, on the side he began taking English lessons.

Soon after returning to Krakow, he dropped in on Jerzy Turowicz and the other editors of *Tygodnik Powszechny*, which he had continued to read even in Rome. He had written an article on the worker-priest movement and the state of the Church in France, based on his trip.

Says Turowicz, "He supported the idea of priests' working, which was always very controversial. The problem was that many [priests who worked] became Leftists or communists. Some even married and left the priesthood. In most cases, we refuse to publish articles when a priest brings them in, but this one was interesting and well written." Not only did Turowicz accept the piece, but "the Holy Spirit enlightened me to put it on page one."

Wojtyla's article blamed France's loss of religion on its lust for material wealth and warned that the same could happen in Poland. He urged Polish priests to be the servants of their parishioners and to stop taking fees for services like weddings and funerals.

Publication of his poetry soon followed. Wojtyla also began dropping by for performances and discussions at the newly reorganized Rhapsody Theater, just down the street from his church, and even helped the troupe assemble souvenirs to raise money. By all accounts, he remained silent and aloof regarding politics. People thought him uninterested in the struggles that were shaping the Cold War. There was not much he could have done in any case.

After Mindszenty was condemned, the anti-Church campaign spread from Hungary to Poland. March 14, 1949, the Polish government wrote to the Church's governing bishops, or "Episcopate," in Warsaw, complaining that priests were "cooperating with various criminal, anti-state groups that are agents of Anglo-American imperialism."

The letter put Wyszynski at a crossroads. He could have accepted the communists' invitation to a showdown, as Mindszenty had. Instead, he assigned some bishops to negotiate with state officials to find a modus vivendi, a way to live peacefully under Soviet domination while preserving as much independence for the Church and freedom for the Polish people as possible.

The "hidebound hierarchy" (in the CIA's phrase) opposed him. Some bishops supported the Western-funded anti-communist guerrillas who were still fighting in the forests. Among those most opposed to Wyszynski's position was Cardinal Sapieha. "We have no brave people—they want to make agreements," Sapieha grumbled to a young American aid worker he met in Rome.[3] Now eighty-two, Sapieha had grown ever closer to the aging Pope Pius XII, who also thought no deals should be made with communists.

July 2, 1949, Pius declared that he would excommunicate any Catholic who joined or contributed to a communist party, or published or wrote anything that advocated communism. As if that wasn't enough, he also forbade priests to marry, bury, take confession from, give communion to, or otherwise assist anyone who *helped* communists. He even pressured the Italian government into firing communist civil servants.

Meanwhile, the Polish government used the offer of jobs and scholarships to lure Wyszynski's clergy into "Pax," a state-sponsored organization of "patriotic priests" and Catholic laymen. Priests who did not join Pax risked being jailed on trumped-up charges. The government took over Church hospitals, audited churches, and fined priests large sums for minor discrepancies.

In Czechoslovakia, Archbishop Josef Beran, who had spent the war in German camps, was imprisoned by the Russians with all his leading bishops. Eleven of the country's thirteen seminaries were closed. In two nights of police maneuvers, convents and monasteries were emptied, and soon eleven thousand persons were being held in prisons or labor camps for their Catholic vows. Church schools were closed, and Church lands confiscated. As in Poland, the remaining clergy were invited to join an organization that promised government-paid benefits.

Soviet officials toured the region trying to sell the new regime to workers. They boasted that "unemployment—the inseparable companion of capitalism"—was now gone for good. Medals, vacations, and praise were awarded to miners and other laborers. "Long live the glorious working class!" exclaimed a typical speech—and part of a worker's job was to applaud. "Long live the unbreakable Polish-Soviet friendship! Long live the Leader and Teacher of the Soviet Nation, the Great Genius of Mankind, Generalissimo Stalin!" The communist-controlled press published every word, filling papers with articles glorifying loyal workers.

What the controlled press didn't report was that the five-year agricultural plan was failing dismally, as a third of the farms refused to deliver their produce.

In January 1950, the government press began alleging that goods donated to the Polish branch of Caritas, an international Catholic charity, were being sold on the black market. Priests were said to be living the high life on donated funds, while only a tiny part reached the needy. The government seized Caritas and imposed a new administration composed of members of the Pax "patriotic priests" movement. Newspapers carried lurid tales of drunken priests and nuns coercing children into sex at a youth home, while dishing out bad food and no medical care.

It's unlikely that anyone swallowed these stories whole. But they did play successfully on widespread resentment about the comforts and privileges of the clergy. Many Poles complain even today that under communism, clergy were second only to Party members in the affluence they enjoyed. Everyone could see that nuns, rather than tending to the needy, were often employed to tidy the comparatively spacious living quarters and serve the relatively well-stocked tables of communities of priests. So when the communists stirred the pot with phony stories, real letters flowed to newspapers, criticizing the

Church. The true problem wasn't theft or debauchery, but rather a popular sense that the priesthood was often beneficial rather than sacrificial.

For this and other reasons, many sincere idealists, both clergy and laymen, joined Pax, even though its mass meetings ratified government action against the Church.[4] Among the important young Catholics with socialist inclinations who joined Pax was Tadeusz Mazowiecki, future friend of the pope, and Solidarity's choice to be prime minister of Poland after communism.

Another, Andrzej Micewski, who was among the Pax members appointed to take over Caritas, later became Wyszynski's authorized biographer. Micewski still defends his Pax membership. "You must understand that Pax was the only public organization in which you could be active as a Catholic," he says. "There were no other opportunities for people like us to become involved." Even Jerzy Turowicz, Wojtyla's friend and editor, helped run a group that supported the government on peace and German issues, though it didn't oppose the bishops on Church issues as Pax did.[5]

The Cold War momentum grew with each exchange of insults. After the State Department warned of danger to Americans in Poland, Ingersoll Rand, which had just sold the Poles some mining equipment that they were not yet trained to run, reneged on its promise of technical assistance. Other companies did likewise. One American priest in Warsaw on an aid mission wired home in a panic from the U.S. embassy that he was about to be arrested. (He wasn't; generally, Westerners weren't harmed by the police-state repression.)[6]

Wyszynski ordered priests to stop attending meetings critical of the the Church. February 12, 1950, he had a message read from every pulpit in Poland, including Wojtyla's: "The Episcopate has done much and is willing to do more to maintain peace. . . . There are, however, limits we bishops cannot cross if we wish to be faithful to the commandments of God. . . . I call on you to pray for those who persecute and insult us. To no one let us repay evil for evil, but on the contrary let us do good to those who hold us in hatred."

Wyszynski pursued a campaign of persistent reasonableness, aiming to retain his and the Church's dignity against all provocation. Consciously or not, it was the same tactic used in the old Oriental martial art known as t'ai chi ch'uan, in which one absorbs and dissipates the force of a powerful enemy rather than thrusting against it. He wrote Bierut that he shared the communist boss's wish to keep priests out of politics; he expressed "surprise" at Pax's attempt to draw priests *into* politics. It looked, he said, like a "war against religion."

Although the government's public response was a diatribe, accusing the Church of seeking to restore the "regime [of] capitalists and big landowners," privately Bierut seemed impressed. He proposed precisely the kind of deal

Wyszynski had requested: "While recognizing the pope as authority . . . in religious matters, the Episcopate will be directed in other matters by the *raison d'état* [political purpose] of People's Poland." Would Wyszynski sign?

The primate surveyed the dismal scene before him. Germany and other issues separated him from the Vatican. Pax had ignited suspicion among his priests. Average Catholics were, in the words of an American diplomat, "mentally and morally torn asunder . . . confused and bewildered."[7] Suddenly, Polish communist officials were summoned to Moscow,[8] after which word spread that they might create a "Polish National Church," which would placate people's thirst for religion but would operate under government control, severing ties with the Vatican.

Faced with this prospect, Wyszynski, with small adjustments, accepted Bierut's deal, the first that a Catholic leader had ever cut with a communist. He would, "in accordance with Church teachings," instruct priests to "foster among the faithful respect for the laws and prerogatives of the state." The pope would be "supreme authority" in "matters of faith, the moral order, and ecclesiastical jurisdiction," but in "other matters" the Episcopate "must act in conformance with the *raison d'état* of the Polish government." In return, the government guaranteed continued Church participation in national life. It would keep religious instruction in schools and recognize Catholic organizations, universities, and publications, so long as they obeyed laws that applied to everyone else.*

The deal's most important point, however, was its mere existence. As anti-communists would loudly complain, the Church, by signing it, had recognized the legal authority of a communist government. American officials ridiculed Wyszynski as a coward, a fool, or both.[9] But by the same token, the communists recognized the legal authority of the Catholic Church. What Wyszynski accepted in 1950 represented a tactical retreat from a position that was fast eroding anyway. While surrendering no fundamental principles, it bought him time to try to unify the country and strengthen the Church's hand.

Knowing that Cardinal Sapieha and Pope Pius XII would view the agreement as a sellout, Wyszynski held up signing it until Sapieha was off to Rome,

---

* In other significant points, the bishops pledged to "encourage the people to work . . . for reconstruction of the country," to punish clergy found guilty of antistate activity, and to urge Pope Pius to recognize the former German territories as Polish. The Church would also accept the idea of rural cooperatives, a compromise that Bierut was trying to sell to the Soviets in place of the collectivization of small farms, which almost no one in Poland wanted. For its part, the government guaranteed that students, soldiers, and hospital patients would have access to priests.

intending specifically to ask Pius to stop Wyszynski from making a deal with the Polish government. When news of the completed deal reached Sapieha there, his octogenarian temper exploded. "I do not know what did they do!" he kept fuming to Father Michael Zembrzuski, an American aid official.[10] Wyszynski later told the whole story to a Polish friend in Rome, not knowing that his friend had become an American spy and was filing reports that are now available at the U.S. National Archive.[11]

Wyszynski's friend told U.S. agents that Sapieha brought back to Poland "an extremely stiff and disapproving message from the Vatican, chiding the [Polish Church] hierarchy for capitulating to the state." Pius informed Wyszynski that "although the agreement was inherently bad," it would stand because "it was signed and publicly acknowledged.... The Vatican, however, expects more resolute resistance on the part of bishops in the future."[12]

Pius was particularly embarrassed by the agreement because he had just published a "White Paper" denouncing communists as enemies of the Church in Eastern Europe. There is also evidence that the Vatican was still working secretly with Western spy agencies.*

Previously classified U.S. documents now reveal that Pius was so furious that he plotted to remove Wyszynski and send a replacement to Poland to take a tougher line. According to U.S. intelligence, the intended replacement was Vojciech Turowski,[13] a Pole and head of the Pallantine religious order.[14] First,

---

* At about this time, the communist government of Romania expelled the papal nuncio there—Archbishop Gerald O'Hara, an American and good friend of Cardinal Spellman—charging him with spying for the West. The Vatican indignantly denied the charges, and O'Hara continued doing Vatican diplomatic work. Recently, however, impressive evidence has appeared that suggests O'Hara did use his Vatican positions on the CIA's behalf. Virginia Snyder, a private detective in Delray Beach, Florida, was hired in 1987 by two women claiming to be the lover and daughter of Archbishop O'Hara, from Savannah, Georgia, where O'Hara was bishop from 1935 through the war. In searching for his estate on their behalf, Snyder found persuasive evidence in support not only of the women's claims, but also of O'Hara's close friendship with senior CIA officials. These contacts were described by independently interviewed sources in the United States and Britain, where O'Hara was serving as a Vatican representative when he died, in 1963. Roy Cohn, a lawyer for and friend of Cardinal Spellman with long-standing CIA ties of his own, was identified as having come to England with a CIA official whom O'Hara had known in the U.S.; the two men closed a large, active bond account that O'Hara had kept at a London brokerage, as well as his safety-deposit box. My own interviews with Snyder's sources and my examination of her documents leave me reasonably convinced that O'Hara was involved with the CIA.

Turowski was to return to Poland as bishop of Czestochowa, a major Catholic center because of the revered Black Madonna shrine there. Then Wyszynski was to be called to Rome and kept there while Turowski took over as primate.

But a funny thing happened when Turowski arrived to take his place as the new bishop of Czestochowa: he was given only a temporary visa, then shipped back to Italy by the Polish government. An Italian diplomat was shocked when he tried to discuss this with Wyszynski. He expected the primate to be outraged by this communist interference in Church affairs, but instead, Wyszynski's secretary, a priest, defended the expulsion of the new bishop. Allied intelligence suspected that Wyszynski had seen through Pius's ruse and conspired with the communists to boot out the new man, foiling the Vatican's planned coup d'état in Warsaw. In any event, the hostility that had once burned between Pius XI and Sapieha was now rekindled between Pius XII and Wyszynski.

The Americans were angry that Pius's plan failed,[15] but they had other fish to fry. In Korea—which, like Europe, had unexpectedly stayed divided along World War II occupation lines—Soviet-trained troops from the north invaded the south. As in Berlin, Truman resisted Stalin's attempt to overrun a U.S. ally. With UN support, the President sent troops to Korea. America was back at war.

3

Wyszynski and Sapieha always set aside their differences when facing the government. They jointly protested communist violations of the April 1950 agreement, including the mass firing of teacher-priests from the schools. But many Polish priests still gossiped that their two leaders were split and that the Vatican had turned hostile under German manipulation.[1]

Wojtyla tended his flock at St. Florian's, seemingly oblivious to such infighting. The Jagiellonian students who stopped by to talk to him included not just Catholics but communists and those who went along with the communists to benefit their careers. "He was very open-minded," says Jerzy Turowicz of *Tygodnik Powszechny.*

Wojtyla wrote down students' questions and his answers, and gave a copy to Father Suder, his former seminary classmate. Suder and others began using the notes as an illegal manual for talks with youth, covering such topics as "the origin of man, whether God existed, [and] Christian love."[2] Wojtyla had constructed what amounted to an underground anti-communist catechism that achieved dangerously wide circulation in the early 1950s. He also took young parishioners to the outskirts of Krakow after school to play soccer; this, too, violated communist regulations on the formation of youth groups. Some priests were arrested for doing what Wojtyla did.

For Karol Tarnowski, then an aspiring philosophy student, Wojtyla remains unique among priests he has known. "His confession lasted an hour," Tarnowski says. "It was a big, personalized, philosophical discussion. He treated me as a man, very seriously."

To the relief of many, Wojtyla shortened his sermons. He continued to ignore politics in favor of cosmic moral ideas, a lucky coincidence between the way his mind worked and the practicality of living in a police state. His articles in *Tygodnik Powszechny* dealt with "faith, religion, morals, the Church," Turowicz says.

Even though Wojtyla avoided politics, it was agreed he should publish his writing under a pseudonym.[3] He picked "Andrzej Jawien," the name of the protagonist in a popular novel about a young Catholic intellectual experiencing a crisis of faith. His poems remained passionate, but were philosophical, never narrative. A later reviewer noted that they were "about the nature of man" but nonetheless devoid of "individual human beings."[4]

Acquaintances from these days recall Wojtyla's shyness and his shabby-looking secondhand cassocks.[5] Despite their many meetings, even Turowicz never learned of Wojtyla's tragic childhood.

The first week of October 1950 was one of those quiet turning points of history that pass unrecognized at the time. It is worth mentioning because it looms so large in retrospect.

That week, the United States won an overwhelming victory in its (and the UN's) war in Korea. U.S. General Douglas MacArthur had staged an amphibious invasion behind North Korean lines, then routed the enemy out of South Korea and chased it well into the north. The aggressing army was shattered, and its industrial base broken. U.S. forces now had the opportunity to establish a new, more defensible boundary.

Instead, President Truman allowed General MacArthur and the newly created CIA to push on. Their aim, it's now clear, was to overturn the 1949 communist revolution in China. MacArthur met privately with former Chinese dictator Chiang Kai-shek, who had taken his remaining army to Taiwan. Chiang and the CIA launched a secret guerrilla war against China, attacking from bases located mostly in neighboring Burma.

China, which correctly blamed the Korean war on the Soviets, repeatedly demanded a friendly Korean buffer between it and any new American forces. If MacArthur's troops reached the Korea-China border, China said, it would enter the war. MacArthur may even have wanted that, figuring he could then A-bomb China.[6] There was no public or congressional discussion of the new agenda; Truman himself may not have realized that the Korean goalposts had been moved back. But when U.S. troops reached the border, China kept its word and unleashed its vast manpower.

The immediate, tangible result was that the U.S. victory in Korea was reduced to a tie; nearly fifty thousand Americans were killed (90 percent of U.S. casualties in Korea came after China attacked); and the seeds were sown for the Vietnam war, which began a few years later. But the most important result was *in*tangible: U.S. foreign policy, governed largely by the Constitution for the previous 160 years, was implicitly redefined.

Instead of fighting wars to accomplish finite objectives, the U.S. now entered a permanent state of war, to maintain the upper hand in a conflict that was assumed to be endless, against a global communist onslaught that was thought to be coordinated but was in fact inflated out of all reality.

The U.S. government created an informal, untitled new branch of the military that transected existing branches and demanded secrecy in its work, no matter how lethal or costly. Some operations were managed by the Pentagon, others by the CIA. A warlike propaganda apparatus sustained fear among voters and also in Congress, which appropriated fabulous sums without requiring specific accounting. All other policies of the world's strongest country were subordinated to the conduct of this permanent war.

Strains of this policy had been growing for years. But the first week of October 1950, the policy gained the upper hand with the President. The new U.S. attitude meant fundamental, involuntary change in the life of every human being—big-businessmen and revolutionaries, villagers in Third World countries that weren't named yet, and even the priests at St. Florian's Church in Krakow.

In December 1950, all Polish citizens were ordered to exchange their old birth, employment, and marriage certificates for new ones. Long lines and confusion swamped the country. Although called a census, the result was to assign everyone to a neighborhood committee. These committees, endemic to communist countries, were run by resident busybodies who monitored people's behavior and contacts and enabled the government to control travel.

The last privately owned business enterprises were snuffed out as agents closed down entrepreneurs who were still trying to operate from home after their plants had been seized. Since the communist production system couldn't stock the government's retail stores, which were often empty, the free market emerged on its own as a black market.

Otherwise honest citizens who would never have stolen money or broken the law grew to rely on illegal goods, which were swiped from government warehouses and sold on the sly. Networks were developed of friends and relatives who worked in various state enterprises and slipped each other needed goods. Ordinary life became full of secrecy and illegality. Despite all the splendid dreams of Karl Marx, that was how communism invariably worked.

Many workers had believed at first that the system would improve their lot. Instead, they soon found themselves working harder, earning less, and, perhaps worst of all, having to listen to the lies their children brought home each day from communist-run schools.

As the economy stalled, the communists' one remaining popular issue was the resurgence of West Germany with the help of American capitalists and former Nazis. Exploiting this, Premier Bierut unilaterally named Polish bishops as permanent administrators of dioceses in the former German territories. (The administrators installed by the late Cardinal Hlond had been provisional.) In order to preserve the principle that only the Church could assign bishops, Wyszynski had no choice but to appoint the men Bierut had named. Many Poles applauded the government for forcing the issue because it promoted Polish interests against Germany, even if it did usurp Church power.

Only the pope was supposed to appoint bishops, however, and Pius still wanted the dioceses in German hands. Wyszynski worried privately that Pius would fire him on sight during his forthcoming trip to Rome.[7] April 2, 1951, he boarded a train, carrying a handful of Polish soil and a picture of the Black Madonna. On his arrival in Rome, he met with an old friend, Wlodzimierz Sznarbachowski, for the first of many conversations between them. Wyszynski didn't know it, but Sznarbachowski, too, was a spy. The primate's deepest confidences were passed on in reports stamped "SECRET" (mostly now available at the U.S. National Archive). He said Poles approved of his deals with Bierut, considering them necessary to keep the Church independent and to "preserve the Polish nation."

Wyszynski waited days to see the angry pope, meanwhile facing the secretary of state, Dominico Tardini. "The trouble is Tardini," he said later. "He has no understanding of communist society, the conditions we are living in."[8] Later Wyszynski told Cardinal Franz König of Vienna that he had had "a rough time in Rome" but had finally "convinced Pius" that the deals with Bierut had been "right for the Church."[9] He said Pius had given him the same authority he had given Hlond to bypass Rome in making appointments. But for twenty more years, the Vatican continued to call the former German dioceses by their German names and to refer to their Polish bishops as temporary administrators.[10] Meanwhile, the Polish communist press branded the Vatican "an enemy of peace and democracy" and "a direct assistant of the American warmongers."

Now seventy-five, Pope Pius decided to shelve an idea two cardinals were pushing, to convene a second Vatican Council. (The first was in 1869–70.) Cardinal Alfredo Ottaviani, who policed the world for heresy as head of the Holy Office, wanted a council to combat "the great accumulation of errors that are being diffused," and also to clarify that Mary's physical body, like Jesus', had gone to heaven along with her soul (the "Assumption"), and that she had become "Queen" there. Deciding to bury the controversy rather than magnify it with a council, Pius simply condemned the errors and proclaimed Mary's status infallibly.[11] (Some say this was the only time a pope has spoken infallibly; some say there were other times. Unfortunately, all the sources are fallible.)

In May 1951, Jerzy Turowicz replaced Father Piwowarczek as top editor at *Tygodnik Powszechny* because the police had grown suspicious of Piwowarczek's ties to a Western-led resistance movement. Turowicz says he knew about the secret Western contacts, but doubts that Wojtyla did. The big news in Krakow that summer was the opening of a huge steel mill that the Russians had financed in the suburb of Nowa Huta; some forty thousand workers were moved off farms into new apartment projects as the government sought to create a proletarian worker class in the country's most tradition-bound Catholic area. Car and bicycle plants were coming soon.

For Wojtyla, the summer also brought personal news: his happy pastorship was under threat. Father Ignacy Rozycki of the Jagiellonian University philosophy faculty, having taught Wojtyla in the seminary and read his theology dissertation, had decided that Wojtyla was meant to be a scholar, not a pastor. Rozycki had persuaded Sapieha to send Wojtyla to the Jagiellonian for a second doctorate, this time in philosophy.

Wojtyla protested that he had already sacrificed the contemplative life he had wanted; now they should let him enjoy being a pastor. Sapieha waved off his pleas, but Wojtyla remonstrated so passionately that the cardinal promised him one more audience.[12]

He didn't get it: Sapieha died July 23, 1951. Wojtyla was doubtless among the 250,000 people who attended the funeral despite communist efforts to minimize the event. Wyszynski, in his oration, again asked for peace with the government but promised that the Church would resist new attacks.

Wojtyla had to be thinking about his own crisis. He loved his job. He had set new records for giving retreats. He took students to the Tatra Mountains south of Krakow, skiing in winter, hiking in summer. He had baptized 229 babies and married 160 couples, a great satisfaction. He had grown close to the group at *Tygodnik Powszechny*; about twenty staff members attended his 7:00 P.M. Mass at St. Florian's and once a month stayed for supper. Wojtyla liked listening to Turowicz and his colleagues discuss politics and Church-state relations, though he rarely said much himself.[13]

Going back to school now would mean the end of all this. "It's more than a doctorate," he moaned to his seminary-mate Malinski. "It means embarking on an academic career, and I don't see myself as an academician. I can't imagine not carrying on some kind of pastoral work."

He appealed to Sapieha's replacement, Archbishop Eugeniusz Baziak, for permission to split his time between school and St. Florian's. Baziak shook his head. "I won't agree to any half-and-half solution," he said. "You will not be allowed to do pastoral work except with my personal permission on each occasion."[14]

Baziak even decreed that Wojtyla move in with Father Rozycki, who had a first-floor flat on a narrow street literally in the shadow of the Wawel. Malinski describes Wojtyla's new room as "large, dark . . . hung with huge reproductions of stained glass windows [made] by a friend of Father Rozycki's." Wojtyla's unwanted mentor was also his domineering roommate and decorator. He was trapped.

Rozycki even selected Wojtyla's thesis topic: the ethical system of German philosopher Max Scheler. The first task was to translate Scheler's massive book *Formalism and the Ethics of Substantive Values* from German into Polish.

"Look what I've got to cope with," Wojtyla complained to Malinski. "I can hardly make it all out, my German is poor, and there are a lot of technical terms I don't know how to translate." Besides that, he had been made an assistant professor and had to teach classes.

Still, he made the best of circumstances he couldn't change—as he always would. Soon enough he was telling Malinski that Scheler "opens up a whole new world, a world of values and a fresh view of mankind." Every Wednesday at 8:15 P.M. he was allowed to return to St. Florian's to lead a discussion on ethics. He continued to take student groups to the mountains and said weekly Masses at St. Anne's, the huge Gothic basilica that dominates Krakow's market square.

In Poland's rigidly controlled communication system, the Church was an island of permitted interchange. Caution still had to be exercised because the government had spies and hidden microphones, and even bishops could be (and sometimes were) jailed for sedition. But Wyszynski and his bishops regularly discussed events with unusual freedom. Wyszynski also sent his priests, as a group, messages that the censors would never have allowed to be printed in public. While each priest knew that his name was on a folder in a secret-police office somewhere, he could read the primate's messages in church on Sunday, and even add some words of his own in the same spirit, and expect to get home safely.

Stalin wanted to preserve the myth that religion was allowed, so long as it was loyal. What was forbidden was any challenge to the official pretense that communism was the best way to govern society, and that the Soviet Union was a model of communism. For all Poles, life was, in part, a game: to say what needed saying in a way that would allow them to continue saying it. Church-men played this game in public.

Wojtyla, and all Poland, received an education in communications from Wyszynski. The primate turned the communists' propaganda style against them, using words they favored, like *freedom* and *justice*, to construct messages that conveyed the very opposite of what the communists meant by those terms. If he wanted to attack a particular aspect of communism, such as disrespect for God, Wyszynski found a similar aspect of capitalist society and attacked that. Poles knew what he meant.[15]

Wyszynski couldn't supplant the government, which came at gunpoint, but he aimed over the long haul to engage it persistently and constructively—to refuse to go away. Each message, each homily, advanced his purpose of cementing the participation of the Church in the life of society. He found virtues that he and the communists both admired, such as discipline and con-tribution to the community. When the government promoted a valid cause—say, more work on the harvest—Wyszynski made sure to have his priests help from the pulpit, but in ways that subtly endorsed private, not collectivized, farming. Churchmen lent prestige to many communist campaigns for interna-tional peace.

Historically, neither communism nor Catholicism had put much stock in free expression. Just as Wojtyla returned to his studies, Catholic academics in Poland were hit from both sides. New rules came down implementing Stalin's decree that the purpose of universities was to "build up . . . the cadre of the people's intellectual leadership . . . in the fight for . . . socialism." No less daunting was Pius XII's encyclical *Humani Generis*, which condemned evolutionism and other common beliefs. Thinkers on Polish theological faculties who ventured beyond strict Thomism were now muzzled by both Rome *and* Moscow.

When the government offered to publish the work of Pax members in an effort to lure more priests to join that movement, Wyszynski prohibited clergy from publishing articles or books without his permission. When Wyszynski himself wrote an article for *Tygodnik Powszechny* criticizing a new constitution decreed by the government, the censors banned not only the article but the whole newspaper, cutting off its supply of printing paper. The government even launched a campaign against Christmas, calling instead for "New Year's trees" and "New Year's gifts."

It was in this atmosphere that Wojtyla returned to academia to study Max Scheler (1874–1928), a disciple of the philosophical school known as phenomenology.

4

Because Wojtyla studied phenomenologists and has written about them even as pope, he is constantly called one. In fact, he never was—at least as most phenomenologists use the term.

Scheler, Wojtyla's subject, was a student and disciple of Edmund Husserl (1859–1938), known as the father of phenomenology. Husserl and Scheler, both Germans, had been fascinated by aspects of the work of Immanuel Kant (1724–1804), another German, who is often considered the greatest philosopher of recent centuries. Like Plato, Aristotle, Augustine, and Thomas Aquinas before him, Kant was heavily concerned with ethics—choosing right from wrong. But he also thought (as did the others) about the nature of knowledge itself.

Kant tried to distinguish between what really happens and what we perceive. Plato had used an analogy to explain his view: reality occurs behind our backs, and we observe it as shadows projected on a wall in front of us, like a primitive movie. These perceptions are what Kant called phenomena (in contrast to pure ideas, which he called noumena). Husserl devoted himself to the study of perceptions—hence the name of his school, "phenomenology."

Unlike the traditional greats, however, Husserl was among a growing number of philosophers for whom the knowledge process was the primary focus, not just a sidelight. In part, this fascination with process was a reaction to modern science—an effort to relate its discoveries to the world of Plato and Aristotle. But to some minds, it also diverted philosophy from essential ethical questions and reduced it to hairsplitting.

Husserl dismissed the distinction between reality and perception. For him, reality *was* what people perceived. This issue has sometimes been reduced to the question: If a tree fell in the forest and nobody heard it, did it really fall? To Thomas Aquinas, it certainly did fall; God heard it, if nobody else. But to

Husserl, it didn't fall—or, at least, it doesn't matter whether it fell. Reality is rooted in human consciousness, and what counts is how your mind handles your perceptions.

Wojtyla reveled in his exposure to phenomenology, as he generally did in new ideas. But he was fundamentally at odds with what it sprang from: the modern concentration on the knowledge process. Wojtyla traced this trend—as others have—to the French philosopher René Descartes (1596–1650), who agonized for many years and hundreds of pages before finally deciding that he existed, because who else had been thinking about it, if not he?

In a 1994 book, *Crossing the Threshold of Hope*, John Paul II painted Descartes as the villain in the history of philosophy. When an interviewer asked why God didn't reveal himself clearly enough to persuade doubters, the pope berated the question as "characteristic of modern philosophy—the history of which begins with Descartes, who split thought from existence.... How different from the approach of Saint Thomas, for whom it is not thought which determines existence, but existence ... which determines thought!"[1]

Thomas believed that natural law, certain and immutable, preceded human thought. He was a religious thinker for whom God was critical. Husserl didn't invoke God. Like Descartes, Husserl was trying to decide whether *anything* is certain, given the limitations of human thought. Husserl wrote that to best study phenomena, one should isolate them from all preexisting ideas, a process he called bracketing. Only the object under study mattered. Obviously, this process conflicted with Thomas's ideas on natural law.

Phenomenology might never have taken off—and almost surely wouldn't have landed on Wojtyla's plate—had it not been for Søren Kierkegaard (1813–1855), a Dane. Although Kierkegaard's books weren't translated in time to influence Husserl, several of Husserl's students—including Scheler, Wojtyla's subject—did read Kierkegaard and decided that his philosophy, called existentialism, would allow Husserl's ideas to be applied to the study of ethics.[2]

Kierkegaard was a devout Christian (Protestant) and was fed up, just as Wojtyla would be, with the thread of philosophy running from Descartes, which asked how we know we exist, whether a tree really fell if nobody heard it, and so on. Kierkegaard believed that what matters is not what you know, or how you explain it, but *what you do*. To be a Christian, act like one.

Kierkegaard was aflame with mystical passion, like Jan Tyranowski and Saint John of the Cross. He is the writer mentioned here whom one would think Wojtyla would be most attracted to. But for some reason—maybe the scarcity of translations, or that he was a Protestant and Wojtyla's schools were Catholic—Kierkegaard didn't seem to catch Wojtyla's attention.[3]

Kierkegaard's invention, existentialism, holds that you define yourself by what you do while you exist, rather than being defined by some ideal that pre-dates you.[4] In one swoop, his philosophy threw out Aquinas's baby (natural law) and Descartes's bathwater (an obsession with thought processes). Ironi-cally, existentialism mostly bypassed Kierkegaard's fellow religionists and was popularized by novelists such as Frenchmen Jean-Paul Sartre, Albert Camus, and André Gide, who were more Marxist than Christian.

Pope John Paul II and his friend, French Cardinal Jean-Marie Lustiger, once confessed to each other that they had felt a youthful attraction to those authors in the 1940s, around the time John Paul went to France.[5] This is especially ironic because existentialism was among the common beliefs that Pius XII expressly condemned in *Humani Generis.* Pius later condemned it a second time to placate Cardinal Ottaviani, who wanted existentialism denounced at a Vati-can Council. Despite their condemnations, the future Pope John Paul II was about to seize on existentialism and turn it in a new direction.

Husserl's most famous disciple was Martin Heidegger (1889–1976), whose work combining Husserl with Kierkegaard won him Husserl's philosophy chair at the University of Freiburg when Husserl retired. In the 1930s, Heidegger tramped about in a Nazi uniform. Ironically, a second Husserl disciple, Edith Stein (1891–1943), was born Jewish. Although she converted to Catholicism and became a Carmelite nun, she was murdered by the Nazis at Auschwitz; John Paul II has initiated her path to sainthood.

Scheler, Wojtyla's subject, was Husserl's third major disciple. He was born to Protestant-Jewish parents but converted to Catholicism at age fourteen, say-ing he was attracted by the ceremonies. It certainly couldn't have been Catholic moral teachings that appealed to him:[6] though a brilliant student, popular teacher, and fiery lecturer, Scheler preferred sex and booze. He was banned from the University of Munich for moral turpitude.

While Benedict XV preached that World War I was morally indefensible, Scheler (who was saved from the trenches by bad eyesight) took to writing public-relations tracts for the kaiser, demonizing Anglo-American democracy as well as (after 1917) Russian communism. He renounced Catholicism; though he complained of philosophical fine points, his resignation from the Church was timed to allow him to divorce his second wife and marry a third. Husserl eventually asked to be disassociated from him.

It's surprising that anyone would expect a scoundrel like Scheler to appeal to the punctilious Wojtyla; Rozycki and other university scholars may simply have wanted a first-rate young mind like Wojtyla's to grapple with a modern philosophical movement like phenomenology in order to keep the faculty up to date.[7] But theological historian George Hunston Williams offers another reason for Wojtyla's being assigned to study Scheler: in spite of all Scheler's faults, he suggests, Catholic authorities may have hoped to turn him into a weapon against Kant.

Kant, having decided that people were incapable of accurately perceiving an outside message from God, decided to think out his own ethics and, in his case, basically ended up reproducing the Golden Rule from the Bible. But his do-it-yourself approach contradicted Thomism: others working out their own ethics might arrive at a more sinister ideal. Because Kant's popularity among scholars threatened the Church, several Catholics had tried and failed to discredit him, using Scheler's critique. Perhaps Rozycki thought that Wojtyla would be smart enough to succeed.[8]

But if that was the plan, Kant once again escaped. Wojtyla liked Scheler's passion and felt his method; phenomenology—with more emphasis on feelings than Husserl—could be useful to a Christian ethicist. In the end, though, he rejected Scheler just as other Catholics had—something consistently overlooked by phenomenologists wanting to claim the pope as one of them.

It is important to know *why* Wojtyla rejected Scheler: he said that because Scheler's phenomenological method was limited to the life experience of the philosopher, it could not logically vindicate all Catholic ethical teaching as revealed in scripture and in the Church's pronouncements. In other words, Scheler's approach failed because it could not validate Catholicism's array of preexisting conclusions.

Professor Williams calls Wojtyla's dissertation "slight" and claims it ignored much of what Scheler actually said. Others complain that by playing Catholic doctrine as a trump card, Wojtyla removed himself from the rules of reason and thus from philosophy.

The dissertation does display a fundamental gap between Wojtyla and Scheler. As put succinctly by the pope's former philosophy student and colleague Halina Bortnowska, "Phenomenologists cannot believe in natural law. You cannot be a phenomenologist and a Thomist at the same time." By traditional standards, the pope must be counted a Thomist.

But for Wojtyla, traditional standards may not be enough. After long analysis, Monsignor Richard Malone of St. Charles Borromeo Seminary in Philadelphia has concluded that Wojtyla, rather than rejecting Scheler completely, just criticized him. Malone thinks Wojtyla was undertaking a long-term project to marry Thomism and phenomenology, hard as that sounds, and that he made significant advances before the papacy interrupted him.

Wojtyla got his second Ph.D. He wasn't through with either phenomenology or existentialism, however.

5

"One day in April 1952, when we had known Father Wojtyla about a year, someone said the crocuses were blooming at Zakopane," recalls Danuta, a student of Wojtyla's at the Jagiellonian. "It turned out a lot of us had never seen crocuses, and Father Wojtyla hadn't, either. We agreed to go look," even though Zakopane was in the mountains, two hours south of Krakow.

"Five of us girls turned up at the station on Saturday night," Danuta says. "Some boys were to have come, too, but they were prevented by exams. Father Wojtyla agreed to take us just the same, though at that time it was almost unheard-of for a priest in lay clothes—he always wore knickerbockers on those occasions—to be taking a party of girls on an overnight excursion. But off we went.

"It was on this trip that we decided with his permission to call him 'Uncle' in public, as it would have caused a sensation if we had addressed him as a priest. We saw the crocuses. The sun was shining, but there was still snow on the ground. After that, we went on day trips to all sorts of places."

The name "Uncle" stuck with him. It appeared to be a sign of endearment, but students say it was really camouflage to keep Wojtyla from being jailed for running an unauthorized youth group.[1] Former students remember the trips vividly. They felt close enough to Wojtyla to kid him about his tendency to "switch off," or start meditating, in the middle of something; they didn't let him lead on bicycle trips for fear he would steer into a tree. He was often off alone gazing into the distance—"thinking or praying, I don't know," Danuta says.

When Wyszynski became a cardinal, in January 1952, the government responded with new arrests of clergy, including elderly priests, for even minor antigovernment comments. Parents were threatened with loss of their jobs unless they affiliated their children with a new government youth group. The Rhapsody Theater was closed, and its actors blacklisted from all but menial work (even though Wojtyla, as "Andrzej Jawein," had promoted its productions in *Tygodnik Powszechny*). Wyszynski was summoned by the government and ordered one day to do more paperwork, another day to register Church duplicating machines, another to teach courses on communism in seminaries. His bishop candidates were rejected.

Perhaps this was the central moment of Wyszynski's leadership: he refused to act harassed, instead finding ways to keep the Church alive. The annual Church pilgrimage to the Black Madonna at Czestochowa in August was a religious observance the government had pledged to respect, so Wyszynski gave it all the political impact he could without crossing the line. "He changed the Czestochowa tradition," says one Catholic.[2] The number of pilgrims swelled far beyond the few tens of thousands who had come to pray in the past.

The pilgrimage was no longer mainly about religion. The heart of Wyszynski's homily at Czestochowa August 15, 1952, could have been endorsed by any lover of freedom, yet it stayed within the bounds of communist rhetoric. He spoke of "human rights . . . family rights: the right to . . . the choice of life, to a vocation. . . . The rights of the nation . . . to history, language and culture." Officially, the communists endorsed all these rights; by repeating them, Wyszynski reminded everyone that they weren't observed.

Later, to the editors at *Tygodnik Powszechny*, he summed up his vision, quite different from that of Western anti-communists: "From my first moment in command . . . the government was hostile to me. But that could not influence my attitude toward the government. Many of their so-called social achievements are permanent"—including, he said, redistribution of the ownership of industry and large estates. "The Polish Church is not going to fight for restoration of . . . even its own farms. . . . We showed in Dachau and in the Warsaw Uprising that we know how to die for the Church and for Poland. Today we have to show . . . the ability of the Church and Poland to live. I want my priests . . . in the pulpit, in the confessional—not in prison."[3]

In November 1952, police burst into the Krakow archbishop's palace (where Wojtyla had hid from the Germans) and arrested Archbishop Baziak and a paddy wagon load of priests on charges of subversion. There followed Poland's biggest communist show trial.[4]

Only after the fall of communism in 1989 was the likely cause of the Krakow curia raid revealed. Krzysztov Kozlowski, the post-communist police minister (until then an editor at *Tygodnik Powszechny*), says he got a call from aides who were searching police archives after forty-four years of communism. They had found a pouch seized in the 1952 raid and thought Kozlowski should see it.

"I found it marked 'Top Top Top Secret,'" Kozlowski says. "It was a very dramatic moment for me. We opened it on my desk. There was the smell of the human body in the grave. There were papers, rosaries, notes." It was the remnants of the Katyn massacre of 25,700 Polish leaders in 1940—and proof of Stalin's guilt, despite continuing Russian attempts to blame the massacre on Hitler.

"In the last year of World War II, an unknown, anonymous person came to the Krakow curia with envelopes from graves in Katyn," Kozlowski says. "The personal belongings of those killed. Sapieha got them and kept them. There were dated notes to the moment of April 1940. Nothing later." Thus, all the victims died *before* the Germans reached Katyn. Somehow the Soviets learned of this proof and were determined to seize it.[5]

Wyszynski vowed to free the arrested priests. "We may have the right to sacrifice ourselves," he said, "but we may not sacrifice the dioceses. When bishops and priests disappear, so does the Church." After days of often humiliating discussion, he persuaded the government to drop charges against Baziak and some others. In exchange, he agreed to replace Baziak in Krakow with a bishop more to the government's liking.[6]

The trial began January 21, 1953. It was an era in which many U.S. dissidents were likewise facing court proceedings for subversion, though usually with less draconian results. Father Andrzej Bardecki, a *Tygodnik Powszechny* editor who covered every session of the Krakow trial, says some accused priests were tortured with days of sleep deprivation and cold-water dousings.

He also acknowledges that some of the government's charges were valid. Priests were in fact secretly exchanging information with Western agencies, particularly Radio Free Europe, a CIA operation that over the next thirty years would constitute perhaps the most important puncture point in the Iron Curtain. Based in Munich, Radio Free Europe fed on secret contacts in the Eastern Bloc[7]—including, later, Karol Wojtyla.

Death sentences were handed out, later commuted to long prison terms. Stunning new orders came down that from now on, all Church personnel changes were to be cleared by the government. After Stalin died, March 5, 1953, censors—who until now had only deleted material—ordered *Tygodnik Powszechny* to print a eulogy. Turowicz refused in a loud argument. The paper was shut down.

At Easter, Wyszynski began weekly lectures in his cathedral on the theme of "Christian socialism." Before overflow crowds, he accused capitalism of reducing people to mere factors of production. Socialism must not make the same mistake, he said. He offered the government a "good" socialism, in contrast to the kind it was now administering. A political officer from the U.S. embassy noted, "The cardinal defined the political crisis as one in which all states are degenerate [and] regard the citizen as their enemy. . . . It was clear that the audience was following his every word with close attention," and many took notes.[8]

Throughout the year, Wyszynski preached patience: "He who has recourse to violence ... may conquer bodies but not souls," he said. "Violence is the confession of his weakness." He wrote Bierut a widely discussed letter reviewing the Church's faithfulness to the 1950 agreement, and the government's violations.[9]

Where was Wojtyla during the sensational trial and its aftermath? He was at his books and with his students, keeping his thoughts on the crisis to himself. "Wojtyla never played a political role" in these years, says *Tygodnik Powszechny's* Turowicz. The evidence supports this statement.

Yet he influenced his students' thinking. When they went skiing, most, coming from professional or aristocratic families, expected to travel in the first-class section of the train. But Wojtyla steered them to second class instead, saying, "Let's go with the people." He took them to the shrine at Czestochowa for Easter and several times to the mountains south of Krakow for hiking.[10]

One day that June 1953, Wojtyla tramped up the old wooden stairs to the *Tygodnik Powszechny* office in Krakow and found Father Bardecki disconsolate. Many times Wojtyla had climbed those same stairs to give Bardecki seven or eight typewritten pages of poetry or an article he wanted published. Now he plopped down in a chair, knowing the presses were silent.

Bardecki had just returned from Warsaw, where he and other editors had pleaded for a resumption of publication. Instead, the government had turned over the newspaper to patriotic priests and forbidden the staff any contact with Wyszynski. Wojtyla waved off Bardecki's account of the political details and asked about the finances and family circumstances of each of *Tygodnik Powszechny's* out-of-work editors. As Bardecki recited one tale of woe after another, Wojtyla pulled an envelope of bills from his pocket and placed it on the desk. It was half his monthly salary. Wojtyla said he wanted it distributed to the editors.

After that, every month, without further discussion, Wojtyla delivered between a third and a half of his own salary to be divided among the unemployed journalists. Bardecki told others what Wojtyla had done, and by the end of summer, the pastor at a nearby church and some members of the curia were following Wojtyla's example. The other priests, Bardecki observes, were paid more; Wojtyla was "so poor, just starting out."

With *Tygodnik Powszechny* in enemy hands, the priests' donations sustained the original editors. During the Solidarity repression of the 1980s, underground journalists still talked about Wojtyla's gesture, which had fed the courage of journalists in the 1950s.

6

Romuald Kukolowicz, the son of Catholic intellectuals from the Laski circle, worked as a clerk but had done underground printing during World War II. Some friends from those days, now students at the Jagiellonian, approached him, raving about a young professor whose lectures on Catholic ethics and communism were inspiring and ought to be published. Did Kukolowicz know anyone who could do it?

Kukolowicz found an underground printer in Lublin. His friends arranged for him to pick up the manuscript from the professor—Wojtyla—at a convent in Krakow. As the manuscript was typed, edited, and published, there were more meetings between Kukolowicz and Wojtyla, but little small talk. "When I saw him it was always [to discuss] what to publish and how," Kukolowicz remembers. "It was a very strict conspiracy."

Some 250 reams of printing paper were stolen by the members of this "conspiracy" from the state institutions where they worked. A World War II press was used, requiring each page to be rolled by hand over a typed matrix. Kukolowicz calculates that his friends had to press some 112,750 sheets of paper separately to make the book. It was published in two volumes, a year apart, with only 200 to 250 copies in each edition—loose pages in an envelope, to be bound, if desired, by the recipient. Copies went to priests who taught students in all the major cities of Poland.

"They weren't given [directly] to students because of the need for secrecy," Kukolowicz says. "Police agents infiltrated the classes. If the security forces found such a book in your apartment, you would be subject to ten years in prison."

The work, called *Catholic Social Ethics,* is nowhere described in *Kalendarium* or any other available literature; Kukolowicz's is the only copy I have encountered. The Vatican confirms his story. To my knowledge, this is the book's first public disclosure,[1] and it belies much that has been written about Wojtyla in recent years.

Bishop Tadeusz Pieronek, now secretary of the Polish Episcopate but in 1954 a student in Wojtyla's social ethics course at the Jagiellonian, remembers being stunned to learn that Father Wojtyla had written a manual, several copies of which were passed around at the school.[2]

"It was impossible to publish a manual in those days," Bishop Pieronek explains. "All printers were registered by the government. Even typewriters were registered, but authorities allowed you to type. The university had a library, but the books were not accessible to the average reader. You can't imagine how libraries looked. Till the 1980s, whole lists of books were banned."

As a priest in the 1970s, Pieronek visited Cardinal Wojtyla for dinner and found parts of that old manual on a bookshelf in the dining room. "We learned about capitalism for the first time from Wojtyla's text," Bishop Pieronek recalls. "He tried to explain each system."

Catholic Social Ethics reinforces the notion that Wojtyla was a Thomist; it asserts at its inception that Aquinas's natural law "allows theories of ethics" to be stated with "scientific" precision. It also shows that by age thirty-three, Wojtyla had adopted unreservedly both the welfare-state economic ideas and the courage of Cardinal Wyszynski. No longer a novice or small-parish priest, he instead marked himself in this book as a serious, innovative thinker with his eye on the world.*

"The main task of the Catholic social ethic is to introduce the principles of justice and love into social life," Wojtyla wrote in the first volume, on politics, dated 1953. Tracing economic history from feudalism to the industrial age, he endorsed the notions of a working class and a class struggle. But he stressed that class should be among a person's secondary loyalties. Primary was the family, the success of which depended on its "close cooperation" with the Church and the state. "The nation, as the natural society, must be respected," he wrote, but "the common good demands" a balance between "loyalty to the nation . . . and, on the other hand, avoidance of overzealous nationalism."[3]

Government had "a superior function" that was "very useful in achieving the common good of society." Its power "comes directly from society, indirectly from God."

Wojtyla condemned "individualism," a word that he and other European scholars used to refer to unregulated capitalism. "Individualism and totalitarianism," he declared, "remain opposed to the principle of correlating the individual good and the social good, which Catholic ethics accepts."

"Justice and love" must govern international relations as well, he wrote: "War is evil. It should be avoided even as a last resort to restore justice between countries, because it may result in even greater evil and injustice than it combats."

* Kukolowicz would allow me to photocopy only portions of the text, though I looked over all of it with my principal Polish associate and translator, Professor Nina Gladziuk. Kukolowicz went on to be a trusted assistant to Wyszynski in important affairs to be discussed later in this book. He is married to a former nun, a longtime friend of Wyszynski's who is a professor at the Catholic University at Lublin. It is clear from the text that the portions of *Catholic Social Ethics* that I could not obtain merely elaborate on points in the very detailed table of contents, which I do have. I am grateful to my translators: Dr. Gladziuk, Dr. Anna Kubiak of Warsaw, Jerzy Kopacz of Krakow, and Joanna Tyrpa of Cranford, New Jersey.

His statement on war went significantly beyond other current Catholic teaching, which allowed war if all else failed. Although many anti-communists would later try to co-opt Wojtyla into their military policies, he condemned war unequivocally in 1953, even as a means to correct injustice, because he believed it tended only to create new injustice.[4] (He did not, however, dispute Catholic teaching that violence could be used to repel violent attacks.)

In a chapter on Marxism, Wojtyla saw beyond the system that tyrannized his own life, and into the issues that would later present themselves to him as pope. He wrote:

> The relentless materialism in Marxism contradicts Catholicism, [which] sees man as spirit and matter in one, [and which] proclaims the superiority of the spirit. . . . Ethics is . . . the science of spiritual good, such as justice or love, that provides the material activities of human beings with specifically human values. This gives ethics primacy [over materialism] in economics or biology.

But, he added, "The goal of these thoughts is not to criticize Marxism entirely." He explicitly embraced Marx's essential theory, that "the economic factor . . . explains, rather substantially, the different facts of human history. . . . Criticism of capitalism— . . . the system of exploitation of human beings and human work—is the unquestionable 'part of the truth' embodied in Marxism."

In 1993, John Paul II would provoke mocking headlines when he criticized Poland and other post-communist countries for accepting pure market economics from the West and thus abandoning the "grain of truth" in Marxism. Although many thought the pope was reversing himself, he was in fact using almost the same words he had used forty years before in class lectures and in his book, and had been using ever since.[5]

Wojtyla separated Marx's *analysis* of economic exploitation, which he largely accepted, from Marx's *solutions,* which he rejected. "The Catholic social ethic," he wrote in 1953, "agrees that in many cases a struggle is the way to accomplish the common good. Today . . . a class struggle . . . is the undeniable responsibility of the proletariat."

Not only is class-conscious revolution compatible with Christianity, he argued; it is sometimes *necessary* to Christianity. What is incompatible is Marxism's subjugation of the individual human spirit to a grand economic design *after* the revolution.

In *Catholic Social Ethics,* Wojtyla set down rules for social struggle that are strikingly similar to those that would be enunciated less than a decade later by the Reverend Martin Luther King, Jr., in the United States. Wojtyla and King each believed the struggle should be aimed at persuasion, not at violent, Marxist-style upheaval. Wojtyla wrote:

> Demonstrations, protests, strikes, and passive resistance—all these are means of class struggle that need to be considered appropriate. The struggle for rights, after exhausting all peaceful means . . . is a necessary act of justice that leads only to the achievement of the common good, which is the goal of social existence. . . .
>
> It is clear that from the view of the ethical assumptions of the Bible, such a struggle is a necessary evil, just like any other human struggle. . . .[6] It is also evident from the Bible that struggle itself is not the opposite of love. The opposite of love is hate.
>
> A struggle in a specific case does not have to be caused by hate. If it is caused by social and material injustice, and if its goal is to reinstate the just distribution of goods, then such a struggle is not [hatred]. . . . Social justice is the necessary condition for realization of love in life. . . .
>
> Many times Jesus Christ has proven that God's kingdom cannot be achieved in man without a struggle. . . . Achievement of social justice is one element of achieving God's kingdom on earth.

Wojtyla made a major distinction between revolution within a country and international war—though in some ways, the distinction seems paradoxical.

> Revolution causes much more damage than war, because the unity of the natural society—the nation or state—is much greater than the international unity of humanity that gets torn in war. . . . Hatred for those who are close to us is much more dangerous and inflicts more damage than hatred for people who are further removed.

Yet war, he said, isn't permissible and isn't likely to improve conditions. Revolution, though best avoided, *is* permissible and *can* improve conditions:

> Can the opposition that brings down [an unjust] government surpass all the damage that was caused by an armed struggle, and thus make the revolution ethically justified? The answer is yes. . . .
>
> It can be accepted that the majority of the people who have taken part in revolutions—even violent ones—have acted on their convictions, in accordance with their consciences. . . .

Such a struggle is a necessary evil. Although it does not have to be an act of hatred ... such a struggle undoubtedly provides an opportunity for acts of hatred. . . . One can hate negative characteristics of human beings. But one cannot hate the human being himself. . . .

Marxism ... does not see any other way to solve the burning social issues. . . . Catholicism sees the possibility of solving ... social issues by evolutionary means. The struggle of the oppressed classes against their oppressors becomes the stimulus for the evolution to proceed faster. . . .

The class struggle ... grows stronger when it meets resistance from the economically privileged classes. Pressure from the class struggle should bring appropriate changes in the socioeconomic system.

Although Marxism saw struggle as inevitable and desirable,

Catholicism cannot accept struggle as the principal ethical dictate. . . . Regardless of all the factors that set people apart in society ... there exist deeper factors that foster unity and solidarity.

His biggest problem with Marxism, though, wasn't its advocacy of struggle but its opposition to the institution of private property. Grappling with this forced him to think through, perhaps for the first time in print, what Saint John of the Cross had said about material wealth. The question must have crossed his mind before: if Saint John had been right about abandoning physical property, why weren't the communists right about it? The answer, Wojtyla decided, lay in distinguishing worthy ideals from practical possibilities.

Marxism, he wrote, sought

a classless society. To achieve this order, one must get rid of private property because it is the only source of class opposition. . . .

While the Church clearly sees and proclaims the need for reform of the socioeconomic system, it does not consider necessary a radical upheaval in attitude toward property. . . . The re-creation of the socioeconomic system may be achieved while maintaining the institution of private property, and should be based on the enfranchisement of the proletariat.

His rationale for private property differed from that of free-market theorists, and what he wrote about it makes for fairly explosive reading in the 1990s:

The Church realizes that the bourgeois mentality, and capitalism with its material spirit, are contradictions of the Bible. According to the tradition of . . . monastic/religious life, the Church also can appreciate the idea of communism. . . . Communism, as a higher ethical rule of ownership, demands from people higher ethical qualifications.

After a subsection headed "The Objective Superiority of the Communist Ideal" (the text of which I was unable to obtain), Wojtyla noted,

At the present state of human nature, the universal realization of this [communist] ideal . . . meets with insurmountable difficulties. Private property is suited to human nature. The goal that should be pursued is to achieve, in the system based on private property, such reforms as will lead to the realization of social justice. The class struggle leads to this. . . .

Revolution is not the doom of society, but at most a punishment for specific offenses in socioeconomic life.

Wojtyla wrote that "ethical evil is caused" not by those wishing to rebel but "by those factors of the socioeconomic system that have spawned the need for a radical movement."

The second volume of *Catholic Social Ethics*, published the next year, was more specifically concerned with "rebuilding the economic system [and] defining the many moral obligations of owning and using property." Its premise was: "Because private ownership of property is ethically good if the property is used appropriately, individual owners and especially the state should carefully watch its use."

Regarding labor, Wojtyla again rejected strict free-market doctrine, returning instead to the ideal of the poet Norwid, that "work cannot be treated as merchandise." Regarding capitalism, he said,

An economic enterprise based on capital is ethically justified if it contributes to social prosperity. But if its main goal is to maximize the profit of the owner, then it is ethically wrong. . . .

The entire tradition and teaching of the Church is clearly opposed to capitalism as the socioeconomic system of life, and as a general value system.

The exchange of goods complements the economic process. . . .
Therefore it is ethically justified, like production, so long as it does
not lead to unjustified, speculative profits. . . . A just profit depends
on a just price for merchandise, which is determined by using an
appropriate value theory. Determination of the price is a function
of society. . . .

[Because] money . . . is very important in the socioeconomic
process . . . the state should supervise monetary and credit policies
for the good of the whole society.

Among the essays listed in the index that were *not* available to me were the
following:

"The Role of the State in Price Determination"
"The Ethical Meaning of Private Ownership in Relation to the Social
    Character of the Property"
"The Negligence of [Owning] Excessive Goods"
"The Natural Causes of Economic Inequality"
"Economic Inequality as a Result of Immoral Behavior"
"The Stance of the Catholic Church against Liberalism"*

Wojtyla said that collecting interest on loans "is ethically justified, given the
current state of the world's economy." But he said interest rates should be limited not by what the market will bear but by ethical considerations. His introduction promised to set down "conditions" for determining interest rates, but
I couldn't obtain the section in which he defined those conditions.

He was very concerned with pay. "The profit gained from work in the form
of compensation is the main factor in the just division of the income of society," he wrote. And "the just solution to the problem of pay is the principle of
family pay."

He has championed the "family pay" concept ever since, arguing that the size
and needs of a worker's family should influence the amount of wages or salary.
While this idea was somewhat Marxist (Marx said, "From each according to his
abilities, to each according to his needs"), Wojtyla rejected the determination of
compensation by need alone. "In determining family pay," he wrote,

* "Liberalism," in the European terms Wojtyla used, means a pure, free-market economy. It should not be confused with the American usage of "liberalism" to mean a welfare state, which Wojtyla generally advocated.

one should consider the economic state of the enterprise and of the whole country. An entrepreneur has a right to a reasonable, moderate profit, considering both his own work and his financial investment ... for example, for renting land. ...

The common good is best achieved when individual members of society evenly attain material prosperity. So we must strive to limit luxury and excessive wealth.

The society must use all ethical means to save its members from poverty and lead them to prosperity. Society should take special care of those in poverty.

Rather than allying him with market capitalists, these views ring closer to those of supporters of "liberation theology," a Catholic movement that Wojtyla would later encounter in Latin America, which sought to redistribute capital. After several years of intense reading of Wojtyla's published words as both priest and pope, I cannot cite an instance of his saying anything to contradict what he said in his 1953 book.

7

In 1953, the Czestochowa pilgrimage saw its greatest year of growth.[1] Instead of the old once- or twice-in-a-lifetime trip to pay religious respects, it had now become an annual event, with teachers leading whole classes on a four- or five-day trek to the site, sleeping at farmhouses along the way. Families joined children. Some priests organized whole villages.

"For the first time, there came to be something the communists could not control," says the writer Zygmunt Kubiak. "Not thousands, like in Tiananmen [Square, in China], but one or two million people." They heard Wyszynski continue his carefully worded challenges to the government. He was truly transforming Poland's ancient aristocratic Church into a popular one.[2]

A month later, September 25, Wyszynski spoke to an overflow crowd at a Warsaw church about Saint Wladyslaw, who defied the government out of conscience; the crowd understood that the primate was really talking about a Polish bishop who had just been sentenced to twelve years in prison, along with three priests and a nun, for "espionage and currency offenses," allegedly at the direction of the U.S. embassy. Another crowd was expected to hear Wyszynski the next day at a different church.

Sometime around midnight, however, heavily armed police burst into the archbishop's palace, roused Wyszynski from bed, and told him to bring his belongings and come. He refused to bring anything. "I came to this house poor and I will leave it poor," he said. When his pet dog bit one of the arresting officers on the leg, Wyszynski himself bent down and treated the wound with iodine. As he left, a nun threw a weatherworn coat over his shoulders; only in the car to the police station did he realize she had pulled from storage the coat left behind by a bishop friend who had been murdered by the Germans at Dachau.[3]

By morning, the population was abuzz with the news. The main communist newspaper said the bishop jailed for espionage had confessed and that "beyond any doubt" Wyszynski was guilty, too.

Within weeks, eight bishops and nine hundred priests were locked up. Many signed compromising statements under vague threats of physical harm. U.S. Secretary of State John Foster Dulles cabled his ambassador in Warsaw asking why Poles didn't revolt; the ambassador reminded him that Poland was surrounded by Soviet troops and permeated by secret police.[4]

One unplanned consequence of Wyszynski's arrest was to make a fixture of Radio Free Europe, which until then was only an occasional nuisance to the communists. Broadcasts now began each day with the announcement that it was "Day 2," then "Day 3" of Wyszynski's arrest, and so on for months, followed by new developments. Radio Free Europe's tentacles shot swiftly into almost every Polish household and stayed there.*

In the fall of 1953, a U.S. diplomat was sent around Warsaw to report on the retail economy. Poles wouldn't buy the clothing for sale because their fit and appearance were "terrible," he wrote. Warsaw's main department store, "open only two years, is in an amazing state of decomposition, with rotting floors and an overall patina of grime." As in every communist country, common household items from spoons to washboards appeared in stores only sporadically and attracted long lines when they did. Bureaucrats slashed prices to move

* A similar device was used twenty-six years later on U.S. television when Iran seized American diplomats in Teheran. Each night at the same time reporter Ted Koppel announced that it was Day 14, Day 97, and so on, of "America Held Hostage." By the time the diplomats were freed, Koppel had hooked an audience for a permanent program, *Nightline.*

the clothing and chastised bakery-shop managers for not stocking the required thirty-two varieties of bread according to state recipes.

American operatives recorded complaints all over Poland about a government seemingly blind to its own citizens' concerns:

"First they promote our priest to be a bishop against his will, and then they lock him up because he won't do as they tell him."

"The regime is having a terrible effect on schoolchildren, who have no respect either for their teachers or their parents. They play truant from school, and the parents are powerless to help."

Easter Sunday, 1954, Wyszynski noted in his diary (fading in and out of the royal "we"), "We celebrated Mass in our little prison chapel, without a procession. People bereft of religious joys sit like birds with their wings tied back. We pity such people. Today I risked saying to the deputy . . . 'I wish you much joy and happiness.' He responded in a whisper, 'Thank you.' We stopped for a moment at the desk of the guard on duty. We implored him to fight off sorrow since it was not proper for victors to wear such glum faces. When Christ rose from the dead, he revealed so many possibilities to men that we no longer even care about our present situation."

Meanwhile, Polish officials wrote each other memos asking how farmers could be expected to plant when factories hadn't shipped any fertilizer.[5]

Wojtyla, like Wyszynski, continued to make the best of the cards life dealt him. He hadn't wanted to be a parish priest. Then he relished it so much that he fought his transfer to academia. Once at the Jagiellonian, he brought the intensity of his contemplation and the intimacy of his pastorship to his new task. He even took a part-time second job in the fall of 1954, teaching philosophy at the Catholic University in Lublin, which continued to operate independently into the communist era by professing to be open to all schools of thought. As it would for twenty-five more years, the government denied Wojtyla the job title "Professor," shortchanging him with the junior grade of "Docent." He didn't seem to mind.

Unbelievably, amid the misery that was Poland, Karol Wojtyla arranged for himself what for his taste was the life of Riley. Had the communists departed and he inherited a fortune, it's doubtful he would have chosen to change much. Sure, his students had to pass around limited copies of his text surreptitiously, but he probably thought—correctly—that the exercise was good for their characters.

He said what he thought about communism and capitalism to the people who mattered to him. Besides his university work, he lectured to various meet-

ings of priests and nuns and was a favorite after-dinner speaker at informal
gatherings. He likely never dreamt of having a global audience and so didn't
notice the lack of it. Better clothes or food he would only have given away.

His vacations were abundant and custom-designed; he probably would have
pitied anyone ossifying on a cruise. Winter weekends he went skiing, while
most of July and August he spent in his favorite environment—Poland's mountains, lakes, and rivers—hiking and canoeing with his favorite companions,
college-age students.[6]

"He treated forty or fifty of us as his family," says one.[7] Trips ranged from
long weekends to three-week excursions, with fifteen to twenty students along
each time. From the Tatras in the South, they ventured to the northeastern lakes,
as far as one could get from Krakow inside Poland. In two weeks, they would
cover two hundred miles, sometimes carrying canoes or kayaks as well as all their
provisions. "He was very strong," says former student Karol Tarnowski.

Wojtyla was so strong, in fact, that in 1954 he won an award from the Polish Tourist Society for the number of kilometers he had hiked, with bonus
points for hikes made in winter. In May 1955, he entered an international
kayaking competition in Poland; he ripped the hull of his boat on some rocks
and barely managed to push it across the finish line before it submerged, dous-
ing him thoroughly.

His one regret was probably that he and his students had to hide their
adventures. "Police asked students where they were going on vacations," says
former student Stanislaw Grygiel. "It was OK to go to the mountains, but the
presence of a priest had to be secret. Careers might be hurt."

Were they afraid? "Who was afraid was absent," Grygiel laughs.

Wojtyla sought participants from outside the intelligentsia class that filled
the universities. Up to half his groups came from vocational schools. "He had
sympathy for solid [laboring] jobs," Tarnowski says. Yet in a way, the group
was *all* "intelligentsia"; Wojtyla just defined it by intellect, not by parentage.

"Uncle"—the name had stuck—"would have an early bath while we were
still asleep, and went canoeing by himself at about six. He said Mass every
morning at an altar consisting of two boats turned upside down, with two pad-
dles lashed together to form a cross. Then we had breakfast and spent the rest
of the day afloat, with a short break for lunch and a main meal in the evening.
[Then] we sat around a campfire and sang," with Wojtyla sometimes making up
new words to old songs in the folk tradition. Prayers and hymns preceded bed.[8]

"There was a constant, permanent discussion on philosophy," says one
camper, himself now a professor.[9] Says Tarnowski, also a professor, "He took
one person to be with him in the canoe"—changing several times a day—"and
talked about moral questions. They were intense discussions," often on "ethi-

cal questions between men and women. I never met a man who had so balanced a view of the dignity of both sexes."

Yet Wojtyla framed gender issues differently than Western feminists (or antifeminists) do now. "The very important role of the woman, the basis of her dignity, was to be a wife and mother," Tarnowski remembers. "For a man, the most important thing was to know his responsible role in the family, to be a father. He didn't discourage women from being engineers or doctors. But he taught mainly how to prepare for and succeed in marriage."

Wojtyla was changing his focus again, and doing it so comfortably that the change was hardly noticed. Almost as soon as he had completed his second doctorate, he set aside the weight of metaphysics (which he would resume later) and steered his attention and curiosity back to his consuming, lifelong interest in the family. It was, perhaps, his way of continuing the pastoral work he hadn't wanted to leave, even as he carried on his professorship.

One participant in the outings says he wondered for years why Wojtyla was so dedicated to the student groups. "It was an enormous expenditure of energy on a bunch of young people" who didn't always listen. Years later, Wojtyla explained it to him: "It's important to set up a model of how Christians should live—people who are not priests, but still Christians."[10]

Maria Tarnowska—a fellow teenage camper then, and now Karol Tarnowski's wife—says she was able to talk to Wojtyla, as to no one else, about her parents' impending divorce. "I would come to see Father Wojtyla maybe three times a week in his house," she says. "He knew how to listen. There are not very many people who can."

She blamed her parents' separation on the extreme misbehavior of her father, whereas Wojtyla tried "to get me to love each parent. He talked about there being evil in the world. He got me [to] thinking that my father had been in concentration camps during the war, and this could mark him so as to make him [behave] this way. I found in Wojtyla a new father." Once, she says, at Wojtyla's suggestion, she held a party for friends at his apartment, because "I could never invite friends to be around my father."[11]

These were the rules Wojtyla laid down for a successful marriage, according to Karol Tarnowski: "Fidelity. Be truthful. Friendship before marriage. Know your partner well before engagement."

At preparation sessions, couples were taught to see beyond what attracted them and to confront each other's negative side openly. "The problem of faithfulness is the ability to support the negative side of the partner," Wojtyla would tell them. In addition, Maria Tarnowska says, he would advise "that you never intervene in the personal, religious life of anyone, even your spouse. It is not possible to share that with anybody."

"I later had a lot of difficulties in my marriage," her husband says. "But I had a conviction that one must not give up on it. It is worth a fight."

The former students I spoke to who had been on these trips say that to their knowledge, none of the group has been divorced, though the divorce rate among Polish Catholics is quite high.

During the mid-1950s, Wojtyla gave an annual Lenten retreat for high schoolers in Rabka, a mountain village south of Krakow, at the invitation of their religious teacher—Mieczyslaw Malinski. "He spoke of matters that were really too advanced for them," says Wojtyla's former seminary mate. "But I could tell he was holding their attention. Afterwards, he would stand by the door and talk to them in a joking way about everyday matters. He announced that he would be free after lunch if anyone wanted to go to confession or have a chat. This was not the usual custom." Later Malinski would see Wojtyla strolling with one student after another up and down a line of pine trees. He even shared his new poems with the students.

"Next year when I asked the young people whom they would soonest have again of all the priests who had given Lenten retreats, they replied, 'Father Wojtyla.' " So Wojtyla came six years running, Malinski says, following mostly the same schedule. He would dine in the evening with the pupils' parents; mornings he would work alone, saying he could get more done in the quiet of Rabka than in Krakow. Eventually, some pupils went to Krakow or Lublin to study with him.[12]

At the universities, Wojtyla's popular courses in introductory philosophy and ethics were taught entirely from the perspective of Aquinas and natural law, students say. Phenomenology wasn't discussed. He regularly took students hiking at Kalwaria Zebrzydowska, the Stations of the Cross in the forest, where his father had taken him as a child.

"It was known among the seminarians that Wojtyla was under the influence of Saint John of the Cross," says Monsignor Bronislaw Fidelus, now second in command of the Krakow curia, who was a student of Wojtyla's in 1956 and 1957. "He never spoke about it openly. But everybody knew, and there was a run on books of Saint John of the Cross. They were hard to get until the supply adjusted."

Sometimes he took students on ski trips, but more often he went alone. Jan Zajac, now a priest near Oswiecim, holds up a map of his native Tatra Mountains and says, "There is not a single mountain on this map that has not been climbed or skied by Karol Wojtyla, often disguised around half-day meetings at monasteries or convents."

According to Wojtyla's childhood friend Jerzy Kluger, it was on one such trip near Rabka that he decided to ski a particularly virgin area, where wild boars and wolves still roamed and even natives sometimes got lost. A local priest warned him that he needed a companion and paired him with a teenager, a brilliant student and expert skier who knew the remote area well and whom the priest wanted in a seminary. And that, Kluger was told, was how Wojtyla met Stanislaw Dziwisz, whom he not only delivered to the priesthood but who became his private secretary from around 1965 to this day.

8

In February 1955, Nikita Khrushchev, sixty, gained the upper hand in a power struggle that had consumed the Kremlin since Stalin's death, two years before. Khrushchev, a peasant's son, had worked in the mines and factories of his native Ukraine until age thirty-five, when the Party sent him to Moscow for formal education. He worked his way up the Party ladder fast. He helped execute (an apt word for it) Stalin's purges and became fairly close to Stalin.

But after Stalin's death, he chose a different path, more in accord with his background. Khrushchev was probably the closest thing the Soviet Union ever had to the kind of leader Karl Marx envisioned for his successful revolution— not a power-mad maniac, but a real worker hoping to improve the lot of working people. As Khrushchev gradually took over in 1955, fresh air circulated.

In Poland, Catholic prisoners were released, the Pax movement declined, and Wyszynski was moved from his cold, wet, secret holding pen to a convent where he could correspond and read newspapers.

At once, though, Khrushchev faced a Church-related problem in far-off Vietnam, where independence fighters had just thrown out the French colonialists. The Soviets had armed the independence fighters after the United States refused to help them. When it became clear that the Soviet-allied party would have the most votes in the national election scheduled for 1956, the U.S. sought to prevent the election. Once again it turned to Cardinal Spellman of New York, who, as cardinal, visited and blessed practically every dictator who sought U.S. aid in the global fight against communism.[1]

During the Vietnamese independence war, Spellman had housed a Vietnamese Catholic, Ngo Dinh Diem, in a monastery in New York State. There, Diem had gained the personal support of Spellman's powerful friends, including Catholic Senators John F. Kennedy and Joseph R. McCarthy. To block unification, Diem was later flown to the south, which was being administered by

former French allies pending the election. The U.S. also secretly sent in guerrilla teams to sabotage the north, which was administered by the Soviet allies.
Civilians in the north, especially Catholics, were encouraged to flee to the
south, and many did (despite a team from Pax, the Polish "patriotic" Catholic
group, sent in by the Soviets to persuade them to stay).

The problem for the U.S., however, was that most Vietnamese were *not*
Catholic. When Diem and the Catholics took power in the south, it angered
the Buddhist majority, whose support was needed if communism was to be
resisted. The U.S. stopped the unification election, but in doing so spawned
what would be the longest war in U.S. history.[2]

Early in 1956, perhaps invigorated by his new surroundings, Wyszynski conceived his big idea. Nineteen sixty-six would be the thousandth anniversary of
Christianity's arrival in Poland. Wyszynski decided to mark the occasion by
dedicating the nation to Mary, to deliver it from political subjugation. More
important than the event itself was what would proceed it: a "Great Novena."

Catholics have a tradition of "novenas"—nine days or years of prayer leading up to some event. To rally the nation's spirit, Wyszynski decided that each
year until 1966, prayers would focus on a different one of the patriotic vows
taken by King Jan Kazimierz at Czestochowa three hundred years earlier, before
his defeat of the invading Swedes. Day and night in his cell, Wyszynski
planned religious services that he knew would harbor enormous political
significance.[3]

As Wyszynski schemed, Wojtyla traveled southern Poland giving inspirational speeches. En route to one remote convent, thirteen-below-zero (Fahrenheit) cold delayed his train eight hours; arriving at two A.M., he walked from the
station and probed half an hour in the snow for a way in. Finally rousing a nun,
he caught a few hours' sleep, gave his talk, and then probably went skiing.[4]

That same month, February 1956, the Communist Party of the Soviet
Union assembled for a historic congress. Khrushchev shocked party leaders by
dropping all pretense and assailing Stalin as a murderer, hypocrite, and sexual
pervert. He released documents showing that Lenin had planned to decentral-
ize communist rule with local and ethnic autonomy, and that Stalin had
betrayed him.

Stalin's Polish protégé, Premier Boleslaw Bierut, was invited to the congress
to hear this news firsthand. At some point in the proceedings, Bierut dropped
dead; foul play was suspected but never proved. Other Stalin loyalists left office
as word spread of his "desanctification" and Khrushchev solidified his own
leadership. In Poland, members of the old, homegrown socialist parties dared

to challenge the Stalinists who had subdued them in 1948 and jailed their leader Wladyslaw Gomulka.

That June 1956, workers in Poznan, a town 175 miles west of Warsaw, went wild, set fire to a prison, besieged Party headquarters, overturned state cars, tore down Soviet flags, and paraded through the streets chanting, "We want bread!" More than two hundred people died (including some police); many more were injured.[5] As the army quelled the violence, Gomulka supporters declared that the workers had valid grievances. The former Stalinist leaders were replaced.

In August, one and a half million Poles came to Czestochowa on the annual pilgrimage. From his detention, Wyszynski arranged for a bishop to announce the Great Novena and read King Kazimierz's message to Mary, which began, "Queen of Poland! Today we renew the vows of our ancestors." There followed a list of promises, essentially to keep the Christian faith and put Poland "under Your control in our personal, family, professional, and social lives." After each vow, a million and a half voices roared back, "Queen of Poland, we promise!"

Wrote Andrzej Micewski, "The scene was incredible, astounding, and difficult for anyone who did not experience it to imagine.... The nation, represented by the Episcopate and a million pilgrims, pledged itself to Mary, while the communist authorities stood by helpless."[6] Word reached a "radiant" Wyszynski the next morning. No doubt the news also reached Wojtyla, who had just returned to Krakow from a student canoe trip.

A general atmosphere of crisis preceded the Polish Party's annual meeting October 19–21, 1956. Gomulka wanted to become premier and oust the Soviets from leadership positions in the Polish army; China's communist leaders (though still Soviet allies in Washington's eyes) urged Poland to join them in declaring independence from Moscow.

It was a landmark month in the Cold War. As Khrushchev pondered how to end Stalinism without destroying communism, and Wojtyla took an extended bicycle trip with students, yet another crisis diverted attention. Egypt, a Soviet ally, had seized the Suez Canal, and France and England began plotting with Israel to return the canal to international control. Khrushchev pledged to help defend Egypt. Radio Free Europe, staffed with Eastern European political refugees, seemed to embolden its listeners toward revolt.

October 19, 1956, the day of the big Polish Party meeting, dawned grim in Warsaw. A Soviet division rolled toward the city. Factory workers, armed to meet it, inflicted several casualties. Suddenly, out of the threatening sky dropped the plump, unlikely figure of Khrushchev himself, who flew in with his four top ministers (including defense and foreign). Khrushchev literally screamed at Gomulka at the airport. But his troops halted their advance on the city. All day, Poles and Russians were in and out of meetings.[7]

Gomulka emerged the Polish leader, but with a contingent of pro-Moscow men on the Central Committee to watch him. Some hated Soviet officers were booted off the Polish general staff, but the Soviets' military domination remained clear. Collectivized agriculture was ended. (An estimated two hundred thousand farmers had been jailed for not cooperating.) Existing collectives would be split back into individual farms. The state remained the only supplier of seed and equipment and the only legal buyer for produce, but everyone knew the black market would be open for business in the morning.

In an atmosphere in which black-market potatoes seemed like free enterprise, Gomulka seemed like a nationalist hero. Several hundred thousand people—Warsaw's largest gathering before Pope John Paul's visit in 1979—assembled to cheer Gomulka's victory speech. Millions more listened on the radio. "Gomulka himself was surprised by the degree of his support," says Jan de Weydenthal, an official of Radio Free Europe. "The choice was just Polish versus Russian."

Gomulka promised a more pragmatic economy. He welcomed a "progressive Catholic movement," and called it "a poor idea that socialism can be built only by communists." Sensing a new mood, the Polish Academy of Sciences ended the Marxist monopoly on teaching posts. The Catholic University at Lublin got a new rector, and Wojtyla was appointed director of the ethics department. Just two days after standing down Khrushchev, Gomulka met with Catholic laymen to negotiate the release of Wyszynski.

But the Soviets hadn't given up on a forceful demonstration of authority; they just wanted an easier target. Hungarians closely followed the Polish crisis on Radio Free Europe, and by early October, crowds were protesting in Budapest streets. The Hungarians, like the Poles, weren't demanding Western-style capitalism, just a more common-sense socialism, run by Hungarians. This was not just because the total overthrow of communism was thought impossible; it was also because a big part of the population (without elections, no one knows *how* big) genuinely wanted a socialist government.

On the day Gomulka triumphed in Warsaw, student-led crowds swept through the streets of Budapest demanding free press, free travel, free education, the abolition of capital punishment—and an end to Soviet occupation. Within a few days, local hero Imre Nagy, whom the Soviets had earlier deposed as communist premier, was restored. He asked troops to calm the demonstrations, but instead they joined in. Soviet forces in Hungary lost control. October 26, 1956, the rebels declared an independent government.

That same day, Gomulka's emissaries visited Wyszynski at his convent. Everyone seemed to sense that time might be short. The primate offered to publicly accept Gomulka's government if the government would drop its insistence on appointing Church personnel, free a list of jailed churchmen, and reactivate the Catholic press. Some details were refined, and a deal was struck.

John C. Whitehead, then a young investment banker from Goldman, Sachs & Company in New York, says he was vacationing with his wife in Austria that month. At breakfast one day, "We were suddenly confronted with a bearded, disheveled refugee from Hungary" who said he had come to the café to meet a "friend."

The friend turned out to be the same Austrian oil-company executive the Whiteheads were there to meet; the disheveled Hungarian was a rebel leader. He asked for radios, trucks, boat motors that could outrace those of Russian police boats, and other guerrilla paraphernalia.

"I was so caught up in the drama of the crisis meeting that I cut short our vacation and returned to New York," Whitehead says. Through Goldman, Sachs—perhaps the most lucrative private banking house on Wall Street—he reached out to corporate America. Robert Sarnoff, the president of NBC, donated radios; an executive at the Outboard Marine Corporation pledged boat equipment. Pan American World Airways agreed to fly everything to Vienna, free. Whitehead called the oil-company executive, who met the shipment and trucked it to the guerrillas at the Hungarian border.

Within seventy-two hours of the breakfast encounter, Whitehead says, the goods were in Hungarian hands. "It was all illegal. We defrauded our Customs and evaded their Customs. I assume the statute of limitations has expired. I was caught up in the heroism of the revolution." He says he acted entirely on his own and only afterward went to the CIA, through a friend who worked there, and filed a full report.

Whitehead—brilliant, practical, and profoundly patriotic—will reenter our story thirty years later, on leaving the chairmanship of Goldman, Sachs, to oversee American diplomacy in Eastern Europe at the end of communism. In the interim, he founded and ran a relief organization with William Casey, a venture capitalist and later director of the CIA. Their group, the International Rescue Committee, specialized in Cold War action zones: Vietnam, Cuba, Cambodia, and Czechoslovakia (in 1968, when the Soviets invaded), among others. Whitehead's "charity" work was effectively off-the-books U.S. government work, often done with government cooperation. He says he had "an emotional tie to the captive nations," and no doubt he did.

But debate has raged for years over whether the Hungarians in 1956 were baited into a trap by hints of full-scale American support that Washington never intended to deliver. The Hungarians either stumbled or were led into a tragic error.

October 30, 1956, crowds freed Cardinal Mindszenty, and Premier Nagy demanded an end to the Soviet alliance. That same day, as the Soviets were being challenged in Europe, Britain and France seized the Suez Canal, and Israeli forces thrust across the Sinai peninsula. Egypt screamed, but the Soviets didn't rescue their ally (they, too, welched on promises), and World War III didn't happen.

Instead, November 1 and 2, eight Soviet divisions poured into Hungary. One by one, Hungarian rebel radio stations issued their last pleas for Western intervention, then went silent. About sixty-five hundred Hungarians were killed. Nagy was (after a delay) executed. Mindszenty took diplomatic refuge in the American embassy.

In Poland—where the lesson of Hungary would be remembered for decades—Wyszynski met officials and toured the country, counseling calm. November 4, at a Warsaw church, he gave his first postrelease sermon. "Atmosphere emotionally charged, congregation in tears," the U.S. ambassador cabled Washington.[8] Wyszynski said, "The call today is not for the sacrifice of death, but for the much more difficult sacrifice of plain toil, out of love for the country. The call [is] to work and to order, application to daily tasks, rather than to martyrdom and resistance."

Religious classes were restored in public schools as an after-hours elective. *Tygodnik Powszechny* was returned to Jerzy Turowicz and the other former editors. Parliamentary "elections" were scheduled, and a non-communist minority was approved to run, including Turowicz and half a dozen of his socialist-inclined Catholic friends—most of whom were Wojtyla's friends, too. Wyszynski urged Poles to vote and did so himself. The government let him speak on the radio at Christmas.

Convinced that their minority representation was genuinely welcomed, Turowicz and other newly elected Catholic parliamentarians issued a conciliatory statement: "We do not wish to minimize the differences both in fundamental views and in methods of action . . . between Catholics and Marxists. We desire within the . . . system to cooperate in everything that is good, moral, and creative."

But it was still communism. Red tape plagued parents who tried to enroll their children in religious classes. It tied the hands of chaplains who tried to gain promised access to hospitals and prisons. Censorship still bound the Catholic press, and clergy who were freed from prison were sometimes kept from their pulpits.

9

"How much filth there is among us!" Wyszynsky began his sermon February 2, 1957. "We protest against the filth in books and in the press and against increasing pornography." The sermon opened a new campaign—not against erotica (for communists were generally as prudish as priests about such things) but against Western consumer goods and communist attempts to copy them. Repeated throughout the Polish Church, it was a campaign the government may well have supported.

"In the press we can see fashionable dolls and frivolous ladies whose costly dresses are . . . awakening unnecessary desire among peacefully working people," Wyszynski said. "We cannot afford this now. We are a destitute nation. . . . For-eign people [have] sometimes made money from our poverty and misery. Now, when we can work, let us reject luxury and waste. . . . How can foolish women enjoy their silk dresses, which are frequently quite indecent and shocking at that, when so many mothers have no shirts for their children?"[1]

Among other things, the campaign illustrated the difference in outlook between the Polish Church and anti-communist Wall Streeters like John Whitehead and William Casey.

Wojtyla helped lead an important movement that blossomed in the new, freer environment: Catholic Intelligentsia Clubs were organized in half a dozen major cities, a lasting framework in which intellectuals regularly exchanged ideas. In Krakow, says Stanislawa Grabska, then his student and later a club president, Wojtyla was "a kind of guru, a minister of souls, a charismatic professor."

He still addressed various groups, and in December 1956 escorted some Catholic doctors to Czestochowa. To pass the time, he got to talking with Dr. Wanda Poltawska, a Krakow psychiatrist. It was a chance conversation that would touch the world.

Dr. Poltawska mentioned that her husband specialized in medieval manu-scripts. A happy coincidence, Wojtyla said—he was just now struggling with a medieval manuscript at the university, and would her husband have a look at it?

So, Andrzej Poltawski recalls, his wife arranged a meeting. He no longer remembers what the manuscript was; Wojtyla had come down with the flu and Dr. Poltawska insisted on treating him, despite his aversion to medical care and other pampering. Soon they were all friends. Her real medical specialty, it turned out, was not the flu but sex—a subject large in Wojtyla's thoughts and in those of his students. She subscribed completely to the Catholic ethic: no sex outside marriage, and no contraception inside it. But she had gone beyond all that, and in a way that would fascinate Wojtyla for life: she aimed to validate Catholic teaching scientifically.

The Poltawskis have remained close to Wojtyla to this day and vacation with him almost annually. They traveled in Poland until he became pope, then began staying at the papal summer home at Castelgandolfo. When I met them, in the summer of 1994, they were packing for their customary two weeks there.

Dr. Poltawska at first declined to talk to me, saying she believed her relationship with Wojtyla/John Paul should stay confidential, and that if I wanted to learn about him I should content myself reading his poetry. But she agreed I could talk to her husband. After listening to us for two hours from the next room of their surprisingly dark and shabbily furnished (by Krakow standards) apartment[2] right off the city's market square, she joined us.

I learned that over the years, Dr. Poltawska and her clinic have advised many couples on sex, compiling much data. She has formulated two arguments against contraception, one religious, the other medical. "The use of contraception leads to neurosis," Poltawski asserted. I asked for supporting data and was told that Dr. Poltawska had written numerous articles demonstrating this. Poltawski didn't have copies, but typed out a bibliography for me of three articles, all in obscure publications for which he didn't have addresses, all evidently put out by Catholic rather than scientific groups. The only one the New York Public Library or the Library of Congress could locate for me was a three-page tract published by a Church-run antiabortion group in Maryland. The article contained sweeping assertions and a few borrowed anecdotes, but no quantified research by Dr. Poltawska, nor any information on contraception.[3]

I asked Poltawski if some common forms of contraception were covered by his wife's research. "All those means are harmful," he replied. "Coitus interruptus is more natural, but certainly leads to neurosis, frigidity, secondary frigidity [a term Catholics use for male impotence], and so on. It is not natural even though there is no chemistry in it." With any form of contraception, he said, "you bring some harm to fertility, to the health of the person."

As to the religious argument against contraception, he said that the Bible declares the sexual act must be open to procreation. He stressed that procreation wasn't the only reason for sex: "Sexual intercourse in matrimony does contribute to intimacy," and sex between older or infertile couples "is no less valuable" than between fertile couples. "The important thing is not whether

you want children, but whether you are open to them" if God wills it. Artificial contraception "excludes absolutely the child."

I asked why his wife approved of birth control through the so-called rhythm
method—limiting intercourse to a woman's infertile periods—but ruled out
attaining the same end by surer means. Shouldn't an ethical test focus on intent?
Poltawski explained that the virtue of the rhythm method lay precisely in its
uncertain effectiveness. "If you believe that at this time you should not have
another child, you are entitled to [limit sex to] the infertile periods," he said.
"But even so, you must leave the final decision to God."

I pointed out that condoms were also unreliable as a means of birth control,
as he himself had said moments before. Didn't condoms also leave pregnancy
"in the hands of God"?

"It is a very subtle difference," he replied. "You are applying means you
shouldn't apply." And that was as scientific as he would get.

Our conversation established that Wojtyla had contributed to Wanda
Poltawska's convictions, as well as vice versa. Over and over, Poltawski used the
Greek word *ascesis* as another cornerstone of the Catholic sexual ethic and said
Wojtyla also used the word regularly. It means self-discipline through self-
denial.

"Abstinence itself is valuable," Poltawski said. "The main idea of the philosophy of Karol Wojtyla is that you must learn to master yourself. In terms of
learning to master your life, that means natural family planning. My wife was
once asked why she holds him in such high esteem. She said she sees in him an
absolutely pure person, who fully masters his reactions."

Poltawski thinks his wife's interest in the sexual field came from her experience as a prisoner at the Ravensbrück concentration camp, in Germany, during
World War II. "For years, she was fighting for her human dignity," he says. "In
sexual intercourse is the dignity of the woman and the man. The important
thing is your attitude. What my wife tries to show is that contraception is, first,
medically bad, and, second, unnecessary. It is only good for those firms that
make a lot of money putting [contraceptives] on the market. My wife also
thinks that contraception naturally leads to abortion. The contraceptive attitude is an attitude against the child. When some form of contraception doesn't
work, it [leads] to abortion."

He also noted that many common means of contraception amount to abortion in Catholic eyes, since they work by intervening after the sperm has fertilized the egg.[4]

As the Poltawskis became close social friends of the future pope, these ideas
were batted about repeatedly, with mutual receptiveness. Although Wojtyla

also enjoyed discussing ancient literature with Poltawski, it was Dr. Poltawska's Catholic doctors' group that Wojtyla took under his wing. He attended meetings almost weekly and sometimes long conferences as well.

Wojtyla enjoyed travel, shunned sleep, and arranged his schedule to accommodate those tastes. He regularly caught the night train from Krakow to Lublin, arrived early in the morning, prayed up to an hour at a monastery where he was spiritual adviser to sixty nuns, then headed for class.

Students apparently adored him, and an unusual number grew to be standouts. "The thing that made ethics interesting," says one—Father Zenon Modzelewski, who runs a Church publishing house in France—"was that he talked about sex and love. He gave very human examples of ethical problems, very different from the Marxism we were surrounded with."

He was known for his sense of humor. One student, later an editor at *Wiez*, swears that Wojtyla once slid down a stair railing in his cassock in front of his students. Another time, a clerk had to bring Wojtyla a message in the middle of a lecture and was so embarrassed that he knelt while presenting it. Wojtyla responded by kneeling to receive the message. After everyone had a good laugh, Wojtyla addressed the messenger and the students alike on the equality of all people before God.[5]

After lectures came meetings with nuns, dinners with various groups, and long, informal evenings with students, drinking tea, then walking slowly in the cold to the station together. A midnight train would deliver him in the wee hours to Krakow, where he would face a regular workload the next day.

At these evening sessions, the sexual talk often became explicit—a rare occurrence in Poland. "Wojtyla was a personal friend. We had the deepest confidence in him, and he was older," says Krzysztov Kozlowski, later a *Tygodnik Powszechny* editor and post-communist police commissioner. "We talked about life in a communist future. We talked of love, that to love is to be fully responsible for the other person. At this time, Karol Wojtyla was not at all interested in political affairs."

May 6, 1957, huge crowds at the Warsaw railway station saw Wyszynski off to Rome for his first meeting with Pope Pius since his captivity. He and Gomulka had talked past midnight about the trip, with Wyszynski continuing to play his government off against his pope. Gomulka did not understand that Wyszynski's relations with Pius were strained. The prime minister wanted the cachet of a formal concordat between his government and the Vatican, and he assumed that Wyszynski did, too—and would promote the idea to Pius.

Wyszynski let Gomulka believe this, not even hinting that the last thing he wanted was for his tormentors, the communists, to have a direct line to his nonunderstanding, unreliable "protector" at the Vatican; it was a link that could only undercut Wyszynski's independence. Gomulka also had no sure sense of the Great Novena plan; later, when its political dynamic unfolded, he assumed that Pius had forced the plan upon Wyszynski, an idea that Wyszynski didn't disabuse him of.[6]

Wyszynski's imprisonment had brought him fame. Crowds greeted him at each stop. In Rome, Pius blessed him. Perhaps more important, however, he visited Vienna, where he became friends with the new archbishop, Franz König. Soon afterward, König sent his secretary to Poland to see how the relatively rich Vienna diocese could help. She immediately began shipping heating coal to Polish convents, but Wyszynski told her that the real problem was not heat but light: "Russian culture was overtaking Polish. Polish intellectuals needed exposure to the outside world."[7]

König began inviting Polish intellectuals to Vienna and housing them there. The program lasted three decades. Karol Wojtyla expanded it to allow four thousand Poles, largely of his personal selection, to visit Austria—a wellspring of the Solidarity revolution.

10

Wojtyla continued to write regularly for *Tygodnik Powszechny*, but this was not the way for him best to endear himself to the primate of Poland. Back in Stalinist days, when the Church and the government were practically at war, Wyszynski had accepted help from the socialist-inclined Catholics in Krakow who ran *Tygodnik Powszechny*, probably the communist world's only lively press. But now the liberal ideas he read in it often made him bristle, and its evenhanded debate of the government's abortion policy infuriated him.

By 1957, Turowicz's newspaper had spawned two affiliated magazines. *Znak*, or "Sign," was as much a social movement as a publication; the Catholics who had been elected to Parliament, including Turowicz, called themselves the Znak group. And a sister publication, *Wiez*, or "Bond," was actually run by former members of Pax, including Tadeusz Mazowiecki.[1]

Wyszynski was so angry that he bypassed Archbishop Baziak (who was back in charge of the archdiocese after the government's attempt to remove him) and called Turowicz and other editors directly to his Warsaw office. Wyszynski launched a tirade. Catholics had to start speaking as one and representing the Church, he said. He berated one of the Znak parliamentary group for writing articles too kind to the communists.

He also laced into another editor, Jacek Wozniakowski, an art history professor and Wojtyla crony who later gave Wojtyla a blow-by-blow account. Wojtyla seemed glad to hear that Wozniakowski had urged the primate to be lenient and had argued that *Znak* benefited the Church.[2]

The problem ran deeper than mere editorial policy. There was high tension between Poland's two big archdioceses, and Wojtyla's friends were the target of Wyszynski's anger.

Wojtyla thought he had left such problems behind when he took off with students for the lake region in the summer of 1958. But a telegram summoned him back to Krakow. A vacancy had opened in the Krakow curia with the death of an auxiliary bishop a few weeks before. People in the Church had been speculating about a replacement. Suddenly, Archbishop Baziak told Wojtyla that he was it. The news came as a surprise: after all the struggle it had taken to push him back into academics, a new move to administration hadn't seemed likely.

Wojtyla calmly told Baziak that he would have to return to his students in the lakes region "to say Mass for them on Sunday." When he told the campers, he later recalled, "They asked me if I was no longer to be their 'uncle.' I reassured them."[3]

How had the appointment come about? "Baziak went straight to the Vatican behind Wyszynski's back," Father Malinski says. He adds that Wyszynski would not likely have selected Wojtyla because the primate "liked pastors, not academics. He liked people he knew well personally." This certainly did not include Wojtyla. And Wojtyla's identification with the radical Catholics at *Tygodnik Powszechny* and *Znak* would have sealed the case against him.

Nor would Wyszynski likely have understood a new bishop who, ten weeks before his consecration, stuck to his usual schedule of nature trips. And a good thing he did, for among the first-time hikers he got to know during that stretch was an important future collaborator in Znak and Solidarity, Bohdan Cywinski of Warsaw, who had been asked along by a student friend.

"Everyone looked forward to Priest-Professor Wojtyla," Cywinski remembers. And then he learned one reason—the surprisingly frank talk about sex: "He was trying to introduce very tough standards of morality [to] all these young people. No intercourse before marriage. All of us tried to dispute this issue. We were not easy listeners. Members of our group were sexually active and said so. But he was our spiritual guru. He depicted an ideal of sexual rigor as analogous to sports achievement. Everybody can achieve. Asceticism was a normal, regular idea to us."

Cywinski was so inspired by the challenge and camaraderie of that first trip that he attended further outings with Wojtyla every chance. He found that though Wojtyla promoted sexual abstinence, he was otherwise first in line for adventure: "Sometimes we would meet in winter. When someone didn't have ski shoes, Wojtyla said, 'What size are you?' and returned with a spare pair."

September 28, 1958, Baziak consecrated Wojtyla a bishop, at the Wawel. The service was packed with friends from Wojtyla's many former lives—country folk, colleagues from the Tyranowski and theater circles, fellow underground seminarians, former parishioners from St. Florian's, journalist colleagues from *Znak* and *Tygodnik Powszechny.*[4] Baziak allowed Wojtyla to continue as chaplain to students at the Jagiellonian and as ethics professor at Lublin.

Among the new bishop's close friends was Przemyslaw Mroczkowski, an English-literature professor. Mroczkowski's daughter Katarzyna, now a translator in Krakow, says the first time Wojtyla appeared at their house with a purple bishop's cord around the sleeve of his cassock, her younger brother Tomasz burst out excitedly, "Oh, have you become a railway worker?" since they, too, wore black coats with purple stripes. She says Wojtyla, not missing a beat, confirmed the boy's suspicion and went on to describe for him the trains he rode.

Wojtyla's elevation to bishop didn't end his availability for volleyball games, either, she says. "It was always a lot of fun when he came. He talked to the children, he didn't just sit with the grown-ups." That was quite in contrast to the mood she remembers when Wyszynski came visiting; the primate was "a little bit stiff. Nobody told any jokes when he was there." She says that though she knew Wyszynski for years, she never realized he had a warm or humorous side until she was called upon to translate Micewski's biography of him. Not so Wojtyla; she still has the handwritten note he sent after her first communion, which travel prevented him from attending.

Bohdan Cywinski once told Wojtyla that the difference between him and Wyszynski was that people genuinely liked Wojtyla; they weren't afraid of him. "That's the way it should be," Wojtyla replied.[5]

Friends say Wojtyla accepted three perquisites from the bishop's job, and no more. He got a separate canoe and tent on camping trips; a reading light and folding desk were installed in the rear of the car he traveled in; and his mother's and brother's bodies were brought from Wadowice to be buried with his father's in Krakow.

Marek Skwarnicki, poetry editor at *Tygodnik Powszechny* since 1957, says Wojtyla was the only bishop ever to come to him with a poetry submission. "Mr. Marek," he says Wojtyla asked, quite in earnest, "should a bishop publish poetry?"

Skwarnicki reassured him—but adds now, "Wojtyla's poetry was not easy to understand. He always said, 'Don't tell me about the quality. Tell me what impression it made on you.' "

It wasn't long before Wyszynski began a subtle rebellion to let the world know he was angry that Archbishop Baziak had imposed such a bishop on him. When Wojtyla kept a speaking date at the Warsaw Catholic Intelligentsia Club, an official from the curia heckled him: Why had a "foreign" bishop been brought in without clearance by Wyszynski's office? he asked. The disturbance was brief, but everyone understood the protest.[6]

A visiting bishop from Warsaw complained to an official of the club's Krakow branch, Andrzej Wielowiejski, that Wojtyla swam with students wearing only their "slips." (That the words for "lingerie" and "swimsuit" were identical is a fair reflection of the prudity surrounding swimsuits at the time.) Wielowiejski says he merely responded, "You want that they go swimming *without* their slips?"

A face-to-face confrontation between Wyszynski and Wojtyla finally came at an Episcopate meeting. Wyszynski was lecturing in his usual formal style. Wojtyla, also as usual, was in the back row, reading. Noting the new bishop's apparent inattentiveness, Wyszynski grew ever more irritated. At last he said, "Now Bishop Wojtyla is going to tell us what we are talking about"—whereupon Wojtyla looked up and recounted everything Wyszynski had just been saying.[7] It was the first of many times this would happen; Wojtyla's capacity to concentrate on two things at once amazed bystanders and infuriated people like Wyszynski.

Around the time of Wojtyla's consecration, Archbishop König of Vienna visited Poland, where he had been sending coal and other donations. Radio Free Europe had announced his schedule, so crowds greeted his train at the Czech-Polish border. "Everyone was laughing and talking," he says, when way in the back, he noticed "a shy young priest." Handshaking his way through the crowd, König arrived at the priest and asked who he was. "I was surprised to learn he was the new bishop and he had come to greet me."

As they started to talk, Wojtyla asked König "not to speak German, but please speak Italian or French. He said his knowledge of German was weak." König quickly gathered that Wojtyla's German was excellent, but that the Nazi occupation had soured his ear for the language. König spent the night in

Krakow, trying to get to know Wojtyla. "If anybody that day would have said to me he would be the pope," König now laughs, "I would have said he was crazy."

October 9, 1958, Pope Pius died. Bishop Ernest Primeau of Chicago found himself seated next to Wyszynski at some event during the funeral week. So many of Chicago's Catholics were of Polish origin that Primeau kept up with affairs there. He asked Wyszynski about "this fellow Wojtyla," the new bishop he'd read about.

"Oh," replied Wyszynski, "he's an opportunist."[8]

After deadlocking through ten ballots over three days, the electors settled on Cardinal Roncalli, who chose the papal name John XXIII. At seventy-seven, he seemed a compromise who would warm the seat while contesting factions gathered strength for a new vote in a few years. Wojtyla didn't know Roncalli personally but certainly knew who he was: for fifty years, while serving in Vatican diplomatic posts and as archbishop of Venice, Roncalli had worked on a pet project, a five-volume biography of Saint Charles Borromeo (1538–1584), leading light of the Church's Reformation-era Council at Trent. The fifth volume had just been published. Borromeo was Wojtyla's namesake saint.

Apparently no one guessed that Pope John's fascination with Church councils might have consequences beyond the literary. Only three months after his election, Pope John dropped a bombshell on Vatican Secretary of State Domenico Tardini just as the pasta was being served at lunch. "Our soul was illuminated," he later recalled, using the customary papal "we," "by a great idea which we ... received with indescribable trust in our Divine Master. A word, solemn and binding, rose to our lips. Our voice expressed it for the first time: 'A council!'

"To tell the truth," Pope John said, as he recalled waiting anxiously for Tardini's reaction, "we feared we had aroused perplexity, if not dismay. . . . But a clear expression appeared on the cardinal's face. His assent was immediate and exultant, the first sure sign of the Lord's will."

Soon the neophyte bishop of Krakow and more than twenty-five hundred colleagues around the world received instructions to prepare to travel to Rome for a new council of bishops, the first in ninety years.

If Wojtyla didn't like giving up pastoral work for academics, one can imagine how he felt about switching to administration. But as before, he spiced his new work with lecturing and personal appearances that enabled him to retain human contact. Every day or two he visited this town or that throughout southern Poland, shoring up spirits, giving Masses or funerals, and visiting shut-ins. When a group of doctors or lawyers wanted a talk, or awards needed handing out for achievements by Catholics young or old, in city or village, and a bishop was requested to lend weight to the occasion, the junior bishop took the call.

Government hostility resumed as Gomulka, now accustomed to office, no longer found the Church an aide in governing. Religion was once more removed from the schools. Wyszynski's microphones were seized as he addressed holiday crowds. The Czestochowa pilgrimage was harassed.

All this seemed the furthest thing from Wojtyla's mind, however. The only time he was drawn into a major Church-state fracas was to restore calm in April 1960, when rioting broke out at Nowa Huta, the new industrial town outside Krakow. In more conciliatory days, the Gomulka government had approved the workers' request to build a church; now the religious affairs minister, Zenon Kliszko, in Warsaw, ordered a school built on the site, in the center of town. When government workers arrived to remove a fifteen-foot cross marking the spot, crowds gathered. Stones were thrown at attacking police. Some people were hurt, and a policeman was killed by a tram.

Wojtyla came to the town to announce that the local party boss, Lucjan Motyka, had apologized to Archbishop Baziak and promised that the cross could stay.[9] Declared Wojtyla, "Your parish priest called for you to keep calm today. Now I am asking you myself. One should avoid reactions of destruction and provocation."

11

In 1960, Wojtyla's work on sexual ethics with Dr. Poltawska bore fruit. Together they started the Family Institute, designed to educate laymen; within a decade it had become part of the theology department at the Jagiellonian. Also in 1960, *Znak's* book division published Wojtyla's first above-ground book, *Love and Responsibility*, a long essay on how people ought to treat each other in general, interwoven with a manual on how they should respond to sexual desire. The book even included charts of the female fertility cycle so readers could try to control childbirth using the rhythm method.[1]

Love and Responsibility stresses that neither enjoyment nor procreation alone can justify a human sex act. Sex must always be a step in a profound relationship with a person of the opposite gender, which transcends the act itself. Wojtyla condemned both "utilitarians" like Freud, who focused on pleasure, and "rigorists" like the British Puritans, who wanted sex limited to procreation. He said sex should be open to both procreation *and* pleasure. He encouraged efforts to enhance enjoyment, especially of one's partner. But above all, he said, the act must always be part of the biblical instruction to love.

Although *Love and Responsibility* doesn't mention it, the Church once thought otherwise. In Saint Augustine's day, Rome held pretty much the same narrow view that the Puritans later did.[2] Thomas Aquinas loosened up only a little on the value of sex outside of procreation. The Church began to focus on love as a basis for sex only relatively recently. Thus, while Wojtyla's attitude toward sex appears restrictive by 1990s standards, by Church perspective it was robust and healthy—a night-and-day departure from Augustine's dark picture of sex as inherently sinful.

In his introduction, Wojtyla said he had been moved to write the book because "the rules often run up against greater difficulties in practice than in theory," and a spiritual adviser must be "concerned above all with the practical."[3] His camping-trip observations had allowed him "to see how feelings of attraction gradually developed into love," Malinski says. "He was there when couples took the decision to marry."

Others say Dr. Poltawska helped Wojtyla write *Love and Responsibility.*[4] Her fingerprints are visible in the text. One passage vividly describes the "organic disorders," "frigidity," and "outright hostility" that may result if "the engorgement of the genital organs at the time of sexual arousal . . . is not terminated by detumescence, which in the woman is closely connected with orgasm." The pope thus specifically endorsed female orgasm (which, doctors now say, increases the chance of pregnancy). Another passage warns that "a sexual urge prematurely awakened . . . can become the source of neurotic disturbances." There is constant mention of neuroses—all material that appears to have come from Dr. Poltawska.

Love and Responsibility advises that some sexual problems call for a "sexologist or psychiatrist," but it warns against doctors who "have a narrowly biological view of things. . . . There are times when the doctor's advice is just what turns the patient into a neurotic." The book repeatedly argues for sex education, of both the nuts-and-bolts and the ethical varieties. Teaching about sex from childhood is an "indispensable requirement of correct behavior and health. . . . It is often necessary to relieve people . . . of the widespread conviction that the sexual drive is something naturally bad."

The book says a person can find God either through a loving and sexually active marriage or through celibacy. But it says celibacy is rewarding only if one is consciously aware of being celibate as a means of expressing love. Mere lack of a sex drive accomplishes nothing because "continence cannot be an end in itself."

Adultery is defined broadly, to cover any sex without marriage—"a boundary . . . crossed not only by those who aspire to what expressly belongs to another, but just as surely by anyone who seeks what is not his own." As for birth control, *Love and Responsibility* says that even "responsible family planning"—the rhythm method—cannot be used to avoid having children altogether. It is merely a device for timing them optimally and for allowing even married couples to experience at times the self-disciplining benefits of celibacy.

The book says couples should normally have more than two children, so a family can grow—but that children should never be sought for economic benefit. Interestingly, Wojtyla asserted that the rhythm method not only can but *should* be used at times, lest a couple "see their family increase excessively"—an acknowledgment that "excessive" birth is possible. Although he wrote that his book was not the place for a debate on world population, he took some potshots at Thomas Malthus, the economist who first warned that unchecked population growth could produce poverty. (Wojtyla dismissed Malthus as "an Anglican clergyman," which Malthus had been early in life.)[5]

Professor Williams of Harvard has noted that under Wojtyla's sexual ethic, anyone who is not either a priest or part of a traditional Catholic family with Mom, Dad, and children gets only a few quick admonitions, no real counseling. Wojtyla lumped homosexuality with bestiality as "perversions." (Since he wrote *Love and Responsibility*, scientists have found evidence that homosexuality may often have a natural genetic basis.) The book's one reference to masturbation says, "Lack of training in the correct attitudes may cause a variety of aberrations (such as infantile and adolescent masturbation)." Widowhood and aging aren't discussed.

Although *Love and Responsibility* argues familiar points of Catholic morality, its main line of reasoning is not traditional at all. Instead of just scolding his readers about forbidden acts, Wojtyla unveiled a theme that would underlie his philosophy throughout his life and become his hallmark weapon in the Cold War: individual human dignity.

Wojtyla wasted no time in conveying that his sexual lessons were mere adjuncts to his main theme, that each person's dignity must be respected and that no one should be made an object of use by another. The first chapter, "The Person and the Sexual Urge," begins with a section entitled "Analysis of the Verb 'To Use.'" Wojtyla argued that sex outside marriage, or inside it without openness to pregnancy, is "using" someone else for one's own sexual relief—even if the relief is mutual.

His main argument against premarital sex and contraception was that no matter how much care one takes to please one's partner, such acts are selfish and exploitative. They treat the partner as a thing, not as a person, and can never reflect love. Love, he said, requires a lifetime commitment spanning many acts of sex, which, taken as a whole, remain open to procreation.

For him, the principle of human dignity explains why marital separation is sometimes a necessary evil, whereas divorce isn't:

> If the parties to a marriage merely withdraw from it, and from their conjugal and family life together, and do not conclude marriages with other persons, there is no breach of the personalistic order. The person is not degraded to the status of an object of use, and marriage preserves its character as an institution.

Many Poles and others who later embraced the human-dignity argument as it applied to politics were unmoved by its application to sexual ethics. And however one judges its philosophy, *Love and Responsibility* did not succeed as a popular guide for couples.

"*Love and Responsibility* is his most readable book, but it's not easy," observes his former student Halina Bortnowska. Cardinal König's secretary Lonny Glaser, who was just getting to know Wojtyla when *Love and Responsibility* came out, calls the writing "very hard to understand." Only face to face, she says, does Wojtyla come across as an inspirational force.

Even after he was pope, *Love and Responsibility* sold poorly. Another former student, Father Zenon Modzelewski, had it translated and published in France, thinking it would be "an important book for young people." But of two thousand copies printed, Modzelewski says he could sell only thirty-three: "It did not have the same popularity as his university classes. It was very difficult to read."

Also in 1960, Znak published what would become Wojtyla's best-known play (written under the pseudonym "Andrzej Jawien"), on the same theme.

The Jeweler's Shop uses Kotlarczyk/Theater of the Word style. Characters talk to the audience, only rarely to each other, using few props and little action. The jeweler, an offstage purveyor of wedding rings, seems to be God (who never speaks directly in Wojtyla's plays or poems). In the play, a faithful widow and her dead husband, a victim of war shortly after the birth of his son, are depicted as better parents than another husband and wife who are both alive but do not love each other. The second couple would divorce except that the jeweler (God) refuses to buy back their wedding rings. Although the play doesn't specifically admonish against a widow's remarrying, it suggests a woman was virtuous in not taking a new husband—just as Wojtyla's father never considered taking a new wife.*

From 1960, *The Jeweler's Shop* lay moribund until its author was elected pope. Then it was quickly produced for Italian and Swiss television, and again at a New York church in December 1994.

Like Wyszynski, Wojtyla was learning to use a metaphorical language that oppressed peoples have used throughout history to speak what was forbidden. Black slaves in the American South found they could get away with assembling for the ostensible purpose of practicing the Christian religion, when a discussion of politics by even a small group was unthinkable; so they scoured Judeo-Christian literature for material with politically charged messages.

In their songs and stories, black slaves favored tales like that of Moses and the exodus from Egypt, and Lazarus, an afflicted beggar who found glory in heaven while the rich man who had tormented him on earth burned in hell. This isn't to say the slaves were insincere in their Christianity, any more than the Poles were; but anyone who attended the meetings, listened to the stories, and heard only the religious content was missing the essence of what was happening.

Similarly, Wyszynski gave Poles a sense of their rights by reading them the communists' own propaganda about freedom. Because Wojtyla's metaphoric language was rooted in academic philosophy, for a long time his message was less perceptible than the messages of the American slaves or Wyszynski. Beginning with *Love and Responsibility*, Wojtyla emphasized the notion that each person had a distinct dignity as a creation of God. This dignity, he said, could not be disclaimed and should not be violated by anyone. Others, from Vatican theologians to Ann Landers, had argued against casual sex. But Wojtyla's reasoning—that sex only for pleasure violated an individual's dignity—was largely original.

Emphasis on the individual flew in the face of communism, which saw a world of masses and classes. At some point, this became a conscious factor in Wojtyla's style. The question is, when? Some who knew him well[6] say that unlike Wyszynski, Wojtyla did not consciously launch public political attacks

---

* In *Love and Responsibility*, Wojtyla quotes Jesus as saying that marriage is part of earthly life and doesn't exist in Heaven, meaning that a widow is free to remarry. But he adds, "to remain a widow or widower is ... altogether praiseworthy since (among other things) it emphasizes more fully the reality of the union with the person now deceased."

until the 1970s; others say earlier. What's important is that the communists—who jailed Wyszynski for his political content in 1953—did not recognize the political content in Wojtyla's speeches and writings until 1964 or later. His government file was still clean in that decisive year of his life.

But some of those listening to Wojtyla heard an anti-communist message in his public comments very early on. "He did not criticize," says his friend Maria Tarnowska. "That was Wyszynski. But when you talk about the liberty of a child of God, it is always political."

His sermon titles from those days sound innocuous: "God Is Someone," "Christianity Is the Religion of Choice for Free People," "Prayer," "Sin," "Love." But in them, "he accented human rights," says Father Bardecki, who quietly began transcribing the sermons and hiding them. "The rights of nations to be independent. He was against censorship. It was his constant topic."

12

Father—now Bishop—Alfred Abramowicz of Chicago was sent to Poland in 1960 by a Church-sponsored aid committee to find out what the Poles needed. He was saddened to see how backward the country was, with "farm vehicles [running] on wooden wheels." He gave Wyszynski fifty thousand dollars that he brought in hundred-dollar bills (causing quite a commotion at airport customs).[1]

"But the universal joke," Abramowicz recalls, "was that what Poland needed was freedom."

Abramowicz marveled at Wyszynski's public homilies: "He would talk for an hour without notes. And you could stand up high and never see the back of the crowd. There was never any applause. That would have been seen as demagoguery. But you could see in their eyes an approval of what he was saying."

Remarkably, Abramowicz and other Americans who went to Poland on Church or relief business say they tried and failed to interest the U.S. government in their work. Even as the United States undertook huge covert wars to beat back revolutions in Southeast Asia, as it traded threats with Khrushchev over Berlin, and as it laid plans to invade Cuba, the State Department did not want to talk to churchmen going to Poland. Apparently, after the debacle in Hungary in 1956, the U.S. gave up challenging communism in its Eastern Europe stronghold.[2]

Pope John XXIII was pushing for a friendly dialogue. John, the old man the cardinals had appointed to serve as caretaker while they resolved their deadlock over policy, had betrayed their intention a second time. After his stunning order for a new Vatican Council, he quietly set about reversing the entire anti-communist policy of the Piuses. John aimed to end the Cold War; his tactic was to treat the communist and anti-communist sides equally. Never assume that people with bad ideas are bad people, he said; always be ready to listen.[3]

The new policy put Wyszynski in the middle of a Vatican struggle. Holdovers from Pius's curia thought the Polish primate was still too cozy with the communists, while John XXIII, aiming to make peace, found him (or at least his legend) too combative. In the ultimate irony, the new pope wanted to remove Wyszynski for the exact opposite reason that Pius XII had wanted to remove him.

Cardinal John Krol of Philadelphia, who watched affairs in his Polish ethnic homeland closely, told me that Pope John "wanted Wyszynski to come to Rome in retirement." But Wyszynski refused, telling John, "The communists will criticize until they have only bishops who are loyal to [them]." "He wanted to stay as a thorn in the side of the communists," Krol said.[4]

Pope John backed off, deciding that getting into a confrontation and possible scandal over Wyszynski wouldn't be the best way to start the peace process. But neither did he choose Wyszynski to be his chief instrument in the new Eastern European policy; instead, he drafted the relatively young Cardinal Franz König of Vienna. König's earlier decision to build quiet bridges to Eastern Europe had produced expertise without hostility, and now it paid off.

Pope John sent König to Yugoslavia in 1960 for the funeral of an imprisoned cardinal.[5] Konig says he "was stunned" that the Yugoslavs even gave him a visa; evidently it signaled warming on a high level.* On his next trip to Rome, König says, Pope John volunteered, "Why don't you go see Cardinal Mindszenty? Maybe we should invite him to the Council." König replied that the Hungarians would never agree to such a visit. Said Pope John, "Go to the railroad station and buy yourself a ticket. Leave it to us to open the frontier for you."

"I don't know what he did," König says, "but I got a promise from the Hungarian embassy I could go whenever I wanted."

He had a harder time of it talking his way past American officials to get to Mindszenty's quarters on the third floor of the U.S. embassy, and a harder time

---

* Barely had König arrived in Yugoslavia when he was nearly killed in a car crash. He describes waking up in a white hospital room, staring for days at a photo of dictator Tito on the wall, and resolving to work for peace. Western news accounts suggested the accident was a staged assassination attempt; König says that's impossible, and that a truck happened by just as his car skidded.

still when he at last reached the cardinal. Turning on the radio full blast to foil eavesdroppers, Mindszenty said he could not understand why the Americans didn't just invade Hungary and drive out the communists.

König wondered at Mindszenty's grasp of reality. By this time he had decided that everyone wanted Mindszenty out of Budapest: the communists, Pope John (who knew Mindszenty wouldn't be allowed back if he came to Rome), and the Americans (for whom his presence at the embassy had become a giant headache). König says he resolved on the spot to countermand Pope John; he just conveyed a papal greeting and left without mentioning the Council.

"My feeling was that it was better for the Church if he remain there," König says.

Khrushchev publicly welcomed Pope John's invitation to thaw relations. The Soviets even lifted a ban on papal writing to encourage distribution of a peace encyclical John XXIII had written. Wyszynski seized the chance to order books printed abroad with the pope's picture on the cover. "Wyszynski brought in books by the hundreds with [the] encyclical of John XXIII," Bishop Abramowicz says. "But they also included the encyclical by Pius XI in which he condemned communism, and the encyclical of Leo XIII on labor." For a while, a lot of banned reading got in behind John XXIII's picture.

It appeared that relations between the primate and his youngest bishop had also warmed somewhat: Wyszynski formally appointed Wojtyla "protector" of *Tygodnik Powszechny* at the end of 1960. But he soon began pressuring Wojtyla to crack down on the Znak group, even though they were now Wojtyla's steady publishers. Wyszynski publicly disavowed the group on behalf of the Church, complaining particularly about *Wiez* editor Mazowiecki, the future prime minister.[6] Wojtyla walked a tightrope, trying to be loyal to both Wyszynski and Znak.

Znak was now planting seeds that would sprout many years later. An editor named Stefan Wilkanowicz used the warmer climate to reach out to Catholic organizations in the West, as well as sympathizers elsewhere in the Eastern Bloc. One day, as he was leaving St. Anne's Church in the Krakow market square, Wilkanowicz was surreptitiously approached by a couple from Prague who were seeking entree to Catholic circles. He arranged for them to write for *Znak* under a pseudonym and quietly introduced them around, most significantly to Wojtyla.

After that meeting, Wojtyla began ordaining Czech candidates for the priesthood, secretly, in Krakow. Clandestine priests returned from Poland to Czechoslovakia without either of the two governments' knowing what had happened. The Czech Church had been nearly dismantled by the communists; now, through Wojtyla, it secretly rebuilt itself with help from the stronger Polish Church. Eventually, in 1989, the daughter of the Czech couple who first approached *Znak* editor Wilkanowicz in 1960, became free Czechoslovakia's first ambassador to Poland.[7]

At Christmas 1960, Wilkanowicz organized a spiritual seminar for students in the mountains. A talk by Wojtyla was to highlight the event. Wojtyla "came in late in the evening, and said, 'Let's start with singing.' We sang Christmas carols for an hour—mostly folk carols, not Church music," Wilkanowicz recalls. "Then he said, 'That's enough for today—and for the conference,' and went back to Krakow" without ever giving the talk.

Two months later, however, Wojtyla delivered a lecture during Philosophy Week at Jagiellonian University that Wilkanowicz thought important enough to reprint in *Znak*. In it, the young bishop etched out a new line of thought, flowing from his book on sex and love. He now aimed to link existentialism—the belief that action defines the person who acted—with Christianity. (As noted earlier, this was the intention of the original existentialist, Kierkegaard, a Protestant whose philosophy was secularized by modern novelists and banned by Pope Pius XII.)

In his lecture, Wojtyla disposed one by one of other philosophers' ideas: Descartes's "mechanistic conception," Kant's "undue subjectivism," and phenomenology's "undue stress on consciousness," as well as the "psychologizing subjectivism" of the Thomist revisionists. Relating all this philosophy to politics, he called for a middle way between "selfish individualism and faceless collectivism."[8]

For the rest of the 1960s, Wojtyla continued to explore the idea of philosophy built around action. The ultimate result was his book *The Acting Person*. Whether or not he foresaw it, his new approach would generate the philosophical language with which he would confront communism.

Wojtyla had to budget time for all this deep thinking. He was still responsible for minor chores for the Episcopate. He went to the theater when his wartime colleague Danuta Michalowska opened a one-woman show (which eventually toured the world). After saying Mass for the twentieth anniversary of the reopened Rhapsody Theater, he took part in a celebratory performance of a Mickiewicz play. For a month he was badly ill with mononucleosis.

Then *Love and Responsibility* reached the Roman curia. Wilton Wynn, a veteran *Time* magazine correspondent in Rome, says that cardinals he knew "were shocked that a priest should so freely speak of things like sexual pleasure and orgasm." But the commission reviewing sexuality issues for the upcoming Vatican Council summoned Wojtyla for advice. He rejoiced in reacquainting himself with Rome after thirteen years.[9]

That spring, 1961, Pope John followed recent papal tradition by issuing an encyclical on social issues on the ten-year anniversary of Pope Leo XIII's groundbreaking 1891 social encyclical *Rerum Novarum*. Pope John's social encyclical, *Mater et Magistra* ("Mother and Mistress"), was the most noteworthy since Leo's original. It welcomed the abundance of modern society but lamented the growing gap between rich and poor. It called for increased state ownership of property, increased activity by international social organizations, and increased aid from rich countries to poor ones. It downplayed the importance of private property.

Whether or not it was John's intent, the encyclical advanced his peacemaking. Khrushchev praised the encyclical publicly (as he had the earlier peace encyclical). On the pope's eightieth birthday, Khrushchev sent him effusive wishes for "success in his noble efforts." Pope John, over what are said to have been objections from his curia, seized the opening and responded warmly, saying he would pray for peace and for the people of the USSR.

Soon this sweet-talk produced a dividend: bishops from Soviet satellite countries would be allowed to attend the Vatican Council.

13

June 14–15, 1962, the monthly Episcopate meeting in Warsaw dragged on till three A.M., discussing the Vatican Council, now less than four months away. What the bishops most remembered, however, was Wyszynski's joyful announcement that the communists, in this new era, had finally agreed to let Baziak become the "ordinary," or permanent, official archbishop of Krakow.

Wojtyla was delighted that his benefactor Baziak, who had suffered years of manipulation in and out of temporary leadership would now likely be rewarded with a cardinal's hat.

Except that minutes after the seventy or so weary prelates broke up their marathon meeting, Archbishop Baziak dropped dead of a heart attack in his hotel room.

The shock of Baziak's death, after the long approval process and on the eve of the Council, delayed the naming of a successor. Someone had to be in temporary charge of the archdiocese, however, and rules called for a vote of the "Cathedral Chapter"—an official advisory council made up of a couple of dozen priests and a few bishops appointed by the sitting archbishop. A month after Baziak died, the Cathedral Chapter designated Wojtyla to run the archdiocese—possibly because he was unlikely to get the job permanently.

For one thing, Wojtyla had just turned forty-two. Krakow was one of Poland's two major archdioceses; Sapieha himself, for whom the job of archbishop had been practically a birthright, had not assumed it until he was fifty-eight. Also, as explained by Wojtyla's fellow seminarian and friend Father Mieczyslaw Malinski, "There was a rule that an auxiliary bishop doesn't become an ordinary in the same diocese."

Malinski says that he and Wojtyla "talked about it all the time. We thought he would be nominated an ordinary in some other [smaller] diocese after the Krakow matter was settled." Wojtyla seemed anything but anxious about it: ten days after he was designated by the Cathedral Chapter, he took off on a three-week canoe trip with ten students (who say they talked mostly about the Vatican Council).

Besides the tangible barriers to Wojtyla's getting the job permanently—his youth and the fact that he was an assistant in Krakow—there were even stronger intangible barriers, such as Wyszynski's aversion to the brainy, sometimes socialist-oriented Znak group. Lucjan Motyka, the local party boss at the time, sensed that "Wyszynski was a populist followed by a crowd of countryside folks, common people. Wojtyla was an intellectual, followed by an elite. There was no love between them."

And Wojtyla had antagonists right in Krakow. A U.S. intelligence report on him[1] said he "had . . . serious difficulties with some members of the Krakow . . . curia. The . . . curia traditionally considered itself to be a privileged and independent body. The position in which Wojtyla found himself was very difficult . . . because as a former [manual] worker, he did not have 'connections' or sufficient authority among the rather snobbish clergy, among whom . . . many . . . were secretly jealous of his career."

The intelligence report even quotes Wojtyla as telling friends, "Well, what can I do? When Cardinal Sapieha, who was born a prince, looked at them from his height, they were afraid of him. But I, a former worker, simply cannot impress them in the same way." (The report, written in 1968, concluded that by then he had "gained the authority by his work and personality.")

Halina Bortnowska, now a prominent Catholic laywoman, was on Wojtyla's staff in 1962; she was doing a second doctorate under him and also working as an editor at *Znak*. To her, Wojtyla seemed an improbable choice for archbishop because "he was not a typical Polish clergyman. It was not typical for a Polish clergyman to be interested in Saint John of the Cross. We are mostly ritualistic people. He was private, mystical. Very few people in the clergy really listen."

Shortly after returning from his canoe trip that summer of 1962, Wojtyla made a fateful venture to the Party office just a few blocks from the square in the old city of Krakow. He apparently went on his own initiative, taking only his secretary. Fate had it that the first secretary in Krakow, the man Wojtyla was to see, was Motyka.[2] Motyka says he was then—and remains now—an enlightened, anti-Stalinist communist.

Even though his patron, Gomulka, increasingly adopted Soviet tactics, Motyka says he "never considered getting out" of the Party because quitting "wouldn't do any good for my country"; his replacement would have been "some hard-liner. The Russians wanted us to copy their system, and we were trying to convince the Russians we were raised in the influence of Western culture."

Coming from a family of artists and writers, Motyka had heard all about Wojtyla from his neighbors, the Kwiatkowskis, and others. But he still didn't expect Wojtyla to ask to see him. "There had been no such case, that a real bishop had visited the committee," Motyka says. The issue that sparked the encounter seemed minor: the government operated a dozen colleges in Krakow and needed dormitory space, so the City Council had taken over an underused seminary dormitory, thinking its twelve residents could go to one of the other two seminaries in town. Says Motyka, "Wojtyla arrived with his secretary. I offered them coffee. And Wojtyla asked to keep the seminary."

"Why are you coming to see me?" Motyka says he replied. "Your problem is with the City Council."

"Yes, we know," Wojtyla said. "But we also know where the true decisions are made. You have the influence."

Motyka was impressed.

"You were educated in Krakow," Motyka said. "Let's do a Krakow bargain." This was a generally understood Polish term for an informal division of a contested item. "Since the seminary is not fully using the building, each will get half. It would be easy to separate it."

"Wojtyla agreed," Motyka says. "He was very relaxed, smiling. So I took the opportunity to talk about other issues as well."

Motyka was responsible for what the communists called social deeds: the government would pay half the cost of materials for local projects if the community supplied the manpower. Some called this forced labor; to Motyka, it was community service. He wanted priests to encourage "social deeds" by their parishioners, but the priests said the new bishop wouldn't let them recommend such work.

"Why won't you give permission?" Motyka asked.

"Because you put this request to the priests," Wojtyla replied. "Every time you go directly to the priests, I consider it an attempt to undermine my authority."

So Motyka asked Wojtyla to approve. But Wojtyla still balked. He complained that such work was deliberately scheduled for Sundays "to make public life seem as if God didn't exist."[3]

Finally, Motyka says, "I understood he was not interested in having his priests do this kind of organizing. I didn't want to make a problem of it. The meeting ended on friendly terms."

Motyka says that when he phoned Warsaw about the dormitory compromise, he got such an argument from a Party functionary there that he decided—again fatefully—to send the Central Committee a full report of the meeting. It became the most prominent item in Wojtyla's government file. Motyka attributed the visit to "his confidence in himself as an actor. He thought he would make a good argument."[4]

Wojtyla, too, talked about the meeting. Andrzej Wielowiejski, his friend from the Catholic Intelligentsia Club, says Wojtyla knew it "was the first case of a bishop's visiting a communist leader. The communists respected him more for this."

Under procedures long agreed to, Wyszynski would submit to the government three names of possible replacements for Baziak, in order of preference. A similar list would eventually go to the Congregation (department) for Bishops at the Vatican, which would make a recommendation to the pope, who would decide.

It made no sense to submit names formally to Rome until they had been cleared by the government. This was not a situation invented by communists; governments had claimed a veto over bishop appointments since closer to the birth of Jesus than to the birth of Marx. (Indeed, it surprised the Vatican two hundred years ago when the American ambassador to France, Benjamin Franklin, told an emissary that his government would break with normal procedure and not say a word about who could or couldn't be bishop because the Constitution forbade it.)[5]

Wyszynski never consulted Wojtyla about Baziak's replacement.[6] Many people close to Wojtyla in 1962, several from the Znak group,[7] say that

Wyszynski submitted at least one list of three names to the Ministry for Religious Affairs in Warsaw, and that Wojtyla's name wasn't on it.[8] The Party Presidium—a committee of eleven men—would vote on the nomination, but the other ten would likely rely on the advice of Zenon Kliszko, the minister for religious affairs. Kliszko, from the early Gomulka group, had been imprisoned with Gomulka from 1949 until 1956, when Khrushchev allowed their rehabilitation.

Examining the files of each candidate, Kliszko was fascinated by Motyka's report of the meeting with Wojtyla over dormitory space. "Kliszko favored Wojtyla," says Kazimierz Barcikowski, later a Party boss in Krakow.[9] "They hoped because of his experience with physical labor he would understand socialist issues and negotiate with the State better than Wyszynski."

Others in the Party[10] thought Wojtyla's "internationalist and academic concerns" were less threatening than Wyszynski's nationalism. According to Father Malinski, the government thought that if Wojtyla was selected, "he might become a red cardinal to Wyszynski's black cardinal. His university lectures promoted the idea that government should intervene to help poor people."

Barcikowski says Kliszko became determined to put Wojtyla in the Krakow archbishop's slot, in direct opposition to Wyszynski's determination to keep him out.[11] "There were prolonged negotiations," agrees Archbishop Bronislaw Dabrowski, longtime secretary of the Polish Episcopate. When asked whom Wyszynski wanted, Dabrowski will only say, "Wojtyla was always one of the candidates."

14

Like his visit to Motyka's office, the Second Vatican Council was timed luckily for Wojtyla's rise. To this day, the Council means different things to different people. Conceived during Pope Pius's time as a way to harden dogma and quell dissent, for Pope John the Council became instead an *aggiornamento*—a bringing-up-to-date with changes in the world.

Many churchmen, however, liked the status quo—and not just the stereotype curmudgeons in the Roman curia. The American Church was riding high. It had its first Catholic President, John F. Kennedy, who seemed likely to be reelected. Central cities, largely Catholic and run by Catholic-led political organizations, were still healthy sites for business and amusement, not yet gang turf.

Polish, Italian, and Irish Catholic immigrants now made up the American middle class, and the future wave of poor Catholic immigrants from Latin America was still a trickle.

Catholic dioceses, flush with wealth, built churches, schools, and community centers as fast as architects and workmen could be hired. These dioceses were ruled—not just overseen—by strongman cardinals like Spellman in New York, Stritch in Chicago, and McIntyre in Los Angeles, and by fathers Bing Crosby and Barry Fitzgerald in the movies. What needed reforming?

Many American churchmen did want to say Mass in English instead of Latin; Mass in the local language was one of the changes being discussed. Many also supported Father John Courtney Murray, an American theologian, in his campaign for the Church to reverse its policy favoring Church-state alliances.

Popes had sought alliances with government ever since Emperor Constantine made Christianity the official religion of Rome in the fourth century; as recently as 1936, General Francisco Franco had invoked his alliance with the Church to smash republican opponents in Spain. Now, however, the Church's policy of allying with governments had become an embarrassment to American Catholics. Worse, it was an ideological albatross for Eastern European churchmen who fought communist control by emphasizing the separation between Caesar and God.

For a decade, Father Murray, pointing to the American Church's success, had spoken out on behalf of those who hoped the Vatican would renounce its pro-theocratic policy and accept Church-state separation. Kennedy, as a candidate in 1960, had turned to Murray to counter Protestant complaints that Kennedy was a stalking horse for an American Catholic theocracy.[1]

Rome's answer to Father Murray's popularity was to order him not to publish or speak without prior Vatican approval. Shortly before the start of the Council, theologians Karl Rahner of Germany and Henri de Lubac and Yves Congar of France—favorites of many Americans because they advocated similar changes—were notified by Rome that they, too, were not to publish or speak without clearance. Such discipline was itself an unspoken issue at the Council; the muzzled theologians, including Murray, were invited by delegates to attend as advisers.

Protestants looked to the Council for democratization that could help reunify Christianity. Bernard Pawley, the Anglican Church's representative to the Council, called the papacy "a totalitarian form of government widely regarded as a tyranny" and accused Catholicism of "an arrogant and censorious ... attitude to the world."

To judge by recommendations submitted to the Council by delegates, many bishops hoped to reverse the centralization of power in Vatican departments that had been ordered by the First Vatican Council, in 1869–70. There were proposals for a college of bishops that would share power with the pope, and colleges of priests to share power with the bishops within each diocese, as well as proposals calling for more power for lay believers.[2]

But in these suggestions lay the seeds of disappointment for many Catholics and continuing strife for the Church. What inspired the drive for decentralization wasn't an abstract theory of governance but popular discontent with Church policy on one issue.

Sex was to divide the Church. As Wojtyla had noted in *Love and Responsibility*, many churchmen—he among them—believed that the Church's attitude toward sex was not merely wise but derived from the revealed word of God, and thus not subject to change.

Wojtyla's submission to the Council's preparatory commission was inspired by his developing philosophy of personal action. As one Catholic scholar sums it up, Wojtyla urged "emphasis on the inalienable liberty and responsibility of the person" as "the basis of all documents of the Council."[3]

Wojtyla was hardly the first philosopher to stumble on the idea of individualism. What was significant was that he had zeroed in on the one most vulnerable point of communism: not military potential or consumer production, but human identity. And he asked his fellow churchmen to keep that foremost in mind as they charted policy.

The twenty-five Polish delegates were allowed to bring only five dollars each to Rome, but once there, they lived off fifty thousand more raised by Bishop Abramowicz's organization in Chicago. Archbishop Krol hand-delivered the money in cash to Wyszynski.

Another, less welcome, surprise on Wyszynski's arrival could only have exacerbated the friction between him and Wojtyla. Pamphlets were widely and anonymously distributed to arriving bishops complaining that Wyszynski and his Polish delegation were devoted to a "cult of Mary" and bent on sabotaging Pope John's plans for reform at the Council.

Steaming, Wyszynski wrote in his diary that the pamphlets were the work of the liberal *Tygodnik Powszechny*–Znak crowd from Krakow, though he did not mention Wojtyla.[4] (Turowicz absolutely denies this and blames the communists.) Wyszynski asked Wojtyla and two fellow Polish bishops to reassure delegates from other countries that the "propaganda" in the pamphlets was false.[5]

Just as Wojtyla was leaving for Rome, his good friend and chief adviser on sexual matters, Dr. Wanda Poltawska, was diagnosed with cancer. X rays showed a large tumor growing in her colon. Surgery was scheduled, but her doctors weren't hopeful.

Wojtyla turned immediately to Padre Pio, the priest claiming supernatural contacts, whom he had visited in 1947. Wojtyla wrote Pio a passionate letter—some say he also visited him—and asked Pio's prayers for Dr. Poltawska. "She is a woman of forty ... who spent five years in a concentration camp during the war," Wojtyla said. "Now she is in danger of losing her life [to] cancer."

Eleven days later, Wojtyla wrote again to Pio, thanking him and reporting that Dr. Poltawska had been "instantaneously cured."[6]

Andrzej Poltawski confirms that "there was a diagnosis of cancer" in his wife, and that "it disappeared" after Wojtyla wrote to Pio. He says there was no treatment; when new X rays were taken, the tumor had simply vanished.

Was it Padre Pio's prayers that cured her? I asked him. "I don't know," he replied. "I think so."

Did Dr. Poltawska think Padre Pio's prayers had cured her and saved her life? He nodded. "I think so."

Wojtyla also related the incident to Father Bardecki of *Tygodnik Powszechny.* "He wrote to Padre Pio to pray for a person with cancer, and the person was healed," Bardecki told me in 1994. At least partly because of this event, Pope John Paul II has initiated the sainthood process for Padre Pio.

∽

"John XXIII had the idea the Council would last a few months," says Cardinal Alfons Stickler of Austria. But the curia wanted to send the reformers home even faster. Led by Cardinal Ottaviani, head of the Holy Office, the Vatican staff had ground all the proposals for the Council into a proposal (or "Schema") of their own for the bishops to ratify.

"The curia wanted to wrap up the Council in two weeks," says Father Theodore Hesburgh, then president of the University of Notre Dame, who was in Rome as an interested spectator. "There was an enormous struggle. The first day of the Council there was a revolution. The French and German and English liberal bishops said, 'We didn't come over here to rubber-stamp this.' They put the curia in its place."

The man most scholars credit with leading this revolt and enabling the dramatic four-year reexamination of the Church that followed, was Cardinal

Joseph Frings of Cologne, Germany. Frings was one of the ten cardinals Pope John had designated as presidents of the Council. (Wyszynski was another.) Seeing what the curia had done, Frings and two colleagues[7] invited an international group of leading bishops to the house where Frings was staying, and proposed that they discard the curia's agenda and start over.[8]

All this is noteworthy because the young man Cardinal Frings (who was blind) relied on to draft his proposals and help sharpen his ideas was Father Joseph Ratzinger, who thus was crucial in rescuing Pope John's vision of the Second Vatican Council. "Cardinal Frings chose Ratzinger as his only theologian," says a colleague.[9] With Ratzinger's help, Frings delivered one of the most stirring speeches in the four years of the Council, calling for Ottaviani's Holy Office to reform itself and to conduct fair trials with the right of self-defense instead of muzzling theologians with sudden, draconian judgments. For this, Frings was rousingly applauded.

Wojtyla got to know Ratzinger at the Council, and two decades later, as John Paul II, appointed him to *head* the Holy Office (now renamed the Congregation for the Doctrine of the Faith). And Ratzinger became the most controversial figure (other than the pope himself) in the John Paul II administration, often accused of being a new Ottaviani and undermining the very reforms that—few people remembered—he helped stir as a young firebrand.

Thanks largely to Frings, the nearly three thousand bishops[10] did no business that fall, but rather became acquainted and reorganized themselves to do business later. Wojtyla revisited his favorite mountain retreat from student days and stayed at the Polish College—closed when he was a student—while Wyszynski put himself in other Polish-run quarters a mile away. "We Polish bishops were something of a curiosity, like the black bishops," Wojtyla told Malinski. "People wanted to hear from us how the Church fared in the Eastern Bloc."

The bishops trembled with people everywhere through late October 1962. President Kennedy announced that the Soviet Union was building missile batteries in Cuba capable of striking American cities, and he ordered the U.S. Navy to board and search all Soviet ships bound for Cuba. It was the scariest week of the Cold War.

It ended when Khrushchev seemingly gave in, turned his ships around, and dismantled the missiles. The world wasn't aware—because the United States didn't want it to be—of two major factors in Khrushchev's decision. First, Moscow was hopelessly outgunned, possessing only a handful of nuclear missiles to America's hundreds.[11] Second, in exchange for backing down, Khrushchev got secret deals that largely satisfied his goals in putting missiles in Cuba to start with: the U.S.

pledged not to reinvade Cuba and promised to withdraw its own missiles along the Soviet border, in Turkey.

Neither side, however, foresaw the biggest consequence of the crisis: Khrushchev's opponents inside the Soviet Union quietly resolved that they would not deal from weakness the next time. Far more money would be earmarked for arms, by both sides.

But with the crisis over, America's Thanksgiving holiday that November was especially heartfelt. As Polish-American nuns in Rome served up a traditional turkey dinner, Bishop Aloysius J. Wycislo of Green Bay, Wisconsin, sat across from Wojtyla, who "was effusive in his praise of U.S. Catholic Relief aid in Poland after the war" but bewildered by his first look at apple pie à la mode. "What a strange custom," he remarked: putting ice cream on—"what did you say *that* was?"

At a reception celebrating his eighty-first birthday, John XXIII spoke privately with Wyszynski about the Krakow archbishop's vacancy and another open bishop's chair. Wyszynski replied with a note the next day proposing names for the other diocese, but saying, "Krakow will have to wait . . . because of the general situation."[12]

A week later, Wyszynski met with Religious Affairs Minister Kliszko, who had come to Rome to see the Council firsthand. Kliszko was still holding out for Wojtyla.

As the Council adjourned in December 1962, intending to reassemble the next fall, Pope John sent an emissary to Khrushchev to seek freedom for an imprisoned Ukrainian archbishop. The emissary reported an amazing conversation in which Khrushchev acknowledged his "religious past" and continuing feelings.[13] He made confessions to the pope of a sort not duplicated until another Soviet leader, Mikhail Gorbachev, said similar things to John Paul II twenty-seven years later.

Khrushchev's words in 1962, spoken right after the Cuban missile crisis, suggest that he might have been open to a far greater departure from Stalinist tyranny than the West supposed. The Church that had supported the tsars was gone, he said. "We have no more difficulties with the Church, and we could even go so far as to protect it if it keeps away from politics." Then he added, "It is clear that all religions should be tolerated and all ideologies and philosophies *and even parties*" (emphasis mine). He promised to send the imprisoned archbishop to Rome, and even proposed opening formal diplomatic relations with the Vatican.[14]

There are reports that President Kennedy, on learning what Khrushchev said, was tempted to ask Pope John to try to mediate peace. But because of his own Catholicism—still suspect to American Protestants—he felt he couldn't deal with the Vatican. He did pursue the opening by offering compromises on a nuclear-testing treaty the U.S. and USSR were negotiating. His concessions, though, were met with a fusillade of accusations from American Cold Warriors that he was selling out U.S. national security. Kennedy then hedged his compromise, and the treaty was put out of reach.[15]

Khrushchev could be viewed, accurately, as the dictator who in 1956 sent troops into Poland and Hungary, and in 1962 tried to put missiles in Cuba. But he could also be viewed, accurately, as the most reasonable likely Soviet leader, a man sincerely worried about the future, who might have been lured to an open door leading out of the Cold War without the West's having to risk much to find out.

Instead, Kennedy gave in to his political opponents. (In fairness, they were holding his civil-rights and other bills hostage.) Khrushchev complained that he had been embarrassed in front of his hard-liners after offering his own concessions on the weapons-test treaty. His rhetoric turned bellicose again.

With Soviet militarists resolved to catch up and American militarists resolved to stay ahead, and no major politician willing to risk his career by striking out in the opposite direction, the world was plunged into a spectacularly destructive arms race whose economic devastation and physical danger long outlasted the Cold War. And the retention of personal political power, on which both Kennedy and Khrushchev had staked so much, lasted neither man very long.

15

Wojtyla understood that many Poles who would not be in church otherwise came because of communism—and he told his fellow bishops that in January 1963. Ironically, he identified a challenge that he would one day face as pope:

> Religion isn't compulsory anymore. On the contrary, it's prohibited. As such, it fulfills the need for freedom, but only for a short time. In the long run, you can't treat religion as an occasion to show your own independence....
>
> A sort of Catholicism of asylum is being created. People are seeking the Church as a hiding place, for the qualities they can't live without.... Meetings at Mass give...them a feeling of strength and security.... Christianity is being made by administrative means.

Defeating communism would not be enough, he said. The challenge was to convert what he called administrative Catholics into real ones. There had to be a genuine triumph of the Church over men's souls.[1] Wojtyla had already set for himself a task that would leave him disappointed at the miracle he would accomplish.

As Wojtyla grew, Wyszynski, now sixty-two, shrank. Some men, as they age, gain a liberality of vision not evident in their early years—like Pope John. Most grow narrower, though, and Wyszynski was among these (as, in some ways, is Wojtyla himself). At the same meeting in which Wojtyla gave his memorable talk about administrative Catholics, the primate revealed a confidential report he had written to the Vatican, built around the astonishing assertion that communists were behind the disagreements at the Council—even the movement in favor of local-language Mass.

The communists' "technique," Wyszynski warned, "is to ... form cells of disunity among the faithful [, to] split the bishops into two blocs ... by cleverly contrived distinctions between 'reactionaries' and 'progressives.' " For page after page he went on, attributing every criticism of the Church to communism. He seemed to have lost all the liberality of his youth, when he had chided the aristocracy for using the "communist threat" as an excuse not to reform itself.

Wojtyla supported local-language Mass and many other proposed changes that Wyszynski condemned. Wyszynski's tirade blaming all this on communism must have unsettled him,[2] especially after someone in the Roman curia leaked it to the Western press, where it got big play.[3]

Pope John, however, was undeterred. Into the Vatican he welcomed Khrushchev's son-in-law, a Soviet newspaper editor who was traveling in Rome. Their meeting was front-page news worldwide. John's policy was becoming known as *Ostpolitik,* an opening to the East, favored also by some German politicians. Cardinal Ottaviani and others in the curia objected loudly. When the Christian Democratic Party in Italy declared an "opening to the Left," bringing Socialists into the government, Ottaviani even helped some lay Catholics form a new, more staunchly anti-communist party.[4]

Ignoring Ottaviani's explicit opposition, Pope John issued an encyclical, *Pacem in Terris* ("Peace on Earth"), which broke precedent in many ways. Instead of being addressed just to Catholics, it was addressed "To All Men of Good Will" (including communists; John sent Khrushchev an advance copy). The encyclical used words strikingly similar to those Wojtyla had used in his university classes on communism and would later incorporate in his "germ of truth" speech as pope: communist movements, said *Pacem in Terris*, "contain elements that are positive and deserving of approval."

Although rooted in "false philosophical teachings" about the nature of man, communism could change and should be worked with, Pope John said. He accused both sides in the Cold War of violating human rights, particularly among Third World peoples. Whereas Kennedy and Khrushchev were squabbling over limiting certain kinds of testing, *Pacem in Terris* urged an outright ban on nuclear weapons.

Soon after the encyclical was released, John McCone, Kennedy's CIA director, a Catholic and a member of the Church-sponsored anti-communist group the Knights of Malta, visited Pope John. He tried to persuade the pope to stop being evenhanded. John declined, publicly reasserting his "confidence" in "all peoples." On Kennedy's orders, McCone then sent James W. Spain, a CIA undercover agent posing as a scholar, to infiltrate the Vatican.

Lying about who he was, Spain interviewed many churchmen, according to his report, which was made public in 1978. He reported "fear that [Pope John] is politically naive." Among the "handful of liberal clerics" who supposedly "unduly influenced" the pope were Father Murray, the American supporter of religious freedom, and Father Robert Tucci, who would later be appointed by Pope John Paul II to run Vatican Radio. Among the anti-communists who Spain said were worried by Pope John was Monsignor Paul Marcinkus, an American in the curia who would one day lead the Vatican Bank into scandal.

Spain submitted his report May 13, 1963, and within five days the President had not only read it but jotted notes all over it. Kennedy then called Cardinal Richard Cushing of Boston and asked him to assure Pope John of Kennedy's faith in him. But John was already bedridden with suddenly advancing cancer; he died two weeks later.

Wojtyla had kept the two-room apartment near the Wawel where he had been ordered to live with Father Rozycki in 1951. To it he brought friends from the Catholic Intelligentsia Club, *Znak*, and *Tygodnik Powszechny* to discuss the Council. He fed articles about the Council to Turowicz, who was by now Wyszynski's bête noire.

By some accounts, it took arm-twisting to persuade Wojtyla to move from his apartment into the archbishop's palace. But that is where he was when Cardinal König arrived for another visit, during which he toured the archdiocese with Wojtyla. Their developing friendship is noteworthy in that König was widely regarded as a "liberal," having promoted Pope John's *Ostpolitik* in Eastern Europe over curia objections. He even brought the controversial theologian Karl Rahner—a favorite of pro-change Americans—to the Council as his adviser after the Holy Office had ordered Rahner silenced. If this bothered Wojtyla, he never let on. Later, König would be his chief supporter for the papacy.

16

June 21, 1963, the conclave of cardinals elected as their new pope Giovanni Montini, the archbishop of Milan, who chose the name Paul VI.[1] Paul was as close to having been groomed for the job—and as far from being a simple small-town boy—as could be. His father was editor of a major Catholic newspaper, and his mother was the foster daughter of the mayor of Brescia, a large city. Pope Paul grew up in a house filled with top clerics and politicians. One brother became a doctor, the other a senator and leader of Italy's Christian Democratic Party.

Pope Paul was the family's contribution to the priesthood. After ordination, he was sent—not to a humble parish—but to the school for Vatican diplomats. After several foreign postings, he became chief document-writer for the secretary of state, Cardinal Eugenio Pacelli, who became Pope Pius XII. Later, when the future Pope Paul clashed with Cardinal Ottaviani, Pius removed him from the Vatican and made him archbishop of Milan, Italy's industrial capital.

At the Vatican Council, Montini and Ottaviani continued to differ, but the future pope was on the winning side on such issues as local-language Mass and Father Murray's religious-liberty movement. With Paul's election as pope, the opponents of change were routed. So upset was Ottaviani's circle that one ally and friend, Cardinal Giuseppi Siri, commented, "The smoke of the devil has penetrated the Church." Siri himself would be the curia's favorite candidate for pope fifteen years later, when John Paul II was elected. Surviving members of the circle still maintain that Paul split the Church.[2]

Paul immediately signaled to the world that he would continue Pope John's *Ostpolitik* opening to the East. The first non-Catholic dignitary he received after his election was Archbishop Nikodim, head of the Russian Orthodox Church, which Stalin had put under the control of the Soviet government.

After long years of silence between the two churches, Paul offered "my hand in friendship."*

But the Khrushchev thaw was now over. In Poland, harassment increased. Soldiers tried to run priests' cars off the road, and authorities found and shredded sixty thousand books Wyszynski had imported from Paris about his Great Novena program. Only half the bishops who requested visas for the 1963 Council session received them. Wojtyla had to fight again over government efforts to seize seminaries.

Right after Wojtyla returned to Rome for the Council, Father Bardecki was visited in Krakow by Stanislaw Stomma, one of the Znak group in Parliament. Walking in the park, out of hearing of microphones, Stomma pledged Bardecki to keep a secret from their old friend Wojtyla. Religious Affairs Minister Kliszko, whom Stomma had got to know in Parliament, had talked to Stomma about the archbishop's job.

"He said he [had] already rejected seven candidates," Stomma informed Bardecki. "Cardinal Wyszynski kept contacting him. Kliszko said that only when the candidate was Wojtyla would he approve."

Bardecki asked why Kliszko was so intent on Wojtyla.

"He thinks Wojtyla is politically inexperienced and will be easy to deal with," Stomma said. Stomma had told Kliszko that Wojtyla avoided politics and was close to the Znak editors whom Wyszynski detested.

It suddenly struck Bardecki that Kliszko and Wyszynski shared the same opinion of Wojtyla; it was why Kliszko wanted Wojtyla in the archbishop's

---

* I have tracked down and now feel confident in dismissing various published reports that Nikodim was a secret agent of the Soviet KGB or the CIA or even a covert Catholic bishop. Among the main contributors to these stories was Peter Hebblethwaite, a widely published Catholic journalist who died in 1994. Hebblethwaite was particularly esteemed by Catholics who disagree with Vatican policy on sexual issues, but he also often wrote with sketchy sourcing about matters that were persuasively denied to me by everyone who seemed to be in a position to know. These denials rarely found their way into his articles. When I tried to question Hebblethwaite, he refused to talk to me. Eventually, I discounted his undocumented words, which explains why some other things he wrote are not repeated in this book.

Father John Long, head of the Vatican's Russian Institute, and Cardinals Edward Cassidy and Johannes Willebrands convincingly refute speculation on Nikodim by Hebblethwaite and others. Willebrands particularly controverts widespread reports that in order to obtain Eastern participation in the Council, he promised Nikodim that communism would not specifically be condemned. By the best accounts I could find, communism was not condemned only because Pope John, Pope Paul, and most of the bishops opposed adopting such a position.

seat and why Wyszynski wanted him out of it, but it was the same opinion. And, Bardecki smiled to himself, "both Kliszko and Wyszynski were wrong."[3]

For the fall 1963 Council session, Wojtyla brought some young scholars to Rome with him to help him with research. Among them were at least two women, Stanislawa Grabska and Halina Bortnowska. Grabska had wanted to continue her theological studies after finishing at Lublin, but had little hope of doing so, being ineligible by gender for the priesthood. She was stunned when Wojtyla, who hardly knew her, awarded her a scholarship he had been given to distribute to a worthy Pole by the dean of a major Catholic university in Belgium. Wojtyla had learned of Grabska's desire and read her work. "The Church needs lay theologians," he told her.

Considering how few women had anything to do with the Vatican Council besides cooking and cleaning house for its members, Grabska's presence there as a theologian was a strong statement by Wojtyla.

He "treated us as family," says Tadeusz Pieronek, another of Wojtyla's young scholars and now a bishop and secretary of the Polish Episcopate. They toured Sicily with him, and "when it was time to go, Wojtyla was lost in prayer," Pieronek says. "He had a reputation for not being punctual, [for having] a very unrealistic idea of how long it would take to get from where he was to where he was going. The students wanted him punished by missing his plane. But the local archbishop held up the plane so he could catch it."

The Council did not disrupt Wojtyla's habits. He regularly stopped on his way into the assembly hall in St. Peter's to pray in a side chapel. Years later, Cardinal Albino Luciani—the future Pope John Paul I—reminded Wojtyla that during the Council, "we were sitting fairly near each other and you never stopped writing."[4] Wojtyla penned letters, poems for *Znak* (about Rome, about Saint Peter, about African bishops he met), scripts for Vatican Radio, notes for a book. When a break came or a session was adjourned, Wojtyla prayed until the crowd thinned, then walked out swiftly. He seemed oblivious to the hard politicking that sometimes went on around him.

Wojtyla laid out his own vision of the Council in a talk he gave at the Polish College that fall 1963. Vatican II was called because of "a crisis," he told students. Society had become

> oriented toward consumption and blind to altruistic values. The
> Church was becoming less effectual.... The gulf between it and
> the world was widening. Religious faith was in conflict with science

and technical progress.... Atheism, materialism, and indifferentism were on the increase.[5]

This was a surprisingly broad view for someone from a country with a controlled press. Wojtyla put himself squarely on the side of the "reformers" at the Council. The men he singled out for praise were mostly supporters of major change, among them Hans Kung, with whom he later, as Pope John Paul II, would have a major falling-out.

> There's a process of decentralization in Church institutions. The primacy of the Pope is unimpaired ... but the national episcopates have begun to play a bigger part.... There's a new relationship between the center and the periphery.... The role of the laity in the Church must be upgraded, and ecumenism developed on an unprecedented scale.

He spoke of "putting an end to Constantinism—the close alliance between Church and State." And, he said, the Church

> must be de-Westernized. Peoples with ancient cultures of their own naturally resist Christianity if it comes to them in Western European dress. It must be Africanized, Indianized, or Japanicized by infusing a Christian content into those cultures. This is a slow and difficult business.

October 21, 1963, in his first speech (or "intervention") before the Council, Wojtyla sided with the reformers in a major controversy: a move to make believers, not priests and bishops, the paramount focus of the Church. He urged the Council to revise a major document because in the existing draft, "the Church appears authoritarian.... It is essential to stress that the laity do not fulfill their duties as members of the People of God by ... the mere passive possession of the faith."[6]

Merely using the new phrase "People of God" made a statement by adopting the reformers' rhetoric. Half a century before, Pope Pius X had called the Church "an unequal society" in which "the multitudes of the faithful have no other duty than to let themselves be led."[7]

But while Vatican II struck a friendlier tone, it's important to note that power wasn't transferred. Putting the believers first in a document about Church structure was symbolic; neither Wojtyla nor the majority supported another proposed change that many people mistakenly believe was a part of

Vatican II: a notion called collegiality, which would have reduced the pope from an autocrat to just a presiding bishop. The Council compromised by urging greater participation by the college of bishops, but said that ultimately the college could act only "with its head, the Roman Pontiff, and never without this head." Catholics who favor decentralization have accused John Paul II of reneging on the collegiality decreed by Vatican II, but in point of fact, there was none to renege on.[8]

Wojtyla's students lionized him and remember Wyszynski as a crotchety curmudgeon—a remarkable transformation from the Wyszynski who had joined the Episcopate as a colt bucking the aged Sapieha. When the Polish contingent assembled in Warsaw right after the 1963 Council session, Wyszynski abruptly punctured the enthusiasm by condemning the new local-language Mass: "They will not understand it in Polish. The mystery should be in a mysterious language," he said.

Then, in what must have been a conscious affront, Wyszynski specifically complained of the change Wojtyla had spoken out for—the notion of the Church as God's People.[9] This may have been Wyszynski's last sputtering blast at Wojtyla. He knew something that no one else in the room did.

October 17, 1963, in Rome, Wyszynski had been called in by Cardinal Antonio Samore, the Vatican secretary of state.[10] Like chief executives everywhere, popes sometimes prefer to deliver only good news firsthand. Samore was assigned to lay down the law from Pope Paul to Wyszynski: Krakow—maybe the most devoutly Catholic city in the world—needed a full-fledged archbishop. Wyszynski said he had been proposing names to the government for more than a year. Samore told him he should now propose them to the Vatican as well.

Wyszynski knew that if he gave Paul a list of unapproved candidates for the Krakow job, it could inspire the direct communication he dreaded between Rome and the Warsaw government. That in turn might even lead to a formal concordat, which would reduce the power of the Polish primate. Seeing the realities, Wyszynski wrote in his diary that he would propose Wojtyla.[11]

Barely two weeks later, he was presented with his first cause for regret. Stanislaw Stomma, head of the Znak group in Parliament (who had talked to Father Bardecki in the park), enraged Wyszynski with an article he published in one of the Krakow magazines that Wojtyla protected. The article promoted Gomulka's wish for direct relations with the Vatican, not even mentioning Wyszynski's opposition. To make matters worse, the Italian press picked the story up. Wyszynski shot a smoldering complaint to Turowicz, and it's hard to imagine that he didn't trade words with Wojtyla over it as well, though there is no record of it. The primate was losing leverage over the archbishop-to-be.

When the Council session ended, December 4, as the rest of the Polish delegation went home, Wojtyla headed for Israel and Jordan with an international group of bishops selected by Pope Paul, all traveling at papal expense. It was a grand experience. They visited the site where Christians believe Jesus had his Last Supper, over the spot where Jews believe King David is buried. They walked the street where Jesus is said to have carried his cross. As he would do on trips everywhere, Wojtyla sought out resident Poles, particularly priests. They sang Polish Christmas carols in Bethlehem and visited churches attended by Polish refugees.

As he returned to Krakow, he got the news of his appointment. December 30, 1963, Pope Paul signed papers appointing Karol Wojtyla metropolitan archbishop of Krakow.

Two days later, Paul shocked the Italian Church by abolishing what for hundreds of years had been known as the Papal Court. Some three hundred laymen assembled before the pope as they did each New Year's, only to be told that their titles, inherited from antiquity, were being revoked. Church jobs would be open to people of all classes. And the concordat policy was changing, Paul said. The Church would no longer "put its hope in the privileges offered by civil authority." Catholicism was winding down as a state religion.

Wyszynski's bickering with Turowicz and Mazowiecki (the editor of *Wiez* and future prime minister) had become constant. The primate accused *Znak* of patronizing the communists, and his irritation only grew when his own Warsaw Catholic Intelligentsia Club embarrassed him by supporting *Znak*.[12]

Wojtyla wanted unity with Wyszynski, particularly on the Great Novena plan and in their common response to government harassment. So he sent his editors to Warsaw on a peace mission. But positions only hardened. Twenty years earlier, Wojtyla had tried and failed to bring peace to two warring theatrical groups, both of which he liked; now, as archbishop, he tried and failed to make peace between his Krakow friends and the Warsaw Episcopate.

In the midst of the dispute, March 8, 1964, at the packed Wawel cathedral, Wojtyla was officially installed as archbishop of Krakow. "It is impossible to enter this cathedral," he said in his sermon, "without fear and awe. . . . It speaks to us of our whole history. . . . The Church of Krakow has borne me as a mother bears her son."

The history he spoke of was literally draped on his body. In a new twist on his famous penchant for secondhand clothing, he wore a golden outer cloak (chasuble) from Anna Jagiello of the sixteenth century, a hat (mitre) and cross (crozier) from two seventeenth-century bishops and another ornament donated by Queen Jadwiga in the fourteenth century, and used the chalice of a bishop from the reign of King Sigismund I (1506). A fellow priest commented to Malinski, "There cannot be many ordinaries in the world with such treasures at their disposal."

Wojtyla's new standing with Wyszynski was perhaps best expressed by Wojtyla himself a few years later, after he received his inevitable cardinal's hat, when he was in Rome and trying to find an Italian counterpart to ski with. Told that no Italian cardinals skied, he replied that 40 percent of the Polish cardinals skied. His companion, an Italian cardinal, stammered that Poland had only two cardinals. Wojtyla said Wyszynski counted for 60 percent.

Their styles were radically different. "To see Wyszynski, you needed to send a letter and get an appointment. To see Wojtyla, you just went to the curia and waited in line," says Stefan Wilkanowicz, the longtime editor of *Znak*. "When people came to him with problems, he seemed more interested in the person than the problem. He found it hard to stop conversations, so he was always late for other appointments"—sometimes hours late, without calling to reschedule.

Now that he was boss, Wojtyla frequently scheduled meetings at Kalwaria Zebrzydowska, the beautiful forest retreat he knew from childhood.[13] As soon as the business was done, he would go off alone, sometimes taking five hours to walk the five-mile Stations of the Cross. According to one priest, "The locals knew this lonely pilgrim, who greeted them with a friendly smile, exchanged a few words, and then continued his journey of prayer."[14]

Foreigners found him strangely guarded. Bishop Abramowicz of Chicago marveled at the way Wojtyla forced him to do all the talking when they met. "All he'll do is keep asking, 'Why?'" Abramowicz says.[15] Edward Piszek, a Philadelphian who made a fortune after founding Mrs. Paul's, the frozen-seafood company, says that when he journeyed to Poland to donate a mobile hospital to his ethnic homeland, Wojtyla "kept demanding why was I there," as if "he thought I was some kind of secret agent or something." Wojtyla kept up his guard even among friends. "It is not his style to discuss things," says Halina Bortnowska, his former student and Vatican II assistant. She says she wouldn't have known of his growing influence within the Church if others had not told her.

Along with other changes, many delegates to the Council wanted to relax the Church ban on contraception. The matter had been prominent on Pope John's agenda.

Contraception and abortion were often lumped together in the public mind because the Church forbade both. But there was a big difference. The Church considered abortion a violation of God's explicit commandment against killing; once it was determined that a soul was created when the sperm entered the egg, there was no room for negotiation. But in the case of contraception, even the Church acknowledged that the biblical message was merely implicit, in such instructions as to populate the earth.

This implicit message had been enough for Pope Pius XI, who banned any interference with the natural process of procreation. Pius's logic certainly covered the new birth-control pill, which altered nature. But Pius hadn't known about the Pill to ban it, which now gave an excuse to those who wanted to reopen the debate: after all, the natural means of human transportation was the feet, but no one argued that the bishops should forgo trains and planes and walk to Rome.[16]

The public seemed to welcome the Pill as it had earlier welcomed the polio vaccine. In the United States in 1964, former Presidents Eisenhower (Republican) and Truman (Democrat) were honorary cochairmen of World Planned Parenthood, and President Johnson repeatedly endorsed taxpayer support of birth control during his successful reelection campaign. Polls showed that American Catholics overwhelmingly embraced the new pill, as a loophole that allowed them to live in peace with both their Church and their common sense. Catholic and non-Catholic attitudes throughout the West agreed.

Pope John had appointed a committee of three priests and three laymen to study the issue and propose options for the Council. Cardinal Leo Suenens of Belgium had urged the Council to remove the ban on the Pill, saying, "Let us avoid a second Galileo case. One is enough."

In June 1964, Pope John's commission reported indecisively. On the one hand, it declared that the Pill was exactly the kind of contraceptive Pius XI had been speaking of; on the other, it pointed out that his message had not been presented infallibly, and so new discussion was appropriate.[17] Paul, deeply troubled, thanked the commission and began stewing over what to do.

Weeks later, he quietly removed birth control and the whole "problem of conjugal morality" from the Council's agenda. A spokesman said Paul would appoint "a proper commission of doctors, biologists, sociologists, psychiatrists, and theologians" to study the matter but "has reserved to himself the final decision."

Pope Paul's *Ostpolitik* policy also went from hope to hard times very quickly. In September 1964, Cardinal König seemed to have negotiated a deal to install Vatican-approved bishops throughout Hungary, where five of fifteen bishops were in jail and seven others barred from their jobs. But the deal was scrapped after October 16, 1964, when Khrushchev was toppled in a Kremlin coup. The new communist leader was Leonid Brezhnev, a power-seeker, not a *mensch.*

Meanwhile, two student communists at Warsaw University, Jacek Kuron and Karol Modzelewski, published an "Open Letter to the Party." Its spirit accorded with that of radical student movements that were forming from Berkeley to Paris to Beijing. The letter accused communists of betraying the working class. It said Soviet-style state control wasn't the "social ownership" Marx had talked about. It urged Polish workers to start a new party and build a true socialist state.

The government sent both young men to prison for three years. It wouldn't be worth mentioning except that Poland, and Karol Wojtyla, would hear a lot more from Jacek Kuron and Karol Modzelewski.

17

The Vatican Council session of 1964 appears to have marked the transformation of the new archbishop of Krakow into an international Church celebrity. With the issues of Church organization and prayer service settled, and the sexual issues withdrawn, the Council turned to politics, and two matters of particular concern to Wojtyla.

The first was Father Murray's plan for religious liberty. Wojtyla wanted human dignity and individual rights to form the backbone of a statement by the Council that Eastern Bloc churchmen could take home and wave before the communists. Father Murray wanted something more specific—almost an international version of the First Amendment of the U.S. Constitution. In this, Murray faced formidable opposition. Where Catholics were a majority in a country (as in Spain and Italy), they often wanted to exercise the very power of a state Church that Catholic minorities (as in America) wanted to prohibit.

To win, Father Murray needed the support of European bishops, like Wojtyla, who favored a change in the Catholic position but still didn't accept complete Church-state separation. The argument continued until delegates voted to halt debate September 25, 1964—minutes after Wojtyla's speech.

The speech was fairly convoluted, more appropriate to a philosophy class than to a political debate. It supported a religious-liberty declaration but was vague about the main practical issue. Murray advocated a negative statement, like the First Amendment, which says what government cannot do; many Europeans found this approach coldly antireligious and sought instead a positive statement, encouraging the free exercise of conscience. That idea bothered still others, who said that to urge the free exercise of all consciences was to endorse error, if it was sincerely held.

Where did Wojtyla stand? He certainly rejected the Jeffersonian notion that disagreement is inherent in human nature. Rather, he embraced a contrary ideal, more common to Europe, of consensus on official truth:

> It is necessary that the nexus between liberty and truth be further underlined in the Document.... Liberty is not given without the truth.... The purpose of ... ecumenical activity ... is ... liberation of the whole of Christianity from schisms, which surely cannot be accomplished unless unity be made perfect in the truth.
>
> Thus it does not suffice if ... religious liberty toward the Separated Brethren appears only as a principle of toleration.... Progress in the perception of the truth must be desired at the same time.[1]

He finished in under his allotted ten minutes and got no applause. Even his friend Malinski called the speech "a little dry." Over coffee, he told Wojtyla, "It's a pity you didn't develop the idea of truth and freedom a bit further."

"There wasn't time," Wojtyla replied, and Malinski sensed that his friend "felt he had not managed to put his point across."

But what *was* his point? Catholics were waiting for the Council to decide how far to legitimize diversity of opinion. Wojtyla's assertion that liberty included an obligation to seek truth was interesting for a philosophy student on Mount Carmel, but it didn't answer the question. The U.S. Catholic News Service was so confused by his speech that it released a brief summary saying he had endorsed "full religious liberty from the state." But Wojtyla hadn't been at all clear on that point.[2]

He was among many bishops, perhaps a majority, who wanted a document declaring itself for religious liberty but hedging on important elements of what Father Murray and others thought that meant. Even Archbishop Karl J. Alter of Cincinnati, who followed Wojtyla to the microphone, felt the need to assure skeptics that under the American proposal, "persons do not have a personal right to teach error."

The Church was a long way from endorsing Jeffersonian liberty, even in Cincinnati. Yet Polish Catholics wanted the right to teach publicly what their government said was error. Catholicism had long proclaimed its own teachings to be "the truth"—even though those teachings sometimes changed. Within this context, however, Wojtyla was known as an unequivocal supporter of making a historic statement, and the American delegates considered him an ally.[3]

A commission was appointed to draw up a compromise. Many delegates petitioned Paul to include a condemnation of communism, but Paul rejected that. Wojtyla apparently declined to sign the petition.[4]

Now the Council moved on to the issue Wojtyla had spent the most time preparing for: how the Church should relate to the outside world. From Krakow, Wojtyla had submitted a long memo urging that the Church become a bulwark of human rights not just for itself, but for everyone. He had persuaded the Polish Episcopate to support him in this. In Rome, using his prodigious language skills, he visited delegations from the United States, Africa, Canada, Ireland, and many countries of continental Europe, in a one-man sales show for his idea. Twice he went on Vatican Radio.

During one meeting with Latin American delegates, a clash occurred that would resonate throughout the Church for decades to come. Archbishop Helder Camara of Recife, Brazil, vice president of the Latin American bishops' conference (CELAM), had become a leader in a fight that was splitting the Latin Church. His mushrooming movement, which would later be known as Liberation Theology, argued that Christian principles impelled the Church to drop its long alliance with the Latin aristocracy, whose estates had evolved from the lands seized centuries before by Spanish and Portuguese conquistadors. Camara and his followers said that if the Church truly stood for everyone, it should stand for the poor, who were the majority.

What made Wojtyla's 1964 clash with Archbishop Camara memorable was not just the reverence in which many held Camara, but also the particular experience just suffered by his country. Studies by the Brazilian bishops showed that 87 percent of the productive land in Brazil's fertile northeast was owned by just twenty large landowners. Their laborers, the region's thirty-three million peasants, received little for their efforts but mud huts, disease, early death, and uneducated children headed for the same cycle. Anyone who tried to break the cycle found no land to farm or capital to operate with.

Though the conquistadors had long departed, over the past century U.S. corporations had cut deals with the local aristocracy throughout Latin America to exploit the region's agricultural and mineral wealth. The aristocrats had learned to count on the U.S. military and the CIA to help them put down democratic movements. One such situation had just come to a head in Brazil, which had overwhelmingly elected an administration committed to laws protecting labor and limiting the export of capital. In April 1964 the CIA, working through cooperative American business and labor leaders and the Brazilian military, had fostered a coup that replaced the elected government with a military dictatorship.[5]

Although the CIA's role in the overthrow would not be acknowledged for more than a decade, Archbishop Camara and his parishioners did not need all the details to know that the U.S. was responsible for what had happened. The coup led to twenty years of military dictators who ruthlessly murdered opponents.[6]

One can only imagine Camara's feelings in the autumn of 1964, six months after he saw the first sprouts of the democracy he had worked for crushed by foreign power. Priests and bishops all over Latin America counted on him to champion the cause of the poor as the Council debated the Church's role in the world at large. Throwing him into a room with Wojtyla, who had endured nineteen years of communism in Poland, was like tossing a tomcat into a cage with a bulldog.

According to Wojtyla's friend Cardinal Deskur, Archbishop Camara pleaded "for all Catholic teachers to take a course in Marxism. He said it was the only way to make sure they would understand [the conditions]. Helder Camara was regarded as a prophet. Well, Wojtyla rose, and said, 'I apologize, but I have lived in Poland, and communists treat Poles like animals.' And he went on and gave a great speech. Nobody spoke again of teaching communism."

For years, Deskur says, Wojtyla would return frustrated and angry from meetings with Latin American bishops, declaring, "They have no idea how much liberty people are losing under the communists." For Wojtyla, Deskur says, "this wasn't naïveté, but ignorance. For him, naïveté is simplicity and honesty. Camara, he would say, was ignorant."

Deskur says Wojtyla likewise became angry when he read that American university students were taking up Marxism to protest American military and economic policy. "People do not understand the way Marxism enslaves," Wojtyla would say, waving a newspaper.

In contrast, Deskur says, Wojtyla was delighted by the time he spent with Africans. At the Council, he befriended such future cardinals as Hyacinth Thiandoum of Senegal (who visited him in Krakow) and Bernard Gantin of Benin (who would become a powerful adviser to him as pope).[7]

October 21, 1964, Wojtyla gave his most important and well received speech at the Council. Although it was basically a reiteration of what he had been telling individual delegations for weeks, the words seemed more striking now because he was contradicting an aging pillar of the Church, Cardinal Augustin Bea, who had directly preceded him at the microphone. Bea had argued that the Church should confine itself in its final statement to quoting Gospel to believers.[8]

Now the new archbishop of Krakow demanded the exact opposite: a dialogue between the Church and the *outside* world, specifically addressing communist countries, among others. Clearly referring to what Cardinal Bea had just said, Wojtyla warned against "a soliloquy of an isolated Church."

"At this point," Malinski recalls, "the background noise died down and I realized that the Council had begun to pay attention." Wojtyla continued: "It is not possible to speak at one time to all men . . . in the same language." Without compromising his previous statements that Catholicism was "truth," he called for the Church to adopt a different attitude entirely in addressing non-Catholics. This was a bifocal vision that would continue in his papacy:

> It is not in question that the Truth is already known to us; the issue
> is the manner in which the world will find it for itself and make it
> its own. . . . The Church should speak so that the world sees that we
> are not so much teaching . . . but rather, along with the world, seek-
> ing a . . . just solution to difficult human problems. . . . In beginning
> our dialogue with atheists, we must demonstrate that we are not
> alienated from the world, but precisely because of our faith, we feel
> deeply committed to it.[9]

Recorded Malinski, "I was surprised at the firmness and boldness with which Karol argued. . . . I saw the fathers looking at him as, head bent as usual, he returned to his seat. The hum of conversation grew louder. Unquestionably, his words had made a strong impression."

Wyszynski himself went out of his way to say so at a meeting the next day, telling others to explain communist life just as Wojtyla had.[10] When the debate ended, Wojtyla was among a dozen delegates appointed to redraft the "Church in the World" document for consideration the following year. His copanelists were among the Church's most prominent young theologians, several others of whom would also go on to become cardinals.[11]

From this point, Wojtyla became more important at the Council than Wyszynski. Wyszynski "was perceived as always talking about Poland," says Micewski, his biographer. "Wojtyla was perceived as an intellectual capable of dialogue."

Increasingly, Wojtyla questioned Westerners about their experience under Church-state separation. Once he asked Bishop Wycislo, the Polish-American from Wisconsin, what the American delegates did on their holidays. Wycislo told him that most went sightseeing, but that he himself already knew Europe, and so he instead spent the time playing golf with an American friend who worked at the Vatican, Monsignor Marcinkus.

The name Marcinkus—later the focal point of a Vatican Bank scandal—meant little to Wojtyla then. But mere mention of the sport drew a swift rejoinder. "That golf," Wojtyla snapped, "that's a stupid game. Chasing a little white ball all over the grass."

"On the contrary," Wycislo replied. "The game is quite challenging, and good exercise. You ought to try it sometime." He invited Wojtyla to join them for a golf outing but was waved off.

The next time they saw each other, Wojtyla began pressing Wycislo for a meeting with Father Murray, the American behind the religious-liberty declaration. "You live with Archbishop [Albert] Meyer [of Chicago]," Wojtyla said. "Does he know Father Murray?"

Wycislo grinned. Murray, he said, often played golf with him and Monsignor Marcinkus.

Wojtyla's jaw dropped: "Now I must really learn that game!"

He pledged one day to go golfing with them but never did. Evidently Wojtyla found some other way to get what he needed from Murray. Years later, Wycislo says, whenever people from Green Bay visited Pope John Paul II, they returned to Wycislo saying the pope had inquired, "How is the bishop's golf?"

Wojtyla made a striking impression on many people that fall—including Paul VI. November 30, 1964, Paul invited him in for a private talk and reminisced about the Krakow Church. When Paul remarked that the priesthood's main task was pastoring the working class and young people, Wojtyla recounted his own youthful experiences as a worker. He presented Paul with an album of photographs of a religious dedication in Poland and was surprised by how carefully the pope examined it.

"I tried to interrupt him," Wojtyla recalled to Polish friends, "thinking that not every photo was so important. But he kept looking at them to the end." Meanwhile, Wojtyla was thinking how tired the former Cardinal Montini looked after only eighteen months as pope.[12]

18

Of all the ideas Wojtyla brought back to Krakow, ecumenism seemed to excite him most. He told Father Bardecki to contact Methodist, Baptist, Orthodox, Lutheran, and any other Christian churches he could find. Bardecki learned that the government had been offering privileges to Protestant clergymen in return for their help in campaigns against the Catholics. So Bardecki and Wojtyla decided to throw a dinner for Protestant church leaders.

"It became an annual tradition," Father Bardecki says. "Friendly speeches. No direct political topics, just how to help." Soon Bardecki was invited every month to share a service with one of the other churches. He couldn't receive communion, "but I gave talks. And they gave talks at Catholic services." Wojtyla visited a synagogue in what was left of Krakow's Jewish neighborhoods, and the local Jewish community was brought into the ecumenical circle. Twenty years later, all this would be a big help in protecting Solidarity.

When Wojtyla's prestigious commission met in Italy, he brought with him an alternative text focusing not on theological arguments but on freedom. In the end, the team added some of his text to the overall document but didn't redraw it, as he had hoped.[1]

Through 1965, the Soviet secret police murdered, one by one, the members of an underground network of priests and bishops that had been secretly created in their midst. The network had been left behind by Josyf Slipyi, the Ukrainian archbishop Khrushchev had released to Pope John. (Slipyi was now in Rome, a cardinal.)

"Slipyi ordained one bishop in a hotel in Moscow. That bishop ordained others, so that one became ten," explains Father John Long, a Vatican official long involved in plans to evangelize Russia. But a police agent posing as a visiting Vatican diplomat eventually tricked one of Slipyi's secret bishops into revealing himself.[2] The bishop died in custody days later. His closest contacts were followed. It was now known by both the Soviets and the Vatican— though not by the public or even most churchmen—that Slipyi had set up a network.

While the Soviets frantically tried to identify its members, Zenon Kliszko, now promoted to deputy head of the Polish party, tried to call in the favor he felt Wojtyla owed him. He spent long hours in Krakow courting the puzzled archbishop, then made his intentions clear: Kliszko would see to it that Wojtyla got the church he wanted in Nowa Huta if Wojtyla would take some verbal shots at Wyszynski. Try as he might, though, Kliszko could not get Wojtyla to utter the slightest betrayal of the primate.

Instead, Wojtyla pressed—as Wyszynski was pressing—for a visit by Pope Paul to Poland for the Church's millennium celebration in 1966. Kliszko wouldn't hear of it: a papal visit, he said, would turn out huge crowds that could get out of hand. Wojtyla related the whole affair at the next Episcopate meeting in Warsaw.[3] It was probably then that Kliszko realized he'd been had.

"The government constantly tried to split" Wojtyla and Wyszynski, says Kazimierz Kakol, who eventually took over the religious-affairs ministry. Kliszko tried to provoke rivalries between the two big archdioceses over church construction licenses, military deferments for seminary students, and other issues, but nothing worked. When French President Charles de Gaulle came to Poland, Wyszynski held to his policy of avoiding foreign visitors who might embarrass the government, and refused to see him. De Gaulle then went to Krakow, hoping to meet the other Polish archbishop, but in a show of unity, Wojtyla arranged to be out of town.[4]

Pope Paul looked past every affront from the communists and stuck to *Ostpolitik*. He agreed to bring jailed Czechoslovakian Cardinal Josef Beran to Rome as the Czech government wished. "Beran was a nuisance to the communists," Cardinal Krol told me, waving his hand in disgust. "He was pulled out because the pope wanted peace."

Although often labeled indecisive, Pope Paul could in fact be a man of iron will.[5] A secret report came back from his nearly sixty-member birth-control commission: six favored approving the contraceptive pill, seven favored broadening Pius XI's ban on contraception to include the Pill, and most—more than forty commissioners—wanted to let well enough alone and do nothing.[6] If ever there was an invitation for an indecisive man to ignore a problem, this was it.

But Paul wouldn't. Cardinal Ottaviani, the nearly blind head of the Holy Office, told him that by recommending inaction, the commission majority was risking "confusing the faithful by saying that the Church has been wrong all the time." Paul resolved to act, and thought of Wojtyla.

Pope Paul had declared that the 1965 Council session would be the last. The opening order of business was the redrawn religious-liberty document. September 22, Wojtyla told the assembly that the Church had to go further than the mere tolerance called for by civil law in many countries. He asked the Council to assert that liberty was

> grounded in the dignity of the human person. . . . This ought to be underlined so that our Declaration will be seen to be . . . personalistic in the Christian sense . . . not derived from liberalism.

Father Murray, in contrast, as Church historian Michael Novak records it, "argued that the Church was better off not trying to impose a uniform philosophy, which would only start arguments, [but] merely say it was none of the government's business."

Speaker after speaker felt there should be no document at all. Cardinal Ernesto Ruffini of Italy declared, "As the truth is one, the true religion is one, and to it alone belongs the right of liberty." Cardinal Ottaviani (who had received many votes for the papacy at the 1958 conclave) declared, "Truth and falsehood cannot have equal rights. Those professing a revealed religion have rights over and above" other people's. Cardinal Michael Browne of Ireland said, "The right to spread false doctrine in Catholic countries cannot be given."[7]

Remarkably, in the middle of this debate, Paul flew to New York and delivered one of the best-known speeches in the history of the United Nations. Visibly distressed by the burgeoning war in Vietnam, the head of the same Church that in bygone days had sponsored the Crusades now pleaded poignantly, "No more war! War never again!"

Back in Rome, he was confronted by a Polish rebellion. "All the Polish bishops were angry," says Wyszynski's biographer, Andrzej Micewski. Wyszynski and Wojtyla complained that Murray's version of the document had "a Western point of view." But Paul supported Murray.[8]

November 19, 1965, the Council voted overwhelmingly to reverse nearly two thousand years of Church history on human rights.* Opponents were placated by insertions reassuring them that theirs was "the one true church." Protestants and others complained that this seriously weakened the document, and that vague qualifying phrases, like "within due limits," created loopholes.

Yet most delegates had leaned Murray's way, not Wojtyla's. Historian Novak adds that "Wojtyla was instrumental in getting the [decisive] votes, by saying, in effect, 'Hey, we Eastern Europeans need this to fight communism'— which wasn't a thought in the original debate."

In the nineteenth century, Pope Gregory XVI had called religious liberty a "delirium." Pope Pius IX issued a "Syllabus of Errors" officially condemning the proposition that "the Church should be separated from the state." To say

---

* The final declaration said: "All men are to be immune from coercion on the part of individuals or of social groups and of any human power in such wise that no one is to be forced to act in a manner contrary to his own beliefs, whether privately or publicly, whether alone or in association with others, within due limits.... Government is to see to it that the equality of citizens before the law, which is itself an element of the common good, is never violated... for religious reasons. Nor is there to be discrimination among citizens.... If... special civil recognition is given to one religious community in the constitutional order of society, it is at the same time imperative that the right of all citizens and religious communities to religious freedom should be recognized and made effective in practice."

Every source I consulted gave a different vote count. Most sources say several hundred bishops opposed the declaration.

that what had been damnable error a hundred years ago was now official policy was quite a leap. The Church's ancient exclusive deals with individual governments were now contradicted by the Council.[9] The new document put the Church clearly in the wrong in the torture and execution of countless thousands of heretics—though it would take until the papacy of John Paul II for the Church to begin to admit that.

Although a compromise, the new document provided a major weapon for Wojtyla/John Paul II in his coming assault on communism.

When the "Church in the World" document came up, Wojtyla again spoke out for a broader focus. He said that concentrating on religious conversion, as many bishops wanted, "presupposes the whole work of redemption" and let "the vision of the world as it ought to be prevail over the picture of the world as it is." He urged more concern with the spiritual and material needs of humanity in all its variety. In the end, though, he accepted the compromise of his committee.

His outspokenness put his name in the newspaper, where it caught the attention of a Polish-born Roman businessman: his boyhood friend Jerzy Kluger. Kluger and his father had endured a phenomenal journey after leaving Wadowice—arrested by the Soviets, imprisoned in separate camps in Siberia, put on trains amid a German invasion, and miraculously reunited, they were allowed to go to Palestine, where exiled Poles were organizing for combat. Jerzy fought in the Allied invasion of Italy in 1944, then stayed on to attend college and started a business manufacturing construction materials. Now, deciding that there could not be two Karol Wojtylas, he phoned a message to the Council office, expecting that Wojtyla might drop him a note.

Moments later, however, his phone rang and the familiar voice of his old friend invited him to come for lunch, where he also found Archbishop Krol of Philadelphia. After lunch, Kluger and Wojtyla went for a walk, traded information about where their classmates had wound up after the war, and renewed a friendship they would pick up often during Wojtyla's frequent visits to Rome.

Paul concluded the Council December 8, 1965, by opening wider than ever the fresh-air window Pope John had talked about. The Holy Office, the censor and enforcer of dogma that had once been called the Inquisition, would now be toned down even further and renamed the Congregation for the Doctrine of the Faith. Its famous list of banned books—four thousand titles, by such authors as Locke, Mill, Rousseau, Kant, Milton, Hugo, Defoe, and the twelfth-century Jewish scholar Moses Maimonides, and even the *Larousse* French dictionary—was withdrawn.[10]

In the thirty-odd years since the Council, many Catholics have come to believe that it changed much more than it really did and that John Paul II has somehow rolled back those changes. It has been written, for example, that the Council loosened the Church's sexual code (whereas Paul removed that from the agenda). More accurately, Bishop B. C. Butler wrote, "The Church had been seen as an . . . institution activated, guided and controlled by the papacy and the Roman curia. Without rejecting the elements of truth in that . . . the Council invites us to see the Church rather as a worldwide human family held together by the Holy Spirit."[11]

Adds Father John Navone of Gregorian University, "Every other Church council ended with definitions, and if a Catholic disagreed, it said '*Anathema sit*'—'Let him be damned.' At the end of Vatican II, there were no definitions, no anathemas. The conservatives were worried about the effect on the Church. [But] the Council was concerned with, 'What can the Church do to benefit the world?' "

No words could more accurately describe the attitude of Wojtyla.

Just before the Council adjourned, Wyszynski asked Pope Paul to allow Poland to delay implementing the many changes in Church ritual (which Wyszynski had opposed). Change was "very difficult" under communism, he said, and circumstances were "difficult to judge . . . from afar." Paul, who could easily have taken this as an insult, replied that he expected the changes to be implemented "energetically and willingly" in Poland.[12]

This confrontation with Wyszynski further boosted Wojtyla in Paul's eyes as the Pole he preferred to deal with. Largely at Paul's suggestion, Wojtyla stayed in Rome when his colleagues went home after the Council session. Speaking frequently on Vatican Radio, the archbishop of Krakow swiftly began measuring human rights in Poland according to the new declaration on religious liberty. He described his annual Christmas Eve at Nowa Huta, amid snow, rain, wind, and below-zero (Fahrenheit) cold, when "you had a sort of marsh under your feet." Yet "there would always be thousands of people" singing Christmas carols. Paul gave him a stone from Peter's grave for the foundation of a church in Nowa Huta, and money for construction.

But the real reason Paul kept Wojtyla around may have been the report of his birth-control commission. Paul said the commission's recommendation of inaction wasn't acceptable. They discussed Wojtyla's book about sex, and Wojtyla accepted Paul's invitation onto a new commission to reconsider the recommendation.

No sooner was Wojtyla back in Krakow than he asked Dr. Poltawska to contribute her research and ideas.[13]

Wojtyla further distinguished himself during a dispute between Wyszynski and Pope Paul over the former German territories in Poland. Just before the 1965 Council session, Wyszynski and the bishop of the territories had claimed permanent possession of them for the Polish Church. West German politicians and churchmen, who had not conceded this point, were irate. Pope Paul, following fixed Vatican policy, wanted governments, not the Church, to settle boundaries; he, too, was angry. Even the Polish government, which wanted the land, was angry that Wyszynski made national policy without consulting it.

Seeking peace, the Polish bishops added a special message to the Germans' copy of an invitation they sent to all the bishops' conferences at the Council, to attend the Polish millennium in 1966. The addendum to the German invitation asked to bury the hatchet over World War II, concluding, "We forgive, and we ask to be forgiven."

The "German bishops letter" received wide publicity. After years of Polish suspicion that the German bishops had conspired with Pope Pius against Poland, suddenly the German press accused the Poles of plotting with the *Ostpolitiking* Pope Paul against West Germany. The German bishops' reply was positive, but Wyszynski and his colleagues thought it was less heartfelt than their overture, and were "very unhappy" about it.[14]

Most Poles felt the same way and were at least as interested in the German letters as in the Vatican Council. "It helped Gomulka," recalls a prominent journalist.[15] "People considered it a betrayal of the national interest. The communists had only one issue that made them legitimate—the Western Territories and protection against the Germans."

Wojtyla's role in the affair wasn't clear,[16] but the communists, trying to exploit the episode in any way they could, attacked him. Employees from the Solvay plant, where Wojtyla had worked during the war, were recruited to sign an open letter expressing "indignation" and "disgust" and accusing Wojtyla of forgetting Nazi atrocities. The letter called West Germany "the heir" of the Nazis and charged Wojtyla with usurping the government's right to speak for the country.

Wojtyla's letter of response was extraordinary. From its first biting words, it turned the tables on the communists to teach a lesson on individual dignity. He reproved the workers for exploiting him in what was really propaganda, not a personal communication:

I got your letter of December 22. I was already aware of its contents, as it had been published earlier in Krakow newspapers as an "open letter."

In the beginning of the letter, you remind me of the German occupation times when I worked—as you do now—in the Solvay factory.... That period, so horrible for all of us, gave me a priceless experience—just because I lived through it as a worker, with you and among you....

But reading further the words of your letter, I realized with sorrow that it was not only a heavy public accusation of myself, but also a verdict of condemnation declared in absentia.... I realized you didn't know the facts upon which you condemned me and other Polish bishops.... You just blindly repeated what was published first by the German and later by the Polish press.

He pointed out that the message sent to the German bishops had

included ... a long list of wrongdoing that our nation has suffered in the course of centuries from Germans.... Our supplication for forgiveness, like the supplication [asked of] the German bishops, is in accord with the Gospel.... Human beings, and nations as well, always have something to forgive and something to ask to be forgiven.

He put the best gloss he could on the Germans' reply, saying it "accepted the blame without question." He even suggested that the German bishops and the Vatican Council had acknowledged Poland's rights to the former German territories, though the record doesn't show that.

Then Wojtyla returned to his real point:

I am answering your letter above all as a human being who has suffered a wrong, who was publicly slandered without any attempt to understand his reasons. When we worked together during the occupation time, we had so much in common. The most important [thing] was respect for another human being, his conscience, and his personal and social dignity. I learned so much of it from the workers at Solvay; I don't find it now in your open letter.

Writing with much grief, I defend not only my personal right to respect, but also the right of the people whom I serve as priest and as archbishop of Krakow.... I believe that you will take care to publish my letter. Thus, everyone who reads your letter will also have a chance to read my answer.

Wojtyla knew the workers couldn't publish his letter; the state controlled the press. But his request drove home his message about human dignity and fairness. Christmas Day, he invited former colleagues from Solvay to bring their families to the palace for a special Mass. And he gave a public sermon about forgiving, forgetting, and the letter to the German bishops.

19

Wojtyla was best known for giving intimate advice, not for addressing crowds, as Wyszynski was. "It was a society overwhelmed by police control," says Bohdan Cywinski, his canoeing friend and later *Znak* editor. "Contacts were private. If someone behaved bravely, and then had problems, it was quite easy to find him later at Wojtyla's. There were dozens of such incidents. But you couldn't ask others what Wojtyla had said—you'd be suspected of being an agent."

He occasionally popped in at the *Tygodnik Powszechny* office, and every month or two had the staffs of that paper and *Znak* to dinner at the palace. "For two or three hours" each time, Turowicz says, Wojtyla and thirty journalists "would discuss Church-state relations and problems of the newspaper. He listened carefully, but not taking part in the conversation until the end."

Each issue of each publication was read in advance by censors. Sometimes new articles had to be substituted for censored ones. Some words were banned altogether; mentioning pagans, for example, was said to infringe on nonbelievers, "even if you were talking about ancient Rome," says editor Halina Bortnowska. Wojtyla himself fought a long battle for his publications' right to print the Vatican's new declaration on religious liberty, refusing to allow censors to change or omit a word.

The censors tried to limit press runs to forty thousand for *Tygodnik Powszechny* and fifteen thousand for *Znak*. "But you can do tricks," Bornowska says. "Paper was sold by weight, so we used thinner paper." And since each copy was widely circulated, the actual readership was considerably larger.

Sometimes the problem wasn't the communists but the Church itself. An Episcopate censor tried to block an article by Bortnowska about Edward Schillebeeckx, a Dutch theologian whose controversial book on Jesus foreshadowed a stormy career (he would eventually be disciplined by Pope John Paul II).

Bortnowska complained to Wojtyla, who then "convinced the underling" to allow the article about Schillebeeckx, she says.

To his editors, Wojtyla was a champion of free speech. When a Church official tried to stop *Znak* from publishing an article about German theologian Karl Rahner, who was urging change in the Church, Wojtyla summoned both the censor and *Znak* editor Jacek Wozniakowski to his office. "Does Rahner say anything against morals or religious conviction?" he asked. The two men agreed the dispute lay elsewhere.

"Then even if you disagree with him"—as Wojtyla let it be known that himself he did—"let his ideas be accessible to the reader, and let the reader make up his mind. The [Church's] imprimatur [on the magazine] does not mean that the censor agrees with the ideas of the author. It means only that he agrees there is nothing against morals or religion" in the writing.

Even a book by Father Ratzinger, the Vatican II radical who would later run John Paul II's Holy Office, was banned in other dioceses because of "something to do with life after death," Wozniakowski says. In Poland, only the Krakow diocese allowed its seminarians to read Ratzinger's book. "Now, Ratzinger is the keeper of the doctrine," Wozniakowski smiles. "These things change very rapidly."

By American constitutional standards, the Wojtylan vision of free speech left a lot to be desired; if one can't speak freely about such frequently disputed topics as morals and religion, the ability to speak freely about other matters seems half a loaf.

But in communist Poland, it was a big half. *Tygodnik Powszechny* came out every week, and priests took the pulpit each Sunday. To maintain this alternative platform required not only great will but also temperance, and a determination to stake out and stick to a moral high ground. Wojtyla's administration in Krakow may have benefited the public more through its support for an independent press than in any other way. "It was the only place where one could work without any control or brainwashing," says Kryzstof Kozlowski, a former Wojtyla student at Lublin who joined the staff of *Tygodnik Powszechny*.[1]

Except on publishing problems, however, Wojtyla shied away from discussions with the government; when an official tried to interview him about the German bishops' letter, for example, he barely spoke.[2] "He always told us that these concerns were 'Cardinal Wyszynski's business—I don't like to be involved,' " editor Kozlowski recalls. "If they diverged at all in what they said, the communists would say they were quarreling."

Yet in meetings of the Episcopate itself, Wojtyla did speak out. Once he provoked Wyszynski by urging more study of the "new theologians" (Congar, de Lubac, etc.) who had pushed for change at Vatican II. Wojtyla argued that the government was winning over young Catholics by saying the bishops ignored "progressives" in the Church. But Wyszynski vetoed studying the progressives.[3]

Another time, Wojtyla wanted to differentiate between philosophical atheists, with whom "there is a possibility of real dialogue," and party-line communists.[4] Wyszynski replied tartly that he wouldn't bow to "official atheism" in any guise.

Easter Sunday 1966, Wyszynski's dream, the Great Novena, officially bloomed into the Millennium of Christianity in Poland. Forty thousand people attended an initial Mass at the Gniezno cathedral, 150 miles west of Warsaw. As it would do in each city the celebration toured, the government bused workers and schoolchildren to a competing civil ceremony. Wojtyla's vespers in the cathedral were interrupted by a barrage of artillery-shell explosions that frightened many worshipers away; the bursts turned out to be a salute in honor of the defense minister's arrival at the civil celebration in the square outside.

Then, according to Micewski, "people broke through police cordons to stream away from the secular observance and toward the sacred one." Through all the explosions and tumult, Wojtyla kept leading prayers, exactly as he had persisted in reciting Mickiewicz's poetry at the Rhapsodic Theater while Nazi loudspeakers blared outside.

A day later, more explosions disrupted the service in Poznan as Gomulka arrived outside to give a speech attacking Wyszynski. When the guns died down, Wyszynski said a public prayer for Gomulka. As he climbed into his car after the service, university students raised it to their shoulders (a comment on Polish cars as well as on Wyszynski's popularity) and carried him off in it.

The touring celebration used Pope Paul's picture propped on an empty chair to remind crowds of his forced absence. To show unity, Wyszynski and Wojtyla split each service, one saying Mass, the other the sermon. "Nowhere else is the union of Church and nation as strong as in Poland," Wyszynski wrote in his diary.[5]

Amid the throngs, Wojtyla quietly wrote two poems celebrating human life and the Christian belief in the separation of the body and the soul at death. First, "A Conversation with God":

> The human body in history dies more often and earlier than the tree.
> Man endures beyond the doors of death in catacombs and crypts.
> Man who departs endures in those who follow.
> Man who follows endures in those departed.

> *Man endures beyond all coming and going in himself*
> *and in You.*

And second, "A Conversation with Man":

> *On this point we cannot agree.*
> *He says: man is condemned only to loss of his body. Man's*
> *history seeks nothing*
> *but the body of things: these remain*
> *while man dies*
> *and generations live on them.*
> *But things don't die a personal death,*
> *man is left with the immortality of things.*
>
> *This I say: much of man dies in things,*
> *more than remains. Have you tried to embrace*
> *what does not die and find for it profile and space? . . .*
>
> *Return to each place where a man died; return to the place*
> *where he was born.*
> *The past is the time of birth, not of death.*[6]

In Krakow, Wojtyla protested in vain as the government diverted his street procession from its planned route, leaving throngs of residents curbside, watching only each other. Crowds mocked the government by subtly changing the lyrics of the traditional songs they sang: lines about "the Swedes," enemies from centuries before, were now directed at police. Dozens of students were arrested.

The Krakow ceremony was planned to coincide with the annual commemoration for Saint Stanislaw, the former bishop of Krakow who was murdered in 1079 for resisting a tyrannical monarch. (Wojtyla had starred in a World War II dramatization of his life.) Said Wyszynski in a sermon, "Let us remember that Saint Stanislaw was killed, but he did not kill. . . . Stanislaw fell in defense of the moral order. . . . [He] bravely told those who were in charge: 'It is indecent to do this!' "

Wyszynski's design of the celebration around a dedication of Poland to Mary forged another bond between him and Wojtyla as they slowly overcame their differences. Wyszynski constantly emphasized Mary's role in theology, to a degree that sometimes provoked intellectuals to complain.[7] The elevation of Mary to a position that often seems to outsiders almost the equivalent of that of Jesus is one objection many Protestants have to Catholicism.

Yet Wojtyla, usually the voice of the intellectuals, agreed completely with Wyszynski about emphasizing Mary. Bishop Wojtyla had chosen the phrase *Totus Tuus*—"Wholly Yours," in reference to Mary—as his life's motto; it later appeared on his correspondence as pope. Both men had lost their mothers early and been raised by their fathers. Each had pursued mother figures, human and supernatural, since boyhood. Their campaign heaped Mary with new titles, such as "Mother of the Church" and "Queen of Poland." The primate pointedly praised Wojtyla for reinforcing this emphasis.[8]

Pope Paul VI, who had previously been archbishop of Milan, was being interviewed in 1966 by a journalist he knew from that city when suddenly he volunteered that he was unsure what to do about contraception. His experts on birth control kept disagreeing with his theologians, and his conscience was caught between them.

Coming from a pope, this was an extraordinary confession, and it was widely quoted. Catholics everywhere who wanted the birth-control ban lifted took Paul's uncertainty to mean that no ban was laid down. In Krakow, Wojtyla quickly formed a committee of Dr. Poltawska and several theologians of like mind to advise Pope Paul.[9]

Yet another issue was tearing Paul apart emotionally: the Vietnam war. In the midst of the birth-control controversy, the pope was confronted with public insubordination from his leading American cardinal, Spellman of New York. As Paul worked to start peace negotiations, Spellman went to Vietnam to rally the troops. In widely publicized talks, he told the very soldiers Paul wanted to disarm that they were "holy crusaders" in "Christ's war against the Vietcong."[10]

In November 1966, Paul sent a message with Italian communists visiting North Vietnam, offering humanitarian supplies from Catholic charities to help the North withstand the American onslaught. The Vietnamese accepted, but a massive American bombing of Hanoi rendered relief impossible. Pope Paul reportedly slapped a desk and cried out over the new round of bombing.[11]

Wyszynski felt similar anguish when Paul, behind his back, actually accepted an invitation from the Polish government to visit Czestochowa on Christmas Eve for a belated, government-sanctioned millennium celebration. The communists stupidly overplayed their hand, however, by insisting that Paul endorse Polish rule in the former German territories by visiting them, and the deal was scotched.

Returning to Rome after abrasive meetings with both Wyszynski and the communists in Warsaw, Paul's star diplomat, Monsignor Agostino Casaroli, stopped in Krakow. In a radically warmer atmosphere, Wojtyla took Casaroli to meet the *Tygodnik Powszechny* editors. Bardecki sensed that Wojtyla was now Paul's preferred source of information not only on sex but on Poland and Ukraine as well. (John Paul II would later make Casaroli his secretary of state.)

Wyszynski's only notice that Paul had decided against the Czestochowa trip was a Vatican Radio announcement that the Pope would spend Christmas in Florence[12]—a sign of their decayed relationship. Pushing on with *Ostpolitik*, Paul continued to send emissaries on fruitless missions to deal with Soviet and Polish communists, without Wyszynski.

Pope Paul was doing a better job of dividing Wyszynski and Wojtyla than the communists were. Wojtyla grew ever closer to Paul. To get him to Rome more often, Paul appointed him to the Council for Lay People and the Council for Justice and Peace, two of many new Church bodies created to fulfill the Vatican Council's wish to better integrate the Church in people's lives. Possibly the biggest change these bodies brought about was not in their actual work but in the cross-pollination of the Roman curia by bishops constantly visiting from hither and yon for meetings and exchanging ideas with curial bishops at the dinner table as well as the conference table.

When a consistory for new cardinals was announced for June 26, 1967, it was no surprise that the head of the Krakow archdiocese was among them. But the news was still exciting. Before boarding the train to Rome, Wojtyla meditated a day at Kalwaria Zebrzydowska and wrote in the guest book, by the statue of Mary, "I came to Our Lady of Kalwaria, to whom I have felt close since my childhood, to put everything in her hands."

The consistory drew a hundred thousand spectators on a scorching summer day. As luck would have it, Wojtyla's friend John Krol of Philadelphia became a cardinal in the same group. But Krol had a problem: he wanted to say a Mass of thanks at the Polish village where his father was born, a tiny place with no paved road, but because of his anti-communist writings, the government wouldn't let him in.

Krol told me Wojtyla "asked if he could serve as a surrogate in visiting the parish." The gesture touched Krol, who said the 250-seat church "was jammed inside and out" for Wojtyla's Mass and talk about Krol, "the son of a neighbor."

20

His new cardinal's hat did not diminish Wojtyla's love of exercise, nature, and old clothes. Once, a New Hampshire woman on a ski trip broke her leg and, as she waited for medical attention, was serenaded by fellow skiers; only later did she learn that the one playing the guitar had been a cardinal. Wojtyla once told a reporter in his office, "I wish I could be out there now, somewhere in the mountains, racing down into a valley; it's an extraordinary sensation."[1]

Many churchmen dress with flair despite their calling. In talking to clerics for this book, I regularly saw expensive-looking gold cufflinks on starched shirtsleeves popping out from cassocks. Cardinal Wojtyla traveled in clothes so worn that his driver complained to Malinski of embarrassment: "His cassock is all shiny, he wears a battered old hat," and his only shirts "have been mended over and over." "For many years, he wore just one green coat," says Bishop Pieronek, then his chaplain. "If somebody bought him a new coat, he gave it away"—and he did the same with underwear and sweaters he was given.[2]

Others admired him for not wasting money on clothes. "Cassocks were very expensive," says Archbishop Rembert Weakland of Milwaukee, who visited Wojtyla regularly as head of the Benedictine religious order. "He never looked unkempt, always very neat, adequate." Still, a CIA man noted that in his simple attire, Wojtyla "constitutes a great contrast to Cardinal Wyszynski, who wears his robes with particular majesty."[3]

Wojtyla remained notoriously unrealistic about money. When Bishop Pieronek accompanied him to Rome for the cardinals' ceremony, Pieronek, still under a government limit of five dollars to take abroad, borrowed two hundred dollars from friends. A few days later, Wojtyla offered him fifty dollars "for your needs."

"I said, 'That's great,' but I [already] borrowed two hundred, and it's almost gone.' He was surprised I spent so much," Pieronek says. "He did not need to have any money. Everything was already done for him. He never bought anything. We kidded him about not buying souvenirs. But he never even bought clothes."

Many churchmen I visited for this book seemed to like impressive surroundings and displayed a taste for art and furniture. Wojtyla "literally owned nothing except a few books, and those simply for the purpose of his work," Malinski says.

He continued to do two or more things at once, which some people still thought rude. He liked to attend "all kinds of meetings [and] symposia" around the country, Malinski says, even when he could have sent an auxiliary bishop in his place. But whenever he wasn't speaking, he began reading, writing, or praying.

Lawyer Andrzej Potocki recalls a dinner in Krakow, after which the twenty participants "were sitting at the table discussing things, and he [Wojtyla] said, 'Excuse me,' left the room, brought back a pile of outgoing letters, went through them, corrected some, and signed them. He finished that pile, then got a pile of incoming letters, read them, and made notes. By then it was ten o'clock. He said, 'I think we have to finish now.' Then he summarized the whole conversation—what [Professor Jozef] Tischner said, Bardecki, Turowicz, Kozlowski, Bortnowska, Wozniakowski. Then he gave his own conclusion. Some time later, I was in a meeting with him and I mentioned, 'You know, you have a divisible attention.' He stopped and thought a minute, and said, 'You're right. If I attended a conference and couldn't do anything else, I would get very tired.' "

The archdiocese librarian marveled at Wojtyla's ability to retain what he read. Copies of sermons or articles would come down, written from memory, with instructions to check the quotes. Usually the quoted passage was found almost verbatim in a book, often with Wojtyla's telltale underlining.[4] He still performed marriages and funerals, baptized babies, and visited the distraught. People still regarded him as unusually meditative. He frequently walked the Stations of the Cross at Kalwaria Zbrzydowska alone.

He said Mass at seven A.M. in the chapel that had been Sapieha's, with its ornate red and gold ceiling—the same place the seminarians had gathered the night the Germans left Krakow. Behind the altar on the left was (and still is) a red padded prayer kneeler, a schoolboy-sized desk of dark wood, and a red upholstered chair. There, eschewing the roomy office where other archbishops had worked, Wojtyla wrote and prayed from breakfast till 11:00 A.M., when he left to meet people. He continued to see anyone who showed up with a reasonable cause, regardless of appointment, as time allowed.

But in the afternoon he took more hours alone in the chapel. Sometimes he locked the door, though nuns and priests attending him usually knew not to enter anyway. Occasionally someone would intrude and find him at prayer, his head in his hands, or even stretched out crosslike on the floor. He spent the night in a small back room instead of in the master bedroom where archbishops normally slept.[5]

A Monsignor Dowsilas liked to entertain Wojtyla with jokes, and one became a favorite. It concerned a woman whose husband had just died and whose priest was definitely not the austere sort.

"Shall we come to your home to fetch the body?" the priest asked her.

"Yes."

"Right. That will be a hundred zlotys. And shall we sing the funeral service there?"

"Yes, you'd better do that."

"Another hundred zlotys."

And so it went until the figure reached eight hundred zlotys, whereupon the priest commented, "Well, we've got him as far as the church."

Whenever you wanted to make Wojtyla laugh, Malinski says, you need only say, "Well, we've got him as far as the church," and the joke would come back and crack him up.

CIA reports on Wojtyla included a couple of ski-trip stories. The winter after he became a cardinal—the second-youngest there was—he stayed in a mountain rest home for several days. An elderly priest who was retired there thought Wojtyla was a novice and constantly sent him on errands, fetching tea or a sweater. Wojtyla played out the role, never disclosing his identity. Another time, police held him for hours at a mountain checkpoint, assuming from his tattered clothes that he must have stolen his archbishop's credentials.

Perhaps the most pertinent recollection about Wojtyla at this time, however, is that of his former student Karol Tarnowski: "He never feared the confrontation of theology and the world," Tarnowski says. "He regularly invited people from various fields in the humanities and sciences. He knew all the important experts in literature, history, and physics. He always wanted to know what was new. He was interested in the structure of matter, and the new moral problems created by advances in medicine."

This particularly impressed Wojtyla's friend Jacek Wozniakowski because Wojtyla was not gregarious by nature. "He was always rather shy, sometimes a little awkward, not very social," Wozniakowski says. Wojtyla pushed himself so he could learn. Many powerful people try to shield themselves from challenge; Wojtyla's ability to seek out available experts without ever questioning his own faith showed the extraordinary depth of that faith—and of his self-confidence.

After writing an article criticizing Pope Pius XII for not speaking out about the Holocaust, Father Bardecki brought it to Wojtyla. "It was delicate for a priest to write about a pope," Bardecki said—even a dead one. How could he publish it?

After reading the article, Wojtyla said, "This is a difficult question. There are three truths about every human being. A historical truth—that is the easiest, because you can investigate it. The second one is a psychological truth—the conscience; the only one who knows it is the person himself. And the third truth is the normative truth—truth in reference to moral rules." Wojtyla wouldn't be more specific.

What does he mean? Bardecki asked himself afterward, replaying the conversation in his mind. Then he understood: Wojtyla had subtly given him a new way of organizing the article to make it acceptable. Historical facts could be cited on the side of Pius: Bardecki would note that he had helped many Jews individually and that Israeli officials had later thanked him for that. As for the psychology, Bardecki obtained comments from a former British ambassador who had often visited Pius in the Vatican.

Having touched these bases, Bardecki could then discuss normative truth and make his point—that Pius had a moral duty to protest publicly, and failed to. Bardecki reorganized the article and submitted it to the censors, confident that the communists would be happy to have a priest's confirmation of their long-standing accusations about Pius. But the government rejected the article: still too positive.

Bardecki returned to Wojtyla, perplexed. Wojtyla helped him go over the heads of the local censors and appeal to higher-ups in the Party, who accepted the partial criticism of Pius. The article ran.

Unfortunately, Wyszynski read it and fired off an angry retort to *Tygodnik Powszechny*. He said Pius had told him that papal intervention "would have made the situation of the Jews even worse."

So Bardecki went again to Wojtyla, who he says leapt to his defense, taking full responsibility for the article. "*Tygodnik Powszechny* was a free paper," Bardecki says. "Wojtyla never said a critical word about us. We never asked Wojtyla for permission to print anything." Bardecki says he approached Wojtyla about the Pius article in the first place only because he wanted wise advice—and he got it.

Sometimes wisdom wasn't enough. When the government again closed the Rhapsody Theater in the summer of 1967, throwing Wojtyla's former mentor Mieczyslaw Kotlarczyk out of work, Wojtyla protested all the way to Lucjan Motyka, his old sparring partner from Krakow, who was now the national minister of culture. It didn't help.

Wojtyla wrote to Kotlarczyk that the closing of the theater was a blow "for everybody, especially for culture."[6] For the next decade, as long as Kotlarczyk was healthy, Wojtyla hired him for pay at any chance, to lecture or give seminars. He visited the family regularly, and every November 4, Kotlarczyk's name day, Wojtyla organized an evening of poetry reading by students in his honor.[7]

21

To help meet Vatican II's call for bishops to be more active in the Church, Pope Paul created a representative "synod," or assembly, to convene in Rome every few years. (This was in addition to the social councils, like the ones he appointed Wojtyla to.) Paul reserved for himself the right to set the synod's agenda, to preside over it, and to approve (or not) its findings.

Wojtyla was to attend the first meeting, in September-October 1967. It was expected to address the battle raging throughout the Church about how much independence Vatican II had intended bishops, priests, and laymen to have from the pope. The cry to let priests marry had become so loud that Pope Paul felt compelled to quiet it with an encyclical reiterating his opposition. Thousands of priests sought approval to leave the priesthood but remain Catholics in good standing.

Much as Wojtyla must have longed to help resolve these issues, he and Wyszynski couldn't participate. Soviet leader Brezhnev had pressed Gomulka to crack down on the Church, and at the last moment, Gomulka withheld Wyszynski's passport. He hoped to split the cardinals, but the plan backfired: in a display of unity, Wojtyla said that if one could not go, both would stay home, and they did. A few months later, normalcy prevailed, and Wojtyla returned to Rome.

By staying home that fall, however, Wojtyla missed not only the synod but the conclusive meeting of Paul's expanded advisory panels on birth control. Had Paul been the indecisive man he was reputed to be, this might have had profound implications. A committee of priests, theologians, canon lawyers, and laymen voted overwhelmingly (64 to 4, according to one report) to drop the prohibition. They urged Paul to declare that if a marriage was open to procreation overall, each individual sex act needn't be.

This recommendation went to the supervising commission of cardinals and bishops that Wojtyla was part of. Remarkably, these senior churchmen voted to recommend the report to Paul (8 for, 6 against, and 6 agonizingly abstaining, by the same account).[1] Had Wojtyla been present, he certainly would have narrowed the pro-contraception vote to 8 to 7. To alter the outcome, he would have had to persuade one or more colleagues, but that was a possibility, given his strong personality.

The point is, it didn't matter. The opinions that Wojtyla, Dr. Poltawska, and their group continued sending from Krakow carried more weight than all the commissions Paul had appointed in Rome.

Gomulka seemed to be unraveling under Soviet pressure. In May 1967, Israel, equipped with Western arms, won a smashing victory over Soviet-armed Arabs in the Six-Day War. To appease their angry Arab allies, the Soviets ordered an anti-Semitic campaign to be waged throughout the Eastern Bloc. Early in 1968, Jews were purged from government jobs in Poland on the ground that they supported "Zionist aggression."

The government churned out booklets blaming the Holocaust on a plot by rich West German Jews against their Polish cousins.[2] Mobs desecrated Jewish cemeteries. Of the relatively few Jews left in Poland, some nine thousand lost jobs, and thousands more of their children were expelled from schools. Many families fled, mostly to France. When the Episcopate denounced the anti-Semitism, the communists turned on Catholics. Secret police visited catechism centers, took down children's names, and intimidated their parents at work.

When audiences at a Mickiewicz play in Warsaw began applauding the anti-Russian lines, the Soviets pressured Gomulka into closing the play.[3] Again, the heavy-handedness backfired. Students protested and attracted others into the streets. The government claimed the protests were the work of Jews and broke them up by force, even bursting into churches in Warsaw and Krakow to club and teargas students (obviously not mostly Jewish) hiding there.

Hundreds of students were expelled, all over the country.

It was a time of global turmoil and extremism. Vietnam had produced the worst civilian and military casualties since World War II. In the United States, Martin Luther King and Robert Kennedy were assassinated. The Yippie movement and Students for a Democratic Society roused street crowds that battled police during the Democrats' national convention in Chicago.

American political scientist David Ost makes a persuasive case that the student demonstrators in Poland that spring were similar in their demeanor and rhetoric to student demonstrators in the United States and Paris, who were generally described as "Leftist."[4] To the extent that the Polish protesters had a rallying document, it was the "Open Letter to the Party" written several years earlier by two students, Jacek Kuron and Karol Modzelewski, who still called themselves communists but wanted political freedom along with Marxist economic doctrine.

One contrast between the student rebels in Poland and those in the West was that in the West, workers jeered students and called them traitors; there was talk of a generation gap. In Poland, the working population supported the students, with some factory workers' organizing sympathetic slowdowns (not quite strikes).

The issues were much more fundamental than the closing of an anti-Russian play: 52 percent of the average Polish worker's income went for food, and Gomulka was raising food prices. Private farming had continued under Gomulka, but modernization hadn't, so output stagnated. Ham, bacon, butter, and eggs all had to be exported in large quantities to pay for imports.

One might date the beginning of the Solidarity revolution from Wojtyla's takeover of *Tygodnik Powszechny*, or from the founding of the Catholic Intelligentsia Clubs, or from the 1968 student demonstrations, or from some later event. But it was building.

To some extent, the government was right that the rebels of 1968 had a disproportionately Jewish leadership, though most followers were Catholic. Wyszynski told academic chaplains he was surprised "to find so many thousands of Zionists among the students."[5] Two prominent leaders who were sent to jail for organizing the protest, Adam Michnik and Seweryn Blumsztajn, were sons of Jewish communists from the 1940s. Blumsztajn had been a friend of Michnik's, and of Jacek Kuron's, since boyhood and had gone to prison with Kuron in the famous "Open Letter" incident.[6]

The Znak group of Krakow Catholics rose in Parliament to defend the student rebels. With that one act, they lost forever the trust of the communists. Wyszynski, their longtime critic, called them in and praised their principled stand; he told them Poland didn't need Catholics in high places so much as it needed politicians who would teach the country morality by defending the students. They asked if they should quit Parliament. He urged them to stay and listen. Like Michnik, Blumsztajn, and Modzelewski, they were still socialists, but they insisted on human rights.

The rebellion was smashed. Truckloads of soldiers teargassed students, then moved on factories and removed the "troublemakers" staging slowdowns. The Party was now worrying less about its popularity and more about fortifying its bunkers. Later, on a train to Rome, Wyszynski encountered some young Polish Jews who were being forced to emigrate. They said they hoped to return someday; Wyszynski, touched, told them he hoped they would.[7]

In Munich, Father Joseph Ratzinger, the theologian and aide to Cardinal Frings, winced at the Church's support for the student demonstrators. As he later recalled it, he now began to have second thoughts: the change he had helped spark at Vatican II was being "misused. . . . In the uprising of 1968, the danger became manifest that the faith would be identified with a Marxism saturated with religion."[8]

And in Medellin, Colombia, the Latin American bishops' conference, under the strong influence of Archbishop Helder Camara of Brazil, voted to make the Catholic Church "the Church of the Poor."

July 25, 1968, Pope Paul VI issued probably the best-known encyclical ever, *Humanae Vitae* ("Human Life"). Rejecting the advice of his committees, he reaffirmed a total ban on any form of birth control except the rhythm method. "We remind you," it said, "that to have recourse to contraceptives is a serious sin that offends God, destroys the life of grace, prevents access to the sacraments, and, even more painfully, wounds the life of the couple."

Supporters said he had erected a rock of moral consistency while values were being cheapened elsewhere. Opponents said he had alienated believers and thrown the Church into the political maelstrom that was consuming the rest of the world. Both were right.

Wojtyla would later (as John Paul II) call it "the hardest decision any pope has had to make in this century. . . . The great problem for [Paul] was that his own birth-control commission was divided."[9]

And more than just the commission. As word leaked out that *Humanae Vitae* would be issued, several leading church voices continued to urge Paul to let this sleeping dog lie and not issue the encyclical.[10] Paul listened instead to the cardinal from Krakow.

Although Wojtyla had missed the meeting of the advisory commission, his and Dr. Poltawska's thoughts—in some cases, their exact words—had nonetheless found their way into the text of the encyclical. According to Andrzej Poltawski, the doctor's husband, Wojtyla "didn't literally write *Humanae Vitae.* I don't think that's literally true. But there were some texts, elaborations devoted to those problems, that came from Krakow that impressed Paul VI. I think you may assume that he [Wojtyla] had an influence." Dr. Poltawska herself wouldn't talk about *Humanae Vitae,* refusing even to tell me how many children she herself had. (According to Wojtyla's letter to Padre Pio about her cancer diagnosis, she had four daughters.)

Almost immediately after *Humanae Vitae* was published, open rebellion broke out in the Church. In the United States, 642 priests, theology professors, and prominent laymen signed a petition in support of the right to use contraception. In West Germany, five thousand Catholic laymen declared that they couldn't accept Paul's dictum. French bishops issued a statement leaving birth control to the conscience of individual couples.

At Catholic University in Washington, Father Charles Curran and Professor David Tracy were tried as heretics but allowed to keep teaching by the university senate. Tracy had called birth control "a source of continuing, intractable pain for Catholics. The Church once taught that usury was intrinsically evil, but changed its stance on that. It once tolerated slavery. There is no reason that it cannot change on birth control."

Some of the most respected figures in the Church agreed. In 1994, Cardinal König, now retired, confessed sadly to me in an interview that Paul "could have avoided an insistence on a difference between natural and artificial birth control. If a woman suffers from disease, or differs with her husband, there must be another way."

Right or wrong, *Humanae Vitae* would cast a shadow over the rest of Paul's papacy. "The dissent got to him," friends said.[11]

Yet Wojtyla became ever closer to Pope Paul, who thanked him for supporting *Humanae Vitae*. Their shared belief on birth control was clearly a pillar of their relationship. Paul lamented "the commercialization of Western life," which he considered to be the cause of contraception. Third Worlders, he told Wojtyla, had appreciated the encyclical most.[12]

22

Of all the rebellions of 1968, the Czechoslovakian seemed the most hopeful. Under a popular new Party leader, Alexander Dubcek, censorship began to lift and power to flow to majority will. Priests were freed, and restrictions on the Church relaxed. To Pope Paul, it must have seemed a satisfying triumph for *Ostpolitik*.

But August 21 and 22, Soviet troops poured into Czechoslovakia as they had into Hungary twelve years before. Dubcek was taken to Moscow, and his "Prague Spring" vanished.

Wojtyla had a greater connection to Prague Spring than he could let on. Over the years, he had gradually expanded his secret ordination of underground Czech priests. By 1965, he was also training and ordaining covert priest candidates from communist Ukraine, Lithuania, and Belorus, where seminaries had also been closed. Some candidates sneaked across the border to Poland, while others arranged for secular jobs that allowed them to travel legally; for example, one was a psychologist who regularly visited a Polish health institute. Wyszynski, in Warsaw, was aware of the nature, if not the details, of these activities. Had authorities known of them, they might well have jailed Wojtyla.

The Czech priesthood candidates began seminary work secretly in Poland under Wojtyla and continued studying back home with smuggled materials. They would return to Poland periodically for tutoring, either sneaking across the border or while on approved travel.[1] Polish "hikers" meanwhile crossed the mountainous border illegally, carrying books for covert Czech seminarians who rendezvoused with them. Sometimes Polish priests would pose as hikers to go teach there. It was clear to *Znak* editor Wilkanowicz that Wojtyla personally oversaw these activities, though he was never told the details and dared not ask.

"If somebody came from Czechoslovakia or Hungary and wanted contact with the curia, I would take him to Wojtyla," says Wilkanowicz. "I would never learn what happened after that."

Archbishop Broneslaw Dabrowski, longtime secretary of the Episcopate, knew about the Wojtyla operation, too. "Many young people risked prison," he says, referring to any secretly ordained Czech priest who was found out. Dabrowski recalls a doctor he sent into Czechoslovakia with a load of Bibles, who was caught, "imprisoned and tortured" but still wouldn't disclose the source of the Bibles.

Father Bardecki, himself born in Ukraine, was assigned by Wojtyla to gather intelligence on the Church there. A friend on the Krakow City Council arranged travel papers for him under the ruse that he was visiting a friend in Romania. En route, Bardecki quietly met with covert Ukrainian priests. One worked as a night guard in a park. "People would come to the park at night to confess to him," Bardecki smiles. When another priest got permission to visit his brother in Warsaw, Bardecki arranged for him to meet with Wyszynski, who consecrated him a bishop; this enabled him to consecrate other priests back in Ukraine. Wojtyla was the only other person who knew about this.

Bardecki also visited Ukrainian churches that had no priests. "People went every Sunday, put a cloth on the altar, said prayers, and sang songs. But there was no Mass because there was no priest."

Not long before the 1968 Czech rebellion, Father Jan Zajac, from a mountain area south of Wadowice, was asked by another Polish priest to help smuggle goods across the nearby Czechoslovakian border. Zajac quickly understood that the enterprise had been under way for some time. Prayer and theology books, Bibles and rosaries would arrive in someone's car trunk or hidden on a truck carrying other goods. No one said so, but Zajac could see that with the religious items came literary works and current-events periodicals.

Zajac's job was to recruit mountain parishioners to stow the contraband in their homes or barns for a week or two, until it could be picked up by a motorist or hikers crossing the border. The Soviet invasion didn't interrupt the activity. Zajac soon learned that similar materials were being smuggled to Russia, Ukraine, Lithuania, and Belorus.

He also learned that the man in charge was Cardinal Wojtyla. Occasionally, the smugglers even discussed the operation with Wojtyla, who "was very open and eager" about it, while being "very discreet" with outsiders, Zajac says. Goods arrived in Poland by train and truck from Belgium, France, West Germany, and Italy; often they were smuggled in by tour groups whose visits to the shrine at Czestochowa were organized by Wojtyla.

Hundreds of thousands of books for shipment to Poland were printed by Wojtyla's former student Father Zenon Modzelewski at his publishing house in Paris, run with money from Bishop Abramowicz's organization in Chicago. Modzelewski says he kept large inventories in stock, to be shipped whenever the opportunity arose.[2]

Once an entire freight car's worth of Bibles, mislabeled and sneaked in from the West, was rerouted straight to Kiev, where it was met by the Church underground. Zajac had bribed Russian soldiers stationed in Poland to seal the car as if it had passed inspection. "It was difficult to make contact with the Russians," Father Zajac says, but once you did, "for a couple of dollars you could do anything." The Church made sure that Polish travelers to the Soviet Union took books or religious items with them.

Zajac, who now has a parish near Auschwitz, says Wojtyla ordained more covert priests from abroad than any other Polish bishop. Partly this was "because he had more contacts," especially among Czechs and Soviets, Zajac says. But Zajac also observes that Wojtyla would consecrate Ukrainians, whereas many Polish bishops refused to out of ethnic prejudice. This was an ancient bigotry that had flared up again during the Warsaw-Kiev war around the time of Wojtyla's birth, in 1920; Ukrainian Catholics in Poland—"Uniates"—were often isolated and ostracized.[3] Because Wojtyla entertained no bigotry, he became a clandestine oasis of support for leaders of the nearly half-million Ukrainian Catholics in Poland.[4]

Once, Zajac recalls, Wojtyla came to his mountain area, Niedzweidz, for dinner and a discussion of smuggling. Most priests there, having experienced Czech confiscation of contraband, now detested the new, tightly controlled Czech government even more than they hated their own. One priest recalled that once, on a flight to Rome, when the pilot announced they were over Czechoslovakia, he had visited the lavatory and flushed the toilet "with great pleasure." Replied Wojtyla, "Unfortunately, the plane carries the waste along with it."[5]

In addition to secret ordinations, smuggling, and his protection of an independent press unknown elsewhere under communism, Wojtyla did still more to foster a liberation movement. In an innovative and unusual adaptation of an idea from Vatican II, he organized local synods of laymen on the model of Pope Paul's synod of bishops in Rome. The power of such synods, while minimal as measured by Western democratic standards, nonetheless loomed large in communist Krakow.

Through his synods, Wojtyla gave thousands of educated Catholics the feeling that they were helping set Church policy through committees on liturgy, moral matters, and so on. Soon they took on political issues as well. Many were from "intelligentsia" families that had been accustomed to community leadership for generations but were given no role under communism. The synod reenergized them.

Slowly, a spirit of independence from communism grew out of Wojtyla's Krakow synod. He created committees to discuss and prepare position papers on topics being raised in the Polish Parliament or the bishops' synod in Rome. The objective was to encourage feelings of participation and empowerment, even where no real power existed. Five hundred synod working groups, each with ten to fifteen members, met regularly through the 1970s.

"His vision of the Church was to listen to people, to make local priests more active," says Wilkanowicz, who was on the synod's steering committee.[6] Wojtyla searched for cracks in communist rule where ordinary Poles could affect decisions. He told people to distinguish between *politico sensu largo*, "politics in the large sense," meaning concern for the common good, and *politico sensu stricto*, or "politics in the narrow sense" of who held office. Since the communists guarded *politico sensu stricto*, he encouraged Poles to stick to issues of *politico sensu largo*, where they might change policies and begin to sense power.

On plenty of issues, the synod proposed plans to better Poland in ways that would not offend communist sensibilities, for example, offering financial bonuses for families with many children, building better orphanages, and establishing a program to encourage prosperous families to adopt uncared-for children. The synod pushed for increased funds for housing and a system to make the distribution of apartments fairer. It urged opportunities for part-time employment or more flexible working hours for mothers, and an end to night work for women. On each of these subjects, records show, Wojtyla organized a committee.

He said mothers rearing children full-time "should be treated as working people with a right to a pension." Committees pressed, too, for relocation of retail stores to make shopping easier, better vacations for families (such as a reserved spot on a lake), more medical facilities specializing in pregnancy and birth, more preschools for working families, and pay incentives to encourage teachers, nurses, and social workers to care for problem children. (Ironically, many Western feminists would come to view Wojtyla as an enemy simply because of his stance on reproduction, unaware that for decades he had been battling to fulfill much of their other agenda.)

Wojtyla advised his synod committees to be practical, to come up with precise legislative initiatives that could be proposed by the Znak group in Parliament, which could hope to swing the communist majority behind reasonable, positive, family-oriented policies.

"In the Krakow diocese, it was very effective," Wilkanowicz says. "People became active in community life." Gains were made in Parliament on a few issues, but "the most important achievement was the influence of Wojtyla's social ideas on the Solidarity movement."

In interviews with scores of Wojtyla's former parishioners, I noted almost universal admiration for the difficult, creative line he walked. On one side was a suspicious Wyszynski, determined to admit only the minimum change in the Church required by the Vatican; on the other was the Znak group, which pushed hard for increased popular participation and was allowed some leadership in the synod.

Wyszynski summoned the Krakow editors to Warsaw again when *Tygodnik Powszechny* published an article by editor Turowicz entitled "Crisis in the Church," which said the Church was alienating Catholics by resisting major social trends. Wyszynski accused the editors of helping "the Marxists exploit divisions among Catholics."[7] The editors say Wojtyla supported them unwaveringly but in his own quiet way, masking his advocacy and preaching unity rather than division.

23

Turowicz was right: there *was* a crisis in the Church. Perhaps in no other decade in history has change overtaken Western life as radically as it did in the 1960s.

A decade earlier, in the United States, unmarried couples from good families had trysted, if at all, in car seats or motel rooms; by 1970, even "nice girls" openly shared apartments with boyfriends. A decade earlier, even the "Playmate of the Month" in a magazine intended for adult men could reveal only a partial breast behind a coyly placed arm; by 1970, popular Hollywood stars displayed their naked bodies at any local Bijou. A decade earlier, women were unusual if they sought careers outside the home, other than teaching or nursing. Now many demanded equal opportunity and equal pay for equal work.

A decade earlier, Africans had lived in "the jungle" in places like the Gold Coast and the Belgian Congo. Now they showed up at the United Nations in Savile Row suits, as delegates from the countries of Ghana and Zaire. A decade earlier, blacks in the United States had been required by law to drink from separate fountains, go to separate schools, and occasionally get lynched to solve some unadjudicated crime. Now they were legally entitled to the same treatment as whites.

A decade earlier, America's "friendly neighbors to the south" had been expected to pick coffee beans, nap behind picturesque sombreros, and otherwise do what American-paid generals told them to; now they wanted the right to elect governments that would give them their earned share of their countries' wealth.

A decade earlier, Europeans and Americans who visited each other's countries had been mostly rich people boarding ocean liners with five days' reading; now, popularly priced jetliners made the trip in an afternoon. Television, as well, had suddenly made it possible for most people in the world (to the extent that their governments would let them watch) to see what was going on everywhere else, whether it was a war, a meeting, or some form of entertainment.

Not only were Catholics part of this changing society, but the Church had committed itself at the Vatican Council to connect with society and improve its lot. In Chile, 135 priests signed a protest when the Vatican nuncio bought a splashy home in a swank section of Santiago, "at a time when the majority of Chileans are suffering and many are starving."[1] In Belgium, Cardinal Leo Suenens, a major figure in Vatican II, published a book entitled *Co-responsibility in the Church*, which charged the papacy with not respecting the diversity of Church members and not listening to its bishops. (Wojtyla was among the cardinals defending Pope Paul, in lectures and in an article in the Vatican newspaper.)

At this moment, Wojtyla made his first trip to North America.

For years, Polish-American communities had begged in vain for Wyszynski to visit the United States. In 1966, Father Michael Zembrzuski, who had been meeting Polish Church leaders in Rome since Sapieha, asked Wyszynski to dedicate a shrine for Polish-Americans that Zembrzuski had built in Doylestown, Pennsylvania, near Philadelphia. (President Johnson spoke instead, and 150,000 people came.)

Zembrzuski raised money for Poland at the Doylestown shrine, bringing thirty thousand dollars or more on his regular visits to Warsaw. He also brought scores of deep-pocketed private donors, who carried as much as ten thousand each. These Polish-American donors deserved a return visit by Wyszynski to the U.S., said Zembrzuski, and would give even more if they got one. Similar appeals came from the aid group in Chicago and generous Polish communities across Canada.

The problem was that if Wyszynski, famous for his imprisonment, went abroad (other than on Church business to Rome) and didn't publicly excoriate the communists, it would send a message that life in Poland was OK. On the other hand, if he spoke out, he would probably not be allowed back into Poland. So the lower-profile Wojtyla had to go in his stead.

August 28, 1969, he arrived in Montreal for a Polish-Canadian congress, exchanging greetings with the mayor at the airport in adroit French. He visited churches, universities, orphanages, old people's homes, cemeteries—every place that people with Polish blood could be found. He gave Masses in big civic auditoriums. He did the same thing in nine other cities across Canada.

In the United States, he traveled to cities with large Polish communities or shrines to Mary, including Buffalo, Cleveland, Detroit, Chicago, Baltimore, Boston, New York, Philadelphia, St. Louis, Pittsburgh, Lodi (New Jersey), and West Hartford (Connecticut). Wherever something was ready to be dedicated or blessed, he was asked to do it. Everywhere, Polish-Americans flocked to see him. He thanked them for their aid and praised their efforts to preserve Polish traditions and language in the New World.

Almost everywhere he went, he was the houseguest of local churchmen, of Polish extraction if possible. He met with six cardinals and several dozen bishops. He prayed at the graves of John and Robert Kennedy, of Jan Paderewski (the pianist-composer) and the Unknown Soldier. In Chicago, a near-miracle occurred: "Some priest took him to a haberdashery," Bishop Abramowicz says, and afterward he was seen in new clothes.

His visit boosted Polish-American morale enormously, Cardinal Krol told me: "There was quite a bit of tension" between Polish-Americans and Irish-Americans over church assignments; "the Poles complained they didn't have enough bishops" and even distrusted Church data because it "was prepared by Irish clerks." One in five American Catholics was of Polish descent, but only one in seventeen parishes was run by a Polish-American.[2] After Wojtyla's visit, recalls Father Bednarz of Chicago, Poles "felt they had more of a voice."

Wojtyla found North American ways "a bit strange at first," particularly the receptions following Mass and the constant dinners in his honor, says Bishop Szczepan Wesoly, who accompanied him from Poland. "But he soon realized that if you stand with a glass in your hand, you don't need to drink, and people won't pester you. In Poland there would have been two hours of speeches" instead.[3]

When the mayor of Toronto told Wojtyla that his son was honeymooning in Florida with his Polish-Canadian bride, Wojtyla telephoned the couple to congratulate them, delighting the mayor. In Calgary, however, he spent so long meeting Poles that he was three hours late arriving for a scheduled reception at Edmonton, the next stop. The archbishop and the welcoming committee had left by the time he got there, and when he barely apologized later, they were frosty toward him.[4]

Wojtyla's diary of the trip stuck discreetly to the names of people met and places visited.[5] He kept his impressions to himself. Only when he returned in

1976 did he disclose his real opinion—that the U.S. was greedy and overly commercial, and had come loose from its spiritual moorings.[6]

October 1, 1969, after five weeks in North America, Wojtyla flew directly to Rome for the second synod of bishops. These synods, at which Wojtyla worked and socialized with about a hundred of the Church's elite, were crucial to establishing his stature in the minds of colleagues as an international leader in Catholic affairs. Significantly, Wyszynski was the only Polish delegate elected by his peers this time; Wojtyla attended because Paul appointed him among the 15 percent of delegates reserved for the pope.

With Catholics still looking to the synod to bridge the gap between them and the papacy, Paul struck preemptively to ensure there would be no compromises on issues of morality or authority. He declared that the "most serious and most insidious" danger to human dignity was sex—"an eroticism that has become an epidemic . . . barbarian and subhuman . . . pushed to unbridled and disgusting expressions."

Clearly, Paul saw no possibility that the Church might work with those who were glad to be free of generations of sexual repression and who now needed a new ethic. He wouldn't distinguish recklessness and exploitation from mutual love and joy. Although there's no record Wojtyla spoke out at this moment, Paul must once more have felt, and appreciated, Wojtyla's strong intellectual credentials in his corner.

Paul's approach to the sexual revolution—demanding nothing short of unconditional surrender—was the same as Pius XII's to communism. But the two situations were different. The initial years of sexual freedom had failed to produce a consensus that the new system was not working, as had happened with communism. There were backlashes against practices that people felt had gone too far. But on balance, for all the new miseries that had taken the place of the old, Westerners had decided the new sexual rules were an improvement. They did not want to resubject society to standards of absolute chastity outside of marriage or to forced prudery in artistic or personal expression.

Also, with communism, the Church had shown that it understood and rejected the evils that provoked revolution, and provided practical ways to avoid both extremes. Yet to those fleeing misery under the old sexual ethic, Paul seemed to offer no more than scolding.

The specific agenda of the synod was to define the role of future synods. But Paul tied the bishops' hands on this score, too, by declaring in advance that attacks on his authority were attacks on the Church and that the attackers would have to answer to God.[7] The bishops were torn. They didn't want to rebuke the pope, but the text his curia proposed to them seemed to strip the synods of power. Cardinal Suenens pressed hard for greater democracy.

Wojtyla backed a winning compromise, suggested by Cardinal François Marty of Paris. In the end, the synods got more trappings of power (permanent staff, more frequent meetings) without taking anything away from the pope's authority.

On such trips to Rome, Wojtyla faithfully visited Sophie Skawranska, former archivist to the Polish Episcopate and "a wonderful old Polish woman," according to Archbishop Weakland, who had become her confessor because she lived in retirement with the Benedictines in Rome. Wojtyla regularly passed money to Weakland to make her life more comfortable.

His adopted "grandma" in Krakow, Mrs. Irena Szkocka, died in 1971, at the age of ninety-two. He wrote to and visited her right up to the last. After her death, a relative looked through a volume of the Slowacki poetry she had loved; next to the line "He has made ready the throne for a Slavic Pope," she had written, "This Pope will be Karol."[8]

24

In December 1969, Wojtyla published his book on the significance of personal action. It was his philosophical magnum opus, a decade in the writing. The English edition is titled *The Acting Person*, though the original Polish title translates literally as "Person and Act."

"It was not readable," says his former student Halina Bortnowska. "It needed to be written again and paraphrased. I tried it myself but could not find a publisher for it." Professor George Hunston Williams of Harvard agrees that it is "very difficult to read." At a conference on it at Catholic University in Lublin, one professor declared from the lectern that he had "read the book twice and was not sure" what it said.[1] Others joke that Wojtyla knew he would someday become pope and wrote the book so that priests in Purgatory would have to read it.[2]

It certainly contains a lot of what sounds like philosophical hairsplitting. But jokes aside, *The Acting Person* earnestly sought to bridge existentialism, phenomenology, and Thomism. It attacked Descartes and the trend toward a philosophy of personal process. Asked Wojtyla, "Does man reveal himself in thinking, or, rather, in the actual enacting of his existence?" Reality, he said, is "in the confrontation itself, when [man] has to take an active stand . . . having vital consequences and repercussions." He declared that his goal was no less than "reversing the post-Cartesian [after-Descartes] attitude toward man."[3]

Yet Wojtyla diverged from existentialism by denying that action *defined* man (a formulation that leaves God out of the picture). To Wojtyla, action proves whether an individual lives up to the norm for what man should be—thus connecting existentialism to traditional Thomism, with its preexisting definitions.

One point is clear about *The Acting Person:* in communist Poland, Wojtyla published a book about the importance of each individual. Even if he got away with it only because almost no one understood it, saying it still mattered.

In March 1970, police demolished a makeshift chapel erected by villagers in Chodkow, in southeast Poland, who had been denied permission to build a church. It took dogs, clubs, tear gas, and an ugly scene to disperse the crowd protecting the chapel.

Days later, miners in southwest Poland—an area called Silesia—refused to surface unless they were guaranteed bigger meat rations. When police couldn't immediately fetch them up, nearby industrial workers took heart and struck over increased food prices. The workers' wives then marched through the regional capital, trashing a supermarket and stoning windows at Party headquarters and the police station. Such strikes wouldn't be tolerated by the Kremlin, because they challenged the myth that communism represented the workers. Afraid the Soviets would remove him if the strike spread, Gomulka revoked the price increases, and the Silesian Party boss persuaded the workers to return to their jobs.

Then some priests doing maintenance work discovered hidden microphones behind a painting in the episcopal meeting room and in the heating system of a prominent bishop's residence. Everyone knew the government eavesdropped, but Wyszynski used the occasion to air a backlog of grievances. Responses escalated. When the Church proclaimed a celebration of the fiftieth anniversary of the 1920 "Miracle of the Vistula," the Soviets—who wanted to forget 1920—ordered it stopped. But the celebration was a popular event, and stopping it embarrassed Gomulka. He was now rumored to be in trouble. Ironically, it was again Germany that drove history to the next stage.

In 1969, West Germany had elected as chancellor Democratic Socialist Willy Brandt, a former mayor of West Berlin who had long championed his own version of *Ostpolitik* (some say he invented the term). He pushed the Soviets to settle outstanding issues from World War II. Unlike his Christian Democrat predecessors in West Germany, Brandt was ready to let go of the former German territories and accept the new border with Poland. But in return, he insisted that Germany be recognized as one country, with freer commerce in goods and ideas between the East and West zones.

The Soviets found Brandt's initiative irresistible: a deal with West Germany would make communist rule in the Eastern Bloc seem stable, if not quite legitimate. It promised a flow of sorely needed Western currency. And it would sting the main enemy, the United States, whose new foreign-policy guru, Henry Kissinger, "hated *Ostpolitik* and Willy Brandt from the beginning" (in the words of an aide).[4]

When Brandt and the Soviets came to terms, they tightened a vise around Gomulka, who now had to make a Polish treaty with Germany. To appearances, the terms were just what Gomulka claimed to want: Poland got the disputed territories. But his real need was for a German enemy, without which he would lose his only source of public support.[5] The treaties were signed amid celebration in December 1970.

Gomulka decided that if he had to accept a German treaty, he would at least use the public euphoria to sneak through his food price increases (a vain effort to address shortages). Prices went up just two weeks before Christmas. Outraged port workers in Gdansk rallied in the rail yards; wives and students joined them to march on Party headquarters, singing, ironically, "The Internationale," the original hymn of communist idealism:

> *Arise, you prisoners of starvation!*
> *Arise, you wretched of the earth!*[6]

It was a communist revolution against the communists. Militia sent to stop the marchers were stoned and Party and police offices torched. Crowds blocked the fire trucks. Strikes became riots and spread along the industrialized Baltic coast. Hundreds were injured, and some killed. Gomulka deputized his vice premier to go on television and say that the strikes would be repressed to prevent Soviet intervention. Then he gave fateful orders for the militia to fire on the crowds if necessary.

What happened next was pure Greek tragedy. The mayor of the port city of Gdynia went on the radio to urge workers to return to their jobs. December 17, 1970, many decided to comply. But when they arrived at the shipyard at six A.M., no one had unlocked the gates. Suddenly militia appeared. Primed to obey their new orders, they began shooting the trapped, bewildered, unarmed workers. More than three dozen were killed, and thousands wounded or arrested. Troops also opened fire in Gdansk. Overall, forty-five

workers were listed as dead and 1,165 wounded, though unofficial estimates
of the casualties were much higher.

Where was Wojtyla during this tragedy? December 16 and 17, 1970, he was at
a previously planned conference at the Catholic University in Lublin to evaluate *The Acting Person*. For two days, he heard his work "torn to shreds" (as one
account put it)[7] by respected professional philosophers. With some exceptions,
they politely suggested that the book was incomprehensible because it mixed
jargon from both Thomism and phenomenology.

Obviously unaware of the bloodbath that had occurred in Gdynia a few
hours earlier, Wojtyla gave a final speech in which he appeared to surrender to
his critics. "Any attempt to combine these two philosophies," he said, was so
mistaken as to be "completely out of the question."[8]

Possibly he was being too modest. Monsignor Richard Malone, a theologian
at St. Charles Borromeo Seminary in Philadelphia, contends not only that was
Wojtyla attempting to combine Thomism and phenomenology, but that he
was on the verge of succeeding. Although the criticism had shaken him, he
could have surmounted the problems, Malone believes.

"Being original is difficult," says Malone. "[Wojtyla] is not simply a phenomenologist, he is not simply a Thomist." Rather, Malone says, in *The Acting
Person* Wojtyla showed that phenomenology could infuse Thomism with an
"awareness of consciousness and subjectivity" it didn't have before. "Wojtyla
has to go beyond Thomism to go where he wants to get. You would never have
this consciousness of the individuality of the person without Scheler and Kant.
I've never found any of those things in any Catholic author until [Wojtyla]
came along."

In a preface written in 1977 for an English-language edition of *The Acting
Person*, Wojtyla seemed to acknowledge his continuing effort to combine the
two philosophies. He said he

> owes everything to the systems of metaphysics, of anthropology,
> and of Aristotelian-Thomistic ethics on the one hand, and to phe-
> nomenology, above all in Scheler's interpretation, and through
> Scheler's critique also to Kant, on the other hand.

He did, however, also take pains in *The Acting Person* to set himself apart from
Scheler and other phenomenologists on precisely the issue of Aristotelian-
Thomist absolute truth. He called Scheler an "emotionalist" and said emo-

tionalism had to be "subordinated . . . to truth."[9] Was this the triumph of Thomism over phenomenology, as it might sound, or rather a sophisticated marriage of the two?

For Malone and some others, it was a wedding. The scholars had rebelled at Lublin because Wojtyla had pushed back the borders of phenomenology further than they could follow. "Luckily, Socrates had a Plato who could understand him," Malone says. In fact, he says that when he and a colleague[10] finished an intense study of Wojtyla's work, "We were regretting his papacy, because he could have become a better philosopher. He could have developed these foundations."

25

Edward Gierek, the local official who had peacefully ended the strikes in Silesia, replaced Gomulka as premier December 20, 1970. The Soviets accepted Gierek and dropped their threat of intervention. (Kliszko, who had made Wojtyla an archbishop, was toppled along with Gomulka.) Gierek had grown up in Belgium as the son of a Polish miner and strike leader and returned to Poland to fight in the wartime resistance. Appearing on television after becoming premier, he promised to consult with workers in the future, but said that for now, Gomulka's price increases would stand. He pledged "brotherly friendship with the Soviet Union."

Both Pope Paul and Wyszynski, recoiling from the violence, gave Gierek the benefit of the doubt. Paul urged Catholics not to involve the Church in "bitter" disputes, while Wyszynski told Poles, "We beg of you: do not accuse . . . forgive . . . put your hands to the plow so there can be more bread in our fatherland."

Wojtyla's first statement bore a very different tone. It was issued jointly with Wyszynski and read from all pulpits in Poland on New Year's Day. For the first of what would be many times, as cardinal and pope, Wojtyla seemed to inject resolve into a Polish primate who had instinctively backed down before a show of force. Without timorousness, Wojtyla's New Year's message set down conditions for cooperation with the new government: a bill of

> rights that must be guaranteed. . . . 1. Freedom of conscience and
> religious life. . . . 2. The right freely to shape the culture of one's
> own nation. . . . 3. Social justice. . . . 4. Freedom of expression and

the supply of true information. 5. Material conditions that ensure decent existence for the family and every citizen.

Only two weeks after the debate at Lublin, Wojtyla had become the Acting Person of his book's title. In marked contrast to Wyszynski's earlier forgiveness, Wojtyla implicitly blamed the communists for the killing: "Resort to force does not contribute to maintaining social peace, especially when innocent people, women and children, fall victim," he said.

Gierek began his administration by touring the country and good-naturedly answering workers' questions. But real policy was being made behind the scenes. Gierek's new military chief (and some say puppet-master) General Mieczyslaw Moczar, a leftover Stalinist, met with the Soviets. Within weeks, one Gdansk union leader was murdered, a second narrowly escaped a lethal assault, and other true union leaders were forced from office.[1]

Still, Pope Paul and his diplomat Casaroli wouldn't give up on *Ostpolitik*. In March 1971, Casaroli made the first trip to Moscow by a papal envoy since the 1917 revolution. Although he got no significant concessions, he claimed to have opened a "dialogue" after fifty years of "monologue." He and Pope Paul regularly posed for smiling pictures with Polish communist officials they received in Rome. Neither Wojtyla nor Wyszynski liked it, but if Wojtyla discussed his objection with Pope Paul, he didn't tell people around him.

"Wyszynski was shaped during the fight for Polish independence, before World War Two," says Jozef Czyrek, a foreign minister under communism. "He thought the most important good is an independent state. But in Wojtyla's life, independence was taken for granted. His focus was on what *kind* of state. He emphasized human rights."

By his fiftieth year, Wojtyla's message was being recognized by friends and enemies alike. "There is a great divide between the Catholicism [practiced] between the two world wars and contemporary Catholicism," says Wojtyla's colleague Professor Jozef Tischner of Catholic University in Lublin. "On the face of it, it was the same dogmas, the same prayers. But in fact, these are two different Catholicisms. The idea of humanity was present in the language of the prewar Church, but it didn't occupy such a prominent place as it does now. This was Wojtyla's contribution."[2]

At about this time, Wojtyla persuaded the Catholic Intelligentsia Clubs to start a special section dedicated to human rights. It was led by Tadeusz Mazowiecki, the former Pax member who now edited the magazine *Wiez* under Wojtyla's patronage. "It was dissident activity just to talk of human rights," says journalist Jan Turnau.[3] "Poles had never heard human-rights talk till Wojtyla."[4]

Every year Wojtyla sponsored a weekend conference attended by thirty or forty potentially influential people. The stated purpose was "to encourage them to speak and think clearly," says Marek Skwarnicki, the poetry editor of *Tygodnik Powszechny*, who helped organize the affairs. While critics of Wojtyla's own writing might smirk at his giving lessons on clarity, what he was really teaching was gumption.

"It was against the law to go to the conferences," Skwarnicki says. "They were using stuff that was published underground." Invitations, on plain paper, were delivered even to jailed dissidents if they might get out in time to attend. "The conferences were for everybody, believer and nonbeliever, Jew, et cetera. The elite from Warsaw, Krakow, Lublin got invited. Those not afraid to come, came." Wojtyla specifically encouraged the participation of women. Topics included theater and poets like Norwid, whose works were largely unavailable. "In the schools, the kids would not know the poets ever lived," Skwarnicki says. To Wojtyla, that was intolerable.

He startled many Catholics by expressing admiration for the jailed dissident Jacek Kuron, a professed atheist.[5] He held a Mass for the Buddhist Dalai Lama and other refugees from Chinese repression in Tibet and sponsored a public tribute to a sociologist he admired, who, like her husband, was an avowed non-believer.[6]

The family was still the most frequent topic of Wojtyla's sermons and retreats. He constantly reiterated the need for both husband and wife to participate energetically in parenting, whatever their outside activities. He continued to push courses to prepare couples for marriage. His appeals to prosperous families to take in single mothers or pregnant women produced a network of homes that helped rear fatherless children. He persuaded some nuns to start a group home for single mothers and persuaded families to donate washing and sewing machines, clothes, and other gifts for its residents.

Nowa Huta still had only one small church, though Wojtyla had created a dozen congregations, each with a priest, that met in the homes of parishioners. Elsewhere, churches that were denied building permits were expanded with materials bought by parishioners on the pretext of improving their houses. Father Bednarz of Chicago came to Krakow to arrange private aid from Polish-Americans who helped the Polish Church, with its twenty thousand priests, remain far stronger than its counterparts in neighboring countries. To avoid communist financial controls, the Americans often brought money to Western

Europe and gave it to traveling Polish clergy to carry home. The travel, often to take educational courses, was itself funded by Polish-Americans.

Amazingly, Father Bednarz, Monsignor John Quinn of Chicago, and Cardinal Krol of Philadelphia (the titular head of their committee) all told me in separate interviews that hard though they tried, they were unable to get U.S. government assistance for their project. "The reason was obvious," Bednarz says. "We had no investments there. The [U.S.] government was never interested. They had their own thing, fighting in Vietnam. They would laugh at you." He says officials told him they couldn't help because "the Russians would squawk."

Poles "had no reason to believe the West was behind them" in their struggle, says former Nixon White House official Hendryk Houthakker (whose Polish-born wife got him involved him in Polish affairs). "Wyszynski and Wojtyla had help from very, very few people" in the West.

Because Wyszynski gave people the impression that Pius XII had written him a blank check to be "the acting pope in Poland,"[7] after Pius's death, apparently not even the succeeding popes realized that his relations with the primate had been strained. Wyszynski exercised power usually held by Rome to appoint leaders of religious orders in Poland.

When Archbishop Weakland, head of the Benedictine order, reported widespread objection to a mother superior Wyszynski had named in Poland, Cardinal Jean Villot, Pope Paul's secretary of state, confided, "We just don't know what powers he has. They came from an oral agreement with Pius XII. Just tell the nuns they better accept the new mother superior."[8]

As Wyszynski grew ever more crochety and authoritarian, he must have presented Wojtyla with countless problems of tact. Yet no one recalls hearing a word of complaint from Wojtyla. "He tried to be very loyal to Wyszynski, which wasn't always easy," editor Bortnowska says. "There was tension and there was talk about it."

Debates were kept internal, says Bishop Pieronek. "They respected each other. The archive shows that all the important documents were drawn up by Wojtyla and signed by Wyszynski."

Wyszynski did, however, block Wojtyla's efforts to establish lay synods throughout Poland on the model of his synod in Krakow. Wojtyla's ideas for Intelligentsia Club projects were often blocked as well.[9]

Yet Weakland says that priests "were willing to look the other way at what they disliked" because they "all felt their strength was in unity with Wyszynski.

You'd visit him and see the priests getting out of their cars and putting their cassocks on because he wouldn't see anybody [a priest] not in one. Then they'd come out and roll up their cassocks to get into the cars again."

26

In September 1971, Cardinal Mindszenty finally agreed to leave Budapest, move to Vienna, and refrain from making political statements. In exchange, Pope Paul promised not to replace him in Hungary.

"A Hungarian prelate living in Rome arranged it," says Cardinal König. "I told the pope, if you want to get him out, I can't do it. Send a Hungarian." To Paul, it was a victory for *Ostpolitik,* and on the eve of the 1971 synod.

The synod was assigned a major task: reversing a trend that had seen twenty-five thousand priests, 7 percent of the total worldwide, resign since Vatican II. Paul again tied the bishops' hands before they started, by instructing them to avoid "overanxiety to adapt to secular ways." This was understood to mean that the celibacy requirement was not to be challenged. Wyszynski told the synod that priests who questioned such teachings as celibacy should be reprimanded. He blamed Western culture and "journalists" for trying "to bring unhealthy parliamentary customs into the work of the Church."

But it was Cardinal Joseph Malula of Zaire, neither a Westerner nor a journalist, who declared that the celibacy requirement for priests was causing a crisis among the African clergy, "even though the mass media have less power among us." And it was Cardinal Slipyi, the hero released from a Soviet prison, who most embarrassed Pope Paul, by observing, "Christ called married men to be his apostles, and the apostles themselves consecrated bishops who were married."

Slipyi was from the Eastern Orthodox minority that had repledged its allegiance to Rome in 1596, while retaining its tradition of a married priesthood. The brotherhood with these so-called Eastern Rite Catholics was uneasy. The Vatican wanted their numbers but banned their tradition of married priests in Western countries for fear the example might tempt other Catholics.[1]

"The protests against celibacy are loudest in [Western] countries where our married priests are not allowed to practice their ministry," Slipyi said. Pressure for a married priesthood didn't come from Eastern influence or from journalists but, rather, from human nature, he argued. He continued to criticize Paul's policies to his face, denouncing *Ostpolitik* and complaining of discrimination against Ukrainian Catholics. Other bishops also challenged Paul by asking for relaxed rules for priests.

Wojtyla defended the pope in his usual refined, intellectual way. Priests should not be like laymen, he said; celibacy was a visible sign of commitment to the priesthood. Paul had to like that.

In the end, the synod voted to retain celibacy, 168 in favor, 10 against (some opponents, such as Malula, left before the vote), and 21 wanting a compromise.[2] In a separate vote to elect bishops to serve on the synod's permanent council of fifteen, Wojtyla was chosen to fill one of three seats reserved for European bishops.

But the high point of the synod for the Polish delegates was a ceremony to beatify, or elevate toward sainthood, Father Maximilian Kolbe. For years Wojtyla had urged Paul to initiate sainthood for about fifty Catholics who had died at Auschwitz (where Wojtyla still said Mass each All Saints' Day), and Kolbe was first. On August 14, 1941, Kolbe volunteered to die in place of a man chosen at random to be locked in a hole and deprived of food and water until death, as punishment for all the Poles in camp. When the man cried out that he had a family, Kolbe, a priest, went instead.

Charter flights brought an odd mix of fifteen hundred Poles to the beatification, including the man in whose place Kolbe had died. Communist government officials sat in front, dressed in mourning coats.

Kolbe's prewar leadership of a chauvinist movement that had been responsible for mob attacks on Jewish-owned businesses added a note of controversy to his beatification.[3] Jews were sensitive about anything Auschwitz-related.[4] But if there was an answer to the complaints, Wojtyla gave it in what was the day's best talk: Kolbe, he said, had not merely saved one man but had shown many other doomed men how to die.

Cardinal Malula had been defeated in the celibacy debate, but it was nothing compared to what awaited him at home. The ruler of his country, Zaire, was a Stalin-like autocrat, and a thief to boot, named Mobutu Sese Seko. Even the CIA, which had conspired with Mobutu to kill his elected predecessor and help him take power, wouldn't have called *him* a saint.[5] But the relationship between Mobutu and Malula personified the problems the Church would face when John Paul II later decided to make Africa the Church's number-one growth area.

By dint of its population, mineral wealth, and agricultural fertility, Zaire was a potential African superpower. But Mobutu chose instead to steal literally billions of dollars in graft, while his malnourished, disease-ridden nation mostly lacked electricity, running water, and medical care. When Zairians revolted, the United States, Belgium, and France all sent troops to save Mobutu's government, and thereby to protect the monopoly rights Mobutu had granted to Western mining companies.

When Cardinal Malula returned home from the synod, he found that Mobutu had closed his residence and charged him with opposing the one-party state. Pope Paul's protests persuaded Mobutu to spare Malula a trial and let him return to Rome, but Zaire's priests were put under watch as "subversive agents" and ordered by Mobutu not even to pray for their cardinal.

While he would later face the mad Mobutu as pope, Wojtyla had already discerned that there was injustice on both sides of the Iron Curtain. Addressing a large Polish audience right after the synod, he essentially endorsed Soviet charges that the West had kept its colonial grip on parts of the Third World through other means:

> the phenomenon called neo-colonialism—meaning the exploitation of nations by other nations, of the poor by the rich, of the weak by the stronger ... injustice felt ... throughout the world ... by nations, and by social groups.[6]

In October 1972, President Nixon's foreign-policy specialist, Henry Kissinger, announced that a settlement had been reached and "peace is at hand" in Vietnam. But weeks passed, and America's South Vietnamese allies refused to sign. Finally, the South hinted that it would go along if it could get an additional concession from the North to make it appear that the holdout had accomplished something. The North refused.

Beginning December 18, 1972, America's biggest war planes, B-52s, flying seven miles over the northern capital of Hanoi and a nearby port, unloaded every nonnuclear bomb they could carry, around the clock for twelve days. Most of the area's population of just over one million people fled to the countryside. More than sixteen hundred were killed, including many schoolchildren and three Polish seamen on a freighter in the harbor. Ninety-three U.S. airmen died, and more than $130 million of U.S. aircraft was wrecked. Nixon resented history's characterization of this as "the Christmas bombing" because, he said, he called a one-day halt on Christmas.

Kissinger's biographer Walter Isaacson, later editor of *Time* magazine, wrote, "Hanoi was bombed in order to force changes in a treaty that the U.S. had already seen fit to accept. The modifications for which these lives were lost were so minor that neither Nixon nor Kissinger would adequately remember what they were. . . . The main reason . . . was . . . to help Saigon save face."[7]

When Pope Paul tried to address the bombing in his Christmas message, he broke down crying. It was, he said, "the cause of our daily suffering." In the United States, Cardinal Krol—no minor anti-communist—was also overcome, and denounced the U.S. bombing.

Eighty-five-year-old Rosa Alexandrowicz was a citizen of Miedzeszyn, Poland, a wide spot in the road southwest of Warsaw. An advocate of country air, she decided, with an invalid priest she knew, Father Peter Jelowiecki of Warsaw, to turn her house into a vacation home for sick and elderly city folk. For ten months they renovated it, ending up with six bedrooms, a kitchen, and a bath-room. In 1971, guests began arriving for stays of a week to six months. Through family or Church contacts, weak, elderly people who had been cooped up in blighted urban rooms were suddenly exposed to trees, birds, and flowers. On Sundays, Father Jelowiecki said Mass around the dinner table; guests' families often came to take part.

This was the kind of initiative Poles frequently undertook. Making money wasn't the object; any enterprise that produced something, even if just a little happiness, was valued on its own account. It brought people in an atomized society together. The Church was often the only institution where Poles could interconnect easily. Sometimes, if they stayed modest, these initiatives suc-ceeded; authorities either didn't notice or were too lethargic or busy elsewhere to stop them. Often, though, they failed.

Word of Mrs. Alexandrowicz's vacation home somehow spread to govern-ment busybodies. February 8, 1973, seven ambulances pulled up, and represen-tatives of the Warsaw City Council burst into the house to declare that they were taking the eleven guests to a government old people's home and demol-ishing Mrs. Alexandrowicz's house as unsafe. Mrs. Alexandrowicz produced a certificate of suitability for habitation signed by her town council.

An argument ensued. Six residents refused to leave. Four agreed to go to the government home, and the eleventh returned to Warsaw with her family.

Over the next four days, government officials tried in vain to persuade the remaining residents to come quietly. Then officials brought papers saying Father Jelowiecki was illegally running a rest home outside his parish, and that the residents hadn't registered their changes-of-address. Everyone was cleared out, and the house was razed.

Mrs. Alexandrowicz curled her eighty-five-year-old fingers around a pen and wrote to various officials, including Party Boss Gierek, asking, "Why, in the thirtieth year of the Polish People's Republic, was I thrown out of my house when it was the best possible place from which to develop this much-needed initiative?"

She got no answer.[8]

In February 1973, Wojtyla, his secretary, Father Dziwisz, and two other Polish bishops flew to Melbourne, Australia, for an International Eucharistic Congress, a Catholic assembly devoted to the practice of, rather than arguments over, religion. As happened now everywhere he traveled, Polish settlers awaited him. Even at a stop in West New Guinea, Wojtyla found a seminary and two missions run by Polish priests and nuns. In Manila and seven Australian cities he watched as Polish clubs put on shows of children dancing polkas and singing Polish songs. He praised them for preserving the culture.

In Melbourne, amid a crowd of 150,000, he showed off his English and made connections among the majority of the world's bishops who didn't attend synods. He went home, as he had left, by way of Rome, where he sat in on more meetings of more committees (now he was part of the Congregation for the Clergy) and took part in a consistory for eight new cardinals, each of whom would vote when the time came to elect a new pope.

His focus was still personal and national. His diary shows he was preoccupied with the Polish presence, even in Australia. The event that apparently made the biggest impression on him[9] was a chance encounter at the Warsaw airport with a mother who was taking her sick son to Rome for treatment. When the boy died months later, the mother wrote to the cardinal that she was losing her faith in God. Wojtyla wrote back asking her to see him if she was in Krakow. She came, discussed her suffering with him, and later credited him with restoring her faith. He confirmed her second son in his chapel.

Bishops and cardinals he met on his travels began coming to Krakow for events such as the annual tribute to Saint Stanislaw. He encouraged youth groups to visit from Western Europe and made sure Auschwitz and the cell of Father Kolbe was a standard tour stop.

Just before Easter 1973, Wojtyla went undercover in civilian clothes, over the mountains, across Czechoslovakia, and into Hungary to see the situation there and to minister to Polish workers at a sugar mill. On his arrival, he pulled a cassock from his pack and put it on. According to Father Jan Zajac, who helped arrange the trip, "If the Hungarians [had] discovered him, they probably wouldn't have done anything, but the Czechs would have harassed him, held him, and confiscated his belongings."

Wojtyla also fired a shot on behalf of Pope Paul, publishing a book, *At the Bases of Renewal: A Study of . . . Vatican II.* Systematic and nonargumentative in tone, it made its point by showing that the radical changes some Western churchmen attributed to the Council were simply not in the documents.

Two other books published around the same time had more definitive consequences. One, published underground, was by Bohdan Cywinski, Wojtyla's old canoeing friend and philosophical disciple, who had just been made editor in chief at *Znak*. Cywinski's book, *A Heritage of Rebellions*, linked the Catholic intelligentsia's stand against the occupation forces in the 1800s with the student-worker uprising of 1968.

Fatefully, a copy fell into the hands of Seweryn Blumsztajn, one of the student leaders from a Jewish-communist background who had gone to jail for their part in the 1968 uprising. Cywinski's book was a revelation to Blumsztajn: the Catholic intellectuals, who he had always considered reactionaries and adversaries, in fact shared the same thoughts and experiences as his own group.

"The mutual understanding was with regard to basic moral values," he says. "Human rights and freedom." Blumsztajn was so excited by Cywinski's book that he passed it to his fellow rebels Adam Michnik and Jacek Kuron, and on his own decided to try to meet with Cywinski and others from the Catholic Intelligentsia Clubs. In the back of his mind, however, questions lingered: Didn't Catholic aristocrats still want to reimpose the old feudal system? "If communism was going to be overthrown, the first victim was going to be the working class," he feared. But he began seriously studying the Catholics' ideas.

Cardinal Mindszenty also came out with a book: his memoirs. He knew well that it broke his vow of political silence. But in his rage, he published it anyway—and at a particularly bad time for both the Vatican and Wyszynski. It had just been announced that Casaroli would make an official state visit to Poland early in 1974. Wyszynski, frightened as ever that Pope Paul was preparing a concordat with the communists behind his back, rushed to Rome. Paul promised him that nothing would happen without the Episcopate's agreement, but Wyszynski remained uneasy.[10]

Then, February 5, Mindszenty's memoirs arrived, pages smoldering. Immediately, Paul VI declared the Budapest bishop's job vacant, named a replacement, and ordered Mindszenty to move to Rome.

It got ugly. Mindszenty publicly accused the Hungarian Church leaders Paul appointed of being communist pawns and said the Vatican had betrayed the faithful. The Vatican released an unsigned statement saying Mindszenty had a "not entirely religious concept" of being primate.

Two days after Mindszenty was brought to Rome amid a loud public contretemps, Casaroli landed in Warsaw for his state visit. Wyszynski was at his absolute best, pretending that Casaroli's talks with Polish officials were exactly what he wanted, while at the same time constantly asserting that his Episcopate, not Rome, ran the Church in Poland. They said Mass together in the cathedral, and Casaroli left Warsaw with nothing much changed.[11]

May 6, 1974, three months after he was replaced in Budapest, Mindszenty dropped dead of a heart attack.

Casaroli continued *Ostpolitiking.* He visited the Kremlin, lunched with Castro, pursued any opening. Posters on walls near the Vatican screamed, "Excommunicate Casaroli, the Red Excellency of Compromise."[12] He answered his critics bluntly: "A Church deprived of liberty and forced to continual compromise is always better than no Church at all."

Wyszynski was in between. "We often hear it said," he argued, "that it is a fine and glorious thing to die for one's country. Sometimes it requires a greater heroism to live, to endure, to hold out for years on end and to work."[13]

27

At this point, it might be well to pause and take stock of the political philosophies we have encountered. Four ways of opposing tyranny have been advocated, and a look at the other three will help in illuminating Wojtyla's.

Mindszenty's way was unconditional opposition. It sounded noble—and was. Mindszenty was the hero of early anti-communism. But he was crushed, reduced to an ineffective corpse, long before he actually died. Hungary, like Poland, was about two thirds Catholic when the communists came. When they left, a triumphant Polish Church is what chased them out; the Hungarian Church was a beaten shell.

A second way of opposing communist tyranny, America's, was rigid, like Mindszenty's. But instead of choosing a rigid moral high road, as Mindszenty did, the United States took a moral low road: when challenged, it exercised deviousness and physical strength before other means. The U.S. decided that to beat the enemy, it had to outplay him at his own game. This legitimated lying, to the point where, as in Moscow, the truth was regularly lost sight of.

The U.S. sponsored wars, assassinations, election fixes, or other mayhem in more than three dozen countries.* Often (as in Brazil and Zaire) it used force to overthrow elected governments. It installed dictatorships that murdered

---

* Since World War II, as far as is publicly known: Afghanistan, Albania, Angola, Australia, Belize, Brazil, Cambodia, Chad, Chile, China, Costa Rica, Cuba, Dominican Republic, Egypt, El Salvador, Greece, Grenada, Guatemala, Haiti, Honduras, Indonesia,

political opponents wholesale. American officials from the President down denied responsibility. Besides tyrannizing their countries politically, these U.S.-backed governments often thwarted free enterprise as well, favoring bribery, nepotism, and price-fixing.

In 1974, just as the folly of Mindszenty's approach became most clear, the folly of Washington's was displayed, too, as the U.S. extricated itself from its longest war ever, in Vietnam. The public had been lied to about it throughout; even the boat attack that had persuaded Congress to approve sending combat troops in the first place turned out to be a fraud.[1] More than fifty-eight thousand Americans and a million Vietnamese died to support a series of South Vietnamese governments, none of which shared the ideals the United States said it was fighting for.

Instead of learning from this disaster, the U.S. in that same year, 1974, plunged into its second-longest war—smaller but even more futile—helping one ethnic group fight another in Angola. Again, the U.S. government lied to voters about how the war started, blaming communists forces when in fact the U.S. intervened first.[2] In private, Kissinger said the U.S. fought in Angola mainly to prove it was still tough after the defeat in Vietnam. Tens of thousands of Angolans, many of them children, died or lost limbs, and another potentially prosperous African country was devastated.

The ultimate proof that American policy was misguided is that the U.S. achieved its goals only after it lost the wars. Other states in the Vietnam region, instead of falling like dominoes, as had been predicted, stayed capitalist and became the world's premier area of economic growth.[3] Democracy increased, while insurgencies waned. After the Angolan war, the U.S. discovered that its natural ally—in terms of both commerce and human rights—was the side it had waged war against, which then won a free election. U.S. negotiators found themselves in the embarrassing position of begging their former wartime ally, a dictator, to lay down his U.S.-supplied arms and obey the voters.[4]

American policies were often as self-defeating as they were unjust. The diversion of money and brainpower to create a global military behemoth left the U.S. debt-ridden and less competitive. The long increase in American living standards ended. America's sacrifice of its own noble values was perhaps the greatest casualty of the Cold War.

John XXIII and Paul VI promoted a third way of fighting communist tyranny. Despite obvious differences, their *Ostpolitik* had much in common

Iran, Iraq, Italy, Korea, Kuwait, Laos, Lebanon, Libya, Nicaragua, Pakistan, Panama, the Philippines, Saudi Arabia, Somalia, Vietnam, and Zaire. My books *Endless Enemies* and *The Crimes of Patriots* provide further details.

with the pacifism of the British philosopher Bertrand Russell and an array of Ban-the-Bomb groups in the West. Basically, they thought a satisfactory long-term compromise could be reached with communism, and they blamed continuing hostilities on an inadequate commitment by the West to reason and goodwill.

This policy—seeking peace and an end to the arms race through mutual understanding—had enormous advantages over the American approach. It didn't kill any one. It didn't cost anything, except for Cardinal Casaroli's airplane tickets. *Ostpolitik* was also based on the highest ethical values. It didn't require deceit and didn't degrade its practitioners.

The problem was that it also didn't free anybody.[5] Despite its lofty aspirations, its result was to let things be. This was fine for people in the West but tough on populations living under totalitarian governments.

Although repeated differences have been cited in these pages between the views of Wyszynski and Wojtyla, their approach to the communists was similar enough to constitute a fourth way of facing tyranny. It had a lot in common also with the methods of Mohandas Gandhi in India and Martin Luther King, Jr., in the United States, in that it worked by moral force. (Wojtyla had read many of Gandhi's writings, beginning in the 1950s; as pope, he paused on a trip to India to pray where Gandhi's body was cremated.)[6]

The Wojtyla way of fighting communism rejected physical violence while demanding unflagging resolve. Unlike the pacifist way, this method embraced a higher good than peace alone.

Among its many contrasts with the American policy was that it consistently marshaled resources rather than squandering them. It viewed human life as the end rather than the means—something to be saved, not spent. Each potential confrontation was evaluated against the long-term goal, which was always the promotion of something, not the mere destruction of its opposite.

Wyszynski and Wojtyla understood that success depended most on their conveying a clear vision of the values they were promoting. They never lay aside their values to gain a temporary or tactical advantage.

Unlike Mindszenty, they knew how to listen and when to keep their mouths shut. They pursued what understandings they could. They set their own timetable and avoided inopportune showdowns. Unlike the government of the United States, they never promoted what they did not believe. And unlike the pacifists, they never let either their adversaries or their own followers forget what they believed and what they were struggling for.[7]

The aim was not victory, but a better world *after* victory.

And it worked. Thank God.

28

Wojtyla's magnum opus, *The Acting Person,* survived the scorching criticism it received at his university. In September 1972, a Polish scholar visiting New York gave a copy to a phenomenology lecturer at St. John's University there, Anna-Teresa Tymieniecka. A slender, strawberry blond, Polish-born aristocrat, Tymieniecka had left home in 1946, studied in Switzerland, and later moved to the United States, where she married Hendryk Houthakker, a Dutch-born Harvard economics professor whom President Nixon appointed to his council of economic advisers.

The two professors lived on a quiet, suburban street in Belmont, Massachusetts, lined with enough trees that if one fell, someone would likely not only hear it but feel it. Although their house looked much like others on the block, it—and the Houthakker-Tymieniecka summer home in Vermont—also served as headquarters for the World Phenomenology Institute, the World Institute for Advanced Phenomenological Research and Learning, and the International Husserl and Phenomenological Research Society, all of which Tymieniecka ran.

Recently, Tymieniecka had faced opposition from her fellow phenomenologists: she believed action told more about a person than thought, whereas Husserl, the founder of the school, had held the reverse, and most scholars in the field sided with him.[1] Tymieniecka, however, was not burdened by self-doubt. "I have founded a sort of school of phenomenology [with] a philosophy of action," she says. "The deepest questions which Husserl sought to answer unsuccessfully to the end of his life, I am solving them. He could not. I can."

Convinced that life was in the doing, but surrounded by advocates of thinking, she was immediately taken with *The Acting Person* and pronounced it "a great find!" Till then, she says, her work "did not seem to have aroused much attention by fellow phenomenologists. Here, at last, was a kindred spirit . . . a scholar who started into philosophy through action."

Two academic conferences were being planned on related themes, and Tymieniecka got permission to invite Wojtyla. Her invitation was so enthusiastic that the delighted cardinal asked her to visit him in Krakow. She accepted, arriving in July 1973.

"This is a great book!" she says she told Wojtyla about *The Acting Person.*

"He was amazed," she says and quotes his reply: "I'm surprised, because when my book was discussed in Lublin it was completely torn to shreds. I lost all confidence in it."

"They don't know philosophy!" Tymieniecka reassured him. In meetings on successive days, he agreed to write articles for her "World Institute" publications and a paper for a conference in Montreal, though he begged off attending. So she herself introduced his paper at the conference, with high praise. The next winter, she was back in Krakow with a contract, which Wojtyla signed, for her to publish an English translation of *The Acting Person.* Wojtyla appointed his own translator.

But Tymieniecka believed the book needed more than translation. "They had published a book in unprintable condition," she says. "Sentences without end, punctuation completely wrong. I was the philosophical editor, rewriting the book with him. I remained in Krakow several weeks." Before she left, Wojtyla agreed to allow her to reprint a paper he was about to deliver in Switzerland. She calls their work a "rare form of collaboration."

It was, at least, an unusually intense relationship, and it lasted for years. As in his relationship with Dr. Wanda Poltawska, he also became friendly with Tymieniecka's husband. Professor George Hunston Williams, an early John Paul biographer and a friend and neighbor of Tymieniecka's, asserts that the pope's relationship with her seemed for his part to be based on "erotic energy, though not acted upon." He says the same erotic energy was responsible for Wojtyla's "unusual number" of "cross-gender friendships"—including with the female students on his camping trips. Williams says these were willful brushes with temptation and that Wojtyla's successful navigation of that temptation proves that in his celibacy, he "was reliable, not the contrary."[2]

Wojtyla's first public appearance for Tymieniecka was in April 1974, on a phenomenology panel she headed at a conference in Italy. Stefan Wilkanowicz, the *Znak* editor, attended, and thought Wojtyla gave an even better talk a few days later. Afterward, Wilkanowicz and a professor friend went up to congratulate Wojtyla. "Someday you will become pope," the professor said.[3]

Replied Wojtyla, "You're crazy."

Just partially. He had the character. Traveling to Italy for the conference, Wojtyla had stopped off to give a funeral oration for a Czechoslovakian cardinal, in defiance of a ban officials had imposed on such orations; he calculated, correctly, that they wouldn't provoke an incident by arresting him. He also was slowly becoming more aware of the world. Visiting West Germany later in 1974, he was surprised—and revolted—by what might seem the routine commercial excesses of Western society.

"Friends told him to just walk down the street and see what was in the movies and shops," Father Bardecki says. He came back grim, declaring, "*Love and Responsibility* says there are three aspects to sex—physiological, psychological, and ethical. The West focuses only on physiology."

During ceremonies in honor of a Nazi war victim, Wojtyla impressed every-one with his fluent German. At a reception afterward, he was congratulated by Jan Novak, a former Polish war hero and now the beleaguered director of the Polish branch of Radio Free Europe in Munich. The radio agency had just been scandalized by revelations that it was a CIA operation, with an agenda other than honest broadcasting. Some congressmen were demanding that it be closed, which would have deprived hundreds of millions of Eastern Europeans of their daily lifeline to news. In the end, the agency would be saved by being removed from the CIA and put under a publicly accountable panel of broad-cast professionals, as it could have been in the first place.

Now, Wojtyla lifted Novak's spirits. "I recognize your voice," he said. "I lis-ten to you every morning as I shave."

Both Wojtyla and Novak then headed to Rome for the bishops' synod. Meeting Casaroli, Novak said he worried that Wyszynski, who was about to turn seventy-five, might have to retire. Casaroli assured Novak that Wyszynski would stay on, but he added, "Don't you know that behind Wyszynski we have one of the most powerful intellects of the Church?"

"I had never thought of Wojtyla that way," Novak says. "Wojtyla always stayed in Wyszynski's shadow. I once saw them crossing St. Peter's together, and at first I mistook Wojtyla for Wyszynski's chaplain because he walked a few steps behind him. Then I saw he was a cardinal, too."

Novak then visited with Bishop (now Cardinal) Deskur, the highest-ranking Pole in the curia. Deskur seemed anxious about Pope Paul's declining health. "Every pope tries to designate who should be his successor by making his choice as well known as possible" among the cardinals, Deskur said. "But this pope is not doing it. The only one he promotes is Wojtyla, a Pole, who doesn't have a chance."[4]

There is further evidence that Paul was pushing Wojtyla for the papacy. Paul's secretary, Monsignor John Magee, has told many people that by around 1974, Paul had decided he wanted Wojtyla to succeed him[5]—though, notably, Magee is quoted as saying this only *after* Wojtyla was elected in 1978. More impressive, Wojtyla's friend Jerzy Kluger, visiting the papal summer home at Castelgandolfo soon after Wojtyla was elected, noticed that the chapel was dominated by a large painting of a famous Polish scene, the Swedish siege at Czestochowa. Kluger joked that the new tenant, John Paul, had wasted no time in customizing the chapel. But John Paul told him that Paul VI had installed the painting, saying, "It will serve my successor."

Paul generally offered Wojtyla preferential treatment, and Wojtyla responded conspicuously. For the 1974 (fourth) synod, Paul named Wojtyla the official "relator," charged with presenting a jumping-off paper and concluding comments. Overwhelmingly, the bishops had wanted to address the topic of family life in the aftermath of the birth-control encyclical, but Paul refused to discuss it and selected instead the comparatively bland issue of evangelism.

Even then, the bishops couldn't agree on a compromise between those who favored a uniform Church service and those who wished to see local traditions brought in. The synod was widely considered a disappointment, even a failure. But Wojtyla, in his summary, called it the best synod yet and lauded Paul for his leadership. Although in the past Wojtyla had supported the incorporation of different cultures into ritual, so that Catholicism wouldn't appear to be mainly a "Western" religion, his synod summary, in seeming deference to Paul, indicated a preference for uniformity and central authority over local tradition. Paul hastened to embrace what Wojtyla had said, warning that "it is dangerous to speak of diversified theologies according to continents and cultures."[6]

Wojtyla did go out of his way, in his speech, to praise the three Third World continents: Latin America for its concern with human liberty, Africa for its desire to make the Church indigenous, and Asia for improving relations with non-Christians. Then, perhaps with his walking tour of Frankfurt fresh on his mind, he derided Western Europe and North America as places that had been Christian in the past but had now adopted secularism as a way of life.

While proponents of collegiality accused Pope Paul of turning synods into a mere rubber stamp, the 1974 synod marked yet another milestone in Wojtyla's rise. Paul began using Wojtyla's fellow Pole, Cardinal Deskur, as a relay to get the Krakow cardinal's opinion on important matters. Deskur says Paul sometimes noted on files, "Don't decide until Cardinal Wojtyla has given his opinion."

Before returning home from the synod, Wojtyla took some priests who had accompanied him from Krakow to visit the grave of Padre Pio.

Trouble, however, was brewing between Paul and Poland in the unlikely town of Camden, New Jersey. Doubtless inspired in part by *The Washington Post*'s exposure of the Watergate scandal, Camden's diocesan Catholic newspaper uncovered a scandal of its own, involving Wyszynski's old friend Father Michael Zembrzuski.

In order to build his big shrine in Doylestown, Pennsylvania, near Camden—the one that had been dedicated by President Johnson when Wyszynski couldn't come—Zembrzuski had not only collected donations but sold bonds. Catholics of modest means had invested their retirement savings, impelled by religious devotion but certainly also expecting to get their money back with the promised interest. And they weren't being paid.

Carlton Sherwood, a reporter for the Camden church paper, learned that a large bank in Minneapolis had gone to court demanding payment on behalf of three thousand bondholders. Zembrzuski asked Cardinal Krol for a $1.5 million loan to pay the overdue interest. So Krol sent an accountant to examine the shrine's books. They were a mess. Krol went straight to Pope Paul. If the bank filed suit, he explained, an embarrassing scandal would become national news in the U.S. To prevent that, Krol proposed that the matter be investigated within the Church and straightened out quickly and privately.

But Paul misjudged ethnic sensitivities in the United States. The investigators he appointed were Irish-Americans, while Father Zembrzuski and the others being investigated were all Poles. The Irishmen—Bishop George Guilfoyle of Camden and Father Paul Boyle, head of the Passionist religious order—knew nothing of Zembrzuski's long years of travel to Rome and Warsaw, during which he had comforted Wyszynski and collected millions of dollars for Polish relief. Guilfoyle and Boyle showed Zembrzuski little mercy in their report: millions of dollars borrowed from American Catholic families was missing and unaccounted for.

They said Zembrzuski's "friendship with a woman, whom he supported generously with monastery funds, gave rise to many rumors and accusations." Sherwood got hold of their report and wrote about it.[7]

As the 1974 synod began, they hired the large international accounting firm of Peat, Marwick & Company to conduct a thorough—and secret—audit at Doylestown. Father Zembrzuski was transferred to another monastery and his supervisors, the heads of the Pauline order in Poland, were replaced. Wyszynski took this as a direct assault on his perceived special authority as "acting pope" in Poland. Piqued, he saw Poles and Polish institutions under attack.

In the midst of all this, the Vatican, again without Wyszynski's agreement, signed a treaty establishing formal relations with the Polish government. Wyszynski was so angry that when Pope Paul's nuncio, Archbishop Luigi Poggi, arrived in Warsaw, he didn't go to the airport to greet him. He warned his bishops, in words that can hardly have stayed secret from Pope Paul, that "responsibility for the Holy Church in Poland falls on the Episcopate." Bishops were to guard against Poggi's interfering in their affairs and particularly to keep him from interceding from long-running talks with Gierek over a bishop's vacancy.[8]

Poggi, a diplomat for the Vatican since 1945, was unfazed by Wyszynski's outburst. In Krakow, he met with Znak editors and then went with Wojtyla to a forest outside town to discuss something so "confidential" that Poggi says it is still a secret—one more indication that Pope Paul trusted the cardinal in Krakow more than the one in Warsaw.

∽

Jan Novak was ousted from Radio Free Europe in 1975; American officials said his pro-Polish jabs at U.S. policy had irritated West Germany.[9] But others from the radio began meeting Wojtyla when he left Poland, which now occurred increasingly. The meetings were kept secret to protect the Church in Poland.[10]

Gradually, the nonpolitical Wojtyla was being politicized. Says Krzysztof Kozlowski, the *Tygodnik Powszechny* editor, he "realized he would succeed Wyszynski, and that he must learn politics." His personal style showed when the Episcopate assigned him to write an all-pulpits letter protesting the lengthening of the Polish school day, a transparent attempt by the government to disrupt afternoon Catholic religious classes.

"In the past, the [protest] letter would have been just about religious instruction," says Wojtyla's friend Bohdan Cywinski. But Wojtyla used the opportunity to expand the topic into "how to teach national history—how to stop lying in school. He was thinking of things like Katyn [the Soviet massacre of Poles that was officially blamed on Germany]. The letter said schools must educate human beings in accordance with the right to truth."

In the end, the fight evaporated; the government couldn't find enough buses, teachers, or classrooms to carry out its plan.

29

Of the many topics the bishops debated, money never seemed to be one. The Vatican lived mostly from the endowment it got in the 1929 treaty with Italy, now multiplied many times by inflation and investment success. Another ten million dollars a year came from voluntary contributions by Catholics around the world, known as Peter's pence, a medieval practice that had been revived when the papacy lost its vast estates to a reunified Italy in 1870.

Most of the wealth that would show up on a proper audit of the Church consisted of historic buildings, plazas, and art; their value was enormous but of little use in paying bills. "The income-producing holdings of the Vatican," Father Andrew Greeley has noted, "are perhaps a little larger than the endowment of Harvard University and substantially smaller than the book value of the Ford Foundation. A tidy sum . . . but scarcely fabled wealth."

Not worrying about money came easily to Wojtyla. It was both a personality trait and a philosophy. But Pope Paul, with his political/financial family background, paid enough attention that he eventually grew dissatisfied with the stagnant investment returns delivered by the Vatican agency managing the

1929 treaty money. In 1968 and 1969, Paul revamped the Vatican's two financial arms. The agency that supervised the 1929 treaty money and paid salaries
and other Vatican bills was labeled the Administration of the Property of the
Holy See, or APSA.

The other financial arm was the Vatican bank, or IOR, which Pius XII had
organized in 1942. Bishop Wycislo and Archbishop Sapieha had found IOR to
be a convenient channel for American relief funds to Poland after World War II.
Cardinal Spellman of New York had used IOR to secretly help the CIA manipulate the 1948 Italian election. Mother Teresa used IOR to minister to the poor
of Calcutta. And Vatican clerks and janitors kept accounts there to pay bills.

Later, after two huge scandals, hordes of financial detectives and investigative reporters from the West would try to unravel APSA and IOR. It would be
among the most publicized and poorly understood episodes of John Paul II's
papacy. The investigators tended to overlook the unusual circumstance in
which the two institutions had been founded: the Vatican was both an independent state and an autocracy. As long as the sitting pope stayed satisfied,
nobody had to write anything down or inform anyone of what was happening.

The answer to many questions that would later be asked about Vatican
finances is that *nobody knew.* The information had gone to the grave with a pope,
or with a papal adviser who didn't tell the pope what he was doing. There was
less deceit than people imagined. On the other hand, the irresponsibility of it
fairly boggled the mind—which is one reason crooks felt invited.

APSA (or its predecessor) had invested the 1929 treaty money in an unusual
way, buying a controlling interest in various firms, including construction companies and manufacturers of everything from spaghetti to pharmaceuticals.
Ordinarily, investment funds prefer to own small blocs of shares in a great
number of companies, both to gain the safety of diversification and to leave
management in professional hands. But the Piuses wanted to control the management of the companies they invested in, in order to govern their morality.

IOR followed the same policy as APSA. It bought controlling interests in
banks, both in Italy and abroad. And it wasn't clear to outsiders—one suspects
it might not have been clear to several popes—whose money IOR was investing. A bank has two kinds of money: its own capital and the funds it is holding for depositors. To protect depositors, Western governments require banks
to maintain their capital—the owners' investment—as a percentage of total
funds; the Vatican, as an independent autocracy, had no such requirement. No
record has ever been disclosed of what capital, if any, IOR started with or
maintained; no record may exist.

In the bank's early days, its operations were all supposed to have some connection to "works of religion" (the English translation of the name whose

acronym is IOR). Even helping the CIA rig the 1948 Italian election was ratio-
nalized as having such a connection. But eventually the bank began to take
deposits, transfer funds, and do other banking business for friends of friends
of Church employees—clients whose closest connection to religion may have
been going to Easter Mass. People saw that IOR had a big advantage: since it
was on Vatican soil, it wasn't subject to Italian financial controls. Italy's tax col-
lectors and criminal investigators didn't know how much money IOR's clients
had or where outside the country they took it.

For many years, IOR was run by an aristocrat friend of Pius XII's, who
retired about when Paul VI took over. His two chief civilian underlings at IOR
stayed on, as did an aggressive tax lawyer and businessman he had brought in as
a consultant: Michele Sindona, whose base was in Milan but whose roots and
birthplace were in Sicily. Sindona had started in business in Sicily with Mafia
help. The significance of this seemed to pass everyone by.

Early on, Sindona persuaded IOR to invest money to help him buy a prominent Milan bank, which IOR then used to store and transfer funds. Sindona
was friendly with the archbishop of Milan, Cardinal Montini, who would
become Pope Paul VI. The Sicilian could be a powerful friend: when the archbishop and future pope undertook to fund a retirement home, for example,
Sindona raised two million dollars from businessmen in one day.[1]

When Paul became pope, he decided to change the unusual investment
strategies of APSA and IOR. Not only did their policy of owning whole companies sacrifice safety, it also didn't accomplish the original purpose of avoiding controversy, as disputes inevitably dogged large businesses. (There was even
a rumor, apparently false, that APSA's pharmaceutical company manufactured
birth-control pills.) Paul resolved to diversify the portfolios of APSA and
IOR—in itself a wise move. But for counsel he turned to his banking friend
Sindona, the Mafia ally. Paul seemed delighted to learn that the two civilian
bank administrators he had inherited from Pius XII also liked Sindona.

Early in Paul's reign, Sindona bought out most of IOR's holdings in a Swiss
bank and a second Milan bank, leaving IOR a minority position in each, with
a seat on the board. In early 1969, through complicated arrangements, Sindona
also raised funds to buy most of APSA's stake in its big construction company,
as well as its stakes in the pasta manufacturer and two other businesses.*

---

* In a grand twist, Sindona quickly resold much of the construction firm—Società Gen-
erale Immobiliare—to Gulf & Western Industries, an American company that also
owned Paramount Pictures. Paramount then made the *Godfather* movies, which portray
fictional high-level financial conspiracies between the Mafia and the Vatican, specifically
involving a construction firm called . . . Immobiliare.

Paul also wanted to install a strong overall boss at IOR, someone he could trust. He picked Monsignor Paul Marcinkus, an American who went about as far at the Vatican as his hale-fellow, well-met personality could take him. Nonsense has been published that because Marcinkus was born in Cicero, Illinois, headquarters of Al Capone, he had some tie with the American Mafia. In fact, he was the son of a Lithuanian-born window washer and was enrolled in seminaries from the age of thirteen. After his ordination, Marcinkus headed to Rome for studies and, it would turn out, his career.

At six foot three and a muscular 230 pounds, he excelled at all the American school sports and was a lifelong golfer. He learned Spanish, French, and Italian. After school, he went to work for the Vatican secretary of state. As he drove around Rome, Father Marcinkus would do favors for people—including Archbishop Montini, the future Paul VI, then a colleague at the secretariate of state. "I used to see him walking around the grounds and I'd give him a lift in my car," Marcinkus told the *Chicago Tribune* later. "We got along well."

After diplomatic postings in Bolivia and Canada, Marcinkus returned to the Roman curia a veteran. He kept an apartment big enough to allow him to play enthusiastic host to visiting Chicago churchmen, who brought him crates of steak and lobsters as gifts.[2]

The Church offers many levels of ambience to its priests and bishops. They get modest official salaries, but that often has little to do with how well they live. Some, like Wojtyla, give away what they get. Another cardinal, Franz König of Vienna, says that before he retired, he was paid three hundred dollars a month plus free room and board; he neither smoked nor drank, so he gave away about $120 a month and used the rest on books, travel, and cleaning for his five suits (because he didn't like to buy new ones). He vacationed in Florida, but churchmen can travel cheaply if they room and board in church quarters. He drove a Mercedes because the company discounted the cost.

Some priests, however, seem to think nothing of taking substantial gifts—whether opulent goods or thousands of dollars in cash—from wealthy parishioners, not for charity but for their own comfort. They live in swank private apartments. Some diocesan residences are very comfortably decked out.

Most such quarters in Poland—particularly the archbishops' palaces in Warsaw and Krakow—are modest, sometimes surprisingly threadbare. Other countries are more prone to luxury. In Rome, even a monsignor with a good job in the curia seems able to live comfortably and dine well if he wants to.

There is a clear difference, though, between accepting personal gifts from parishioners seeking a churchman's attention and taking a payment specifically in connection with the expenditure of Church funds—that is, a bribe. Those who later suspected Marcinkus of corruption never offered evidence that he took a single wrongful dime (or lira). He probably didn't. But he wasn't especially discerning about people who did. He liked their company and sharing their amenities. No one would have mistaken him for an ascetic.

During Vatican II, Marcinkus had been a natural to run a kind of visitors' bureau to make sure the American delegates got the extracurricular activities they needed. That was how he began golfing with Bishop Wycislo and Father John Courtney Murray, author of the declaration on religious liberty. When the Chicago diocese later built a residence in Rome for American priests working in the curia, Marcinkus got the job of organizing it.

He and Montini continued to lunch regularly, even after Montini became Pope Paul. He also struck up a friendship with Paul's secretary, Monsignor Pasquale Macchi, with whom he sometimes went to restaurants after the pope had gone to bed. After Paul was frighteningly jostled by overzealous crowds on a Middle East trip in 1964, it was decided that he needed somebody beefy, with street smarts, to handle security. Who better than Marcinkus?

On Paul's next trip, to India, security worked smoothly under Marcinkus's supervision. Then he translated for Paul at a meeting with President Johnson; from then on, he was indispensable. Without any thought of relieving him of his bodyguard duties, Paul gave Marcinkus the added task of overseeing the Vatican bank. Marcinkus owed no allegiances to the Italian businessmen who, Paul could see, were running the bank and its affiliated companies almost as personal feifdoms. Yet Marcinkus could get along with the businessmen—or with anyone else, for that matter—with his meaty handshake and hearty howdy-do.

Later, after the scandals, Marcinkus asserted that when the IOR job was offered to him, he replied, "You must be out of your minds! . . . I have no experience in banking!" But then, he explained, "I don't believe that I have the right to refuse."

As for formal training: "I didn't have any time. . . . When I came into this job, I went to New York. I went to Chase Manhattan for a day or two; I went to a place to see how stocks and stuff operated; I went to Chicago, and friends introduced me to people at the Continental Bank—they gave me a kind of three-day course, taking me through everything. I spent another day at a trust business. Then I spent the whole day in a small bank seeing how the operation worked. That was it. But what kind of training do you need? . . . I was always one for figuring out systems and numbers. . . . As for financial experience . . . let's say I counted the Sunday collection and never got it wrong!"[3]

Contrary to some of what has been written, there is no evidence that

Marcinkus knew Michele Sindona before Paul gave him the IOR job. There is no evidence he had anything to do with Sindona's takeover of APSA and IOR properties up to that time. But Marcinkus met Sindona quickly. Chicago's Continental Illinois Bank, where he went for training, was run by a friend and associate of Sindona's.[4] Moreover, it was not in Marcinkus's nature to be suspicious of people with money or to confine important relationships to stuffy offices when there were restaurants, golf courses, parties, and villas.

Soon after Marcinkus took over IOR, Sindona told two friends, both Italian businessmen, about his influence at the Vatican. They were Licio Gelli and Umberto Ortolani, who ran a secret Masonic lodge whose members included high-level corporate executives and politicians. (The Masons are a largely Protestant group that some Catholics joined against the wishes of their Church.) Through the lodge, Gelli and Ortolani organized many illegal activities, including the funneling of bribes from corporations to politicians so the corporations could flout the law.

One lodge member, Roberto Calvi, was an ambitious executive at Banco Ambrosiano, perhaps Italy's most prominent privately owned bank. Calvi approached his lodge friends—Gelli, Ortolani, and Sindona—with a plan to secretly buy up shares in Banco Ambrosiano and gain control of it. Soon Calvi was becoming chummy with Marcinkus.

Like many other political and corporate officials in the lodge, Calvi would later go to jail for his activities. But in 1969, and with all these schemes still secret, Marcinkus welcomed his company. As far as he and Pope Paul were concerned, any friend of Sindona's was fine.

Five years later, in the summer of 1974, a genial young American priest who taught in Rome was invited to a cocktail party and found himself talking to Mark Antinucci, a native Sicilian. Antinucci, a tall, dark, Anthony Quinn type, said he had made a small fortune in business in the United States and was now multiplying it in Italy. He introduced himself as a partner of Michele Sindona, the big banker with entree at the Vatican. By now almost everyone knew of Sindona, who had recently added to his collection of banks in Italy and Switzerland by buying control of America's twentieth-largest bank, the Franklin National in New York.

The young priest, John Navone, gently tried to ascertain what Antinucci actually did for Sindona. "Investments," was the only reply he could get. But when Antinucci learned that Father Navone was from Oregon, his ears pricked up. Did Navone know Yamhill County?

Very well, Navone said.

"I just bought a ranch there!" Antinucci exclaimed. "I want you to come to dinner and tell my wife all about it." After giving Father Navone the location and time, Antinucci added a curious afterthought: "Wear your collar."

When Father Navone arrived for dinner, he found himself seated directly across the table from Archbishop Marcinkus, president of IOR. It came out that Marcinkus regularly played golf with Antinucci and knew his partner Sindona. (After Sindona bought the Franklin National Bank, Marcinkus had told him, "Hey! You operate over there like you operate here in Italy, you'll end up in jail."[5] Yet Marcinkus didn't break off their relationship.)

By the time Father Navone met him at the dinner party, years had passed since Marcinkus first lunched with Sindona and his friend Roberto Calvi.[6] They now knew each other well. Calvi had climbed the ranks to become general manager of the giant Banco Ambrosiano and had given a good job there to the inexperienced son of one of Marcinkus's top civilian assistants at IOR. Even at this stage, however, Marcinkus probably didn't understand what Sindona and Calvi were doing, or how he was helping them. They simply proposed deals to him, and he went along.

What Sindona and Calvi were really doing was stealing funds from the big, reputable banks they managed and using the funds to secretly buy shares in each other's banks. The idea was to gain hidden control over billions of dollars belonging to unsuspecting depositors from Milan to Manhattan. To get away with stealing funds, Sindona and Calvi hid their activity behind layers of front companies and made the transactions as complicated as possible.*

The hidden ownership of the front companies in these transactions wasn't stated in the legal documents. The underlying interconnections were pieced together only later, during years of investigation by professional financial sleuths. What is significant is that the front companies gained credibility for their other dealings by doing business with IOR, whom everyone trusted.

As Sindona and Calvi came to control the funds of more and more bank depositors, they bribed Italian government officials through the secret, corrupt

---

* An example: an affiliate of Calvi's Banco Ambrosiano in Liechtenstein, through a subsidiary in Luxembourg, loaned Calvi money to buy control of a bank in the Bahamas (on whose board Archbishop Marcinkus sat). The Bahamian bank, through another loan, then financed the purchase of shares in a Swiss bank that Sindona had bought control of from IOR. Sindona then kicked back part of the money he received on account of the Swiss shares to Calvi as a "commission"—though the money had come in the first place from depositors at Calvi's bank. It's okay not to understand this; no one was supposed to.

Masonic lodge. Again, there is no evidence at all that Marcinkus knew of the bribes. But under his leadership, IOR invested ever more heavily in the stock of Calvi's Banco Ambrosiano.

Calvi and Sindona needed to do business at "offshore" institutions where they could hide money from Western bank auditors and government regulators. They chose Switzerland and the Bahamas largely because those countries offered secrecy. IOR also offered secrecy—not because its founders had intended to hide criminal schemes, but because it answered only to a pope and an archbishop, who had studied Mariology while other bankers were studying accounting.

In 1971, Calvi set up his private bank in the Bahamas, a place known for its lax banking laws and cheaply bribed public officials. Of $2.5 million in original capital, Archbishop Marcinkus signed up IOR for a 20 percent share. He then deposited another $16 million of IOR funds—a lot of money for the Vatican bank—to help Calvi's Bahamian bank get started. To oversee this investment, Marcinkus joined the Bahamian bank's board of directors.

Archbishop Marcinkus told me in a series of phone chats from his retirement home near Phoenix that he would answer my questions after he resolved some "personal problems."[7] After two years, he withdrew the offer and denied he had ever made it. But back in his Vatican days, he informed colleagues that he had invested IOR money in Calvi's Bahamian bank and joined its board because the profit potential seemed good.

Others note the golf is also good in the Bahamas in December, when the board met. But sources including Cardinal Egidio Vagnozzi, whom Paul appointed to supervise Church economic affairs, have confirmed that the pope was urging his money managers to make more profit. "We are a poor church," Paul told them.[8]

Marcinkus got this message and began fishing for profits in odd waters. IOR money was given on account to a Sindona company that hired a shady Los Angeles stockbroker to invest it. The broker used the IOR money to manipulate stock shares; a federal judge cited both the Vatican and the stockbroker for violating U.S. securities laws and made IOR repay three hundred thousand dollars in profits.[9] Marcinkus even talked, apparently unwittingly, to two Italian men who were trying to fence $950 million in counterfeit bonds for some American Mafiosi. He denied buying the bonds and wasn't charged; the gangsters were sent to jail.[10]

Although Father Navone knew nothing of these details when he met Archbishop Marcinkus at the dinner party, he still sensed that something was not right. When the party broke up, Antinucci, the host, had a secretary drive Navone back to his quarters at the Gregorian University, where he taught theology. On the way, as they passed new building after new building, the secretary would point and say, "They're all Mr. Antinucci's."

A week later, Father Navone flew home to visit his mother in Seattle. Over breakfast, he glanced at the *Seattle Post-Intelligencer*, and his jaw dropped. The FBI had discovered that Yamhill County, Oregon, where Mr. Antinucci from Sicily had just bought a ranch, had become the Northwest's regional distribution center for illegal drugs from Mexico. Who was this Antinucci, anyway?[11]

Navone had cause to ask himself that question again a few months later, when Italian bank examiners announced that Sindona's two Italian banks were insolvent. They had been looted by Sindona of nearly four hundred million dollars, which money had been shipped abroad in loans to other companies he secretly controlled. With Sindona's Italian banks unable to provide funds, insolvency quickly rippled through his empire. A week later his Franklin National Bank in New York collapsed with a shortfall of two billion dollars, the largest bank failure in American history to that time. Depositors were paid by the Federal Deposit Insurance Corporation, backed by American taxpayers. Sindona's Swiss bank also failed.

Sindona was convicted of enormous frauds. Much of the money was unrecoverable, lost in deals that couldn't be untangled. Prosecutors in the United States and Italy also pinned on Sindona the financing of six hundred million dollars' worth of heroin imported into the U.S. by the Gambino Mafia family, as well as the gunshot assassination of an Italian government official who had been assigned to try to locate money Sindona had hidden away. Sindona, Pope Paul's old friend and benefactor and now Marcinkus's, faced imprisonment, effectively for life.

Back in Italy, Father Navone got a Christmas card from Antinucci declaring, "I am no longer a partner of Michele Sindona"—an odd sentiment for a Christmas card, Navone thought.

Amazingly, Calvi's career wasn't touched by the scandal. Although he was known to be friends with Sindona, their business ties remained hidden to outsiders. Somehow the illusion was created that Calvi came into IOR *after* Sindona, as a sort of honest replacement for the thief. In truth, of course, the two men had been hand-in-glove before Archbishop Marcinkus took over IOR.

The Vatican's losses in the bank failures were either insured or relatively small. Besides, Sindona had bought a lot of assets from the Vatican at good prices back when Pope Paul decided to diversify. No one seemed to realize what this meant: the Vatican had been paid profitably with money Sindona had stolen from public depositors in his banks.

Archbishop Marcinkus stayed on at IOR, a papal favorite despite this appalling trail of scandal. And he continued dealing with Calvi as if nothing had happened.[12]*

Among the cardinals, the man who would ultimately have to deal with the IOR mess, Karol Wojtyla, was particularly—even spectacularly—ill equipped to do so. Worthy projects he promoted—a Krakow hospice, for example—sometimes languished because he never considered how they might be paid for.[13] Bishop Pieronek, the curial staff chief on whose shoulders it fell to carry out Wojtyla's plans, recalls that once, when the cardinal was "visiting someplace in Poland, someone put an envelope in his pocket [containing] ten thousand zlotys, which was then a lot of money," a donation for some project. "He forgot the money was there." Later, "he went to Czechoslovakia, [and] the border guards found the envelope and accused him of smuggling."

Wojtyla was not generally absentminded; when something mattered to him, he attended to the slightest detail. On one occasion, irritated by an article that appeared in *Wiez*, he phoned a priest who he knew was the uncle of the author and asked him to enlighten his nephew. For a play featuring his former leading lady, Halina Krolikiewicz Kwiatkowski, he advised on the cathedral stage sets, right down to the artwork; then he came to watch. When it came to money, however, Wojtyla had a weakness that was just the opposite of many other men's: he simply never thought about it.

30

One manifestation of the "progress" that Wojtyla so mistrusted was the movement of populations from farm to city. As agriculture came to depend more on machines than on manual labor, family farmers sold (or lost) land to big agribusinesses. Under capitalism and socialism alike, rural family life was shattered; generations went their separate ways. This sort of upheaval had been painful enough in the United States and Western Europe, but now it was under way throughout the Third World, where industrial growth hadn't cre-

---

* Although a longer list appears in the endnote, I want to pay prominent tribute here to the two best books I know on Vatican finances: *The Money Changers* by Charles Raw and *The Calvi Affair* by Larry Gurwin. Gurwin was also personally helpful to me. His book is the more readable of the two, though the Raw book—partly because it was written after the main investigations were over—is more definitive, one of the most relentless investigative jobs I have ever seen on any subject.

ated a multitude of city jobs. The result was a blight that Wojtyla would face as pope, when he turned the Church toward the poor regions where its greatest potential growth lay.

He was particularly attuned to this crisis because, alone among the countries of Europe, Poland had felt the same pull in the 1970s. As a result, Wojtyla and Wyszynski began to articulate a Jeffersonian agrarian romanticism coupled with an Old World Catholic morality—a philosophy Wojtyla would carry with him to the Vatican.

Western banking was a culprit in this scenario. Banks had developed what seemed to be a profitable business lending money to Third World dictatorships that were part of the U.S. anti-communist program. The banks reasoned that U.S. military power would make it easier for them to collect from such dictators than from individuals. But Polish Party Boss Gierek decided that he, too, could tap these loans to jump-start Poland's flagging economy—not realizing that so long as the economy was socialist-driven, it would continue to flag. The notion of an influx of money was so attractive, however, that Gierek's Soviet masters let him borrow it.

Unfortunately, these loans tended to turn any orderly retreat from family farming into a rout, forcing dictators to export more produce just to meet their loan payments. Had the loan money been invested by entrepreneurs building viable businesses, new wealth might have been created, to repay the loans and leave a profit—the way borrowing is supposed to work. But under dictators, the money was more often stolen or squandered, as it was in, say, Zaire and Brazil.

The loan system did in the American bloc what socialism had done in the Soviet bloc: Government price-fixing encouraged plantation farming for export and made family farming even less viable. This in turn exacerbated the tendency of youth to move to cities and join the electronic culture of music and television, while the family farms died with their parents. Many countries lost the ability to feed themselves as masses of people in their prime working years abandoned the fields and gathered, strangers to each other, in cities that were unable to support them either economically or spiritually.

Poland's industrial base was geared to export to the Soviet Union. To repay the Western loans, family farms were pressured to convert to large ham and dairy export operations. Wyszynski and Wojtyla were dead set against this. They undertook a campaign in 1975, declaring,

> The flight from villages to towns . . . is a marked cause for unease in our nation today. . . .

Love for the land demands that we stay on this soil. . . . Do not
flee from the villages, do not flee from the farms. Stay and raise the
standard of life. . . . Stay like a tree, rooted in the soil of the homeland, so that our nation will not be pushed around within its ethnic
borders as a result of underpopulation and insufficient union with
the soil.

"Underpopulation" referred to Wyszynski's fear that Polish independence
was threatened by Russian and German population growth. Poles who moved
to cities had fewer children; they were also more subject to government control.
The so-called debt trap was one more global problem that Wojtyla could relate
to from firsthand experience.

In 1976, Wojtyla was vested by Pope Paul with a singular honor: during Lent,
he would lead Paul and about eighty curial officials, including many cardinals,
in a weeklong spiritual retreat. To prepare for the twenty-two lectures he would
give, Wojtyla characteristically turned less to libraries than to the outdoors. He
went on several mountain skiing weekends (always with a Church function to
justify the trip)[1] and stayed at Kalwaria Zebrzydowska, the Stations of the
Cross in the forest. In Rome, he drove straight for Mentorella, his mountain
sanctuary since student days. All his favored hideaways were so rugged that just
climbing the steep driveways to the buildings might tax the fainthearted; once
there, Wojtyla would disappear up miles of lonely trails.

Pope Paul's "retreat" was spiritual rather than geographical, taking place
entirely within the Vatican. Even at age seventy-eight, Paul took the willful suffering of Lent so seriously that he wore a bristly hair shirt and thorns under his
cassock (he did this on other solemn occasions as well, which helps explain his
pained expression in many photographs). But beyond that, he also now suffered
from osteoarthritis in his legs and neck, and had to be helped to his seat.

Wojtyla structured his talks around the fifteen "mysteries" described in the
Catholic faith, concerning Jesus's birth, death, and resurrection. He addressed
the burgeoning conflicts within the Church, entitling the lectures as a whole the
"Sign of Contradiction," after a prediction in the Gospel of Luke that Jesus
would spark disagreements. Published later as a book, the lectures were
described even by cardinals as difficult.[2]

Yet as ever, Wojtyla inspired those who were on hand to hear his words much
more than he did those who merely read them on paper. The talks emphasized
his view that Christianity embraced all the world, that Jesus' death brought

about the "birth of 'the new man,' whether or not man was aware of such rebirth and whether or not he accepted it." He compared the contemplation of Catholic religious orders to that of "the desert Bedouin ... and perhaps the Buddhist ... as he purifies his thought, preparing the way to Nirvana."

Wojtyla also displayed his fascination with science and his quest to find there a common ground for all religions. He compared the infinity of God to the concept of infinity in mathematics.

He introduced an idea that would later preoccupy him as pope, that the very beginning of the Bible was "the key to understanding today's world. ... It may sound a trifle strange," he said, "but I think it is true that today one cannot understand either Sartre or Marx without having first read and pondered very deeply the first three chapters of Genesis." He dwelled on the temptation of Adam and Eve by the serpent, who for him became a real devil. "The history of mankind," he said, "will be subject to rule both by the Word and the anti-Word, the Gospel and the anti-Gospel."

He told stories of Poland and seldom missed a chance to flatter Pope Paul, quoting him constantly and rebuking his critics. He even compared the opposition to Paul's birth-control encyclical to the rejection of Jesus.

He painted despairing pictures of all "the so-called 'three worlds' " of humanity: totalitarian ("the age of a new enslavement"), democratic ("where men have grown sick from too much prosperity and too much freedom"), and Third World ("where millions endure hunger and live in conditions of dire poverty").

31

Vatican events such as the synods and the Lenten retreat made Wojtyla a leader in the Church. Given that his travel held such peril for communism, I repeatedly asked former Polish communist officials why they let him out of the country. It turns out the Soviets used to ask the same question.

Polish delegations were hauled to Moscow throughout the 1960s, '70s and '80s, even to see Brezhnev himself, according to former Polish Foreign Minister Jozef Czyrek. "We were constantly asked about this suicide: Why do you allow this kind of political activity within the Church? It wasn't a disagreement; they just did not comprehend it. And we always answered that Poles are overwhelmingly Catholic, and religious beliefs cannot be regulated."

Jerzy Kuberski, ambassador to the Vatican under the communists, says the Soviets constantly insisted "we had to get rid of the Church. It was the source of all the Polish problems." But even the families of communists still believed in Catholicism, he says. When the time came for a child to be baptized or take first communion, they would go to a relative's village where they wouldn't be recognized by coworkers and hold the ceremony there. "Life had two layers," Kuberski says. "We lived in such confusion!"[1]

In Warsaw, a popular joke was that Party Boss Gierek drove the biggest car in the world: the seat was in Warsaw, the backrest in Silesia (the mining district), the brakes in Gdansk (the strike center), and the steering wheel in Moscow. Another joke held that it was easy to be a good Catholic and a good communist at the same time, because Catholics believed but did not practice, and communists practiced but did not believe.

As Wyszynski aged, even he gradually acknowledged the need for Wojtyla to step up. He knew Poles were disappointed by his passive response when the Soviets forced new, ideological clauses into the Polish constitution. On a visit to Krakow, he spoke to Wojtyla for the first time in the personal, familiar usage of the Polish language, omitting formal titles. Touched, Wojtyla felt the baton slowly being passed.[2]

A watershed came June 17, 1976, Corpus Christi Day, an annual celebration of the Eucharist that is much bigger in Poland than it is in the West. Offices and factories empty for a few hours, and priests have the ear of the country just as they do on All Souls' Day, except on this day the mood is festive. In communist Poland, the day acquired significance as the only time people could legally gather in the streets for anything other than a communist event. Kazimierz Barcikowski, former Party first secretary for Krakow, says that among his annual duties was thinking up new ways to ruin the Corpus Christi Day parade.

Two events fueled a confrontation in 1976. That spring, young people had organized, as they had in 1968, into a "Student Committee of Solidarity"; members were jumped and badly beaten by police, and one was killed. And the government imposed last-second changes on the course of Wojtyla's procession, to keep it away from the main market square.

The procession stopped four times, and "each of [Wojtyla's] four homilies was increasingly outspoken," says Krzysztof Kozlowski, the *Tygodnik Powszechny* editor. As always, Wojtyla kept to religious language, but his meaning was unmistakably political. When he lectured on "Satan, the Prince of Darkness," people understood that he was referring to communism. Censors barred *Tygodnik Powszechny* from reporting it, but Radio Free Europe did a story, and all Krakow talked about it.

Wojtyla's increasing militancy reflected that of the nation. Just a week later came the first rumble of the revolution that would ultimately overthrow communism in Europe. The government announced food price increases of 39 percent. Workers struck at the huge tractor factory at Ursus, near Warsaw, and at the metal works at Radom, sixty miles to the south. Party headquarters were burned. Strikes soon spread throughout the country. Workers at Ursus and Radom were pushed through gauntlets of club-wielding police,[3] and twenty-five hundred were jailed. A priest who came to administer last rites to the wounded was murdered by police. The specter rose of the 1970 massacres in Gdynia and Gdansk.

The next night, the government rescinded the price increase. But it refused entreaties, including one from the bishops, to drop charges against those jailed. In what would prove to be a big mistake, the government chose instead to put on a show of toughness. A new minister for religious affairs, Kazimierz Kakol, extended censorship to almost all priestly writing, even memos. Znak's political headquarters was closed (though not its publication office), and passports were withdrawn from Znak officers. New rules limited evangelizing to the confines of churches.

Instead of being intimidated by the harassment, however, Catholic intellectuals scurried to form new clubs and alliances, to replace Znak and try to free the jailed workers. They began circulating copies of an article published from exile in Paris by Adam Michnik, the Jewish former communist who had helped lead the 1968 student rebellion. "In today's Poland," Michnik wrote, "the Marxist-Leninist doctrine is . . . an empty shell, its gestures nothing but an official rite." He called for popular resistance.

At this crucial juncture, on July 23, 1976, Wojtyla boarded a plane for his long-planned second extended trip to North America.

Wojtyla led nineteen Polish bishop delegates to an International Eucharistic Conference in Philadelphia, in connection with the two-hundredth anniversary of American independence. Anna-Teresa Tymieniecka, determined to remedy the fact that "no one had ever heard of the philosopher Wojtyla," booked him for a lecture at Harvard.

She and her husband, Harvard professor and former White House adviser Hendryk Houthakker, were given an extraordinary amount of the cardinal's time. Yet they remain miffed that he delayed his arrival at the Harvard guest house to stay with Polish priests in New York and Boston, forcing the cancellation of events they had planned. "The way he behaved himself was unruly, not the way of a great statesman," says Houthakker.

Wojtyla spent his second and third days in the United States at the World Institute for Advanced Phenomenological Research and Learning, headquartered at the Tymieniecka-Houthakker summer house in Vermont. They spent hours polishing and rehearsing his speech. His "spoken English was still rather rough," according to a Polish-American scholar they invited along.[4]

The next day, Wojtyla was supposed to lunch in Vermont, then drive to a reception at the residence of Cardinal Humberto Medeiros of Boston. "But at noon," Tymieniecka says, "Wojtyla is on a raft on the pond and doesn't want to leave. When he finally got out, [Father] Dziwisz [his secretary] had no dry pants for him." Wojtyla wound up three hours late for Cardinal Medeiros's reception, Tymieniecka says, and wore a plain black cassock because he didn't stop for his cardinal's outfit.

On the other hand, Thomas Crooks, then head of the Harvard Summer School, says Wojtyla was "one of the most impressive men I've met in my life, an absolutely radiant personality." Crooks remembers that when he showed Dziwisz and Wojtyla their quarters, Wojtyla remarked that Dziwisz had been given the bigger room. Crooks was momentarily mortified, thinking he had slipped up—then realized he was being teased.

Crooks remembers telling the Boston archdiocese that Harvard usually paid speakers five hundred dollars, and asking how much to give Wojtyla.

"Don't give the cardinal any money! He can't handle money!" the excited voice came back. Crooks thought he'd saved $500. "But you can give it to the chaplain," he was told—and Dziwisz got the stipend.

The speech at Harvard was one Wojtyla had delivered earlier, in Switzerland; it said that both Marxism and capitalism were essentially materialistic and that only Christian spirituality could cope with the alienation of modern society.[5] It went over well, though much of that seems due to Wojtyla's personal charm, prominently on display at a reception afterward; among those having tea with him was Zbigniew Brzezinski, who would soon be President Carter's national security adviser.

Wojtyla also spoke at Catholic University in Washington. Jude Dougherty, dean of philosophy there, met him at the airport and vividly remembers their drive to campus. Wojtyla, he suddenly thought, was a possible pope. "I had met enough cardinals to know the pool is not all that great," Dougherty says.

The two men discovered they agreed on several issues that separated them from most American churchmen: "The impoverished state of the Church in America" is the way Dougherty recalls Wojtyla's phrasing it. They concurred that "Vatican II had wreaked a lot of havoc. The spirit unleashed then" had reduced the incentive to be a priest. New standing was being given to theological dissidents; too much traditional ritual had been shed.

"The American bishops especially didn't seem to have much backbone, or willingness to stand up to trendiness," they concluded. "Maybe I was doing most of the talking, but he was agreeing," Dougherty says. Wojtyla talked knowledgeably about the case of Father Charles Curran, a Catholic University professor who had challenged Pope Paul's birth-control encyclical and now, with faculty backing, was resisting the school's attempts to fire him for it. Wojtyla said the U.S. needed "a stronger Episcopate" to control such errant members.

Archbishop Weakland, from his travels as head of the Benedictines, also sensed that Wojtyla and other Poles had "very negative notions about Americans—that the U.S. is superficial, not intellectually profound." Clear as was Wojtyla's opposition to Nazism and communism, he was also out of step with the eighteenth-century philosophers who had set the tone for Western democracy. He "looks at the Age of Enlightenment differently than we do," Weakland says. "He's much more critical of it. His works and thinking were definitely more anti-capitalism, anti-Enlightenment."

Wojtyla's uncomfortable fit with the American milieu seems further illustrated by his strange relationship with Tymieniecka and Houthakker. Despite the extraordinary time he allowed them, they were irritated when he backed out of a Washington dinner Tymieniecka had arranged for two dozen "dignitaries" and a meeting Houthakker had set up with President Ford. (Wojtyla later said he didn't meet Ford, who was running for election, because it "might be given a political interpretation.")[6]

Wojtyla spent several more days at their World Institute/summer house at the end of his trip, only to dismay Tymieniecka by not having rewritten *The Acting Person* as she wished. "The work was arduous and extremely slow," she later wrote. "Each phrase . . . had to be discussed. . . . All this led to long-winded arguments." For example, Wojtyla "absolutely insisted on" using the word *mirroring* to mean one thing when she told him it meant something else entirely in another branch of philosophy.[7]

But before he left, she got his signature on contracts giving her "all rights of translation in all languages" to *The Acting Person* and calling her edition "the definitive version."

Wojtyla traveled to Detroit, Buffalo, Miami, Phoenix, Los Angeles, and San Francisco. Everywhere, there was heavy emphasis on Polish-Americans. He also deepened his relationships with American church leaders he would later deal with as pope; Cardinal John Cody of Chicago and Archbishop Joseph Bernardin of Cincinnati would repay his visits to them with visits to Krakow.

Wojtyla had remarked to Cardinal Krol that he "thought American Indians should be interested in Catholicism because they have similar beliefs." So Krol took him to some Indian camps in the Southwest, where they honored early Indian Catholics and urged the appointment of an Indian bishop.

In Chicago, Bishop Abramowicz, who toured parishes with him, says, "He just couldn't understand why the neighborhoods kept changing. You'd show him a [traditionally] Polish parish, and today it was half Negro. I remember taking him through Hyde Park, a nice section, and some of the black belt, full of garbage [and] vandalism. He kept asking why. I told him it was basically racism. And poverty and economics. You couldn't get an answer or an opinion from him. Just why the white man got the job and the black man didn't."

Throughout his U.S. travels, Wojtyla was bothered by what seemed to him an absence of nationhood. In *Tygodnik Powszechny*, he wrote,

> Belonging to a nation of fathers and forefathers reaches deep into the conscience of man, requiring truth about himself. . . . This is a real problem in the structure of American society. The extent of this problem is demonstrated today by the so-called Black Question. I have not noticed any average American—even of the WASP type—express the words "American Nation" with the same conviction that an average Pole in Poland speaks of the Polish nation.[8]

At the Eucharistic Congress in Philadelphia, Wojtyla spoke in English to forty thousand listeners at Veterans Stadium, recalling the Polish volunteers who had fought in the American Revolution and the dismemberment of Poland itself at about the same time. He also spoke at a massive Polish-American celebration at the shrine Father Zembrzuski had built at nearby Doylestown. The Doylestown event, however, couldn't have been as happy as it looked; financial clouds continued to gather around Wyszynski's old friend Zembrzuski.

Wojtyla's handling of the Doylestown scandal revealed a nonchalance about financial wrongdoing that would play an important part in his papacy and even in the Solidarity revolution. It was ironic, considering that he advocated tighter control of priests in other areas.

A few months before Wojtyla came to the U.S., Pope Paul received the report he had ordered on the Doylestown shrine from blue-ribbon investigators and accountants. They warned Paul that criminal prosecution was possible. The Pauline order had sold $4.3 million in bonds and raised $5 million more in donations for the shrine, which was originally to cost $3.3 million; now, still unfinished, the structure was appraised at only $1.3 million. Where was the rest of the money?

Pauline monks everywhere took vows of poverty befitting the desert hermit who had founded their order (not the Paul of the New Testament). In America, however, Paulines had cars, credit cards, checking accounts, and expensive modern appliances. According to reporter Sherwood's articles, Zembrzuski and other monks lived like corporate executives, jetting frequently to Poland and elsewhere. A few monks who had wanted to maintain their poverty vows told the investigators they had been rebuked for it by their high-living colleagues.

Although the Paulines had declared assets of $21 million to sell the bonds, the shrine now was nearly $8 million in the red, the accountants said. Cardinal Krol agreed to raise $5 million to pay back the bondholders while trying to keep the scandal quiet. The editor of the diocesan newspaper that had exposed the whole mess was fired. Reporter Sherwood left, too—but was hired by the Camden *Courier-Post* to develop the story for a mass audience.

Father Zembrzuski was ordered by Paul's Irish investigators to turn over his credit cards and car keys and get on a plane to Rome at once. He refused and went to Poland instead, where he met with Wojtyla and Wyszynski two months before Wojtyla's American trip.[9]*

August 23, 1976—two weeks after Wojtyla spoke at Doylestown—Zembrzuski got written orders from Paul's investigator, dismissing him from the Pauline order for violations of canon law.[10]

Wojtyla learned of this at the end of his cross-country trip. He headed home via Rome, where he met Wyszynski and went with him straight to Pope Paul to appeal. Immediately after the meeting, Paul ordered the charges against Zembrzuski withdrawn—an amazing decision, apparently not based on any challenge to the facts. The notion that ideology shouldn't disrupt

* In an interview at the Doylestown shrine June 29, 1993, Zembrzuski told me: "If I had money, I had to put it into this building. These huge buildings cost very much money, $6.6 million between 1963 and 1969. I built all this. I raised it from people who wanted the shrine. And I borrowed the rest. The bonds were ten- to fifteen-year bonds. I thought they would be paid off. When the Vietnam war was going strong, just as this building was half built, prices went up. Money got tight. Interest rates were up. We had expected it would cost $3 million. We couldn't stop then or the original investment would all have been lost. So we borrowed more. Now we have enough income to run it. Bishop Guilfoyle and Father Boyle [the Church investigators], they couldn't understand the mentality of Polish people. They are not Polish. They take an entirely different approach." I asked Zembrzuski why he had been removed. "I found it was better to go away," he said. "It's an internal matter."

investigations of suspected wrongdoing was another aspect of America that Wojtyla rejected.

As in many coverups, the Doylestown matter appeared over, but it was a long way from over.

No sooner had Pope Paul appeased the Polish cardinals over Zembrzuski than he undercut some of their painstaking work in Czechoslovakia in an apparent effort to appease the Czechoslovakian government. When the government promised to ease up on the official Church, the Vatican sent an envoy to Czechoslovakia to halt some of the underground activity Wojtyla had helped foster.

Especially poignant was the case of one secretly ordained bishop, Jan Korec, who had spent 1960 to 1968 in prison and now practiced his priesthood while working as an elevator repairman. Korec was handed papal orders to stop ordaining priests and, he says, engaging in some other secret activities. Korec (whom John Paul II would make a cardinal) told Pope Paul's men that the Czech government would double-cross them in any efforts at appeasement. He was right: it refused to approve the new bishops it had said it would. When communism fell, in 1989, ten of thirteen Czech dioceses had no bishops.

What Wojtyla was told of the new directive hasn't been disclosed. But contacts between his Krakow intellectual friends and their Czech counterparts continued, as did his own quiet contacts with Korec. His secret ordinations of Czechs didn't stop for long if they stopped at all.[11]

32

Poland itself had become a cauldron by the time Wojtyla returned September 5, 1976. In late August, a new wave of strikes brought more arrests. As in the past, the bishops promised that if the government would free the prisoners, the Church would urge citizens to work harder for the economy. But such deals between Church and state were relics of a fading framework.

Events were spinning forward exactly as Wojtyla had been pushing them. In the public consternation and anger over the mass arrests of workers, the two camps that would eventually produce the Solidarity revolution had finally intertwined. Seweryn Blumsztajn, the Jewish student radical who had gone to jail in the protests of 1968, had begun talking to Bohdan Cywinski, Wojtyla's friend and editor, whose underground book about Catholic rebellion had fallen into Blumsztajn's hands a few years before.

Blumsztajn's friend Joanna Szczesna, also Jewish, says Cywinski's *A Heritage of Rebellions* had become "a bible for my generation. It showed that if you fight for your freedom as one family, differences are not important. You could cooperate."

Blumsztajn's mentor Jacek Kuron—who had gone to prison in 1964 for his open letter urging fellow communists to rebel—had found his own match in Cywinski's friend Antoni Macierewicz, a Catholic. By American standards, these men were radical, not conservative. As a student protester, Macierewicz had sympathized with Marxist movements in Latin America that resisted American-backed dictatorships.

In late summer 1976, Macierewicz and Kuron brought together about twenty friends from their respective circles and formed an illegal, underground organization to help the arrested workers and their families. It was called the Workers' Defense Committee (in Polish, Komitet Obrony Robotnikow), or KOR.

The result was just what Wojtyla had worked toward: a political movement related to the Church but outside the Church, encompassing all Poles in the fight for human rights. KOR's first concern was collecting and delivering money to help the families of arrested workers. More than two hundred such families were sustained on aid raised immediately by KOR.

Then KOR turned to journalism. It was, after all, in large part an outgrowth of the Znak publications in Krakow, which had nourished freedom for two generations and were now being muzzled by the government. Unlike the Znak publications, however, KOR made no pretense of passing censorship. Beginning in September 1976, KOR issued typewritten bulletins reporting on workers who had lost their jobs and on court cases of those who had been arrested.

But typewritten bulletins couldn't circulate widely enough. One KOR member, Miroslaw Chojecki, a chemist, volunteered to make printing dye. He also thought he could build a press with a wooden frame. A visiting professor from Japan who was heading home told Chojecki he could complete the illegal printing operation by supplying matrixes (a printing term for pliable, lightweight molds that can produce many copies). After that it was merely a matter of finding people traveling from Japan who could smuggle in the matrixes.

When the Episcopate met in November 1976, it felt pressure to act, not just for the thousands in jail but for the thousands more who had been blacklisted from their jobs because of the strikes. News that Gierek had been honored in Moscow for his aggressiveness made Poles even angrier. But Wyszynski, now in declining health and facing surgery, was increasingly forced to withdraw from events.

As the bishops assembled, KOR's cofounder Antoni Macierewicz was taken for a meeting that his KOR colleagues said was very important—with Cardinal Wojtyla. There was no substantive discussion, Macierewicz says; Wojtyla just greeted him affably, chatted awhile, and affirmed his best wishes. But for Macierewicz, the message was clear: Wojtyla was encouraging the work he and KOR were doing and would help as he could. In session, with Wojtyla in the lead, the Episcopate demanded amnesty for arrested workers and warned the government that an "embittered people" would not produce goods.

By early 1977, secret KOR chapters were spreading among students. Kakol, the minister of religion, started court proceedings to seize the Znak publications on the ground that they were working with KOR. In fact, the editors had tried to keep a formal separation, with Cywinski, for example, declining to be a member of KOR. But there was no denying the KOR leaders were the close friends, political allies, and news sources of the Znak editors. Wojtyla's intellectuals were openly organizing a mass movement.

Meanwhile, an interview with Wojtyla, taped in Krakow, was broadcast on Italian television. Father John Navone marveled at the way Wojtyla "was able to say everything between the lines. He was able to tell you what an oppressive situation this was with extreme cleverness. He said, 'There are certain fundamental human freedoms that every society should afford its people.' He pressed the boundaries of discretion just to the point where they couldn't pounce on him. I thought then, what a glorious thing if that man could be pope."

Many people saw the same interview, some of them cardinals.

As Wojtyla battled communists, he was also challenged by the split growing in the Church since Pope Paul's birth-control encyclical. In this battle, too, his sympathies were clear, but he deftly kept his lines of communication open to the other side.

Many of Europe's top churchmen, including most of the editorial board of the influential Swiss-based theological journal *Concilium,* believed that Vatican II had created a permanent spirit of change that transcended whatever the Council had actually voted on. Prominent on *Concilium*'s board were two men Wojtyla had singled out for praise during Vatican II, Yves Congar of France and Hans Kung of Switzerland.

But now, as journalist Wilton Wynn wrote, "It seemed that traditional teachings of the Church had suddenly come under fire from some of its most noted theologians.... Some saw the virginity of Mary as only symbolic. Others stressed the humanity over the divinity of Jesus. There was widespread pressure for Church approval of divorce and remarriage, of abortion, of premarital sex in the context of true love."[1]

In March 1977, Pope Paul acted decisively to try to halt this push for continuing change. When Munich's Cardinal Dopfner died, Paul broke with custom to fill his seat with someone from the usually separate world of academia: Father Joseph Ratzinger, the theologian notable for his work with Cardinal Frings at Vatican II. Paul—and everyone else who was paying attention—knew that Ratzinger was now a leader in a group of theologians who had banded together to resist the push for change. They had started their own magazine, *Communio,* to promote Vatican authority. Ratzinger had even resigned from an advisory post in the German Episcopate, saying that the bishops were trying to make synods into a "Church parliament."

Especially worrisome to the *Communio* group was the case of Kung, who had defied an order by the Congregation for Doctrine (the updated Holy Office) to stop teaching that laymen might bless the Eucharist at Mass in emergencies. Worse, Kung was being widely hailed as a hero for his rebellion.

Many Christians had proclaimed their independence from the Church's teaching authority in the past, of course; these people were called Protestants. "What was new in this rebellion," said journalist Wynn, "was that the rebels did not leave the Church. They remained Catholic and insisted that they were good Catholics."[2]

Some in Ratzinger's *Communio* group believed that this kind of dissent seriously jeopardized the faith in a sexually decadent West. When Ratzinger was rocketed from the classroom to a major job in Church management, it was a clear statement. But Paul's adversaries, particularly cardinals Hume of England and Suenens of Belgium, quickly demonstrated that there would be no halt to their protests: they complained anew that bishops weren't consulted enough on papal decisions. In this fight, Wojtyla was perceived as tending toward the *Communio* side, but quietly, not as a leader. (He tried to launch a Polish edition of *Communio,* but communist censors blocked it.)[3]

Rome was definitely getting perilous. Wojtyla, who had just navigated challenging ski slopes, twisted his ankle attending a Vatican committee meeting and was laid up for two days. Anna-Teresa Tymieniecka, in Rome hoping to see him, pounced, and says she kept him in editing sessions the whole time he recovered.

May 7, 1977, the leader of the student opposition at the Jagiellonian was beaten to death a few blocks from Wojtyla's office and residence. Almost everyone blamed the secret branch of the police, which attributed the death to an accidental fall.

After a massive funeral march, Wojtyla gave the service, during which he said the student "fell victim to the hatred of the democracy movement among the students." It was a stunning public accusation by Wojtyla that the government was responsible.

A Catholic Intelligentsia Club official and many young people suspected of KOR sympathies were arrested. But instead of being intimidated, KOR members were galvanized. Poles from all walks of life seemed ready to follow. KOR was alluded to at the annual celebration of the martyrdom of Saint Stanislaw. May 15, fifty thousand people came to see Wojtyla consecrate the church he had finally won for Nowa Huta.

Soon after the service, he was confronted with a momentous personal decision. Bohdan Cywinski, his friend of two decades and now the editor in chief of *Znak*, appeared in his office. On being told of the problem, Wojtyla suggested they go for a walk in the woods.

Cywinski had always kept a discreet distance from his friends who ran KOR, trying to protect his besieged magazine. After the murder of the student leader, KOR had decided to stage a hunger strike. But its leaders had all been arrested at the funeral and jailed: Kuron, Blumsztajn, Michnik, Macierewicz, and eight others. Joanna Szczesna, the remaining "staff" of the KOR bulletin, was hiding with friends.

Now Cywinski's colleagues had sent word from prison that it was up to him to organize the hunger strike and maintain KOR's visibility as an active rallying point for opposition. It was a huge challenge, he told Wojtyla. If he led a hunger strike, "I would first have to give up my work, running the most important Catholic periodical in this country." Otherwise the government would seize the whole magazine group. The staff at *Znak* had already declared that if he got political, he would have to quit. "I have a wife and two children," he added. Jail was also a possibility now, and people were occasionally killed.

"Which values are most important?" he kept asking Wojtyla. "The circle around me [at the Znak group] is all against this. They say nothing is going to come of this. 'You're risking your family, your magazine, and your life.' "

Wojtyla let him talk it out, then presented the decision as a series of alternatives. "If you decide to take part, it will endanger your family and magazine," Wojtyla said. "On the other hand, if you take part, you will testify to those very values that are most important now. You will testify to solidarity with those who are in prison. The decision is up to you."

"He always said, 'The decision is up to you,' " Cywinski recalls. "And he would always say he knows nothing about politics. Then he would say, 'But the

Ursus workers, and Radom workers—some had ten-year [prison] terms.' " The tilt of Wojtyla's seemingly balanced list of values was clear. "After two hours of discussion, I had no doubt what to do," Cywinski says.

Around the same time, without consulting Cywinski, Tadeusz Mazowiecki, editor of the other Znak monthly, *Wiez,* also came to Wojtyla, with exactly the same problem. He had been asked by the same jailed friends to break ranks at the publication and join a hunger strike. He came away from Wojtyla feeling the same commitment Cywinski did. "Wojtyla understood that the struggle for freedom was not just for the Church but for everybody," Mazowiecki remembers.

One week later, Cywinski and seven friends went to a prayer service in a historic church in the heart of Warsaw; when the service ended, they didn't leave. Soon afterward, Mazowiecki, outside, declared that the eight were on a hunger protest against the government and that he would act as their spokesman. It was one of the most dramatic and important moments of the long struggle against totalitarianism. No one but the two of them knew that the cardinal of Krakow had prodded them into their stand.

33

Every citizen of Warsaw knew St. Martin's Church, the site for the hunger strike. It had been built in 1352, only to be destroyed by the Germans during the Warsaw Uprising almost six centuries later. The rector and many parishioners had died in the ruins.

To widespread surprise, Stalin had permitted its reconstruction from 1951 to 1953, with the labor of Catholics who wanted the storied church back. Stalin, though, intended the rebuilding as a propaganda gimmick, and when it was finished, he gave the rebuilt church to the Polish Ministry of Education for offices.

St. Martin's had gone back to being a church as part of the deal Wyszynski struck for his release from prison in 1956. To give it special status, Wyszynski entrusted it to the nuns who ran Laski, the woodland camp he had loved from World War II. A revolving contingent of Laski nuns stayed on the St. Martin's compound. For its rector, Wyszynski chose Bronislaw Dembowski, a young priest close to both Laski and the Warsaw Catholic Intelligentsia Club. Among Dembowski's top student protégés was Bohdan Cywinski, who a year later would hook up with Father Wojtyla of Krakow on a canoe trip.

Dembowski learned of the 1977 hunger strike not from Cywinski, however, but from "a colonel of the secret police" who "came to visit and told me that some people who are not of a stable character wanted to organize a hunger strike and were considering St. Martin's." Dembowski figured that "there were probably fourteen or fifteen people at the meeting of KOR where it was decided, and probably one of them was an informer."

He wasn't fazed. "Conflict was unavoidable," he says. "The totalitarian government saw itself as ruler not only of the economy and politics but also of the mind and soul. I used to say in my sermons, I am not in opposition to the government. I have a thousand years of Polish history. The government is in opposition to *me*."

A few days after the police colonel visited, "Cywinski, my old friend, came and asked what the reaction would be if some people didn't leave church after Mass. I answered, 'So what? I couldn't do anything about it.' " Both men knew without having to say it that police would have a harder time breaking up a demonstration in a church.

So one night the group filed into the service carrying sleeping bags. Among them was a priest, Aleksander Hauke-Ligowski, who Father Dembowski knew was a first cousin of Prince Philip of England; that would further protect them. Besides him there was a writer (Stanislaw Baranczak, now a professor of literature at Harvard), a sociologist, an engineer, and, among the others, Ozjasz Schecter, a onetime communist and father of the jailed Jewish KOR leader Adam Michnik.

Father Dembowski spent the night with the men in his dressing room; the women slept in the chapel. Though not announcing it, the strikers planned to stay eight days. "I am against an open hunger strike," Dembowski says. "A strike is a kind of dialogue. If you say it's till death, then it's blackmail, not dialogue."

News of the action raced through Warsaw: Anyone not plugged into gossip heard about it on Radio Free Europe the next morning. The government was apoplectic. Police ranted about Church rules to Father Hauke-Ligowski's superior, who replied, "He asked me for leave and told me he would spend it in a church praying and fasting. This is in accord with Church rules. If it's a political crime, arrest him. But beware! He's a cousin of Queen Elizabeth!"

Officers then went to Father Dembowski, as they would continue to do each day of the strike. He was warned that he would be held morally responsible for "all the bloodshed it would cause." He responded that he was "not afraid of the striking people," just "of the police" if they tried force.

Wyszynski issued a single brief statement: "The Church knows the law of asylum." This constituted clear but nonprovocative support.

A growing crowd kept vigil outside St. Martin's around the clock, despite police efforts to disperse them. Western reporters mingled with them, conducting interviews, which provided another measure of protection. Masses at the church overflowed all week.

The strike was more than just a public-relations coup; it was an important personal experience for the strikers, who, like Cywinski and Mazowiecki, had each confronted his own moral dilemma about participating. The group's ranks swelled to fifteen. One new participant was Joanna Szczesna, who came out from hiding to join her colleagues. "I wanted to protest," she says, "but the second reason was to defeat my own fear."

Each striker would emerge taller, readier for the next time.

On the final morning, suspecting that police provocateurs were in the crowd to stir violence, Father Dembowski led the tired—and hungry—strikers out through a back door to waiting cars.

Thanks to the strike, the international press started reporting again about the workers imprisoned since the summer before, whose arrest had inspired KOR in the first place. Two months later, July 22—the Polish national day—the jailed workers were released.

More important, a precedent was set for taking successful, enterprising action and getting away with it. In the revolution that brought down communism, the St. Martin's hunger strike was the equivalent of the Boston Tea Party, or of Rosa Parks's refusal to give up her seat on a Birmingham city bus to a white person.

Cywinski lost his job, but his family wasn't left penniless after all. Wojtyla called him in as soon as he was back in Krakow and offered him a new job compiling a history of the Church under communism. On the spot, the cardinal handed Cywinski his first monthly pay envelope, containing seven thousand zlotys—about what he had been receiving at *Znak*.

For Corpus Christi Day a few days later, Wojtyla arranged, as usual, to hang a biblical quotation across the main outdoor altar. This year, the banner said, " 'Your efforts will not be in vain.'—KOR I." "KOR" was the usual abbreviation for the Polish spelling of the New Testament book of Corinthians, from which the quotation came. But the population of Krakow broke into a broad grin at the first sight of it. No one in town missed the point that the cardinal had just endorsed the hunger strike, to the government's face, in a way so clever the government was rendered helpless to respond.[1]

But the government wasn't finished. Immediately afterward an arsonist torched the cloister at St. Martin's where the nuns lived and worked. More than a dozen blind women had to be evacuated. "They could have been killed," says

Sister Ruth Wosiek, who helped save them. The roof and top floor of the two-story annex were destroyed.

KOR responded by spreading its roots to Czechoslovakia, where a rock group called Plastic People of the Universe was put on trial for violating censorship. A playwright, Vaclev Havel, and 1,250 other intellectuals—many of whom had been trafficking in ideas with Wojtyla's Krakow group—signed a protest demanding human rights. That document became known as Charter 77.

Pope Paul, however, still believed goodwill would solve the problem. June 9, 1977, right after the hunger strike and other displays, Paul welcomed Janos Kadar, head of the Hungarian Communist Party, into the Vatican to celebrate a new agreement between them. With a straight face, he declared that they were "crowning . . . a slow but uninterrupted process" that had brought the Church and the Hungarian communists "closer together." Paul acknowledged that "many people are critical of the [Vatican's] initiative in this rapprochement," but with high praise for Kadar, he hailed "the promise of new progress toward more advanced goals" of working together "in the service of noble causes" to help "all mankind."[2] Kadar's spirit of "positive cooperation" was news to a lot of Hungarians.

That summer, 1977, Adam Michnik published a book in Paris, *The Church, the Left and Dialogue.* As a child, he wrote, he had hated the Church for forcing unwanted Catholic religious training on him. His own ideals remained secular and socialist. But the Church now appeared in a different light to him as it joined in the fight for individual rights, against totalitarianism: "Reason, law, civilization, humanism—whatever they are called—have sought and found . . . a new meaning and new strength. . . . This source is Jesus Christ. Belief in the divinity of Christ is a matter of grace which is not granted to everyone. But belief in the inviolability of Christ's commandments is everyone's duty."[3]

Wojtyla received an honorary doctorate June 23, 1977, in Mainz, Germany, where he stayed with Cardinal Hermann Volk; Volk visited him in Krakow two months later. In Paris, Wojtyla spoke to expatriate Poles and stayed with Cardinal François Marty. Each cardinal would vote and talk to other voters at the next conclave.

Pope Paul again refused to let his synod tackle the sex issue, instead assigning the topic of child education. Wojtyla spent time meeting cardinals. Whether he was consciously campaigning can only be wondered at, but he had never before been such a social butterfly. Deskur, the top Pole in the curia, hosted gatherings without particular agenda, at which Wojtyla hobnobbed with cardinals from around Europe.[4] He went to Milan to lend his support to Cardinal Giovanni Colombo, under seige by parishioners for banning rowdy at-home baptism parties.

34

As the synod broke up in November 1977, Polish Party Secretary Edward Gierek followed the lead of his Hungarian counterpart and paid an *Ostpolitik* visit to the Vatican. In Rome, Gierek threw a bizarre reception for Italian Prime Minister Giulio Andreotti, a proud Vatican insider. Guests included Cardinal Casaroli, other Vatican officials, and a number of Italian communists.

One can only imagine how Wojtyla must have felt two days later, when Gierek, standing next to Pope Paul, declared that there was an "absence of conflict between the state and Church," only cooperation in "the great national goals." Not arguing, Paul added his own conciliatory address. So fawning were the speeches that the official Polish press printed every word.

Because *Tygodnik Powszechny*'s weekly deadline fell six days after everyone had read the speeches in the official press, Father Bardecki decided to print only a summary. He was stunned when the government then accused Wojtyla of sabotaging the peace by omitting the remarks from his Church paper. Although Wojtyla had known nothing of Father Bardecki's decision in advance, scores of letters poured in accusing him of censorship. It was obviously a communist campaign, but to what end?

The top staff from *Tygodnik Powszechny* gathered at the archbishop's palace December 21 to discuss it. After Mass and dinner, the conversation was animated. The Party had once portrayed Wojtyla as reasonable, in contrast to the reactionary Wyszynski; now it was the other way around. Wojtyla said little, and the meeting broke up at eleven.

Bardecki, upset at even innocently having caused such a ruckus, took a walk in the park despite the frigid cold, arriving at his apartment building at around midnight. Briefcase in hand, he headed for the gate. Suddenly two big men, hats pulled low over their eyes, rushed around the corner and asked him the time. Startled, he looked at his watch, only to feel the first blows on his frail form. He remembers only pain, then dogs barking, approaching fast, and the two men fleeing.

Another priest found him blood-soaked. Rather than trust a public ambulance, he phoned a *Tygodnik Powszechny* secretary to take Bardecki to the hospital.

Teeth were missing and bones, including his nose, broken. Doctors said he almost died from internal bleeding. The beating exactly paralleled the one the student leader had died from seven months before, a few blocks away. Only a chance approach had saved Bardecki's life.

As soon as Bardecki got home the next day, Wojtyla came to see him. "You got that for me," he said. It was "a political event." He promised the Church would supply lawyers to help with the investigation. Bardecki filed a full report with police; four months later, the prosecutor notified him that the perpetrators couldn't be found.

KOR's underground newspapers—anonymous and not subject to government or Church censorship—were a lot livelier than Bardecki's could be. They exposed secret government plans and other shenanigans uncovered by KOR members.

KOR also started a "flying university" in Warsaw, similar to the one Wojtyla had attended in Krakow during the German occupation. There were informal classes in history, sociology, economics, and other subjects, minus the Marxist-Leninist filters. Professors from the Polish Academy of Sciences by day agreed to come to people's apartments by night to teach honestly. Once, Michnik was scheduled to speak; word spread so fast that the police heard and—again—arrested him.

The fever of rebellion also spread. Flurries of newsletters were passed around, bearing no sign of where they came from, with titles such as "Manifesto of the 59," "Letter of the 14," "Memorandum of the 101," and so on. People made home duplicating machines out of the wringing attachments on washtubs. In Gdansk, KOR members launched an underground labor newspaper called *Robotnik*, "The Worker."

One evening that spring, Cywinski organized a meeting between Wojtyla and the KOR leadership at an apartment in Warsaw. Cywinski, Jacek Kuron, Antoni Macierewicz, and two others talked for nearly four hours with the cardinal. Mostly they sought his help in expanding the "flying university." It had been a great success, but it was still a gimmick; they wanted to make it an institution.

By rebuilding a historical consciousness among Poles—something Wojtyla had long advocated—KOR could build a political opposition. KOR wanted the Church to provide cover for a much better organized flying university to start up in the fall, and it wanted Wojtyla to authorize this. Courses and lectures would be scheduled at churches all over Poland, so police would be reluctant to break in.

A social breakdown almost ruined everything. "Kuron tried to dominate the talk" and "was a little surprised that Wojtyla was so reserved," Macierewicz says. Macierewicz and Cywinski knew of Wojtyla's inclination to hold his tongue, "especially when meeting spontaneous, powerful people like Kuron. There was a psychological conflict to the degree that we were trying to stop Jacek, feeling he was hindering a successful agreement."

Macierewicz and Cywinski left the meeting feeling certain they could count on Wojtyla to provide Church cooperation; Kuron left feeling confused and frustrated.[1] There's no evidence the government ever learned of the discussion or discovered that Wojtyla was supporting a KOR leader, Cywinski, with monthly envelopes of cash.

KOR didn't have to wait long for an answer to its appeal. A few days later, on Corpus Christi Day—May 25, 1978—Wojtyla declared himself publicly, in his main sermon before tens of thousands of people massed in downtown Krakow:

> We pray for our Motherland, looking at her entire past. The past that was great and difficult; the past that brought tears to whole generations. Whole generations bled and carried fetters! Our Motherland is so much more valuable to us because the price of freedom was paid by so many generations. We will never give up this past! We will not allow it to be torn from our souls! It forms our identity even today. We want our young people to know the whole truth about our nation's history. We want the legacy of Polish culture to be transferred to new generations of Poles without any deviations!
>
> A nation lives by knowing the truth about itself. A nation has a right to know the truth, and a right to fight for it! Most of all, it has a right to expect the truth from those who teach.

As always, Wojtyla's every word was within the bounds of communist rhetoric. But everyone, Catholic and communist alike, understood that he was talking about the famous, illegal "flying university." A grass-roots revolutionary initiative had challenged a communist state, and the archbishop of Krakow—increasingly the main spokesman for the Polish people—was publicly endorsing it.

To KOR—and to every priest and bishop who might be asked for permission to use a church as an underground classroom—Wojtyla's sermon was official approval. It was a command as clear as other revolutionaries might give to blow up a bridge or assault a police station. But this was not a revolution that would be fought with violence, which would have been much less effective and probably have brought a quick end to itself. This was a revolution that would be fought—and won—by the word.

Or as Wojtyla would put it, the Word.

Just eleven days later—June 5, 1978[2]—there was a knock on the door of Bogdan Borucewicz, a KOR activist in Gdansk. It was a sturdy man with a walrus mustache who gave his name as Lech Walesa.

During the 1968 protests, Borucewicz, then in high school in Gdansk, had been convicted of distributing illegal materials and had spent a year and a half in prison. The conviction banned him from the state university he wanted to attend—a big mistake by the communists, since it steered him instead to Catholic University in Lublin. There, in 1974, a professor assigned his class to write essays on the Boy Scout movement. Among the prominent former scouts Borucewicz chose to interview was Jacek Kuron, who had just left prison for writing his famous open letter.

Borucewicz immediately fell under Kuron's spell, got his degree in history, joined KOR, and returned to Gdansk to try to enlist shipyard workers in the resistance. He took a port job and placed an advertisement in KOR's underground newspaper, *Robotnik,* seeking people interested in unionizing. Boldly, he included his address.

A few days later, in walked Walesa. Walesa had taken part in the 1970 Gdansk shipyard strike, and at the age of twenty-seven had been elected to a leadership committee, just before the strike ended in a bloodbath. Six years later, frustrated, he had stood up at a meeting of Gierek's stooge union and challenged its leaders. He argued that a new piecework system that the government claimed raised wages actually reduced them, as the time allotted for tasks was constantly being shortened, forcing workers to labor at impossible speeds to attain the supposedly high wages. When managers heard of his speech, they fired him.*

Walesa had taken a job with a small construction and repair concern. Reading about the St. Martin's hunger strike had inspired him to try unionizing again, he said.

Says Borucewicz, "He literally came over and said something like, 'Hello, I'd like to join a union.' My answer was, 'OK, I'll come see you.' " Borucewicz

---

* To be fair, many American corporations, including Joseph Coors Brewing and Texas Instruments, were doing the same thing at about the same time to workers who advocated unionization.

thought that going to workers' homes instead of inviting them into his own helped protect him against the secret police. He—and the rest of Poland—were later shocked to learn that Walesa, while speaking out for unions, occasionally talked to the secret police himself and told them more than he should have about his compatriots.[3]

That summer, a celebration was held in Milan for the tenth anniversary of Pope Paul's birth-control encyclical. Wojtyla gave a speech and met more cardinals. Then he went canoeing for three weeks, ducking back to Krakow only once for meetings. Fellow campers from the 1950s now had children of their own, so the trips were opened to families. "He was still wonderfully fit," says one veteran of both the 1958 and 1978 trips. "The lake is nearly nine hundred yards across, but he could swim to the other side and back without stopping."[4]

35

Due to illness Pope Paul missed Easter ceremonies in 1978 for the first time. In May, Italy legalized abortion, free on request in the first trimester of pregnancy. Then, Paul was criticized for his inaction during the terrorist "Red Brigade" kidnaping of former Italian Prime Minister Aldo Moro, and seemed unsteady at Moro's funeral.

Paul died August 6 of a heart attack during Mass at the papal summer residence at Castelgandolfo, in the hills near Rome. How his successor, Pope John Paul I—Cardinal Albino Luciani of Venice—was elected is, in part, the story of John Paul II's election.

Three weeks was allotted between Paul's death and the opening of the conclave, so the cardinals could gather in Rome to discuss the state of the Church. Of 111 cardinals, only 11 had voted for a pope before. Speculation and manipulation over a new pope had quickened with Pope Paul's deteriorating health. Priests and bishops of the curia even handed out dossiers accusing some candidate they didn't like of shady business deals or keeping a mistress. Cardinals couldn't help noticing such stories.

Promoting any candidate was supposedly prohibited in their conversations, but, as with criticizing communism in the Soviet bloc, words were found to convey prohibited messages. Cardinal Jean Villot of France, the *camerlengo* (a caretaker appointed by each pope to supervise proceedings after his death), organized formal meetings every morning in rotating small groups.

Lacking any superior human authority, cardinals talked more openly. They revealed concerns over being cut off from the pope's decision making, over the financial problems and the scandal at IOR, and over the agony of the Church in the communist bloc. Wojtyla spoke on Poland and was forced in turn to listen for the first time to details of Vatican finances.[1] Afternoons, though, he disappeared to a house some priests had rented at the seashore thirty minutes from Rome.

Seventy-five cardinals, two-thirds plus one, were needed to elect a pope. Favorites named by assorted handicapping sheets were all Italians and veterans of the curia; none was among the pastoral bishops who advocated new policies on sex and gender. Yet when churchmen talked about the most influential cardinals, rather than those most likely to be elected, they tended to name pastors, men who won elections at synods, mostly non-Italian, like the college of cardinals itself.

After the conclave, people would recall hearing occasional talk of Luciani or Wojtyla as candidates. But it's hard to find mention of either one in accounts written *before* they were elected. The head of Vatican Radio later said that many non-Italian cardinals asked about Luciani's health, suggesting that he was the compromise Italian favored by non-Italians.[2]

"Cardinals didn't travel as much [then] as now," says Cardinal Silvio Oddi of Italy. "They didn't know each other as they do now." Although he first met Wojtyla on a trip to Poland during Vatican II, Oddi says he really got to know Wojtyla only in the days preceding the August 1978 conclave—and then only because Wojtyla prodded him. Oddi served on the Congregation for Sacraments, and says Wojtyla approached him about an unusual marriage situation that had arisen in Poland. After discussing the problem, they just kept talking.

"I was one of the cardinals already thinking that the nationality of the pope does not necessarily have to be Italian," Oddi says. As he talked to Wojtyla, he says, he thought of Wyszynski as a candidate. "But Wyszynski was very old. And thinking of Wyszynski brought to mind another Pole."

No doubt Wojtyla had many such conversations.

Of seven previous conclaves in the past century, only two had taken as long as four days (for Pius X in 1903 and for Pius XI in 1922). One (Pius XII in 1939) had been decided in a day.

August 24, 1978, the day before the conclave was to begin, Wojtyla went to Mass at the Polish College with Father Malinski, his old seminary mate. Malinski prayed aloud: "We beseech thee, oh Lord, by the intercession of Saint Bartholomew whose feast we are celebrating, to bring it about that Cardinal Wojtyla is elected Pope."

He says Wojtyla stayed motionless, hands clasped, while someone offered a prayer for another cause. Finally, Wojtyla said, "We beseech thee, almighty

God, that if a man is chosen pope who does not believe himself capable of bearing the heavy responsibility of being the vicar of thy Son, thou wilt give him courage to say, as Saint Peter did, 'Depart from me, for I am a sinful man, oh, Lord.' But if he should accept the burden, we beg thee to grant him enough faith, hope, and love to bear the cross thou layest upon him."

Late the next afternoon, Wojtyla and his colleagues found their quarters in the area where they would be quarantined until they made their decision. The conclave was sealed and draped.[3]

Based on his prior inspection, Father Andrew Greeley compared it to "the enlisted men's section on an aircraft carrier." The plastic dining chairs, he went on, "look like a discount-store bargain sale. The rugs they put in the Sistine Chapel . . . are cheap felt and will be filthy after the first group of cardinals walks down the aisle to vote. Each cardinal is issued one roll of toilet paper, two ballpoint pens . . . and maybe ten sheets of writing paper. . . . Each also gets a plastic wastebasket out of a dime store, a washbowl and pitcher, a red plastic glass, a tiny bed lamp, one hard-backed chair and an even harder-looking [prayer] kneeler. To make it clear that he ought to get out in a hurry, he gets only one bar of soap and two very tiny towels, which will drive the Americans up the wall. A second-class *pensione* it is not. The beds are the worst I think I've seen since the seminary, and they ought to be because they were borrowed from a seminary . . . very narrow, with thin, hard mattresses over wire mesh."

In other words, they were much like the quarters Wojtyla had requisitioned for himself in Krakow after declining the finery of his predecessors. But there was also heavy cigarette smoke in the narrow hallways. Fresh air came only during after-meal walks in the courtyard.

In the morning, after Mass and a light breakfast, the cardinals were crowded for balloting onto hard chairs jammed together before hard tables, occupying about half the Sistine Chapel. "I don't think I want to be a cardinal after all," Father Greeley concluded. "Considering their average age (68.7 years), there is almost a cruelty in the harshness."

Yet there were also the Michelangelo frescoes, and the grandeur of the mission. Each voter received a card at the top of which was printed *Eligo in summum pontificem*, or "I chose as supreme pontiff." The cardinals were instructed to disguise their handwriting. They paraded in order of seniority to the altar, where each knelt, prayed, rose, and then stated, "I call to witness Christ, the Lord, who will be my judge that my vote is given to the one who, before God, I consider should be elected." Then each placed his folded card on a plate, slid it into a chalice, bowed, and returned to his seat. All told, the process took an hour. Three cardinals at a table scrutinized the voting. One would unfold a card, tally the vote on paper, and pass it on. The third to receive each card would read the name aloud and pierce it through.

How the voting goes is perhaps the biggest secret of the Church. Cardinals who willingly told me many other things I suspect they weren't supposed to, who would even begin to hint at the voting patterns, would catch themselves before they got specific about the vote and rebuke me for asking. But they did hint. And there are diligent contemporaneous accounts.*

No one was surprised that the vote seemed to pit Cardinal Giuseppe Siri, the hard opponent of change at Vatican II and ever since, against the rest of the field, who wanted kinds and degrees of change. But Siri could count on only about one fourth of the votes. The papacy would ultimately go to someone who would discuss change but wasn't pushing hard for it.

Wojtyla was among those getting votes—"a small but significant number," he would later tell *Time*'s Wilton Wynn over dinner; "four or five," he told another journalist.[4] He told Wynn that the votes came mostly from German-speakers, possibly including König. When he heard his name called, he said he felt "a severe agitation" approaching fear.

The surprise was that Luciani was making at least as strong a showing as the other so-called moderates, including the betting favorite, Cardinal Sergio Pignedoli, who ran a Vatican congregation. On the first ballot, Greeley says Luciani ran a clear second to Siri—a sign that in choosing their "moderate," the cardinals wanted to end the recent string of curial popes, who had family connections to the Church and spent their careers climbing the rungs of Vatican departments.

As national Churches were created in former colonial countries, the ranks of diocesan cardinals had increased, until now, for the first time, they outnumbered curial cardinals. In retrospect, no one should have been surprised that such cardinals thought the world needed a pastor more than it needed another administrator.

Luciani was the son of a migrant worker and a maid. Coming from Pope John XXIII's home district, Venice, he had been a favorite of John's and the

---

* The best accounts of both 1978 conclaves are probably those of Father Greeley and *Time* magazine correspondent Wilton Wynn, who were at the Vatican working the cardinals—and, importantly, their staffs—as hard as possible to get the lowdown while memories were fresh. Although not a journalist, Greeley had a sense of American journalistic standards. I have tried to temper my reliance on both men's reporting with what information I could obtain during my own talks with the cardinals who were present and, in a few cases (such as Beni Lai's), with the former trusted staffers or confidants of those cardinals. I have also drawn on contemporary press accounts that either seemed informed rather than speculative or that could be verified, particularly those in the *Tablet* (London).

first bishop John ordained after becoming pope. He then ran a small diocese north of Venice, Vettorio Veneto, where he supervised each parish and priest individually. Even in Venice, where he had been archbishop since 1969, he had a reputation for walking among the parishes and shunning all symbols of wealth.

The proceedings were slowed by the tradition that the votes from each ballot be burned immediately, and that the crowd in St. Peter's Square be kept abreast of the election through bursts of black smoke from the chimney: when a ballot produces a new pope, a chemical is added to make the smoke white.

Halfway through the second ballot of the morning, it became clear that Luciani was gaining support. At lunch, cardinals from distant lands sought information about him. By the fourth vote that afternoon, the only significant protest ballots were blank. Luciani was approached by the *camerlengo*, Cardinal Villot, and asked if he would accept. He replied, "May God forgive you for what you have done with me."[5]

Villot then asked by what name he wished to be called. New names had become a tradition after 1009, when someone named Peter was elected pope and decided it would be presumptuous to call himself Peter II. Luciani chose to make a statement with an unusual combination of two names, emphasizing that he admired and hoped to continue both the change associated with John XXIII and the restraint on change associated with Paul VI.

The careful balancing of his opening speech left few clues as to his intended direction. To those who opposed change, he promised that he would be "careful . . . to ensure that an impulse, generous perhaps but out of due time, does not distort the content and meaning of the [Vatican] Council." But to those who favored change, he pledged "to see [to it] that conservative and timid forces do not slow down the magnificent thrust toward renewal and life."

There were tantalizing hints—but only hints—that John Paul I *might* have seen a way for the Church to accept some contraception. Italian churchmen considered him a voice for interpreting the birth-control encyclical with less ironclad language than Paul's. And just two weeks before his own election, he had made some startlingly undoctrinaire remarks that the cardinal-electors must have read. The occasion was the birth in England of the first test-tube baby, Louise Brown. When her parents could not conceive normally, an egg taken from her mother was fertilized with her husband's sperm in a laboratory dish—in vitro—and planted in her uterus. While the process was hailed by scientists and infertile couples around the world, Pope Paul had condemned such "unnatural" behavior.

Luciani had approached the event as a pastor, not as a theologian. "I send the most heartfelt congratulations to the English baby girl whose conception was produced artificially," he declared to inquiring newspapermen. "As for her parents, I have no right to condemn them. . . . They could even deserve great merit before God for what they wanted and asked the doctors to accomplish."

When he was questioned on this seeming diversion from doctrine, Luciani sounded a coy retreat. He said he hadn't yet found reason to change the Church's position. It seemed to leave the door open.

Almost from the beginning, there was evidence that the cardinals—however much they were guided by the Holy Spirit, as they said—had made a dreadful mistake. They had not misjudged the new pope's virtues: he was kind, holy, conciliatory, and made a great public impression. With his warm smile, he seemed more accessible than any pope in memory, certainly in contrast to the withdrawn Paul. The cardinals had wanted all that. That was the pastor.

But emotionally, physically, and intellectually, the job seemed to overwhelm him. Venice was deceptive, prominent more because of its history and beauty than because of its current size or power, which was second-rate. Luciani had neither the experience nor, just as important, the support staff that most men bring with them into positions of high power. His personal secretary was a thirty-nine-year-old country priest who said his duties in Venice had been only to "answer the phone and the door, and type . . . and . . . give alms for the poor." All decisions were left to Luciani.

The secretary, Don Diego Lorenzi, was simply unable to cope with the Vatican, to judge from what he told British author John Cornwell, who investigated the death of John Paul I with Vatican authorization. Lorenzi fled to see friends whenever he could. John Paul I soon asked Pope Paul's secretary, Monsignor John Magee, to stay on, a telltale sign that the new pope couldn't take control. His only other entourage was a couple of bumpkins who disrupted the papal office by bringing friends in to gawk and take snapshots. He agreed to dismiss them.

Archbishop Marcinkus, who met with John Paul I and was a close friend of the holdover secretary, Monsignor Magee, told Cornwell that the new pope didn't "even know where to start" with the paperwork that the secretary of state dumped on him each day. In contrast to the leisurely pace in Venice, where he walked in the square or took rides in the country, Marcinkus said now, "He comes in here . . . and everybody's calling him. . . . 'You've gotta get this, gotta get this. . . . What about this?'

"One of the reasons I went to see Luciani," Marcinkus said, "was that there were certain funds, foundation moneys . . . and I tried to explain what was available to him. But he couldn't care less!" The pope just said, "Thank you, thank you, very good, very good."

Nothing went right. As had Paul VI before him, John Paul I invited Archbishop Nikodim, head of the Russian Orthodox Church, to be his first ecumenical visitor. As they met, September 5, 1978, Nikodim fell dead at the pope's feet, from his fifth heart attack.

By that time, John Paul I was having medical problems of his own. A longstanding circulatory problem got worse. His legs swelled so much that he couldn't wear shoes, only slippers. He took to walking for hours on the rooftop garden to help his circulation. Once, the wind was so strong that confidential papers blew out of his hand, sending guards on a dangerous mission leaping from rooftop to rooftop, like villains in a bad movie, to retrieve them. After that, the pope's walks were confined to his study.

Remarkably, the Vatican seemed to pay little attention to the health of its chief executive. His medical records were somewhere in transit between Venice and Rome, with one doctor thinking he had given up responsibility and the next not yet ready to assume it. This may confound Americans, accustomed to a President who often seems to have the Johns Hopkins faculty waiting in the next room in case he sneezes. But the Church is so concerned with its mystique of perfection and divine protection that secrecy and privacy often come before health care for its leaders.[6]

No professional was supervising John Paul I in taking medicine he needed daily to control a blood-clotting tendency. A nun kept track of his pills. Anticoagulant medication must be used with great care, as too much can lead to unstoppable internal bleeding, while omitting doses can cause a pendulum swing the other way, making a quick, fatal brain or lung clot likelier than ever.

Each week into his papacy, John Paul I seemed emotionally more erratic. He asked others what to do, asked his secretary, Lorenzi, to say Mass while the Pope served as altar boy, and made repeated, ominous references to his own impending doom. When he invited an old friend, Father Don Germano Pattaro, to visit, as relayed to author Cornwell, "Pattaro was completely mystified. . . . Luciani, the Pope, was totally disoriented. . . . The Pope told Pattaro he didn't know whom to turn to because he didn't know how anything worked and whom he could trust. He was utterly lost. They prayed together and talked; Luciani seemed reluctant to let him go. . . . It seemed to Pattaro that John Paul was just clutching at anybody he had known in his life up in [Venice]."[7]

36

While John Paul I struggled, Wojtyla and Wyszynski made their third trip to West Germany in four years. Cathedral crowds were the largest since the 1963 visit of President Kennedy.

In Poland, KOR had made critical leaps. On the tenth anniversary of the August 1968 Soviet invasion of Czechoslovakia, KOR leaders including Kuron, Macierewicz, and Michnik sneaked into the mountains to plan strategy with leaders of KOR's Czechoslovakian counterpart, Charter 77—including Vaclev Havel. Whether Wojtyla, who was at that moment meeting cardinals in Rome, knew the arrangements in advance isn't clear. But in Michnik's words, "A photograph shows the future president [Havel] seated side by side with future cabinet ministers and parliamentarians. At the time, we were all criminals, pursued by the police."

For a year, Miroslaw Chojecki had been publishing an underground KOR newspaper with his homemade ink and press and the printing matrixes smuggled in from Japan. A lot of hand-pressing was required, however, just to turn out two hundred copies. Aiming higher, Chojecki found sources who could procure enough paper illegally from government stocks to allow him to print books—*if* he could get better printing equipment.

In late summer 1978, another KOR member, Zbigniew Romaszewski, found the needed equipment through an acquaintance—the chief political officer at the American embassy. The embassy was being renovated and was auctioning off old furniture. Two used mimeograph machines weren't listed among the sale items because printing equipment was tightly controlled by the Polish government, but the Americans could deliver them to Romaszewski as part of the sale.[1]

Once Chojecki had the printing machines, he smuggled a message to Aleksandar Smolar, a Jew who had fled to Paris in the anti-Semitic purges of 1968 and was printing a Catholic magazine there for shipment to Poland. Chojecki asked Smolar for a machine that could reproduce printing matrixes electronically, a standard item in the West. Paying for it from his business, Smolar smuggled it into Poland, boxed and labeled as a french-fried-potato machine.

With that in hand, Chojecki was able to churn out three thousand pages an hour of better quality than his previous two hundred hand-pressed sheets. In September 1978, he christened his illegal enterprise the Nowa Publishing Company and began printing uncensored books, including literature and poetry, as well as KOR bulletins.

His main problem lay in sneaking the needed quantity of raw paper into his apartment and the printed paper out, without arousing suspicion. So KOR developed a network of about ten people who were willing to let their homes be used to store paper smuggled from government plants. They took turns allowing Chojecki to bring his printing machine into their homes when time came to publish a book. He would work a week without leaving, then move the printer to the next site as the printed pages were being folded, bound, and carried out in small lots. As with most of the Polish revolution, money wasn't a major problem; people gladly paid five times the normal price of a book for the privilege of reading uncensored writing.

More important even than the books, however, Chojecki began hiring and training printers who could come to the chosen sites and help with the work. Starting with half a dozen, he soon had a hundred skilled people working for him. KOR officials told Charter 77 officials, and soon Chojecki was in Czechoslovakia, where he set up a network of fifteen underground printers. Then some Hungarian visitors to Poland were brought to meet him, and he taught them the operation, too.

September 29, 1978, probably a little after five A.M., a nun who had been the servant of Luciani/John Paul I for eighteen years noticed that he hadn't come out of his bedroom for his tray of morning coffee. She knocked, called his name, then finally entered.

He was sitting up in bed and appeared dead. Terrified, the nun wakened her superiors. Together, as a sort of committee, they roused the pope's two secretaries, who were supposed to be up but were sleeping late (if you can call 5:25 A.M. late).

A few hours later, in Krakow, Monsignor Dziwisz, Wojtyla's secretary, rushed in with news of the pope's death as Wojtyla breakfasted with thirteen priests. The cardinal stirred his tea for a minute, then, still silent, went to the chapel and prostrated himself on the floor.[2]

Wojtyla's diary records his going about his day as if nothing had happened: visiting a new housing project, saying the rosary with some sick and elderly people in their homes, stopping by to thank a couple for allowing religious classes to be conducted in their home despite government threats to tear it down. But on his return to the archbishop's palace, Wojtyla seemed preoccupied by the situation in Rome. "Everyone noticed he was much absorbed," says Bishop Bronislaw Fidelus. "It's hard to explain, but it was on his face."

Confronted with the puzzling and embarrassing death of an unprepared and poorly attended-to pope, the Vatican did what many powerful organizations do in a crisis: it lied. Because someone thought it was indecorous for a nun to enter the pope's bedroom, even to try to save his life, the Vatican said Secretary Magee had found the body. Since popes are supposed to be serene, it was announced he had died of a heart attack in bed while meditating on a religious book, *The Imitation of Christ*, by Thomas à Kempis.

But like most such webs of lies, this one quickly unraveled when people asked perfectly natural questions. For example, a heart attack would produce at least brief trauma and other symptoms that the Vatican denied had occurred. Since an autopsy was considered unseemly, the body was embalmed without one.

The tabloid press lifted off. A distraught public believed the worst. People passing the pope's body on display before the funeral screamed, "Who did this to you, who did this to you?" Magee, the holdover secretary from Paul VI, read so many outrageous suggestions that he had murdered the pope that he fled Rome for Ireland.

Inevitably, an author, David Yallop of England, produced a book, *In God's Name*,[3] asserting that one of six people (he wasn't sure which) killed John Paul I because the new pope was investigating their corrupt dealings.* The book was a best-seller.

A few years later, Pope John Paul II gave his blessing and cooperation to John Cornwell to reinvestigate the death. Cornwell had written for Catholic publications, and John Paul II hoped he would end the controversy once and for all.

In *A Thief in the Night*,[4] Cornwell ripped Yallop's book to shreds. He said that many interviews for *In God's Name* had been conducted not by Yallop but by "researchers" who, when interviewed, couldn't confirm disputed information. Other information had been misstated, such as Yallop's suggestion that morticians had been called to the Vatican before the body was officially "found" and that they had disputed the doctor's estimated time of death (about eleven o'clock the night before).

What gave Yallop some credibility was that he had reported, as few had, the hostilities and deceptive practices that were rife within the Vatican. Had there been a murder, Yallop's book certainly highlights some motives. But after Cornwell was done, Yallop was left without evidence that a murder had taken place—a fact he may now recognize. When I wrote asking to speak to him about the discrepancies, his agent responded that she had discussed it with him, and "perhaps the less said, the better."

---

* The six unfairly accused men were Archbishop Marcinkus, Cardinal Cody of Chicago, Vatican Secretary of State Villot, Roberto Calvi and Michele Sindona (the crooked bankers), and Licio Gelli, head of the crooked Masonic lodge.

Cornwell prodigiously and valuably recorded the testimony of the key witnesses, who had apparently not been interviewed before. But the Vatican and John Paul II couldn't have been pleased with his work. Cornwell mounted a clear case of medical neglect, the facts consistent with a death caused by inappropriately dosed medication. There remained unresolved questions about the strange circumstance in which the body was found—propped up in bed, as if reading, with no sign of trauma. Witnesses from the security staff fairly ruled out any unusual comings and goings that night. But Cornwell had no sure reason to believe the account of two persons who were clearly at the scene— the secretaries who said they hadn't seen the pope between the time he went to bed and the time the nun found his body.

Cornwell concluded his own investigation with a hypothetical guess: that the secretaries had found the body, perhaps collapsed on the floor, the night before. Then, embarrassed by their own lapses in responding to the pope's medical warning signals, they restaged the scene to make it look as if he had died quietly, reading. This might also explain why they slept later than normal.

We still don't know exactly what happened. The death of John Paul I, like most of his papacy, revealed unbecoming mismanagement at the Vatican. The result was the death of a good man, which might well have been prevented, and a continuing, widespread, unwarranted public suspicion that the pope was murdered.

Sunday, October 1, 1978, two days after the death, Cardinal Giovanni Benelli gave a sermon in France about the next pope. Benelli, a longtime curial official and now the archbishop of Florence, was credited with persuading many non-Italians to vote for Luciani in the August conclave. Now he said the next pope should be relatively young, healthy, and a proven administrator, but with pastoral experience. This was generally taken to be a reference to himself.

That night, Wojtyla eulogized John Paul I in the huge church in Krakow's market square. Afterward, Bardecki approached and asked permission to publish the eulogy in *Tygodnik Powszechny.* Wojtyla told Bardecki to edit it for him, as he was leaving for the funeral. Bardecki thought he "behaved strangely— asked me to pass greetings to friends as if he did not expect to return soon from Rome."

The next evening, Wojtyla and his secretary, Monsignor Dziwisz, brought Cywinski an envelope containing three months' pay—twenty-one thousand zlotys—and apologized for missing the previous month in all the confusion. They had chatted half an hour when Dziwisz suddenly asked if Wojtyla had the two thousand zlotys needed to pay the airport tax the next morning. Wojtyla never knowingly had a dime and didn't now. Embarrassed, they asked Cywinski to return two thousand zlotys so Wojtyla could catch the flight to Rome.

This time there was no need for weeks of meetings about the state of the Vatican. But in the two weeks before the conclave, Cardinal Siri noticed that Wojtyla seemed much tenser, declining afternoon trips to the seashore.[5]

König says he asked Wyszynski who he thought would be a good candidate, and was told, "I see none." Wyszynski thought the papacy would and should stay in Italian hands.

"Perhaps Poland will have a candidate," König suggested.

"Nonsense," said Wyszynski. "The communists always wanted me out of Poland. It would be a great triumph for them."

"Perhaps another cardinal," König said. Wyszynski seemed never to have considered Wojtyla.

"Oh, my goodness, he's far too young," Wyszynski replied.[6]

No, he wasn't. Already factors were falling into place that would make Wojtyla the ideal compromise candidate to be the first non-Italian pope in centuries. König reports receiving letters from priestly colleagues even in Italy, saying that the supply of premier Italian candidates was exhausted and that it was time to look abroad.

Siri was still the candidate of the curial authoritarians. But why should anyone think Siri could get more than the same 25 percent he got a month before? The key to the election may lie in the thoughts of Siri's closest friend and supporter, Cardinal Silvio Oddi.

"König has written that he was the man who anointed Cardinal Wojtyla," Oddi says. "Well, he was probably thinking he was. Certainly some cardinals were suggesting [Wojtyla's] name, and others were saying 'Why not?' I was one thinking, we should have a pope against communism. More cardinals were asking me privately, 'Who do you think would be a good pope?' I was thinking that having the courage to pick a pope from a communist country would be a blow against them. The cardinals supporting Wojtyla were saying we must fight against communism. We were convinced that this man was capable of doing something to not permit communism to go on."

And that was the pivotal issue, he says.[7]

It would be nonsense to say anti-communism was at or even near the top of the list of characteristics the conclave wanted in a pope. Wojtyla wouldn't have been under consideration were it not for his character, his faith, and numerous other factors—including the self-defeating bickering going on among the Italians. But at decision time anti-communism is what made him many people's second choice. Even Oddi, though, acknowledges that none of them imagined how decisive his election would be.

☙

Saturday, October 7, 1978, an Italian newspaper printed an interview with Cardinal Siri that he had believed wouldn't be published until after the cardinals were sequestered. In the interview, Siri belittled John Paul I as a tool of his curial handlers. The remark sparked a minor scandal.

How many people have destroyed themselves by trusting Italian journalists isn't on record, but it must be a lot. In this case, the sword cut two ways. Word spread that Benelli, Siri's chief Italian rival, had goaded the newspaper into publishing the interview prematurely. Both Siri and Benelli came away looking puerile and unpopelike.

Wojtyla spent the day at the Mentorella mountain shrine. The three Polish priests he brought with him gave out along the way, and he ascended the last miles to the mountain peak alone, as he often did. He was considered a probable Benelli voter. Greeley and Wynn both say that Sunday, October 8, Benelli's secretary met with Wojtyla, Bishop Deskur, and several other high Polish prelates gingerly seeking support and hinting that if Benelli faltered, he would throw support to Wojtyla; Deskur denies attending any such meeting.

A few days later, a dozen influential non-Italian cardinals, usually considered leaders in opposition to the curialists, held a critical meeting. These men favored change but, perhaps except for Suenens, not radical change. Among them, Greeley lists, and König confirms, Cardinals Willebrands of Holland, Lorscheider and Arns of Brazil, Alfrink of Belgium, Tarançon and Narciso Jubany-Arnau of Spain, Marty of France, and a few others. The same group, König says, "met from time to time. We had several talks about who was a possible candidate. We were interested in going beyond a conservative line." Cardinal Krol sometimes attended.

"The first point of interest was nationality," König says. Because there was still a Cold War going on, and dozens of countries wanted no part of it, no American could be considered. "France was impossible," König says, "and with Germany, there was the war, Nazism and all that." Cardinal Hume's Britishness was less a problem because the Anglican Church, not the Roman, represented Britain; but on issues, Hume seemed almost as strident as Suenens. And "Brazil was considered too far away," König says.

He concedes, "The ideas of cardinals before the conclave are not very rational. But it was a feeling. My interest was Wojtyla. I tried to suggest that he was a possible candidate. A very gifted man. Not everybody felt as I did at the time. Some said he was a little bit isolated in a communist country. Many cardinals had a wrong idea that bishops behind the Iron Curtain had to fight only for their Church, that they had no time for other problems."

It was suggested that Krol could probably deliver American votes for Wojtyla and that the German cardinals would be practically unanimous for him. The Spanish cardinals seemed to like him. Even Suenens, who differed with Wojtyla on theology and intended to cast his first vote for Benelli, left the meeting "moderately certain that Wojtyla would be elected" (Greeley's words) and happy about it. Wojtyla would be the youngest pope in 125 years. But who wanted another conclave soon? A consensus seemed to be that the Italians deserved a day to find a candidate but wouldn't make it.

Friday, October 13, the day before the conclave, Bishop Deskur, Wojtyla's old friend, suffered a major stroke. Wojtyla and other Poles in town gathered at the Gemelli Clinic, a Roman hospital, where Deskur lay near death. At four-thirty Saturday afternoon, Wojtyla joined the other cardinals behind the locked doors.

By consensus accounts, Siri led the first ballot, but with fewer than 50 votes. Benelli was close, but their totals were unlikely to grow. The remaining votes were scattered among Italians and non-Italians. Wojtyla got a handful. Unable to waste time, even in a conclave, he was seen with his nose in a Marxist journal.[8]

Benelli's supporters continued to hope. Greeley says Benelli led the second ballot. At the lunch break, however, Siri's supporters decided that if their man couldn't win, they would at least block Benelli. They buttonholed fence-sitters, particularly from abroad. Benelli's last push was the third ballot; it failed. By the fourth and final ballot of the day, Italians hoping to elect one of their own had lined up behind the aging Cardinal Colombo of Milan, but not nearly enough for victory.

As cardinals talked, a bit tensely, over dinner that night and in the garden afterward, Wojtyla was primed to reap votes from all sides. The supposed "liberal" bloc saw him as one of theirs because he was a non-Italian, pastoral-minded intellectual who loved discussion and shunned Church intrigue. Their antagonist, Siri, also turned to Wojtyla because "he was very conservative" about changes in the Mass and priestly behavior.[9] On communist issues, too, Wojtyla was uniquely positioned to attract both hard-liners and *Ostpolitikers*: who could doubt either his opposition to communists or his ability to deal with them?

Wojtyla himself told Wynn, "By the beginning of the second day, it all had become clear. I could feel that the Holy Spirit was working among the cardinals, and I could sense the outcome."

"On the second day, his name began to rise," König says. "On the next vote it grew solid. After lunch, a very big majority." Greeley says he passed 20 votes on the first ballot, 40 on the second, 60 on the third. By the last vote of the second day, the eighth overall, he passed 76 votes and was said to have neared 100.

Again, Cardinal Villot asked a colleague if he would accept the papacy; this time the answer, while pious, was unequivocal. Again Villot asked for a name. Much has been written about Wojtyla's choice of "John Paul II," and what it meant about where he aimed to take the Church. Though the name was ambiguous, Wojtyla was not.

Wojtyla's choice of name may have been a characteristic act of decency rather than a policy statement. Whatever else was happening, a pope had just died after thirty-three days. The Church was still in shock. Taking the man's innovative name was probably the best available way to recognize a fallen comrade.

Once again, the cardinals lined up to congratulate the new pope. At Konig's turn, he says, Wojtyla looked at him earnestly and asked, "How did it happen?"

"Holy Father, we're bound by secrecy," König replied, producing Pope John Paul II's first laugh.

Wojtyla embraced Wyszynski to keep him from dropping to his knees. Later Wyszynski told Siri, "I have lost a friend." Siri assured him that Wojtyla would still need old friends along with the new.

In Krakow, Bohdan Cywinski thought he had lost his two thousand zlotys for good, but he didn't mind.

Anna-Teresa Tymieniecka

Zbigniew Bujak

Father Jerzy Popielusko

Adam Michnik

BOOK FOUR

ARMAGEDDON

1

As John Paul II took office, a new semester began. Following his leadership, churches across Poland opened their doors to KOR's "flying university." Fliers were handed out openly on university campuses, and seventy well-known scholars endorsed the program publicly. As many as two hundred people turned up for lectures.

An intellectual revolution was under way. Befuddled authorities were afraid to enter churches, but did at times arrest scheduled lecturers on the street, or at the railroad station if arriving from out of town. Nothing like this had happened before under communism.

Determined as John Paul II was to push the revolution forward, his overriding call right now was to seize the reins of the Church. He altered papal routine with each new day. He plunged into crowds to shake hands and greet people after his weekly "general audiences" (open to the public). He warmed up to Italian communists, who in the 1976 elections had come within 2 percent of being the leading party in Italy. He was particularly cordial toward Giulio Argan, the first communist mayor of Rome, who had draped the city in welcoming signs for him. John Paul pledged to aid Argan on crime, employment, and a "guarantee [of] the right of every family to have a house."

The new pope took his job as bishop of Rome more seriously than had any pope in memory. Every Sunday, and on many holidays, he visited one or another parish and consulted with the (initially) startled priests about local problems. He quickly scheduled a meeting with all the city's priests, in which they aired their complaints: dwindling numbers of clergy and too little money. But if they were hinting that the priesthood should be made easier in order to attract more priests, they lost. John Paul reiterated, for the first time as pope, his belief in the importance of priestly celibacy and dress codes:

> We are necessary, immensely necessary, to our fellow men, and not in a part-time way, like employees. We are necessary as those who bear witness and awaken in others the need to bear witness. Let us not imagine we are serving the Gospel . . . if we seek to laicize our way of living and acting and eradicate the external signs of our vocation.

Within weeks he called in the heads of religious orders, whose members had increasingly taken to wearing civilian clothes for their largely civilian work. He said priests and nuns should

> be recognizable . . . in the streets as men and women who have given up everything worldly to follow Christ. . . . People need signs and reminders of God in the modern secular city, which has few reminders of God left.[1]

The Sunday after his inauguration, forty thousand of his Roman flock drove to meet him at Mentorella; he was now ferried by helicopter. Several thousand trekked up with him to where the cypresses met the blue sky. "This is where man opens himself to God in a special way," he said, "far from everything, yet close to nature, where he can talk intimately with God."

When he visited the tombs of Italy's guardian saints, Francis of Assisi and Catherine of Siena, tens of thousands showed up to catch a glimpse of him. He preached, shook hands, kissed babies.

The Vatican domestic staff, like the security men, were thrown off guard. Popes had customarily eaten alone or with a secretary. This one wanted guests for breakfast, lunch, and dinner—even after his friends from Poland had gone home. He worked eighteen-hour days and could schedule multiple meetings in an afternoon, not needing time to gear up for just one. Vatican diplomats on routine visits to Rome were startled to find themselves being grilled by a pope about local conditions. "It struck me he was making an enthusiastic effort to learn about parts of the world he was unfamiliar with," recalls Bishop (now Cardinal) Edward Cassidy, then the envoy to Bangladesh and Burma.

Amid all this, John Paul still read his former students' doctoral theses; a month after his inauguration, he returned two, with critiques. His speeches were regularly printed in the Vatican newspaper, *Osservatore Romano*, with his *I*'s and *my*'s left intact. Even he had trouble getting used to his victory; speaking

French to one ecumenical group, he said *"nous"*—"we"—then paused to stress that he meant "all of us here."

To introduce his ideas to *Osservatore Romano* readers, he selected two articles from earlier years to be reprinted. His choices, from a lifetime of writings, said a lot about his priorities. One was his defense of *Humanae Vitae*, the birth-control encyclical. The other was an essay arguing that Jesus addressed each of humanity's four billion people individually, and that there were no abstract "masses" in the Marxist sense.

His first recorded formal action on a political matter, November 8, 1978, was another sign of his priorities. Without making any public disclosure, he reversed Paul VI's decision and put the Pauline order, and Father Michael Zembrzuski's insolvent and mismanaged shrine in Pennsylvania, back under Cardinal Wyszynski's control. John Paul then ordered the stunned American investigators, Bishop Guilfoyle and Father Boyle, to submit a final report. They did, several months later. Again they advised that the Paulines should expel Father Zembrzuski and the priests loyal to him. The pope rejected their report.

"Zembrzuski won," Boyle said later—and blamed the "political situation in Poland."[2]

"The Polish pope, he helped us very much," Zembrzuski says now. "He knew very well this situation. In a very short time the whole thing was finished."

Not quite.

Before his papacy was a month old, John Paul acted secretly on another controversial issue that had lain dormant: he pledged to make a major Church institution out of Opus Dei, an international Catholic society whose many adherents see it as a model for mankind but whose many opponents call it—in Father Andrew Greeley's words—"dishonest and untrustworthy." While Opus Dei professes to be wholly aboveboard, important facts about it are kept clandestine—such as who its members are, and, for a long time, the pope's 1978 commitment to it.

Opus Dei ("God's Work") was founded in Spain in 1928 by Father Josemaría Escrivá de Balaguer and began to expand at about the same time that Jan Tyranowski, Wojtyla's early religious mentor, was forming his Living Rosary in Krakow. Opus Dei shared many principles with the Living Rosary, which helps explain its appeal for John Paul. Besides adherence to the Catholic religion, these principles included a Spartan rigor in daily life, yet a purposeful rigor, aimed at academic learning and self-understanding.

Unlike Tyranowski, however, Father Escrivá drove people to learning not for its own sake but rather to serve Catholicism in careers. He sought mainly good-looking, highly intelligent followers who would excel professionally in fields like banking, journalism, and commerce. Also unlike Tyranowski, Escrivá aspired on a grand scale: by the time he died, in 1975, he had recruited seventy thousand members on six continents, who, he said, "daily resolve to make the doctrine of Christ known by their own example."

Opus Dei said most members were married, 2 percent were priests, and others were single and pledged to celibacy. Members often lived together in austere quarters, with space allotted for work, sleeping, prayer, eating, sanitation, and not much else. At best there might be a recreation area; sport was valued as part of a fitness regimen, but just having fun was generally frowned on.

Even today, Opus Dei's lay members—known as numeraries—are expected to turn over their income to the organization, and are given pocket money. All incoming and outgoing mail must be read by a spiritual director, who also must approve any courses members take, and even what they may read. Members confess only to Opus Dei priests. Outsiders sometimes have trouble understanding how Opus Dei members—stylishly groomed, seemingly urbane, and skilled at exciting work—can cheerfully defend all this, as if there were nothing unusual about it.

Recruitment is aggressive and covert. The target is not told at first why someone is suddenly befriending him, or the nature of the "center" where he is invited for a lecture, or what is entailed in joining.[3] Opus Dei is sometimes accused of being a cult. (A cult, of course, could be defined as any religious organization whose followers are more enthusiastic about it than *you* are about *yours.*)

Opus Dei has also been accused of fascism because it aided, and was encouraged by, the Fascist dictatorship of General Franco in Spain. This is another difference between Escrivá and Tyranowski, who risked his life to defy a Fascist dictatorship—though Escrivá did reject, absolutely, the violence that fascism employs. Violence, he said, was not "an apt means for . . . winning a [dispute]. Error is to be fought with prayer, . . . study, and persuading others to study."

In 1969, Opus Dei members took over most cabinet posts in the Spanish government in an effort to put a respectable face on Franco's dictatorship.[4] The group survived a scandal when it was exposed that agencies under Opus Dei control had awarded large grants to secret Opus Dei members who were accused of having misused the money.

Pope John XXIII officially recognized Opus Dei as an institute of the Church. But he, and Paul VI after him, consistently refused to do what Escrivá really wanted—to make Opus Dei the equivalent of a religious order, its priests reporting directly to the Vatican, independent of local bishops. Opus Dei couldn't *be* a religious order, because most members were laymen. But Escrivá wanted to exploit a previously unused provision of Church law for something called a personal prelature, which would accomplish the same thing. His request drew vigorous opposition from bishops, particularly in Britain and France, where Opus Dei was active and resented.

After Escrivá died in 1975, his successor, Monsignor Alvaro del Portillo, continued to lobby Pope Paul for a personal prelature. He wrote that Opus Dei members "now operate . . . 475 universities and high schools on five continents; 604 periodicals, reviews, and scientific publications; fifty-two radio and TV channels; thirty-eight news agencies; and a dozen [film] production companies." A personal prelature, he said, would "make it possible for the Holy See to use a mobile (and exceptionally well trained) force" to evangelize "circles of civil society and professional activity."[5] The memo seemed to imply what Escrivá had repeatedly denied: that Opus Dei members were covert agents, infiltrating society with an agenda that they hid from their unsuspecting employers and customers.

Had Opus Dei's members not been skilled and dedicated, they would not have attained the powerful jobs they held. The members I have met all display exceptional talent at their work and rectitude in their lives. Other than the financial scandal in Spain, no misconduct has surfaced. But Opus Dei bothered enough people that popes were inclined to keep it in its place—until November 15, 1978.

On that date, John Paul promised del Portillo "no further delay" in getting a personal prelature. The new pope acted under the guise of sending greetings for Opus Dei's fiftieth anniversary, though the anniversary had passed weeks before John Paul's election.

Years later, when other Catholics learned of Opus Dei's new status, rumors spread that John Paul owed a secret debt to Opus Dei. Some said Opus Dei had promoted him for the papacy and paid for his travels. No evidence of this has been offered, however. Cardinal Wojtyla had no unaccounted-for expenses; his travel, as a guest of churchmen, was inexpensive, and Poles everywhere had begged to pay for it. Opus Dei had supported Cardinal Siri for the papacy in newspaper advertisements—not Wojtyla, who seemed to prefer the rival Benelli.

There is no evidence either in *Kalendarium* (his official history) or elsewhere that Wojtyla paid much attention to Opus Dei before his papacy. He prayed at Escrivá's tomb in Rome before the 1978 conclaves, and once attended an Opus Dei–sponsored conference; but he prayed at somebody's tomb or shrine every few days, and went to hundreds of conferences.

Still, the Vatican never answered my repeated inquiry as to when, if ever, John Paul met Escrivá. The two men happened to have come to Rome for the first time within weeks of each other in the winter of 1946–47. Wojtyla, with his respect for asceticism, would have been interested in Escrivá's movement. Did they meet? Did that influence John Paul, before his papal chair was even warm, to rush through secret approval for Opus Dei's controversial request for a prelature? The answers to these questions are probably innocent, but they can't be relayed here because no one will provide them.[6]

In the same few days during which he forgave the multimillion-dollar misfeasance at the Paulines and guaranteed Opus Dei its special status, John Paul also reached out to revive the career of a bishop whom Paul VI had all but excommunicated: Marcel Lefebvre of France, who had revolted publicly against Vatican II. Paul had banned Lefebvre from priestly work in 1977 for continuing to train and ordain priests in pre–Vatican II, Latin-language style.

"We beg our brother . . . not to commit yet another grave act of disobedience," Paul had said about the ordinations, stressing the personal "sadness" and "suffering" that Lefebvre caused him. But Lefebvre defied Pope Paul, as he had for years, and continued his mutinous ordaining of priests.

Why would John Paul II, a stickler for unity and obedience, grant this willful insubordinate a thirty-minute private audience and publicly embrace him before and after it? Whatever John Paul's intention, it backfired. Lefebvre abused his goodwill, later denouncing Popes John XXIII and Paul VI for having "destroyed . . . the faith [with] liberal-communist Council reforms." Lefebvre said that by receiving him, John Paul had set him free to "reject the magisterium of those popes." But even after Lefebvre thus slandered John Paul's two namesakes, he was not disciplined; instead, he was invited back to the Vatican for more talks.

As in the cases of Father Zembrzuski and Opus Dei, the new pope's impulse to resolve the Lefebvre problem merely postponed it. Each situation was now a time bomb set to go off later in his administration.

2

After the inauguration euphoria, the Polish government reversed itself and said a papal visit home would be impossible. "They had lots of trouble trying to convince the Soviets," says Archbishop Poggi, the nuncio for Eastern Europe.

Poggi badgered Gierek. "You have weighed what the pope's visit would mean," he said, "but have you also weighed what preventing the Polish pope's visit would mean? It would cause a great outrage. The pope wouldn't swallow this denial. He would speak out against it."

This was no idle threat. John Paul had begun to unravel *Ostpolitik* from almost the moment he took office. He had dispatched Poggi to Hungary to light a fire under Cardinal Lekai, Mindszenty's replacement. Lekai was told to be more vigorous and to "make the witness of his Church more effective."[1] Now Poggi's orders from the pope were to ride Gierek until a visit to Poland was approved.

John Paul proposed another, even more sensational policy switch that the curia talked him out of. The new pope decided to spend his first papal Christmas in Bethlehem, scene of *the* first Christmas. Cardinal Casaroli, still the top Vatican diplomat, broke into a sweat. Bethlehem was on the West Bank of the Jordan River, he pointed out. Formerly in Jordan, it had been held by Israel since the Six-Day War. The Vatican didn't recognize Israel.

Well, said John Paul, let's recognize it now. His Jewish friends had encouraged that all along.

Casaroli sputtered. There was no mutually accepted boundary. The Vatican couldn't recognize Israel for the same reason it hadn't recognized the Polish-German border before a treaty was signed. Such a policy was needed to avoid endless temporal disputes.

On this point John Paul, proving he was not impervious to argument, gave in.[2]

Almost at once, though, the Carter administration handed him the kind of peacemaking opportunity popes seek but rarely get. The dictators of Chile and Argentina, both notorious for murdering their political opponents, were threatening war with each other over three little islands at the southern end of the long border they shared. Even as wars go, this one seemed ridiculous.

Carter's national security adviser, Zbigniew Brzezinski, sensed that the real issue wasn't islands, but rather, a concept that Carter was trying to introduce into international diplomacy: human rights. Carter had begun to shut off U.S. military aid to countries run by murderers and torturers, though people everywhere still disbelieved he was serious about it. American Cold Warriors, eager to continue supporting anti-communist dictators throughout the Third World, ridiculed Carter as naive. The dictators themselves were furious at having their pipelines to the U.S. taxpayer cut.

"My impression was that both the Argentine and Chilean military wanted to divert [Carter] from his human-rights policy," says Robert Pasztor, a Brzezinski aide who handled the problem. "And there were people in the U.S. government who were eager to get Carter to drop his policy and get closer to these governments. The issue from my perspective was, how do we retain our human-rights policy and at the same time reduce the prospects for war? And it occurred to me on the eve of Christmas, it might be resolved by the pope."

John Paul readily agreed. Chile and Argentina, predominantly Catholic countries, accepted Vatican mediation, and the war was averted. The human-rights policy, the dream of both Carter and the pope, stayed in place.

At Christmas and New Year's, John Paul told gatherings:

> Where there is no justice ... there can be no peace.... Where there is no respect for human rights ... there can be no peace, because every violation of personal dignity favors rancor and the spirit of revenge.
>
> Recourse to arms cannot be considered the right means for settling conflicts.... It is not permissible to kill in order to impose a solution.... The din of battle dominates history. But it is the respites from violence that have made possible the production of those lasting cultural works that give honor to mankind.

John Paul also wrote to his former flock in Krakow, reminding them again of Saint Stanislaw's "magnificent example of concern about people, which we have to compare with our indifference ... and despondency." Krakowians couldn't read the Christmas message, however; censors banned the references to Stanislaw, and *Tygodnik Powszechny* refused to run an altered version. An entire issue of *Wiez* devoted to the meaning of the pope's election was also banned.

John Paul fired back immediately to establish that he was no longer Cardinal Wojtyla and would no longer be subject to Polish censors. The very next Sunday, as Western TV cameras captured his weekly prayer service from his apartment window overlooking St. Peter's, he assailed the Polish government's repression of information. Then, having named Bishop Franciszek Macharski to succeed him in Krakow, he brought Macharski to Rome for a Mass in the Sistine Chapel and had the sermon—on Saint Stanislaw—broadcast on Vatican Radio "to reach the whole Church in Poland, all dioceses and parishes."[3] Then he ordered a Mass beamed home in Polish every Sunday afternoon, whether the communists liked it or not. Poles would hear what their pope had to say.

John Paul invited Soviet Foreign Minister Andrei Gromyko to the Vatican for an unusually long talk, two hours, to ask (according to Gromyko) whether Soviet citizens had freedom of religion. Gromyko wrote in his memoir that the pope had accepted his assurance that Soviet religion was free.[4] John Paul told reporters the next day that it was "the most tiresome" audience he'd had yet as pope.[5]

That very day, Zbigniew Romaszewski—the KOR leader who had secretly obtained printing equipment from the U.S. embassy in Warsaw—was in the Soviet Union. Romaszewski, a physicist, had received permission to attend a professional conference there, but says his real purpose was to meet and "link operations" with dissident physicist Andrei Sakharov. Sakharov, who had helped build the Soviet hydrogen bomb, was now an outcast for protesting the police state.[6] Romaszewski and Sakharov arranged to correspond by secret courier.

Unable to attend the papal inaugural, French President Valéry Giscard d'Estaing sent as his personal representative André Frossard, a devout Catholic journalist he knew. Like others in the crowd, Frossard was electrified by John Paul's phrase "Do not be afraid." He decided this message wasn't intended only for people under communism: "I saw it also addressed to the communists' own fear of humanity. And to Western people afraid of communism," he says.

Frossard immediately phoned his newspaper in Paris: "This pope does not come from Poland. He comes from Galilee." Determined to meet John Paul, Frossard passed his business card the next day to Monsignor Dziwisz. What happened next is what happened over the years to many people lucky enough to capture John Paul's attention.

Frossard was invited to a papal speech, after which security men called him and a few others backstage for a brief papal greeting. As John Paul left, Dziwisz whispered in Frossard's ear, "Be at the 'Bronze Door' on the right of St. Peter's at six forty-five tomorrow morning. Be on time."

Frossard was there by six-thirty. He was met by men from the Swiss Guard, a Vatican honor group that has worn the same brightly striped, oddly clown-like costumes for centuries. (Tourist legend ascribes their design to Michelangelo.) Frossard was walked down a corridor and up to a small private courtyard one story above St. Peter's, surrounded by Secretariat of State offices. From the courtyard he caught a small elevator, operated by a nun, to the fourth floor, the site of senior officials' offices—and the papal apartment.

In the apartment's white marble chapel, Frossard found the pope already before the altar, deep in prayer. A replica of the Black Madonna stared down from the wall. The papal household quietly assembled, and at seven, the pope began Mass. When it was over, he came up, took Frossard by the arm, scolded him playfully for not bringing his wife, and said, "Come, we shall talk." In the next room waited a Polish-Italian breakfast spread of rolls, jams, sliced ham and cheese, and coffee.

Frossard was stunned by the pope's detailed questions. John Paul had read up on his guest—knew that Frossard's father had been a French communist leader, and that Frossard, like the pope, had favored the French worker-priest movement. John Paul praised Frossard's book *God Exists, I Have Met Him*, which had sold well in Europe but not in the United States, and they confessed a shared conviction that "Americans lack seriousness."

Suddenly the pope said, "We must write a book together, you and I. Ask me questions." Frossard almost fell off his chair.

"He said he wanted to make his ideas and his self known," and that he preferred a book to a television interview because "a book would penetrate the conscience. Pictures flee, a book stays. He had written books on philosophy and theological questions, but wanted something understandable to a lay person." Frossard persuaded the pope to let him plan his questions before they continued.

In scores of irregular meetings over two years, they put together a book of papal insights, *"Be Not Afraid!"* [7] Although it was built around Frossard's questions, the pope, in his usual style, substituted philosophy for personal information whenever he could. The book sold well in Europe, but—as its authors would have predicted—bombed in the United States. (In 1994, John Paul responded similarly to questions from an Italian journalist and produced a book not discernibly more interesting or better written than the one with Frossard; yet it became a raging American best-seller, *Crossing the Threshold of Hope.*)

Meanwhile, John Paul's election had also spurred Anna-Teresa Tymieniecka's publisher to race *The Acting Person* into a hot market. Professor Potocki, John Paul's translator in Krakow, kept trying to warn the pope that Tymieniecka, in his opinion, was making "a number of changes very much going away from the intentions of the author. Her idea was to make Wojtyla a phenomenologist, which simply wasn't true." But the pope was busy.

Vatican minions cabled Tymieniecka not to publish—that rights now belonged to the Church. She says a consultant double-checked her work, and "further delay . . . was impossible."

January 2, 1979, Potocki received proofs in the mail from Tymieniecka with instructions to correct and return them by December 31—two days before. Still seeing what he thought was distortion of the pope's views, he fired back revisions. But he says he was told the book had already gone to press. [8]

3

Among the first challenges facing John Paul after his election was the every-ten-years meeting of the Conference of Latin American bishops, known as CELAM. The pending meeting in Puebla, Mexico, was crucial. At the previous meeting, at Medellín, Colombia, in 1968, the bishops had radically departed from their traditional alliance with the oligarchies and military regimes of the region. Led by Archbishop Helder Camara (with whom Wojtyla had argued at Vatican II), CELAM had voted to side with the poor, under the banner of Liberation Theology. Pope Paul had accepted that decision.

Since then, turbulence had swept the region. In many parishes, the Church gave the poor courage to assert their rights. Landless workers, demanding more reward for their labor, were terrorized by armies protecting the oligarchs' estates. Government treasuries were drained to repay foreign bank loans, the proceeds of which had disappeared into relatively few private pockets. Many in the U.S. blamed the turmoil on Fidel Castro, the Cuban dictator, who hoped to exploit the situation by encouraging communist revolution.

In a heavily Catholic region, the policy decisions of the new CELAM meeting loomed large. The bishops might decide to continue to support the poor or might revert to an alliance with the oligarchs, whose families were well represented among the bishops. Some still said the Church could be on both sides at once, though the sides saw themselves in a life-and-death struggle. Even among bishops, angry voices abounded, and Vatican leadership could be pivotal.

John Paul I had decided to skip the meeting, which was originally set for October. He feared he couldn't master the problems and should just leave them to the Latin bishops. The Vatican curia advised John Paul II to stay home as well, and edit CELAM's proposals from the safety of his office.[1] But this pope's characteristic response was to reschedule CELAM when he could attend, and to call in a Spanish tutor every morning until then.

In January 1979, the new pope got his first sight of Latin America, stopping two days in the Dominican Republic en route to Mexico. It was soon clear what a difficult task he faced. He spoke of ancient history—how Columbus founded the first colony in the Americas there, in 1492—but he avoided recent history—a U.S. invasion in 1965 to stop the country's only elected president in fifty years from taking office. American sugar companies had accused the electee of communist influence. As twenty thousand U.S. troops protected the sugar companies' grip on the Dominican economy, the Vatican, indirectly, shared in the profit: the biggest plantations were owned by Gulf & Western Industries, which had put up the money used by Michele Sindona, the mobster, to buy assets from the Vatican. But the paradox passed John Paul by. He instinctively attacked social and economic unfairness, but seemed oblivious to the power relationships behind it.

In the slums of Santo Domingo, he told vast crowds:

> To make this world more just means, among other things, making sure there are no children without sufficient food, without education; that there are no young people without suitable training; that there are no peasants without land [most Dominican farmers were plantation employees] . . . ; that there are no systems that permit the exploitation of man by man or by the state; that there is no corruption; that no one lives in superabundance when others, through no fault of their own, are in poverty . . . ; that the law protects all alike; that force does not prevail over truth and right, but truth and right over force; and that economic or political matters never prevail over human matters.[2]

In Latin America, this was no small undertaking. It would require overthrowing the established order—and overthrowing U.S. policy. The elected Dominican president, Juan Bosch, had been blocked from office by U.S. troops for trying to implement exactly what the pope was now advocating: laws to limit foreign ownership of Dominican farmland and require corporations to share their profits or land with Dominican farm labor. As in Poland, it was one thing to decry injustice, another to address the forces responsible.

The Mexican trip was the first of the papal journeys that became a John Paul II trademark. There was a chartered Alitalia jet with the pope up front, two dozen aides in the compartment behind him, and 150 or so others, mostly journalists, in the rear. The pope granted informal interviews on the plane, and kissed the ground upon arriving. He bantered amiably in local dialect, was always ready with a good-natured quip, yet never soiled his dignity.

There were almost nonstop events from dawn to late evening. Separate meetings were scheduled with government leaders, local priests and nuns, local parishioners, Polish immigrants, youth groups, local non-Catholics, and whatever special-purpose organizations were appropriate to the locale. There were open-air Masses attended by hundreds of thousands of people. He traveled the eighty miles from Mexico City southeast to Puebla, site of the CELAM conference, standing in a specially constructed open car—a prototype of what later became known as the popemobile—waving to the throngs that lined the highway.

All this was to be repeated everywhere he went for fifteen years, until a broken leg forced him to slow his pace. The show—and it *was* a show—attracted enough journalists paying their own way on the plane to help support the trips.

What John Paul lacked in Latin America wasn't courage. The CELAM conference he had chosen to attend was a hornets' nest. Many, maybe most, bishops wanted to encourage vigorous social activism. In nearby El Salvador, Archbishop Oscar Romero had just excommunicated the country's president over the constant murder of priests and laymen by Salvadoran troops. Three Chilean bishops headed to CELAM were stoned at the airport by the secret police,[3] who had already tortured and killed thousands of political opponents of U.S.-backed dictator Augusto Pinochet. Brutality against priests was reported in Brazil, Ecuador, Argentina, Bolivia, Uruguay, Nicaragua, El Salvador, Paraguay, and Guatemala.

Supporters of Liberation Theology, including many cardinals and other international Church figures, said they wanted the Church to be the "unifying factor of all Latin American societies, and . . . the liberating force which alone can ensure full participation and justice."[4] Official CELAM documents denied that Liberation Theology was mostly political, and endorsed the movement as "the birth of a new kind of civilization." Liberation Theology had inspired Church human-rights groups to begin registering atrocities that previously went unrecorded. Dictators were embarrassed, and businessmen said they feared a papal visit could provoke rebellion.

But on his first trip to Latin America, John Paul brought a message from Eastern Europe: a warning against communism. Flying to Mexico, he still saw Liberation Theology through the lens of Poland's Pax movement, as a front for communists who sought credibility by associating with priests. He misread the situation.

Nowhere could he have found Catholics more oppressed or in need of spiritual help. Yet the evil of communism was not the particular evil they suffered from. Despite his past denunciation of the excesses of capitalism, here in the region where capitalism was most out of bounds, he told his priests to ignore it:

> You are priests. . . . You are not social or political leaders or officials
> of a temporal power. . . . Temporal leadership can easily be a source
> of division, while the priest should be an . . . agent of unity and
> brotherhood.

It was a remarkable message from the patron of the hunger strike and "flying university." John Paul, who had told the Polish clergy to stand up for justice, was telling the Latin clergy to mind their manners. But he had been

alienated by the theological tone of some in CELAM. In his main address, he
warned the delegates that they were

> teachers of . . . not a human and rational truth, but the truth that
> comes from God. . . . Some Christians portray Jesus as a political
> activist, a fighter against Roman oppression, even as one involved
> in the class struggle. This idea of Christ as a political figure, a rev-
> olutionary, as the subversive from Nazareth, does not tally with
> the Church's teaching. . . . He opens his message of conversion to
> everyone.

Puebla, where the pope was speaking, was near the border with Guatemala,
where literally tens of thousands of citizens had been murdered in recent years
for the economic benefit of large landowners. Yet John Paul told the churchmen to stick to "a Christian idea of liberation," not an "ideological" one. He
even equated several kidnapings by rebel groups in South America with the
government-sponsored bloodbaths.

The Mexican press, among the freest in Latin America, reported his
remarks critically. Cardinal König observed that the pope had paid too much
attention to a minority of conservative Latin bishops. Brazil's Cardinal
Lorscheider followed John Paul to the platform and said what he had not:
"The injustices . . . domination by a ruling few . . . hinder liberation and the
formation of man."

What John Paul had meant to do, according to his friend Marek Skwarnicki
of *Tygodnik Powszechny*, was relate the message of his old hero Brother Albert: the
pastor's role was to follow the flock to the revolution, not to lead it. If that was
the pope's intention, though, he misjudged the effect of his words.

But he listened to his critics. Stung by the unexpected negative reaction to
his opening speech, he changed his tone the next day to address hundreds of
thousands of Indians at Oaxaca:

> The pope wants to be your voice, the voice of those who cannot
> speak or who are silenced; the defender of the oppressed, who have
> the right to effective help, not . . . the crumbs of justice.

He spoke of "the deprived world of the rural areas . . . the worker, who by
the sweat of his brow waters his affliction." He said the worker

> has the right to be respected, not deprived of the little he has
> through manipulations that at times amount to real thefts.

It is necessary to initiate, without delay, agricultural reforms. ... The Church defends the legitimate right to private property, but it teaches no less clearly that private property always carries with it a social obligation.... If the common good requires, there must be no doubt about expropriation itself, carried out in the proper manner.

As in Poland, he decried "the flight from the countryside to the cities" and the "overcrowding in houses unworthy of human peoples." He assailed

leaders of the powerful classes, which sometimes keep land unproductive and hide the bread that so many families lack. The cry of the destitute and above all the voice of God, the voice of the Church, [tells them] it is not just, it is not human, it is not Christian.

At a stop in a wealthier district, he said,

I call with all my strength on those who have means, and who feel they are Christians, to renew their minds and hearts, promote greater justice, and even give something of their own, so that no one will lack proper food, clothing, housing, culture, and work.

For seven days he toured Mexico. His plane circled Guadalajara for an hour while hundreds of thousands of people below flashed mirrors reflecting the sun. Never did he return to the negativity of his first days.

At a prison, he recited prayers over a loudspeaker with twenty-four hundred inmates. At night, students serenaded him under his window. In Monterrey, factories stopped and workers flocked to hear him advocate trade-unionism and environmentalism. He was saying now what many bishops had wanted him to say all along:

Those who have the fortune to work wish to do so in more human and secure conditions, to participate more justly in the fruit of the common effort.... They want to be treated as free and responsible men, to take part in the decisions that concern their lives.... It is their fundamental right to freely create organizations to ... promote their interests.

The task is complicated today by ... unjust commercial and financial circles, the rapid exhaustion of some resources, and the risks of irreversible contamination of the ... environment.

He denounced American firms that hired migrant Mexican labor in order to "offer lower wages, reduce social-insurance and welfare benefits, and provide housing unworthy of a human being."

Ambivalence would dog his Latin American policy for eight more years, until the Liberation Theology fight was settled. But John Paul never lost the vision he painted in Santo Domingo and rural Mexico: families had a right to work their own land or, if they chose employment on the land of others, a right to modern amenities and a proper share of the profits.

The Latin bishops produced a 230-page report condemning both Marxism and market capitalism. Perhaps with John Paul in mind, they observed that "the fear of Marxism prevents many from confronting the oppressive reality of liberal capitalism. Faced with the danger of one sinful system, some forget . . . to fight the reality inherent in the other sinful system." The delegates called for "an international statute regulating the activities of multinational companies."*

4

March 9, 1979, Vatican Secretary of State Jean Villot died at age seventy-three. His timing gave John Paul a graceful chance to appoint his own management team.

Cardinal Casaroli replaced Villot, which was widely misinterpreted to mean that *Ostpolitik* would continue. In fact, *Ostpolitik* had died the day John Paul was elected. The pope would be his own foreign secretary. But he was astute enough to realize that as the first non-Italian pope in 455 years, he needed an Italian secretary of state, both to placate the Italians in the curia and to steer his decisions through their arcane politics. Casaroli had spent his career in the curia and had relatives in high Church jobs. John Paul had known him for years—knew where they differed (which didn't matter because John Paul would set his own policy) and where they agreed.

For specific anti-communist work, John Paul chose another agent, Jozef Tomko of Czechoslovakia, and rocketed him through the curia to give him the stature he needed for the job. Tomko was swiftly made a bishop and given the

---

* The bishops could be accused of unfairly equating liberal capitalism with oligarchical dictatorship—just as democratic socialism was sometimes unfairly equated with Stalinism. A market is not free when land is controlled by a minority whose means are violence rather than a social contract.

official title of standing representative of the bishops' synod. Brzezinski says that when John Paul became pope, Tomko took over the "operational" aspects of dealing with the Eastern European underground Church.

Brzezinski recalls being invited to Tomko's office on a visit to Rome and meeting a covert priest from the Soviet Union. The priest held a cover job as a factory worker and had been sneaked into Italy on a ruse. Tomko questioned the priest about conditions in the USSR in front of the obviously impressed U.S. national security adviser.

Tomko (who said he wanted to be interviewed for this book but couldn't find time) must have known about Wojtyla's secret ordinations of Czechoslovakians and probably shared Wojtyla's feelings when Pope Paul weakened the underground Church during *Ostpolitik*. (Tomko is among the pope's closest advisers; in 1985, he was made a cardinal and put in charge of the Congregation for Evangelization.)

Also in the 1979 reshuffling, John Paul moved to restore the priestly discipline he constantly talked about. He hastened the resignation of dying American cardinal John Wright, whose management of the Congregation for the Clergy had never been forceful, and substituted Silvio Oddi, the old curia hand who takes credit for bringing Siri supporters around to voting for Wojtyla in the conclave.

"When I was appointed," Oddi says, the pope "called an audience to tell me what was expected of me: to make sure priests didn't change the habit [clerical dress] and to work in favor of a good catechism. Those two things." Oddi was specifically directed to halt projects by several national bishops' groups to write their own catechisms. "We profess the same faith in all countries and should have the same catechism," the pope told him. Oddi began by inviting suggestions from priests worldwide. Neither man could have guessed that twelve years would pass before the new catechism was issued.

What may have touched off the catechism crisis was a dispute within the Dutch Church, which became public while John Paul was touring Mexico. Reports said a majority of Dutch bishops had declared that abortion, homosexuality, and priestly celibacy were still open issues; a minority disagreed.[1]

John Paul believed that before the Church could accomplish the good he envisioned, it must end such disputes and define itself more certainly. To a world adrift, he wanted to speak from a rock, not from a portable soapbox. As journalist Wilton Wynn put it, he "wanted the little old lady in the pew to know what her Church stood for."

He also sought every opportunity to establish individual moral accountability for the consequences of action, a cornerstone of his *Acting Person* philosophy. He felt that growing denial of responsibility at all levels of society underlay a social breakdown. This one issue, personal responsibility, explains, at least in part, his policies on everything from land ownership to birth control.

In the first of what were to be annual Easter week letters to priests, he declared that the days of easy resignation were over. Paul VI, with what he said was a heavy heart, had allowed 31,324 priestly resignations, of 32,357 applications; John Paul I granted two hundred more in his mere thirty-three days as pope. No more. John Paul II linked the unreliability of priests to the increasing breakup of families.

> It is a matter here of keeping one's word to Christ and the Church.... Difficulties, temptation do not spare the priest any more than they spare any other Christian.... Our brothers and sisters joined by the marriage bond have the right to expect from us ... the [same] witness of fidelity.[2]

When it came to giving their word, the pope wanted people to focus on what they said, not on the loopholes available for escape.

Improving relations with Jews was also high on John Paul's agenda. The pope sought to redress a long history of Vatican anti-Semitism. Back in 1555, Pope Paul IV had banned Jews from business, tortured and humiliated them in public entertainments, and burned many alive, claiming they had "fallen into eternal servitude by their own guilt" in Jesus' death. As late as 1870, popes kept Jews in ghettos; Garibaldi's conquering troops freed them. Vatican II finally exculpated Jews in Jesus' death, but the potential goodwill from this act was lost when many bishops vigorously opposed it.

Since his childhood in Wadowice, John Paul had been driven from the heart on this issue. Inviting the heads of Jewish organizations to the Vatican, he pledged that differences over whether Jesus was the Messiah wouldn't prevent "fraternal dialogue and fruitful collaboration."

But the meeting was doomed from the start over a new issue: Israel. John Paul was blunt about the problem. He believed that Jerusalem, the formerly divided city that Israel had captured in the 1967 war, should "be effectively guaranteed as a center of harmony for the followers of the three great monotheistic religions." He wanted the UN to open Jerusalem to all and restore the rights of its former Palestinian residents. Everyone knew, however, that Israel had made Jerusalem its capital and was determined to hold on to it. This issue would frustrate the pope for many years in his quest to heal Christian-Jewish divisions.

✌

Three days after this meeting, John Paul released his first encyclical, *Redemptor Hominis* ("The Redeemer of Man"), defining the state of mankind as his papacy began and suggesting the breadth of his ambitions. The speed of preparation (five months) and scope of the work were extraordinary. Unlike other papal documents of the recent past, it was written by the man who signed it.

Redemptor Hominis began unusually for papal documents, with personal comments (mostly pretty bland) about recent popes and the papal election. It concluded with a fairly standard appeal for the Catholic faith. But the middle third was a tribute to the individual ("each one of four thousand million human beings") and a pungent critique of modern life.

Under both capitalism and communism, it said, man had become "the slave of things, the slave of economic systems . . . and the slave of his own production." Fear had become

> the main chapter of the drama of present-day existence. . . . The man of today seems ever to be under threat from what he produces, from the work of his hands, and even more from the work of his intellect and the tendencies of his will. All too soon . . . it is simply taken away from the person who produces it [, and] it turns against man himself.

Man "often seems to see no other meaning in his natural environment than what serves for his immediate use and consumption." God wanted man to be the "master and guardian" of nature, not the "exploiter and destroyer" of it:

> A civilization purely materialistic in outline condemns man to slavery, even if at times this occurs contrary to the intentions of its pioneers. . . . The person who, on the one hand, is trying to draw maximum profit, and, on the other hand, is paying the price in damage and injury, is always man.

"In the sector of trade," the pope said, "the laws of healthy competition must be allowed to lead the way." But there must also be an

> immediate redistribution of riches. . . . The task requires resolute commitment by individuals and peoples who are free and linked in solidarity. Too often freedom is confused with . . . the instinct for

combat and domination, whatever ideological colors they are covered with.

If he had said *that* to the bishops in Mexico, they might have been happier.

A few days later, at his general audience, he attacked "the excessive growth" of television in wealthy countries, as if he had meant to include television in his encyclical. TV, he said, hampered

> development, particularly in children. . . . The child lives on sensations alone, seeking new ones all the time . . . and often remains intellectually passive; the intellect does not engage in the search for truth; the will remains bound by habit.

John Paul suggested giving up television for Lent. He asked TV executives to relinquish "your adherence to program planning geared to instant success and maximum audience ratings."

Within days, he delivered a similar message to physical scientists meeting in Rome. Addressing them in French and Italian, he said, "The universe has a harmony in all its parts. Every upsetting of the ecological balance brings harm to man." Scientists, he warned, should "not treat nature as a slave, but . . . consider it as a sister called to cooperate."

He saved particularly strong words for soldiers, whom he addressed repeatedly. The morning after his return from Mexico, someone had scheduled a visit to the Vatican by the directors and staff of the NATO War College. What these visitors expected to hear can only be guessed at, but the pope bluntly told them to find other work:

> Sensitivity to the immense needs of humanity brings with it a spontaneous rejection of the arms race, which is incompatible with the all-out struggle against hunger, sickness, underdevelopment, and illiteracy. . . . Reflect on the sacredness of human life, on the exigencies of justice, and on the unacceptability of violence.

Later, he told another visiting group of ten thousand soldiers that to be good Christians, and protect security and liberty, they would be better off joining an international peacekeeping force instead of a national army.[3]

When a new group calling itself Ex-Combatants for Disarmament held its initial meeting in Rome, John Paul invited seven hundred members to the Vatican and commended them as "realistic and courageous." He condemned the giddy spiral of armaments under the pretext of the threat of potential enemies. . . . It is always a question, it is said, of defending oneself, of avenging violated rights. It is often a part of the truth. But how many skillfully camouflaged lies trigger off conflicts, the . . . results of which have already been calculated?[4]

His words eerily foreshadowed tragedies about to unfold in Afghanistan and Central America.

5

John Paul sometimes seemed obsessed with the word *solidarity*, which he had always liked. In his general audience of Holy Week 1979, he used the word six times in the first three paragraphs, and again later: "solidarity with the suffering . . . solidarity with our brothers . . . If we live in conditions of freedom, we must suffer all the more for the oppression of societies that are deprived of freedom."

Yet he refused to see—or have any other Vatican official see—José Esteban Gonzalez, the national coordinator of the Human Rights Commission in Nicaragua, an intensely Catholic country. Esteban had come to Rome carrying several thick volumes documenting killings, torture, and imprisonments-without-trial by the government of dictator Anastasio Somoza. While the Nicaraguan human-rights worker waited in vain to make his case, visiting Hungarian and Polish churchmen were feasted and welcomed.

Then the long-suffering Archbishop Oscar Romero of blood-soaked El Salvador arrived for his scheduled periodic visit to the pope. He was kept waiting day-to-day for a week. In his diary, he recorded his worry over the money he was spending on taxis to the Vatican.

Just a few years before, Romero had been "very conservative. His friends were mostly the privileged and powerful," according to Father Vincent O'Keefe, an American Jesuit official in Rome who often dealt with him. Romero even removed Jesuits as teachers in his seminary for being "too progressive." Then Romero's friend Father Rutilio Grande was murdered.

Grande "was a quiet man, not a radical," O'Keefe says. He had a parish among the poor and "helped them set up cooperatives and get loans. He gave good retreats. He was machine-gunned in 1976 on his way to say Mass, with his altar boy and sacrostan [assistant]. It was a turning point in [Romero's] life. He began a much closer association with poor people. He began giving powerful sermons. The papal nuncio wrote unfavorable reports—said Romero was being manipulated by Jesuits and Marxists."

When General Carlos Romero (no relation) was installed as president of El Salvador, he asked for a celebratory Mass in the cathedral; Archbishop Romero refused. Says O'Keefe, "Some bishops wanted it. [Archbishop] Romero said it would confuse the People of God. The next day, the newspapers had a picture of the new president drinking a champagne toast with the nuncio."

In his pastoral letters, Archbishop Romero, like the pope, stressed that priests must keep "the overall perspective of Christian salvation," and "not let themselves be ensnared by political polarization." At the same time, though, Romero said God's word must be applied to human needs—just as Wojtyla had argued at Vatican II. "The economic, social, political, and cultural hopes of men are not alien to the definitive liberation achieved in Christ," Romero wrote.[1]

Many Latin bishops, often from landowning families, complained to the Vatican, in one official's words, "not that Romero was a communist, but that his position could help a Left solution."[2]

When John Paul finally received him, May 7, 1979, Romero immediately sensed, according to his diary, "that negative information about my...mission...had preceded me at the Vatican." He reported the murder of Father Octavio, one of half a dozen priests who had been killed recently by government-sponsored death squads. John Paul advised "great prudence in making concrete denunciations."

Said Romero, "I explained to the pope that there are situations like that of Father Octavio in which it is necessary to be concrete because injustice and violence have been concrete. The pope recalled his own situation in Poland where he had to deal with a non-Catholic government, and stressed the importance of unity among the country's bishops. I replied that I also desired this, but unity could not be simulated. It had to be based upon the Gospel and the truth."

The pope held his line. According to Romero, "He thinks it better to stay with principles, because there is a risk of making errors or mistakes with specific accusations."[3]

Back in El Salvador, Archbishop Romero said Mass at a church where, only five days before, government troops had shot twenty-three dissidents dead. "We don't seek revenge," he preached. "Only conversion. Violence seems like a daily ritual, like the air that we breathe. But violence and hate are not the force. Love is the force."

John Paul also chose to go slow in South Africa, another area where millions of people endured economic and political servitude to a rich minority. There, though, his actions had much less influence on events than they did in Latin America.

"He had a real concern for the situation, but a conviction that our bishops in South Africa were handling that very well," says Cardinal Edward Cassidy, the Vatican diplomat there, who discussed it with the pope in Rome that spring of 1979. South Africa's biggest white church, the Dutch Reformed, supported the minority white government and, in Cassidy's words, was "rabidly anti-Catholic." John Paul thought a vigorous campaign by Catholics against racial discrimination would only heighten interfaith tension and weaken Catholic influence.

The argument was logical, though probably not persuasive to black South Africans, who were confined to ghettos, with second-rate schools, jobs, and pay scales. The pope persistently refused the South African government's requests for a papal visit, because, Cassidy says, "The opinion of the bishops in South Africa was that it would appear we were giving support to the government."

The pope feared no such confusion about going home to Poland to support another majority in its oppression by a minority government. Party Secretary Gierek finally agreed to the visit after what he has said was an angry phone clash with Soviet Premier Brezhnev. "How can I not receive the Polish pope?" Gierek argued. "What do you imagine I can tell the people?"

"Do what you want, so long as you and your party do not regret it later," Brezhnev told him, and hung up abruptly.[4]

John Paul had proposed coming in May, for the nine-hundredth anniversary of Saint Stanislaw's murder. Gierek, wanting to avoid any connection to Saint Stanislaw, proposed August instead. They settled on June. But as soon as the dates were set, the wily pope simply issued an apostolic letter moving the celebration that year from May 15, when it actually fell, "to the week beginning with Whitsunday and ending with Trinity Sunday"—which happened to be the week he would be in Poland. (If the communists could rearrange history at will, why not the pope?)

John Paul began bringing up Stanislaw in public appearances. Church newspapers printed his poem on Stanislaw.

Hours before the pope's departure, U.S. Secretary of State Cyrus Vance visited the Vatican while in Europe on other business. Remarkably, Vance seemed oblivious to the landmark Cold War event about to unfold. Treating his stop with the pope as a social call, Vance brought his wife and didn't mention the Polish trip.[5]

The Czechoslovakian government paid the pope's journey more attention, imprisoning eleven members of Charter 77 so they couldn't exploit the occasion. One secretly ordained priest, Michael Gono, later died of injuries inflicted while Czech police "questioned" him.

Also just before he left Rome, John Paul was given his first look at the Vatican budget by Cardinal Egidio Vagnozzi, whom he had appointed to supervise it. Even if he didn't understand all the numbers, the pope understood what Vagnozzi told him: "Holy Father, if things continue in this way, the Holy See will be bankrupt in five years."[6]

6

The flight from one political universe to another took less than two hours. The most important change John Paul brought—the empowerment of the Polish people—began even before he arrived. Parish by parish, the Church organized an army of marshals to keep order during public gatherings. Ordinary lay Catholics replaced police physically and, more important, in people's minds.

"It was the first time people could gather in such masses, for their own purposes," says Ewa Krasinska, who later became a Solidarity fighter and is now a Polish diplomat. "One could sense in the street that people were somehow united. The police stood aside. People had a feeling they could decide things for themselves."

This mood change was precisely what the pope had aimed for, says Bohdan Cywinski, who met privately with him on the trip. "He knew he could cause an enormous change in the way people thought. The [immediate] political results were of secondary importance."

Even high communist officials felt the euphoria. One, Mieczyslaw Rakowski, later prime minister, recalls, "The choice of a Pole for a top job made us a main nation. People were comparing this moment to centuries of our having no place in Europe. I remember a sign on a building, 'We Greet the Deputy of God on Earth.' "

As usual, John Paul knew how to convey his message in words the communists couldn't argue with. Arriving at the airport, he thanked Gierek politely for allowing the trip, but said, "peace and the drawing together of peoples" depended on "respect for the basic rights of the nation . . . political self-determination for its citizens and formation of its own culture and civilization."

Events were televised in hopes of discouraging live crowds, but crowds came anyway. Hundreds of thousands lined the pope's route into Warsaw. TV coverage showed only close-ups of speakers or small groups of listeners—never the vast crowds, which were the highlight of many events. Coverage was relegated to a secondary channel whose weak signal couldn't reach Lithuania, Czechoslovakia, or East Germany.

In the photographs of John Paul's open-air Mass that afternoon in the huge Victory Square Park in central Warsaw, you can't see a blade of grass, so thick are the crowds fading into the distant trees. Estimates ranged up to one million. Directing not another word of thanks to the communists, he skewered them for an hour. Five times in the first few minutes he spoke of Paul VI's disappointment at not being allowed in Poland, adding, "With it he went to his grave."

Recounting proud moments of Poland's past, he continually referred to Stanislaw, then said, "Christ cannot be kept out of the history of man in any part of the globe, at any longitude or latitude." At that, a press account said, "The applause started and went on and on, in waves . . . dying down in one part of the square and starting up elsewhere."[1] Father Bednarz, who flew in from Chicago, remembers, "He couldn't talk for the next ten or fifteen minutes. People were singing hymns, chanting 'We want God!' Finally, he said, 'I already have a reputation in Rome for talking too long. Let me finish."

And he did, almost poetically, referring time and again in new ways to the significance of his being there—and of having Mass said at all on the main common ground of Warsaw. Even his references to the unknown soldier, buried a few yards away, seemed to take back the identity of the country for its people, away from the Soviet occupiers. It was the kind of speech, and reception, that any politician lives for.

Gierek watched it all, frightened, from the hotel overlooking the square. According to a senior Vatican official with him,[2] "He'd had some troubles with the Soviets over the visit, and he was afraid an uprising could be triggered." Gierek warned the official, and Wyszynski, that the Soviets might react violently. The two churchmen took his concern to John Paul, who the next day made a televised stop at a memorial to Soviet soldiers, a sign to placate the Russians.

For nine days, the pope didn't waste a minute, addressing one gathering after another. In Gniezno, before another crowd that overflowed the range of wide-angle camera lenses, he declared:

> Is it not Christ's will . . . that this pope, in whose heart is deeply engraved the history of his own nation and the history of neighboring peoples, . . . should reveal the developments that have taken place in this part of Europe?

In each city, it was "this Polish pope" or "this Slav pope," repeated many times in each talk. Individuals who had been isolated, atomized under the communist system, were suddenly galvanized into a united, patriotic citizenry. "This Polish pope . . . comes here to speak . . . before Europe and the world, of those often forgotten nations and peoples. He comes here to cry with a loud voice."

Others from Eastern Europe found their way in through border gaps in the high mountains. People in the crowds held up signs bearing messages such as "Holy Father, Remember Your Czech Children." He would point and respond that he would "remember the Czechs and Slovaks . . . the Slavs, the Croats, the Slovenes, the Bulgarians, the Moravians, the Russians, and the Serbs"—all now Soviet subjects.

And with each national name, "this Slav pope" would pause for cheers, the way entertainers do at resorts when they mention various hometowns. He began reciting the list at almost every stop, letting the cheers of obviously illegal émigrés tell everyone that communist rule could be flouted.

Sometimes he lampooned the communists sarcastically. Once, after naming the Eastern European nationalities, he added, "I trust that they hear me. After all . . . freedom . . . of information . . . has been thoroughly guaranteed." ("Each time I can," he later explained, "I put the Polish government face-to-face with the Polish constitution.")[3]

When the day's official ceremonies ended and the pope retired to the local bishop's residence for food and (supposedly) rest, more crowds would gather outside, often singing Polish songs. John Paul would appear at a window or balcony and give yet another talk. In Gniezno, he sang and exchanged remarks with some forty thousand people for an hour and a half. A British reporter remarked that the nonverbal communication between the pope and the crowds was "as intimate as if the two sides were sitting in one small room. He cannot bring himself to leave."[4]

At Mass in Czestochowa, crowds swelled beyond range of the loudspeakers. Many in back listened on portable shortwave radios. Members of Western radio crews were passed overhead by the crowd, row by row to the front, to get better sound. Referring to the Black Madonna, John Paul talked of

hearing the beating heart of the nation in the heart of the Mother. How many times has it vibrated with the laments of the historical sufferings of Poland, but also with the shouts of joy and victory! . . .

Every threat . . . against the family and the nation has its source in our weakness. . . . Before Our Lady of Jasna Gora [the Black

Madonna] . . . this is what I am entrusting to you. Do not succumb
to weakness!

The Western press repeatedly misreported John Paul's visit as a continua-
tion of *Ostpolitik* and detente. That wasn't the message Poles got. When the government barred the pope from several sites he wanted to visit, including the
labor tinderbox of Silesia, he found miners and workers elsewhere. Don't abandon farming in the push for industrialization, he urged: "The right to the land
does not cease to be the basis of a healthy economy and sociology."

He told them to do their own thinking:

> Any man who chooses his ideology honestly and through his own
> conviction deserves respect. The real danger for both sides—for
> the Church and for the other side, call it what you will—is the
> man who does not . . . listen to his deepest convictions, to his
> inner truth, but wants only to fit, to float in conformity, moving
> from Left to Right as the wind blows. . . . The future of Poland
> will depend on how many people are mature enough to be non-
> conformist.

He prayed at Auschwitz and at Birkenau because "it was impossible for me
not to come here as pope." Passing by memorials in twenty languages, he
stopped before the one in Hebrew and said, "The very people that received
from God the commandment 'Thou shalt not kill' itself experienced in special
measure what is meant by killing."

Where he went, the world's press followed. He led them on a tour of his boyhood home in Wadowice, lunched at the parish house with Monsignor Zacher
and others, and said Mass on the town square for thirty thousand—more people
than lived there. He also publicly embraced Father Zembrzuski of Doylestown,
flouting the recommendations of his American investigators. Cardinal Krol, who
had worked with the investigators, was on hand and watched dumbstruck as the
pope and Wyszynski brought Zembrzuski into their official entourage.

If that was the low point of the trip, the inevitable high point was Krakow
at the end of the week. By then the nation had learned the intended lesson: the
communists were their masters only if the people themselves allowed it. The
pope had freed them to gather and express themselves. On the other hand, he
displayed an exact sense of limits, in one instance stopping a potentially violent confrontation.

Some fifty thousand university students and chaplains, some from as far
away as Russia and Lithuania, showed up for one scheduled meeting and at the

pope's invitation brought crosses to him to be blessed. Then some students brought in a big cross that had been erected at the Jagiellonian and torn down by the government. They asked John Paul to bless it and promised a student march that night to restore it. Knowing that trucks of police were parked just out of sight, ready for any trouble, John Paul blessed the cross but directed the students not to try to replace it or cause a scene. Shamed, they agreed. Then he deftly revived the festive mood for everyone.[5]

He held a reception for Janina Kotlarczyk, his theatrical mentor's widow, who was now wheelchair-bound. When she addressed him as "Your Eminence," he replied "Stop that!" and insisted she call him Karol as she always had.[6]

In the evening, his former student flock in Krakow gathered outside his window at the palace, under circumstances none had dreamed possible. Their generation would make up the fighting core of Solidarity. A vivid account comes from Thomas Brand and his wife, Katarzyna Mroczkowska-Brand, whom Father Wojtyla had bounced on his knee as a child when visiting her father, a professor.

"He arrived from some ceremony around 10:00 P.M.," Brand recalls. "Everyone was waiting, hoping for a few words. There were TV lights in front of the palace. The motorcade went inside. He came out and said that he was hungry and wanted to eat supper and would be back."

When he returned, Brand laughs, Archbishop Noe, the schedule-keeper who always accompanied John Paul, "tried to restrain him as he leaned out to us, as if he was thinking the pope was going to fall out the window. The pope said, 'What's wrong with you people? A citizen of your city disappears eight months ago and you have never even come to look for him!' "

"It was magical, surreal," says Mroczkowska-Brand. "He was so full of joy and happiness—talking, joking, singing—and he just couldn't stop. Till 2:00 A.M. He would start by saying, 'I'm just going to tell you all good night, because you're tired and I'm tired. But do you remember that song we used to sing . . .' And then he'd start. He asked us to let him catch a few winks, and the crowd would shout 'No!' They would shout questions—'Will you come back?' 'Don't leave us, we need you.' 'Don't you think you're more needed here than there? You have better friends here.' He would turn serious, and say a prayer and sing a religious song. But half were just songs from around the campfire.

"I remember wishing he would have taken a political stroke," she says. "But I know now it would have triggered a bad reaction. When you grew up under that system, you learned all sorts of ways to say things without really saying them. All sorts of slang expressions for the police that everybody knew. He said, 'How do you like the way our friends in blue are treating you? Isn't it funny how sweet they are being now?' It was always joking, but the allusions were clear. 'Isn't it nice to feel that *they* are afraid of *you* now?' He always knew just when to push hard to demonstrate the power of the people, and when to back off. It was a sensational feeling. When anybody tried to get him to do anything overtly political—and there were definitely such moments, [when people urged,] 'Use this power now, just crush them now'—his response would be, 'I know how you feel, but I can't do it in this way. I'm with you. Trust me. But I can't do that now.'

"And there was this feeling of a whole city being on fire, of sitting on a pile of powder and they were handing him the matches. And he was saying, 'I'm going to tell you how to use this power in a different way.' And he would go on toward the spiritual."

The next day, Sunday, John Paul officially ended the Saint Stanislaw celebration with a Mass that *Osservatore Romano* claimed was attended by three million people. Some in the audience let go balloons bearing the sign of the anticommunist resistance from the 1940s. To the crowd, and to millions more listening on television and radio, the pope said:

> All of life assumes the aspect of . . . a large number of tests of faith and character. . . . Saint Stanislaw has become in the spiritual history of the Polish people the patron of these tests. . . . From every victorious test the moral order is built up. From every failed test moral disorder grows. We know very well from our entire history that we must not permit, absolutely and at whatever cost, this disorder.

Then he held aloft the box containing the preserved skull of Stanislaw, displayed each year on his day, and said:

> You must be strong, dear brothers and sisters. You must be strong with the strength that comes from faith. So as I depart, I ask you to accept once again all that spiritual heritage that is called "Poland," with faith, hope, and love. . . .
> I ask you that you never despair, never grow weary, never become discouraged;
> that those roots from which we grow are never severed;
> that you keep your faith despite each of your weaknesses, that you always seek strength in Him, where so many generations of our mothers and fathers found it . . . ;

that you never lose that freedom of the spirit for which He has liberated man;

that you never spurn that love . . . expressed by the cross, without which human life has no roots and no meaning.

I ask this of you.[7]

As John Paul boarded his plane with an entourage that would definitely not be searched, tagging along was Father Bardecki, carrying the collected Krakow sermons of Cardinal Karol Wojtyla. They would now be published, in Rome.

Vatican diplomat Luigi Poggi, now a cardinal, was in the pope's entourage and says the Polish trip "was the beginning of the Solidarity movement, the beginning of nonviolent opposition. From then on, the government had to negotiate. The mere fact that it negotiated weakened its position."

Nina Gladziuk, then a graduate student, now a professor: "We saw each other for the very first time, after decades of communism. We saw we were united. There were millions like us. We discovered community, solidarity, and power."

Jerzy Turowicz, editor of *Tygodnik Powszechny:* "His election, in a rather drab period, was like a light, totally unexpected. And after his first trip [to Poland], everybody was, for the first time in forty years, able to manifest openly what he thought. Before, people thought, 'Well, I myself think this way but perhaps no one else does.' Now people were able to see they were unanimous, and if they were unanimous, they were strong."

Konrad Bielinski, then a graduate student and later a leader of Solidarity: "[That week] we had the feeling that the communists didn't exist. Even in state-owned shops, there were pictures of the pope. The whole country was ruled by the pope, not the communists. Crowds were nice to each other. There were no guards pushing. It was a practice in self-organization."

Jozef Czyrek, a communist official and later foreign minister of Poland: "John Paul II constantly talked about the dignity of the human person, human rights. He said exactly the same thing when he was archbishop, but after he was pope, he had a big impact on government decisions."

After the pope left, the Intelligentsia Clubs discussed his messages. Says Stanislawa Grabska, whom Cardinal Wojtyla had enabled to get a theology degree despite her gender, and who was then president of the Krakow club: "There was new hope, and faith in nonviolence. Many young people had wanted a frontal assault. Young workers and even some young intelligentsia thought, 'Nonviolence is good only up to the moment we have a weapon.'

Political events could have developed as in 1970, when they went to burn down the police stations or communist party offices. But during all his visits, he was teaching us that we have to stick to the ethics of dialogue. We have to be for something, not against anything. I know many nonbelievers who became followers of the Church. He not only taught people their rights, but also how to achieve them."

Wojciech Arkuszewski, later a Solidarity leader: "He made the Church fashionable."

Father John Navone, the theology professor: "He revolutionized Vatican diplomacy. Before this man, the Vatican would negotiate the right to build a church, appoint a bishop. What this pope did was request freedom of speech, the right to form organizations—the kind of thing that would help everyone."

An editorial in the London Catholic newspaper *The Tablet:* "Never before in Christian history has the world seen such a confrontation of spiritual force and material power as in the pope's visit to Poland. One man came to a state surrounded and dominated by the most formidable militant atheistic regime that has ever existed, armed with every weapon. . . . Had he been a local prophet with the same vision and message, he might have been bundled away into a forced labor camp. . . . But the pope walked into a tyranny which could not touch him. . . . Every utterance, prepared or spontaneous, was a challenge to a system that has nations enslaved. . . . One man seems to have demonstrated what manhood means."

7

That summer, 1979, John Paul appointed his first cardinals, mostly big-city archbishops, but two of them Poles—Macharski, his replacement in Krakow, and Ladislaw Rubin of the curia. There was also a secret appointee (unusual but not unprecedented), identified in 1991 as Gong Pin-mei, archbishop of Shanghai, China.

July 9, John Paul met for the first time as pope with the leadership of the Knights of Malta. Ostensibly a charitable organization dating from the Crusades, the Knights were mostly militant Cold Warriors from the West who constantly pushed anti-communist causes. The Knights are worth mentioning because many prominent businessmen and spies have been members, and stories persist that the group wields mighty behind-the-scenes power at the Vatican.

But unlike Opus Dei, which really did gain powerful influence with the pope, there's no evidence the Knights are more than a collection of wealthy people with a strident political agenda not shared by John Paul, but who contributed so much money and made so many pious remarks, that he gave them the occasional ritual they wanted at the Vatican.

Former CIA directors William Casey and John McCone (both Wall Street lawyers) joined the Knights, as did Alexandre de Marenches, head of French intelligence. Former CIA Chief William Colby said he turned down an invitation because "I'm a little lower-key." Another member was Count Umberto Ortolani, who ran the secret Masonic lodge that fixed deals for crooked bankers Michele Sindona and Roberto Calvi.

The longtime leader of the Knights in the United States, until his death, in 1995, was Peter Grace, head of W. R. Grace & Co., whose vast international operations often served as a cover for CIA activities. Grace's controlling shareholder (with almost a third of the shares) was the Flick family of Germany, which flourished under Hitler and whose patriarch was convicted of war crimes. Through the older generation of the Flicks, Peter Grace put many defeated Nazis on the company payroll.

Knights of Malta leaders in Rome play at nineteenth-century-style royalty, wearing fancy ribbons and medals and calling each other "Prince" and "High Eminence." But their occasional meetings with John Paul appear to be ceremonial courtesies. A Vatican official, after consulting with the pope, assured me that the Knights had "not much influence. They run some hospitals, historic things."[1]

In mid-July, John Paul followed usual papal practice and adjourned to the summer residence in the hills at Castelgandolfo. He installed a swimming pool ("cheaper than another conclave," he told reporters), then began boning up for a scheduled October trip to the United States. The unusual roster of advisers he chose may reflect just how badly he needed advice about America.

Among his first visitors were Anna-Teresa Tymieniecka and Hendryk Houthakker. "He had an entirely wrong conception of the United States," Houthakker says. "He thought we were all money-grabbers. He thought there was no interest in anything else. And he was going to tell us." Tymieniecka and Houthakker say they looked over the pope's proposed speeches and persuaded him to tone them down. "They would have offended many people," she explains. But when Houthakker tried again "to convince John Paul that capitalism had merit," Houthakker says, the pope "was not very receptive."

Apparently John Paul still harbored doubts about Tymieniecka's work on *The Acting Person*, because he asked his next visitors at Castelgandolfo, Andrzej Poltawski and Dr. Wanda Poltawska of Krakow, to evaluate it. Poltawski says they advised him, just as translator Potocki had earlier, that her work needed major repair. Before anything was done, however, the book was out.[2]

Although the Vatican still officially denied Tymieniecka's right to publish the book, *Osservatore Romano* gave it a splendid review. Philosophy scholars from Marek Skwarnicki in Poland to Ralph McInerny at Notre Dame, however, were irate. "Tymieniecka tried to turn him into a flaming phenomenologist," McInerny says. "Explicit references to Thomas Aquinas in the Polish text don't show up in the English text. The context is left out." Arguments were thrashed out in the pages of the *Times Literary Supplement* in London, but the pope himself stayed aloof.

Tymieniecka says she "ran into real hot water" by telling *Time* magazine that John Paul was a phenomenologist. "This is a complex and extremely involved philosophy. The Poles were absolutely furious at me. They were very, very narrow-minded." As late as 1994, when I spoke to her, she alluded to disputes over the book and said, "This is not finished yet." But for all the squabbling, her husband, Houthakker, says *The Acting Person* "has produced only a few thousand dollars in royalties. It is not a best-seller."

Before the Poltawskis left Castelgandolfo that summer of 1979, Andrzej Poltawski says, John Paul asked his wife, Wanda, "to read some texts" on the United States and advise him for his coming trip there. The pope continued to be confused, or put off, by most Americans, and his best American friend, Cardinal Krol, seemed to have lost influence over the Doylestown case. The Poltawskis of Krakow, much as he trusted them, may not have been the best source of advice for him.

Another visitor at Castelgandolfo that summer was Father Hesburgh, then president of Notre Dame, the preeminent Catholic university in the United States. It was their first meeting, though Hesburgh had often visited Paul VI. He recalls, "I went in [to John Paul] with six points that were very important to me," about a theological institute Hesburgh ran.

The pope "had one book on his desk, an atlas," Hesburgh says. "He wanted to know where I'm from. I said the archdiocese of Fort Wayne [Indiana; Notre Dame is in South Bend in that archdiocese]. And he thought I was from Fort Worth [Texas]. I spoke to him in Italian, but he saw this as an opportunity to speak English. I came in with six points and didn't get through to him with any of them."

Hesburgh says that over the years, he could never get John Paul engaged in a good conversation. "One time I had just come back from China, and started to talk to him about the Church in Peking. He just brushed it off, [saying,] 'patri-

otic Church,' meaning loyal to the government. It was obvious he wasn't interested in talking about the Church in China." Hesburgh, unaware that John Paul
had secretly appointed a Chinese cardinal, misjudged the pope's interest in
China; the point, though, is that John Paul brushed off a major American
Catholic academician as not worth listening to.

Another American, Avery Dulles, would seem hard for the pope to ignore,
for two reasons. First, he is the jowly, physically imposing tintype of his father,
John Foster Dulles, perhaps the most influential U.S. secretary of state in this
half century. His uncle Allen molded and ran the CIA. Avery Dulles also is a
well-publicized Catholic convert and priest, and a widely published theologian
on university faculties in Rome and New York (Fordham); he had been
appointed to a papal advisory commission. Yet Dulles told me in 1994 that
he'd met the pope just three times, and "he's never indicated he recognized me.
I don't think he knows who I am."

Further evidence of a knowledge gap about the U.S. is John Paul's odd intervention in a bishop's appointment in Milwaukee in 1979. After the appointment had cleared all other hurdles, the pope objected to a report the prospective
bishop had written on the ordination of women. Milwaukee Archbishop Rembert Weakland, who is nothing if not a mediator, volunteered to negotiate a
revision to the report that might salvage the appointment. The pope approved
it, but only on condition that the changes appear in the *Milwaukee Journal*, which
had publicized the original report. "He probably thought we could get anything
we wanted in the Milwaukee papers," Weakland smiles. Luckily, he adds, the
Journal printed a story.

Archbishop Weakland says John Paul "didn't quite understand the ethos"—
the guiding character and beliefs—of the American nation. "When he came
over here, he stayed in Polish parishes and settlements. He would go from Polish enclave to Polish enclave. They would feed him Polish food, sing him Polish folk songs, dress in traditional ways; the Mass would be in Polish. And to
some extent they were guilty of giving him the feeling the United States was an
extension of Europe."

In his early appointments of American bishops, Weakland notes, John Paul
tried to preserve ethnic-origin groups under the leadership of one of their
own. But over the years, the ethnic criterion for bishops faded. Still, John Paul
didn't lose his fundamental skepticism about the Age of Enlightenment. He
believed that he and many others, even though they lived in political and economic deprivation, had found a happiness that Americans were missing,
despite all their freedom and economic achievement.

Marcus Lefebvre, Catholic chaplain at Edinburgh University in Scotland,
says, "The Polish pope's true challenge to us in the . . . West [is] to reconsider

not so much such particular items of our philosophy as our attitudes to money, sex, pleasure, abortion [or] women's rights, as [to reconsider] the whole liberal philosophy that makes them possible."[3]

On the other hand, the Enlightenment ethos had made the U.S. a great country and beacon for mankind. The saddest part about John Paul's difficulty communicating with the dominant American culture was that each side had things to say that the other needed to hear.

As America prepared to receive John Paul, the Gannett News Service ran reporter Carlton Sherwood's exposé of Father Zembrzuski and the Doylestown shrine scandal. By that time, Sherwood had augmented his original information about the missing millions with details of a cover-up: the Vatican had squelched attempts by American bishops to fix the mess and bail out the bondholders.

Six months later, Sherwood's articles were awarded the Pulitzer Prize for meritorious public service. For an exposé of wrongdoing in the Catholic Church to win the highest honor for public service was surely one more thing John Paul would never understand about the United States.

8

John Paul was a loyal advocate of the United Nations, whose then secretary-general, Kurt Waldheim, a Catholic, wanted him to speak there. Time and money dictated that a trip to the UN include stops in some of the dioceses that were seeking a papal visit and could pay for one. The United States was home both to the UN and to the Church's richest donors.

Another logical stop was Ireland, where John Paul wanted to preach peace. Young Irish Catholics had turned increasingly to violence to try to drive British forces out of six Northern Irish counties that were still part of Britain (which relinquished its eight-hundred-year hold on the rest of Ireland in 1922; British settlement had created a Protestant majority in the North). A month before the pope's trip, the guerrilla Irish Republican Army blew up a fishing boat, killing a prominent British lord and his family, and then ambushed and killed eighteen British soldiers.

John Paul flew to Dublin, the capital. He kissed the ground, held his usual rash of meetings, and visited Knock, where some people said Mary had appeared in 1879. He had planned then to stop in the war-torn North, but canceled when the Protestant political leader, Ian Paisley, threatened a general strike. Instead, John Paul helicoptered to Drogheda, near the border, and addressed the fighting from there. Before hundreds of thousands of people, he denied that the conflict was "a religious war between Catholics and Protestants." War, he said, wasn't a Christian undertaking:

> Christianity does not command us to close our eyes to ... unjust
> social or international situations. What Christianity does forbid is
> to seek solutions to these situations by hatred.... Violence destroys
> what it claims to defend: the dignity, the life, the freedom of
> human beings.
>
> On my knees, I beg you to ... return to the ways of peace. You
> may claim to seek justice. I, too, believe in justice and seek justice.
> But violence only delays the day of justice. Violence destroys the
> work of justice.

He told Ireland, like Poland, to find salvation in its traditions. In a Dublin park, before a crowd announced at a million and a quarter people—more than a third of Ireland's population—he warned against

> trends [of] present-day civilization and progress.... The very capa-
> bility of mass media to bring the whole world into your homes pro-
> duces a ... confrontation with values that until now have been alien
> to Irish society.... Human identity is often defined by what one
> owns.... When the moral fiber of a nation is weakened, when the
> sense of personal responsibility is diminished, then the door is open
> ... for violence ... and for the manipulation of the many by the few.

In Boston, the pope was greeted by First Lady Rosalynn Carter, some other dignitaries, and a pelting rain. Before half a million very wet people on the Boston Common, he chose a theme more reminiscent of Mrs. Carter's husband than of any other politician of the era:

> Faced with problems and disappointments, many people will try to
> escape from their responsibility: escape in selfishness, escape in sex-
> ual pleasure, escape in drugs, escape in violence, escape in indiffer-
> ence and cynical attitudes. But today, I propose to you the option
> of love, which is the opposite of escape ... perhaps in some special
> service to your brothers and sisters, especially to the ... poor, the
> lonely, the abandoned, those whose rights have been trampled on or
> whose basic needs have not been provided for.

If it wasn't difficult enough preaching spirituality to Americans, torrential rains followed the pope's plane to New York. At the UN, he faced the memorable standard of Paul VI's 1965 speech. He could match Paul's line "No more war—war never again!" only by repeating it, which he did ("I, who come from the country on whose living body Oswiecim was constructed, say...").

Without naming names, he rebutted both Soviet and American justifications for the development of new weapons:

> In alleging the threat of a potential enemy, is the real intention not, rather, to keep for oneself a means of threat, in order to get the upper hand?... Peace tends to vanish in favor of ever new forms of imperialism.

He proposed that resources be shifted away from weapons, toward promoting the UN's Universal Declaration of Human Rights—the same idea that President Carter was struggling to promote. The pope's vision of human rights was Rooseveltian, not Reaganesque:

> the right to life, liberty, and security of person; the right to food, clothing, housing, sufficient health care, rest, and leisure; the right to freedom of expression, education, and culture; ... the right to choose a state of life, to found a family, and to enjoy conditions necessary for family life; the right to property and work, to adequate working conditions and a just wage; the right of assembly and association; the right to freedom of movement, to internal and external migration ... and the right to political participation.

He reiterated in a separate UN message that government action was necessary to secure these rights. He praised "social security systems" that "make an important part of [a country's] wealth directly available for common use ... apart from any logic of competition and exchange."[1] He objected to any economic enterprise "when the aim pursued is the perfection of the work rather than the perfection of the worker who carries it out."[2]

John Paul's overriding political cause was to stop the governance of human beings as if they were primarily economic units. "Market forces," he said, "are never natural, but always constructed by people." They could "play their beneficial role" only when they functioned "under ... individuals ... who are free, equal, and linked by solidarity, and under ... moral norms that are binding upon everyone."[3]

With rain still coming down, John Paul spoke at a black school in Harlem, and (in Spanish) to a crowd at a street corner in the South Bronx, and at

Yankee Stadium nearby. The pope praised Americans' "well-deserved reputation for generosity." But he urged them to search for "the structural reasons
which foster . . . poverty in the world and in your own country." The reasons,
he said, lay "within the framework of your national institutions." Christians
must bring about

> a decisive break with the frenzy of consumerism, exhausting and
> joyless. It is not a question of slowing down progress, for there is no
> human progress when everything conspires to give full rein
> to . . . self-interest, sex and power. We must find a simple way of liv-
> ing. . . . It is not right that the standard of living of rich countries
> should . . . maintain itself by drawing off . . . the reserves of energy
> and raw materials that are meant to serve the whole of humanity. . . .
>   You must never be content to give [poor countries] just the
> crumbs from the feast. You must take of your substance, and not
> just of your abundance, in order to help them, and . . . treat them
> like guests at your family table.[4]

It was not a message likely to please Americans. Over the next thirteen
months, they would nominate and elect as President Ronald Reagan, whose
economic message was almost the precise opposite of John Paul's. Still, the
pope drew capacity crowds—three hundred thousand at Battery Park, near
Wall Street—despite the continuing downpour.

At Shea Stadium, in the Brooklyn archdiocese, Monsignor Tony Bevilacqua
"arranged for a big trailer to be outside if he wanted to wash or change. My job
was to walk him from the car to the trailer. His cassock was soaking. I asked if
he wanted to change. He said, 'No.' The poor man looked so tired and so wet!"

In Philadelphia, John Paul warned students at a seminary that they needed
"firm conviction" before they undertook the priesthood, because they couldn't
back out. Archbishop Marcinkus was still in charge of travel arrangements, and
Cardinal Krol took devilish delight in defying Marcinkus's instructions to limit
the dinner crowd to a dozen: Krol invited twenty-five, and arranged for a boisterous Polish songfest.*

---

* One song seemed to follow John Paul everywhere, about a highlander who left the
mountains "for bread" but missed home. Polish groups the pope visited around the
world prepared versions, some changing "for bread" to "for the Church" or "for you, O
Lord," which was Cardinal Krol's version. The song followed John Paul as "The Missouri Waltz" once followed Harry Truman, but whereas Truman eventually grew sick of
the Missouri song, John Paul never showed weariness of the one about the highlander.

The next morning, however, Krol and John Paul closeted themselves for a long meeting. Hours later, as the pope left town, Church lawyers agreed to a deal with the Minneapolis bank that had threatened suit over the Doylestown shrine. The Church paid $4.2 million to settle the bond debt, and the bank promised to stop talking to the press. Father Zembrzuski and his supporters resumed charge of the shrine.

"The pope blundered," says Monsignor Salvator Adamo, the editor who lost his job for uncovering the scandal. (He has since become a pastor in Haddonfield, New Jersey). "They [the Church] tried to frighten the bondholders into waiving interest due them—more than a million dollars." Adamo credits Sherwood's Gannett series with forcing the Church to pay off its debts. Left unasked, and unanswered, was whether any of the $20 million or so that the accountants said was squandered or mismanaged was in fact secretly "donated" to the Church in Poland.

Reporter Sherwood had already moved on to Chicago, where Father Greeley had another mess for him to clean up. Greeley had decided that Sherwood, having proved his mettle in Doylestown, could now unseat the autocratic Cardinal Cody, who could then be replaced by Archbishop Bernardin. The Gannett News Service approved the assignment, and Greeley had begun to tell Sherwood why Cody was unfit to serve.

Chicago was also the pope's next stop. Cody had refurnished his deteriorating residence for the visit and gave the pope a hundred thousand dollars in cash, in a rosewood box, for charity. The U.S. Bishops' Conference gathered in Chicago to greet John Paul. Addressing them after dinner, he thanked them profusely for their donations but admonished them that he expected strict adherence to doctrine on abortion, contraception, divorce, and sex. In his customary fashion, he had combed through the U.S. bishops' own statements to gather quotes to support his points.

Even in the quotes he selected, however, the American bishops' tone was unmistakably different from his own. The bishops repeatedly offered sympathy and hope to Catholics who failed Church standards. "Homosexual orientation" wasn't a sin, they assured gays; only "homosexual activity" was. Rebukes were similarly hedged for the divorced. The distinction was subtle but persistent. The pope insisted on absolute duty to a moral code, regardless of life's difficulties; the bishops stressed sympathy with the difficulties.

John Paul's public sermons in Chicago, including one to a huge gathering in the Loop, dwelled on the sexual-morality issues that did not play well in the United States (or most countries). But he was determined to bring the big, recalcitrant American Church under control. A showdown came in Washington, when it talked back.

On his second day in the capital, the pope met with representatives of America's nuns. Chosen to welcome him was Sister Theresa Kane, superior of the Sisters of Mercy order and head of the Leadership Conference of Women Religious—a sort of nuns' union. An unabashed feminist, she wasted no time before complaining about the "intense suffering and pain" of "half of humankind." Women had "heard the powerful messages of our Church," she said, and felt entitled to be "included in all the ministries of the Church"—not least the priesthood.[5]

Politely but firmly, the pope replied that Mary was the model for women: "Without herself being inserted into the hierarchy . . . of the Church, [she] made all hierarchy possible because she gave to the world the shepherd and bishop of our souls." Disregarding what else the pope had said about women, some interpreted this remark as an instruction to the whole gender to be satisfied as a ladies' auxiliary to male achievers.

Privately, John Paul seethed at Sister Kane's insubordination. On his return to Rome, he gathered the Mothers General of all major nun orders and instructed them to send a chastening message to the American group. As for Kane, "she has never been forgiven. She's anathema as far as the pope's concerned," according to Thomas Fox, editor of the weekly *National Catholic Reporter.*

At his open-air Mass on the Washington Mall, John Paul continued to explain the Church's unpopular reproductive code:

> Decisions about the number of children [to have] and the sacrifices
> to be made for them must not be taken only with a view to . . . com-
> fort. . . . It is certainly less serious to deny . . . children certain com-
> forts or material advantages than to deprive them of brothers and
> sisters who could help them to grow in humanity.

To Catholic university professors and theologians, he repeated his seemingly contradictory views on academic freedom. On the one hand, he said all universities need "freedom of investigation" because science requires "a surrender to objectivity." But in the next breath, he added that Catholic universities must "safeguard" the teaching of the hierarchy because "it is the right of the faithful not to be troubled by theories and hypotheses that they are not expert in judging."

It seemed like the theory of freedom of a Lenin or Castro: the scholar is free, provided he agrees with the master. (A few months later, the pope added that there should be no contradiction between "the search for truth" and "the certitude of already knowing the source of truth." The purpose of knowledge, he said, is "the light it helps to throw on your reason for living. In this domain everyone needs certitude.)"[6]

∽

The pope's visit with political Washington was more polite but no more harmonious than his visit with Catholic Washington. At the White House, before Congress and several thousand invited guests, he praised the United States for its dedication to human dignity but urged the leaders around him to disarm, not build new weapons. Again, an American audience applauded papal instructions that it had no intention whatsoever of heeding. After exchanging whispers with Carter to make sure it was all right, John Paul gave a blessing in Latin.

His private meeting afterward with the Carters was apparently more ceremonial than substantive. Again, John Paul's mistrust of Americans cost him an opportunity. When I was offered a chance to submit some written questions to the pope through Joaquin Navarro-Valls, his press aide, I asked whether he and Carter had ever tried to coordinate their lonely and innovative crusades to make human rights the new cornerstone of international relations. Surprisingly, John Paul didn't remember that Carter was especially concerned with human rights, or that they ever communicated about it. (Carter declined to be interviewed.) They parted, a potential alliance unexplored.

John Paul did open his trust to one American official, however: a fellow Pole. On his way out of the White House, he invited a startled Brzezinski to come that afternoon with his wife and three children to the nuncio's house, where the Pope was staying. Brzezinski sputtered that he was scheduled to spend the afternoon chauffeuring his kids to soccer games and the like (it was Saturday) but that he would round them up. Delighted that the national security adviser's children were engaged in a good Polish sport, the pope rescheduled the impromptu invitation to the Brzezinskis' convenience.

He went off to address the Organization of American States, telling ambassadors from El Salvador, Guatemala, Brazil, Chile, Argentina, and other murderous regimes that it would be "gross deception" for them to call themselves Christian if they violated their citizens' rights over a "concern for national security."

Then he shut himself in with Brzezinski, sometimes alone, sometimes with family, for up to three hours. Brzezinski will say only that they discussed the Soviet Union, the pope's concern over the swiftness of change in the Church, and the pope's plan to visit Turkey later in 1979. John Paul teased Brzezinski about a published report, attributed to the Soviet KGB, that Brzezinski had engineered John Paul's election, using Cardinal Krol as an agent. "You elected me, you come see me," the pope said, inviting Brzezinski to Rome.

"What's striking when one talks to him is his time frame," Brzezinski says. "He really talks in a perspective of a hundred years from now. Even about communism: when I was talking about how to undermine them soon, he was talking about a long-term trend. He always said it would come out okay, but it bothered me that he was talking in terms of a hundred years, longer than was important to me."

At one point, Mrs. Brzezinski urged the pope to "listen to the prayers of American women" for a bigger role in the Church. The pope replied enigmatically that he respected "the reality of womanhood." This was the day before his explosive meeting with Sister Kane, who said more bluntly what Mrs. Brzezinski said politely.

As he was preparing to fly home, the pope himself remarked to a reporter for the Catholic press, "I don't think the venerable cardinals knew the type of man they were electing."[7]

That fall, 1979, the pope began a highly unusual transformation of the papal general audience every Wednesday into a yearlong seminar on a single subject—even though the crowds were largely tourist and changed week to week. The topic was Adam, Eve, and sexuality—the same topic that had inspired John Paul's first above-ground book and his long friendship with the Poltawskis. "He had written a [new] book, *The Theology of the Body*," explains Andrzej Poltawski. "He was working on it around the time of his election. But popes don't normally publish books. So he decided to divide it into short segments and preach it at this series of audiences."

His gist, again, was that the opening chapters of Genesis defined humanity. Speaking in the style of a college lecturer, not a preacher, he quoted everything from scripture to Carl Jung, the pioneer psychiatrist. Genesis, he said, revealed that man was more metaphysical—made up of ideas—than physical. The biblical use of the word *knew* to mean "had intercourse with" was not a euphemism or mistake; rather, sex and knowledge were bound together in the original definition of man:

> Sex not only decides the physical individuality of man, but defines at the same time his personal identity.... The one who knows is the man and the one who is known is the woman-wife.... In the "knowledge" of which Genesis speaks, the mystery of femininity is manifested and revealed completely by means of motherhood.[8]

The separate creation of man and woman showed significant differences between the sexes. Humanity was born with both original sin and original innocence, suggesting that good and evil were competitively matched in the struggle for men's minds.

As in many other matters, the press, when it paid attention at all, often conveyed the wrong idea of the pope's thought. John Paul spent many weeks analyzing a phrase from the Gospel of Matthew, quoting Jesus that "everyone who looks at a woman lustfully has already committed adultery with her in his heart." (The phrase became famous in the United States when President Carter said in an interview that he had committed adultery in his heart.) To John Paul, the passage had

> key meaning for the theology of the body. . . . The man of lust does not control his own body . . . as the man of original innocence did. . . . Self-mastery, essential for the formation of the human person . . . is . . . shaken to the very foundations. . . . Man is ashamed of his body because of lust.

Adultery thus encompassed not just *whom* one approached for sex, but *why*—whether one was merely succumbing to lust or was instead also expressing the feelings of a loving relationship. In this way, the pope said, a man could even commit adultery with his own wife. It was a meaningful thought, but became the butt of humor.

John Paul continued to steer Poland and Latin America down separate tracks. That fall, when Chilean bishops came to Rome for the routine visits all bishops are asked to make every five years, he didn't mention the bloody repression of their countrymen, but just told them to stay away from politics:

> You are not a symposium of experts, nor a parliament of politicians. . . . You are pastors of the Church. . . . Future priests must be formed so they are . . . clearly aware of their specific mission [and] will not be tempted . . . to adopt methods . . . geared to merely temporal aims.[9]

Yet that same week, he created a secret Church news service to evade communist censorship back home. Monsignor Bogumil Lewandoski, a Pole on the payroll of the Congregation for the Clergy, would direct the group, which would work from the Foreign Press Office in downtown Rome. Lewandoski in turn recruited Father Konrad Hejmo, the youth-magazine editor who had seen the nuns dancing in Poznan on the night of John Paul's election. Hejmo had already been brought to Rome to study Italian.

Now, Hejmo would live in a pilgrims' center that was being established for visiting Polish churchmen a few blocks from the Vatican. He would translate the pope's speeches into Polish, collect news from Polish visitors and the foreign press, and smuggle everything home. Plenty of couriers could be found in the swelling stream of Polish pilgrims ostensibly coming to Rome for religious reasons on invitation from the pope.

"A few religious speeches of the pope could be published in Poland, but not the politically sensitive ones," Hejmo says. In the burgeoning underground press operated by KOR, the only limit on what could be published was what could be learned. Lewandowski's team, on the Vatican payroll in unobtrusive jobs, now took care of providing the news.[10] The material was then fed to a priest in Wyszynski's office in Warsaw, who began typing a bulletin.[11]

Father Jan Zajac was also now on the Vatican payroll, as director of administration for the Papal Theological Academy in Krakow; meanwhile, he continued to expand the smuggling operation Cardinal Wojtyla had started him in. Contraband now regularly reached the Soviet Union. A committee of expatriate Poles was formed in London to raise money to buy books for the "flying university," and to pay salaries to professors who lost their official jobs for participating.

9

October 16, 1979, John Paul's first anniversary in office, the *Tablet* called him "without doubt the outstanding personality in the free world." Said Harvard professor George Hunston Williams, "No pope before John Paul II has produced such a cascade of documents, from addresses . . . to encyclicals, almost all drafted . . . by him." Ordinations to the priesthood had increased worldwide for the first time in six years. Contributions from the world's churchgoers— "Peter's pence"—had risen dramatically after a long decline, and everyone could see that donations jumped wherever the new pope visited.

John Paul had taken to heart Cardinal Vagnozzi's warning about Vatican finances the previous spring. November 5, he convened the first meeting of the full college of cardinals in more than four hundred years for a purpose other than electing a pope.[1] After four days of talks, a communiqué was issued revealing that 1979 income from the Vatican endowment would fall $20.2 million short of meeting expenses, and that Peter's pence wouldn't make up the difference as it once did.

The councils and commissions called for by Vatican II had strengthened the Church enormously, but they had also ballooned its expenses, while producing no new income. A council of fifteen cardinals was appointed to find ways to raise money and, if possible, cut expenses. Cardinals Krol and Joseph Höffner of Cologne were its leaders—the two most generally believed to be wise in the ways of finance.

Some cardinals asked whether the Sindona mess at IOR had been fixed. They were assured that it had been.

With the cardinals still in Rome to talk finance, John Paul disclosed his surprise choice to fill a vacant bishop's job in Orléans, France. Most surprised was the appointee: a pious, contemplative parish priest, Jean-Marie Lustiger. Lustiger had been baptized in Orléans and knew the city. But he still thought John Paul had made a mistake, and quickly wrote him: "I said, 'My parents were born in Poland, Jews. I was born a Jew. My family was mostly killed by the Germans in the camps. I am in France. You never heard of anti-Semitism in France?' It was a very provocative decision. I never got a response to the letter."[2]

Separated from his parents by the war, put in predominantly Christian schools, Lustiger converted in 1941, at age fourteen. Months after his bishop's appointment, he asked Monsignor Dziwisz, John Paul's secretary, about it, and was told it resulted from long prayer by the pope. "That was for me a great security," Lustiger says. "It told me there was no lobbying; it was his decision."

Stunning as the Lustiger appointment was, the speech John Paul gave later the same day to the Pontifical Academy of Science was almost as surprising. On the one-hundredth anniversary of Albert Einstein's birth, the pope made an admission perhaps unprecedented:

> The greatness of Galileo is comparable to that of Einstein, something recognized by all. The difference is that today, in the presence of the college of cardinals ... we are honoring Einstein, whereas Galileo was made to suffer a great deal ... by the men and the organization of the Church.

On the spot, John Paul appointed a commission to reinvestigate the 350-year-old case of Galileo, who was threatened with burning unless he renounced his notion that the earth revolved around the sun. The pope hoped that the "faithful recognition of wrongs ... will dispel the mistrust that in many minds still prevents a fruitful concord between science and faith." Later, he spoke of

> those notorious conflicts that arose from the interference of religious authorities in ... the development of scientific knowledge.

The Church remembers this with regret, for today we realize the errors and shortcomings of these ways.[3]

He was so interested in what his science academy was doing in general that during the days of meetings that followed, he several times dropped in unannounced to listen to the discussions.[4]

Sunday, November 18, 1979, the Vatican announced a trip to Turkey at the end of the month (the same trip the pope had discussed with Brzezinski). Turkey was a mass of contradictions. Its ancient Christian history had been eclipsed by an ascendant Islam. Communism was resisted for the alien idea it was, yet national pride was wounded by the government's alliance with the Christian West, and the presence of U.S. military bases, to oppose communism.

Five days after the announcement of the pope's trip, twenty-one-year-old Mehmet Ali Agca was smuggled out of a Turkish prison by friends from the Fascist-style youth group he had joined in high school. Agca had been imprisoned after admitting to the assassination of a prominent Istanbul newspaper editor the previous February, when the pope was in Mexico. The editor Agca shot had campaigned for Islam to adapt to modern life and Western learning.

Agca's Fascist group, the Gray Wolves, was associated with a strongly nationalist political party that opposed such Western ways. Its hundreds of thousands of members literally howled like wolves at meetings. A few days after Agca's escape from prison, the murdered editor's newspaper received and published a letter from Agca, saying: "Western imperialism has . . . dispatched to Turkey in the guise of a religious leader the Crusade commander John Paul. Unless this untimely and meaningless visit is postponed, I shall certainly shoot the pope."

Whether John Paul or his banker/security chief Marcinkus was even aware of Agca's threatening letter is uncertain. But from that moment, Agca eluded police. He traveled secretly through a dozen countries in Europe where the Gray Wolves had contacts among likeminded paramilitary groups. He would surface only much later, gun in hand, at the Vatican.

John Paul was coming to Turkey to meet the bearded Orthodox Patriarch Dimitrios I. The Orthodox had broken off from Catholicism in 1054, to be headquartered in Istanbul (then known by its Christian name, Constantinople). It was calculated in 1979 that there were about seventy-six million Orthodox believers worldwide, though when communism ended and believers behind the Iron Curtain revealed themselves, these estimates roughly doubled.

John Paul had told Brzezinski that "the time had come for closing the schism between" the two churches. "From the very beginning the pope had the sense that this [trip] was an enormous opportunity for the Church and Christianity in general," Brzezinski says. It was a mission that would cast tragedy on years of his papacy.

John Paul and Dimitrios exchanged greetings, gifts, and platitudes about the importance of their meeting. They visited tourist spots together, including the Topkapi Museum and the ruins at Izmir. They shared a church service and jointly lamented their inability to say Mass together because of their differences. In the end, though, it was like all the many ecumenical initiatives of John Paul's reign: full of talk about the need to resolve differences, with no discernible progress toward agreement on any major difference. For now, John Paul saw value in dialogue itself.

Soon after he returned to Rome, the pope sent a delegation headed by Cardinal Willebrands on a similar ecumenical mission to another Orthodox land now under a non-Christian administration: the Soviet Union. For twelve days, Willebrands traveled in Odessa, Leningrad, and Zagorsk. "I preached in their churches, I had meetings with their theologians," he says.

Willebrands insists that missions like his to Russia, and the pope's to Turkey, were "very successful," despite the lack of progress toward reunification of the churches. "There have been missionaries in Asia for four or five centuries," he says. "Do you think it has been unsuccessful because Asia isn't Christian? I do not. When Peter and Paul died in Rome, there were very few Christians. Were their lives unsuccessful?"

John Paul did try to use what influence he had in Islamic countries to persuade Ayatollah Ruhollah Khomeini, the new leader of Iran, to release sixty-five American hostages who had been seized by Iranian mobs. Khomeini treated the pope's supplications as a joke, asking where he had been when the Western-backed shah was committing crimes against the Iranian people.[5] Later, John Paul's negotiators scored one measurable success, recovering for the United States the bodies of several soldiers who were killed trying to rescue the hostages.

10

Unable to budge the Orthodox Dimitrios or the Moslem Khomeini, in December 1979 John Paul moved forcefully to bring fellow Catholics into line. He was still determined that the "ladies in the pew" would know what their

Church stood for. What happened over the next few months became a principal controversy of his papacy.

First the pope summoned to Rome the Dutch theologian Edward Schillebeeckx, whose unorthodox depiction of Jesus he had allowed to be described in *Znak* years earlier. Thirty of Schillebeeckx's prominent colleagues at the magazine *Concilium* protested the pope's summons. "The authorities of the Church, who publicly uphold the rights of man, should themselves respect...those rights within the Church," they said. "Disciplinary sanctions are no way to help a theologian review his position."

John Paul disagreed. The trials he began in December 1979 of Schillebeeckx and others amounted to an ideological purge, but differed from totalitarian purges in that the subjects could always declare themselves Protestant and go on with their lives. They were also given honest hearings. And the pope took care to respect their humanity; he was truly purging ideas, not people.

That was emphasized a few days before Schillebeeckx's hearing, when a French theologian assigned to the examining team declared on Vatican Radio that Schillebeeckx was a heretic. According to Wilton Wynn, John Paul telephoned the head of the radio service and ordered him to apologize to Schillebeeckx; there was to be no talk of heresy, and Schillebeeckx was to be treated courteously.[1]

At the hearing, Schillebeeckx was served coffee as three theologians questioned him. His defense counsel, the dean of his theology school at Nijmegen University, was stationed outside and called in occasionally to be asked about specific points. On the second day, Schillebeeckx agreed to clarify certain positions. Later, the Congregation for Doctrine—surely speaking for the pope—pronounced the clarifications unsatisfactory. After more written haggling, some of Schillebeeckx's views on the priesthood were declared "at variance with the teaching of the Church." But he kept his classroom.

A few days after the Schillebeeckx hearing, the Congregation for Doctrine condemned the book *Human Sexuality: New Directions in American Catholic Thought*, which had been commissioned by leading bishops, edited by a priest, and published by the leading U.S. Catholic publisher, the Paulist Press. The book was said to view sex outside the context of marriage and procreation. From now on, churchmen were not to publish it, use it, or recommend it.

The Congregation then declared that Professor Hans Kung of Switzerland had "departed from the integral truth of the Catholic faith, and therefore can no longer be considered a Catholic theologian." Kung, a hero of Vatican II, had challenged papal infallibility and suggested that in a pinch, laymen could perform priestly functions; he had declined invitations to explain himself in Rome.

The *Concilium* editors accused Cardinal Ratzinger of Munich of orchestrating Kung's downfall. Ratzinger even canceled university lectures scheduled in the Munich area by Kung and Father Johannes Metz, a supporter of Liberation Theology. Students protested, but the German bishops as a whole asserted that "the pope [was] obliged to act" against Kung, and that Kung himself had "interpreted the fact that the Church had not withdrawn his authorization to teach as a sign that the . . . Church was not sure of its position."

It's worth noting that Kung continued teaching at, and drawing a salary from, the same university (Tübingen, where Ratzinger had also taught). He was merely switched from the theology faculty to the secular faculty. He couldn't supervise priesthood candidates, but they could attend his lectures and pursue doctorates under him.

Kung called himself a "human-rights" victim and published a plea for other priests to revolt against the hierarchy. "One parish priest does not count in the diocese," he exhorted. "Five are given attention: fifty are invincible."

The pope wrote the German bishops a public letter:

> Has a theologian who does not accept the teaching of the Church in its totality the right to teach in the name of the Church? . . . We must not delude ourselves that another, more secular model of the Church would respond more adequately to . . . the world. . . . [We need] certainty about the faith she holds, and we should be profoundly fearful lest our belief in the gift of Christ, which guarantees that faith, namely infallibility, be cast into doubt.

In a speech in Turin, John Paul said the world faced a choice among three movements that were "in acute conflict." One was Marxism. The second—Kung's model, he implied—was "rationalism, Enlightenment and scientism . . . the so-called . . . 'liberalism' of Western nations, which brought with it the radical negation of Christianity." The third choice was Christianity.

Debate raged among Catholic intellectuals over how much uniformity should be expected from teachers at Catholic institutions. It was a major philosophical demarcation. Many wanted classrooms to be forums for ideas, while others wanted them to provide a rock of certain truth.

Professor Jerzy Janik, John Paul's former student and camping companion, remains angry that so many Western Catholics backed Kung and Schillebeeckx. "People in the West suffer from a democracy paradigm," Janik says. "Democracy was such a success as a political system that people in the West consider it a criterion of truth—[that] truth is something decided by vote."[2] Says Stefan

Wilkanowicz of *Znak*, "The West distrusts institutions, but Poland needed strong institutions."

Ironically, the victory that liberalism was to claim over communism was won by a man who did not believe in liberalism. Yet even Cardinal Bernardin, Father Greeley's hero and in many ways a son of the Enlightenment, defended the sanctions that John Paul was meting out: "If we really believe in the Church, we have to accept that within the Church is a teaching authority given by Christ," he said.[3]

In barely a year, John Paul had swept through the concerns of the Church, defining firmly, precisely, and consistently rules that had been politely debated or ignored for a decade under Paul VI.

Pushing on, he reshaped the Italian Church into something more religious and less political. In Venice, Turin, and Milan, he appointed cardinals who were thinkers more than doers and who had not previously appeared to be on the corporate ladder. The Milan appointment that December was particularly striking; to run Italy's largest archdiocese—five million parishioners and twenty-four hundred priests, John Paul named Carlo Martini, the rector of Rome's Gregorian University. Martini was a Jesuit and so, being outside the hierarchical diocesan system, had never been a bishop. John Paul had known him many years as a scholarly colleague who spent his spare time working in the Rome slums with Mother Teresa's nuns. By the 1990s, Martini was often mentioned as a candidate to succeed John Paul.

The night of December 27–28, 1979, a hundred thousand Soviet soldiers riding on an awesome array of modern armor poured into the beautiful but dirt-poor land of Afghanistan. Aside from the sickening brutality of it—probably a million Afghans (nobody even knows) were killed in the ensuing repression—the invasion was epochally stupid: it changed the Cold War map forever, to the Soviets' disadvantage.

Like the Americans in Vietnam, the Soviets had blundered into Afghanistan thinking that a little bit of killing would suffice. After years of jousting with the United States for influence there, in April 1978 the Soviets helped a small band of Afghan communists stage a coup and take over the country. But like Vietnam, Afghanistan refused to cooperate in its subjugation. By December 1979, popular rebellion had spread to the point where without Soviet troops, the twenty-month-old puppet regime would fall.[4]

As much financial damage as the Vietnam war did, the U.S. at least had a cushion to absorb it. The Soviet Union was always just a poor country pretending to be rich, hiding behind the facade of a big military. Also, the communists' only prestige lay in the notion that they were defending the world against American imperialism. Many Soviet soldiers expected to be welcomed into Afghanistan as heroes. When, instead, they discovered that almost the entire Afghan population hated them—and when Soviet families saw bodies come home and heard tales from returning veterans—a positive self-image was shattered, much as had happened to Americans in Vietnam. And just as the Soviet government had much less money to lose than the American, it had less credibility as well. And it squandered its skimpy reserves just when John Paul posed a real threat to it.

The pope's annual New Year's peace message for 1980 was written before the Afghan invasion, but was a fitting commentary:

> It has become more and more the custom to analyze everything in social and international life exclusively in terms of . . . power, and to organize accordingly to impose one's own interests. . . . As long as selective support is given to certain forms of violence in line with interests or ideologies, . . . restraint . . . will periodically give way in the face of . . . the suicidal exaltation of violence.

John Paul continued his disciplining of the Church into 1980. Four days before the filing deadline, the pope ordered a Massachusetts congressman-priest, Robert Drinan, not to run for reelection. Father Drinan, a Jesuit and a Democrat, was a voice in Congress for aid to the poor and against military support for dictators. He said he opposed abortion, though some Catholics complained that he had refused to exclude abortion from publicly funded medical programs.

After appealing the pope's order to no avail, Drinan obeyed "with regret and pain." He said, "I am certain I was more influential as a priest" during his six years in Congress "than in my previous fourteen years as dean of Boston College Law School."[5] Father Robert J. Cornell, a professor and former congressman from Wisconsin who planned to run again, was also told not to. A Vatican spokesman said the pope "not only asks those priests already in politics to withdraw, but also requests them not to make inflammatory political statements or take sides on sensitive political issues."

The press noted that one priest was a Colorado state legislator, and another on a county board in New York State. A nun was mayor of Dubuque, Iowa, and others were in the Arizona and Rhode Island legislatures. Three priests were in the Spanish Parliament, and a fourth was a town mayor near Barcelona. John Paul's mentor Sapieha had sat in the Polish Parliament until Pius XI forced him out. Before World War II, many Hungarian bishops had served in Parliament, and priests had run important government departments.[6] In the Philippines, Cardinal Jaime Sin had called himself a "critical collaborator" in dictator Ferdinand Marcos's seizure of power.

The Vatican insisted it was merely upholding canon law in the Drinan and Cornell cases, not targeting anyone. But canon law calls for discretion; though it bars priests from taking "an active role in political parties," it allows exceptions where "the need to protect the rights of the Church or promote the common good requires it in the judgment of the competent ecclesiastical authorities." Father O'Keefe, the Jesuit official, says Father Drinan's candidacy had been approved before each election by the U.S. Episcopate and Boston's cardinal.

Many people thought the pope's policy varied by region. His effort to keep priests out of Western Hemisphere politics made so much news that the president of the Italian Chamber of Deputies asked for equal treatment, calling on the pope to stop Italian priests from campaigning against abortion, which had been legalized in Italy in 1978. Abortion, of course, was against the Catholic religion; but so was murdering farmers to steal their land, which some governments were doing in Latin America, with U.S. aid.

In Germany, the governing Social Democrats complained about a letter the German bishops had ordered read from all pulpits during a Parliamentary election. Beyond the Catholic issue of more liberal divorce laws, the German Episcopate criticized "dangerously high state debts" and the growth of government bureaucracy. These remarks paralleled the campaign themes of the opposition Christian Democrats, and Germans got the message that the Church backed the Christian Democrats (who lost the election).

John Paul took no action in Italy or Germany, where priests spoke out but didn't actually become members of political parties.

11

Next, the pope decided to bring the increasingly prominent Archbishop Romero of El Salvador into line. On another visit to Rome, in January 1980, Romero recorded in his diary the pope's warning that a victory by "the popular Left" could bring retribution and bloodshed.

Back home, in a homily February 17, Archbishop Romero asked President Carter to stop new U.S. military aid to El Salvador. As he did each week, Romero listed new death-squad victims and told where each had died. This wasn't politics, he said, but the Gospel. Two days later, the Church radio station in El Salvador was bombed, then the library of the Catholic university. Romero began rotating his place of sleep; he told friends that fear often kept him awake all night anyway.

The pope, too, was disturbed. Sometime around March 20, 1980, Cardinal Silvio Oddi, then head of the Congregation for the Clergy, sat down with the cardinals who ran two other major congregations—Franjo Seper of the Congregation for Doctrine and Sebastiano Baggio of the Congregation for Bishops—with orders to make a plan for Romero and report back to John Paul.

"My Congregation wanted that Romero would go to another diocese because he was acting without responsibility," says Oddi, making this public for the first time in an interview. "The [Salvadoran] government interpreted his doctrine to be in favor of communism." Cardinals Oddi, Seper, and Baggio also discussed "two or three [other] bishops" whom they considered to be "too engaged, not in agreement with the Holy See," Oddi says. It was unanimously agreed to reassign Romero "somewhere else in Latin America." Baggio was sent to discuss it with John Paul.[1]

Sunday, March 23, 1980, unaware that he was to be removed from his job, Romero recounted in his sermon "a very tragic week." The government had routed striking brewery workers, killing some. The group behind the strike was too extreme, Romero allowed, but that was because "they are not allowed to take part in normal political activities.... They are persecuted and often killed.... The country is ... in a prerevolutionary stage. The basic question is: how can we find a way out of this crisis with the least violence? The main responsibility here lies with our rulers."

Romero had collected news clippings about the pope's speeches denouncing terrorism in Italy (where John Paul had just given the funeral for a prominent judge who had been assassinated). "If the pope were here in my place, he would not only speak of the cruel killings ... in Italy, but would dwell, as I am doing, on the many killings [in El Salvador] every day," Romero said. "The bodies of four peasants were found on eighteen March, two in Estapan and two in San Miguel. On nineteen March, the bodies of three peasants were found at five-thirty A.M. after an operation by the military in San Luis...." And so on.

Romero appealed "to those in the National Guard, the police and the garrisons. Brothers, you belong to our people. You are killing your own peasant brothers.... No soldier is obliged to obey an order that goes against the Law of God.... In the name of the Lord and of his long-suffering people whose laments are heard in Heaven every day, I beseech you, I beg you, to stop the repression."

Archbishop Romero was shot through the chest the next day as he said Mass in the chapel of a hospital. His words as he lay dying were "May God have mercy on the assassin."

Expressions of reverence for Romero's courage and dedication to others poured forth from around the world—from everyone but his boss. John Paul's telegram to the president of the Salvadoran Episcopal Conference expressed grief at the "sacrilegious assassination" but contained not one word of praise for the slain archbishop. (He described Romero only as "zealous.") That same day, John Paul released an open letter to a papal nuncio held hostage by revolutionaries in Colombia, conveying "all my admiration for the example of fortitude, calm, and prudence you are giving."

The pope began his general audience that week "happy" to announce a coming trip to Africa. Then he continued his discourse on sexuality, which in other weeks he had set aside to discuss major events. In his closing remarks, he again condemned the violence of the Romero assassination but still said nothing good about Romero.

Palm Sunday—March 30, 1980—as the pope addressed the crowd in St. Peter's, 125,000 people, including thirty foreign bishops, gathered in the square outside the San Salvador cathedral for Romero's funeral. John Paul meanwhile declared his "heartfelt grief and deep concern" for martyrs who had died that week—in Chad, not in El Salvador.

John Paul's treatment of Archbishop Romero, and his continued treatment of Romero's memory, are an injustice like no other he has done anyone. Cardinal Oddi says he doesn't know whether Cardinal Baggio was able to arrange Romero's dismissal with John Paul in the few days before the murder. But Archbishop Weakland of Milwaukee expresses a consensus of high churchmen when he says, "It is as much as certain that after this pope, Oscar Romero will be canonized a saint."

The pope's good friend, philosophy and economics professor Rocco Buttiglione, calls Romero "a martyr of the Catholic Church, [killed] defending human rights." The *Tablet* editorialized, "It is possible that Romero's assassination . . . may come to occupy in Latin America the kind of place that Becket's martyrdom enjoys" in Britain.

Or, perhaps, Saint Stanislaw's in Poland.

Not until years later was it acknowledged that Romero was murdered by soldiers sent by Major Roberto d'Aubuisson, an avowed Nazi admirer who operated under American protection and whose party later came to power in El Salvador under American auspices.[2]

Romero's funeral exemplified what he had been up against. As Cardinal Ernesto Corripio Ahumada of Mexico finished his homily, there was a loud explosion; priests said they saw a firebomb dropped from the roof of the nearby National Palace. Then shooting erupted, also coming from the palace.

The vast crowd panicked in the hail of bullets; forty persons died, mostly crushed to death.[3]

The funeral was never completed. The coffin containing Romero's body, which rested on the cathedral steps during the tumult, was buried quietly. A government statement blamed the violence on "Left-wing groups." Ten foreign bishops quickly contradicted the government account based on what they had seen, adding, "We feel today more than ever in solidarity with [Romero's] prophetic mission."

Father O'Keefe, the Jesuit leader, says some American cardinals "were radicalized by being shot at during the funeral. Cardinal [James] Hickey [of Washington, D.C.], Archbishop [John] Quinn of San Francisco—they dove for the ground in their priestly vestments."

At last, after that, John Paul issued a statement noting "the particular witness" in which Archbishop Romero "united his life with the service of the poorest and the most underprivileged." Still, the pope literally protested more about the Polish government's plan to build a road limiting crowd access to the Czestochowa shrine than he did about the shooting war being waged against his Church in El Salvador.

That spring, Carter visited John Paul in Rome. After they discussed Jerusalem and Iran, the pope brought up Central America, but offered only vague platitudes about spreading "the justice and the peace of Christ." At least in public remarks, neither man mentioned U.S. military aid to El Salvador and Guatemala.[4]

Judge Atilio Ramirez Amaya, who was assigned by the Salvadoran government to investigate Archbishop Romero's murder, quickly fled the country after two nearly successful attempts on his own life.

12

May 2, 1980, John Paul took off for the continent where his priests were having the most trouble with sexual issues, but which was also the most fertile field for converts. If the Church was to grow, Africa was the likeliest place.

Millions of black Africans were adopting monotheistic religions—not always in place of traditional multigod animism, but often superimposed on it. Many practiced native religions Saturday night and either Islam on Friday or Christianity on Sunday. Ministers, mullahs, and medicine men met coming and going at homes where someone was seriously ill. It wasn't hypocrisy; it was a decision not to leave any bets uncovered.

Traditionally, black Africans were freer in their sexual practices than Mediterranean peoples, Christian or Islamic. But neither Islam nor the rapidly expanding Protestant denominations made such an issue of sex as did Catholicism. Chastity and other sexual rules constituted a big handicap for Catholics in the competition for converts in Africa.

A case in point was that of Father Hans Lotstra, a seminary teacher in Kenya, where John Paul was to stop. In June 1976, Father Lotstra had been asked by Kenya's bishops to produce a code of medical ethics for a family-planning program the Kenyan government was initiating with international help.

While one of Africa's wealthier countries, Kenya was also among the few with a population problem. Largely because of better health care, population growth was among the world's fastest—nearly 4 percent a year. Fathers had so many surviving sons that farms were cut into smaller, less viable units with each generation. At stake were not only human beings but the world's last great populations of elephants, lions, rhinoceroses, giraffes, zebras, and antelopes, which needed forest and grass for food. The only way to get new land for human crops was often to invade animal sanctuaries.[1]

So the government was acting. But how were Catholic doctors to reconcile their faith with their new medical responsibilities under family planning? After much discussion, Father Lotstra proposed a compromise: Catholic doctors should tell patients that the rhythm method "is normally most in accord with human dignity." But they could also "give couples an objective explanation of other methods and their respective merits and demerits."

Father Lotstra's guidelines stressed that "certain fundamental moral values must be safeguarded: mutual respect, self-sacrifice, generosity, marital love." Beyond that, however, "refusal to cooperate with" programs that merely gave information "would deprive many sincere people of badly needed advice and support."

Kenya's bishops told Father Lotstra that "the competent authorities in Rome" had approved his proposal with minor changes, which were made. It became Kenyan Church policy. But in July 1978, a London newspaper published parts of it. Within days, the Vatican nuncio in Nairobi told Father Lotstra that his policy had been overruled "at a level at which error was no longer possible." According to Father Lotstra, the nuncio stressed the difference between what was proclaimed from the pulpit and what was "whispered in the confessional."[2]

The Kenyan hierarchy then declared that Catholic doctors couldn't be associated with family planning beyond the rhythm method. By chance, a drought soon began, and food grew scarce for the first time in memory in a land generally known for its bounty. Father Lotstra complained that the new Vatican policy lacked "compassion."

His story illustrates the moral dilemma faced by many priests, and the unease felt even by some archbishops, over enforcement of the birth-control ban. In this instance, newspaper publicity seems to have forced bishops to conform to a Vatican policy that they evidently would have bent in private. A month before John Paul's African trip, a prominent magazine published by the East African Episcopate printed an article saying as much—and even suggesting that polygamy might be accepted where it was part of local culture. Fortunately for the Episcopate, the pope didn't learn of the article until he was back in Rome.[3]

Besides the barrier of sex, John Paul faced a political barrier in Africa. But he was determined not to let that stop his evangelizing, either. In Zaire, over the nine years since "President-for-life" Mobutu Sese Seko had declared war on Catholicism, a truce had evolved. Cardinal Malula was back at his post. Just before the pope arrived, Malula married Mobutu to a girlfriend; the dictator had wanted John Paul to perform the ceremony, but the pope drew the line at that.

Mobutu still stole the national wealth, forbade unionizing and dissent, and occasionally used the Western military to help him put down rebellions. But John Paul set all that aside, addressing Mobutu as "Your Excellency" and expressing "satisfaction at our new dialogue." The pope had come "to strengthen and encourage . . . my brothers"—the fifty-five local bishops, all but seven of whom were now black.

Malula openly expressed his disappointment that John Paul passed up a two-hour "Zairian Rite" Mass that had been arranged, featuring drums, spear-carrying dancers, and a rhythmic recitation of the Lord's prayer. The pope said he hadn't yet mastered the languages, but may also have feared that the spontaneity would go too far and contradict the message of orthodoxy he was sending elsewhere.

Nor could Malula have been thrilled by the public Mass John Paul gave the next day in French, stressing chastity. Malula had long argued, as far as one diplomatically could in the Church, that strict sexual rules doomed Catholicism in the fight for converts in Africa, and that celibacy made it hard to recruit priests. Instead of de-emphasizing those rules, however, the pope promoted retreats and support groups to help people remain chaste. He told priests and bishops the papacy would not "release you from any responsibility. On the contrary, it will drive home to you your responsibility."

The pope did back down on clerical dress: after a few days in the equatorial sun, he stopped reprimanding priests who wore shorts and distinctive crosses instead of normal collars. At his main open-air Mass in Kinshasa, nine people died and many more were injured when crowds surged against a fence; he learned about it only later. He took a rain drenching in good humor and visited a leper colony. He spoke out for democracy in neighboring Zimbabwe, where European settlers had gained Western support for a white minority government by claiming they were fighting communism.

But he didn't speak out for democracy in Zaire. When he talked to students at Zaire's university, he seemed unaware that Mobutu's police had just beaten and evicted hundreds of their classmates, killing many. In an airplane interview,[4] he spoke of a different standard, which allowed him to ignore Mobutu's crimes:

> Sometimes perhaps politics is sinful, and sometimes there are sinful governments. But . . . it gave me great joy to see peoples who a few years before had been subject to colonial power finally enjoying their own sovereignty. Perhaps it was an imperfect sovereignty, not yet translated into democratic principles. But at least these people are their own masters.

In another interview,[5] he emphasized that to him the economic power of the former colonial countries was more to be feared than the political power of black African dictators:

> Having lived in a country . . . subject to the aggression and influence of its neighbors, I have a deep understanding of Third World countries—this other type of dependence, especially economic. I have spoken about it many times with African leaders. I understand what exploitation is, and I have opted [to side with] the poor . . . and defenseless. The powerful ones of this world do not always think well of such a pope. Sometimes they are even angry with him. They want free rein.

This other standard—that it was better for dictators and exploiters to be native-born—was the only one that might explain the farewell speech the pope gave alongside Mobutu, expressing his "feeling of deep joy" at the "historic way on which you are starting here." In Kenya and the Ivory Coast, where other dictators were gradually eliminating democracy, the pope was similarly kind.

He constantly praised traditional African society. In Ghana, he called it

> a conception of the world in which the sacred occupies a central
> position; a profound awareness of the link between nature and the
> Creator; . . . a sense of family and community.

"Preserve your culture," he told Africans, "and offer it as your contribution to
the world." Repeatedly, he said the West must learn not just to give to Africa
but also "to receive from African peoples [who] need . . . to give: their heart,
their wisdom, their culture, their sense of man, their sense of God, which are
keener than in many others."

He stressed the importance of farming, and staying on the land instead of
moving to the cities. Outside of church, he seemed to enjoy the drums and col-
orfully dressed native dancers; at times he swayed to the music. In several countries, he consecrated local bishops in public ceremonies, underscoring the
Church's turn to indigenous leadership.

He barely acknowledged Africa's magnificent animals, making only a quick
stop at one park—less time than he spent meeting the archbishop of Canterbury, head of the British Church, when their paths crossed in Ghana. He
stopped half a day in arid Burkina Faso to promote international "solidarity"
to bore wells, adapt crops, and plant trees to stop the southern expansion of
the Sahara Desert. He urged weapons researchers "to direct your work toward
the search for new means to combat desertification." (As a direct result of his
visit, $9.2 million was raised in Germany for a "Sahel Fund" to be run by
Africans appointed by local bishops' conferences.)

The pope's stamina remained awesome. He came in from touring at eleven
P.M., still met half an hour with local Poles (who seemed to be everywhere)
before going to bed, then was off again at dawn. He traveled as if he were campaigning for office, yet always to spread ideas, not, like a politician, to win popularity.

Before boarding his airplane home, he gave Africa this advice:

> Be yourselves. Guard against both Western materialism and
> Marxist ideological solutions to your economic and political
> problems. . . .
>   There is a great temptation to . . . acquire at a high price arms
> for populations that need bread, to want to seize power by setting
> some ethnic groups against others . . . or else to succumb to the
> intoxication of profit for the benefit of a privileged class. Do not
> get caught up, dear African brothers and sisters, in this disastrous

mechanism. . . . You don't need to imitate foreign models based on contempt of man [Marxism] or on self-interest [pure capitalism].

Back in Rome for his sixtieth birthday, John Paul received apparently sincere congratulations from Polish communist leaders, who seemed surprised—and delighted—that he had stood on principle. He had spoken out against new American military installations in Europe. He had denounced an American plan to build a neutron bomb—a weapon that would kill people with radiation while leaving buildings intact, the ultimate triumph of commercial over human values. He had opposed President Carter's boycott of the Moscow Olympics that summer, punishing athletes to protest the invasion of Afghanistan.

John Paul had not become quite the agent of Western interests the communists had feared.

13

With barely time for laundry the papal road show was off again—for Paris, both to rally the local Church and to address UNESCO, the United Nations Educational, Social and Cultural Organization, headquartered there.

The problem of the French Church was the exact opposite of the problem of the African Church. There was hardly any competition: three of every four Frenchmen were baptized Catholic. But in France, faith itself was on the wane. Only 15 percent practiced.[1] Annual ordinations had dropped from 550 in 1968, after the euphoria of Vatican II, to a mere 120 in 1979. French government leaders had distanced themselves from the Church since Charles de Gaulle accused it of courting Fascists during World War II. No pope had crossed the border from Italy to France in 176 years.

For his main appearance apart from UNESCO, John Paul chose the working-class neighborhood of St. Denis, a typical area of lapsed Catholics. As in Rome, the mayor was a friendly communist, and welcomed the pope by saying that Christians and communists were "side by side" on the big issues of economics and peace. The pope talked about how to mix work and family—a problem for everyone in his audience, and a plague on modern life.

The loss of traditional family roles had caused anguish, he said. Communist and capitalist societies alike had pushed women outside the home, not because they chose a profession, but merely to bring in money. He spoke of "the woman who works in a factory, at a tiring pace, and who is constantly concerned about being with her children and her husband." He called for "the rights of the family" to "be deeply inscribed in . . . every code of work."

The next day, at a youth rally, he was asked to identify the most important problem regarding justice and peace in the world. He declared it was the moral obligation of the richer countries of Europe and North America toward the poorer countries to their south. As always, he seemed to have the most fun when he was with young people, dropping the formality of his office; before long, they were singing songs together.

He used the big speech at UNESCO to launch yet another major theme of his papacy: the promotion of culture as a primary value at least equal to the dominant emerging value of commerce. During its dismemberment, Poland had "conserved its national . . . sovereignty, not by depending on . . . physical power, but by depending on its culture," he said. Culture had proved "a greater power than all other forces."

He asserted that there was a common European culture, based on Christianity. It unified West and East, "from the Atlantic to the Urals." Now, however, this culture was under threat from "the materialism of our age and the decline of moral values." Championing culture over material wealth soon brought the pope head to head with science:

> In spite of the undeniably noble intentions of scholars and scientists, the future of mankind and of the world is radically threatened . . . because the marvelous results of their researches . . . continue to be exploited—contrary to the demands of morality—for ends which have nothing to do with science, for purposes of destruction and death. . . .
>
> Up to now it has been said that nuclear arms have had a deterrent effect, and this is probably true. But will it always be so? Nuclear arms are being perfected with each year and are being added to the arsenals of a growing number of countries. The world cannot go on like this for long. . . .
>
> We must convince ourselves of the priority of the ethical over the technical, of the person over things, of the . . . spiritual over the material.

Watching on television was the new bishop of Orléans, Jean-Marie Lustiger. "When I heard that address, I thought communism was finished," he says. "It was very audacious. For the first time, I heard somebody say that the economic fight was not paramount. Culture was the upper structure of reality, the real matter of history. It was Marxist language inverted. I said, 'He dares to say that! He will be understood by people on the other side.' "

Soon, in Germany, John Paul elaborated on this theme, asserting that all the harm religion had inflicted on science in centuries past was now being returned in full measure by science upon religion. Science was in control, and

> the world . . . becomes a mere complex of phenomena that can be . . . examined with reference only to its functionality. . . .
>
> The progress of humanity must be measured not only by the progress of science and technology, but also and chiefly by the primacy given to spiritual values and by the progress of moral life. So it is deplorable [that] legitimate pluralism is often confused with neutrality of values. In the name of misunderstood democracy, people think they can increasingly do without ethical norms, and . . . the moral categories of good and evil in public life. . . .
>
> It is as if knowledge and scientific research stretched out toward the infinite, only to snap back to their origins. The old problem of the connection between science and faith has not become outdated with the development of modern sciences; on the contrary, in a world more and more imbued with science, [faith] manifests . . . vital importance. . . .
>
> In the past, precursors of modern science fought against the Church with the slogans Reason, Freedom, and Progress. Today, in view of the crisis . . . of science, the battle fronts have been inverted. Today . . . the Church takes up the defense for reason and science. . . . Both parties must continue listening to each other. We need each other.[2]

In Hiroshima, the city most devastated by science, he said science would destroy culture unless three temptations were avoided:

> The first is the temptation to pursue technological development for its own sake as if one should always do what is technically possible.
>
> The second temptation is to subject technological development to . . . the logic of profit, or nonstop economic expansion . . . with no care for the true good of humanity. . . .
>
> Third . . . is the temptation to subject technological development to the pursuit . . . of power, as when it is used for military

purposes, and whenever people are manipulated so that they may be dominated.[3]

When the lights of Rome interfered with the view from the century-old Vatican observatory, John Paul commissioned a new observatory in Arizona. He wrote its director:

> Religion is not founded on science, nor is science an extension of religion.... While each can and should support the other as distinct dimensions of a common human culture, neither ought to assume that it forms a necessary premise for the other.... Science can purify religion from idolatry and false absolutes. Each can draw the other into the wider world ... in which both can flourish.[4]

It was clear, though, which one he favored in a conflict. He condemned, without exception, the rapidly growing practice of in vitro fertilization, which offered a chance at parenthood to the estimated 15 percent of couples trying to conceive who were infertile. "The procreation of a person must be the fruit and the result of married love," he insisted. "The conjugal act is inseparably corporal and spiritual."[5]

Thus he settled an issue that had divided his two predecessors. But John Paul II's formulation went beyond Pope Paul's in that it required sexual pleasure as an integral part of procreation. Unless both pleasure *and* openness to procreation were present, there could be neither pleasure *nor* procreation.

Journalist Wilton Wynn asked John Paul how he could make such sweeping doctrinal rulings. Replied the pope,

> Some modern scientific and medical developments are apt to make of the human person a product, an object. We insist that the human person ... must always be considered the subject. That is the basis for our teaching, the absolute standard.[6]

Many people rejected the pope's conviction that moral values could be defined with the certainty of science. Yet many of these same people shared his fear that science had run amok and needed governing. Many were also the same people who welcomed his attempt to impose moral values on capitalist economics.

If the pope could not set moral standards for everyone, it was nonetheless his job to make everyone think about them.

14

At some point, John Paul had come to the conclusion that Liberation Theology deserved a more sympathetic understanding than he had thought when he took office. He demonstrated that beginning June 30, 1980, during twelve days in Brazil, the world's largest Catholic country, with 123 million people.

The Romero affair may have impressed him, or he may have listened to the two Brazilian cardinals who were active in Liberation Theology, Paulo Evaristo Arns of São Paulo, South America's largest city, and Aloísi Lorscheider of Fortaleza, in the primitive Amazon Valley. (Lorscheider had been an important supporter of John Paul's election.) Or perhaps the pope simply saw what was before his eyes.

The Jesuit priests of Central America had just accused the American-backed government of Guatemala of killing 3,252 civilians in ten months; the government then threatened to kill all the Jesuits, too, branding them "Marxist."[1] Dictator Pinochet had seized Chile's Catholic university and fired seventeen professors after a study was published indicating that his policies hurt poor people.

The summer before, Sandinista rebels in Nicaragua had driven dictator Somoza into exile. John Paul's own Nicaraguan bishops had unanimously refused Somoza's request to meet with them in his hour of crisis, telling him his troops should stop killing innocent people, and accusing him of having "an obvious disregard not only for God but for all sense of human love." When Daniel Ortega and Violetta Chamorro, members of Nicaragua's new Sandinista leadership, came to the Vatican, John Paul praised their new literacy program, though cautioning them to respect the rights of Catholics to religious education.[2]

In Brazil itself, a decade after an American-assisted military coup overthrew the democratic government, the dictators still called Catholic priests "subversive . . . the most active enemy of national security."[3] After the government tortured and murdered a prominent São Paulo television journalist, Cardinal Arns formed an important ecumenical partnership with a Presbyterian minister, Jaime Wright, whose brother had also been tortured to death by the military. Their joint funeral for the journalist (who was Jewish—a rabbi also participated) drew nearly forty thousand people, overflowing the São Paulo cathedral.

In 1979, a new military government under General João Figueiredo had declared an end to the torture and murder, and did, in fact, reduce them. But Figueiredo also granted amnesty to guilty soldiers even as Church workers and union organizers were still being killed. Shortly before John Paul arrived in 1980, Cardinal Arns and the Reverend Wright conceived a daring plan to document the terror, with the help of sympathetic lawyers who had access to government archives.

With money Wright got from the World Council of Churches, they hired a staff and began sneaking government files, batch by batch, to be photocopied at a nondescript office they rented. Risking their lives through the early 1980s, they chronicled the violence. As with Jews and the Holocaust, they believed that what was set down and remembered was less likely to be repeated. Uncertain of John Paul's sympathies, Arns kept the work secret from the Vatican.*

In the weeks before John Paul's visit, the Brazilian Episcopate, led by Cardinal Arns, supported a metalworkers' strike in São Paulo. General Figueiredo accused Arns of having incited the action. A human-rights lawyer for Arns was stabbed and nearly killed. The government publicized ridiculous charges that Cardinal Lorscheider had robbed squatters in a land deal (much as the Polish communists had once charged priests with stealing charity funds).

With Church-state relations at rock-bottom, Arns and Lorscheider asked the pope to avoid General Figueiredo and go directly to the impoverished Amazon region. But John Paul's style, more effective, was to begin officially in the capital, Brasilia. Speaking in Portuguese after seven weeks' study, he first talked cordially with Figueiredo but then challenged him before the crowd:

> Every country has the duty to safeguard its peace and internal security. But it must in some sense merit that peace by ensuring the welfare of all and respect for their rights. Where justice is lacking, society is threatened from within. This does not mean that the changes required should be realized through violence, for violence merely paves the way for a violent society, to which, as Christians, we cannot subscribe. What it does mean is that there are social changes, sometimes very profound ones, that must be brought about . . . by peaceful reforms.

The bluntness of the pope's speech must have shocked the general. Had John Paul retained the attitude of his first days in Mexico the year before, he might have gone after Arns and Lorscheider instead; now, he supported them, telling a youth gathering:

> Do not hide your desire to transform radically those social structures you find unjust. You say, and rightly, that it is impossible to

* The story of this enterprise was beautifully told by journalist Lawrence Weschler in *New Yorker* articles that became the book *A Miracle, A Universe* (New York: Penguin, 1990).

be happy if one sees that a multitude of one's brothers lack the
minimum necessary.... When I was young, I lived by these same
convictions. God willed that they should be tried in the fire of war,
the atrocity of which did not spare my family. All this ... taught me
that social justice is not genuine unless it is based on the rights of
the individual, and those rights will be truly recognized only if the
transcendent dimension of man, created in the image and likeness
of God ... is recognized.

Everywhere he spoke, he described the "subhuman conditions" he saw. Of
those who were well off, he asked, "Do you not feel the pangs of conscience on
account of your riches and affluence? Man's worth is measured not according
to what he has, but according to what he is."

In a dramatic gesture in a Rio de Janeiro slum, he removed a papal ring from
his finger and donated it to the community. John Paul also appealed for development aid from North America. Noninterference in the affairs of other
nations, he said, did not mean "indifference to the fate of peoples whom
nature and circumstances have so disfavored."

He still told priests that their primary work was "spiritual ... in the domain
of souls." But he added that they "cannot be dispensed from ... works of
charity and the defense of justice." This was his attitude toward the Polish
priests in the St. Martin's hunger strike, a long way from the tone he had used
in Puebla, Mexico, when he seemed to bar priests from politics.

In strike-plagued São Paulo, the pope told workers:

> An exclusively economic logic, ... corrupted by crass materialism,
> has invaded all fields of existence, ... threatening families and
> destroying all respect for the human person. Factories spewing forth
> their effluents deform and contaminate the environment and render
> the air unfit to breathe. Waves of immigrants crowd into degrading
> hovels where many lose all hope and end in misery. Only too often
> development becomes the large-scale version of the parable of Dives
> and Lazarus [on the unjust treatment of the poor by the rich].

Then, as hundreds of thousands looked on, the pope dramatically brought
to his side Cardinal Arns's human-rights lawyer, in a wheelchair from the stab-
bing and beating that everyone knew was the work of the government. John
Paul embraced him and had him read a Bible passage. This was, again, the kind
of political statement the pope might have made in Poland.

He concluded the trip with several days in Lorscheider's territory, the Amazon, where traditional farmers were being routed off their land by agribusinesses. He spoke as loudly as one man could about "indigence, undernourishment, ill-health, illiteracy, insecurity." He referred to the Lazarus story repeatedly. He told Brazilians that despite property rights,

> the demands of the common good take precedence over private advantage. . . .
>
> To take [farm workers] from their native soil and set them off on an uncertain exodus toward the great metropolises, or else not to guarantee their right to the legitimate possession of their land, is to violate their rights as men and sons of God. . . . Just agrarian legislation is required. . . . The land is God's gift for all men.
>
> As far as priority needs are concerned—food, clothing, housing, medical care, basic education, professional formation, means of transport, information, recreational possibilities, religious life— there should be no privileged classes.

This was radical stuff.

On Brazilian television and before a vast live audience, John Paul even embraced his old antagonist Archbishop Camara, known to supporters as a father of Liberation Theology (and to the Brazilian military as the "Red Bishop"). John Paul brought tears to some eyes when he proclaimed, "This man is the friend of the poor, and my friend." To assist him at the Mass, John Paul brought to the altar the mother of a priest who had been "disappeared" while working for human rights.

Before flying home, he scolded the country's bishops behind closed doors. In their required five-yearly reports, he said, "I have been struck by the extent to which many of you lament the lack of deep faith" among Brazilians. In contrast, the pope said he had found the Brazilian people to be "religious, good, and . . . naturally Christian." It was up to the bishops, he said, to reach out to them.

> Your vocation as a bishop forbids you . . . any contact with political parties, any subjection to this or that ideology. . . . But it does not forbid you, on the contrary it almost invites you, to be close [to] and at the service of all men, above all the most handicapped and the dispossessed.[4]

The trip should have been the basis for a workable consensus to solve the Liberation Theology problem. But it was not to be.

15

Returning home, John Paul was jolted by one unexpected reaction to his constant preaching about unionism. Mariano Cerullo, an engineer at Vatican Radio, went to Secretary of State Casaroli with the signatures of 90 percent of the Vatican's eighteen hundred civilian employees, declaring that they wanted a wage increase, their first since 1972.[1] And there were no written rules at the Vatican, so employees in some offices had to work longer than those in others to earn the same pay. They wanted a union contract. John Paul told Casaroli to work one out.[2]

Another, more important union was also formed that summer.

Alarmed by the growing power of the Polish freedom movement, the Soviets had tried to crack down on KOR in 1980. Mikhail Suslov, Brezhnev's second-in-command, had flown in from Moscow to take over the quadrennial Party meeting in Warsaw in January, and had insisted that Gierek get tough. Arrests of KOR members and other protesters increased; officials accused of being too lenient were replaced.

But the crackdown ran head-on into the spirit John Paul had brought to the Polish people. The spark was struck at, of all things, an art exhibit. Huge crowds waited in line for up to three hours in Krakow to see a show of three hundred "patriotic" paintings dating from the twelfth century. The last two were incendiary. One showed the pope, muscled like an athlete, hands folded under his chin—one a fine intelligentsia hand, the other a gnarled worker's hand. The final painting, of a helmeted worker, face defiant, was labeled "Pole '79." Socialist poster art had been turned against communism.

"This exhibit was the most dramatic patriotic event in decades," says Janina Jaworska, an art historian who helped organize it. It was crowded, she says, for "the same reason our churches were so crowded in those years, as a protest." Only fear that the crowds might riot kept the police from closing down the show.

July 1, 1980, with everyone talking about the exhibit, the government raised meat prices. Rumors spread that Polish meat was being diverted to Moscow for the Olympics. Strikes began in town after town. KOR members helped organize them, and advised local workers' groups of their rights under communist law. Among those organizing the workers in Gdansk was Lech Walesa, the electrician who had signed up the year before with KOR's union organizer, Bogdan Borucewicz. That July, Walesa was jailed for forty-eight hours and Borucewicz for two weeks, but they didn't stop organizing.

When both were free, Borucewicz took Walesa and two others to meet KOR founder Jacek Kuron in Warsaw. Walesa brashly began arguing with Kuron—"the worker vs. the intellectual," one participant says.[3] It foreshadowed conflicts to come. But Walesa was dynamic, a magnet for fellow workers and a sure bet to give colorful interviews to the Western reporters who came to Borucewicz wanting to talk to a unionist.

Robotnik, the underground KOR newspaper, was now everywhere. Its articles became dinner-table conversation and helped spread the strikes, as did Radio Free Europe through its daily action reports.

A crisis arose in mid-July in Lublin. After the auto-repair, dairy, tea, and poultry plants were shut down, rail workers cut the link to Moscow. Gierek appeared on television to warn of the danger involved in disturbing Poland's Soviet "friends." The government ended the strikes by raising pay and agreeing to union elections, though not to a truly independent union.

Gierek flew to Brezhnev's vacation home to report that the strikes were over, but found the Soviet premier "rather unpleasant."[4] In Gdansk, unionists complained that the Lublin workers had caved in too soon. Police hunted for the KOR leadership.

In late July 1980, the two most prominent fugitives, Jacek Kuron and Adam Michnik, met. "Jacek, like me, was very uneasy about the situation in Gdansk, where they seemed to have some pretty wild ideas," Michnik later recalled.[5] One "wild idea" was for "independent and self-governing trade unions. . . . Jacek knew this was impossible in a communist system. . . . I was supposed to go to Gdansk to explain to them that it was senseless to insist on such a demand. Since I was known and rather liked there, perhaps I might have convinced them. Fortunately, I was arrested." So Michnik went back to jail, and the Gdansk leaders never learned of their folly.

August 7, 1980, government managers at the shipyard fired Anna Walentynowicz for her participation in Borucewicz's union. *Robotnik* headlined the story: she was a thirty-year employee, only five months from retirement. At six o'clock on the morning of August 14, workers at the shipyard struck, demanding her reinstatement. A strike bulletin signed by Borucewicz and two others was widely distributed. By eight, the whole city knew, including Walesa (who had been forced to find work elsewhere). He hopped a streetcar and pushed his way through the crowds to the shipyard gate, which had been sealed by police. He found a low wall and, displaying a great sense of drama, scaled it.

He had dreamed of this day, he later wrote. He thought "we needed a year or two more of hard work to prepare. But events had overtaken us. We no longer had any choice but to go on."

Using his natural charisma, the respect he had earned during earlier protests, and his identification as a worker rather than an intellectual, Walesa took charge. The demands were expanded to include his own and some others' jobs back as well as Walentynowicz's, plus a big pay raise and a monument to the victims of the 1970 violence. Suddenly, the eyes of the world were on Gdansk.

Bishop Pieronek was vacationing in the mountains with John Paul's secretary, Monsignor Dziwisz. Descending from a peak, they turned on their radio and heard of the strike. In an instant, Dziwisz was on a special phone line to the pope, who had kept up with strike news all summer through visiting Polish groups.

Priests, even from Warsaw, "went to the shipyard spontaneously," one recalls.[6] "We were prepared because of the teaching of John Paul in 1979, and his voice from Rome on Radio Free Europe. The shipyard workers were active young Catholics."

The Soviet ambassador in Warsaw hounded Gierek. Brezhnev phoned to say Gierek had a counterrevolution "on your hands, and you should grab them by the snout." Gierek replied that the problem was strictly economic.[7]

Wyszynski was at that moment in Czestochowa for the annual pilgrimage. To the surprise and confusion of many, his sermons urged restraint. "We have to see that everyone can obtain his daily bread," the primate said. Strikers understood that he was telling them to go back to work. That night, they almost did, negotiating a tentative deal with the government that promised a raise, reinstatement of the fired workers, and no reprisals.

According to American political scientist David Ost, who interviewed the main participants, the person most responsible for scotching the deal—and thus sustaining the strike—was Alina Pienkowska, a shipyard nurse, union organizer, and the future wife of Bogdan Borucewicz. She exhorted the strikers not to return to work until the government met the demands of strikers at nearby sites including Gdynia and other Baltic towns. By this time, transport and communications workers had also struck, and ships were lining up to enter the gridlocked harbor.

At first, Walesa sided with those who wanted to take the government's deal, declare victory, and go home for the weekend. Then, according to his autobiography, he was shocked to see demonstrations and graffiti in the shipyard signaling that workers wanted "solidarity" with their comrades elsewhere and a true victory over the government. Many called him a traitor for backing the settlement, saying he had sold out.

Among Walesa's gifts was a keen sense of atmosphere. "A strike is a crowd reacting in its own changeable and unpredictable ways," he wrote later. "In the midst of a crowd, before it becomes a mob, I know instinctively what most people want." Suddenly, he changed his stance and vowed he would be the last to leave the shipyard.

"Solidarity was born at that precise moment when the shipyard strike evolved from a local success ... to a strike in support of other factories ... in need of our protection," he wrote.[8]

Wyszynski again urged restraint. Workers could strike for adequate pay, he said, but had to act responsibly. Bishop Pieronek, who was in the thick of it, insists that Wyszynski had not talked to the pope, whose pictures the workers had already hung at the entrance to the shipyard.

Why had Wyszynski turned reluctant? Some say his concern for Polish independence over Polish democracy led him to fear Soviet intervention. Others think illness had already warped his faculties, leaving him increasingly influenced by his longtime secretary, Jozef Glemp. At any rate, for the pope and primate not to have talked to each other during such a crisis—when a direct phone line was open to Monsignor Dziwisz—suggests problems between them.

By the time Wyszynski spoke, however, the workers wanted more than money. They wanted recognition of an independent regional trade union to negotiate with state enterprises on behalf of workers. Nobody came out and said so, but if it stood, it would clearly be the antithesis, and ultimately spell the end, of communism.

How the union came to be named Solidarity is disputed. Walesa says it was an ironic reference to something the government shipyard manager said. Ost says it was the name of a newsletter. But anyone who has read or listened to the speeches of John Paul II knows that the pope planted the term in a lot of minds.

Wyszynski's effort to ice the strike was met the next morning by the publication in an underground newspaper of a long, influential article by Antoni Macierewicz, the KOR co-founder. It left no doubt where the KOR intellectuals—the pope's friends—stood. Macierewicz's words fairly sizzled off the page: "The formation of free trade unions is of fundamental concern for the whole country. Without them, the crisis will run on forever, ruining the economy."

Macierewicz said KOR stood ready with "a program of necessary changes" and "the beginnings of an authentic political infrastructure." The authorities, he said, "are no longer in a position to govern. But they are still strong enough to do harm." What society needed, he asserted, was "not ... street disturbances, but . . . authentic representatives, . . . free elections [for] a parliament that represents the people, upholds the law, and controls the administration. . . . Such a direction is recognized by the [statement of] the Gdansk shipyard workers." And he asked for the support of the Church.

At this decisive moment, John Paul himself issued an open message to Wyszynski, prodding him and reminding everyone that the Polish crisis was foremost in the world's news accounts. With no talk of restraint, he urged "the Polish Episcopate led by its primate" to help the nation win "social justice and . . . the protection of the inviolable rights to its own life and development."

That same day, a chastised Wyszynski sent a secret emissary to Walesa, offering the Church's services. The emissary was none other than Romuald Kukolowicz, who had printed Wojtyla's first book underground in 1953 and had since become a friend of Wyszynski's. Three times that week, Kukolowicz shuttled information between Gdansk and Warsaw.

In direct response to John Paul's call, leaders from more than fifty intellectual workplaces in Krakow met at a steel plant to organize an independent trade union there. In the forefront was the president of the Intelligentsia Club, Andrzej Potocki, the pope's translator.

Similar meetings were held throughout Poland. Professors of economics and social work from around the country poured into Gdansk to help the strikers negotiate what was now seen as a major economic restructuring. Solidarity was intertwining the gnarled laborer's hand and the fine intelligentsia hand clasped under the pope's chin in the painting in the June exhibit. Walesa and his fellow workers, and Borucewicz and his fellow KOR members, were now one team.

August 23, 1980, with the whole country engaged, the number of government enterprises on strike around Gdansk rose to four hundred. The critical concession came: Gierek said the government would drop its insistence on controlling the union it negotiated with, and would deal instead with the regional committee the strikers chose, led by Walesa.

But Gierek had a secret weapon, and he played it again: Wyszynski. The two met August 26, and again Gierek threatened Soviet intervention unless Solidarity backed down on the rest of its demands. Again without consulting the pope, Wyszynski appeared on national television, paired with a government political commentator, and asked the strikers to accept the government offer and return to work. The primate even scolded the workers, saying they should do a better job of feeding the nation before making more demands.[9]

A senior Vatican official, close to John Paul then and now, says the pope was deeply dismayed over Wyszynski's performance, believing that "perhaps because he was old, he was giving in."

Without John Paul's instinct that the time was ripe, that Wyszynski had to be overridden, and that the weight of the Church now had to be thrown behind Solidarity, it all might have ended right there. But the pope came through hours later, at his general audience. With many Polish visitors—and the world's press—on hand, and the Gdansk strikers listening at their radios, he reiterated unequivocal support for the Polish workers who were meeting "the great and very important problems of our country."

The compromise the strike committee reached with the government August 31, 1980, provided for a democratic, independent Solidarity union to represent the workers' interests. After a fiery debate that caused at least one leader to storm out, Solidarity decided to placate the government by explicitly disavowing a political agenda and recognizing the Party's continued control over the state.

The compromise precisely followed John Paul's long-standing prescription for organizing society. Like his program for the Krakow synod in the early 1970s, it assumed that if the various interested groups, such as families or workers, were fairly represented, the system would change by itself. If the people controlled social and economic decisions, it mattered little whether the Party kept political office.[10]

Specific job issues were either settled or left for later. Walesa signed the agreement with an oversized souvenir pen from the pope's 1979 visit, with the pope's picture on top. John Paul's reaction, according to a senior official who was with him when he heard the news, was "God has won."

The government quickly declared that the Gdansk accord would apply only in the Baltic region; its terms would not be matched elsewhere. This was almost an engraved invitation for Silesian coal miners and steelworkers to strike for equal terms, and they did.

September 6, Gierek was replaced as Party secretary by his deputy, Stanislaw Kania. Five days later, Kania himself threw in the towel and agreed to recognize independent unions around the country.

In mid-September, leadership from thirty-five local unions from all over Poland met in Gdansk to create a national structure. No one had directed it, but they were all called Solidarity.

The government resisted as it could. It arrested union leaders or threatened their jobs. It offered improved housing or a car to those who quit Solidarity. Phone service to Solidarity offices was disrupted. Despite the harassment, membership grew by the millions. Unions of teachers and health-care, textile, transport, and metal workers renounced their government affiliation and declared themselves independent branches of Solidarity.

16

In choosing the topic for his first bishops' synod, in 1980, John Paul wasted no time; he assigned the bishops the sex-and-family issues they had wanted to address for a decade, the issues Pope Paul had barred them from discussing.

Most people agreed that disintegration of the traditional family had contributed to, if not caused, an explosion of lawlessness, drug use, disregard for community, lower educational and living standards, and the general malaise that the pope termed the alienation of modern life. Yet in the midst of the synod, the American public elected the first President to have committed the Catholic sin of divorce, Ronald Reagan. The divorce, and Reagan's seemingly hollow relationship with the children of his second marriage, would have crippled his candidacy a few decades earlier, but were hardly mentioned in 1980. Most of society in the United States and elsewhere had come to accept the Reagans' family problems as typical.

With no politician seeming eager to spearhead a movement to restore the family as a stabilizing unit of society—at least with any considered, comprehensive program—the pope volunteered.

To that end, his synod was clearly designed to ratify Church policy, not to prolong what had already been a full debate of it. Dissent on birth control was barred in advance by John Paul's "relator," Cardinal Ratzinger (in the role Wojtyla himself had played for Paul VI). The pope also precluded a public report; instead, the synod would give him a private message, which he could publicize if he chose.

Still, some dissenting bishops did speak their minds—and some may have wished later they hadn't. Cardinals Hume and Derek Worlock of England and Archbishop John Gran of Norway spoke up on behalf of well-meaning Catholics who violated Church teachings. Archbishop Gabriel Zubeir-Wako of Sudan said the Catholic marriage code "remains alien to peoples' lives." Archbishop John Quinn of San Francisco cited surveys of U.S. Catholic opinion and suggested, "Unless one is willing to dismiss the attitude of all these people as obduracy, ignorance, or bad will, this widespread opposition must give rise to serious concern."

Later that week, the Vatican released "some clarifications" from Quinn—a rambling statement in which he seemed to eat his words. "Neither I nor the American Bishops' Conference" want to change the birth-control doctrine, he concluded. Quinn says he made the clarification without prompting by the pope or other officials,[1] but Thomas Fox, editor of the *National Catholic Reporter,* says, "I know Quinn believes the pope never forgave him for" speaking out at the synod. "Quinn's advancement ended that day," Fox says.

The bishops who questioned Church policy weren't cranks; their peers had elected them as representatives. On the other hand, none offered any concrete alternative policies, and when the time came to vote, reports say only about a dozen opposed John Paul's program. The bishops did urge the pope to "hold fast to the law of gradualness." In releasing their statement, he added his rebuttal: "The law of gradualness does not mean there are gradations in the law."

A few weeks later, he told a German audience:

> It is believed that the Church sticks firmly to her norms only out of obstinancy, and that this is in contradiction to that mercy of which Christ set us the example. . . . The hard demands of Jesus—his saying "Go and do not sin again"—are ignored. . . .
>
> Compromise does not count. What is important is only that unity which the Lord himself founded.

Even after this, some continued to doubt Church law on birth control, and to talk as if the door were still open to changing it. But anyone who thought the law could be changed while this pope or his appointed bishops ruled the Church merely proved his own inability to listen.

As its first emissary to John Paul, Solidarity sent Tadeusz Mazowiecki, the former editor of *Wiez* who had stood up for the St. Martin's hunger strikers on the encouragement of Cardinal Wojtyla. Mazowiecki delivered a firsthand account of Solidarity's formation and returned from Rome with an enthusiastic papal blessing.

Wyszynski also went to Rome in the fall of 1980, having been diagnosed with a spreading, terminal lymph cancer. Travel was already so difficult for him that instead of making him come to the Vatican, John Paul paid an unusual visit to Wyszynski in his quarters in Rome.

The very day Wyszynski returned to Warsaw, Solidarity received its promised legal charter. Walesa and his entourage went directly to Wyszynski's palace for a celebration. Wyszynski reminisced about his own union work in the 1930s and urged the formation of a farmers' Solidarity, which the government had so far rejected. After a while, Wyszynski asked Walesa to join him and his liaison, Kukolowicz, privately.

Wyszynski advised Walesa to go to Rome for the pope's blessing. Then, according to Kukolowicz, he said, "But another trip awaits you. To Moscow. If you do not get the permission of the Russians, your movement's life will be short."

Walesa declared that he would go to Rome but not to Moscow. The shipyard workers he represented were sick of the Soviets' invasion threats, he said. They felt defiance, not deference. He was so adamant that Wyszynski dropped the issue.[2]

The CIA had developed an extraordinary Polish source: Colonel Ryszard Kuklinski, who was on the team that laid military plans with the Soviets. His cooperation was so secret that information from him went straight to CIA director Stansfield Turner, and then only to Carter, Brzezinski, and Vice President Walter Mondale. Nobody wrote down his name. He was completely trusted.

In October 1980, word came that the Soviets were thinking of intervening in Poland to crush Solidarity. East German leader Erich Honecker had written to Brezhnev demanding immediate action: "Any hesitation will mean ... the death of socialist Poland," he said.

To the extent that the communists could have won in Poland—probably small—Honecker was right. Brezhnev called an emergency meeting of Warsaw Pact countries.[3] He had three hundred thousand troops already camped in Poland. But he also had to worry about his position in Afghanistan, where he was finding that the more rubles and lives he spent, the worse the situation got.

Carter and his war team pored over CIA reports that fifteen Soviet divisions were set to roll into Poland December 8 or 9, hoping not to have to fire a shot while Polish police arrested the Solidarity leaders. The White House planned to respond by creating a crisis elsewhere: signing an anti-Soviet treaty with China and blockading Cuba were both considered.

Brzezinski's priority, however, was to warn the Poles. The evening of Sunday, December 7, 1980, he called the pope in the middle of the Italian night. "The switchboard operator at the Vatican practically flipped," Brzezinski says. "Dziwisz came on the line. I said, 'I'm calling from the White House on a very urgent matter and need to speak to the pope.'" Thirty seconds later, Brzezinski says, he had his only phone conversation ever with John Paul, and told him what Washington had learned; he will not disclose the pope's reply.

Joaquin Navarro-Valls, now John Paul II's press secretary, was then in Warsaw as a Spanish newspaper correspondent and remembers "journalists certain each night as we went to bed that the next morning there would be tanks in Victory Square. Solidarity said, 'No, they are not going to come. You'll see.' "[4]

Wyszynski again urged surrender, arguing that "not all justice and peace can be provided by the present world." Solidarity leader Kuron published a statement of resolve, but repeated the pledge given at Gdansk that Solidarity wouldn't try to dislodge the communists. The pope renewed his support, and the crisis—which appears never to have been as close to the edge as Washington thought—evaporated.[5]*

December 16, 1980, the memorial to the victims of the 1970 violence, promised in the Gdansk agreement with Solidarity, was unveiled. Party leaders including President Henryk Jablonski shared the platform with Cardinal Macharski (John Paul's successor in Krakow) and Lech Walesa. A week later, a strike over meat rations was settled with an agreement to let Solidarity administer the rationing. The people's union was now taking over the functions of government, exactly as John Paul had dreamed.

The pope beamed a Christmas message home on radio and television. After some Chopin and traditional Polish prayers, he talked of Solidarity:

> All that has been accomplished in the past few months—this work
> of unity, peace, mutual respect, and understanding—is not di-
> rected against anyone. It is not "against," but "for": for construc-
> tion, for renewal, so that everyone might be able to take part more
> fully [and] consider himself a promoter of creativity, work, duty,
> [and] joy in the construction of the common good.[6]

He also revealed action he had taken to support his vision at UNESCO of a single European culture "from the Atlantic to the Urals." Saints Cyril and Methodius, who had spread Christianity to Eastern Europe a thousand years before, were being promoted to joint patron saints of Europe, alongside the existing patron saint, Benedict, an Italian. Eastern Europe would thus be on a par with Western Europe in the eyes of the Church.

This may seem remote symbolism to non-Catholics, but it was a major encouragement to Poles, who, through John Paul and Solidarity, were struggling to reclaim their self-esteem after centuries of subjugation. Poles still

---

* After checking with the pope, Navarro-Valls categorically denied for me a report by journalist Carl Bernstein in *Time* magazine that John Paul told Brezhnev he would fly to Poland if the Soviets invaded.

speak of the elevation of Cyril and Methodius as a milestone in the overthrow of communism.

From the beginning of the Cold War, the AFL-CIO had maintained an office in Paris to support the work of anti-communist unions internationally. The curmudgeonly George Meany, who had battled socialists to become president of the American labor movement, continued confronting socialists abroad. He worked closely with the CIA under Democratic Presidents Truman, Kennedy, and Johnson, all Cold Warriors who were politically allied with U.S. unions.[7] When KOR was formed to defend striking Polish workers, the Paris office made contact with Adam Michnik and Jacek Kuron.

But times had changed. Under Reagan, the U.S. government became an antagonist of labor. And Lane Kirkland, a graduate of the Georgetown University School of Foreign Service, had succeeded Meany, a trained plumber, as AFL-CIO president in 1979. Kirkland was still committed to helping international labor, but unlike Meany he didn't view the U.S. government as a likely ally. "Once Solidarity surfaced, we were in fairly constant contact," Kirkland says. The AFL-CIO sent tens of thousands of dollars in supplies to Solidarity—"Whatever they asked for." But, Kirkland declares, all of it was his members' money; not a dime came from the government.

By much evidence, the AFL-CIO recognized the importance of Solidarity and Poland long before U.S. government officials from either the Carter or Reagan administrations did—except, of course, for Brzezinski. And even Brzezinski seemed to regard Solidarity as just another card on the Cold War table, not as the way out of the game.

Kirkland and his staff decided they needed a representative in Poland. Figuring an AFL-CIO official might embarrass Solidarity and feed Soviet fears, they sent Bayard Rustin, a veteran civil-rights organizer the AFL-CIO had often cooperated with. But even Rustin proved too high-profile for Walesa, who agreed to meet unobtrusively only with Rustin's young assistant.[8]

17

A federation of socialist-communist Italian trade unions happened to share a building in Rome with the Polish cultural institute, which had expanded after John Paul's election. Like the communist mayor with whom John Paul got on so well, these Italian unions opposed Soviet dictatorship. They saw Solidarity for what it was: an idealistic, socially minded organization designed to put power truly in the hands of the people, democratically.

Beginning with the shipyard strike in August, these Italian unionists sought ties with the cultural institute's director, Father Hieronim Fokcinski. They sent representatives to Gdansk as soon as practical, and hooked up with Solidarity units all over Poland, offering advice and office equipment. They brought Solidarity leaders, particularly those from small towns, to Rome for training in how to organize and negotiate. They even served as the official hosts when a team of Solidarity workers (as distinct from the intellectuals), headed by Walesa, visited the pope January 15, 1981.

Glorious as the visit was, it revealed a rift within Solidarity and a power-hungry streak in Walesa that later threatened the revolution. Walesa ordered Anna Walentynowicz—the union leader whose firing had precipitated the August strike—kept off the delegation to Rome: colleagues say he wanted no threat to his stature as sole leader of Solidarity's workers in dealing with its intellectuals.

Walentynowicz and her friends were outraged. The intellectuals knew she lacked Walesa's ability, but they thought she had earned her share of the glory. "We forced Walesa to take her with him," Borucewicz says. "But it created a bad atmosphere, severe conflict."[1]

Unaware of that, John Paul welcomed Walesa alone into the papal library and closed the doors for twenty-five minutes; neither has said what they discussed. Then Walesa's wife, father, and union colleagues joined them. Before leaving Rome, all were asked back.* In public ceremonies to which a Polish government representative was invited, John Paul again stressed that Solidarity was not "directed against anyone . . . not against anything," and that it "does not have a political character."

He understood and supported the compromise in Gdansk that had allowed Solidarity to live—the separation of the social movement from party politics. It fulfilled his dream of a politics in the larger rather than the stricter sense. Solidarity, he said, was

> a collective effort to raise the morality of society. . . .
>   Against the background of terror operating in various countries,
> which does not spare the life of innocent men, this way of acting

---

* Among the Italian labor leaders whom the Solidarity group spent time with was Luigi Scricciollo, who pleaded guilty eighteen months later to spying for Bulgaria. Some Westerners have seen this as evidence that Bulgaria (thus the USSR) was responsible for separate plots to kill Walesa and the pope. But nothing Scricciollo was accused of or confessed to related to any such plots, and no harm has been suggested from anything he learned from the Solidarity entourage. Walesa was cagey by nature when talking to anyone.

> free from violence and arrogance, which seeks solutions along the
> way of mutual dialogue and ... keeps in mind the common good,
> is a credit both to ... Solidarity and to the ... state authorities.

A few weeks later, a major moral victory was achieved. National negotiations had broken down over the length of the work week, an issue postponed by the Gdansk accord. Solidarity declared a one-day strike. To resolve the dispute, the government shared with the union previously secret data showing why the country needed more work time. After seeing the numbers, Solidarity conceded the time. It was a milestone in setting a precedent for joint decision-making.

The very day Solidarity negotiators won this victory, January 30, 1981, President Reagan, ten days in office, held a strategy session of his top foreign policy team. Secretary of State Alexander Haig gave a traditional hardline speech about beefing up military power to contain the Soviet Union. CIA Chief Casey fired back that containment—the American policy since 1946—should be shelved. Reagan declared that Casey was right: increased military power was now to be *used*, to roll back, not merely contain, Soviet influence.[2]

Times had been changing ever since the Soviet Union's December 1979 invasion of Afghanistan. Throughout the election year of 1980, the Carter administration had jettisoned the policies of its first three years, including on human rights. This was more than just a routine election-year shift to the center to appeal to borderline voters. Fate had dealt Carter a series of improbable setbacks, none of which he was particularly responsible for, but all of which played to Reagan's strength. And Carter lacked the conviction to navigate the storm with his own compass.

The hostage-taking in Iran had followed twenty-six years of American intervention there, beginning with the CIA's 1953 overthrow of an elected government and installation of a shah, or king, to protect the interests of Western oil companies.[3] The Iran policy could have boomeranged into antiAmerican violence at any time. Luck occasioned it at the precise moment necessary to elect Reagan (with 51.6 percent of the vote) and change American history.

Americans were frustrated by not having an efficient level of force to rescue the hostages Iran held. Meanwhile, the crisis tripled the price of oil, and drivers had to wait in line to buy gasoline. Energy-driven inflation ravaged the economy. Then the Iranian turmoil helped lure the Soviets into neighboring Afghanistan. Carter expressed bewilderment and betrayal and seemed to think the Soviets had triumphed in Afghanistan. Misreading their disaster as his own, he panicked.

Reversing an economic policy that had been oriented toward working families, he raised interest rates, which helped the holders of capital instead. He launched a major weapons buildup, diverting public funds from other needs. He withdrew from the Olympics and restricted East-West commerce. During Carter's last days in office, leaders of the U.S. Catholic Bishops' Conference came to the White House and pleaded with him to stick to his human-rights standards and not resume aid to the Salvadoran military. Four American Catholic churchwomen—three nuns and a lay volunteer—had just been raped, mutilated, and murdered by U.S. "allies" in El Salvador, whose troops also attacked two group homes for priests. Carter turned the bishops down and resumed military aid to El Salvador.

Reagan called his own program conservative, though it brought the most radical shift in American government at least since Franklin Roosevelt. His team came to Washington committed to raising military spending beyond Carter's imagining; throwing aggressive firepower behind generals in Latin America, Africa, and Asia who would protect the owners of wealth against workers seeking a greater share of it; and putting the entire machinery of the U.S. government at the service of the market economy.

The Reagan group would later claim an alliance with the pope in all this, though in both domestic and international matters, Reagan's commitments directly confronted beliefs that John Paul had held all his adult life and had reiterated tirelessly throughout his papacy. The pope's heart lay in Poland and the countries around it, yet in the well-documented words of historian Raymond Garthoff, "Policy toward the communist countries of Eastern Europe was low in the interest and priorities of the Reagan Administration in 1981."[4]

After Reagan's election, the U.S. Bishops' Conference voted to prepare "pastoral letters" on the main issues. The choice of men to draft the letters—Archbishop Weakland (on the economy) and Archbishop Bernardin (on war), both of whom had long been outspoken—made clear that the bishops were on a collision course with Reagan. One Catholic historian wrote, "For the first time in memory, the Catholic bishops, once thought dependably loyal to strong anti-communist administrations . . . would begin to examine the morality of the country's . . . defense and . . . economic system."[5]

As the administration changed in Washington, John Paul installed a new man of his own there, aiming to give the American Episcopate the backbone he had said it needed during his visit as a cardinal in 1976. He recalled Jean Jadot, an easygoing archbishop who he thought had allowed U.S. Catholic teaching to splinter out of control,[6] and named Archbishop Pio Laghi, then fifty-eight, as his new representative (not a nuncio because Congress, under Protestant pressure, had banned U.S. relations with the Vatican in 1867).

As soon as Laghi took over in Washington, he began rejecting names submitted by American dioceses for bishops' vacancies. Previously, popes, including John Paul, had almost always appointed candidates from the list submitted, even if not the first choice. Under Laghi, that changed.[7]

In large part because of the U.S., where 24,400 marriages had been annulled in 1979 alone, the Pope ordered the Church body that considers applications for annullments (called the Sacred Rota) to stop making the process so easy. The permanence of marriage was to be upheld. Father Andrew Greeley wrote that American Catholics were "frustrated, angry, and disappointed" that at the synod, their bishops had backed down from dissent on family issues. He said Laghi's appointment was designed "to prevent any future honest statements" like the one Archbishop Quinn had recanted at the synod. The pope's "image is very low among most American Catholics," Greeley added.

There were complaints, too, that Laghi had just spent six years as nuncio in Argentina, where the Church had been conspicuously quiet during a reign of terror. A human-rights group turned up contemporaneous accounts that Laghi gave a pep talk to soldiers at a concentration camp for political prisoners, though Laghi himself denied having done this, and reiterated his opposition to violence.[8]

John Paul also perceived that discipline had been lax in France, and decided to replace Cardinal François Marty as head of the Church there. Yet none of the three replacements the French bishops proposed appealed to him. The pope's own choice, a monk, didn't want to leave his monastery.[9]

He sought suggestions, even from André Frossard, the French journalist with whom he was writing a book. When Frossard was too bashful to reply, John Paul observed, "There is a remarkable person in France"—Lustiger, the new bishop of Orléans. Frossard immediately exclaimed that Lustiger had been his parents' parish priest years earlier, and was wonderful.

The appointment stunned France. Questioned by the press, Lustiger said he still considered himself to be a Jew and had a "dual affiliation." Catholics and Jews both protested, but Lustiger didn't shrink from it. He called each priest from the archdiocese in to meet him, in groups of a dozen—some sixty two-hour meetings. He chafed at the administrative work and delegated much of it. "I have no intention of allowing myself to be turned into a manager," he said. "I like traveling in the Metro."

Like the former archbishop of Krakow, Lustiger was criticized for being an inattentive administrator. But also like Wojtyla, he believed his job was to give intellectual direction to policy. His grasp of ideas is universally admired. He readily acknowledges that after the war he was "impressed by the communist vision," though he didn't consider joining the communist party because it was antireligious. "French intellectuals had very confused ideas," he says.

"As a youth, like everyone, I believed in [Albert] Camus [the existentialist novelist] and his circle. I would see them at conferences." But their blindness to Stalinism put him off. In the end, he, like Cardinal Wojtyla, was more impressed by the writing of Soviet dissident Alexander Solzhenitsyn. Now Lustiger thought Solidarity was fulfilling "what Solzhenitsyn wrote."

Having visited the Americas three times and roamed Europe and Africa, stopping off in Rome in between to put the Church in order, the papal caravan left for Asia in February 1981. In Manila, the mere prospect of his trip—and its promise of international press coverage—had induced Ferdinand and Imelda Marcos to lift the decree of martial law by which they had ruled for nine years. But whatever his system was called, Marcos remained a dictator, promoting corruption that benefited his friends and devastated most Philippine citizens.

John Paul praised the "recent initiatives" on martial law and apparently decided not to push Marcos further. His sermons focused on family and reproductive issues and honored Filipinos who had been murdered trying to spread Christianity to Japan in the seventeenth century. The Marcoses spent $1.2 million to impress the pope with frills such as coordinated outfits for the invited guests and fancy imported food. Church officials told the New York Times it "fulfilled their worst fears that in a country of great poverty the pope would be surrounded by official luxury."[10]

Imelda Marcos and an entourage of forty socialite friends from abroad (including Cristina Ford, wife of the car tycoon) flew ahead of John Paul as he island-hopped. Taking advantage of crowds assembled to see the pope, Mrs. Marcos strutted her friends and delivered her own speeches. The pope bore it without public remark, even when the roar of her four airplanes taking off drowned out his homily on the island of Mindanao. U.S. diplomats reported that public reaction to her sideshow "was unfavorable."[11]

According to Philippine Cardinal Jaime Sin, John Paul was offered nine schedule options for his tour there and picked the most demanding. In five and a half days, he said seven public Masses, gave at least ten other formal speeches, and talked before twenty ad hoc groups. Then he stopped in Guam, where he amazed the citizenry by speaking in their native Chamorro; he had practiced for hours with tape recordings. Next he became the first foreign dignitary to address the Japanese Parliament in Japanese.[12] At Hiroshima and Nagasaki, he used nine languages to reiterate his feelings about nuclear war.

Although General Douglas MacArthur had predicted in 1945 that Japan would be Christian within ten years, Catholics made up only 0.5 percent of the population when John Paul visited. With so few Catholics to fill the pope's schedule, Gene Pelc, Marvel Comic Books' representative in Tokyo, got to meet him—and presented him with what Marvel billed as the first religious comic from a major secular publisher, a life of Saint Francis of Assissi entitled *Francis, Brother of the Universe.*

Pelc says the pope thumbed through it, looked up, and said, "Well, why can't John Paul II be number two?"

Pelc wrote headquarters in New York, and a cartoonist was hired. The resulting product at first outraged Vatican officials, but the pope quieted them by expressing his delight. His picture was on the comic book's cover, right below that of Spiderman (who had outlived Captain Marvel to become the Marvel company's main hero).

A refueling stop in Anchorage, Alaska, on the way home produced probably another papal first: a dogsled ride in the airport snow.

As John Paul toured the Philippines, a Spanish priest in Guatemala went to console the families of thirteen farmers who had just been tortured and murdered by soldiers. On his arrival, the priest, too, was murdered. The next day, the U.S. government—which had armed and guided the Guatemalan military since the CIA overthrew democracy there, in 1954—announced increased arms aid to El Salvador, despite appeals from many churchmen, including Archbishop Romero's replacement, Archbishop Arturo Rivera y Damas.

CIA Director Casey called on Archbishop Laghi, the new papal representative in Washington, for the first of what would be half a dozen meetings in Laghi's office. Casey brought along William Clark, another Catholic, who would become Reagan's national security adviser.

"They wanted to know about the U.S. bishops' opposing intervention in Latin America," Laghi recalls. "They would come [and say], 'Why is the conference of bishops so much against the President?' "

Laghi says he would merely smile and reply, "These are moral issues."

At Reagan's request, Laghi made an appointment for General Vernon Walters, a covert diplomat who had served Presidents spanning four decades, to go to Rome to meet privately with John Paul. Walters, another Catholic, had long advocated the administration's new, get-tough policy. He was well aware that John Paul actively opposed that policy. "That's why President Reagan sent me," he said when I asked him.

"Basically, President Reagan wanted the pope to be well informed," Walters says. "Once every three or four months, I would go to Rome and talk about what we were doing and why. There were maybe a dozen meetings" in all, always in the papal apartment, each lasting up to an hour, though John Paul never invited Walters for a meal.

Walters says he won't break his promise to keep private what the pope said. But he says John Paul listened, not criticizing American policy except occasionally to point out the threat of nuclear weapons to mankind. He let Walters do 80 percent of the talking.

"He would ask questions," Walters says. "He was always very grateful for the information I was giving him." This included reports on new Soviet weapons and prison camps—"things that might be of particular interest to Poles," says Walters, who showed the pope some highly secret spy-satellite photographs to back up his words.

In its early months, the Reagan CIA lacked contacts with Solidarity, according to author Peter Schweizer, who was allowed extraordinary access to Reagan administration foreign-policy officials, and previously secret files, in order to write a book defending their actions.[13] Admiral Bobby Ray Inman, Casey's second at the CIA, remembers "a conscious decision not to get CIA involved in support for Solidarity. The line through the American unions was effective, and the CIA would only compromise it."[14] Its domestic agenda now kept the administration from any close alliance with Kirkland's AFL-CIO.

Killing and terror in El Salvador and Guatemala escalated as death squads accurately perceived that they had a license from the new administration in Washington to kill not just revolutionaries but political opponents. Secretary of State Haig testified to Congress that the rape and murder of the three American nuns by Salvadoran soldiers might have been justified because they "may have tried to run a roadblock . . . and there may have been an exchange of gunfire"—suggesting it was the nuns who had opened fire.

Archbishop Rivera y Damas, Romero's successor, visited John Paul. Their talk remains secret, but on emerging, Rivera y Damas squarely blamed the Salvadoran government for the bloodshed. He told reporters that the Salvadoran opposition Reagan was targeting wanted only peace, legal recognition, and the release of prisoners. These were precisely the demands that KOR and Solidarity had made in Poland.

18

The Soviets were determined to get rid of Solidarity.

In February 1981, the Central Committee in Poland named a general, Wojciech Jaruzelski, the new premier. Within a month, Jaruzelski, Party leader Kania, and two fellow leaders were summoned to the Kremlin. Waiting for them there was practically the whole Soviet government, led by Brezhnev, secret police boss Yuri Andropov, Foreign Minister Gromyko, and Defense Minister Dimitri Ustinov. All agreed it was "particularly urgent to give a firm, resolute rebuff [to] anti-Socialist activities"—obviously meaning Solidarity.[1]

Three days after the Polish leaders returned, they began an anti-Semitic campaign aimed at splitting the Church from the KOR intellectuals. There was still a perception that KOR was primarily Jewish, though the leadership was at least equally composed of John Paul's old Krakow Catholic intellectual group. Government newspaper articles and staged demonstrations decried "Zionist terror" but failed to stir the reaction the communists sought.[2] Workers from Solidarity even restored desecrated Jewish monuments.

When anti-Semitism failed, police attacked Solidarity representatives—Catholics—who were protesting the refusal of the Bydgoszcz town council to recognize a farmers' Solidarity.[3] Farmers had been sitting-in at Bydgoszcz municipal buildings, and the Solidarity men went to help. Police clubbed them, hospitalizing three. Dozens of farmers were injured in the ensuing melee.

Admiral Inman, then at the CIA, says the Bydgoszcz violence was "staged" by communists to give the Soviets an excuse to intervene. He says the Soviets "were pressuring [Jaruzelski] to invite them" but didn't want "to come against Polish opposition." If the Bydgoszcz violence was a provocation, it worked: Solidarity scheduled a national strike for March 31 in protest. "Millions of workers stocked supplies, studied strike instructions and prepared for a long-term occupation of the factories," wrote one scholar.[4]

Wyszynski met Jaruzelski and, according to intelligence reports that Inman says the CIA accepted, the primate "dropped to his knees, took hold of [Jaruzelski's] uniform, [and] begged him never to invite Soviet troops [or] use Polish troops against Polish citizens."

But the two sides were still at an impasse. Solidarity demanded recognition of the farmers' union and punishment of the police in the Bydgoszcz melee. The government wouldn't yield. John Paul cabled the union to waive the strike deadline and keep talking. Meanwhile, without telling Solidarity, he also called in the Soviet ambassador to Italy for a two-hour meeting March 28, and through him began secret negotiations with Brezhnev. Records of these tense exchanges were discovered in 1994 by researchers combing old East German secret-police files. The files indicated that the Soviets planned to invade if Solidarity struck.[5]

As Warsaw Pact troops maneuvered near Poland's borders, Wyszynski summoned the Solidarity leadership, told them of his talk with Jaruzelski, and said they should "not abandon our position, but acknowledge that the implementation of our objectives is not possible at present."

Solidarity agreed not to strike. Wyszynski advised the pope, who then offered a no-strike pledge to the Soviet ambassador if the Soviets pledged not to invade. Brezhnev accepted. On the eve of threatened intervention, March 30, 1981, Walesa reached terms with the government representative, Vice Premier Mieczyslaw Rakowski.

Accounts at the time and recent histories all say Walesa gave in to prevent a Soviet invasion. The actual events, however, suggest that on the contrary, once the Soviet army was at bay, it was the Polish communists who gave in to Solidarity. The formal deal, signed April 17, stayed secret. But on May 12, the long-sought Solidarity of private farmers was legally chartered. Solidarity had accomplished its main objective—some surrender![6]

Apparently the deal was concluded behind the backs of both the CIA and the Soviets, and John Paul helped. April 23—after the secret accord was signed—CIA Director Casey visited the pope. According to a 1996 memoir by Casey's deputy Robert M. Gates, Casey thought the crisis was still alive. Gates writes that John Paul told Casey "that Moscow could not tolerate very much more . . . and that . . . a tactical withdrawal by Solidarity . . . was the only way to avoid suppressive measures."

But the pope must have known the terms of the agreement, which he was crucial in obtaining. Today, his spokesman, Navarro-Valls, downplays the April 23 Casey visit. He says Casey brought his wife, and that "there are no written records and the conversations were short."

Father Fokcinski recalls John Paul buoyant at about this time, visiting his cultural institute and crediting Solidarity for enormous changes. Visitors from Solidarity, coming to Rome as religious pilgrims, passed through the institute regularly, swapping stories "on what was really happening in Poland," Fokcinski says. "We passed information to the Vatican, and vice versa."

May 9, 1981, John Paul created a Pontifical Council for the Family, to encourage care for abandoned children, promote courses in preparation for marriage, and sponsor research on family issues.

Two days later, Monsignor Dziwisz visited Wyszynski, now gravely ill in Warsaw, who sent back word of his preferred successor.[7] As Dziwisz returned to the Vatican, the Turkish political assassin Mehmet Ali Agca wound up a year and a half of travel. In Rome, he checked into the Pensione Isa, then a twenty-dollar-a-day hotel (since upgraded).

After a wave of violence during his first year as pope, John Paul had published an essay on terrorism:

> All over the world people live in constant terror and anxiety. I myself, I the pope, have to be guarded and surrounded by police agents when I cross the streets of Rome to visit a parish. . . . My God! Such a situation should be inconceivable.

It had, in fact, been a thousand years since a known papal murder. (In the tenth century, one was smothered and another strangled.)

Wednesday afternoon, May 13, 1981, Agca joined the crowd in St. Peter's Square for the weekly general audience. At its conclusion, the pope rode his usual circuit around the square in the popemobile, an open vehicle resembling a racing hot rod with an elevated roll cage that the pope could hang on to while standing. As John Paul looped the northern colonnade, near the Bronze Gate entrance to his quarters, Agca held aloft a nine-millimeter pistol and carried out his eighteen-month-old published threat to "shoot the pope." A nun, Sister Lucia Giudici, grabbed Agca—who seemed to make no serious struggle to get away—and turned him over to security guards.

The four-mile trip to the Gemelli Polyclinic, a large hospital, took eight minutes by ambulance. André Frossard, the French writer, who interviewed John Paul as he recuperated, said the pope, though weak, stayed awake the whole time, praying aloud and remarking that 5:00 P.M. May 13 was just when three shepherd girls had reported seeing Mary at Fatima in 1917.[8] (It was among the most famous sightings of Mary, who, the three girls said, delivered several predictions about the future of the world.)

Dr. Francesco Crucitti, one of three chief surgeons at Gemelli, was treating a patient at another hospital when a nun rushed to tell him that the radio reported the pope had been shot and was en route to Gemelli. Crucitti followed a wrong-way lane to Gemelli through rush-hour traffic, picking up a police escort as he drove. He arrived to find John Paul already anesthetized and on the operating table.

"His blood pressure was OK, but falling rapidly," Crucitti says. With one look, he knew he could save the pope, though the wounds "would have been fatal if untreated." A bullet had rendered the first knuckle of John Paul's left forefinger permanently immobile. His colon was badly ripped. But the most damaging bullet, entering near his navel, had missed by one tenth of one inch a major artery that would have caused death if severed. The bullet tore five serious wounds through the pope's upper intestine; repairing them required four hours of surgery.[9]

When John Paul woke, he asked Dziwisz if he had yet said the day's schedule of prayers. Assured that he had, he forgave the gunman. Then he told his doctors to involve him in all decisions.[10]

Italian politicians of every stripe flocked to Gemelli. The Socialist president booked a room for the night to be near the pope. Brezhnev wired, "I am shocked by the attempt on your life and wish you a rapid and complete recovery."

Agca looked like central casting's idea of an Islamic terrorist: thin, dark, short hair, sullen expression, hungry eyes, permanently needing a shave but without a real beard. It was soon learned that he had stopped for a month or two in Bulgaria in the summer of 1980 (before Solidarity). There was speculation that he might be one of many lowlifes who ran heroin from Western Asia to Europe through Bulgaria, and arms back the other way. The Vatican immediately explored the possibility that either the Soviets or Latin American radicals had plotted to kill the pope; the Latins were soon excluded for their lack of contact with Agca.[11]

"Poles from the beginning were convinced deep down that Agca had been sent by the Russians," observes Jan de Weydenthal of Radio Free Europe. "It was not supported by any evidence, but the perception greatly increased the power of the pope." On the other hand, Dr. Crucitti says that during the convalescence, "Never did anyone in the pope's presence say a word about a possible plot. They may have suspected one from what was in the newspaper, but that's it."

Claire Sterling, an American living in Rome who had just written a book on international terrorism, was interviewed by *People* magazine about the shooting. She blamed it on Moslem resentment of the West and said the pope had made "a terrible mistake" by visiting Turkey in 1979. "Some people are saying that the Russians plotted this because of the pope's role in Poland, but I think that's crazy," Sterling said. "There would have been a better getaway plan. . . . I could envision a small splinter group of Moslem fanatics with Agca among them . . . but more likely, he made the final decision alone." The investigation would take many turns but eventually produced grounds for a solid conclusion.

The pope quickly brought staff from the Vatican in to the hospital. Soon cardinals and other Church officials were coming and going. The following Sunday, he could not have been happy to read that Italian voters had kept abortion legal by 68 percent to 32 percent.

Learning of Wyszynski's worsening condition, the pope called May 25 from his hospital bed to the bed in the Warsaw archdiocese where the Polish primate lay dying.[12] Archbishop Dabrowski recorded Wyszynski's end of the conversation. In a weak voice, taking heavy breaths, Wyszynski said (the ellipses that follow are pauses, not omissions):

"Father ... Father ... I am very weak. Very. Thank you for the rosary, which cheers me up, Father. We are united because of suffering. Let's pray for each other. ... The Holy Mother is between the two of us. The whole hope lies in her. ... Father, I kiss your foot. ... Bless me. ... Bless me. ... [He crossed himself.] Father ... Father ... bless me once again. Amen ... amen ... amen."[13]

Flags with black trim flew from public buildings. The government and Party sent respectful messages and declared public mourning. At the funeral, Solidarity and the government militia both provided marshals.

On the fringe of the crowd of honored guests was Father Zenon Modzelewski, the former student of John Paul's who had emigrated to Paris in the 1960s and ran a publishing house for books to be smuggled back to Poland. He had been summoned by Wyszynski to his deathbed, and now clutched what the primate had given him there: the diary Wyszynski had kept during his imprisonment from 1953 to 1956. Modzelewski would sneak the manuscript out with some cardinals who wouldn't be searched; he had no idea how powerful the work would become.*

The pope returned to the Vatican June 3, 1981, and within thirty minutes was at the window blessing the crowd. Within weeks, though, he was back in the hospital with a chronic fever and a serious lung infection. His life again in danger, he chose to make an extraordinary physical connection with his faith.

19

Today's Vatican was built on the spot where early Christians said they buried Peter, the first pope, in about 64 A.D. It was a popular Roman grave site. Under

---

* During John Paul's 1979 visit to Czestochowa, Joseph Dembo, a CBS News crewman covering the trip, was taken by Church officials for an exclusive look at the Black Madonna. The chapel where the painting is usually displayed had been sealed off that day because of the crowds. But on opening the door, they discovered a lone figure on his knees, praying. It was Wyszynski. I think of this image whenever I hear cynics express doubt about the sincerity with which high churchmen hold their faith. One ex-Catholic American newsman who has written extensively about the Church told me that at the level of cardinal, "most of them don't even believe in God." The evidence I saw in three years of research was quite the opposite.

St. Peter's, you can still tour the ancient tiled rooms where Roman families entombed their relatives inside walls, under what were then open skies. They would come with picnic baskets to remember departed loved ones with a celebratory meal, even sharing the feast by pouring wine and food down a tube to the bodily remains. In about 160 A.D., with Christianity still banned, Pope Aniceto quietly marked Peter's believed grave site.

"The Vatican" was the name of the hill housing these grave sites. As hills do, it eroded. To shore it up, Christians built a series of buttressing walls downhill from Peter's grave site. In 312, Emperor Constantine, who legalized Christianity, began work on a basilica to honor Peter. To even its foundation, workers leveled the hill, creating drainage problems that plague caretakers to this day. By the end of the sixth century, Constantine's basilica was crumbling, so Pope Gregory I built a new one over it. In 1119, Pope Callisto II built a new altar over the old. Nearly five hundred years later, the whole basilica was razed and replaced, and Michelangelo designed the soaring dome that visitors see today.

With each addition, care was taken to build the new church directly over the old, so that if you dropped a plumb line from the peak of Michelangelo's dome, it would, in theory, pass through altar upon altar to reach the bones of Peter.

In 1940, Pius XII decided to find out. Occupying Germans were told that the workmen carrying dirt from the Vatican basement were addressing the drainage problems. Bones were found. But instead of calling in experts, Pius— who may have lacked John Paul's faith that science would confirm religion— showed the bones to his doctor, who decided they were probably Peter's. After the war, Pius declared they probably were, though he acknowledged he couldn't prove it "with certainty."

Scientists got involved, Pius notwithstanding. The diggers he hired had uncovered one of the early buttressing walls, which was adorned with graffiti about Jesus and Peter. Professor Margherita Guarducci, an archaeologist, noticed a hollowed-out compartment behind a crack in the wall. A workman from Pius's original crew told her that the compartment had contained bones wrapped in a gold and purple cloth (not the ones Pius's doctor had examined), which had been stored upstairs. Then, in 1953, Guarducci read in a newspaper that a priest who had worked on Pius's excavation claimed to have found a fragment of the graffiti wall containing the words *Petrus Eni*—"Peter is within"— and had been keeping it in his room all that time.

Excited, she took a look and concluded that the bones in the gold and purple cloth must be Peter's. She had two other archaeologists test dirt traces on these bones, and they matched dirt taken from the grave directly under the altar, which had contained the bones Pius thought were Peter's. Tests she arranged by several Italian university professors showed that the bones Pius had accepted had belonged to three people (one a woman) and were of different dates. But the bones in the gold and purple cloth were from one man, who had died in the first century.

Professor Guarducci theorizes that during an early persecution, Christians had dug up Peter's bones for fear they would be desecrated, and secreted them in the wall nearby. She says Pius's excavators, finding Peter's original tomb empty, as if looted, gave Pius bones from nearby graves. The Vatican says the bones Pius identified did come from Peter's tomb, but may have been decoy bones substituted by the Christians who hid the originals in the buttress wall.

In any event, Pope Paul declared in 1968 that the buttress-wall bones were Peter's. Most people didn't realize that he had changed Pius's findings. To a skeptic, the evidence is impressive but inconclusive. It rests largely on the word of an amateur excavator, a priest who kept a purportedly monumental archaeological find in his room and then wrote about it in a religious magazine,[1] where the popular press picked it up. Some scholars who have read the graffiti don't think it actually says *Petrus Eni*; they say it could just as well be a fragment of the phrase meaning "Peter in peace" or even "Peter is *not* here." Still, the Guarducci theory is the best anyone has come up with.

Paul had scientists encase the bones in acrylic boxes and rebury them in the original grave directly under the dome—except for some fragments he wanted for his private chapel. Professor Guarducci recalls that Paul took nine fragments, and says, "The request . . . surprised me a little. . . . The pope had promised to respect my wish . . . that the unity of the relics might be respected. It appeared intolerable to me . . . that . . . the authentic relics of the Apostle might become confused in the great number of false relics existing in the Vatican or elsewhere."

In 1981, for the first time, the bone fragments were removed from the Vatican, when secretaries brought them to John Paul's hospital room as a holiday for Peter approached. But one could also imagine John Paul, on the precipice of death himself, wanting in a sense to hold his predecessor's hand if the journey came.[2]

Professor Guarducci says the bones were returned to the Vatican a few days later—but where? When I asked the pope's old comrade Cardinal Deskur about this story, he told me that the pope couldn't have had Peter's separated bone fragments brought to the hospital—because Deskur himself had them! At his behest, the nuns who serve him (he is wheelchair-bound) took me and my wife to the chapel in his apartment, in a separate building from the pope's at the Vatican. They showed us a plaque to which were affixed small objects that looked like bone fragments, which we were assured were Peter's.

Cardinal Deskur insisted that there were no other bones save the ones in Peter's grave, and that these hadn't left his quarters. "The pope knows they are in my chapel," he said. My query to Navarro-Valls came back with a politely hedged pointer to trust Professor Guarducci in this matter.[3]

At the end of June 1981, readers of *Tygodnik Powszechny* were surprised to find a long, bland interview with Jozef Glemp. Back in 1966, Glemp had caught Wyszynski's eye after returning from canon law studies in Rome, and had been appointed the primate's secretary. In 1979, he had been raised to bishop just as Wyszynski began to falter.

Right after the interview appeared, Poles were even more surprised to learn that John Paul had named Glemp primate of Poland, acceding to Wyszynski's last request. The Glemp appointment appears to be the one decision John Paul clearly came to regret, one of few he might even think twice about. But as Cardinal Deskur told a friend years later, "The pope was ill. The pope was cheated."[4]

Agca was turned over to Italian authorities under the 1929 treaty, quickly convicted, and sentenced to life in prison.

Meanwhile, his victim had improved enough to start arguing with his doctors. The surgery on his intestines had required a colostomy—a bowel bypass that sends waste through an opening in the side, to a pouch that needs continual attention. The doctors wanted John Paul to rest at Castelgandolfo and then return to Gemelli in September to have the colostomy closed and normal function restored.

"He said he was not going till it was closed," Dr. Crucitti says. "About five doctors tried to persuade him." Cardinal Krol, suspicious of Italian medicine, sent a favorite doctor from Philadelphia to check on the case. The doctors warned that if the colostomy was closed while any infection remained, it could flare up and threaten the pope's life. He calmly—"He is very calm all the time," Crucitti says—stayed put. "He felt more safe from illness in the hospital than at Castelgandolfo," Crucitti says.

By early August 1981, Krol says, John Paul told the doctors, "I want you to give me as thorough an exam as you can and tell me why you should not close the colostomy. I am the subject of this situation, not an object." Saying he felt "half alive and half dead," he ordered the colostomy closed.[5]

"We had to respect his will," Dr. Crucitti says.

20

To clean up an old joke, if you owe a bank $3 million, the banker has you by the throat. If you owe the bank $300 million, you have the banker by the throat. By the summer of 1981, Roberto Calvi's relationship with Archbishop Marcinkus, John Paul's banker/security chief, was approaching that of a $300 million debtor.

Under their arrangement, the flow of money was largely circular. Various companies with nondescript names, all in Calvi's secretly controlled empire, would deposit money in IOR (the Vatican bank). IOR would then lend this same money back out to other Calvi-controlled companies. On paper, the assets and liabilities balanced: IOR owed a lot of money, but the money was owed right back to it. IOR booked a profit on each deal by charging slightly more in loan interest than it paid on the deposits. Sometimes IOR collected a fee for moving money internationally or performing some other service.

Ultimately, however, it was money Calvi was embezzling from the big Banco Ambrosiano, of which he was president. If the scheme was interrupted, and the Calvi companies that owed money to IOR didn't pay, IOR would be stuck with a large book of debts. On the surface, these debts would just be to other Calvi companies, but it wasn't that simple. Those companies had in turn used their IOR deposits to secure loans from Ambrosiano and other big banks. These big banks relied on IOR to pay if the companies they had lent money to failed.

By acting as an intermediary in so many transactions, IOR helped Calvi hide his thievery from auditors, from other executives at Ambrosiano, and from the legitimate banks that Ambrosiano owed money to. Exactly what Archbishop Marcinkus understood of the situation is impossible to state. He has denied wrongdoing and won't answer questions. But he did have a ringside seat at a spectacular fraud that owed much of its success to his acceptance.

There were plenty of reasons a prudent man might be suspicious of Calvi. In March 1981, police had raided the headquarters of the secret, corrupt Masonic lodge. Its leaders, Licio Gelli and Umberto Ortolani, had fled abroad. Calvi had paid Gelli and Ortolani a mind-boggling two hundred million dollars. Much of this was spread around as bribes, but much may have just been laundered, then returned to Calvi in secret bank accounts.

Calvi was among the first persons to be investigated after the lodge was raided. Although at first the prosecutors couldn't prove his embezzlement, they did establish that he had sent cash outside Italy in violation of currency-exchange laws. So during the summer of 1981, Calvi was convicted and jailed before being freed while the case went on appeal.

Despite having been sentenced to four years in prison and fined fourteen million dollars, Calvi kept his job at Ambrosiano—a testament to how commonly Italy's currency-exchange laws were violated. Wrote financial journalist Charles Raw, "One reason Calvi got away with [his fraud] for so long is that many people thought he was merely smuggling currency, like everybody else."[1]

Still, some banks that Ambrosiano did business with in other countries began to cut off credit. Calvi's fellow executives, and Italian banking officials, squirmed. Archbishop Marcinkus and the two lay professionals he depended on at IOR—Luigi Mennini and Pellegrino de Strobel, both holdovers from the Sindona era—may also have become suspicious and wanted out.

In August 1981, with Calvi already in deep trouble, a flurry of negotiations produced a stunning and deceitful new agreement between him and IOR. The negotiations started when a major Italian bank sought a new guarantee from IOR that it would pay the debts it owed to the companies Calvi secretly owned. There were indications that both the big bank (Banca del Gottardo) and IOR's chief accountant, de Strobel, suspected that something illegal was afoot; they took pains to exchange documents through privileged Vatican diplomatic pouches via Switzerland, thus shielding their correspondence from investigators.[2]

Instead of signing the guarantee that the other bank was requesting, IOR made a deal with Calvi. IOR gave letters to Banco Ambrosiano reaffirming that it was responsible for ten companies in Calvi's secret network, in Luxembourg, Liechtenstein, and Panama. The letters specified, "We also confirm our awareness of their indebtedness toward yourselves." The ten companies whose debts IOR thus guaranteed owed Ambrosiano or its subsidiaries $1.3 billion. To give some measure of how staggering this sum was, when the Vatican finally published a financial statement in 1991, it showed a total annual income of $109 million. Against that figure, a $1.3 billion debt begins to conjure up images of St. Peter's Square being auctioned off to real-estate developers.

To be sure, much of the $1.3 billion was also secured by other, larger banks. But even if the other banks paid, IOR's share would be around $300 million—and the letters implied that IOR stood behind the whole $1.3 billion. Even as quickly as Calvi ran through cash, the letters afforded him substantial breathing time. IOR also gave him additional letters appointing him IOR's "attorney-in-fact" to manage the companies it accepted responsibility for.

This new Vatican imprimatur was an enormous boon to Calvi. One thing IOR got in exchange—and maybe the key to the entire deal—was Calvi's written promise to pay IOR what he owed it, roughly $300 million, and end their relationship by June 30, 1982, nine months away. Giving Calvi the letters of guarantee might allow him to keep going long enough to borrow (or steal) sufficient funds to pay IOR and extricate it from the mess.

IOR also extracted another price for its gift to Calvi: outrageously, it took back a secret letter from Calvi stating that IOR didn't have to pay any money that might be claimed as a result of the letters IOR gave him. In other words, Calvi got letters saying that IOR stood behind his debts, and IOR got back a letter saying that the letters it gave Calvi didn't count. The only purpose of such a mutually negating exchange would be deception, so that Calvi could extend his credit by showing his letters from IOR without revealing that he had simultaneously canceled them out.

And that is exactly what he did. This let him bilk more people. (As a fig leaf against fraud, IOR made Calvi promise not to show the letters outside Banco Ambrosiano, but it's hard to believe anyone took this promise seriously; Calvi certainly didn't.)

Journalist Charles Raw uncovered another incentive for the Vatican bank to have issued its letters to Calvi. Among the maze of documents later turned up by authorities, Raw found a $20 million payment to IOR from one of the ten Calvi companies it took responsibility for. The $20 million was recorded as a down payment on the purchase of a construction company IOR owned, but the construction company wasn't sold, and the $20 million wasn't returned.

Calvi's friend Sindona told Raw from his prison cell that Calvi had paid IOR $20 million for giving him the letters. And Calvi told an associate, who secretly tape-recorded the conversation, that there was "enormous danger" if a $20 million payment at about that time were traced. "It would make the world explode," Calvi said.

Raw concludes that the $20 million payment—allegedly for shares in a construction company that wasn't really sold—"may well have been intended as a fee [to IOR] for the letters." Judging from the evidence, Raw may well be right.[3]

And on the day that Archbishop Marcinkus's managing director, Luigi Mennini, signed the letters for Calvi, he also ordered $3.5 million in IOR funds paid to a numbered Swiss bank account; the next day the $3.5 million was moved to yet another account, this one controlled by a mysterious and sinister man named Francesco Pazienza—a top-level contract agent for Italian military intelligence, a friend of Italian and American political leaders, socialites, and Mafia figures, and an all-around manipulator. Pazienza would soon be heard from again.

As the Calvi-IOR negotiations played out, Solidarity continued to grow in the direction John Paul had mapped for it, as a social-economic force independent of both state and Church. The union's national commission issued an "Appeal to Society," calling for "institutions that will guarantee working people influence" over how the state was managed. The idea was to formalize cooperative arrangements that had already been experimented with: Solidarity would end strikes over the size of rations if it could oversee the distribution of rationed goods. It would work more days if it could determine what was produced on those days.

This noble plan ran into trouble almost as soon as it was announced. First, Solidarity's own miners voted not to surrender their economic demands for the good of the country, as the plan required. Worse, unbeknownst to the union, Brezhnev ordered Poland put under martial law, ending Solidarity altogether.

Colonel Kuklinski, the CIA source in the Warsaw Pact high command, warned Washington of Brezhnev's plan, reporting that Polish-language leaflets containing martial-law orders had already been printed in Moscow. But CIA Chief Casey suspected that the plan was a ruse, planted with Kuklinski's group to uncover the spy in their midst.[4] Unlike Brzezinski the year before—whose first impulse on hearing a report of Soviet intervention had been to warn the Poles—Casey just sat on Kuklinski's messages.

John Paul's first speech on leaving the hospital was in Polish, an appeal for "Christian solidarity." As the Solidarity union's first congress opened September 5 in Gdansk, with a Mass by Primate Glemp, the pope told fifteen thousand visitors to Castelgandolfo that a free and independent Poland was necessary for world peace. Father Jozef Tischner, the Krakow theologian and papal friend (who some say was John Paul's real preference for primate), said daily Masses at the Solidarity congress. When the Polish government wouldn't give the AFL-CIO's Lane Kirkland a visa, he sent a priest friend from Catholic University in Washington to Gdansk to read his speech for him.[5]

Three candidates challenged Walesa for the union presidency, all promising greater militancy and accusing Walesa of selling out their economic demands. He told them they underestimated the government's power. He barely won election. The membership also voted, over Walesa's opposition, to support similar independent unions in other communist countries, a resolution that further infuriated Brezhnev.

The Soviet premier's problems were growing. Even before Solidarity adopted its official policy of going international, members from the KOR faction had continued to meet secretly in the mountains with leaders of the Czech movement Charter 77, including Vaclav Havel. Their communiqués, broadcast on Radio Free Europe, gave new courage to people throughout Eastern Europe.

Thanks to KOR in Poland, several underground periodicals and at least seven hundred books were now circulating illegally in Czechoslovakia. Eight

Czechs were jailed for distributing underground literature that fall.[6] Many
Czechs understood that the pope had been the wellspring of this journalistic
rebellion since his Krakow days. Czechoslovakia's cardinal/primate, Frantisek
Tomasek, prodded by John Paul, ended years of silence by protesting govern-
ment human-rights abuses and the lack of a Church press. KOR also steered
Hungarians into underground publication and other activities.

John Paul referred again and again to the "great spilling of blood" of World
War II, which he said had earned Poland its independence. "The Congress of
Solidarity that has just begun [is] an important deed in the life of Poland," he
declared.

In Chicago that fall of 1981, the efforts to oust Cardinal Cody reached a cul-
mination. Carlton Sherwood—the Gannett reporter who had won a Pulitzer
Prize for uncovering the Doylestown shrine scandal—had grown increasingly
frustrated that Father Greeley didn't back up his allegations of financial misconduct by Cody. Furthermore, Sherwood's research had led him to a stunning
discovery: someone with access to Greeley's files[7] had found damning tapes and
correspondence between Greeley and his publisher before the 1978 cardinals'
conclaves. There were references to a conspiracy to fix the papal election and
the need to "get" Cody.

Then, just as it began to seem that Greeley, not Cody, might be the culprit,
the story took a new twist: an employee in the Chicago archdiocese discovered
what Greeley had known in his heart all along but couldn't prove: there really
were improprieties in Cody's management! Federal prosecutors obtained documents showing that Cody had lavished hundreds of thousands of dollars on a
woman in Boca Raton, Florida, whom he called his cousin but who wasn't
related to him. Her son, a broker, had received fat diocesan insurance contracts.

The Chicago *Sun-Times* and its rival the *Tribune* competed in a newspaper war
with front-page headlines about Cody, his finances, and the plot to get him.
Greeley admitted, with appropriate embarrassment, that his earlier statements
had been "fantasies."[8]

John Paul II responded to the news of a federal investigation of Cody just
as he had responded in the more private case of Doylestown. In his view, the
Church should be spoken of only positively. He would take no action against
Cardinal Cody that might encourage the press or the prosecutors. Cody was
seventy-four, a year from retirement, and had bad arteries. The Holy Spirit was
left to settle the Chicago problem.

Cody died the next April, 1982. The federal investigation against him was
suspended.

21

Agca's bullets had delayed the economic encyclical that it was now customary for popes to issue each decade on the anniversary of Leo XIII's *Rerum Novarum* in May 1891. Leo had put the Church on the side of labor unions. In 1931, Pius XI had reversed course, condemned strikes, and said the state could dictate work and pay. In 1961, John XXIII returned the Church to the side of unionism. Paul VI kept it there in 1971. And no one was surprised that when John Paul II was finally able to issue his encyclical, in September 1981, he continued to champion the rights of labor.

In the history of these encyclicals, his *Laborem Exercens* ("On Human Work") was probably the deepest philosophically and surely showed the most personal commitment. The word *solidarity*—with a lower-case *s*, but precisely chosen—lay scattered about the pages like seeds in a field. As he had from the beginning, John Paul rejected the ideologies behind both sides in the Cold War. By now the communists were used to his criticism, but Catholics who supported the new Reagan administration in the United States and expected an ally in the pope were stunned and angered by what they read.[1]

John Paul condemned the aspect of capitalism that treated work "as a sort of merchandise that the worker sells to the employer." To him, work was still the noble human undertaking he had described in his poem about splitting rocks in the quarry. To treat it as an interchangeable commodity was "opposed" to "Christian truth," he said—thus renouncing the system under which Western countries had become industrialized.

In the twentieth century, capitalism had been modified to benefit the working majority, with such additions as social security and workplace-safety rules. The system had continued to produce bountifully. But now Reagan and British Prime Minister Margaret Thatcher were seeking to restore capitalism to its pure form, making John Paul's encyclical poignant in its timing.

When pure capitalism had prevailed, the pope said, it

> strengthened and safeguarded . . . the possessors of capital alone. . . .
> It did not pay sufficient attention to the rights of the workers, on
> the grounds that human work is only an instrument of production,
> and that capital is the basis . . . and purpose of production.

In other words, pure capitalism judged the merit of an enterprise only by the financial profit it returned. To John Paul's reading of the Christian faith, this was wrong. It had led to a system of injustice and harm that cried to heaven for vengeance. . . . The workers put their powers at the disposal of the entrepreneurs, who, following the principle of maximum profit, tried to establish the lowest possible wages for the work done. . . . Little attention was paid to the safety and health of the workers.

In response, labor unions had been formed—"worker solidarity"—which "brought about profound changes." Apart from the economic benefits of unionism, the pope praised innovative arrangements under which "workers can often share in . . . joint ownership, . . . running businesses, controlling their productivity," and sharing profits. What John Paul advocated was precisely what the Solidarity leadership in Poland had just proposed in its "Appeal to Society" (which wasn't surprising, considering the pope's influence on Solidarity's ideas).

Labor unions had succeeded on a local level, he said. But new developments threatened to drive society back to the old, unjust system. "Large, transnational enterprises" again threatened to "treat work as . . . merchandise, or as an impersonal force needed for production. . . . We must . . . recall a principle that has always been taught by the Church: the . . . priority of labor over capital."

Both capitalism and socialism, he said, were guilty of a

> fundamental error [in] considering human labor solely according to its economic purpose. . . . Christian tradition has never upheld . . . the right to ownership of property . . . as absolute and untouchable. . . . The right to private property is subordinated to the right to common use, to the fact that goods are meant for everyone.

In "suitable conditions," he said, some means of production should even be put under community control ("socialized"). But the Marxist system of "converting the means of production into state property" was "by no means equivalent to 'socializing' that property"; state ownership merely substituted a politician for a capitalist, without necessarily improving the lot of the worker. "Socializing" was completely consistent with private ownership, but required that "both those who work and those who manage or own the means of production must in some way be united in a community."

> In the Church's teaching, ownership . . . could . . . never . . . constitute grounds for social conflict [with] labor. The means of production . . . cannot be possessed against labor. . . . The only

legitimate title to them—whether in the form of private ownership or in the form of public or collective ownership—is that they should serve labor. . . .

Recognition of the proper position of labor . . . demands adaptations in the right to ownership of means of production. . . . The position of "rigid" capitalism must undergo continual revision . . . from the viewpoint of human rights. . . . Labor is in a sense inseparable from capital; in no way does labor accept the separation and opposition that has weighed upon human life in recent centuries as a result of merely economic thinking.

He called labor unions "indispensable . . . for . . . the just rights of working people . . . even if in controversial questions the struggle takes on a character of [conflict]."

When John Paul wrote this, Reagan had just defined his own policy by firing government air-traffic controllers who went on strike, and hiring nonunion replacements. He then radically changed the enforcement of labor laws to allow private companies, too, to eliminate unions and freely apply their capital in the most economically efficient way. American union membership and power plummeted in the years of Reagan's presidency. His social philosophy encouraged companies to lay off managers and professionals when seniority pushed their pay levels above those of younger replacements. This in turn devalued the uniqueness of a manager's work, too—all in contradiction to the pope's teaching.

For all his support of unions, however, John Paul cautioned that strikes were "a kind of ultimatum . . . legitimate in the proper conditions," but not to "be abused, especially for political purposes." For the most part, he discouraged confrontation; he preferred "associating labor with the ownership of capital" through "a wide range of intermediate bodies with economic, social, and cultural purposes . . . bodies enjoying real autonomy" from political authority. He foresaw "living communities" whose members would be "encouraged to take an active part."

This was a utopian vision—but not an abstract one. He was describing his dream for Solidarity. (It was also a dream common to many Liberation Theologians.) The pope surely had Solidarity in mind when he wrote in his encyclical:

The person who works desires not only due remuneration for his work; he also . . . wishes the fruit of this work to be shared by himself and others, . . . to be . . . a sharer in the responsibility and creativity . . . to which he applies himself, . . . to . . . know that . . . even on something owned in common, he is working "for himself." This awareness is extinguished . . . in a system of excessive bureaucratic centralization, which makes the worker feel that he is just a cog in a huge machine moved from above.

Laborem Exorcens urged community action to ease the pain of unemployment during the transition to more automated production. It warned that "the heritage of nature is limited and . . . is being intolerably polluted" by shortsighted economic policy. And it demanded relief for women, whether or not they chose careers. "There must be a social reevaluation," he said,

> of the toil connected with [motherhood] and of the need that children have for care, love, and affection. . . . It will redound to the credit of society to make it possible for a mother to devote herself to taking care of her children without inhibiting her freedom, [and] without [her] being discriminated against psychologically or practically. . . .
>
> This in no way implies the exclusion of women from the world of work or from social and public activity. Human work is not merely a question of economics; [it] involves personal values. . . . The true advancement of women requires that labor should be structured in such a way that women do not have to pay for their advancement [in a chosen field] by abandoning [child-rearing].[2]*

2 2

A stroke felled Father Pedro Arrupe, leader of the Jesuits, in August 1981, accelerating a crisis in the Church's largest order.

---

* Along with his philosophy, the pope offered some economic forecasts. He was correct that living standards would taper off in the United States and Britain, but wrong in predicting that the wealth lost by the richer nations would benefit the Third World. Environmental deterioration in the next decade would not be quite as bad as he feared, though perhaps that was because the West took much of his advice about regulating pollution. John Paul was most wrong in predicting a crisis over rising commodity prices; as the political confrontation over oil ended, commodity prices shrank.

Now thirty thousand priests strong, the Jesuits were founded by Saint Ignatius of Loyola in 1534. In recent decades, they had been accused of "Leftist" views. Probably more than most orders, they had adopted secular dress and ways. John Paul had decided during his first summer as pope, in 1979, that radical change was required to bring the Jesuits into line with his ideas. This was shortly after they had elected the immensely popular Arrupe to his fifth term as leader. The Sandinista revolution in Nicaragua that summer may have helped bring the Jesuits to the pope's attention: Jesuit priests participated in it.

John Paul had ordered Father Arrupe to call Jesuit leaders from fourteen countries to Rome, and had told them their conduct had caused "confusion in the Christian people and concern to the Church." Without going into detail, he quoted the record, which he had obviously combed, to show that Popes John XXIII and Paul VI had also criticized the Jesuits, "especially as regards the austerity of religious life, . . . secularizing tendencies [and] discipline."

"This was a shock from out of the blue—a very important meeting," says Father Vincent O'Keefe, the New Yorker who was Arrupe's longtime deputy and friend. The pope "was concerned that we were upsetting the People of God." But Arrupe, at least in his formal reply, didn't seem to comprehend the severity of the rebuke.

"We have tried . . . to understand [and] to recognize our limits," Arrupe said. "We are certain that we shall receive from this meeting with Your Holiness . . . a confirmation and an encouragement for the whole Society of Jesus." The pope gave him nothing of the sort, only a continued tongue-lashing.

Afterward, discouragement began to sink in. Arrupe wrote Jesuit supervisors worldwide that "a call to attention from three popes leaves little room for doubt that it is the Lord himself who . . . expects something better of us." He began talking to friends about retiring early and finally notified John Paul he would call a special congress to elect a successor.

Again, Arrupe had misread the pope, who summoned him immediately and said he was "surprised and displeased. . . . I am asking you not to do it for the good of your society and the Church." He said they would discuss the future after he returned from his African trip. But six months passed, and Arrupe heard nothing.[1]

Arrupe was, like the pope, an almost larger-than-life figure. He was a Spanish Basque, like Saint Ignatius. As a priest in Japan during World War II, Arrupe had been imprisoned in Hiroshima. A former medical student, he tended to the wounded the day the bomb was dropped, and afterward wrote one of the great descriptions of its horror. The stroke hit him exactly thirty-six years and one day later.

He lay frustrated, able to think but mostly not to talk or defend himself against the complaints he faced. William Wilson, a wealthy Reagan campaign supporter who had just been appointed to represent the White House at the Vatican, boasted that the Jesuits were getting a new leader because he had complained of their work in Latin America.[2] Probably much more influential were some European Jesuits, particularly Spaniards, who had urged John Paul not only to fire Arrupe but to block O'Keefe, his heir apparent, from taking charge.

"A lot of European Jesuits felt Americans weren't the real article," says a senior Church official in Rome who is familiar with the complaints. "Americans knew only English [as a language]. They ran big schools. O'Keefe had a sense of humor, and worked with ABC-TV [on news], so they thought he wasn't serious."

Two months after Arrupe's stroke, O'Keefe's secretary broke in on a meeting at Jesuit headquarters to announce that Vatican Secretary of State Casaroli was headed over to see Arrupe, now home from the hospital. On arriving, Casaroli at first barred O'Keefe from the room but then called him in.

"Father Arrupe's trying to tell me something, and I can't understand him," Casaroli said.

O'Keefe listened, then told Casaroli, "He said he wants to introduce you to Father Dezza." O'Keefe wondered why they were talking about Paolo Dezza, a seventy-nine-year-old retired rector of the Jesuits' Gregorian University. But as Casaroli went off to see Dezza, Arrupe showed O'Keefe the letter Casaroli had brought. O'Keefe went pale as he read it. The pope had appointed the aged Dezza to organize a Jesuit congress to elect a new leader. O'Keefe asked what role this left for him.

"You stay, you stay," Arrupe replied. But the next morning Dezza announced that he had been asked by the pope to run the Jesuit order until the congress. O'Keefe was out. A pope had suspended the constitution of a religious order for the first time in many decades, and imposed his own rule.[3]

O'Keefe brought the matter up with Cardinal Eduardo Pironio of Argentina, head of the Vatican department that supervised religious orders. Pironio was just as stunned as O'Keefe was. "He was out of the loop, that was pretty clear," O'Keefe says of Pironio. "He heard it over the radio and wept. He was a dear friend of Arrupe and had not even been consulted." Pironio was soon out of his own job (and didn't respond to my requests for comment).

The *Tablet* of London spoke for many when it said of Arrupe, "Historians will probably recognize him as the greatest general of the [Jesuit] society since Ignatius himself, and certainly the best loved. Now half-paralyzed in a wheelchair . . . what he sees and hears must give him intense pain. The recent papal action is a brutal insult both to him and to his colleagues."

The *Tablet* also observed that those happiest must be the dictators to whom "the Jesuits have offered eloquent, effective and formidable opposition. To tame that opposition . . . would be a major triumph for some of the harshest and most un-Christian governments in the world"—from Latin America to China, where a dozen Jesuits had just been arrested.

Soon, eighty-three international Jesuit leaders convened with John Paul at a villa near Rome to plan the congress the pope wanted. "There was anger in the air," says one official. "You could feel it. I know the pope felt it. He said he admired the reaction of the Jesuits, that they had obeyed. He had been led to believe there would be open rebellion." Many Jesuits felt insulted that the pope had expected disobedience.[4]

Using four languages, John Paul renewed his instructions to avoid political activity that would compromise priestly duties. He praised Father Arrupe cordially but said Vatican II should be carried out "through . . . listening to the spirit of the Pentecost . . . not according to personal criteria or psychosociological theories."

When it was over, Father Giuseppe Pittau, now head of the Gregorian University, told the press, "We have for a long time been the light cavalry, which goes ahead. Now we must dismount in order to persuade those who have remained behind, so that the Church can advance as a whole." But he also said he worried that Jesuits held many civil jobs where there were "no laymen around" to take over.

As if in his spare time that fall of 1981, still recovering from his wounds, the pope studied, adjusted, and approved a new code of canon law that Pope John XXIII had ordered twenty years earlier. It had been working its way through the curia all that time, and still would not take effect until the fall of 1983.

John Paul also undertook a crusade for "the abolition of all nuclear arms," which was becoming a crusade for many bishops as well. This was one irritation that Washington couldn't blame on the Jesuits. Reagan, who was committing unprecedented sums to U.S. nuclear forces, fumed over a referendum in California to freeze nuclear weapons, backed by Archbishop Quinn and other California prelates.

The bishops of Belgium voted 12 to 1 to condemn a Reagan plan to put new nuclear weapons there and in other European countries. More than three hundred Chicago priests bought a full-page advertisement in the *Sun-Times* protesting both the arms race and the administration's reduction in spending for social services.

The National Council of Catholic Women, meeting in Kansas City, voted overwhelmingly to support John Paul's "tireless work for disarmament and the abolition of all nuclear weapons." The group voted down a proposal to "support Reagan administration military policies . . . in the fight against communism." It was the first criticism of U.S. military policy in the organization's sixty-one-year history.[5]

Even those bishops the administration most counted on—Cardinal Terence Cooke, Cardinal Spellman's friend and successor in New York, and Cardinal Krol—had now joined the opposition. Krol volunteered to speak at an antinuclear rally in Philadelphia. Two Montana bishops[6] opposed the proposed construction there of a giant missile system originally designated the "MX," but which Reagan liked to call "the Peacekeeper." Bishop Leroy Matthiesen of Amarillo, Texas, urged workers at a nuclear-bomb assembly plant there to consider resigning; eleven diocesan bishops in Texas endorsed his statement.

Cardinal Sin of the Philippines wrote a public letter criticizing Reagan for arming dictator Marcos's soldiers, enabling them "to kill their fellow Filipinos," while at the same time Reagan cut off Philippine food aid.

There is no record the pope objected to any of these statements; rather, his own vast, published record is filled with the same thoughts. After Bishop Roger Mahoney of Stockton, California, stirred a controversy by asserting that "no Catholic can ever support or cooperate with . . . policies . . . which . . . intend to use nuclear weapons, even in a defensive posture," John Paul promoted him to cardinal/archbishop of Los Angeles. The pope encouraged Catholic youth groups to join the European disarmament movement even as Washington worked hard to undermine the movement.[7]

Arms opponents even published an old Wojtyla poem, "The Armaments Factory Worker":

> *I cannot influence the fate of the globe.*
> *Do I start wars? How can I know*
> *whether I'm for or against?*
> *No, I don't sin.*
> *I only turn screws, weld together*
> *parts of destruction,*
> *never grasping the whole,*
> *or the human lot.*
>
> *I could do otherwise (would parts be left out?)*
> *contributing then to sanctified toil*
> *which no one would blot out in action*

to belie in speech.
Though what I create is all wrong,
the world's evil is none of my doing.

But is that enough?

When the Reagan administration made news by planning for the aftermath of nuclear war,[8] including such details as mail delivery, the pope released a statement—obviously aimed at Reagan—in which he disparaged "recent talk about winning or even surviving a nuclear war." Such talk, he said, flew in the face of the gruesome prospective casualty figures produced by his Pontifical Academy of Science. He wrote Reagan and Brezhnev in "profound anxiety," urging progress at their arms-control talks in Geneva; where neither side had offered serious concessions.

Americans, however, seemed to pay as little heed to the pope's military pronouncements as to his birth-control pronouncements.[9] Bishop Matthiesen conceded that after three months, not one worker at the Texas nuclear bomb plant had quit on principle.

Poland returned to center stage in the fall of 1981. Secretly preparing for martial law, Moscow had General Jaruzelski—already prime minister and defense minister—appointed Party leader as well, a concentration of power unseen since Stalinist days. The thin, uniformed Jaruzelski cut a striking figure, always in sunglasses, which gave him a Hollywood look but were in fact necessitated by an eye condition requiring limited light.

On his orders, police arrested Solidarity members for handing out union literature. He sent military teams to two thousand towns to take over food distribution and "maintain order," and introduced a bill banning strikes, inviting a new confrontation with Solidarity. Primate Glemp begged Parliament not to pass the bill, and Walesa begged his members to forgo strikes voluntarily, hoping to avoid a showdown. But workers wanted action. Living standards had been dropping due to a reduction in imports, as Jaruzelski diverted hard currency to repay Western bank loans.

November 2, 1981, Soviet officers announced at a meeting of the Warsaw Pact command staff that someone had leaked plans for martial law in Poland to the Americans. Colonel Kuklinski, the CIA's source, tried to hide his quickening pulse. Immediately after the meeting, he sent a prearranged signal to his CIA contact, and in four days he and his wife and son were whisked out of Poland to assume new identities in the United States.

What neither Kuklinski nor the Soviets knew, however, was that for all the risks he took, the American government still rejected his information. Consumed with stamping out dissent in El Salvador and overthrowing the new government in Nicaragua, the Reagan team paid little attention to Poland.

John Paul continued to try to keep Europe focused on the long term. He had organized a Vatican conference that fall, 1981, on "The Common Christian Roots of Europe," looking beyond the Cold War for ways to equalize the status of Eastern European culture with that of the West— extending the campaign that had raised Cyril and Methodius to co–patron saints of Europe. He chose scholars from his former university at Lublin to help plan the affair; Solidarity intellectuals were among 225 attendees, from two dozen nations.

On the very day Colonel Kuklinski was arranging his escape, the pope electrified the scholarly conference by minimizing the importance of the "Iron Curtain." He declared that the European continent was united by "a painful moral uncertainty [that] goes hand in hand with the disintegration of family life." He cited popular modern histories like *Decline of the West* by Oswald Spengler and *Crisis of Civilization* by Johan Huizinga. In the audience, American Catholic scholar Michael Novak sat rapt: the pope was defining Europe not as a place but as "an idea, a set of values," says Novak. "It was absolutely clear that he meant to reunite Europe."

As the scholars listened to the pope in Rome, General Jaruzelski, Primate Glemp, and Walesa met in Warsaw for what was announced as the first in a series of "domestic summits." (It turned out to be the only one.) Eager to show Jaruzelski that Solidarity was trustworthy, Walesa shut down four big wildcat strikes by going to the factories and personally persuading the strikers to return to work. Other Solidarity leaders complained that he was patronizing the government.

According to Romuald Kukolowicz, the Church emissary to Solidarity, Walesa also changed his mind and decided to travel to Moscow, as Wyszynski had suggested, to seek Soviet acceptance for Solidarity. Kukolowicz says Walesa asked him to arrange the trip. The Soviets told Kukolowicz to work through their embassy in Rome. There, throughout repeated meetings, the Soviets put Kukolowicz off, while he phoned reports to Papal Secretary Dziwisz.[10]

As Kukolowicz waited, John Paul made one of the most important appointments of his papacy: Cardinal Ratzinger to succeed the aging Cardinal Seper at the Congregation for the Doctrine of the Faith, the old Holy Office.

Ratzinger, the former youthful firebrand of Vatican II, could be counted on to clamp down on doctrinal dissidents with the vigor of someone who had been there.

The appointment gave new heart to the dwindling, tradition-bound wing of the curia that had opposed the Vatican II reforms. Cardinal Oddi was delighted: "Ratzinger came to Rome [in the 1960s] with a group favoring new things," Oddi says. "But he came to understand that these theologians were asking too much, and he abandoned them."

The "liberals" were less happy. Although Ratzinger's role was chief theologian, he would affect politics as well—for example, in his belief that Liberation Theology perverted Church doctrine. Cardinal König, John Paul's biggest supporter at the conclave that elected him, says he repeatedly told the pope during their occasional lunches that he was concerned that dissidents and Liberation Theologians were being treated too harshly. Under Ratzinger, the harshness would only intensify.

Ratzinger was, like the pope, brilliant and a fast-riser (only fifty-four). Ratzinger noticeably lacked John Paul's charm, athleticism, and charisma, but they bonded nonetheless. "I can't tell now what is [the pope] and what is Ratzinger," says Archbishop Weakland (who has felt their criticism). Weakland stresses that Ratzinger is "fair, not politically motivated. He knows the literature." The problem, Weakland says, is that Ratzinger shares John Paul's "anti-Enlightenment, antirationalist thinking. Intellectually, the relationship reflects the love-hate relationship the Poles have with the Germans. The pope defers to Ratzinger. When a meeting is about to close, it is Ratzinger who can add a last word if he wants."

John Paul told Ratzinger on appointing him that his German nationality had been pivotal in his selection. According to Father Karl Becker, the longtime friend and adviser whom Ratzinger had me interview as a stand-in for himself, the pope emphasized that Germany wielded a disproportionately large influence on theology. Because the German government pays for Catholic and Protestant theology schools (other religions are too small to qualify), "publication and study are greater than in other countries," says Becker. Even Liberation Theology was developed in Germany, where its pioneers, like Father Leonardo Boff of Brazil, studied. Ratzinger "knows all the opposition," Becker says—a point the Pope cited in explaining his appointment.

Asked about Ratzinger's seeming transformation, at least in reputation, since Vatican II, Becker says, "Not Ratzinger changed but the time changed." Ratzinger, he says, thinks Vatican II lacked "profound effect because of the confusion afterward."

23

November 22, 1981, John Paul managed his first working trip since the shooting, to a parish in a nearby town. He also talked to visiting Polish bishops about another trip to Poland the next summer.

Two days later, in Warsaw, Soviet Marshal Viktor Kulikov, commander of Warsaw Pact forces, visited Jaruzelski.

November 30, Jaruzelski declared an economic plan for 1982 that imposed strict central control, without consulting workers as promised in the Solidarity agreement.

December 2, Polish police in helicopters forcefully ended an eight-day sit-in strike by students at Warsaw's firemen's school. That night, two Soviet embassy officials in Rome invited Kukolowicz to an elegant restaurant for dinner. After lots of wine, food, and talk about friendship, Kukolowicz says he asked for an answer about Walesa's proposed mission to Moscow.

"They said, 'Now there is no time for such meetings.' I said, 'So, when?' The answer was, 'We will let you know.' At the time, I didn't understand it. Only after December 13 did I understand."

The next morning, December 3, Solidarity's leadership met. Government microphones picked up every word. "A confrontation is inevitable," Walesa said; the union must "dethrone" the government. The group voted to insist on a "provisional" government including Solidarity representatives, to be followed by free elections.

Over the weekend of December 5 and 6, Walesa and his three top advisers met with Glemp and two senior bishops. The gathering showed just how much the opposition owed to one man: John Paul. Walesa's team consisted of Tadeusz Mazowiecki, the pope's former Krakow editor, who now edited the Solidarity newspaper; Andrzej Wielewiecki, another old papal friend who headed the Catholic Intelligentsia Club the pope had fostered; and Bronislaw Geremek, a Jewish history professor whom John Paul had just welcomed to Rome for the conference on Europe. Glemp and the bishops all reported to John Paul.

The churchmen said they feared an awful communist retaliation unless Solidarity backed off. Walesa agreed, but said his members would replace him if he softened his stand.[1]

The next morning, the government published Walesa's taped remarks about "dethroning" it. The union said his words had been taken out of context.

December 10, the Soviet Politburo formally debated whether to take over in Poland. One official said Jaruzelski would impose martial law within a few days,

but KGB Chief Yuri Andropov and others replied that Jaruzelski was still unde-
cided. Notwithstanding that, the military was adamant that "one Afghanistan is
enough for us."[2] A consensus formed even among the hard-liners—including
future premier Konstantin Chernenko—that Soviet forces shouldn't intervene,
and Brezhnev declared they wouldn't.[3] There is no clear record of whether
Brezhnev relayed this to Jaruzelski. But Mark Kramer, Director of the Harvard
Project on Cold War Studies, says, "All the Politburo transcripts and everything
else I've seen suggest that they were desperate not to go into Poland. I think if
Jaruzelski had done what Gomulka did in 1956 and stood up to the Russians,
he could have gotten away with it." But Jaruzelski didn't.

December 11, Miroslaw Chojecki, founder of the Polish underground
press, gave a private lecture at the State Department in Washington. He had
left Poland to display his wares at a book fair in Germany and then proceeded
to Canada, where Mazowiecki (the editor) told him some unions had offered
to donate much-needed paper. Once in North America, Chojecki took the
opportunity to visit his uncle Jan Novak, the former head of the Polish section
of Radio Free Europe, who had retired to Washington. Novak arranged the
State Department meeting for him.

Chojecki, unaware of the warnings the CIA had received from Colonel Kuklinski, assured U.S. officials that a crackdown on Solidarity was unthinkable.
His assurances reaffirmed the administration's own belief that the communists
wouldn't act.[4]

That evening, Friday, December 11, the Solidarity leadership council began
a scheduled three-day meeting at the Gdansk shipyard. Militants quickly took
over. With Walesa saying little, the council voted to demand a national referendum in February leading to free, open elections for Parliament. Discussion
began on plans to seize and "socialize" (as the pope meant it) factories and
television.

Just before they called it a night, at one A.M. Sunday, December 13, Walesa
pulled aside the men he called "the two Zbigs," Zbigniew Bujak and Zbigniew
Janas; each was the elected representative of workers at a major industrial plant
in the heartland. The phone and telex had stopped working, Walesa said.
Something seemed strange. A source in the police—it didn't occur to the Zbigs
then to ask how Walesa came to have a source in the police—had told him
something was up. He said the Zbigs ought to be careful going home.

So instead of returning to their hotel, Bujak and Janas went to the station
to catch the all-night train back to Warsaw. A hotel where some Solidarity
leaders were staying was visible from the train platform. Suddenly, Bujak and
Janas saw the hotel ringed by police. One by one, their friends were taken away
as prisoners.

Descending to the street, Bujak and Janas encountered Walesa's driver, who told them Walesa had been grabbed at his home. The two Zbigs decided to go separately to the homes of nonactivist friends where police wouldn't look, and to meet the next evening at the cathedral. (Why didn't the police watch the train platform? I asked. "You overestimate the skills of our police," Janas smiled.)

In Warsaw, shortly before midnight the phone rang at the apartment of Konrad Bielinski, a graduate student. Inspired by John Paul's 1979 visit, Bielinski had gone to Gdansk during the shipyard strike that created Solidarity, and started a newsletter. Now he was editor in chief of the Solidarity regional newspaper. His girlfriend and deputy editor, Ewa Kulik, who was finishing a doctorate in literature, had just moved in with him. The phone call was from Warsaw Solidarity headquarters. The phone and telex had been cut to the Gdansk office where the big meeting was being held. Something was wrong. Still clutching the phone, Bielinski heard a knock on the door. In an instant, burly cops were hauling him away.

Across town, another police team arrived with a warrant at Kulik's old apartment, but left without finding her. The police who came for Bielinski didn't know the woman in his bed was Kulik, and left her free. Thus, an out-of-wedlock arrangement the pope would have frowned on helped save Poland. (John Paul would be pleased to learn that fifteen years later, the couple seems happily married.)

With Bielinski gone, Kulik tried to phone friends. The lines were dead. Eager for news and knowing that the police would eventually return for her, she hit the streets. A taxi took her near the Solidarity office. Seeing a police cordon, the terrified driver dumped her on the street and drove off. She walked from one friend's to another's. Not just unionists had been arrested, but intellectual sympathizers as well, including an actress she knew. She hoped to find workers assembling to sit-in at factories, but the factories were dark. At Jacek Kuron's, she learned that police had taken Kuron's wife and son along with him.

Then she began seeing tanks in the streets. At that point, the newspaper-woman in her took over. She decided somebody had to record what was happening and publish it.

Archbishop Dabrowski, secretary of the Polish Episcopate, was awakened at one A.M. by a knocking on the window of his room near the cathedral in the old section of Warsaw. Looking out, he saw the president of the local Solidarity. Dabrowski opened the door and was told that "everybody" was being arrested. Could the Episcopate do anything?

Dabrowski reached for the phone to call the vice premier, his contact on a Church-state commission, but the line was dead. As he and the Solidarity officer talked, in came the Episcopate's press aide, Father Alojzy Orszulik. For months, Orszulik had been typing out and printing an underground news bulletin containing information smuggled in by the secret Polish press agency the pope had set up in Rome.[5]

They were still debating what to do at five o'clock, when a man from the Ministry of Religion came to the gate to announce the imposition of martial law. Dabrowski called Primate Glemp on an internal line. Glemp was preparing to drive to Czestochowa to address a youth conference. Incredibly, Glemp told Dabrowski and Orszulik to handle the martial-law situation by themselves, and proceeded to Czestochowa. There was no hint of cowardice, as shown by Primate Hlond when he fled the Germans; Glemp's desertion seemed, rather, an act of sheer witlessness.

At six, with the primate gone, a bishops' delegation walked over to the vice premier's office, where they found no one to talk to but soldiers (who whispered to Dabrowski a common greeting at Mass: "May Jesus Christ be praised"). That morning, instead of saying the usual Mass, Dabrowski and the bishops invited government opponents who hadn't been arrested to come to the archbishop's palace for strategy talks. All day, they debated what to do and sent messages demanding to see Walesa.

A taped speech by Jaruzelski had been repeating itself on television and radio since first light. Most Poles awoke, saw soldiers in the street, turned on television, and heard Jaruzelski. Solidarity had brought Poland to the brink of civil war, he said. Now the government had suspended Poles' right to strike, protest, assemble publicly, or leave the country. Only essential phone lines were open, and they would be monitored. A 10:00 P.M.–to–6:00 A.M. curfew was decreed. Government and the administration of major workplaces were in the hands of a temporary military council.

People instinctively went to Church that morning, "not so much for prayer as to hear what its policy would be," noted a visiting Briton. "At the nearest church to our home, there were queues down the front steps and along the street. We stood outside in the snow listening to the service over the loudspeakers as the priest appealed for calm. Then the hymn 'O Lord, Make Our Homeland Free Again,' the words of which the whole congregation knew by heart."[6] Since the German occupation, the hymn's original words had been banned, officially changed to "O Lord, Bless Our Homeland." In the 1970s, however, the government had stopped enforcing the ban, and one by one, churches had returned to the original words.

Today, long after communism's fall, Jaruzelski and his team still protest their innocence. They say—despite Soviet Politburo minutes showing a decision not to invade—that the Soviets would have come in, and that in declaring martial law, Jaruzelski chose the lesser evil. It is what Quisling said when he fronted for the Nazis in Norway.

Rocco Buttiglione, a young philosopher and economist (now a political leader in Italy), had gotten to know John Paul during his recuperation from Agca's attempt on his life. An international Catholic youth group Buttiglione helped lead, Communion and Liberation, frequented both Castelgandolfo and the Vatican with songfests in which the pope participated vigorously. Members of the group visiting Rome from Poland, Latin America, or elsewhere joined in. Banter and story-telling would go on for hours—just as when Wojtyla met students in Poland—until Dziwisz at last dragged the pope away.

Now, as news of martial law hit Rome, Buttiglione and others in Communion and Liberation were frightened to learn that many Polish friends had been arrested. "We were afraid they might be killed," recalls Buttiglione, who had visited Poland with his group. Poles in Rome, afraid of seeming cowardly, showed "absolutely crazy courage, saying, 'We will make an uprising and we will hang all the communists.' We were afraid it would get out of control. Then on Sunday the pope appeared at that window."

Buttiglione was among the exceptionally large crowd that jammed St. Peter's for the weekly noon prayer from the papal window. Free radio was waiting to beam the pope's words past the censors into Poland. "Nobody could imagine what he would say," says Buttiglione. "There were stupid stories in the Western press that he would go to Poland if the Russians came. This is exactly what he did not want.

"He said, 'Enough Polish blood has been shed in this century. Through dialogue, all can still be saved. No more blood.' In the West, it seemed to be a religious thought, but in Poland it was absolutely clear. To the communists, he was saying, 'Don't kill the prisoners, and there will be no uprising.' To the people of Poland, he was saying, 'We can still handle this through dialogue.'

"It was a strategy of nonviolence," says Buttiglione. "It took eight years, but eventually it led to the downfall of communism. Often in the West, nonviolence has been synonymous with cowardice—'Better Red than dead.' Now it was something more, a strategy. It was a way of showing respect for your adversaries—adversaries, not enemies—but with a constant demand on their moral conscience."

Later, when the pope went for his regular Sunday visit to a Roman church, Italian Foreign Minister Emilio Colombo met him with intelligence reports from Western diplomats. In his homily, the pope asked for "many prayers and much solidarity."

At about six P.M. December 13—or Twelve-Thirteen, as the beginning of martial law became known in Poland—Primate Glemp came motoring back from his youth conference. By then, Archbishop Dabrowski and the other bishops had talked the government into releasing thirty agriculture professors and some literary figures who had only tangential connections to Solidarity.

The primate, arriving in the midst of this, "asked what he should do," Dabrowski says. "Everyone told him he must say Mass the next morning, and speak to the people, to avoid a bloodbath."

While Glemp prepared his speech, Dabrowski and Father Orszulik, the press officer, were told they could finally see Walesa. They were escorted to a villa near Warsaw by a police colonel, who particularly irritated them and whom they would remember years later. They had been promised a private talk with Walesa, but the colonel insisted on listening in.

They told Walesa not to give up. "We will take care of the victims," Dabrowski promised.

But Walesa seemed to have lost touch with the reality of his situation. He shouted back at the surprised churchmen, "They [the government] will come to me on their knees!" By Walesa's own account, the churchmen "disapproved of my lack of Christian humility."[7] Walesa asked them to arrange a meeting for him with Jaruzelski. Dabrowski says he tried, but after that evening, the communists wouldn't even discuss such a meeting.

In Krakow, Cardinal Macharski had invited those Solidarity leaders who were still free to the palace. He asked them to organize a committee to distribute aid to the prisoners and their families.[8]

Back in Gdansk, Zbigniew Janas went to the cathedral, as arranged, to meet Zbigniew Bujak. As Janas scoured the crowd, worried, a priest motioned for him to follow. Bujak was waiting in the priest's quarters. Some other priests had found him on the street the night before and brought him home with them. Janas joined Bujak in accepting the priests' hospitality for a few days, then returned to Ursus, where he represented the fourteen-thousand-member Solidarity unit at the big tractor factory. He was to arrange a long-term underground existence for himself and Bujak as fugitives.

Arriving in Ursus, he learned from a priest that his brother and sister had been caught and jailed. His parents were distraught. Janas hid in the basement of a church.

In Warsaw, Ewa Kulik located some friends who had a duplicating machine and paper. "The first thing we decided was to publish" who had been arrested and who was still at large, she says. "Then to organize the underground." They determined that Bujak was the highest-ranking Solidarity officer on the loose, and so would be in charge—if anybody could make contact with him.

Then news arrived that Bujak's deputy, Victor Kulerski, was also still free. "Somebody knew somebody who knew a priest in Ursus who knew where Kulerski was," Kulik says. So she went to Ursus and left a message for the priest. Eventually, he brought Kulerski to her. They agreed that she would return in a week with false identification papers for Kulerski, Bujak, and others.

Back in Warsaw, Kulik moved into an apartment occupied by friends who were not likely to be on any police list. She began compiling lists of other safe apartments—many would be needed—and looking for photos of people who resembled the fugitive Solidarity members, to be used in making false credentials.

She encountered a young priest, Jerzy Popieluszko, a counselor to student groups. "Somebody told me he knew where the Solidarity legal board was hiding," she recalls. He gave her an address. Until then, she had never heard of Popieluszko; he would soon be one of Poland's most famous people.

24

"Don't offer your heads; the price of human life will be very low," said Primate Glemp in his homily the next morning. Even some bishops privately criticized him for sounding weak.[1] "Glemp thought Solidarity was doomed to failure; he thought it was too liberal and open-minded," says Aleksander Smolar, a Pole in Paris who became a major Solidarity voice at the BBC.

Cardinal Laszlo Lekai, primate of Hungary, lined up with Glemp, urging Poles to surrender to "political reality." He said that Solidarity, like the failed Hungarian revolt of 1956, had been provoked by "an excess of injections of hope from the West," and that Poles should be grateful for communism's good points, like free medical care and old-age insurance.[2]

Countering this defeatism, the pope sent courage to the desperate, scattered remnants of Solidarity—just as he had infused strength at the formation of

KOR, at the St. Martin's hunger strike, and at the Gdansk strike from which Solidarity was born. Appearing unscheduled that Monday before five thousand Poles gathered in Rome, John Paul called not just for peace but also for "the rights of man and of peoples."

Workers around Poland staged sit-down strikes. The police engaged in some violence—seven miners near Katowice were killed—but more often merely surrounded plants and arrested strike leaders.

Ewa Krasinska, then a translator of English literature, now a Polish diplomat, was among the members of the writers' union branch of Solidarity who weren't arrested and who convened at the union office: "They cut off all petrol supplies, but people came. All the phones were cut, but people from all over Warsaw knew, and they came."

As people told their stories, it emerged that policemen had been frightened by their superiors' claims that Solidarity would murder them in a revolution unless the police acted first. "People were arrested in nightclothes in midwinter," Krasinska says. "A six-month-old baby was taken to an orphanage when his mother was thrown into prison." Union negotiators eventually won release for the child's mother and for some elderly and sick prisoners.

Donations of food, clothing, and medicine for the prisoners and the families they had left behind poured into the writers' union office. Since the office would inevitably be raided (and was, after three days), someplace else had to be found to store the goods for distribution. Krasinska went to the cloister at St. Martin's Church, where the hunger strike had taken place. It was centrally located and had spacious quarters for the caretaker nuns from Laski.

Thirty-seven years earlier, during World War II, the same group of nuns had allowed young Father Wyszynski to use Laski as a secret hospital during the Warsaw Uprising. Now the nuns told Krasinska that Solidarity could use the cloister, and the remote, forested Laski, as secret supply depots during martial law.

In Washington, despite months of forewarning, the Reagan team was taken completely by surprise.[3] Miroslaw Chojecki, Solidarity's underground press czar, says his uncle Jan Novak arranged a meeting for him with Richard Pipes, Reagan's expert on the USSR and Eastern Europe. Chojecki says that "Pipes wanted to learn what was happening" but offered no support and made no requests.[4] At Novak's house, Chojecki met Brzezinski (Carter's former adviser) and some others out of government; they formed a Solidarity Foundation, which eventually raised modest but helpful sums for Polish relief.

Archbishop Dabrowski had arranged daily radio contact with the pope through covert Radio Free Europe representatives in Warsaw (not official correspondents). Dabrowski had tried to meet Radio Free Europe officials on the sly whenever he was out of Poland, just as Wojtyla had, so communication channels were ready when martial law struck. Messages went through the secret Warsaw contacts (Dabrowski still won't name them) to Radio Free Europe in Munich, and then to the Vatican. With papal encouragement, Dabrowski continued to plead with authorities for the release of prisoners, mostly in vain.

Bohdan Cywinski, John Paul's old canoeing companion and KOR founder, was in Rome on December 13. After Solidarity was recognized, Cywinski had temporarily set aside the book on Church history that Cardinal Wojtyla had commissioned from him after the hunger strike, and had gone to work as Mazowiecki's deputy editor at the Solidarity newspaper. When authorities clamped down on the paper in the fall of 1981, John Paul brought Cywinski to Rome to finish the book, with funding the Pope arranged from Communion and Liberation, the youth group that Rocco Buttiglione was associated with.

The team that would sustain Solidarity was drawn from a fairly tight-knit circle around the pope. Earlier in the month, when Cywinski's wife, a painter, had visited him from Warsaw, the couple was invited for a private dinner at the papal apartment. The pope blessed a rosary and gave it to Mrs. Cywinska as a gift for the woman who was watching their three children in Poland that week: Maria Wosiek, a founder of KOR, whose sister was a nun at Laski. Mrs. Cywinska returned home December 11 and gave the rosary to Maria Wosiek. The next night, Wosiek clutched it as police dragged her to prison. She was taken with other "intellectual" prisoners to quarters in Poland's far north, used by the army as a summer resort but frigid and unheated in the winter. She says the rosary from the pope brought her warmth.[5]

Monday, December 14, Cywinski, still in Rome, couldn't reach his family. When he called Monsignor Dziwisz to schedule his weekly meeting with the pope, he was told to come right over.

"I was shocked" upon entering the room, Cywinski says. "I think he [John Paul] had aged a few years in terms of his looks." There was no talk of the Soviets or the Cold War, Cywinski says. "It was not a moment for political reactions. For the pope, his political reactions grow out of his moral reactions." Together they pondered how to get aid to the imprisoned and other needy souls in Poland.

Help soon came from Wanda Gawronska, the longtime Rome resident from a prominent Polish family whose socialite contacts had enabled Poles to see the pope's inauguration on television. Now she once again turned on her charm and energy, this time to help her countrymen fight martial law. At a high-powered dinner party December 15, she persuaded Italy's postal minister to let relief packages to Poland be mailed free, and talked Parliamentary leaders of both the governing Republican Party and the Socialist Party into starting a fund for Polish relief.

And—at the same dinner—she says she also cajoled a Fiat truck executive into allowing free use of a tractor trailer, largest size, to haul goods to Poland. How did she acquire such powerful contacts? "We're a big family," she smiles. "They were friends of my sister's."

Members of the Reagan administration's foreign-policy team have claimed that in the days after martial law, they began a covert operation in Poland with Vatican cooperation. They say this operation sustained Solidarity and was important in bringing down the Soviet Union. The story has been generally accepted in books and articles.

The team's scribe, Peter Schweizer, has written that the operation began at a meeting President Reagan called, so high-level that it was attended only by him, Vice President George Bush, CIA Director Casey, National Security Adviser William Clark, the secretaries of state and defense, and two other top national-security officials. Schweizer gained exclusive access to most of these men, and he says Clark and Defense Secretary Caspar Weinberger also reviewed his manuscript before publication. According to his account, East European expert Pipes proposed the program to support Solidarity, and Reagan ordered it put into action. Pipes told Schweizer, "No formal intelligence action was taken. It was feared it would leak. This was a highly secret operation, handled 'off the books.'"

But the story of how America kept Solidarity alive, despite its myriad of high-level sources, appears to be untrue, an attempt—successful to this point—to rewrite history and steal credit for work really done by the Poles themselves.

What Pipes evidently didn't tell Schweizer was that probably the most potent guerrilla soldier in the Polish opposition—Miroslaw Chojecki—sought the administration's help that week and was brushed off. Chojecki—the father of the Polish underground press, and an instrumental force in the underground presses in Czechoslovakia, Hungary, Lithuania, and the USSR—says he walked into Pipes's office a few days after martial law was declared, but got nothing. (Pipes says the only meeting with Chojecki recorded in his diary took place the day *before* martial law; either way, the result was the same.)*

Chojecki had crossed the Atlantic at the suggestion of Mazowiecki, Walesa's top adviser, to collect a donation of printing paper from some Canadian labor unions. If U.S. officials wanted to start an operation to help Solidarity survive, where better to begin it than with Chojecki? But Chojecki says no U.S. official ever tried to contact him after he visited Pipes.

Schweizer wrote that after the meeting with Reagan and the others, Casey "raced back to Langley [CIA headquarters] . . . his Olds sped down the George Washington Parkway"—and called Cardinal Casaroli, John Paul's secretary of state, in Rome. According to Schweizer, "The assassination attempt on the Pope and the declaration of martial law had affected [Casaroli] deeply," and he pledged to cooperate with the CIA. Schweizer provides no details of any cooperation.[6]

Nor does he explain why Casey "raced" through Virginia to call Rome, when Casaroli was right there in the White House. Schweizer says his high-level sources didn't tell him, but three days after martial law was declared, Casaroli, returning from a religious event in Mexico, kept a long-scheduled appointment with President Reagan (who had already telephoned the pope). Emerging from the meeting, Casaroli told reporters, "U.S. authorities do not have enough complete and sure information" to evaluate the situation in Poland.[7] No one has suggested that a covert operation was discussed that day; given Casaroli's continued commitment to *Ostpolitik*, it seems unlikely.

I could find no evidence that Reagan administration officials ever undertook any effective operation to help Solidarity, or that the pope, Casaroli, or others at the Vatican cooperated with them in any such work. There is, in fact, as we shall see, abundant evidence to the contrary.

The facts suggest that the long war against totalitarian communism was finally won not by men in dark suits in command of violent armies, but by one

---

* Pipes says he remembers only the group meeting in the State Department (already described), about twenty-four hours before martial law was imposed, when Chojecki, in Pipes's word, "pooh-poohed" the possibility of a crackdown. Chojecki says Novak arranged a second, private meeting with Pipes after martial law. Novak says he was involved in so many meetings that he can't resolve the disagreement.

Pipes says he phoned Chojecki at 9:00 A.M. on the Sunday martial law was announced, and that Chojecki again expressed disbelief about the crackdown. Pipes says Chojecki "was one of the people from Solidarity who misled the government, one of the reasons we were surprised." He says that this was one reason he did not call Chojecki later to offer help. Another reason, he says, is that it was a CIA operation, and so he wasn't in on the details.

man in a white robe with the willing following of an army committed to principle, and to nonviolence.

The day Casaroli met Reagan, Primate Glemp spoke so compliantly that he
was put on Polish radio and TV by the communists. Knowing he had been
widely criticized for weakness, Glemp said he was appealing "to reason, even at
the price of receiving insults. . . . It is not important if the Church is accused of
cowardice." He asked, "even if I have to do it on my knees, that one Polish person not strike another one. . . . The Church will appeal wherever it can for calm,
for an end to fratricidal struggles."

Some Polish bishops wanted to condemn martial law, but Glemp prevented
them from speaking out.[8] He had no such authority over the pope, however;
that night, John Paul urged a crowd of ten thousand to pray "for the people of
Poland, so harshly tested, that their rights may be respected."

Archbishop Dabrowski approached the government for permission to deliver
donations of food and warm clothing to about five thousand prisoners. The
government welcomed the aid, which helped defray its own cost of providing
for the prisoners, but it worried about security: the goods, it said, would have to
be gathered in one place. Father (now Bishop) Dembowski, the longtime vicar
of St. Martin's, volunteered his church as the logical spot for the depot the government was agreeing to. He realized this would legitimize the Solidarity store-
house that was already secretly operating in the nuns' cloister there.

The sticking point was whether the prisoners' families would be included in
the distribution. "The families had no means to make a living," Dembowski
stresses. "The state owned all the workplaces." The government was finally
persuaded. At one point, Dembowski says, a general he was arguing with told
him, "Your file in the archive will be thicker than mine."

An office was set up near the entrance to the cloister, in a room dominated
by a portrait of John Paul. Parishes began delivering donations.

Jerzy Milewski, a physicist, had been elected to the Solidarity leadership council representing the staff at the Polish Institute of Sciences. But as most of the
council was being jailed on Twelve-Thirteen, he was en route to New Orleans
for a conference on lasers. In the days that followed, he watched television pictures of tanks in Poland with other physicists from around the world, and
answered their questions about Solidarity.

Visiting a cousin in Connecticut after the laser conference, he became a sudden celebrity, the highest-ranking Solidarity official available to take part in an

AFL-CIO press conference and a meeting of Polish-Americans. (Chojecki, effective as he was, was an underground publisher, not a Solidarity officer.) Volunteers began asking Milewski how they could help, and he began taking charge.

In Rome, Cywinski continued receiving updates from John Paul and Dziwisz. With their encouragement, he went on Italian national television during prime time to explain the situation. Out-of-Poland Solidarity members, who had been calling each other across Europe, arranged a meeting and press conference in Zurich, where Swiss labor unions had offered help. Cywinski phoned Polish friends to come to Zurich: "I knew three such people. Each of those knew three people. The first task was not organizing aid, but informing the world."

Right off, Cywinski found himself mending a split in the resistance. The Swiss and Italian trade unions were considered "Leftist," while Communion and Liberation (which was funding Cywinski's work) was considered "Rightist." "Whenever Communion and Liberation wanted to help, the trade unions were reluctant, and vice versa," Cywinski says. "Political life in Italy was such that you couldn't do anything together." Back in Poland, Cywinski had helped bridge the gap between the so-called Left opposition of ex-communists and the so-called Right opposition of Catholics, thus enabling the creation of KOR. When the labels came off, people discovered they were on the same side. In Zurich, that happened again.

In the background at the Zurich meeting was someone else who would help everyone work together: Father Giambattista Danzi, a wispy, swarthy, bearded, chain-smoking parish priest who was originally from Italy but had settled in Bellinzona, Switzerland. He already knew John Paul, but what he was to do over the next few years would make him a papal favorite: today his Vatican office and budget are bigger than most cardinals'.

Danzi had joined Communion and Liberation as a student when it was founded in 1954, and later helped organize the Swiss branch. In the early 1970s, after meeting editors from *Tygodnik Powszechny* and *Znak* on trips, he had arranged for articles from Krakow to be reprinted in Italy, and recruited writers in Italy and Switzerland for the Krakow magazines.

Danzi had also initiated annual summer pilgrimages of Italian youths to Czestochowa. Beginning with just a few students, by the mid-1970s Danzi was bringing four hundred youths a year to Poland and introducing them to Wojtyla. Because the Polish government discouraged large groups, he had to arrange for visas to be obtained furtively in batches of five or six. These smaller groups then rendezvoused in Poland. By 1980, because of John Paul's papacy and the new Polish openness, five thousand youths made the trip.

Now, from Zurich, Danzi called Monsignor Dziwisz and asked about taking a truckload of relief supplies to Krakow. John Paul blessed the idea, and
Father Danzi went to work organizing what would be a trail-blazing mission.

Apparently sensing that he and Glemp saw martial law differently,[9] John Paul
decided to write General Jaruzelski without going through the primate.*
December 19, 1981, the pope's letter left Rome with Archbishop (now Cardinal) Luigi Poggi, a senior Vatican diplomat with long experience in Poland.
Flights having been halted, Poggi boarded the all-night train to Poland. Czech
guards detained him and accused him of having a fake passport and bringing
in weapons. (He says he brandished his cross, declaring it was "a real weapon.")
"The guards wanted to offend the pope by offending me," Poggi says. The
entire train was stopped for five hours, with no heat. It reached Warsaw the
next day, but Poggi had to wait four more days for an appointment with
Jaruzelski.

Meanwhile, Poles once more stood in the snow to hear church services and
sing "O Lord, Make Our Homeland Free Again." After more arguments with
the government, Archbishop Dabrowski spent Sunday and Monday in a prison
with Solidarity members. "I told the communists, I am not going to leave the
prison until I see them," he says. Not knowing if they would leave prison alive,
he gave them absolution. When flights out of Poland resumed December 22,
Dabrowski was on the first plane, for Frankfurt, bound for Rome even as papal
emissary Poggi sat in Warsaw, waiting to see Jaruzelski.

Polish workers resumed normal schedules in quiet resolution. Some phone
service necessary for business was restored, but each call was preceded by the
message "Conversation being monitored." Government radio daily asserted
that shortages in stores were due to hoarding by Jews.

December 23, 1981, President Reagan slapped a broad embargo on trade
with Poland and suspended Polish airport and fishing rights in the United
States. He asked allies to join in the embargo. The Vatican quietly spread the
word that the pope believed an embargo would only increase the suffering of
the Polish people.

* In his book *Pope John Paul II,* Tad Szulc reports that the pope was responding to a tape
recording that a Polish UN diplomat from New York brought him, of a meeting with
Jaruzelski on December 16. Jaruzelski is said to have promised economic reforms and no
more bloodshed. According to Szulc, this began a long, friendly correspondence between
the pope and Jaruzelski, leading seven years later to democracy in Eastern Europe. With
sketchy detail, Szulc portrays John Paul, Jaruzelski, and Glemp as comrades in victim-
ization by the Soviets. The facts I have found are at odds with this thesis.

The next day, Poggi finally gave John Paul's letter to Jaruzelski and listened as the general—"very serious, sure of himself"—defended his actions. Neither Poggi nor the Vatican Press Office will disclose the contents of the pope's letter. Jaruzelski offered me an interview in exchange for a large cash payment, which I declined to make.* Kukolowicz says he was told at the Episcopate that the letter disputed Jaruzelski's contention that martial law and mass jailings were necessary to forestall a Soviet invasion: "The message was, there is no choice between a greater and a lesser evil. The choice is always between good and evil."

Early morning on Christmas Eve, Father Danzi loaded a truck of supplies for Poland. The venture was paid for by Communion and Liberation from small collections in Italy, according to Tadeusz Konopka, who assisted Danzi; Konopka, a Solidarity leader and editor at *Tygodnik Powszechny* who had known Wojtyla for years, had been abroad on Twelve-Thirteen and came to the Zurich meeting.

Father Danzi won't discuss the financing of the relief he arranged because "it would compromise the Holy Father himself." For my interviews in his Vatican office, Danzi pulled out his old files and promised to tell all. But on finding occasional papers and notes, he would grow frenzied, tear them dramatically into tiny pieces, and throw them away, refusing to say what they were.

The first truck trip, Danzi says, was made more to obtain information than to deliver the cargo of food and medicine. Like Poggi, Danzi found that the Czech border was the real Soviet barrier to Poland. Arriving there at midday, he spent Christmas Eve being searched and threatened. Christmas morning, a new shift of guards with machine guns tried to persuade him to turn back but finally, after much talk, let him through.

Poland was in "total paralysis," he says. "From the border to Krakow [sixty-two miles] we went through twenty roadblocks [where] our documents were checked." Despite Jaruzelski's argument that he had acted to preserve Polish control, Danzi says he found Czech and Russian guards at television, radio, and postal installations.

Monsignor Bronislaw Fidelus, Cardinal Macharski's second in command, remembers the joy they felt when Father Danzi's truck pulled up to John Paul's old palace. The aid-distribution committee was summoned and told Danzi what to bring in future shipments. Danzi then went discreetly around town tak-

---

* Jaruzelski said two other American journalists doing papal biographies had paid him about a thousand dollars each. One, Tad Szulc, says he was asked for the money but refused to pay because he felt it was unethical; he says Jaruzelski then agreed to see him anyway because of their long relationship from other work.

ing photographs. Shops were empty. Food was mostly black-market, sold for dollars, not zlotys. Each city was isolated; no one knew what was going on elsewhere. "The situation in the hospitals was tragic," Danzi says.

He dashed back to Rome and delivered a report to Dziwisz, whom he then saw regularly. He urged the Vatican to seek stable relations, "to have a clear picture of what was happening, and not the picture given by the regime." Soon he was meeting with John Paul himself.

Konopka and Cywinski followed Danzi back to Rome, where they organized a structure for continued shipments. Konopka joined the others on the payroll of Communion and Liberation, where the pope seems to have had a blank check. "We gathered food, pharmaceuticals, money, clothes," Danzi says, from a multitude of donors in Italy and elsewhere in Western Europe. All three men deny knowing of any contribution by the U.S. government. They say little could have been contributed without their knowing about it.

Cardinal König's secretary, Lonny Glaser, who for decades had been helping Wojtyla/John Paul send intellectuals to Vienna for exposure to the West, now organized relief collections and persuaded the head of a Vienna trucking firm to donate transport. Soon the first of what would be ninety-one truckloads of baby formula, cooking oil, rice, sausages, and medical supplies was on its way north to Krakow. On its arrival, Glaser phoned the delighted pope. A Catholic pharmacist read a newspaper article about the shipment, walked into Glaser's office, and offered to drive his medicines to Krakow in his van.

At St. Martin's Church in Warsaw, trucks started arriving in the weeks after Christmas from church groups in France, Belgium, and Sweden. Then came clothing shipments from Polish-Americans.

The activity amounted to another Berlin Airlift—except instead of being run by the U.S. Air Force on the orders of the President, it was the spontaneous act of a volunteer army that was mostly, though far from entirely, Catholic. The army was inspired by the pope's pep talks about the importance of peace *and* rights "in my own fatherland," which were beamed to Poland and the rest of Europe almost daily. Even if Poles couldn't talk to each other on the phone, they didn't miss a word of the pope on the radio. Interest in his general audiences mushroomed, and attendance doubled.

The Jesuits probably didn't throw the most exciting New Year's Eve party in Rome even under the best circumstances. But this year, the pope's decision to spend the evening trying to encourage a celebratory mood at Jesuit headquarters touched many hearts. It demonstrated again that his fights were always with the error, not the errants. After visiting the bedfast Arrupe, John Paul told a dinner gathering that their former leader had talked "quite well. In fact, he talked more than I did. . . . I did my best to keep my Spanish unmixed."

Trying to add some levity to his past dressing-down of the Jesuits for being too secular, he observed, "I see that my visit . . . has had the happy result of occasioning a good meal. . . . One of the fathers here at the table made it clear that I must not get the idea you eat like this every day."[10]

New Year's Day 1982, crowds in St. Peter's brought "Solidarity" signs. That night, Krzysztov Kozlowski, John Paul's former student and now Turowicz's deputy editor at *Tygodnik Powszechny*, dined in the papal apartment. They talked about the assassination attempt as well as martial law.

"I said the devil is a reality in the world," Kozlowski recalls. "Not just a lack of goodness, but a positive evil force."

"I prefer to use the word *Antichrist*, rather than 'the devil,' " John Paul said. But they agreed that the real villain "was a general evil. It didn't matter if it was the KGB or Jaruzelski."

Kozlowski, who had been in Rome December 13, was flying home the next day: "I was so afraid, I fell on my knees. I felt all hopes were in ruins. I told the pope the biggest danger was that not only I but all Poles will start to hate our neighbors. I was afraid society would be overtaken and ruined by this."

But John Paul was determined that would not happen.[11]

2 5

Early in the new year, a truck from France pulled up to the St. Martin's storage depot. Glemp's office said it was from the pope. Volunteers were thrilled to find, hidden among the clothing and food, a crate of typewriters. From that day, contraband—mostly information, and equipment to reproduce information—was a regular component of the relief supplies.

An underground Solidarity network was already in place to use it. Ewa Kulik had located Solidarity members with a newfound talent for forgery. Fugitives were outfitted with false credentials. Kulik booked safe apartments for them from a list she and others had compiled. The tightest secrecy surrounded Zbigniew Bujak, the highest-ranking leader still at large, and the unofficial head of the underground. He was moved constantly, and usually only Kulik knew where.

The main supply depots were the archbishop's palace in Krakow, St. Martin's Church in Warsaw, and St. Bridget's Church in Gdansk. But committees were set up in towns throughout Poland. Many created hidden depots in the woods to store contraband. Shipments considered too dangerous for St. Martin's were stored at Laski.

Nuns and priests were heavily involved and thoroughly aware, though life held some surprises. Sister Ruth Woziek at Laski remembers trying to prepare a group dinner with a can of tomatoes and soy she had set aside from a food shipment, only to find it contained anti-Soviet press clippings. Hanna Federowicz, a volunteer in the St. Martin's distribution effort, recalls being given back a large jar of jam by the family of one imprisoned Solidarity leader: it contained printer's ink.

"It's impossible that [Father, now Bishop] Dembowski didn't know about" the contraband, says Joanna Szczesna, a St. Martin's hunger striker who became a major underground journalist. Dembowski, then the St. Martin's rector, says that when he visited the depots, he told workers, "Don't tell me what you're doing, I don't want to know." Twice, he says, he entered his confessional and found secretly delivered messages from Bujak, thanking him for the flow of supplies to the underground.

The police immediately began accusing the Church of using the relief shipments as a cover for contraband. Archbishop Dabrowski and Bishop Dembowski repeatedly denied it.

Even though the operation was called the Primate's Committee for Relief, Dembowski says, "I think Cardinal Glemp was not informed." Others agree. Says Hanna Federowicz, "My feeling was that he [Glemp] was not even interested in knowing what I was doing. He maybe visited once a year." She says she and others assumed that "Dembowski was intentionally concealing it from him."

Volunteers say that Glemp's secretary, Monsignor Bronislaw Piasecki (who declined to be interviewed), was a courier on trips to Rome. Ewa Krasinska says Piasecki took the pope a list that her committee had compiled of the internees and how they had been arrested. Many arrest warrants originally listed a prison that had been closed after a fire in September; the name of another prison was written over it. From this change, the committee deduced that martial law had already been planned by mid-September—something the CIA had known but never acted on.

The truckloads of supplies from France were largely organized by Father Eugene Platar, of Caritas, the Catholic charity. Seweryn Blumsztajn, the former student rebel who had helped unite Catholic and Jewish dissidents, had been in Paris to meet with French unions on Twelve-Thirteen. He helped start a Solidarity committee there, which worked with Father Platar.

"The French money was collected from hundreds of different organizations," Blumsztajn says. "Thousands of checks came in." The biggest help, he emphasizes, came from unions on "the Left" that weren't affiliated with the international labor group the CIA supported.[1] Blumsztajn says he saw no indication of any CIA help.

Wanda Gawronska tells a story to illustrate how eager Italians were to help the Poles. The president of a major pasta company offered a donation that she understood to be ten tons of pasta, which would fill 40 percent of the Fiat truck she had procured. When she called to confirm the pickup a day in advance, she learned from an underling that the donation was actually ten *quintale*, a unit of weight apparently peculiar to pasta, which equals only about one ton. She put the trip on hold until she could find other goods to fill up the truck. But when the underling reported the confusion to his boss, the pasta company immediately increased its donation to the full ten tons so the trip could proceed.

Gawronska rode in the cab of the truck. She ignored the cold, the ice, and the strip search that had frightened Father Danzi. "Oh, they undressed you," she laughs. "They did that to all of us." She delivered the goods to Lublin, brought back a wish list from the underground, and started calling donors again.

Zdzislaw Najder, the writer, was also abroad on Twelve-Thirteen, but not to help Solidarity. Najder had left after friends learned that he had talked regularly to the secret police in exchange for permission to travel. He tried to excuse it by saying he had never talked about other dissidents, but KOR founder Antoni Macierewicz, who helped publicize the charge (as he would later publicize similar charges against Walesa), asserts that even general discussions were helpful to the police, and inexcusable.

In partial disgrace, Najder had gone off to teach at his old college in England. Eager to help when martial law struck, he contacted former colleagues at Radio Free Europe, where he had done secret free-lance work over the years. He was asked to come to the radio's Munich headquarters to take over a vacancy running the Polish branch.

In Munich, Najder says he was instantly supplied with tapes of what the pope was saying, even in some private audiences, thanks to "a secret agreement with Vatican Radio. Tapes were taken immediately to Radio Free Europe in Rome and telephoned to Munich."

Maciej Morawski, one of many prominent Poles who emigrated to Paris over the years, became a constant voice beamed home on Radio Free Europe, reading "letters and books smuggled by tourists out of Poland," written by the likes of Kuron, Michnik, and Geremek (the historian the pope invited to the

Vatican). Morawski and Najder, too, say they encountered no evidence of CIA aid to the underground Solidarity effort.

Solidarity relied on millions of Poles, disconnected and spiritless before John Paul's papacy but now gripped by a team fervor. Loyalty to the cause became such a matter of honor that the estranged wife of one Solidarity officer dropped her divorce suit against him when she learned of his arrest. Throughout Poland, police surveillance made furtiveness a sport, uniting the country. So that curfew wouldn't keep everyone home at night, all-night sleepovers became common, sometimes unplanned, often sparking romance.*

Once again, as in centuries past, the Church provided the institutional framework to carry on a dialogue with government, while maintaining contact with those whom the government had imprisoned. The churchmen closest to John Paul were the heart that kept the blood circulating, visiting the arrested and their families, pressuring authorities for their release.

"People never lost heart because they knew they had their defender, their pope in Rome," Monsignor Fidelus says. "People all over the world helped Poland, but most of that sympathy during those years is because of the pope." Father Danzi agrees. He persuaded food and drug manufacturers in Italy, Germany, Austria, and Switzerland to send donations on their own trucks. "Their generosity was undoubtedly due to the fact the pope came from Poland," Danzi says.

The Reagan administration, which made so much noise about defeating the Soviets, was on the sidelines in the critical match. One telling story is related by David Ost, an American political scientist in Poland, who became frightened that his vast archive on Solidarity might be seized by Jaruzelski's men. After much deliberation, he took the archive to the U.S. embassy for safe storage, having removed the names of confidential sources. Certain that the embassy staff would jump to read his notes, documents, and copies of rare underground publications, he was stunned to find "they had no interest in it at all. They gave me a hard time just holding the stuff."

AFL-CIO President Lane Kirkland at last got an invitation to talk to Reagan. He recalls "sitting in the Oval Office and [Reagan's] saying, 'We finally have something on which we can agree.'" Kirkland, doubting that, immedi-

---

* My associate Dr. Janine Wedel, an anthropologist, collected hundreds of such stories about Polish life. See her books *The Private Poland* (New York: Facts on File, 1986) and *The Unplanned Society* (New York: Columbia University Press, 1992).

ately challenged the President to "call the Polish loans that are in de facto default and thereby deprive them of credit." Ironically, $1.6 billion in U.S.-backed agricultural loans were supplying fuel and fertilizer to Polish state farms, while the private farmers who grew three fourths of Poland's crops were being denied aid by their government. Wall Street and the U.S. Treasury were literally financing the imposition of communism.

Kirkland says neither Reagan nor Vice President Bush, in a follow-up meeting, would agree to foreclose the overdue loans. Kirkland later learned from the newspapers that instead, the administration itself had paid off the banks that were lending money to Poland, breaking all precedent by doing so without declaring a default that would truly have set back the communist government. Reagan "not only didn't call those loans, but the taxpayers paid them!" Kirkland exclaims.

Kirkland didn't know it at the time, but it now turns out that Defense Secretary Weinberger originally wanted to persuade Western banks to declare Poland in default, just as Kirkland suggested. But the first banker Weinberger consulted, an executive at Chase Manhattan in New York, talked him out of the idea because Polish default would trigger an "instant replay" of defaults by other countries, particularly in Latin America. The banks would get clobbered. So Weinberger dropped his plan,[2] and the unpaid debt was passed off to the American public. "They were rhetorically committed to fighting communism," Kirkland fumes. "But the conservative parties want to protect the banks."

Kirkland says Reagan never discussed Poland with him again.

Many others also sought to squeeze the Polish communists by cutting off their credit. But since that would hurt ordinary Poles (by halting imports), John Paul had long urged the opposite solution: he wanted banks not to cut off credit but to relax and even forgive past loans. And he specifically wanted this forgiveness extended to Latin America, the very thing the bankers feared. In both Poland and Latin America, loan payments were collected from the sweat of workers who had been given no say in borrowing or spending the money.

The argument between John Paul and Reagan over economic sanctions sparked the closest thing the pope has had to a public tiff with a civil political leader, communists included. The pope had sent what he thought was a confidential, polite note to Reagan in response to the President's phone call and letter supporting Poland. He expressed his opposition to U.S. economic sanctions in his usual euphemistic way, by thanking the President for the "humanitarian and food aid" Americans had sent. Such aid, he said, represented "attitudes that are directed not against the life and progress of Poland [an apparent reference to trade sanctions] but toward supporting the aspirations of her people."

John Paul was reported "stunned" when Reagan publicly claimed that the pope's letter supported his economic sanctions. It was especially embarrassing because the pope had just endorsed a statement by the Polish bishops opposing sanctions on the ground that they always increase popular suffering, while the ruling class finds a way to stay supplied. "The pope was put in the position of either calling Reagan a liar or admitting that he himself had lied to the Polish bishops," a senior Vatican bishop said.[3]

The Vatican issued a statement politely denying support for the sanctions, though American reports still suggested that Reagan's initial statement reflected the pope's true feelings.[4]

Then Reagan did the last thing the pope would have approved of: to punish the Soviets, he unilaterally postponed the start of the nuclear-arms limitation talks John Paul had been encouraging.

January 31, 1982, the administration took its single known action in support of Solidarity: it presented a television program, Let Poland Be Poland. According to Kirkland, "the net effect of it was zero. It spent money, it didn't raise any." Jerzy Milewski, the physicist who was the highest-ranking Solidarity officer in the U.S., says what he remembers most about Let Poland Be Poland is arguments over the administration's decision to invite dictators onto the program as advocates of freedom. Milewski says the only major American official he met while working on the program was UN Ambassador Jeane Kirkpatrick, who he says just shook his hand and said hello.

26

The Reagan administration focused on what might be called Second Amendment aid overseas—that is, helping the recipients keep and bear arms (as discussed in the Second Amendment to the U.S. Constitution). Because of those arms, hundreds of thousands of Latin Americans, Angolans, Afghans, and Soviet conscripts in Afghanistan were killed during the administration's eight years in office.

Solidarity was from the beginning a First Amendment operation: it dealt in words. The First Amendment aid it obtained, from scattered private donors, proved not only more effective than the government's Second Amendment aid but a lot cheaper.

Founded on words, Solidarity needed to publish. The first impulse of Ewa Kulik and others had been to gather and print news. Martial law stilled the underground publishing empire of Miroslaw Chojecki, who was in the United

States, but the hardware and talent he had assembled remained intact. Even when Solidarity was legal, Chojecki had refused to bring his secret publishing network aboveground because he didn't want to submit to censorship.

Before martial law, Chojecki's publications had been not only self-sustaining but profitable, with press runs of up to fifteen thousand copies for his periodicals. With Chojecki, Mazowiecki, Cywinski, and other Solidarity newsmen arrested or in exile, the task of restarting the presses fell to two veteran underground journalists, Halina Luczywo and Joanna Szczesna (of the St. Martin's hunger strike). They used Chojecki's leftover portable presses and accumulated profits to start *Tygodnik Mazowsze* (*tygodnik* meaning "weekly," and Mazowsze being the geographical area around Warsaw).

In his book *Victory*, Peter Schweizer—relying on the senior Reagan officials who gave him his information—claims that the CIA organized and funded *Tygodnik Mazowsze*. Szczesna, Luczywo, and Chojecki, whom I interviewed independently, all not only denied getting any CIA help, but treated the notion as a joke. "That's what we were accused of by the communist regime," Szczesna says.

"We got money from papers we sold in Gdansk, Warsaw, Krakow—fifty to eighty thousand copies a week," Szczesna explains. Each copy was passed around, and people who read them sent money. "In each issue we thanked people for their donations, even small amounts."

Chojecki raised some money in the United States from financier George Soros, the Ford Foundation, and the John D. and Catherine T. MacArthur Foundation. Then he headed for Paris and hooked up with KOR journalist Seweryn Blumsztajn, who was already helping to ship contraband printing equipment to Poland, hidden among relief supplies. Together the two men persuaded a Paris-based Polish literary magazine with a worldwide subscription list to donate a thousand dollars monthly in cash, and to begin publishing a miniature edition that could more easily be smuggled into Poland.

"We didn't need big money for *Tygodnik Mazowsze*," says Chojecki, who advised on its operation from abroad. "We already had paper and printers." Once the newspaper was launched, some of his former assistants also restarted his book-publishing enterprise. Ewa Krasinska, who worked days at St. Martin's Church distributing relief supplies (and collecting the printing equipment that was concealed in each truckload), stayed up nights translating foreign articles to be published in *Tygodnik Mazowsze*.

Soon other underground newspapers sprang up. The most prominent, nearly as big as *Tygodnik Mazowsze*, was run by a flamboyant writer using the pseudonym David Varshawski. Even most of his colleagues in Solidarity didn't learn until years later that Varshawski was actually their friend Konstanty

Gebert, a young Jew who had been fired from his government job for his Solidarity work and now supported his wife and children as an English translator.

Varshawski/Gebert became a folk hero when the first few issues of his newspaper were published early in 1982. For years Poles wondered what he would do next to tweak the government. He published forty thousand copies fortnightly, using a silk-screen process with hand-inked presses. Although slower than Chojecki's process, it needed "zero technology," Gebert says. "If a mimeo breaks down and you don't have a spare part, you're finished." In addition, silk screens could be folded into a suitcase, required no electricity, and were usable "anywhere you don't mind spilled ink," Gebert says.

He says his equipment was mostly procured by a friend, Nellie Nortin, who had fled Poland during the anti-Semitic campaigns of the 1960s and settled in Turin, Italy. They exchanged messages in hollowed-out candles or boxed multirecord opera sets, carried by an Italian trade unionist who traveled back and forth between the two countries. The drop spot was a Warsaw church whose nuns knew Gebert by yet another alias.

Machines, paper, and ink came from Turin concealed in crates of used clothing, brought to a monastery eighteen miles west of Warsaw, where priests, risking arrest, let Gebert use a storeroom. Besides money from newspaper sales, Nortin collected contributions from Italian contacts—mostly "Left-wing," he says. "Their contacts on this end were very conservative Catholic priests and nuns, but it worked out nicely."

Like the Chojecki group, Gebert compartmentalized his printers, distributors, and journalists. Only he knew the whole operation. Like Chojecki, he loaded his small car carefully with paper: too much "would weigh you down and they may catch you," but not enough meant extra trips, which increased the chance of being followed.

He relied on the inefficiency of the police. "For most of them, it was just a job," he says. "They were rigidly organized and poorly motivated. We were sloppily organized and greatly motivated. You can't crack an amoeba. Had we resisted the mailed fist, they would have broken us. But it was like the mailed fist went through a chunk of butter. We were just dripping all over."

Once, some undercover men were following him because of his Solidarity association, unaware of his newspaper work. "I went into a bookstore," he says. "At two o'clock, I saw them look at their watches, turn around, and walk away." Another time, though, policemen attacked him with clubs. They were commonly eighteen- or nineteen-year-old farm boys attracted to uniforms and power. Many believed their government indoctrination and accused members of the underground of being "traitors in the pay of the Germans, the Jews, and the Americans," Gebert says. "Some of the police really thought that if we won we were going to murder their families and give their land back to the Germans."

The "flying university" Wojtyla had helped start was as much a part of the opposition as the underground press was. After the main organizers went to jail, hundreds of volunteers replaced them. "It could only be done on the grounds of a church," says Antoni Macierewicz, who had first brought the idea to Wojtyla. "Every parish in Poland had such a meeting at least once a week. Often it took place right after Mass. They couldn't stop all Masses."

Lectures were strictly factual, but the discussions afterward often turned to the martial-law crisis. Popular topics continued to be the Katyn massacre and Jaruzelski's World War II record of helping the Soviets against Polish nationalists. Meetings were sometimes broken up, and the lecturers arrested, but most proceeded without incident.

John Paul's thirst for news of his homeland seemed insatiable. He regularly invited Solidarity figures who happened to be in Rome to his apartment for Mass, with a discussion afterward. Jacek Wozniakowski, the founding editor of *Znak*, says he passed through Rome on his way to a teaching stint in France; phoning Dziwisz to see if he could be of service, he was told to be at the Vatican in fifteen minutes. He spent almost all day being grilled by John Paul on everything he had seen and heard.

Workers at the St. Martin's relief depot say they were frequently visited by priests, especially from out of town, inquiring after the condition of arrested people and their families. One young priest came by almost daily: Jerzy Popieluszko, dark, boyish, thin, always hunting medicine for his parish.

"Popieluszko started to grow before my eyes," says Father Michael Czajkowski, a friend from the days when both were chaplains to students. Popieluszko's reputation had spread just before martial law, during the week-long sit-in at the firemen's school, where he was chaplain. Although police had sealed off the school, Popieluszko joined the sit-in by being hoisted over a fence, as Walesa had done at the Gdansk shipyard.

Popieluszko was also chaplain at the steel plant that was Warsaw's largest employer. When union leaders were arrested on Twelve-Thirteen, he stayed close to them. "I felt it was then they needed me most," he later said, "in those difficult times, in prison cells, in the courtrooms where I went to hear the trials."[1]

In February 1982, Popieluszko began a "Mass for the homeland" the last Sunday of each month at the church where he was assistant pastor, in a mostly working-class suburb of Warsaw. Despite his benign appearance, he was a dynamic motivational speaker. Like the pope, Popieluszko urged Poles to stand up for their rights though rejecting violence. As word spread, the monthly sermons attracted thousands of listeners, coming not just from all over Warsaw but soon from all over Poland, overflowing the church and even its spacious courtyard. Popieluszko spoke of "a solidarity of hearts" and "a patriotic struggle to reinstate human dignity."

"The communist government wanted Glemp to move Popieluszko," says Father Hejmo, then on the pope's undercover news team. Not only the government but Glemp himself disdained Popieluszko's populist charisma. Glemp ordered the young priest to study in Rome, but "Popieluszko refused to leave Warsaw, saying it would 'be treason to my people,' " according to a priest who knew him well.

Only the Church's red tape saved Popieluszko and his inspirational sermons. Glemp couldn't easily move him because technically Popieluszko was not attached to Glemp's archdiocese. He had been sent to Warsaw by the bishop of Poznan as a professor of theology, and was assigned to a Warsaw church under its rector. Both the bishop and the rector strongly supported Popieluszko, and Glemp preferred to avoid the unpopular high-level showdown that would have been required to send him away.

In Rome, unsure of what to make of this conflict, John Paul asked a visitor from Warsaw, Bishop Zbigniew Kraszewski, about Popieluszko. "I was his tutor in the seminary!" Kraszewski exclaimed. "I assure you he is God's man, no politician." Kraszewski confirmed that the Polish Church was divided over the wish shared by Glemp and the government to remove the young priest from the spotlight.

From his pocket, the pope pulled the rosary he prayed with and extended it to Kraszewski. "Give this to Father Jerzy and tell him the pope is together with him and prays on his behalf," John Paul said.[2]

A close friend, another well-regarded priest, says Popieluszko "was ecstatic" over the rosary and clutched it often as he persisted with his "Masses for the homeland."

At about this same time, reporter Wilton Wynn of *Time* magazine asked John Paul if he would return to Poland in 1982 for the six-hundredth anniversary of the arrival of the Black Madonna, despite martial law.

The pope paused, then said, "Poland. Martial law. Our Lady. Martial law has been in existence since last December. Our Lady has been with us six hundred years."

Wynn pondered, embarrassed. Was that a yes or a no?

"I have answered the question," the pope replied.

27

In mid-February 1982, John Paul toured Africa's biggest country and three of its smallest. Nigeria's population, already nearing one hundred million and on its way to doubling in thirty years, was half Moslem and just 6 percent Catholic. In the national stadium at Lagos, the pope scolded citizens for letting windfall oil wealth rob Nigeria of its dignity. Nigerian governments, both military and civilian, had been dominated by men who saw their power as a means to private gain.

"It is necessary to reject corruption, bribery, the embezzlement of public funds," John Paul asserted. Yet, as in Zaire, he seemed to blame foreigners:

> When Africa as a whole is left to manage her own affairs without pressure or intervention of . . . foreign groups, she will not only astound the rest of the world by her achievements, but will . . . enable other continents . . . to share in her wisdom, sense of life, and respect for God.

The next decade would not justify the pope's optimism. Even though oil wealth freed Nigeria to shape its outside dealings, it was reduced to an ever more corrupt and dictatorial state. The pope was further disappointed when he tried to address the Church's Moslem problem, which was epitomized in Nigeria. Progressing ever southward from a Sahara base, Islam was converting Christians and animists (spirit worshipers) throughout the country.

The pope not only wanted to expand Catholicism, but still dreamed of cooperation among the world's great religions for the spiritual advancement of mankind. Africa, where spirituality was more real and interdenominational lines were more blurred than perhaps in any other continent, seemed the ideal place to start. But Moslem leaders, unable to agree among themselves on a common stance, canceled scheduled meetings with him.[1]

Still, for John Paul, these political and interfaith defeats in Africa were less important than the shared social values he felt there. Africa's "extended family system provides a loving human environment for the care of orphans, the old, and the poor," he noted. "Children are regarded as a blessing and are desired as the crown of marriage." After Nigeria, John Paul visited tiny Benin, Gabon, and Equatorial Guinea (only four hundred thousand people, but 90 percent Catholic).

One achievement of such visits was summed up by a Nigerian journalist who told *Time* magazine, "To many of our people, the pope is a spiritual figure who lives in heaven and comes down to earth in Rome. . . . Just think what it means to them to understand that he is a real person who cares enough to come see them." Another reason for the pope to travel was that he spread his message by making news. Merely by getting on a plane and showing up someplace unusual while 120 international journalists watched, he drew global attention to the Gospel—and to Poland.

Relief goods piled up in the spacious courtyard outside Wanda Gawronska's office in Rome. She had solicited Italian families to "adopt" an individual Polish family and care for it. "The bell was ringing every five minutes with somebody bringing sugar, jam, stockings, pepper—of course, books," she says.

She began working with Tadeusz Konopka, the former *Tygodnik Powszechny* editor who now represented Solidarity in Rome while drawing a paycheck from Communion and Liberation. He arranged for the ink, paper, and other contraband that was hidden among the relief supplies on Gawronska's donated Fiat truck. Learning of her work, John Paul began inviting Gawronska for dinners with him; it turned out he was pushing for sainthood for her uncle, who had died of polio contracted while helping the sick.

The pope, Konopka says, oversaw "a bridge between Poland and Italy." The Polish pilgrims' center, which had opened in 1979 in a former nuns' home a few blocks from the Vatican, became headquarters for the dozens of Polish churchmen who were in Rome at any given moment. It was a beehive of anticommunist sedition. The little house was just across a narrow street from the giant Jesuit headquarters, so pilgrims often stopped Jesuits on the street for directions and shopping advice. Father O'Keefe, the longtime Jesuit official, remembers constant talk among Poles "about meetings with [Cardinal] Deskur and [Monsignor] Dziwisz. They met with the pope. Pilgrims acted as couriers from Rome."

One thing they carried home was money. Father Kazimierz Przydatek, the Polish Jesuit who ran the pilgrims' center, acquired major importance as banker for the operation. "Przydatek helped the Polish people a lot," says Father Fokcinski, who ran the other major Polish institution, the cultural center, a mile or two away.[2] "People asked him to put them in touch with the Vatican because he was in the Vatican every day. He arranged audiences with the pope."

"Father Przydatek would receive money," Fokcinski says. "He was a chaplain at an exclusive hospital here and knew many important people. He took part in many meetings organized by his friends to raise money for Poland."

Among the friends whom Przydatek received large envelopes of money from was Flavio Carboni, a real-estate developer with a yacht, a private jet, a Lamborghini, and a string of beautiful mistresses. Carboni was also a companion and assistant to Roberto Calvi, whose crooked banking empire was deeply intertwined with IOR, the Vatican bank—where Przydatek, like other priests, kept accounts. Carboni's tolls on the fast lane were paid from multimillion-dollar loans his companies got from Calvi's banks.

Calvi had hired Carboni specifically to revive his troubled relationship with IOR, which wanted Calvi to repay the $300 million he owed. How better to mend fences with IOR than to contribute to the pope's favorite cause? So cash went to Father Przydatek, and thus to Solidarity.

Przydatek's friend Carboni had met Calvi through Francesco Pazienza, the Mafia-connected Italian spy who (as noted earlier) received a $3.5 million payment from IOR through a numbered Swiss bank account. Pazienza had ingratiated himself with the Reagan team even before it moved into the White House, by passing it Italian intelligence secrets about President Carter's brother's dealings with Libya; the resulting mini-scandal had helped Reagan in the 1980 election campaign.[3]

Now Pazienza was feeding the Reagan team information about Arabs and communists, while helping Calvi bribe Italian politicians with loans from Banco Ambrosiano. Pazienza's girlfriend, the niece of film producer Dino De Laurentiis,[4] later testified that on a visit to Pazienza's house she ran into Bettino Craxi, head of the Socialist Party and future prime minister of Italy.

Pazienza now professed a deep interest in Solidarity. He says that Calvi gave Solidarity a lot of money, and that he, Pazienza, helped pass some of it along. Associates say he knew Father Przydatek of the Polish pilgrims' center. Przydatek literally ran from the room in midinterview when I asked him about Pazienza and Carboni, and wouldn't answer further questions when I followed him, asking about them.[5]

Father Przydatek worked closely with socialite Wanda Gawronska on her initiative to send relief and political contraband to Poland. Directly or indirectly, Calvi funneled cash to both of them. It was, effectively, Vatican money—money that Calvi owed to IOR, and that IOR would later pay from its capital.

Gawronska says that at one of the many dinner parties she attended, someone brought Calvi over to her, saying, "This is Wanda Gawronska, she is raising money for Poland." She says Calvi apologized for not having his checkbook with him, then pulled a hundred million lira out of his pocket—worth about a hundred thousand dollars at the time—and handed it to her. She says she was stunned: she had never dreamed that anyone walked around with so much cash, and now she feared having to carry it home.

For Calvi, gifts to Solidarity must have seemed a wise way to invest just a tiny percentage of the money he was stealing.

☙

That spring, 1982, Solidarity Radio went on the air from multiple, roving locations. Like the underground newspapers, the radio, over the next years, would persuade Poles that Solidarity lived, and that the communists could not stamp it out. At first, the radio was operated by Zbigniew Romaszewski, the KOR member who had linked up with fellow physicist Andrei Sakharov in the USSR.

In his book *Victory,* Schweizer and his Reagan administration sources claim that Romaszewski used CIA-supplied transmitters and that Solidarity Radio was thus a White House product. This scenario has been widely repeated (by papal biographer Carl Bernstein, among others), but Romaszewski calls it "complete rubbish." So do Ryszard Kolyszko and Bogdan Borucewicz—who really *did* provide the transmitters for Solidarity Radio.

"It was not any connection with the CIA whatsoever," says an irate Kolyszko, now a telecommunications consultant in California. "It was my own initiative. It was a very important part of my life. I am quite proud of it." His wife, a Krakow native, has been a friend of the pope's since youth. Kolyszko built the first transmitter "in deep secret," just before martial law, to help Solidarity leaders coordinate strikes. It fit into an attaché case. Martial law halted the strikes, but when Romaszewski came to him suggesting public broadcasts, Kolyszko still had the transmitter. He built half a dozen more, subsequently used by various Solidarity broadcasters.

Borucewicz, the KOR member who recruited Lech Walesa into the union, thought the radio was such a good idea that he ordered many more transmitters, for use in Gdansk and other cities. They were built, he says, by Solidarity scientists who worked in a plant that made transmitters for the Soviet space program. Some were convicted and jailed for sneaking out transmitters and parts. These men are deeply offended by persistent stories crediting the CIA with the work they did, which was very effective.

"The radius [of a broadcast] was just six or eight kilometers," says Konstanty Gebert, the journalist known then under the name David Varshawski. "But it was announced in the [underground] press that it would come on at a certain time and frequency. They would end the broadcast saying, 'Everyone listening, blink your lights,' and a whole housing development would blink."

As a further show of defiance, when government news programs came on television, people would go outside to prove they weren't watching. They put candles in windows when the government switched off the electricity at curfew.

The most wanted man in Poland, Zbigniew Bujak, depended on Radio Free Europe, particularly on Sundays and Wednesdays, when the pope routinely spoke in public. Invariably, John Paul would give a moment to the Poles—to let them know "that he approves of us, is with us," Bujak recalls now, in his Parliamentary office. (He is a senator.) "For us in the underground, what was important was to hear about Solidarity as existing. Each time, when he would talk about freedom, Polish society, resistance, they were signals of support."

With the help of Ewa Kulik and her supply of secret hideouts, Bujak and four other fugitive leaders met on April 22, 1982, and established themselves as a Temporary Coordinating Commission to decide policy for Solidarity. They knew that since martial law, Solidarity had become an amorphous organization without dues, formal membership, or command structure. In effect, Solidarity was every Pole with hope in his heart.

That hope was fueled by the coordinating commission. Over the months and years, its makeup changed (except for Bujak). But its decisions continued to be disseminated by the underground press and radio.

Bogdan Lis of Gdansk was the commission member assigned to foreign affairs. In tiny lettering, on the fine paper that tailors use to mark alterations, Lis wrote out the committee's first command communiqué and smuggled it to Jerzy Milewski, in New York. The commission officially assigned Milewski the task he had been doing unofficially ever since his laser conference in New Orleans: organizing and running an office abroad to attract political and economic support, and to represent Solidarity, particularly with other trade unions.

Milewski gave up a twenty-five-year career as a research physicist to help run a nonviolent guerrilla movement. Like Chojecki, he had gone to the Reagan administration for help and been brushed off. For years, he corresponded with the coordinating commission using coded computer diskettes, or messages sealed in plastic inside spray deodorant cans that had been opened, resealed, and repressurized.

Radio Free Europe gave Poles another big morale boost by broadcasting Cardinal Wyszynski's prison memoir.[6] Father Modzelewski had published the memoir in France after receiving it from the late primate on his deathbed and smuggling it out of Poland with the funeral entourage. It was read on Radio Free Europe, for forty minutes each night.

Listening to these broadcasts soon became such an event that the government told Archbishop Dabrowski it would allow twenty thousand copies of the memoir into Poland if the readings stopped. At Dabrowski's request, the radio agreed; but when the Russians saw the books, they vetoed the deal. By then, however, the underground press had got hold of the memoir, and it was everywhere. Father Modzelewski soon received a lunch invitation to the papal apartment, from a delighted pope.[7]

Another Vatican lunch was arranged for Zdzislaw Najder, of Radio Free Europe in Munich. The pope told Najder he was "doing a very important job" carrying "great responsibility," and reached out several times to touch him for emphasis. After asking about Najder's family, John Paul said, approvingly, that he knew Najder had run a group that published underground anti-communist pamphlets in the 1970s. "We share a belief in Solidarity," John Paul said. "I am with you."

"What was remarkable about the conversation," Najder says, "was the pope's enthusiasm for Solidarity, his deep emotion"—and also what came across as his strongly critical view of Cardinal Glemp. Although the pope never used explicitly negative language, Najder says, "he pointed out repeatedly that there were differences between the way the two of them thought, and that what Glemp said should not necessarily be construed as representing what the pope thought."

Other sources, including a cardinal who spoke not for attribution, say it appeared that on two trips Glemp made to Rome in early 1982, the pope bawled him out for criticizing Solidarity instead of supporting it. After each rebuke, Glemp went to the Polish church in Rome and delivered a pro-Solidarity message.

Najder even allowed some criticism of Glemp onto the air. During regular meetings with Dziwisz when he was in Rome, Najder was constantly reminded that Solidarity was an expression of John Paul's whole philosophy of civil life. "Solidarity was a trade union that rejected class divisions," Najder says. "The same union belonged to janitors and university professors. That was the basis for it in the pope's eyes—a concern not just with living standards but [with] the whole human condition. Unlike traditional trade unions or political parties, it was both at the same time."

Archbishop Dabrowski visited John Paul soon after Najder did. He says the pope coyly teased him about the depot at St. Martin's Church, which both men knew, but could not say, was being used for more than just relief supplies.

"What are you doing over there on Piwna Street [where St. Martin's is located]?" the pope asked.

"We are trying to answer the questions that life is giving us," Dabrowski says he replied. "He is a very wise ruler," Dabrowski adds. "He does not give unnecessary advice. He just encourages us: 'Do it. Go further.' He always asked if there were any new jokes in Warsaw."

Like other churchmen, Dabrowski was given money to take home from Rome: "At that time, dollars could be sold on the black market. Whenever someone brought me money and wanted some kind of receipt, I said, 'You either trust me or you don't. If you need a signature, take it [the money] away.' At the time, it was impossible to keep books."

28

In mid-May 1982, John Paul sent a friendly delegation to an antinuclear conference in Moscow. The White House went all-out trying to scuttle the conference, calling it a propaganda effort to block American deployment of new missiles in Western Europe. The pope had already denounced the new missiles.

Reagan insisted that additional missiles were necessary because "the Soviet Union does have a definite margin of superiority." Without the missiles, he said, the United States offered "a window of vulnerability." These were among many such remarks, all intended to persuade the public that the Pentagon needed more money to catch up to the Soviets.[1]

Like other Soviet "advantages" over the years—such as the "missile gap" John F. Kennedy had complained of when he ran for President—Reagan's was an illusion. Carter's 1979 State of the Union address noted correctly that one Poseidon submarine carried enough warheads "to destroy every large and medium-sized city in the Soviet Union." From the first bomb in 1945, the U.S. had maintained wide nuclear superiority.

Yet behind the scenes, the White House pleaded with American Protestant leaders to boycott the peace conference in Moscow. Popular evangelist Billy Graham and the leaders of many major denominations defied Reagan and attended anyway. Administration officials called in Archbishop Bernardin and his committee to try to talk them out of their proposed statement on war; the two sides just butted heads. Almost all of Christianity seemed to be at odds with Washington on weapons.

May 13 was the anniversary of both the assassination attempt on John Paul and the 1917 report by three shepherd children that Mary had appeared to them in Fatima, Portugal. The pope spent the day at Fatima, to the discomfort of some Western Catholics who weren't sure they wanted their pope to validate a modern-day miracle. John Paul felt no such apprehension.

"As soon as I recovered my consciousness after the attack," he said, "my thoughts turned instinctively toward this shrine, and I wanted to express here my gratitude to our Heavenly Mother for having saved my life.... In the designs of Providence there are no mere coincidences."

Almost as he said these words, security guards foiled a second assassination attempt, this one by a priest who lunged at John Paul with a knife—a priest who had been ordained illegally by Archbishop Lefebvre, the Frenchman who refused to accept Vatican II. Ever since John Paul began his papacy by trying to make peace with Lefebvre, the Frenchman had continued to assert that the Church was being destroyed by a "Marxist movement" within the Vatican.

In Warsaw, an underground weekly published an open letter from Jacek Kuron, whose months of isolated confinement had cut him off from the spirit of Polish society. He predicted "mass insurrection . . . the overthrow of the government!" and called for a strong, centrally controlled Solidarity. Echoing President Reagan, he said, "If you don't want war, prepare yourself for it." According to Schweizer, Reagan loved Kuron's letter and kept a copy in his Oval Office desk drawer to show to visitors.

In Poland, however, the letter was rebuked. Bujak and a deputy responded by quoting with approval Kuron's own earlier words: "Violence breeds violence . . . and the spiral of terror cannot be broken by terror." From their cells, Michnik and other leaders issued similar rejoinders, compassionate but clear. Says Gebert, the underground Solidarity journalist, "We said that violence, even if successful, was counterproductive. It was extremely exciting, but all it achieved was getting people beaten and in jail, sometimes dead. Our idea was organizing people. That the nonviolent strategy could count on the Church as an ally was very important."

When John Paul's Krakow friend Jacek Wozniakowski stopped at the Vatican on his way back from France, the pope gave him written and oral messages for Bujak and other Solidarity leaders. "Tell these people that I support their fight," he said. "Tell them I am on their side." Bujak and others say the personalized papal messages Wozniakowski painstakingly went around delivering to them were like a blood transfusion, especially in the face of Glemp's lack of support.

At public appearances that he knew would be widely reported, John Paul seemed at times to slip the word *solidarity* into almost every sentence. "There is one characteristic that is a requirement," he told a UN meeting in Geneva. "Solidarity. . . . Today, a new solidarity must be forged . . . an open and dynamic solidarity. . . ."

In late May 1982, John Paul had to decide whether to cancel a scheduled trip to England—the first-ever papal visit there—because of a war brewing in the Falkland Islands, off the coast of Argentina. Although the pope had mediated away Argentina's proposed war with Chile in 1979, the Argentine generals had achieved their war anyway, by grabbing the Falklands, with their sheep ranches and eighteen hundred British settlers. Now Britain was launching an expeditionary force to reclaim the islands, and the pope didn't want to take sides.

The British trip had seemed plagued from the beginning. Just weeks before, a joint commission exploring a merger of the Anglican and Roman churches had broken up after twelve years, claiming progress but not showing much. The Anglicans later said their side had offered to recognize "the primacy of the bishop of Rome" (while denying a scriptural basis for that primacy) but wouldn't give him as much authority as the Catholics insisted on. Compromise seemed impossible.

Although papal trips are normally scheduled in detail months in advance, six days before departure, the pope was still trying to salvage this one. At a Mass for peace attended by British and Argentine officials and churchmen in St. Peter's, he urged negotiations. He begged British Prime Minister Thatcher not to attack, and Argentina to withdraw its troops from the Falklands. Both refused. With three days to spare, Cardinal Hume of England rescued the trip by persuading the two Argentine cardinals to schedule a visit for the pope to Argentina the next month as an equalizer.

At eight A.M. May 28, 1982, John Paul kissed the runway at London's Gatwick Airport. At a joint "Celebration of Faith" at the Anglican cathedral, Robert Runcie, the archbishop of Canterbury, said that Christian unity was "not in the past only, but also in the future." Quoting the fourth-century Nicene Creed, Runcie and John Paul affirmed their belief in "one holy catholic and apostolic Church"—but didn't say *which* Church. Their sermons were designed with a common theme: martyrs of our time. But whereas John Paul chose to talk about Father Kolbe (the Polish priest who had volunteered to die in place of another prisoner at Auschwitz), Runcie chose—Archbishop Romero!

The pope said several open-air Masses in London and Liverpool. Although the crowds were as large as 350,000, they fell far short of the million that had been expected. Many Britons evidently didn't want to be scolded, either for their moral habits or for sending troops overseas to take back islands that had been seized by force (by Britain in 1832, then by Argentina in 1982). Implicit in John Paul's message was a condemnation of the Falklands expedition:

> Wherever the strong exploit the weak . . . wherever great powers seek to dominate . . . there the cathedral of peace is again destroyed. Today the scale and horror of modern warfare—whether nuclear or not—makes it totally unacceptable as a means of settling differences between nations.

In an airborne press conference afterward, when a reporter asked John Paul about Saint Augustine's theory that war could be just under certain circumstances, he replied that the whole notion of a "just war" might have been rendered obsolete by technology.

29

June 7, 1982, John Paul gave a Vatican audience to President Reagan, officially lasting forty-five minutes. It was five days after his British trip, and four days before he left for Argentina. The pope was publicly and privately trying to roll back Israel's invasion of Lebanon the day before.

Carl Bernstein, of Watergate reporting fame, wrote a cover article for *Time* magazine, February 24, 1992, claiming that at this meeting, Reagan and John Paul "agreed to undertake a clandestine campaign to hasten the dissolution of the communist empire." Suggesting that the meeting was a turning point in world history, Bernstein and *Time* dubbed it "The Holy Alliance"—a joint Reagan–John Paul guerrilla action run mostly by the White House.

By all indications, however, the meeting was merely ceremonial. Reagan himself was rebounding from an awful three-day summit meeting in France of the seven non-communist financial powers, at which his fellow heads of state had unanimously repudiated him in his main objective, halting a pipeline to bring Soviet natural gas to Western Europe. The pope had also opposed Reagan on the pipeline, loudly and publicly.

Although exactly what the pope and the President said to each other remains private, persons around them say they talked about the mystical significance Reagan saw in the fact that both had survived assassination attempts in the spring of 1981: an inch's variation in the course of the bullets would have left both men dead.

Reagan's longtime friend and counselor Edwin Meese says that Reagan (who now suffers from Alzheimer's disease) thought that by far the major event of his European trip was his speech to the British Parliament, consigning communism to "the ash heap of history" (and supporting the British attack on the Falklands). "He didn't talk as if he regarded the meeting [with John Paul] as particularly important," Meese says, adding, "I don't think there was any secret agreement." Others who knew the two leaders agree.

Yet the image from Bernstein's article etched itself into the conventional wisdom of Americans, even those who never read it. The *Time* article made big news around the world, and Bernstein got a contract to write a book based on it. If there had been such a "Holy Alliance," its triumph would tend to vindicate the risks taken, and money spent, by Reagan's Cold Warriors. Even the book about the end of communism that is most favored by so-called "liberal" scholars—Raymond L. Garthoff's *The Great Transition*[1]—accepts the notion of a "Holy Alliance" and credits Bernstein with providing "the most full account."

Yes—but full of what?

In both its overall thesis and its details, the Bernstein *Time* cover article was a work of fiction from beginning to end. It laid the foundation for Peter Schweizer's later book; based on the same self-serving, "leaked" fabrications, both works attributed Solidarity's victory to the Reagan White House. Like Schweizer after him, Bernstein wrote that Solidarity's underground press and radio were the products of a White House operation in which the pope was involved. We have already seen that this isn't true, and that the real wellsprings of the Solidarity underground began to flow long before June 1982.

After stating his thesis, Bernstein produced a quote from then Deputy CIA Director Bobby Ray Inman; though the words would have been innocuous in isolation, their placement suggested that Inman supported Bernstein's theory. Inman doesn't. "If there had been a major plan, a major agreement, it most likely is something I would have seen," Inman says. "I never heard of it."

The article did the same thing with Brzezinski, quoting general remarks by him about Solidarity and CIA Director Casey as if Brzezinski backed up what Bernstein was saying. On the contrary, Brzezinski says Bernstein's *Time* article was "baloney! The pope wouldn't discuss that kind of stuff, and Reagan never got into that kind of detail." The Vatican also categorically denies that any such alliance was made that day or ever, and says the meeting "may have" lasted only half an hour.[2]

Bernstein reported that as part of the alliance, Cardinal Krol "frequently met with Casey to discuss support for Solidarity and covert operations." "Absolutely not!" Krol shouted at me indignantly when I read him quotes from the *Time* article. "I never sat independently with Casey. I met him once after I said the invocation at the Republican Convention. It was a greeting, not a meeting." Krol said they never discussed Solidarity ("Absolutely not!") or any other international politics ("Absolutely not!").

Bernstein further stated that Krol met with National Security Director Clark. "Never!" Krol told me. Clark says, "I don't recall meeting with Cardinal Krol on any matter."

Bernstein said the Vatican agreed to help the CIA "deal with the Contras," a violent guerrilla group that the administration had secretly organized to try to overthrow the government of Nicaragua.[3]

He asserted that Cardinal Pio Laghi, then the papal representative in the United States, "played a key role by assuring Contra leaders that the administration delivered on its promises."

Laghi (who is often mentioned as a possible successor to John Paul) denies ever talking to any Contras on behalf of the Reagan administration. To the contrary, he told me that the only meeting he arranged concerning the Contra war was for Daniel Ortega, head of the Nicaraguan government that the Contras and the United States were trying to overthrow; Laghi says he knew Ortega from when he was papal nuncio in Nicaragua, and helped him meet some congressmen.

Cardinal Laghi, like others, says Bernstein quoted him out of context to imply that he was a source for the Holy Alliance idea. Laghi interrupted my questions six separate times to exclaim—as if I might have missed his point previously—"There was no Holy Alliance!" Contrary to Bernstein's assertions, Laghi says he never discussed Poland with CIA Director Casey, and only briefly with National Security Adviser Clark.

Laghi went out of his way to stress for me the Vatican's differences with Reagan. "We are not in the same line," he says. "He [Reagan] fought the Soviet Union, which he saw expanding into Latin America. We are in the line of human rights. This is not our trade, armaments and military." Laghi says Reagan overemphasized the coincidence of the two shootings, and that the President "was superstitious."

Generals Vernon Walters and Edward Rowny, Reagan envoys who periodically briefed John Paul on U.S. intelligence collections, both deny that they and the pope ever discussed taking any action, or that any action was taken as a result of their meetings. "Never did the pope say, 'That's the right thing to do.' None of that," Rowny says. "It was very much just a proper one-way street."

Bernstein reported that as part of the Holy Alliance, Reagan agreed to reverse the American policy of providing birth-control aid overseas. General Walters says it's "silly" to think that Reagan changed U.S. policy on birth-control as part of a papal agreement; Reagan always opposed federal birth-control programs, he says. General Walters calls Bernstein's article "fantastic," adding, "The idea of some sort of Holy Alliance is just not related to the fact."

John Whitehead says he is sure that when he became assistant secretary of state for Eastern Europe three years later, he got all relevant information. He declares, "I would be amazed if there was anything significant that came out of that June 1982 meeting that had to do with Poland. Ronald Reagan never talked about the meeting. He never went to church. Or his wife."

Bernstein's main quoted source for details in the "Holy Alliance" article (apart from anonymous "CIA sources") was Edward Derwinski, a former Republican congressman from Illinois who became secretary of veterans' affairs in the Bush administration. Bernstein says Derwinski met often with Casey to discuss Poland. He quotes Derwinski as saying that as part of the Holy Alliance plan, "Monsignor Bronislaw Dabrowski, a deputy to Cardinal Glemp, came to us often to tell us what was needed; he would meet with me, with Casey, the NSC [National Security Council] and sometimes with Walters."

Dabrowski, Glemp's deputy, who became an archbishop in July 1982, not only denies the Bernstein story but offered me his passports to prove that his only trip to the United States was in 1975, and that he was not in the U.S. when the alleged meetings took place.[4] General Walters denies ever meeting Dabrowski. Former Congressman Derwinski didn't respond to my many detailed fax and telephone inquiries.

"The whole story of my special missions was just made up," Archbishop Dabrowski complains. Worse, he says, he repeatedly complained to the major Italian newspaper that reprinted "the slanders of that American" (referring to Bernstein), but no correction ever appeared.[5]

Schweizer says that after the Reagan-pope meeting, the CIA began pumping eight million dollars a year into Solidarity. Bernstein later reported the identical figure, without naming a source.

The former Solidarity underground workers I have met all say the eight-million-dollar figure is ludicrous. Schweizer attributes the information to Glenn Campbell, former head of the President's Foreign Intelligence Advisory Board, who then became president of the Hoover Institute at Stanford University (which subsidized Schweizer's work). When I asked him about this, Campbell said he had "no recollection" of where he got the figure of eight million. "It may have been an estimate," he said. "We were supposed to be making sure there was no wrongdoing. Casey always told us as little as possible. I've never been to Poland."

Father Hejmo, then running the pope's secret news network, says his operation "didn't receive even one dollar" from Uncle Sam, though individual Polish-Americans donated a little.

Inside Poland, Ewa Kulik, who was hiding Zbigniew Bujak and other leaders, was scraping by on newspaper sales, small private donations, and the aid from abroad already described. She says she is sure no money came from the U.S. government. Of the Bernstein-Schweizer stories, she says, "Somebody who wrote that had not the faintest idea of how things were in Poland."

Grzegorz Pollak, then at *Wiez*, Wojtyla's old Krakow monthly, says he, too, was seeking funds, so that *Wiez* could hire Solidarity journalists who lost their government jobs. "I'm absolutely positive" the CIA wasn't supplying funds, he says.

Others agree, and say Bernstein never tried to talk to them before writing his article. Three weeks after the Reagan-pope meeting, Jerzy Milewski, the laser physicist who officially headed Solidarity's international fund-raising effort, moved his office from the United States to Brussels, on orders from the Solidarity commission inside Poland, because much more money was available in

Europe. Milewski and Joanna Pilarska, a Solidarity officer who was smuggled out of Poland to be his deputy in Brussels, both swear that no money came from the U.S. government.

In fact, Milewski and Pilarska say, they requested a meeting with Reagan, thinking a photograph of them with the President and a few kind words from him would help with their fund-raising. They say the White House, afraid of such publicity, turned down their repeated entreaties, until they were finally allowed to see Reagan three years later, in 1985.

By then, some U.S. taxpayer money was finally reaching them—but all of it, they say, channeled through the AFL-CIO.

Bernstein's *Time* article represented AFL-CIO President Lane Kirkland, who organized that aid, as being "literally... in lockstep with the administration." Kirkland, whose unions were decimated by the Reagan administration, has this to say about the Bernstein article (he is, after all, a labor leader): "It's a crock of shit."

30

One more urgent matter was probably diverting John Paul when he met Reagan: IOR. Banker Roberto Calvi's drama was finally nearing its grim climax.

Back in March, Monsignor Hilary Franco, an American in the Congregation for the Clergy, was asked by an Italian lawyer he knew to meet with a businessman: Flavio Carboni. Franco apparently didn't know of Carboni's playboy life, his work for Calvi, or his passing money to Solidarity at the Polish pilgrims' center. Carboni introduced Franco to Calvi.

"I am undergoing an emotional and spiritual crisis," the famous banker told the puzzled monsignor. "I desperately need your religious guidance. I want to be sure to be received positively at the Vatican bank." Franco tried to help. Since Archbishop Marcinkus was at that moment in Britain with the pope, Franco arranged an appointment with Luigi Mennini, Marcinkus's managing director at IOR, apparently not realizing that Calvi had met with Mennini often on his own.[1]

If Carboni was reaching out to friends of friends—like Monsignor Franco— to get Calvi a Vatican appointment, one can only imagine how he must have pressured Father Przydatek, to whom he had given good money and who really had an entree to the pope.[2] Calvi was desperate. Italian investigators later found records showing that Marcinkus had been exchanging phone calls with Francesco Pazienza, the Mafia-connected military-intelligence agent who worked for Calvi; in one instance, Marcinkus left an "urgent" message for Pazienza.[3]

Meanwhile, Calvi trotted the globe seeking another bank he could coax into his network to keep his scheme going. He wrote a gushing letter to John Paul, though the Vatican says the pope never saw it. Calvi's second in command at Banco Ambrosiano was wounded by a would-be assassin; the gunman, shot dead by guards, was identified as a former business partner of Carboni's.

As late as May 3, 1982, *Panorama*, a leading Italian magazine, carried an interview in which Marcinkus stated, "Calvi is worthy of our trust. I have no reason to doubt him. We have no intention of selling the [Ambrosiano] shares in our possession."

At the meeting Monsignor Franco set up, May 31, Mennini refused Calvi's pleas to extend the June 30 deadline for nearly $300 million in payments to IOR. Mennini probably didn't know that in the nine months since IOR had issued letters guaranteeing the debts of Calvi's companies, Calvi had borrowed an additional $170 million.[4] Executives at Ambrosiano certainly didn't know that the solvency of their giant bank rested on payments due from a network of companies secretly controlled by Calvi, which didn't have the money.

June 10, the night before John Paul was to fly to Argentina, Calvi left a note saying he was tired and going away for a few days. Actually, he merely left one Rome apartment for another, both having been arranged for him by Carboni. Calvi's passport had been confiscated after his criminal conviction, but Carboni had forged him a new one.

The next night, Calvi's wife, Clara, and son, Carlo, got a call from Pazienza in London, announcing that Calvi was being taken to London by professional kidnapers hired by Carboni.[5]

John Paul, meanwhile, was having a terrible time in Argentina. His plane taxied to the wrong spot at the Buenos Aires airport, forcing the bishops who were there to greet him to dash across the tarmac clutching their cassocks "like characters from a Fellini film" (one reporter wrote). Most Argentine priests and nuns supported the Falklands war. As John Paul pleaded for peace, generals hung at his side, and banners urged, "Holy Father bless our just war," and "May God defend our cause because we defend his."

In the war fever, no one talked about the repression that had "disappeared" some twenty thousand Argentine dissidents. A few years later, after partial democracy returned, a commission accused fifteen priests of having taken part in the slaughter—even witnessing and encouraging torture—while most of their fellow clergy stayed silent.[6]

The last day of the pope's visit, June 12, a final battle broke out in the Falklands. The British won, in a rout. Within a week, dictator Leopoldo Galtieri resigned and Argentina began inching toward democracy.

Barely was the pope back at the Vatican, his peace mission frustrated, when officials at Banco Ambrosiano became alarmed over the disappearance of their boss, Roberto Calvi. On June 16, several of them visited IOR, bringing the letters from the previous September, in which IOR pledged responsibility for huge debts owed to Ambrosiano. For the first time, the Ambrosiano men saw the companion letter Calvi had given back to IOR, saying it didn't have to pay. They were shocked.

June 17, the head of Calvi's Italian holding company appealed personally to Marcinkus. Unless IOR paid, he said, the holding company would collapse, as would one after another related company, until ultimately, Ambrosiano itself would fail. When that happened, the public was bound to find out about the letters IOR had given Calvi. "Don't you at IOR want to save your own faces?" the executive asked.

"I made a mistake," Marcinkus replied. "I realize I'm going to have to pay a high price for that personally. Whatever happens to our faces, we just don't have that kind of money."

The executive returned to Banco Ambrosiano with the bad news. Ambrosiano notified the Bank of Italy that it was insolvent. Calvi's fifty-five-year-old spinster secretary read the announcement, walked to the window, and jumped to her death.

The next morning, June 18, 1982, Calvi's own body was found hanging from the Blackfriars Bridge over the River Thames in London. A "blackfriar" is a Dominican priest, and many assumed the choice of bridge conveyed a message. As it turned out, the bridge was more likely chosen because scaffolding erected for repairs made the hanging easier.

Police and newspapermen began scurrying for answers to the question of how so prominent a banker, so closely connected at the Vatican, could have met such an end. *Osservatore Romano* complained that the scandalous stories "offend elementary canons . . . and are completely lacking in seriousness. . . . The insinuations have not spared the person of the Holy Father himself."

Solidarity's new international headquarters in Brussels got a windfall infusion of $1.6 million from French trade unions (mostly socialist ones, opposed to American policy). Jerzy Milewski, running the office, relayed money for radio and printing equipment to Miroslaw Chojecki, who had failed to find such help in Washington. Chojecki in turn smuggled goods to Joanna Szczesna, who was helping run his underground publishing empire in his absence.

"The representatives of five different trade unions were monitoring the raising of this money," Chojecki says. "It is just impossible that all five unions had their loyalties to the CIA." Szczesna agrees that the funds could not have come from American sources without her knowing. Milewski and his aide Pilarska, and Bogdan Borucewicz, their liaison with the underground leadership inside Poland, all concur.*

Expatriate Poles in France sent Chojecki to Marian Kaleta, a sympathetic Swedish optometrist who exported eye-examination equipment. Chojecki put Kaleta in touch with a boat captain in Gdansk who would smuggle goods past customs. After that, print and broadcast equipment acquired in Paris and Brussels began flowing to Kaleta, who smuggled it into Poland either concealed in his shipments of optometry equipment or on the boat that evaded customs.

Monsignor Fidelus, Cardinal Macharski's deputy in Krakow, traveled regularly by car to Rome, where Papal Secretary Dziwisz "told me to give this to this person, that to that person. Money, material, whatever somebody asked for"—including contraband.

The communists "did not make any problem concerning food, medicine, or clothing," Fidelus says. "Most difficult was to bring paper and printing machines. We had to convince them that this material would be used for religious purposes." Fidelus now acknowledges that he turned over the printing supplies to the Solidarity political organization, though—perhaps to salve his own priestly conscience about lying—he says part of every shipment really *was* used for religious literature, if only a small part.

He says Dziwisz had persuaded the Polish authorities to waive customs duties on imported goods, which arrived in twenty-ton truck shipments that Dziwisz also arranged. "Probably each priest in this curia, in each diocese, was involved in this work," Fidelus says.

Many trucks carried up to two thousand dollars in cash, in five-, ten-, and twenty-dollar U.S. bills. The money went into the curia safe, from which Cardinal Macharski withdrew it as needed. Through all the problems with Primate Glemp in Warsaw, Macharski, by all reports, remained a trusted, loyal ally of John Paul's and Dziwisz's.[7]

"A little [money] went a long way in the black market," says biologist Anna Krzysztowicz of Jagiellonian University, who handled cash, relief supplies, and contraband as a volunteer at the Krakow curia. The communists had concentrated on jailing students of law, history, and literature, Professor Krzyszto-

* Seweryn Blumsztajn, the Solidarity journalist working with Chojecki in France, and Bohdan Cywinski, who sometimes visited him there, remember general laughter over communist propaganda that Solidarity depended on the CIA. "We used to joke that our only problem was [that] the CIA *didn't* want to supply us with this money," Blumsztajn says. If I risk overkill on this point, it is because the opposite has been so widely reported and so thoroughly accepted.

wicz says, so her science students were mostly free to deliver goods where they were needed. Funds came from Church collections, in Italian parishes by Communion and Liberation, and around the world by various religious orders— "for the pope's sake," Fidelus says.

Compared to the huge cost of wars being fought elsewhere, Solidarity's First Amendment–style activities required only one million to three million dollars a year, though more money would have helped, says Wojciech Arkuszewski, Mazowiecki's deputy. (Arkuszewski, a fugitive, was hidden during martial law by a Calvinist minister whom he had met at Cardinal Wojtyla's ecumenical events.) "A million dollars could keep a thousand full-time people underground, plus all the people who would cooperate with each of them," Arkuszewski says. Even today, he adds, "If I had five million dollars a year, I could deconstruct China."

Solidarity partisans became angry that the United States wouldn't help. Bishop Dembowski, then a priest at St. Martin's, compares it to the dark days of 1939, when "we did our best with the Nazis and nobody on the Western side helped us. And we remembered that. There can be many beautiful words, but when the bloodshed starts, nobody will help."

Bohdan Cywinski says John Paul himself "was very distant from and distrustful of the United States." Cywinski once stopped by the Vatican on his way back from Brussels, where everyone had complained that fund drives were much less productive in the U.S. than elsewhere. The pope fairly exploded with "a warning to me," Cywinski says.

"Are you aware of how politically interested the Americans are?" the pope said. He was using questions as he often did, to dull the edge of what were really harsh judgments. "Are you aware they are always out to get what they want? Always trying to fulfill their goals?"

Cywinski was rocked back on his heels by this display of emotion from the usually unflappable John Paul. "It led me to believe he couldn't have been working too closely with them," Cywinski recalls with a smile.

Bishop Pieronek remembers hearing "circles of Italian cardinals"—whom he refuses to name—criticizing the pope's preoccupation with "Polish political events." Pieronek protests that "it wasn't politics. It was human morality."

The St. Martin's operation was almost closed down in the summer of 1982 when a not-very-bright volunteer courier from Belgium allowed himself to be followed by police as he carried two undisguised radio transmitters into the church. They were immediately seized.

"We never gave any church, especially St. Martin's, as an address" for undisguised contraband, says Kulik, still angry over the incident. Romaszewski's wife saved the operation by accepting responsibility, going to jail, and allowing her fugitive husband to stay in hiding. The bishops managed to persuade the authorities that the St. Martin's staff was innocent.

But the government postponed John Paul's scheduled visit home. Jozef Czyrek, the foreign minister, came to Rome to deliver the news, telling the pope it "was too early after martial law, too emotional." For an hour and twenty minutes, John Paul "argued for an earlier visit, and said he prayed for releasing the prisoners," Czyrek says. "He stressed that in really difficult times he wanted to be with the people—how important it was for him, and for Poles." In the end, the pope had little choice but to agree to wait until 1983. In exchange for his accepting the postponement, Jaruzelski freed a thousand prisoners, including most women.

August 1, 1982, the anniversary of the Warsaw Uprising, crowds too big for the police to easily disperse demonstrated illegally around Wyszynski's marker in Victory Square. Other demonstrators gathered at a memorial for Katyn massacre victims. Suddenly over loudspeakers came the taped voice of Zbigniew Bujak, still a fugitive. Solidarity lived, he proclaimed. The crowds cheered.

In a Warsaw theater, Halina Mikolajska, an actress associated with Solidarity and only recently released from prison, opened in a classical play; she was greeted each night with an ovation before her performance.

Romaszewski, the founder of Solidarity Radio, was caught and arrested. His colleagues kept the broadcasts running.*

On the anniversary of Solidarity's founding, August 31, police shot dead two nonviolent demonstrators in Lublin and used fire hoses to wash away flow-

---

* Reagan national security advisers Robert McFarlane and John Poindexter told writer Peter Schweizer that Solidarity relied on CIA-arranged coded broadcast messages to secure shipments of contraband. This assertion is denied by Chojecki and Romaszewski, who arranged many shipments; by Bujak and Kulik, who supposedly received the messages; and by de Weydenthal and Najder of Radio Free Europe, who supposedly sent them. Chojecki says that after the two transmitters were intercepted at St. Martin's Church, leading to the arrest of the Romaszewskis, he asked to send coded signals to Poland to ensure better rendezvouses in the future. But he says officials at both Voice of America and Radio Free Europe turned him down, on the ground that hidden messages would betray the integrity of the broadcasts. He understood.

De Weydenthal says it is an important point because the Reagan administration replaced broadcast professionals with politicians in top management, causing a battle within Radio Free Europe. "The new administration wanted to push the limits," he says—to make accuracy take a backseat to political effect. "But once you start to exaggerate, like comparing Jaruzelski to Hitler, you lose trust." Najder and a supervising official confirm this story and say the professional staff held the line against political interference. Radio Free Europe stands as a spectacularly successful example of First Amendment–oriented U.S. aid in the Cold War.

ers placed at the scene. Flowers put on Wyszynski's grave in Warsaw were alternately hosed away and replaced all day. Four thousand demonstrators were arrested, and four KOR members charged with capital crimes, though in the end no one was executed.

Glemp offered to call for an end to the demonstrations if the government 1) released Walesa, 2) announced a timetable for releasing others, and 3) allowed a gradual resumption of a scaled-down Solidarity. The government responded with such a verbal vengeance against the Church as to recall the 1950s. John Paul addressed the Polish question in his first appearance after returning from Castelgandolfo, offering no deal, merely insisting that "Solidarity and Rural Solidarity" must be relegalized and invited into the councils of government.

Hearing of the increased hostilities, Konrad Bielinski—Ewa Kulik's boyfriend, arrested on Twelve-Thirteen—conspired with doctor friends on the outside to feign an illness. Admitted to a hospital, he fled out a service door and was soon reunited with Kulik.

31

John Paul had aimed to make a spectacle of keeping his secret postelection promise to Opus Dei, the controversial international Catholic group. He planned to elevate it to roughly the status of a religious order (by calling it a personal prelature) during a scheduled trip to Spain, the land of Opus Dei's founding, in October 1982. But fifty-five of the sixty-four Spanish bishops stunned him by objecting to the new status. Italian and French bishops likewise voted against it. When Cardinal Joseph Höffner of Cologne, Germany, assigned two Opus Dei priests to parishes, the parishioners wrote so many furious letters— comparing them to "Moonies," among other things—that the priests withdrew.

In England, Cardinal Hume tried to clamp down on Opus Dei after receiving many complaints about it. He ordered the group to stop extracting vows of long-term commitment from persons under eighteen. He decreed that young people wishing to join must first discuss it with their parents, that members must be free to leave without pressure and to consult outside priests, and that all Opus Dei activities must be clearly labeled as such. In a passive show of defiance, Opus Dei's British spokesman thanked Hume and assured him Opus Dei had "always sought" these goals, but promised no changes.

Despite the overwhelming opposition of his bishops, John Paul officially gave Opus Dei its long-sought elevation in status on August 23, 1982. But he did it from the safety of the Vatican.

Why might he have persisted against so much opposition? For one reason, he had said he would. But also, Opus Dei efficiently promoted Catholicism. Fundamentalist Protestant groups competed against the Church throughout the world with enthusiastic, well-scrubbed youth, singing and happy. After fifteen years of the humorless Pope Paul and his hair shirt, John Paul wanted his Church to broadcast a message as upbeat and contagious as the Protestants'.

While Opus Dei members are full of smiley positivism, they *aren't* like Moonies—or like the fellow in that country-and-western song "He Used to Take Acid and Now He Loves God, but He's Still Got That Look in His Eyes." They are smart, reliable, and professionally competent. Now their priests report directly to Rome, without even a pretense of obedience to the local bishops they had ignored for years anyway.

The tens of thousands killed in southern Lebanon since the Israeli invasion in June were a constant source of anguish to John Paul. Israel had invaded in the belief that the Palestine Liberation Organization in Lebanon was behind an assassination attempt on an Israeli official. But the invasion had rekindled the civil war between Moslem and Christian groups that had bloodied Lebanon for decades.[1] After several new months of stalemated slaughter, the UN and U.S. negotiated a peaceful evacuation of PLO fighters and their leader, Yassir Arafat. Then, on September 14, a bomb killed the Christian president-elect of Lebanon and seven colleagues.

The next day, as passions flared, John Paul created a world furor by inviting Arafat, who was in Rome on other business, for a visit at the Vatican. They talked politely for thirty minutes and issued a joint statement condemning terrorism. To Arafat, PLO attacks on Israel weren't "terrorism"; he was engaged in a long, dual struggle, attempting to win a good deal for his people and at the same time to retain the loyalty of those who wanted the total victory that he knew was impossible.*

---

* A top Italian security official, Federico D'Amato, testified that the banker Roberto Calvi's adviser Francesco Pazienza helped arrange the Arafat meeting, though the Vatican denies that Pazienza "was involved in any way" in the arrangements. Pazienza—the Mafia-connected Italian spy and Reagan administration adviser—was by then dealing regularly with Archbishop Marcinkus, who was the pope's security officer as well as his banker. Pazienza himself claims he was a critical go-between for the Vatican and the PLO. Security official D'Amato, who has been called the J. Edgar Hoover of Italy, testified before an Italian Parliamentary probe that Pazienza "had a semiofficial mission mediating between Arafat and the Vatican, and took several trips to Beirut." He also said that Pazienza had close ties with Arafat, and that he—D'Amato—once met the Vatican's UN ambassador and the editor of the Vatican newspaper in Pazienza's home.

Israel's denunciation of John Paul for meeting Arafat was unusually intemperate. It dusted off charges of Pius XII's silence during the Holocaust, accused Arafat of wanting "to complete the work" of Hitler, and said the pope's meeting him "is indicative of a certain moral standard." In response, the Vatican called Israel's statement "surprising, almost incredible . . . an outrage against the truth."

John Paul held Israel accountable for the heavy civilian casualties in Lebanon. On the very day he met with Arafat, Israeli troops swept across the Palestinian half of Beirut, from which the PLO troops had been evacuated. Two days later, Israelis invited angry "Christian" militiamen into Palestinian refugee camps and stood by while they massacred six hundred Moslems, many of them women and children. Hundreds of thousands of Israelis protested their own government's action. By the end of the month, Reagan sent U.S. Marines back to Lebanon to enforce peace, in the hope that Israeli and Syrian forces would leave.

Days later, a Jewish child was killed and thirty-four people were injured in an attack on a Rome synagogue. A high-ranking Israeli rabbi declared, "The right royal welcome that the pope gave the master-murderer has encouraged terrorist groups to do this act." Jewish leaders in the United States and Italy, including Rome's chief rabbi, likewise associated the attack with the pope's receiving Arafat.

Stung, John Paul sent Archbishop Dabrowski and two other Polish priests who had survived German concentration camps on conciliatory visits, first to the hospitalized victims, and then to Israel's two chief rabbis. The appreciation for these visits seemed genuine, and relations started to heal. A few weeks later, John Paul received in the Vatican the brother and successor of the slain Christian leader in Lebanon. The pope pleaded for Lebanon's "genuine independence . . . and sovereignty."

October 8, 1982, the Polish government formally banned Solidarity and replaced it with stooge unions. Stupidly, it did this just two days before a major ceremony in St. Peter's Square to bestow sainthood on Father Kolbe, the Auschwitz martyr. The occasion provided the pope an ideal platform from which to respond.

Once again, the revolution was at a crossroads. When martial law was imposed, Solidarity had nearly twelve million signed-up members, a third of the Polish nation. Considering the families these members represented, Solidarity was nearly unanimous—probably the most popular voluntary organization in world history.

Glemp had accepted the ban on Solidarity and even advised Poles to be satisfied with the new stooge unions. Now, to Glemp's face, and before the nation on television, John Paul revoked his primate's surrender. As so often before, he was not carried along by a popular tide, but rather, he created and sustained a tide when others in power were backing down. With eight government representatives sitting in the front row, the pope turned his sermon into flat-out political activism.

"Depriving the Solidarity union's right to legitimate activity . . . was a violation of the basic rights of man and society," John Paul declared. Nearly screaming at times,[2] he promised that the Church in Rome and in Poland would do "all that is in their power" to save Solidarity. Looking straight at the officials before him, he said, "I wish to address myself to the authorities of the Polish People's Republic. My country does not deserve to be driven to tears and desperation."

It was a Sunday, and all Poland had tuned in to watch. Television had transmitted earlier speeches in the ceremony, including those of concentration-camp survivors, but now the communists cut the audio for John Paul's remarks on Solidarity, and showed crowd scenes instead. Viewers understood what was happening, and turned on Radio Free Europe. Many of the ten thousand Poles in St. Peter's hoisted "Solidarity" banners and sang "O Lord, Make Our Homeland Free Again."

The next day, thousands of Polish workers struck briefly. Many carried "Solidarity Is Alive" signs at their plants. A few days later, a striking worker in Nowa Huta was shot dead by police.

That month, Glemp visited the *Tygodnik Powszechny* office and impressed some editors as "paranoid" and "conspiracist." He said his critics in the Solidarity underground were "enemies of the Church" and accused them of working with the communists against him.[3]

Glemp then attacked one of the few remaining visible wings of Solidarity, the theater workers. Since martial law, actors had mostly boycotted state television. To make up for the lack of entertainment, priests risked arrest by staging illegal artistic performances in churches, in the spirit of Wojtyla's underground performances in World War II. Actors who broke the TV boycott were booed when they appeared in public. (In the same vein, the pope's wartime colleague at the stone quarry, Wojciech Zukrowski, became a pariah for continuing to publish his novels with the government press.)

In this atmosphere, Glemp went to an illegal performance in a church and ordered the actors to end their boycott and return to television because "the people needed entertainment."[4] The underground press went after him. Among intellectuals, he became an enemy. Artists feared he would jeopardize their illegal performances and suspected that the government had won his cooperation by approving new churches and allowing him his own television time on holidays.[5]

At a Christmas gathering, Glemp bypassed the festivities and laced into priests for encouraging Solidarity. Again, accounts from angry priests were leaked to underground newspapers. "At the meeting many priests criticized him [Glemp] to his face for being too close to the government," says de Weydenthal of Radio Free Europe. People began commenting on the pope's failure to display affection for Glemp in public, as he had done with Wyszynski.[6]

In countries around the world, President Reagan, who claimed the pope for an ally, was in fact opposing the Vatican. Like Carter before him, Reagan refused Church requests to stop aiding the military in El Salvador. On the very day of the Kolbe ceremony, Archbishop Rivera y Damas defied the Salvadoran military's command that he remove priests from parishes it said were guerrilla-influenced. Instead, Rivera y Damas praised the priests for staying on after the army had killed so many.

Guatemala's bishops announced that three hundred more Indians had been massacred by government troops trying to move them off their land and into settlement camps. Another five thousand were transferred to the camps under threat of death. Amnesty International counted twenty-six hundred Indians murdered in four months. John Paul wrote the U.S.-backed dictator, General Efrain Rios Montt, asking him to end death sentences by secret military courts.

In Chile, the Church protested the economic policies of the Pinochet dictatorship, which had become a laboratory for Reagan's program, overseen by colleagues of White House economic adviser Milton Friedman. As demonstrations grew, the pope publicly endorsed the Chilean bishops in their protests against both the cutoff of welfare-state benefits and the repression. "We have seen . . . men tortured, executed, imprisoned, or chased out of the country," and a "refusal to engage in dialogue," the bishops said. Pinochet wrote back to John Paul that he needed more time before he could create democracy.

The Argentine Church stated that a bishop who the government said had died in a car accident had actually been murdered by the military.

The International Committee of the Red Cross revealed that the armed men who had kidnaped six missing nuns in Angola were from UNITA, a guerrilla group the Reagan administration was arming and promoting. UNITA also attacked a Catholic mission and seized eighty prisoners, including priests and nuns.

In Washington, the U.S. Conference of Catholic Charities voted to condemn the President's budget cuts for social programs, and disputed his claim that the private sector could fill the gap.

Administration officials, particularly Catholics, were assigned to campaign privately and in the press to persuade the U.S. bishops not to issue their proposed letter against nuclear weapons. John Paul was reminded of Reagan's objections during private intelligence briefings given him by U.S. generals, but he didn't stop the letter; instead he made Bernardin, its author, a cardinal, having given him the country's largest archdiocese, Chicago.[7]

32

As a global scandal grew around the Banco Ambrosiano collapse, John Paul resolved to stonewall in public, as he always had with financial scandals. When a prosecutor in Milan notified the Vatican that Archbishop Marcinkus and his two civilian administrators faced criminal charges, the Vatican returned the correspondence with a protest that its employees were immune from prosecution.

Italian authorities claimed that IOR owed nearly $1.2 billion to the bankrupt Ambrosiano, payment of which would allow restitution to many of Ambrosiano's betrayed customers around the world. As negotiations dragged on, John Paul even helicoptered to meet with the president of Italy, who had publicly demanded a Vatican payment. When the trip was discovered, the Vatican denied it concerned Ambrosiano, but no other explanation seemed likely.

October 17, 1982, the Vatican published, in *Osservatore Romano*, an account claiming innocence in the affair. The Vatican said IOR hadn't received funds from Calvi or the Ambrosiano Group—a flat lie—"and therefore does not have to refund anything." As author Charles Raw reports in *The Money Changers*, "IOR was at that very moment repaying" about $99 million in lira to Italian authorities supervising the bankruptcy. Raw speculates that the Vatican may have wanted to conceal these payments for fear that disclosure would inspire authorities in other countries to demand that IOR pay Ambrosiano debts there as well.

Around the same time, Archbishop Marcinkus gave a Catholic newspaper his only detailed interview on the subject. He declared, "The IOR is and was unrelated to all the operations carried out in the past by all the companies controlled by the Ambrosiano Group. . . . There are no grounds whatever" for saying IOR was used as "a safe channel for exporting capital out of Italy."[1]

In fact, Raw shows in tortured detail that much of the $99 million in lira that the Vatican repaid was money Calvi deposited with IOR precisely so that it *could* be exported from Italy illegally; the money was withdrawn in dollars through an IOR-controlled bank in Switzerland. For Vatican officials who knew about Calvi's deposits and withdrawals not to realize that he was using IOR as a money laundry would indicate not naïveté but imbecility.

Marcinkus must have been worried. According to a detailed report in the *Tablet* (London), he asked William Wilson, Reagan's friend and personal representative to the Vatican, to find out whether the Justice Department was investigating the case. Wilson wrote to Attorney General William French Smith. Even posing as a mere inquiry, such a letter could be seen as an inappropriate attempt to discourage an investigation—and Smith's Justice Department aide, Kenneth Starr, rebuked Wilson for writing it.[2]

Nevertheless, the letter apparently worked. A few weeks after Wilson sent it, Marcinkus was invited to breakfast with Attorney General Smith and his wife at Wilson's house in Rome. Wilson later said that all they talked about was tennis and golf.[3]

Inside the Vatican, John Paul resisted any effort to discipline Marcinkus. Cardinal Oddi says he argued that Marcinkus's continued presence was embarrassing: "Archbishop Marcinkus knew that Calvi was in deep trouble when he wrote those letters [taking responsibility for the Calvi debts]. Marcinkus is morally responsible," Oddi says.

"I was present when one of the cardinals said, 'We ought to remove him,' " Cardinal Krol told me. "The pope said, 'Why?' The pope did not want a man fired on rumors." Krol noted that despite his golf, Marcinkus lived and dressed humbly and drove the same Peugeot for thirteen years.

Ironically, just as he was stonewalling in the Ambrosiano case, John Paul was also undertaking a crusade against the Mafia. He paid the first of many visits to Palermo, Sicily, where priests were as much subject to Mob intimidation as everyone else. He deplored the "barbarous violence" that corrupted the city. He continued campaigning there over the next decade, and the Mafia retaliated: more priests were killed, two churches were bombed, and the pope's own life was threatened. But authorities credited John Paul's well-attended and well-publicized Sicilian sermons with producing unprecedented Mafia defections and courtroom witnesses.

It's not clear whether the pope ever associated that Mafia with the Mafia of Sindona and the Ambrosiano mess, right there in the Vatican. But he did reassemble his cardinals in Rome to discuss the banking problem. He told them he didn't want the Holy See to carry on the economic activities proper to a state. The production of wealth and the growth of income do not form part of its aims. The main source of support for the Holy See must be the spontaneous offerings from Catholics and other men of goodwill all over the world. There must be no resort to other financial means which might not appear to respect the peculiar character of the Vatican.

Had Pope Paul VI said the same thing, it would have been rank hypocrisy; he was the one who had pressured Marcinkus to score profits in the first place. But there is every reason to believe that John Paul really wanted Vatican banking to be carried out in a godly way from now on. Even more important to him, though, it seemed, was that the public never find out what wrongs had already occurred.

He said he wanted "the entire truth . . . brought to light" and would "cooperate" with authorities. Yet he publicly endorsed a new statement the Vatican issued that week, merely repeating the lies of the previous statement. A report Casaroli had requested from several prominent Catholic banking experts was hushed up.[4] That so unhypocritical a man as John Paul could utter such blatant deceits proves that for him, the image of the Church took extraordinary precedence. He would acknowledge error in Galileo's case, but not in this one.

The September 1982 edition of *Reader's Digest* had carried an influential article by Claire Sterling, the American writer living in Rome. Completely reversing her previous position, Sterling alleged that the Bulgarian secret service—and thus, inevitably, the Soviet KGB—was responsible for Mehmet Ali Agca's shooting of John Paul. Few seemed to remember that she had earlier told *People* magazine it was "crazy" to think "the Russians plotted this." Her new allegation that they *had* plotted it was all the more incendiary because Soviet leader Brezhnev died that fall and was replaced by Yuri Andropov, who had run the KGB at the time of Agca's attack.

Sterling had gained popular attention with a high-impact book, *The Terror Network,* which contended that international bombings and hijackings carried out by various nationalist groups were coordinated by the Soviet government. Given the political ascendancy of the Reagan wing of the Republican Party, Sterling's new article found a receptive audience. Her thesis sounded reasonable because the pope so clearly threatened the Soviets, and because the KGB's hands were already so bloody. Supporting her work at *Reader's Digest* and elsewhere was Paul Henze, a former Turkish station chief and White House liaison for the CIA (who didn't, however, disclose his CIA career when writing about Agca).[5]

Slightly embellished, the same evidence was cited by Italian authorities November 25, 1982, when they arrested Sergei Ivanov Antonov, a Rome-based employee of the Bulgarian state airline, and charged him with conspiring with Agca to kill the pope. Warrants were issued to arrest two other Bulgarians who had since returned to Sofia.

Agca, in prison, had given a detailed account implicating Antonov; his account had evidently been leaked to Sterling.

Senator Alphonse D'Amato of New York said in a widely published interview that John Paul himself had concluded the Soviets were behind the assassination attempt. (The Vatican has unequivocally denied this statement to me.)

A week after Andropov took over in the USSR, the Polish government released Walesa. New Year's Day, 1983, the government suspended martial law, though thousands of Solidarity prisoners remained in jail. The pope told a general audience that Poland was still a victim of violence and human-rights repression.

John Paul named eighteen new cardinals, four of them from communist countries. Eighty-eight-year-old Bishop Julijans Vaivods of Latvia became the first cardinal in history living in the USSR; he had never openly defied the Soviets. John Paul also tapped archbishops from Yugoslavia and East Berlin, and—unavoidably because he was primate of Poland—Glemp. In a grand gesture, John Paul made a cardinal of the aged Henri de Lubac, who had been disgraced as a "new theologian" under Pope Pius XII in 1950. Some found this incongruous, but the Vatican explained that de Lubac hadn't departed from orthodoxy as far as did Schillebeeckx and others being disciplined by John Paul II.

Dramatic in his absence was Archbishop Marcinkus, who was due to become a cardinal.[6] The IOR scandal evidently had persuaded the pope to end Marcinkus's career rise, though he would never say so publicly.

33

In his New Year's message for 1983, John Paul complained of an increase in

> what is euphemistically called "limited war" by those who are not
> directly concerned.... Where there have been armed conflicts—
> ...alas, more than 150...since World War II—dialogue did not
> really take place, or else was fortified, made into a snare....

To avoid war ... it is not necessary to give up ... through cowardice or constraint what [one] knows to be true and just, for this
would result in a shaky compromise.... Dialogue is ... the search
for what ... remains common to people, even in the midst of ten-
sions, opposition, and conflicts.

He begged people to respond to conflict with dialogue:

Every man and woman and also you, the young, ... have many
opportunities to break down the barriers of selfishness, aggression, and lack of understanding by your way of carrying on a dialogue every day, in your family, your village, your neighborhood, in
the associations in your city.... Dialogue for peace is the task of
everyone.

But dialogue was not much in evidence, at least with the Sandinista government of Nicaragua, as John Paul set off in March 1983 for a nine-day visit to
all seven countries of Central America (itself torn by "limited war"), plus Portugal and Haiti.

Nicaragua was where John Paul's hope of a happy ending to the dispute over
Liberation Theology began to fall apart. He had dreamed of a consensus that
would support human rights without party affiliation, and support the redistribution of unjust wealth without a Marxist division of society. In Nicaragua, this
dream had seemed tantalizingly close, as the extremes edged toward a center.

After the 1979 Sandinista revolution, vast estates had been seized from the
former dictator and his clique and turned into largely autonomous farming
cooperatives; most Nicaraguans had approved. A state ideology of socialism
hampered business growth, but private activity still dominated the economy, in
both farm and town. A radically oppositionist daily newspaper was printed and
sold, though the censors suppressed occasional articles.

Government-initiated violence and political imprisonment were rare.
Schools and health clinics had opened; the largely illiterate society was learning
to read. From the average Nicaraguan's point of view, the new dictatorship was
better than the old one, and better than others in the region. There was hope
that the elections it had promised might still be held.[1]

Catholicism had played a major role in what was good about the regime. In
contrast to the situations in El Salvador and Guatemala, where priests were
among the nearly two thousand civilians the governments now murdered each
month, in Nicaragua priests ran the ministries of foreign affairs, culture, welfare, and education, and held other high jobs.

Shortly after John Paul ordered Father Drinan and other American priests out of political office, the Vatican prodded the Nicaraguan hierarchy to tell its priests to resign their government jobs as well. But Catholic clerics from many countries protested that in Nicaragua's case, unlike that of the U.S., the priests were vital to hopes for having a peaceful, democratic, and well-run country. So the Nicaraguan bishops agreed to "tolerate" the priests in office "for the time being," based on their promise not to flaunt their priesthood for political advantage.

Friction erupted, however, in the summer of 1982 when Archbishop (now Cardinal) Miguel Obando y Bravo transferred a priest he thought was too pro-Sandinista. The priest accepted the transfer, but his parishioners protested with a sit-in. When Obando y Bravo tried to close the parish, a crowd attacked a bishop who had been sent to remove some sacred objects. John Paul wrote an anguished letter calling for a "union of minds and hearts." Jesus, he said, did not want "an *iglesia popular* [people's church] in opposition to the Church presided over by the legitimate pastors." While the tone of his letter seemed to urge both sides to bend toward agreement, the pope was clearly losing his patience.

Meanwhile, there was an increase in military attacks by the American-organized Contra army based in neighboring Honduras and Costa Rica. Sometimes the targets were military, but the real focus seemed to be on terrorizing society in order to erode support for the government. Defenseless farming cooperatives were ambushed, and many ordinary families lost members to gunshots or explosives.

The Contra war, a centerpiece of Reagan's foreign policy, pulled Nicaraguans back toward the extremes. The worse the war got, the more the pro-Sandinista priests felt obliged to be loyal to the government. At the same time, Thomas Borge, the most doctrinaire communist in the strange mix of Sandinista leadership, accused the bishops of allying with "the rich and the imperialists." Pledging to "obstruct [the bishops] and all others who stand in opposition to the revolution," Borge had his police release secretly taken photographs showing Obando y Bravo's spokesman, a priest, naked with a woman parishioner. Exposed in one snapshot was a dual hypocrisy: fornication in the Church and police-state tactics by the Sandinistas.

John Paul could not stand having his priests associated with such divisiveness, particularly when it was directed against the Church. What finally distinguished Nicaragua from other countries where he encouraged pro-democracy activity by churchmen was that in Nicaragua, priests were not just opposing tyrants; they had *become* Sandinistas. It seemed to supersede their commitment to the Church, which had been the pope's fear about Liberation Theology all along. And furthermore, the Sandinistas were not behaving like a democratic force.

Without development of any common ground beforehand, the pope's trip to Nicaragua was doomed. From the instant he stepped off the plane in Managua, he was engaged in an unseemly manipulative struggle. Sandinista politicians were desperate to exploit this moment in the global camera eye and borrow John Paul's prestige; the pope himself, already stung by the way he had been exploited in Argentina, was equally determined to deny the Sandinistas any sign of partisan support. It led to extreme posturing. Having the priests in office against his obvious wishes made everything worse.

Embodying the problem were two brothers (siblings) whose Christian credentials and sincerity were scarcely open to challenge, yet who had chosen to cast their lot with the Sandinistas. Father Ernesto Cardenal, a former protégé of the renowned Catholic philosopher and poet Thomas Merton, had written nonpolitical works of Christian mysticism to great acclaim; he was now Nicaragua's minister of culture. Father Fernando Cardenal, a Jesuit who had spent years living in shantytowns and pastoring to the poor, was now an education and literacy official.

Father Dezza, John Paul's choice to head the Jesuits, had written Fernando Cardenal just six weeks before the pope's trip, expressing almost slavish admiration and gratitude for his work and "clear witness to your priestly and Jesuit identity." Yet, Dezza said, "though it is possible to exercise a real apostolate in a position like the one you hold, the Holy Father has over and over manifested his will that such offices not be performed by priests." Promising "prayers, . . . admiration and . . . help in all that is within my hands," Dezza asked Cardenal to obey the pope in "a delicate and difficult situation."[2] But both cardinals stayed in office.

Barely had John Paul kissed the tarmac in Managua when he was confronted in the receiving line by Ernesto Cardenal, frail, bearded, and beaming worshipfully up at him from one knee. John Paul had obviously steeled himself not to let any photograph be taken that made him appear friendly to either brother, lest it seem to contradict all his previous efforts to get priests out of political office. So as Ernesto Cardenal reached to kiss his ring, the pope withdrew his hand, put a frown on his face, and shook his finger at the priest—a studied image that the cameras captured in a famous picture. "You must regularize your position with the Church," John Paul declared.[3]

Moments later, Sandinista leader Daniel Ortega gave an overtly political welcome, declaring that "footsteps of interventionist boots echo threateningly in the White House and Pentagon." The two sides were drawing lines and hurling dares, not exploring the way forward that both said they wanted.

John Paul shied away from the children and crowds he normally relished, apparently afraid a camera might catch him smiling in Nicaragua.[4] At the site of his open-air Mass, he was outraged to see, instead of a cross, tasteless pictures of Marx and Sandinista revolutionaries and a banner reading "Thank God and the Revolution." The tone of the pope's sermon was equally confrontational. He urged adherence to the teachings of Rome, against "ideological compromises and temporal options."

Sandinista ringers in the audience began disruptive shouts of "We want peace!" and "Power to the people!" The pope bellowed back, "Silence! The Church is the first to promote peace."

Usually, under John Paul, it was. But not always in Central America. The Sandinistas had legitimate grounds for fearing the Church as a Fifth Column of the Yankee invaders: the CIA was slipping cash to the Nicaraguan Church, apparently without the knowledge of Cardinal Obando y Bravo. (Former CIA Director Robert Gates says it wasn't much money—"maybe $50,000.")[5]

A more substantial threat to the Sandinistas, however, came from J. Peter Grace, who had allied the U.S. branch of the Knights of Malta with a major Contra support group: Americares Foundation Incorporated. Americares was a government-funded private organization that delivered large-scale aid to Washington's partisans in Lebanon and Afghanistan as well as Central America. When Congress banned CIA aid to the Contras, Americares seemed to substitute for the CIA.

Americares was run by industrialist Robert C. Macauley, a friend of both Grace and, since Yale days, Vice President and former CIA Director Bush. Bush arranged for Americares to obtain U.S. government financing; aid was delivered to the Contras through a Guatemalan Knights of Malta official who had worked with the CIA for decades.[6]

The pope became involved, apparently unwittingly, by granting an audience in 1982 to Macauley and his associate Father Bruce Ritter, who ran a shelter in New York for runaway youths.[7] Macauley later said the papal audience had inspired him to found Americares. Father Ritter—after being singled out for praise by President Reagan in the 1984 State of the Union address—was exposed for sexually abusing boys he "saved" at his shelter.[8]

There's no reason to believe the pope connected his courtesy meeting with Macauley and Father Ritter—if he even remembered it—to the sex-abuse scandal or to the killing of Central Americans. But consciously or not, John Paul understood something the White House had missed: in the struggle with communism, Central America, for all its tragedy, was marginal, while Poland was the endgame.

The pope did, however, make a big difference in the lives of seven million Haitians on his 1983 trip. He challenged Haiti's dictator, Jean-Claude ("Baby Doc") Duvalier, to his face, as no world leader had ever done. The Duvalier dynasty was in the twenty-sixth year of its rule, terrorizing the country with murderous "voodoo" witch doctors. But as tens of thousands of Haitians sat witness after Mass, the pope delivered an unusually merciless verbal attack on a national leader.

John Paul referred to the voodoo terror and the mass of starving Haitians who were fleeing to the United States "to seek elsewhere—and often in pitiful conditions—what they ought to find at home." Duvalier's political fortunes declined almost from that moment.

John Paul also touched down in El Salvador, under heavy military guard, and stopped, unscheduled, at Archbishop Romero's tomb, against the wishes of many bishops and the government. He prayed ten minutes, privately, then proceeded to his big open-air Mass, where he urged national reconciliation but did not mention Romero.

Most successful careers are a marriage of talent and luck. Certainly that was the case with Tony Bevilacqua, the Brooklyn monsignor who had thought the newly elected pope was Chinese, then later helped him through the rain at Shea Stadium. Now a bishop, Bevilacqua was assigned by the U.S. Episcopate to raise donations for victims of an earthquake in Italy. He raised so much money that he was sent to the Vatican to deliver it to the pope at a personal audience.

When Bevilacqua returned to Rome with other American bishops for their routine visits in the spring of 1983, he had no idea his next big break was coming. John Paul was worried about a possible scandal over a nun in Detroit. During Bevilacqua's round of meetings, an archbishop in the congregation for religious orders pulled him aside and asked him to solve a problem for the pope. This was the story:

Bishop Edmund Szoka of rural Gaylord, Michigan, had been a controversial choice late in 1981 to replace the eminent John Dearden as cardinal/archbishop of Detroit. Szoka himself says the pope selected him largely because of his Polish ancestry. Soon after he arrived in office, he learned that Sister Agnes Mary Mansour, president of a small Catholic college, was running for the Democratic Party nomination for Congress. Given what the pope had said about clergy in Congress, Szoka called her in and told her, "If you had asked permission, I wouldn't have given it. But now that it's a public thing, I won't stand in your way."

As he explains it now, ordering her to pull out "would have given her a lot of free publicity. I felt she had no chance of winning." What he didn't know was that during her campaign, she had endorsed public funding for abortion. "That was unacceptable," he decided. But Mansour lost, as Szoka had predicted, and he thought he was done with the problem. After the election, he was surprised to get a call from Sister Mansour's mother superior asking if Mansour could accept a cabinet job in the new state administration of Michigan.

Szoka replied that he wouldn't object to her becoming director of education, since that was her field. But for her to run the Department of Social Services would be a problem, because it paid for abortions for the poor. Mansour called Szoka to discuss it, but the busy cardinal delayed returning her messages. Two days later he was stunned to hear the public announcement that she would run the Social Services department.

Szoka called her immediately. He says he told her she could accept "only if she would make a statement that while she couldn't change the law, she didn't approve of it." He says she replied she wanted to think it over, and pray. She denies he posed an ultimatum at that time. But six weeks later—after some politically influential Catholics had complained, she says—he called her in and delivered what both say was a clear ultimatum. But she would neither make the statement he wanted, nor quit her job. She said that while she opposed abortion, cutting off public funds would discriminate against the poor.

Szoka withdrew approval for her to serve, and called on the Sisters of Mercy to tell her to resign either her job or her religious order. But the head of the Sisters of Mercy was Theresa Kane, the nun who had advocated the ordination of women while sharing a platform with the pope in Washington. Kane merely granted Mansour a leave of absence from the order so she could continue her job, while public debate raged over whether the Church was violating Mansour's rights, or Mansour was violating the rights of unborn children.[9]

Complaints reached the Vatican, and it became the pope's problem. Who could move Sister Mansour when Cardinal Szoka couldn't? And who could move Sister Kane when the pope *himself* couldn't—and do both things without provoking further public scandal? Bevilacqua was asked to accomplish this miracle.

He planned carefully, and then went to talk to Sister Mansour with a papal dispensation in his pocket. After much talk, she said that if she was forced to choose, she would give up her religious vows to keep her job. Before she could say anything further, Bevilacqua handed the stunned Mansour the dispensation, and in an instant she was no longer a nun. The matter died relatively quietly. Thanks to his priestly skills—and to Sister Mansour's own sense of propriety—Bevilacqua pulled it off.

A few days later, he voted with a bishops' majority of 238 to 9 to adopt the statement on nuclear weapons that the Reagan administration so bitterly opposed. He says that when the U.S. bishops visited Rome, John Paul said not a word to discourage them. In fact, the pope constantly made the same anti-nuclear pleas in his own speeches.

34

March 23, 1983, President Reagan went on national television to announce a major dedication of public resources: the development and deployment of a space-based antimissile defense system that became known as Star Wars. He said it might end the threat of a nuclear attack on the United States.

In 1982, even without Star Wars, Reagan's military budget had exceeded the total profits after taxes recorded by all U.S. corporations for any year in history. Military spending was 50 percent higher than the combined outlays requested for health, education, job training, agriculture, energy, environmental protection, transportation, natural resources, and law enforcement.

American spending on nuclear-related weapons alone during the Cold War was about four trillion dollars, according to the Brookings Institution. This created a massive public debt, interest on which still throws federal budgets out of balance. (Soviet spending is harder to calculate because labor costs are indeterminable, but it was surely less.) Four trillion dollars dwarfs any other public expenditure, ever. For example, Michael O'Hanlon, Brookings's military analyst, calculates that building the pyramids required ten million man-years; the cost of rebuilding them today with paid labor—at most twenty billion dollars—would be well under the mostly secret cost of Star Wars alone.

Reagan aimed to double Carter's already increased military spending within five years. Even before his 1980 nomination was secure, his backers had recruited executives from major military contractors to plan for the considerable challenge of spending so much money.* A secret defense policy that Reagan approved in March 1982 called specifically for weapons that would "impose disproportionate costs, open up new areas of major military competition and obsolesce previous Soviet investment." The same secret policy precluded any arms-control agreement that would prevent the development of new space-based weapons.[1]

---

* See Andy Pasztor's excellent book *When the Pentagon Was for Sale* (New York: Scribner's, 1995).

Not only does this secret policy mean that the American negotiators at the arms-control talks in Geneva were being insincere (to put it politely); it also means that Reagan misled voters (and the bishops) about his intentions and about American vulnerability. Since then, memoirs of participants have established that the Soviets, through quiet contacts, were trying to engage the administration in mutual arms reduction. The Reagan White House rebuffed these approaches with allegations that the USSR was provoking conflict in the Third World (though it's now clear that the USSR began backing off from Third World activity after it invaded Afghanistan).[2]

If the Soviet interest in seriously reducing arms spending was a bluff, it was one that John Paul sorely wanted the United States to call. But Reagan would not. Soviet officials actually began to fear that the U.S. was preparing to start a nuclear war.[3]

Was Reagan being honest when he said his costly buildup was intended to catch up to the Russians, and defend the U.S.? Or was the program really designed to provoke the Soviets into suicidal overspending and thus end the Cold War, as some of his adherents later claimed? Or was it in fact a way to reward favored businesses and to pump-prime the sagging American economy into robustness (which it did, with the price to be paid later)?

Whatever the answer to these questions, among those who read about the Pentagon's spending were the Solidarity underground leaders. "For six years [1982–1988], our people [back home] asked the same question," says Joanna Pilarska, deputy chief of the Solidarity international aid effort: " 'Everybody says Americans are supporting this place and that place all over the world. Why can't they send us half a million dollars?' Solidarity in Poland demanded ten times as much as we could supply." With enough equipment, she says, "every house would have been a printing house."

Pilarska and her chief Jerzy Milewski say they visited contacts at the State Department, on the National Security Council, and on congressional staffs, saying (in her words), "We need a million dollars annually. What does it mean for you? One tank! One million dollars annually to us is attacking the communists much more!"

Milewski says American officials repeatedly replied that the United States couldn't support "an illegal, clandestine organization." When he asked about the Contras and other so-called covert groups the U.S. backed, Milewski says he was told, "We have relations with the Jaruzelski regime."

Lane Kirkland of the AFL-CIO, which provided Solidarity with the bulk of its American aid, says his conversations about Poland with U.S. officials corroborate Milewski's account. "It was government policy during that underground period to find some way out that did not involve the reemergence of

Solidarity," Kirkland says. "They were continually looking for ways to normalize relations with [the Polish government]."

Undersecretary (and later Secretary) of State Lawrence Eagleburger actually asked Kirkland to have the AFL-CIO recognize the union the Polish government organized to replace Solidarity—the stooge union. Kirkland says he indignantly replied with "the slogan of Solidarity: 'No democracy without Solidarity!'" (Eagleburger says he doesn't remember the conversation, but "if Lane says I said it, I must have. I'm not denying it.")

By 1983, Solidarity morale was ebbing. A year of hard work and suffering seemed to have brought no improvement. Self-arranged aid still arrived at church sites, and Ewa Kulik still ran her "post office" (as she describes it) to inform Bujak and others in the coordinating commission what goods came in so they could be distributed appropriately. But the inflow dwindled, particularly of printing equipment.

Astoundingly, Pilarska and Milewski, in Brussels, say they got so tired of reading about the billions of dollars going to the Afghan guerrillas that they tracked down a representative of the Afghan guerrilla movement. (Like Solidarity, the Afghans had representatives in Western Europe.) They finally reached a high-level operative named Massoud and asked him if the Afghans would divert some American aid money to Poland. Massoud gave them a letter pledging moral support—"but no money!" Milewski exclaims, still angry.

On Lenin's birthday, April 23, 1983, the Soviet Politburo gave Party Secretary Mikhail Gorbachev the honor of making the big annual policy speech. Gorbachev emphasized Soviet economic development but also charged the United States with "interference in the internal affairs of the socialist states, up to and including the mustering of a counterrevolutionary 'Fifth Column' in Poland."

Gorbachev and the Soviets, just like their American counterparts, still didn't understand what Solidarity was.

The pope knew the real story of the Solidarity aid network. So approving was he of the operation that he summoned to his apartment Father Danzi, the priest who had trucked in the first shipments from Switzerland after the imposition of martial law. Because Danzi had been so successful at organizing Polish relief, John Paul wanted him to undertake an important new mission.

Having already encouraged Opus Dei, John Paul wanted to do still more to promote the upbeat evangelizing of youth. He had decided to bring young people from around the world for a "Youth Jubilee Day" in Rome. He gave Danzi a year to organize the event. Danzi's Communion and Liberation group—whose singing, laughter, and prayer had helped the pope recuperate from his gunshot wounds—seemed the model of what was wanted. Danzi and the pope asked Opus Dei to help as well.

In the year that followed, the pope questioned Danzi constantly about Youth Jubilee Day and peppered him with suggestions. It was his pet project. Danzi staged it so successfully that it has grown into a lasting legacy of John Paul, now known as World Youth Day. Through the years, no illness or injury has been able to keep the pope from joining the half million or more high school- and college-age youths who bring their beaming faces and strong voices to these gatherings.

For five months after his release, Walesa discreetly avoided any Solidarity activity. But when the coordinating commission invited him to a meeting April 9, 1983, he resolved to go. In the days leading up to the meeting, however, Bujak narrowly escaped capture in a police trap, and the commission decided he should not attend: he was too precious, an almost legendary symbol that Solidarity lived.

After an elaborate and successful scheme to lose his police tail, Walesa declared he was "impressed by the efficiency" with which Kulik organized the meeting. Still, he agreed that it "was primarily symbolic.... Nothing could disguise the fact that we [he and Bujak] couldn't swap roles."[4]

The effect of the meeting may have been the opposite of what was intended. For most Poles, a meeting with Walesa but without Bujak, and to no real purpose, had lost its thrill. Also, now, the grievances had been muddied. Martial law had been suspended, but what remained felt just like martial law. Walesa had been released, but politically he was a eunuch. Solidarity could speak from secret locations, but ultimately that only reminded people that it couldn't *do* anything.

The evaporation of demonstrations and other activity had a ripple effect on workers' spirits. Daily life returned to pre-Solidarity normality. The revolution was in danger of being over.

But that spring, 1983, Bujak and other underground Solidarity leaders received secret visits from Father Adam Boniecki, a Pole who was organizing and translating the pope's papers in Rome.[5] John Paul had sent Boniecki ahead as a covert scout for his June trip to Poland. Kulik's team supplied clandestine meeting locations, and letters were smuggled between John Paul and Mazowiecki in prison.[6]

Recalls Bujak, "My main goal was to assure [Boniecki] that Solidarity as an organization and an idea is present. It exists. And that must be reflected in the pope's visit. The biggest danger under martial law was treating Solidarity as if it was in the past."

John Paul wrote to the Polish government asking that all political prisoners be released before his visit. The request was refused, on the ground that they would likely commit more crimes—which was true. The government said it would release some prisoners after the pope left.

The government seemed to want to impress people with its power. May 3, the ancient Polish national day, two dozen club-swinging cops burst into the St. Martin's Church nunnery. Barbara Sadowska, a well-known poet and volunteer relief worker there, was beaten bloody, along with five others. Four more relief workers were abducted, and found the next morning in different spots in the woods with broken bones, concussions, and missing teeth. Archbishop Dabrowski protested to his longtime counterpart on the Church-state committee, who in the face of all evidence denied police responsibility.[7]

May 12, Mrs. Sadowska's son, eighteen-year-old Grzegorz Przemyk, was celebrating the end of exams with fellow students when they were arrested. He was recognized as a noted Solidarity figure's son and beaten by police until he died.

Father Jerzy Popieluszko was the one remaining visible hero now that Bujak and his colleagues had become almost phantoms. He comforted Mrs. Sadowska, and people began to associate him with the celebrated case of her martyred son. His Masses drew up to ten thousand people, and many fellow priests grew to depend on his leadership.

"If I needed something for my parishioners, from medicine to shoes, I would go to Jerzy and within a few days I would get it," one priest remembers. "He protested human injustice. He defended people and values, workers thrown out of jobs, people in prison." As far away as Washington, AFL-CIO President Kirkland was touched to learn that Popieluszko had prayed publicly for him.

The pope was Popieluszko's hero. "Everything he preached was in the spirit of John Paul's teaching," says a friend in the Warsaw curia. "He quoted the pope constantly. And the pope was very well informed about Popieluszko. He was a big supporter."

And yet they did not meet. Father Boniecki, on his scouting mission for the pope's trip, visited Popieluszko, whose longing to meet John Paul was obvious. But according to Popieluszko's friend Father Antonin Lewek, and other people who don't want to be quoted, Glemp was still angry at Popieluszko, thought him a troublemaker, and kept him off the papal schedule.[8]

May 13, police picked up the wife of Zbigniew Janas, who had tried to stay politically inactive so she could care for their family. She was badly beaten and hospitalized for a month with spine and kidney injuries. Janas's mother—with a son and daughter already in prison and Janas in hiding—was grief-stricken. But the last straw came when Glemp sent over a nun who accused Janas's wife, to his mother, of marital infidelities.

To this day, Janas's face flushes and his veins bulge as he tells the story. Glemp, he says, supported the government line that his wife had been beaten not by police but by a lover. He says his shocked mother kept asking the nun what she meant, and that the nun suggested that Janas's wife had turned to prostitution to make money.

Janas says only one thing kept him going: some days after the nun visited, leaving his mother nearly hysterical, Father Boniecki flew in from Rome and went straight to the hospital to see Janas's wife, carrying a handwritten letter of support from John Paul. The pope himself "knew of this case," Janas says, still awed. "It was such a moral lift!"

"That year," Janas says of 1983, "divided those who really believed in the struggle against communism from those who gave up. It was more and more difficult to find someone to give an apartment, to give help. Some activists decided to leave Poland."

Konrad Bielinski—Ewa Kulik's boyfriend (now husband), who escaped prison with a faked illness—says that after the government's vague promise to release some prisoners, "we felt Glemp and the hierarchy thought that it was finished. Now, if you [were] in the underground, [they said,] 'It is your choice. We don't help you.'"

35

The third week of June 1983 was the most important of John Paul's papacy. More publicity has been given to his first trip to Poland in 1979, and to his meetings with President Reagan and later Soviet Premier Gorbachev, though these meetings were mostly ceremonial; more publicity has been given to his contraception and abortion stands and his encyclicals.

But the pope's second trip home, little heralded outside Poland, was a turning point of history.

A dream cannot sustain itself without action. And when a dream, once born, dies, people lose the hope even to dream. The pessimism settling over the Polish people in 1983 was deeper even than before Solidarity. The underground had lost its momentum, and Glemp's Church seemed eager to bury it once and for all. If the communists might ever stuff the genie of freedom back into the bottle, now was the time.

As the pope flew to Warsaw June 16, Jasga Wronski, an Italian of Polish descent and member of the European Parliament, summed up many people's expectations: The trip "is bound to raise false hopes and lead to frustration," he told reporters. He predicted a "decline in the pope's image in the people's eyes."

The Polish government planned to use John Paul's visit to demonstrate that the country was "normal." It hoped the West would then drop sanctions and resume investing. Jerzy Urban, the Polish communists' press spokesman, recalls some fear that John Paul might "radicalize his message," but the government felt it could count on Secretary of State Casaroli, the old *Ostpolitiker* (who had negotiated the trip and would come along), to keep the pope "within certain reasonable political borders," Urban says. The meeting the pope sought with Walesa was declared to be out of the question.

Father Ken Doyle of the National Catholic News Service, covering the trip for Americans, reported a "grim scene. Streets were silent and people, though unfailingly polite, seldom smiled. A cloud of quiet cynicism hung over the country. The pope's reception at Warsaw's Okecie Airport was as somber as the gray skies overhead."[1] A French journalist compared this visit unfavorably with the pope's first one, in 1979: "People were happy then. They were cheerful, like children. In four years, Poland has grown much older."

Only a few hundred church, government, and diplomatic officials were admitted to greet John Paul. After kissing the ground, he spoke of Poland's torment, past and present. "I cannot visit all the sick, the imprisoned, the suffering," he said. "But I ask them to be near me with their spirit."

At the cathedral, he said a belated Mass for Wyszynski, whose funeral he had missed. He thanked God for having "spared [Wyszynski] the sad events associated with December 13, 1981." He said he spoke on behalf of "all my compatriots—especially those who are acutely tasting the bitterness of disappointment, humiliation, suffering, of being deprived of their freedom, of being wronged, of having their dignity trampled upon." Outside, twenty thousand people awaited him in the square, chanting Solidarity slogans and repeating, "The pope is with us."

The next morning, in a nationally televised ceremony at his office, General Jaruzelski appealed for normalcy. He promised a return to civil rule and "appropriate humanitarian and legal solutions . . . if the situation in the country develops successfully."

John Paul could have fallen in step with this amiable tone. But instead, he seemed to know precisely the jolt Poles needed. When the premier urged normalcy, the pope shot back that Jaruzelski should honor the deal "so pain-stakingly worked out during the critical days of August 1980." He should recognize Solidarity. John Paul again brought up the sacrifices of World War II, which had earned Poland the right to independence "among the nations of Europe, between the East and the West."

"Between"? Had the pope just renounced the Warsaw Pact and made Poland neutral?

John Paul and Jaruzelski now adjourned for a private meeting, at which only Glemp and President Henryk Jablonski sat in. Scheduled for forty-five minutes, the discussion instead lasted two hours and twenty minutes, and ended with a stunning surprise.

"Jerzy Urban, the government press spokesman, came into the press center visibly upset and angered," says Father Doyle. Urban laced into Walesa as a divisive rabble-rouser, but announced that the pope would be allowed to meet with him. Exactly what John Paul said to Jaruzelski to get the Walesa meeting may never become public.[2]

"The gloves were off," Doyle remembers. "Solidarity, the right to assemble, rights of labor. Obviously the pope had frightened them. It was a surprise to me and a lot of journalists. But the Polish priests said no, they had counted on it."*

Having stared down Jaruzelski, John Paul paid a highly political call to Barbara Sadowska, the popular poet who had been beaten, and whose son had been murdered, by Jaruzelski's thugs. The gesture, beyond just being compassionate, conveyed a dramatic message to the country: Sadowska's association with the outspoken Father Popieluszko was universally known.

Then came an open-air Mass at a stadium designed to hold a hundred thousand people; three hundred thousand showed up. Most had paraded four miles from the city center in parish groups. Gebert, the underground journalist, describes how "parish after parish passed the Central Committee building on the way to the stadium, chanting one word: *Przebaczamy*—'we forgive you'—to the riot police. It was immensely powerful. What the riot police were saying back, through their guns, was, 'We are afraid of you.' " Once again, whether or not they knew it, the Poles were mimicking the tactics of Gandhi and King.

A third of the country watched the Mass on television. At the overcrowded stadium, the crush was "dangerous, frightening," says American anthropologist Janine Wedel. "Some suffered broken ribs and arms. You couldn't move. But when he began, there was absolute silence. When he began to pray, hundreds of

---

* Jaruzelski later gave author Tad Szulc a self-serving account of the meeting, omitting the Walesa issue. Jaruzelski called it "a deep personal experience," during which the pope accepted Jaruzelski's tale of "the burden I had assumed on December 13."[3]

thousands of people outside the stadium dropped to their knees. The atmosphere seemed to change."

His speech hammered on the themes of human rights and dignity. By now, he was quoting the platform of Solidarity (which had been quoting or paraphrasing *him* in the first place). He used the word *solidarity* gratuitously throughout his speech.

The excitement started to come back. Throughout the next day, he continued to stir the country with talks around Warsaw.

A priest from Krakow told Father Doyle, the Catholic journalist, "If this were an Italian pope coming here, he might never act this way. He might wring his hands and be afraid of offending his hosts or saying the wrong thing. But this pope knows the government, knows himself, knows the Poles. The people are beaten down. They're afraid. Their jobs are on the line, and the circumstances have beaten the fight right out of them. What they need is a boost."

An estimated three million Poles attended three open-air Masses in two days at Czestochowa, despite unseasonably chilly, rainy weather. Cardinals Krol and Szoka, and Bishop Abramowicz of Chicago, were among 150 high Church officials flown in.

"The nation is truly free when it can shape itself as a community," John Paul said. "The state is firmly sovereign when it . . . allows the nation to realize . . . its own identity." He spoke of the bishops' work to free prisoners and win back jobs, of the beatings and killings that preceded his trip, and of the need "for the defense of every citizen." Over and over he said the word: *solidarity, solidarity, solidarity.* Crowds leaving the services transformed themselves into Solidarity demonstrations, with banners and slogans.

By this time, "the evolution of Solidarity was not as a trade union, but rather as a nonviolent national resurrection," says KOR founder Antoni Macierewicz. "Sometimes nations organize themselves into states, sometimes into religions, sometimes into armies. This time, a nation organized itself into a trade union."

The resurrection of Solidarity infuriated Jaruzelski, and he determined to stop it. Two government delegates were dispatched to Czestochowa to meet with the trusted Cardinal Casaroli, in hopes that he could persuade the pope to temper his rhetoric. But their meeting with Casaroli was unexpectedly interrupted by John Paul himself, who, in Urban's words, "came in and took over."[4] The pope agreed to tone down his remarks and had the Vatican issue a brief statement that the press was wrong to politicize the trip.

But John Paul had no intention of toning down anything. He proceeded to the Silesian mining area and carried on as before, calling free trade unions "an indispensable element of social life" and describing the 1980 Solidarity accord as a religious event. In Poznan, his Mass was followed by a Solidarity demonstration so big that the police went after the demonstrators with tear gas.

Then came Krakow. Police closed the roads around his route to town from the airport to keep people away. But undaunted, crowds blanketed hillsides more than a mile from the road to greet him.

For the southern portion of his trip, John Paul had invited Cardinal Lustiger of France. Lustiger told the pope he would go to Poland, "but I will not go with you to Auschwitz," where his mother and other relatives had died. Lustiger had never gone there.

"It's difficult to explain," he says. "I don't agree with the exhibitionism of those things. I would have all the journalists and photographers on my back. Auschwitz was not made for television. I have my own memory, my own pain."

"You will go," John Paul told him. "Without forgiveness, there is no redemption." Newsmen would be watching the pope, not his cardinal, he promised.

Lustiger rode to Auschwitz with another French cardinal and a new papal secretary (to help Dziwisz, not to replace him), Father Emery Kabongo of Zaire (now a bishop there). "When we went in," Lustiger recalls, "the others with me were speaking normally." That irritated him. He felt his predictions coming true, his sensibilities offended. The photographers recognized him and the significance of his being there, and snapped away despite the pope's assurances.

"In the car on the way back, no one said a word," he remembers. "I finally spoke to break the silence. And Kabongo, the African, absolutely exploded, and started talking about racism and slavery and exploitation in Africa. What he saw about the Jews made him speak about the blacks. And he told me the pope spoke many times, not only of Auschwitz, but of Africans and racism."

Suddenly the experience took on a whole new significance for Lustiger. He wondered aloud to Kabongo whether Africans, through their suffering, had taken the place of the Jews, as a people chosen by God, not to enjoy a privilege but to bear a burden. They discussed it in the car and also repeatedly, later, with John Paul.[5]

All over Krakow, Lustiger met exuberant Poles returning from Czestochowa, including many youths too young to have connected with John Paul as their local bishop, or on his previous trip home as pope.

John Paul beatified two heroes of the 1863 anti-Russian uprising, including Adam Chmielowski—Brother Albert—about whom he had written so much.

"Everybody was waiting for the word *solidarity*," says William Brand, the American translator who married the daughter of a papal friend in Krakow. "He slipped it in innocently, and all the banners popped up."

Afterward, groups carrying Solidarity banners assembled to march to the next Mass, in Nowa Huta, where Cardinal Wojtyla had fought for years to build a church. As the march began, police helicopters hovered overhead, proclaiming, "This is an illegal demonstration! Go home!"

Of many thousands, not one person left, Brand recalls.

By this time, Jaruzelski was coming unnerved. He sent word to John Paul that he wanted to have a second meeting with him before he saw Walesa and left Poland. Millions watching at home on television were amazed when Urban, the hated communist press spokesman, came on to announce that Jaruzelski was en route to Krakow by plane to remeet the pope. Even now, Urban calls his broadcast "a sensation."

"Jaruzelski wanted a meeting at all costs to balance the meeting with Walesa," says a cardinal in the pope's party who was involved in the negotiations.

They met at the Wawel, the hilltop stone castle by the Vistula that was Poland's ancient seat of government. Accounts of the occasion differ. Mazowiecki says John Paul told him afterward that he had again stressed to Jaruzelski the need to legalize Solidarity and to respect the Polish intelligentsia's link to the Church; Urban says Jaruzelski's notes show that the general did most of the talking, in an attempt to explain the government's position.[6]

What mattered most, though, happened immediately afterward.

While Jaruzelski and John Paul met, a score of invited guests assembled at the pope's old palace, in the Wawel's shadow, where a supper was laid out. The pope arrived and joined them midway through the meal, but he had been seated no more than five minutes when crowds outside began chanting for him.

John Paul went to the window and faced an enthusiastic, celebrating throng—much as he had from the same spot on his first return home, in 1979. As the other churchmen went on with their supper behind him, he again began a dialogue with the crowd. The whole scene struck one visiting high churchman as "astonishing."

More bluntly than in his prepared remarks, the pope encouraged the crowd to stay faithful to Solidarity. Laughing, he joined in on their derision of the government. As the churchmen's eyes widened behind him, and the crowd's spirits swelled, Cardinal Casaroli grew ever more nervous. Finally, as quoted by another cardinal who was there, Casaroli said to those around him, "What's he going to do, start a riot? Each day, I have to repair what he did with the government the day before. This could cause bloodshed!"

Says the other cardinal of Casaroli, "He was [acting] crazy, saying this was not *Ostpolitik*. What the pope was doing with Solidarity was the wrong way."

But others in the room "knew that the pope was not pushing the people to bloodshed," the same cardinal says. "He was only speaking the truth. Casaroli couldn't understand. I was surprised Casaroli spoke so openly, very upset. He was usually very quiet."

A third cardinal present confirms this account: "Casaroli feared it could upset the delicate relations. People didn't expect communism to fall so rapidly and without bloodshed."[7]

If a single decisive moment could be isolated in what was obviously a long and complex struggle—if the defeat of the Soviet system could be associated with a single blow—that moment came, that blow was struck, at the window of the archbishop's palace in Krakow that evening. There was no more confusion about the policy of the Church. The momentum in Poland had shifted again, this time forever. The words were relatively subtle, one basket in a high-scoring game; but the message was a brazenly defiant gesture in the face of Jaruzelski, who could have seen it all from his perch in the Wawel, just as Nazi Governor Frank had once looked down on Cardinal Sapieha from the same spot. Jaruzelski, and the communist system, would never recover.

Says the pope's friend Stanislawa Grabska, head of the Catholic Intelligentsia Clubs, "The nation was on a downer. He picked it up."

The spirit of the pope's nonviolent army, in serious jeopardy only days before, was revived for good by his visit in June 1983. The people of Poland, on the verge of giving up, received instead an epiphany from their pope, a message they wouldn't forget: They could not be defeated by martial law unless they admitted defeat. If they continued to believe in themselves, it wasn't the Soviets or Jaruzelski who had won; *they* had won.

The next morning, John Paul and Walesa (with his family) were helicoptered separately to one of John Paul's favorite old ski spots in the Tatras. A mountain location had been chosen because the government wanted as few people around as possible. Both men understood that Walesa was no longer running an organization, and that police would overhear everything they said.

"Nothing took place during their talks," says Borucewicz, who had recruited Walesa into the union. "What was important was the symbolism." In fact, the pope spent more time talking to Walesa's children than to Walesa himself and, displaying his usual unconcern for physical objects, left behind a sculpture Walesa had brought him as a gift. (Afterward, the communists delighted in using the sculpture to decorate an office overseeing the secret police.)

Spokesmen said the pope fell asleep almost the moment he sat down on the Polish airliner that flew him back to Rome. He was jolted awake fast, however, when he got home and saw a copy of the Vatican newspaper, *Osservatore Romano*, with a front-page editorial misinterpreting what had happened. The article said Walesa had retired from union organizing, apparently at John Paul's request, as part of a new Church-state agreement in Poland.

John Paul's jaw must have dropped as he read: "Sometimes it is necessary to sacrifice inconvenient people in order that a greater good may be created for the community.... By receiving him so privately, [the pope] avoided harming the delicate phase of national reconciliation.... Let us honor Walesa's sacrifice!"

As the false story circulated, the pope phoned Casaroli, whose deputy called in Don Virgilio Levi, the editor of *Osservatore Romano*. Levi offered to run a clarification but was told that the pope wanted him to resign—"Now."[8] Rarely has John Paul acted so swiftly and finally.

On the communist national day, July 22, 1983, Jaruzelski formally ended martial law and released many political prisoners. Many, however, remained in jail, and three-year terms were promised for anyone else who participated in an unapproved trade union or demonstration.

Michnik and Geremek traveled to Prague and Budapest, hoping to encourage opposition groups similar to Solidarity, meeting again with Vaclav Havel and others in Charter 77.[9] The Czechoslovakian and Lithuanian governments handed down long jail terms for some priests charged with assisting underground publications.

With the help of Polish-American Democrats, President Reagan persuaded Congress to withdraw its 1868 ban on relations with the Vatican. Reagan's personal envoy, William Wilson, reportedly told him that formal relations might inhibit the Church's criticism of American war policy.[10] So beginning in 1984, Wilson became a full-fledged U.S. ambassador. But the Church stance on weapons didn't change. Cardinal Laghi, who officially became a nuncio, assessed the change thus: "When bringing messages from the pope, I used to go through the back door. Now I will go in through the front door. I will also wear a better suit."

36

In April 1982, BBC's Rome correspondent, David Willey, received surely one of the most bizarre notes smuggled out of the Holy See in modern times. The scribbled message, delivered by a student, was from Emmanuel Milingo, the archbishop of Lusaka, Zambia, in southern Africa. Milingo said he was being held incommunicado by Vatican authorities in a monastery near St. Peter's. Checking on the story, Willey was amazed to learn it was true—and managed to get in to see Milingo.

Milingo had been consecrated a bishop by Paul VI in 1969. Soon afterward, he began to claim healing abilities, a traditional power of African medicine men. Dozens of Zambians said they had been cured of serious disease by Milingo's laying on of hands, or even by a letter or phone call from him. Thousands flocked to his Masses. He said he was driving away Satan.*

He began preaching on radio. His Masses became ecstatic, boisterous. When the nuncio and Zambian bishops forbade him to practice healing, desperate citizens beseiged him in the archbishop's house. He moved in with an order of nuns; pregnancy rumors led to humiliating medical tests, which proved negative. Finally, Milingo was summoned overnight to Rome, treated like a prisoner, and subjected to psychiatric exams. He was told that if after "theological studies and quiet reflection . . . the doctors find you in good health, and if the Holy See receives from Your Grace all the necessary guarantees . . . you will be allowed to resume your office."[1]

Milingo later wrote in a book that he felt deserted by the Church. He accused it of racial discrimination, and of wanting "to undo me as an African in order to make me a European as a condition . . . of becoming a full Christian." His healing, he said, had been based strictly on scripture and Catholic liturgy, never on African rituals. He stressed that the diseases he healed were "psychosomatic."

After Willey publicized his case, Zambian Catholics held rallies demanding his return, alleging that the pope was persecuting him for political reasons. At a meeting with John Paul in July 1983, Milingo agreed to resign as archbishop of Lusaka. The Vatican announced that he would remain in Rome to work for the Pontifical Commission on Emigration and Tourism. Milingo told reporters the pope had been supportive: "He reminded me that the Church is

---

* This is his description of one case: "There was a woman who had suffered from Mashawe, a common spirit possession in Zambia, for five months. She ate nothing. She feared her child because she did not consider him a human being. She heard voices. She was treated at a mental hospital, but to no avail. At that time I did not know how Satan behaves once he is in possession of someone. Suddenly an idea glowed in my mind. Look three times intently into her eyes and ask her to look three times intently into yours. Tell her to close her eyes the third time and order her to sleep. Then speak to her soul, after signing her with the sign of the cross. The woman was overshadowed by the power of the Lord. . . . The Lord was leading me to the healing of Mashawe. This disease cannot be treated in a hospital. We can heal this disease within our own Catholic Church."

guided by prudence in the matter of healings," and cited Padre Pio as an example of the proper way to handle such abilities. John Paul also promised him a chapel in Rome where he would be allowed to heal on a discreet scale.

Milingo visited Lourdes, France, another place where religious healing met with John Paul's approval. In 1858, a fourteen-year-old girl had reported holding a conversation with Mary there; the pope commemorated anniversaries of the event and clearly believed that Mary had really appeared to the girl. At the site, he said, "sick persons find, if not a physical cure, at least a Christian meaning for their sufferings." Thousands of Catholics reported miraculous cures from bathing in a spring at Lourdes, and a committee of Catholic doctors said it had validated sixty-four of these claims.

Visitors who saw Milingo at Lourdes recalled him as "a simple, unassuming man who knew and loved his Lord."[2] Years later, his healing Masses in Rome drew thousands of worshipers and no untoward publicity. John Paul seemed happy. But some cardinals scoffed at Milingo's detailed descriptions of the devil, or his claim that a photograph of Jesus, bleeding, had unexpectedly appeared when one of his nuns took a roll of snapshots to be developed.[3]

John Paul appointed a committee of American bishops to seek ways to attract more nuns and their male equivalents in the United States. Nuns' numbers were down a third, from 181,000 in 1966 to 121,000 in 1983, and few were young. "Brothers" were down 60 percent, to 7,880. The number of priests was dwindling, too, though less precipitously.

Yet the pope would not compromise with the increasingly libertine society from which recruits had to come. On the contrary, he ordered the committee trying to attract more recruits to, at the same time, impose stricter discipline for those who "depart from the indispensable norms of religious life or . . . adopt positions at variance with the Church's." He still believed that others would be attracted by rigor, as he himself was. Nor would he open new opportunities for nuns by letting them take over priestly duties, such as teaching in seminaries; in fact, he removed several who supervised seminaries.

The National Association of Religious Women in the U.S.—the nuns' union—rebelled, resolving at its annual convention to "stand together" and "not be broken. . . . Our sense of betrayal is profound." Some argued that the decline in nuns and brothers was a healthy sign that more opportunities were open to lay people. One leader accused the pope of being hostile to nuns and of driving "thousands of theologically educated women" to Protestantism.[4]

John Paul called in the world's best-known nun, his Nobel Prize–winning friend Mother Teresa. She said nuns should "turn to our Holy Father with childlike confidence and love.... The ambition to be equal to men in all things, even the priesthood, has taken away that peace and joy of being one with Jesus and his Church."

Many nuns remained upset, and remonstrated with surprising vigor during meetings with bishops across the U.S. Throughout the summer, John Paul met with heads of nuns' orders. He conceded that perhaps he should have consulted American nuns' groups before he created the committee, and that lay dress might occasionally be "required by sensitivity to different cultures." But mostly, as always, he held his ground. And his committee failed to increase recruitment.

The overhaul of the Jesuits ended with a whimper, not a bang, when the order gathered to elect a new leader in September 1983. John Paul had indicated his preference by appointing Father Giuseppe Pittau to be second in command to the aged Dezza. Says Father O'Keefe, who had been Arrupe's heir apparent, "If they had elected Pittau, it would have been kowtowing to the pope. If they had elected me, it would have been a slap in his face. They needed a third way."

The group settled on Father Peter-Hans Kolvenbach of Holland, who slept on the floor, rose at three-thirty in the morning, refused cushioned chairs or any ornaments other than a crucifix, and always kept a window open no matter what the weather. He traveled in second-class railway cars without sleeping berths. At their first meeting, the pope reportedly said, "I hear you like walking," after which they walked for their entire one-hour discussion—then sat for dinner.[5]

The pope's speech to the convention that elected Kolvenbach reads much like the scolding he had given the Jesuits earlier, but his tone must have changed: listeners, including O'Keefe, remember him as conciliatory, declaring, "The pope needs you."

Father Arrupe stayed in his debilitated state until his death, in 1991. Several current Jesuit leaders say that the pope's intervention was more extreme than the situation called for, and that he eventually came to realize that. They say Father Kolvenbach's messages have been scarcely different from Father Arrupe's. Father Gianpaolo Salvini, editor of the Jesuit magazine *Civil Catholica*, suggests that the pope simply finds Kolvenbach easier to ring up and talk to than Arrupe was.[6]

A year later, a crisis in the Carmelite order—the one Karol Wojtyla once wanted to join—was resolved much less painfully. The pope wanted the Carmelites to adopt a new constitution, recognizing some Vatican II changes, but the Carmelites voted it down. When Casaroli ordered them to adopt it anyway, the Carmelite leader, unlike the meek Father Arrupe, expressed "disgust" at the command. Casaroli shot back that any Carmelites who objected should find "other forms of consecrated life." The leader, Father Felipe Sainz de Baranda, advised his thirteen thousand nuns to accept the Vatican decision "despite the judgment we may think" it deserved. They did, and seven months later, Sainz was reelected to another six-year term.[7]

37

To John Paul, the growing Catholic practice of "general absolution" was more than just theologically unsound. It symbolized the spreading disregard for individual responsibility and discipline in human action. This was a trend he was out to reverse, and he devoted the 1983 bishops' synod to that end.

At the root of general absolution lay a problem: the ratio of priests to believers was falling. If every Catholic were really to confess as he was supposed to—as Polish villagers had confessed to young Father Wojtyla—priests would be overwhelmed. But advances in transportation and electronics had produced a solution of sorts, allowing what might be called mass Masses, such as the huge open-air services the pope gave when he traveled. Some priests now offered absolution to everyone present at large gatherings. This practice was especially tempting in Latin America, which boasted 42 percent of the world's Catholics but only 8 percent of its priests.[1]

John Paul thought group absolution turned penance into a mere formality instead of the kind of personal spiritual experience needed to keep believers upright. He said so that summer in a sermon at Lourdes, a shrine that specialized in group absolutions—and that then halted the practice, reluctantly. The pope made the point at the synod by granting sainthood to a nineteenth-century priest who devoted himself to confessions.

The bishops' representatives again had different ideas. Cardinal Arns of Brazil talked of social sin, shared by a group, while Archbishop Henry D'Souza of India raised the specter of "structural sin ... militarization ... international banking policies." Others called for the Church to reconcile itself to parishioners who divorced.

No bishop who offered such thoughts can have been unaware that they directly countered John Paul's fundamental agenda. On the other hand, the bishops present had been elected by peers who knew their views and wanted those views represented. Although the synod's proposals to the pope were again supposed to be secret, Archbishop Worlock of England disclosed that they

included "the valid and lawful use of general absolution in certain circumstances."[2]

The pope held the line on absolution but allowed the bishops to release
some steam with a political statement, which he endorsed, condemning many
economic and military "social sins." He even added new personal appeals to
Reagan and Andropov to end the arms race. But he insisted on "the profoundly
personal character" of penance. Social and structural sin, he said, were mere
analogies; sin was "always a personal act."

In a 140-page public letter, he said the world was suffering from a loss of
the sense of sin. It had come to think of sin as "the mere transgression of legal
norms and precepts." The Church had moved "from too much emphasis on
the fear of eternal punishment" in the past, to, now, "preaching a love of God
that excludes any punishment deserved by sin." He forbade general absolution
except "in cases of grave necessity."

The rise in the divorce rate caused him "deep torment," he said; no one
should feel abandoned. But "truth and consistency" must balance out compassion. Instead of protesting their ineligibility for sacraments, he said, divorced
persons should

> approach the divine mercy by other ways. . . . A soul that lowers
> itself through sin drags down with itself the Church and in some
> way the whole world. . . . Every soul that rises above itself raises up
> the world.

Once more, he called on modern society to let go of psycho-feel-good
excuses and accept the consequences of its actions. All around him in the world
he saw tragedies rooted in this same personal irresponsibility. August 21, 1983,
Philippine President Marcos had his most powerful political rival, Benigno
Aquino, murdered, and denied it. Ten days later, a Korean airliner strayed off
its route from the United States and overflew a Soviet air base; the Soviets,
thinking it a warplane but not checking, shot it down, killing 269 travelers.
Afterward, each side hurled unfounded accusations at the other and pledged
new militancy that increased rather than decreased the risk of accidental war.[3]

October 23, 1983, 241 U.S. Marines died in Lebanon when a suicide
bomber blew up their barracks; President Reagan withdrew his surviving peace-
keepers, their mission left unaccomplished. Two days later, a much larger U.S.
force attacked and overran the tiny Caribbean island of Grenada. (Even little
Nicaragua was six hundred times larger than Grenada.) Eighty-eight people
were killed and 533 wounded in the invasion. Ironically, of dozens of American interventions during the Cold War, Grenada would stand as a singular

instance in which the U.S. left behind a government that was clearly superior to the one it intervened against.[4]

As peace seemed ever more urgently needed, the Soviets walked out of the Geneva arms talks to protest the new missiles the U.S. had introduced in Europe. As the pope lamented in vain all these events, and the direction the world seemed to be taking, Soviet Premier Andropov was setting the stage for new tragedy by tightening the screws on John Paul's homeland. In a scathing letter, Andropov berated Jaruzelski for allowing the Church to be "the patron and defender of the underground." He went on to assert, "The most important thing is to . . . restrict the activity of the Church."[5] About two weeks after Jaruzelski got this letter, his agents acted. Primate Glemp was given a list of "extremist priests," including Henryk Jankowski (Walesa's priest in Gdansk) and Father Popieluszko.[6] Popieluszko was arrested and questioned intensely for forty-eight hours in jail.[7]

Then came worse. Two days later, Glemp called Popieluszko in and upbraided him. In his diary, Popieluszko recorded that Glemp told him, "I have so many troubles with you. The authorities warn me they will not give any licenses to build new churches" while Popieluszko's sermons continued.

"Even during an interrogation at the communist police, I was not treated with such unconditional pressure," Popieluszko wrote in his diary. "I understand Primate Glemp because I know he suffers many troubles from the communists because of me. . . . God, make of my suffering some good for all of us, for the cause."[8]

November 28, 1983, the archbishop of Miami hand-delivered a letter from John Paul to Florida governor Robert Graham, asking him to call off the scheduled execution of Robert Sullivan, a convicted murderer. As executions increased in the United States after a long hiatus, due to some Supreme Court rulings, the pope and the Church acted.

John Paul had acknowledged that Christians had killed wrongly in years past; now he was determined to make the Church stand for the principle that only God had the right to pass final judgment. The U.S. Bishops' Conference had come out against the death penalty in 1974, and in 1980 the vote had grown to 145 to 31. As capital punishment was revived, John Paul began writing governors (who have the power to commute sentences) almost every time an American execution was scheduled. He also acted in other countries where similar routes of appeal existed.[9]

Governor Graham turned the pope down and Sullivan was electrocuted.

A few days later, Cardinal Bernardin, speaking at Fordham University, offered such a dramatic new philosophy on life-taking in general that the *New*

York Times reported his speech on its front page. Bernardin had already led the U.S. bishops to a consensus position against American war policy; based on that success, he had recently been asked by the Bishops' Conference to take over the antiabortion leadership left open by Cardinal Cooke's death in New York.

Now, after what had obviously been years of thought, Bernardin merged a series of atomized Catholic positions into a unified pro-life philosophy. It embraced long-standing opposition to abortion; the opposition to contraception fixed by Pope Paul VI and Cardinal Wojtyla in 1968; the opposition to war that Pope Benedict had enunciated in World War I and John Paul II was now making into a fundamental credo (rescinding Saint Augustine's notion of "just war"); the hardening opposition to capital punishment; and positions on advances in medicine and on social-welfare obligations.

Bernardin's uniform pro-life credo, endorsed by the head of the U.S. Bishops' Conference, was unveiled in his Fordham speech. Although John Paul withheld judgment at first, he would later reformulate the idea on his own. A leading Catholic writer called Bernardin's speech "perhaps the most significant address given by any archbishop in the history of American Catholicism."[10]

"When we *can* do almost anything, how do we decide what we *ought* to do?" Bernardin asked. "When we can do anything technologically, how do we decide morally what we *never* should do?" While the various problems deserved "individual treatment," he said, the "combination of challenges . . . cries out for a consistent ethic of life."

Bernardin knew that his idea would seem schizophrenic in the political arena. Those who shared his opposition to abortion tended to support armed attacks in Nicaragua and Angola, while those who opposed the wars often championed abortion-on-demand. These were, in fact, the actual, respective positions of the Republican and Democratic Party leaders. Bernardin's was a new vision:

"The principle which structures both cases, war and abortion, needs to be upheld in both places," he said. "It cannot be successfully sustained on one count and . . . eroded in a similar situation." He said a uniform focus on life also "translates into specific . . . positions on tax policy, employment generation, welfare, nutrition and feeding programs, and health care. Consistency means we cannot have it both ways. . . . Right to life and quality of life complement each other in domestic social policy."

Bernardin pursued his idea repeatedly over the coming months. In a speech in St. Louis, he said that Catholicism "joins the humanity of the unborn infant and the humanity of the hungry. It calls for positive legal action to prevent the killing of . . . the aged and positive societal action to provide shelter for the homeless and education for the illiterate. A consistent ethic of life does not equate the problem of taking of life ... with the problem of promoting human dignity. ... But a consistent ethic of life identifies both as moral questions. It argues for a continuum."

Anti-Bernardin letters poured into the Vatican from American Catholics who, like their President, argued that government spending on the poor either couldn't be afforded or didn't really help.

Soon after Bernardin's landmark speech, openings caused by death allowed John Paul to fill two other top archbishops' jobs in the United States. The press labeled both his appointees "conservative," and on one, the label stuck: Bernard Law, who moved to Boston from Springfield, Missouri. Law was backed by Opus Dei, was a friend of George Bush,[11] and tended to defend Vatican rulings unconditionally while other bishops searched for nuance.

But John O'Connor, who moved to New York from Scranton, Pennsylvania, was harder to pin down. A Navy chaplain for twenty-seven years, he was a ranking admiral and had written a book in 1968 defending American action in Vietnam, where he had come under fire. But John Paul knew, as many in the public didn't, that O'Connor had changed his mind.[12]

With his military background, O'Connor became an especially effective Church voice on war policy. Appointed to Cardinal Bernardin's five-bishop commission writing a pastoral letter on nuclear weapons, he expressed reservations at first (the letter should call for a "curb," not a total "halt," he thought; he lost), but soon became a pillar of Bernardin's consensus.

He testified before Congress with Bernardin against putting the new American missiles in Europe, against the Contra war and against the U.S. decision to build a new type of rocket that carried multiple independently directed bombs (which he said "mortgaged the future of arms control ... without adequate citizen or Congressional scrutiny"). The son of a union painter, O'Connor outspokenly supported labor unions, and the obligation of everyone to sacrifice to help the poor. His popularity suffered, however, because of his uncompromising opposition to homosexuality in a city with a large gay community, and his defense of an unborn child's right to life in a center of support for a woman's right to abort.[13]

What distinguished Law and O'Connor was not "conservatism," as the word is generally understood politically, but rather their propensity to agree with John Paul's position on ethics: that individual rights must be balanced against strong group norms. This contradicted the thinking of many Americans who called themselves conservative or liberal, but who opposed restraints on individual action.

⌇

That December, 1983, on the five-hundredth anniversary of the birth of Martin Luther, John Paul took a step toward rehabilitating the founder of Protestantism. In Rome, having personally arranged it with the pastor, he became the first pope to preach at a Lutheran church. He praised Luther and declared he could see "from afar the dawn of the restoration of our unity." It was the first papal statement on Luther since Pope Leo X excommunicated him, in 1521.

Glemp's Christmas message for 1983 asked, with almost unbelievable neutrality, for Solidarity and the state to try harder to get along, and for priests to stop interfering in politics. The communists actually praised his words.

John Paul's Christmas message asked the world to

> look upon the unspeakable sorrow of parents ... their children imploring them for bread, which they don't have, but which could be obtained with even a tiny part of the sums poured out on sophisticated means of destruction.

Two days after Christmas, he visited Mehmet Ali Agca in his cell, bringing along Monsignor Dziwisz, two bodyguards, and a photographer. Agca had heard that the pope would pay a Christmas visit to the prison, and had asked for a meeting to apologize. What the two men said to each other was never announced, but rumors swirled. A distant television camera captured part of the visit; based on lip-reading and scratchy sound, it has been reported that Agca said, "First of all, I wish to ask your forgiveness." The pope reportedly uttered the following snippets: "Jesus ... perhaps one day ... the Lord gave you grace."[14]

Frossard, the French journalist, told John Paul that another lip-reader had him asking, "Who wanted my death—who sent you?" The pope laughed and said, "No, not that," but he wouldn't elaborate.

It happened, though, that Father Bardecki of Krakow was then in Rome, and breakfasted with the pope the next morning. He says that when he asked John Paul what had happened, the pope, as usual, replied with a question: "What did it look like?" Bardecki said it looked to him as if Agca were confessing his sins.

"No," John Paul smiled. "Agca is a very superstitious person. He learned in prison that the assault took place on the same day as the revelation at Our Lady of Fatima. And he started reading about this. As he imagined it, it was some kind of mysterious force that made his [assassination] plans fall through. He was living in fear that he would be harmed by this mysterious force. And I said that Our Lady of Fatima would not try to take revenge on him. I was trying to calm him. He was not confessing his sins."

Bardecki says his imagination was suddenly gripped by Fatima, and a mysterious prediction Mary was said to have made there, which allegedly had been
conveyed to the Vatican decades ago. Bardecki says John Paul told him the
Fatima prediction was secret, locked in a safe. In his excitement, Bardecki
neglected to ask the pope whether Agca had acted alone.

38

Throughout much of 1983, Vatican Secretary of State Casaroli had been dealing with separate teams of Italian officials over two seemingly unrelated matters: the $1.2 billion in claims over Banco Ambrosiano, and a new concordat
with Italy to replace the 1929 Lateran Treaty. Italy wanted Catholicism to be
revoked as the official state religion, religious instruction in schools to be
optional, and civil law to replace Church tribunals for marriage and—yes—
divorce.

Around Christmas, Casaroli sensed an unspoken link between the two sets
of negotiations: to get the concordat terms it wanted, the Vatican would have
to pay stiffly for its Ambrosiano misdeeds. Archbishop Marcinkus, still IOR's
president, later said he had "told them right from the beginning, 'You're crazy!
Don't even open up the conversation. If we're not guilty we don't pay.'"[1]

The pope disagreed. As long as there was no admission of wrongdoing, he
felt, the financial problem could be negotiated. Casaroli offered authorities a
"voluntary contribution" of $150 million, which was eventually forced up to
$240 million. Everyone agreed to pretend the payment was a noble gesture—
not the result of pressure over the concordat, or the threat of lawsuits that
would have shadowed the Church's evangelism for years.

Charles Raw's thorough investigation concluded that the Vatican's real loss
was more than double the amount publicly reported. Raw noted that before
IOR paid the $240 million, it had already repaid (as previously noted) $99
million in borrowed lira to Ambrosiano, knowing it could not collect from the
Calvi-related companies it had lent the money to. It also lost a $70 million
deposit at the Bahamian bank that Marcinkus had been a director of. Raw
found $71 million in loans IOR made to two other Ambrosiano affiliates it
couldn't collect from. And IOR's $33 million investment in Ambrosiano stock
was down the drain. The real total was thus $513 million—enough to send
tremors through even Citibank.

Where the money came from has never been disclosed. Vatican sources
informally suggested that the money came from IOR's accumulated profits

over the years; but if IOR was sitting on that much capital, it was bigger than anyone thought. Cardinal Krol, supposedly one of the Vatican's money experts, told reporters IOR would borrow some of the money; if so, it must have intended to repay the loans from future profits, even though John Paul had expressly said he didn't want IOR to seek profits.

The Vatican did get some financial relief from the new concordat with Italy, which was signed by Casaroli and Prime Minister Bettino Craxi a few weeks after the Ambrosiano deal was agreed to.[2] In an arrangement much like the one West Germany had with its Churches, Italy added a box to every tax form allowing citizens to check off eight tenths of one percent of their tax for the Church.

More Catholics gave more money that way than when donations were direct. Only 20 percent of Italian Catholics went to Mass weekly, less than at any other recorded time; increasingly, Catholics were marrying outside the Church, and the Italian abortion rate of 405 for every 1,000 births was second only to that of Denmark in all of Western Europe.[3]

On his way to see John Paul again early in 1984, CIA Chief Casey stopped off at the Afghan guerrilla command in Pakistan with a secret, very unpopelike message: Reagan had authorized U.S.-sponsored land raids by the guerrillas into Soviet territory north of Afghanistan.[4] Much as the Soviet government might deserve retribution, it was a frightening extension of American war action against a nuclear superpower, without congressional approval.

Casey's subsequent stop in Rome is part of the myth of U.S. aid to Solidarity. Former Reagan administration officials have put out a story that Casey couldn't speak with the pope, but met Archbishop Poggi, the Vatican's lead diplomat, briefed him about CIA aid, and won Poggi's endorsement of the American economic embargo against Poland.[5] Poggi himself, now a cardinal, denies this. "I can't remember ever meeting Casey," he says. "I never talked about links between Solidarity and the CIA. I never supported Reagan's sanctions, because ultimately it's ordinary people who suffer. I'm not a Reagan supporter."[6]

John Paul's words at the time corroborate Poggi's assertion. In his annual speech to the Vatican diplomatic corps, which the new U.S. ambassador, William Wilson, attended in January 1984, the pope offered a policy line diametrically opposed to that of Reagan and Casey, promoting increased northern economic aid to southern countries; an independent Palestinian state; and independence for Namibia, an African territory where the CIA was then helping forces fighting against independence.[7] The pope expressed disappointment at the very limited arms deals the Americans and Soviets were discussing, which he soon afterward said "merely regulate an arms buildup" and "are clearly insufficient."[8]

While the White House opposed the pope on policy, the Kremlin denied him permission to go to Lithuania for a Church occasion, and the USSR's Czechoslovakian puppet regime jailed some laymen merely for proposing a papal visit. When Soviet Premier Andropov died February 9, 1984, he was replaced by Konstantin Chernenko, a seventy-two-year-old Brezhnev ally undistinguished in either character or originality.

The U.S. government finally began to help the Solidarity underground in 1984, not through the CIA, but through the National Endowment for Democracy, an independent, bipartisan agency created by the Democrat-controlled Congress at Reagan's suggestion. (Reagan was hoping to gain Democratic support for Cold War projects by allowing the Democrats some influence over them.)

The Endowment for Democracy was semi-covert: its grants, to chosen organizations for specified goals, were publicly disclosed, but how the organizations actually spent the money within that framework remained secret. Much of the money went to Democratic and Republican pet boondoggles,[9] but a relatively puny three hundred thousand dollars a year went to the AFL-CIO, expressly for Solidarity. Beginning in 1984, this constituted a third of the income of Jerzy Milewski's international Solidarity office in Brussels.

"As far as I'm aware, and I think I know," AFL-CIO President Lane Kirkland says, "every bit of assistance that was given to Solidarity from the U.S. [government] was given through us, overtly and aboveboard [through the Endowment for Democracy]. The only thing that was not overt was the means by which we got material into Poland."

Underground journalist Konstanty Gebert says the AFL-CIO money made a noticeable impact, coming as it did just when individual Polish contributions were dwindling because of the Polish economy. But traditional sources of aid still predominated. For example, when Solidarity Radio began breaking into government TV news programs to read its own news—at least once flashing a Solidarity symbol on the screen—it relied on equipment made in Poland by the underground.[10]

Milewski was delighted to get the AFL-CIO's three hundred thousand dollars, but he wondered, "Why not four hundred thousand? Why not five hundred thousand?" On one occasion Brzezinski, now a private scholar, stopped by Milewski's office in Brussels; on hearing how tight money was, he pulled out his checkbook and wrote out a personal donation of five hundred dollars (which touched Milewski).[11]

❧

Ratzinger's office resumed considering applications for priestly resignations (which John Paul had suspended when he became pope). But new, tougher standards cut the approval rate to less than half what it had been under Pope Paul.[12] Priests who quit were not permitted to teach at, or administer, Catholic institutions.

The new standards for priestly separation—more nuance than new language—moved toward the same standard the Church used for ending marriages. Just as annulment posited that a particular marriage never really happened because it had been flawed to start with, so Ratzinger's office looked less at the trouble a priest was having now, and more at whether he could prove he had been unfit for his vow in the first place.

In contrast to his initial orders in January 1981, the pope showed flexibility about the marriage standard itself in a speech to the Sacred Rota, a sort of Vatican supreme court for annulments. He encouraged judges to "find a balance between ... the indissolubility of marriage and ... the complex human reality of the concrete case." The new code of canon law he had approved allowed annulment for a "grave lack of discretionary judgment" about the marriage vow when it was taken. As judges considered this, John Paul said, "the concern to safeguard the ... indissolubility of marriage" must accommodate the "undeniable progress of the biological, psychological, psychiatric and social sciences." What was to be safeguarded was only "a truly existing marriage, not one which has only the appearance of such, since it is null and void from the outset." Each case was to be judged without prejudice; none was to be used as an example, or "as a means for correcting abuses."[13]

Some Catholics now deemed John Paul too easy on divorce, which in the United States and other countries was consuming half of all marriages. Catholic psychiatrist Jack Dominian, writing in the *Tablet*, called marital breakdown "by far the most important pastoral issue which faces the Church." He said he "regretted the energy that the question of contraception has absorbed because ... something truly momentous is at stake. . . . I have been amazed that all the churches have not made divorce the leading social evil of our day."

The Vatican itself continued to show favoritism in granting annulments to those with money and influence. A belated annulment was granted of the first marriage of Princess Caroline of Monaco, whose parents attended John Paul's inaugural. Caroline had married in 1978, divorced in 1980, and—when a Vatican panel wouldn't grant her an annulment—married again in a civil ceremony in 1983. Despite this defiance, when an annulment became necessary in 1992 to help preserve the Catholic crown of Monaco, it was granted. Without it,

Caroline's children by her second marriage would have been precluded from ruling, and under treaty, without a direct heir Monaco would become a protectorate of France, a secular republic. (The Vatican has denied widely published reports that John Paul himself directed the annulment; it says the commission he appointed just took ten years to reach a positive decision.)[14]

Similarly, in 1995, Senator Edward Kennedy, at his mother's funeral, received communion from Cardinal Law of Boston. Kennedy had divorced his longtime first wife in 1983 and married another woman in a 1992 civil ceremony. Cardinal Law gave the Senator communion right after Ratzinger reiterated that communion must be refused to divorced and remarried Catholics. Afterward, Kennedy said his second marriage had been blessed, but he gave no details; the Church wouldn't comment.[15]

39

Archbishop Francis Arinze of Onitsha, Nigeria (who had been lecturing in Ireland when John Paul was elected pope), was on a routine visit to Rome in early 1984 when an archbishop in the curia told him that he was among ten archbishops worldwide being considered for a curial appointment. How would he feel if he were chosen?

"I am neither in favor nor against," Arinze said. "If the Holy Father wants me to work for him in the Roman curia, that's fine. If he wants me to stay where I am, that's fine, too."

The archbishop kept pressing. Which would be better for Arinze? For the Church?

"By this time I was becoming fairly agitated," Arinze recalls. "I said, 'How can I be a judge in my own case? Tell the Holy Father not to worry. I am totally free.' "

Several weeks later, in Nigeria, the papal representative put him through the same routine, then returned to announce that Arinze had been appointed to head the Council for Interfaith Dialogue. Years of working with Moslems and pagans on a continent of major potential growth for the Church made Arinze, at age fifty-one, a logical choice. He was given a booklet for new officeholders and invited to Rome.

At lunch with John Paul, and during two days of meetings with him and others, Arinze learned that in the pope's eyes, his new job was even more important than he had suspected. After John Paul's setback trying to meet with Moslems in Nigeria, he was more determined than ever to have local bishops forge bonds outside the Church, as a way to increase the role of spirituality in earthly affairs. Prodding this outreach was a large part of Arinze's new job.

Arinze's was among a flurry of appointments announced in April 1984, as John Paul fixed the team that would carry out the commands of his papacy for the next decade and more. From now on, to the extent that any one man *could* control the Church, he would.

The biggest surprise was his appointment of another African, sixty-two-year-old Bernardin Gantin of Benin, as head of the Congregation for Bishops, one of the three most critical departments of the Vatican. Now Gantin, by helping the pope choose leadership around the world, would shape the Church as much as would Ratzinger, who helped define its beliefs at the Congregation for Doctrine, and Casaroli, who helped direct its activity as secretary of state.

"Jaws dropped," says Father Thomas Reese, the author of several books about Church administration. Gantin had entered a seminary in the heart of the West African rain forest at age thirteen, and become a priest sixteen years later, in 1951. His own nomination as bishop, six years after that, had come not through the department he now headed, the Congregation for Bishops, but rather through the Congregation for Evangelization of Peoples, a sort of colonial office. His appointment, even more than Arinze's, signaled that under John Paul, Africans were no longer to be considered exotic creatures needing missionaries, but citizens of the Church like any other.

Gantin had mostly stayed away from Benin (population 3.5 million) since a Marxist government took over, in the early 1970s. But he had been welcomed warmly there when he accompanied John Paul on a 1982 visit, a papal stop that honored Gantin's rise in the curia.

In person, Gantin and Arinze could scarcely differ more. Arinze, thin and spry, conveys an unpretentious piety, open and affable. His quarters were the least elegant of any cardinal's I saw, with bare floors and hard wooden chairs. He invited me to visit on a Saturday, when his council was mostly closed. As we chatted, just the two of us, he politely fielded several phone calls (once patiently answering some misdirected questions about the sainthood process), all from people who seemed to have no idea they were talking to a cardinal.

Gantin, on the other hand, hefty and overbearing even in his seventies, seems arrogant, snappish, and about as smiley as the faces on Mount Rushmore. When I began our meeting by recalling fondly my visits to his country as a Peace Corps volunteer, he challenged my honesty because I didn't remember the name of a particular town after twenty-five years.

He insisted he had forgotten how he was notified about his big appointment, and said he had been given no advice on choosing bishops other than to read the charter of his congregation and "rely on canon law." By this standard, anyone who passed a course in canon law could do Gantin's job. Paul VI had brought him to Rome in 1971 to work in the Congregation for Evangelization, and four years later asked him to lead the Council for Justice and Peace. In neither case, he said, did he ask or was he told why; his only agendas had been to "evangelize. Priests evangelize."

Many cardinals and bishops told me that Gantin has better access to John Paul than almost anyone else: hours are reserved each Saturday evening the pope is in Rome, during which they leisurely discuss the world's bishops, with emphasis on vacant posts and bishops arriving for their every-five-year visits. Gantin, however, insisted to me that he met with the pope only "whenever convenient."

John Paul's 1984 reshuffling of his administration quietly shifted some of Archbishop Marcinkus's powers elsewhere, but the pope would neither throw him out nor embarrass him. Archbishop (now Cardinal) Deskur also kept his office and residence, but because of his debilitating stroke, two new men were brought in to handle public relations. One, Archbishop John Foley of Philadelphia, took Deskur's post but wound up in a vague planning role. The other, Dr. (of medicine) Joaquin Navarro-Valls, then forty-eight, was given the title Press Secretary and became the pope's right-hand man for public dealings.

An elegant live wire of energy, Navarro-Valls gave up his career as a surgeon to be a foreign correspondent for a Spanish newspaper, later becoming president of the Foreign Press Club in Rome. His odd occupational switches and Vatican appointment may be explained by his membership in Opus Dei, where he has taken a vow of celibacy. Veterans say he is the first papal press secretary to have a sympathetic understanding of what Western newsmen are trying to do, in a milieu—the Vatican—where parable is often preferred to factual precision. He is the only nonpriest in the pope's comfortable inner circle. His access may be exceeded only by Dziwisz's.

Among a host of other appointments, perhaps the most exciting was that of Cardinal Roger Etchegaray, sixty-one, a stately Charles de Gaulle look-alike who was pulled from his post as archbishop of Marseilles to head the Council for Justice and Peace. It is to Etchegaray that the pope turns for reports on issues like homelessness, racism, or the Balkan war.

Etchegaray is passionate. The crucifix on his office wall is flanked by pictures of Martin Luther King, Jr., and the social activist Pope Leo XIII. He says that in contrast to other areas, where the pope seeks preservation, in the concerns of Justice and Peace, the pope wants change: "It is the showcase of the Church. If you walked down a street and there were stores, if the Roman Catholic Church had a store, you [as a non-Catholic] probably would not go in. But if you looked in the window of the Justice and Peace store, you would go in. Everybody is interested."

Marseilles's cosmopolitan makeup—full of Moslems, Jews, and others— prepared him for this job, he says. He became a friend of the pope's during Vatican II and visited him in Krakow occasionally. Justice and Peace has kept him on the road. "Iran, Iraq, Angola, Burundi, Vietnam—name a trouble spot, and I've probably been there," he said a decade after taking the job. "Cuba twice. South Africa three times. Even if you can't do much, it's important to remind people you're around."

The habits of the John Paul papacy were now firm. When he is at the Vatican, the pope begins each day in private prayer, holds Mass for visitors at seven, followed by breakfast and discussion, then secludes himself for prayer and written work. Private audiences start at around eleven.

Lunch, with guests, follows Roman tradition, starting at around one-thirty with pasta and moving on to meat and vegetables washed down with white wine, of which the pope likes a glass or two. Some guests have noted that on the day of their invitation, the pope's main course was simple Polish fare like soup and pierogis, while guests were served fancy veal or chicken; they left not knowing whether John Paul's stomach was acting up or whether he just wanted Wadowice cooking that day and didn't think the others would like it.

He carried his fondness for sweets to Rome. Wines, pastries, and other treats he serves are often gifts from the many people worldwide who want to show off their wares for the pope. But when a baker once bragged that John Paul loved his special brown bread, the nun who headed his household team told reporters the pope "wouldn't know whether the bread was white or brown. He just tears off a piece while he's talking."[1]

Veterans of such meals say the surroundings are elegant without being ostentatious—a lot of marble and crystal, with a few religious or Polish ornaments. They say John Paul fast-forwards through conversational ice-breaking, gets the talk onto serious subjects, and keeps it there. He rarely calls a halt. Dziwisz, who sits at the head of the table while the pope sits across from his guests, signals when it's time to go.

This Roman lunch is followed by a quiet period of "meditation," then a walk outside. More hours of paperwork or meetings follow, then supper at eight, again, always with at least one guest besides his secretaries. John Paul usually works a while longer before going to bed at eleven.

"He needs his sleep," says Archbishop Giovanni Battista Re, who heads the curial staff. When traveling, if "he can't sleep well, he can't work well the next day." Many visitors remark on how often—even for a pope—John Paul slips into the chapel for prayer. "There's a self-certainty that comes from prayer," Archbishop Re says.

Early in his papacy, guests remarked that John Paul wouldn't look them in the eye. Photographs often showed him looking over the shoulder of the person talking to him, or at the ceiling. Gradually, that has changed. Jozef Czyrek, the former communist official, says that Polish priests often lean one ear toward a speaker while looking away—a habit he thinks comes from long sessions in the confessional booth.

Many papal meal guests are the world's bishops. On their every-five-year visits, each usually gets a private audience of up to twenty minutes and a meal with up to a dozen colleagues. Each brings a written report. If the pope doesn't read them all, he reads summaries drawn up by Gantin's staff. Bishops say the pope is remarkable at remembering them and their particular problems, and leaves most in positive spirits.

For his nonobligatory guests, John Paul prizes intellectuals. Says Professor Rocco Buttiglione, "He asks questions and then lets the experts hold forth. When I was there it was current affairs or philosophy. When people came back from someplace, he would grill them" about what they had seen. Guests have deduced that when the pope seems inexplicably obsessed with a certain topic at dinner—family relationships, say, or the meaning of forgiveness—an encyclical or other papal decision is often forthcoming. He bounces ideas off people without always disclosing what he's up to.

Until a broken shoulder in 1993 forced him to start dictating, John Paul wrote almost everything longhand, in Polish, continuing his schoolboy habit of putting short religious dedications in an upper corner of each page: "To Mary," "To Joseph," "To Jesus through Mary," and so on, often using just initials to abbreviate these messages.[2]

Anything he wants others to look at is immediately translated into Italian, the common language of the curia. All major published work is checked for ramifications by the secretariate of state and the Congregations for Doctrine and Christian Unity. The many routine greetings the pope delivers are prepared by relevant departments. Trusted writers in Vatican agencies are routinely asked to rewrite drafts from other agencies without knowing who wrote them (possibly a cardinal); they are simply told what the pope objects to. He still writes all major documents himself.

Staffers say John Paul rarely loses his temper, and then mostly at deliberate acts, such as the shelling of a marketplace in Sarajevo in 1993. Generally, though, as one curia monsignor says, "I've never seen a person so serene."

After a project, he personally thanks those who worked on it, making at least a telephone call, though staffers note that life in Poland left him permanently suspicious of telephone privacy.

Annually his old school friends from Poland or the Angelicum still troop through his apartment, and he seems to love it. He still reads *Tygodnik Powszechny* faithfully. Deputy Editor Krzysztof Kozlowski says that when the top staff was brought to Rome to celebrate the paper's fortieth anniversary, he thought the pope was merely flattering them when he said he read it every week; later, Kozlowski encountered him on a trip, and was flabbergasted when the pontiff leapt on him like a professor on a graduate student to quiz him about an article he had just written.

John Paul's favorite conversational partner may be Ratzinger, who has the only standing appointment (every Friday) besides Gantin's. Ratzinger and John Paul like to explore the doctrinal aspects of every question, no matter how non-doctrinal it may seem.[3]

Whereas other papacies have engendered rumors that some backstage Rasputin was pulling strings (for Pius XII, a manipulative German nun; for John XXIII, a socialist-inclined secretary), no one thinks John Paul is anyone's puppet. He let Polish churchmen leapfrog over the curia to counsel him—inevitably, they are called the "Polish Mafia"—but everyone knows he's boss.

One "Polish Mafia" member, Bishop Szczepan Wesoly, who has been in Rome since the 1960s, says, "He created a revolution—pulled down the wall of secrecy [previously] around this whole hierarchy, the pope and his entourage. The difference between the Vatican now and under Pius XII is more than you can imagine. Pius left the Vatican two or three times in sixteen years. Paul VI was afraid of crowds. John Paul gets rejuvenated by crowds."

Through the middle years of John Paul's papacy, six Polish nuns cooked and cleaned for him. At his beck were an Italian valet, an Italian driver (with a black Mercedes), and other servants. Once, when some Polish bishops were visiting, Bishop Pieronek says, "the nuns showed us that the pope was wearing knickers that had been patched so often they couldn't be patched anymore [but] insisted on keeping them." Pieronek authorized the nuns to throw out the knickers no matter what the pope said, and get him new ones.

He watches little television—occasionally news or, in the early years, a soccer match, though as papal cares waxed, his soccer interest waned. A few times a year he starts a movie on videocassette, usually breaking off after twenty minutes or so, sometimes to resume it another day, sometimes not. According to his boyhood friend Jerzy Kruger, in 1994 he watched all of *Schindler's List*, Steven Spielberg's masterpiece about the Holocaust in Krakow, in this piecemeal fashion, and at the end pronounced it "very good." Another movie that got full papal attention was *Gandhi*. He occasionally listens to Chopin, favoring Arthur Rubinstein's recordings.[4] Even before his health declined in the 1990s, his vacations were limited to a week's hiking in northern Italy each summer.[5]

Paul VI once wrote in his diary of the "extreme loneliness of the Pope." Commenting in *Osservatore Romano*, John Paul said, "Perhaps I have a different temperament." He has never been short of friends.

It is commonly thought that the pope gave up his daily afternoon walks in the large Vatican botanical garden because of Agca's assassination attempt. But several staff members say he began confining his walks to his private penthouse garden even before the shooting, as he gradually adopted a formality he had never bothered with in Krakow. Father Mario Laurenti, supervisor of the Vatican altar boys from 1980 to 1992, says the pope used to mingle regularly with the boys at play but stopped as "a matter of decorum."[6] "At the beginning, this pope felt more free," he recalls. "People around him got him to stop. It was difficult for him."

At state visits, "everything is scripted," Father Laurenti goes on.[7] "You are told in advance where you will walk, and when." Foreign travel is also carefully staged. For example, two days after the second attempt on his life, in Fatima, John Paul burst as if spontaneously through police lines into a field of Portuguese peasants, shaking hands, defying his guards. But journalist Wilton Wynn later learned from security officials that the precise area of his departure from the road had been planned in advance and made safe. The same thing happened the next day, when the pope, acting as if on a whim, left his route to kiss a child in a wheelchair: he knew where the wheelchair would be.

In Tokyo, as Japanese girls in Polish costume danced before him on a stage, two dancers approached and invited him to join in. Reports Wynn, "The pope looked surprised, seemed to hesitate, and then, with a shrug of the shoulders and a broad grin, took one of the little things by the hand and walked into their circle." But Wynn wasn't touched by this "touching scene": a few hours earlier, by coincidence, he had happened upon the rehearsal, and seen the same little girl go through the same gestures and get the same look of surprise from a priest standing in for the pope. Ever the thespian.

John Paul oversees nine congregations, twelve councils, and scattered commissions and tribunals, each commanded by a resident cardinal. Each has a full-time staff (the Vatican has about thirty-five hundred employees, half of them clergy), plus a board of outside cardinals and bishops, though they rarely all fly in for meetings.

"Being a curial cardinal is a big job," says Cardinal Edmund Szoka, formerly of Detroit. Besides running the prefecture for economic affairs, he is on the boards of five congregations. The Congregation for Bishops meets twice a month, while others may meet every few months. "They take lots of time just reading," he says.

The top few leaders of each agency are invited to the papal apartment for meals at least once a year, and most every few months. The secretary of state, who is just down a marble hallway from the pope, talks to him almost daily. Under the secretary are a *sostituto* (chief of staff) and a foreign minister; since one cardinal can't serve under another, these two archbishops are probably the most responsible noncardinals in the Church. One or more of the three meets with the pope for an hour most days at around 6:30 P.M., often staying for dinner, usually with other guests.[8]

More time is spent selecting bishops than on any other papal decision. John Paul consults anyone handy who might have an opinion, but the biggest influence is Gantin—meetings with him and reports from his assistants, who constantly talk to bishops around the world. At least 80 percent of the time, the pope picks one of the three names on his nuncio's original list.[9]

Some bureaucracies are of John Paul's own creation. For example, in 1982 he established a Vatican Council for Culture, under Cardinal Paul Poupard. (Those who thought it logical for a Polish pope to choose a German—Ratzinger—to defend the faith were not surprised that he chose a Frenchman to oversee culture.) The pope wanted "a synthesis between" culture and faith, just as he had sought one between science and faith. Most of all, the new council was to study the culture conveyed by television and other twentieth-century technologies.

At times, the council got bogged down. Assigned by the pope to encourage practicing lay Catholics to teach in universities, Poupard, among his first tasks, surveyed the world's bishops on their relationships with universities—and was surprised to find that many bishops had no such relationships. Twelve years later, the council was still working on a document addressing that problem.[10]

More decisively, Poupard's council helped carry out the pope's decision to restore Michelangelo's frescos in the Sistine Chapel, grown dark and sooty over the centuries. Courage was required: though John Paul's experts said the colors could be restored without damage, others predicted that the irreplaceable work of the world's most acclaimed artist might be destroyed. The Sistine Chapel restoration, like responding to the bishops' survey, took twelve years, but it finished, by most accounts, a spectacular success.

During that time, John Paul also moved to preserve other Church art treasures around the world. Worried that workmen renovating Church property weren't attending to its unusually rich heritage, he created a commission—overseen by a cardinal, but with an internationally trained art historian atop its staff—and ordered care for fine art to be included with human and financial considerations on every project.

Working through the national bishops' conferences, the commission encouraged each diocese worldwide to set up a committee to maintain monuments, historic buildings, and artworks. Through a problem-solving network, the commission devised ways to comply with a Vatican II mandate that altars must face the congregation, without dismantling valuable old altars. Parishes looking to renovate were instructed on up-to-date designs that would accord with the historical period styles of their churches.[11]

Less successful was John Paul's 1982 decision to build a $5.3 million underground annex to the Vatican Library, to safeguard and display its ancient manuscripts and hand-illustrated Bibles and other books. Many display cases remain empty, and the thirty miles of shelves are poorly arranged; cynics have angered the Vatican by suggesting that the annex was really designed as a papal bomb shelter (unlikely).

Many Vatican treasures are not displayed for tourists. Friendly staffers who gave me a behind-the-scenes tour of the literary archives and private Vatican art treasures said they couldn't show me eye-popping jewels and gold they described in private storerooms.

These riches seem hidden less for security's sake than from a sense of unseemliness. They are relics of a past when monarchs were free to be ostentatious, long predating a pope who prefers patched-up pants and takes to heart Jesus' disregard for worldly wealth. There are stories, with no traceable sources but quite in character, that on taking office, John Paul proposed selling off these riches (at about the same time he proposed recognizing Israel) but was persuaded that such a gesture would provoke ridicule rather than respect, and distract from his other agenda.

John Paul's relationship with Italy's Socialist president, Sandro Pertini, was so close that the two men vacationed in the mountains together in 1984. The pope, then sixty-four, skied while Pertini watched. Their friendship was remarkable, considering that in John XXIII's time, Cardinal Ottaviani had cultivated a new political party because he thought even the Christian Democrats were dangerously far Left. Once, after John Paul visited him in his presidential office, Pertini told reporters, "I said to the pope, 'What is God for you, is for me the conscience.' And the pope replied, 'That is because the conscience is transcendent.' I have always found in this pope a great respect and sensitivity for my socialist faith."

That summer, the head of the Italian Communist Party, Enrico Berlinguer, died after a brief illness. John Paul had prayed for his health and sent an archbishop to the hospital to comfort his family. Berlinguer not only had spoken out in support of Solidarity but had rejected atheism, saying religious faith "can stimulate the believer to carry out the socialist renewal of society." His replacement, Alessandro Natta, was to become the first communist leader to speak on Vatican Radio.

America's top bishops, visiting the White House in 1984, found no such rapport. They and Reagan agreed about abortion, but little else.

40

One more major effort was required of John Paul in Poland before his revolution toppled communism. The obstacle was Primate Glemp. Late in 1983, Glemp determined to press the government's stooge trade union upon society as a replacement for Solidarity. Although it meant tolerating a permanent communist state, he hoped the new union would pacify workers, improve living standards, and restore the Church as the major social counterforce. Glemp sent emissaries to ten top leaders of underground Solidarity, urging them to go along; none would.[1]

January 5, 1984, Glemp met with Jaruzelski for the first time since the pope's visit the year before. No account of the meeting was released, but there was evidence of a deal. The very next day, Glemp publicly denounced the new U.S. missiles in Europe, and several days later, Jaruzelski offered Michnik and other imprisoned Solidarity figures an exit to France.

Again, the underground leaders foiled Glemp's plans. Michnik's response to Jaruzelski's offer—smuggled out of his cell and broadcast on Radio Free Europe—addressed the communists as "vindictive, dishonorable swine," and said, "The very idea that there are people who associate Poland . . . with a prison cell, who prefer Christmas under arrest to a vacation in the south of France, troubles you profoundly."

Also after his meeting with Jaruzelski, Glemp tried to silence his most vocally pro-Solidarity priests, particularly Father Popieluszko, who still drew tens of thousands of listeners from around Poland to his patriotic sermons in a blue-collar area of Warsaw. The primate called in Popieluszko and two other priests whose work for Solidarity angered the government, and told them to "avoid useless friction with the state."[2]

A few days later, at one-thirty in the morning, someone rang the buzzer of Father Popieluszko's second-floor flat in a small building attached to his church. Wary, he didn't leave bed to go to the window. Moments later, a brick with a small bomb attached came crashing in and exploded, damaging part of the room. After this narrow escape, Popieluszko began receiving threatening letters. In his sermons, he tried to quote the pope and Wyszynski, so that Glemp and the government could not accuse him of writing seditious material. Father Antonin Lewek, who today is still at the parish, says Popieluszko repeatedly told him, "They can kill me, but I am convinced that what I do is right for the Church and the homeland."

In late February 1984, Glemp transferred Father Mieczyslaw Nowak of Ursus, one of the pro-Solidarity priests he had called in with Popieluszko, to a distant, rural parish. The Ursus workers protested his removal with a sit-in and hunger strike, but Glemp took off to attend Church meetings in South America. In Brazil, he told Western reporters that Solidarity was "a mixed bag, including... Marxists, Trotskyites... and Party members." He said Walesa had "lost control" and "was manipulated a lot." He trivialized the case of another Solidarity leader, Wladyslaw Frasyniuk, whose severe beating in prison had been reported in the underground press. He said some Solidarity leaders were "not Polish"—an anti-Semitic innuendo that Poles themselves read as an attack on Michnik and other prominent Jews in Solidarity.

In Paris, the exiled Aleksandr Smolar saw to it that Glemp's remarks reached the Polish public through the BBC, where he worked.[3] In Brussels, meanwhile, Jerzy Milewski hit the roof, telling people that Glemp "said Solidarity didn't exist, it was a bunch of Trotskyites!"[4] At a conference, John Paul's friend Bohdan Cywinski denounced Glemp as "not principled."

John Paul began using Jacek Wozniakowski, Znak's founding editor, as a messenger, having appointed him to be a lay member of the Pontifical Council for Culture so he could travel frequently to Rome. Wozniakowski carried word from the pope to Bujak and other jailed Solidarity members, and to Milewski in Brussels, letting them know that John Paul "was very well aware of what they were doing" and spurring them on. "And they would always tell me how good it was that I told them, because other people were telling them the pope disapproved," Wozniakowski says. He won't say so directly, but the "other people" were obviously Glemp and the bishops who supported him.

Glemp returned from Latin America by way of Rome, occasioning a showdown. A furious John Paul kept him waiting three days for an audience.[5] In talks with other Poles in Rome, Glemp continued to complain that the pope didn't understand, and was second-guessing him "from the outside."[6]

Glemp and Jaruzelski now seemed almost allies. Jaruzelski reports praising his relationship with Glemp to a skeptical Chernenko.[7] Another sign of their cooperation was the anti-Semitic literature that began appearing in Polish churches, apparently generated by Church presses. Brochures included the

"Protocols of the Elders of Zion," a well-documented forgery purporting to be evidence of a Jewish plot.[8] The *Tablet* editorialized that Glemp preferred "the picture he knew best, of the Polish stage occupied by only two actors, the State and the Church." That was precisely what the pope had been striving to get away from since the 1960s.

Yet at this critical point, Glemp lured Walesa into his camp, revealing just how far Walesa had drifted from Solidarity's active leaders. Outside Poland, Walesa was synonymous with Solidarity, though he had originally balked at forming the union. Now, at Glemp's urging, he tried to persuade the underground leaders to make peace by killing Solidarity.

By most accounts, the deal Walesa and Glemp proposed would have released the dozen or two top Solidarity leaders still in jail and allowed Bujak and others in the underground to live in open society. In exchange, they would promise to withdraw from all political activity. And Solidarity would be replaced by a "Christian trade union"—which the Solidarity leaders began referring to instead as a "yellow trade union."

Walesa sent emissaries who met with the Solidarity underground commission for thirty-six hours. "The talks were dramatic," Bujak remembers. "All these people in prison were waiting for a statement from Solidarity." Some, particularly Modzelewski and Kuron, were ailing and "could have died in prison. Morally, it was a difficult decision for us." Walesa's emissaries "said we must make this compromise. The Church leadership thought it was reasonable."

At first, the commission was split. Once more, the Solidarity revolution could have been stopped in its tracks. But once more, it was saved by its powerful protector. As luck had it, the commission met just as John Paul was commemorating the fortieth anniversary of the battle of Monte Casino, Italy, in which thirteen hundred Poles had died. It was a public ceremony, broadcast on international television and radio that could not be kept off the Polish airwaves. As at the Kolbe ceremony in 1982, Polish communist and Church leaders squirmed in their seats as John Paul chose to talk about Solidarity: Solidarity was irreplaceable, he declared, and the 1980 accord had to be implemented.

His message resonated throughout Poland. "The pope was saying Solidarity was alive," Bujak says. The Jaruzelski-Glemp replacement union "would have put a tombstone on Solidarity. We were terribly angry at [Glemp], but we knew his opinion was not unanimous." Solidarity's own emissaries returned from prisons saying that to a man, the prisoners themselves had rejected the terms of the proposed agreement. The commission then voted down the deal almost unanimously.[9]

After the government and the Polish primate failed to kill Solidarity in May 1984, there remained only for the movement to realize its own strength, and for the Soviet Union to offer it a chance to pounce. That opportunity was to come sooner than anyone suspected.*

41

The same month the stooge union was rejected, May 1984, John Paul went to South Korea for the two-hundredth anniversary of the arrival there of Catholic missionaries. There were now 1.6 million Catholics (and 5.3 million Protestants) in a population of forty million. In an open-air Mass in Seoul, John Paul made saints of 103 Catholics who had died for their faith in Korea; it was the first canonization ceremony outside Rome since the Middle Ages.[1] He had kind words for Confucius, still Korea's main religious figure.

But the trip was dominated by politics. South Korea's president was General Chun Doo Whan, a staggeringly corrupt dictator. For two hours, as John Paul attended a ceremony with him, a riot raged at a nearby university between police and students seeking open elections. Police tear gas wafted over the papal motorcade at one point, overcoming the archbishop of Seoul.

John Paul fed the fervor for democracy. Ordaining priests before eighty thousand onlookers, he stressed their duty to the "poor and alienated." In a tinderbox of industrial workers in Pusan, he reformulated his constant message that "too often, the human being is treated as a simple instrument of production, a tool that should cost the minimum while producing the maximum."

In Seoul, with his presence on the platform drawing international attention, he handed the microphone to selected young people, who complained of government repression and imprisonment. One by one, they asserted that radical groups existed in Korea only because tyranny did. The pope's own advice was simply not to despair; he let the message come from the Koreans. But without him, they would not have been heard. It took three more years of turmoil and embarrassment before General Chun agreed to hold elections. How much John Paul's visit contributed to bringing democracy to non-Catholic Korea can't be precisely measured, but it helped significantly.

In Papua New Guinea, the pope journeyed to a remote mountaintop to address two hundred thousand people in pidgin. He met with the papal repre-

---

* Bujak praises three people as critical lifelines for the underground: papal friend Wozniakowski and two women from Warsaw—Hannah Federowicz, a volunteer at St. Martin's, and Hannah Krall, an underground journalist—who did not themselves see John Paul in Rome, but who carried messages from others who did.

sentative from nearby East Timor, where he couldn't go himself because of increased violence. Predominantly Moslem Indonesia—under a military dictatorship installed and backed by American aid—had occupied Timor (Catholic, formerly Portuguese). Indonesian troops were carrying out group executions on the instant judgment of makeshift courts, while survivors were herded into concentration camps. John Paul was among the few world leaders to speak out, bringing an international spotlight to injustices that Indonesia's allies—including the U.S.—were helping to conceal.

In Thailand, he met the supreme Buddhist patriarch, then went to the northern border to speak to hundreds of thousands of refugees from Cambodia and Vietnam. A local priest who pastored to the refugees told reporters that John Paul was an effective weapon against "a certain compassion burnout in the world." He said the refugees, who were often separated from parents, children, brothers, and sisters, "feel that the pope's presence will make nations more conscious of welcoming refugees. Then their families can be reunited." In a speech that night, the pope said much the same thing.

One part of the Banco Ambrosiano scandal had so far been kept out of the press: the Polish connection. But as John Paul returned from Asia, prosecutors were threatening to go after Father Kazimierz Przydatek, who had accepted money from Roberto Calvi's agents for distribution to the Polish underground. Przydatek's name appeared in a prominent magazine. "Very fine people accused him of taking money from the wrong people," Cardinal Deskur says. Possible exposure of the money chain was the last straw.

Intimates say that other grievances had built up against Przydatek, and that Papal Secretary Dziwisz was angry with him—which must mean the pope was as well. For one thing, Przydatek was feuding with another Polish priest, whom John Paul had brought to Rome to assist visiting Poles. "It was ambition over who was running things," says Wanda Gawronska, who helped both priests aid the Polish underground. Also, Przydatek had embarrassingly bungled a Solidarity benefit concert he organized in Rome's big Sports Palace: the talent was third-rate, and the expected crowd didn't show up, including the pope. On top of that, Father Bardecki says Przydatek was "absentminded, a poor administrator. Papers were a mess, including the accounting."

As the Ambrosiano prosecutors closed in, Dziwisz talked to Bishop Wesoly, the administrator for Polish clergy in Rome. Since Przydatek was a Jesuit, Wesoly asked Father Pittau, John Paul's choice to head the Jesuit order, "to find a parish for him," Pittau says. Przydatek was shipped quietly to a Jesuit residence in Milan and never charged. Even friends didn't know where he was. His name disappeared from the Vatican yearbook, where he had been listed with thousands of other Church officials since 1978. Father Hejmo was asked to take over the pilgrims' center from him, and still runs it. Years later, when the Ambrosiano case was finished, Przydatek resurfaced in Rome, as a pastor in a parish.[2]

John Paul waded into one controversy after another that summer of 1984. In June, he met with Prime Minister P. W. Botha of South Africa. The meeting was so sensitive that the Vatican felt compelled to issue an unusual, nervous disclaimer, reiterating its opposition to racial discrimination and saying that popes saw leaders "from the most diverse regimes," and that Botha had requested the audience. Still, Anglican Bishop Desmond Tutu, a Nobel Prize–winning hero of the South African democracy movement, called the meeting "a slap in the face to all victims of apartheid." A few weeks later, John Paul quelled some criticism by also seeing the head of the Namibian independence movement that the governments of South Africa and the United States both opposed.[3]

Traveling to Switzerland, John Paul faced five days of protests over his refusal to compromise on doctrine. The head of the Federation of Protestant Churches of Switzerland said it was "hardly tolerable" for the pope to pray for unity of the churches but not share the Eucharist. The Catholic Pastoral Council of Lucerne urged him to permit priests to marry. A priest sharing the pope's platform advocated the ordination of women, and university professors criticized his rebukes to Hans Kung.

In his own talks, John Paul bluntly criticized Switzerland for exporting arms and for refusing to accept immigrants and refugees (unless they were rich or did menial work). Crowds for his masses were way below expectations, the largest being forty thousand people.

An ocean away, meanwhile, the U.S. Episcopate released a ninety-five-page study saying the reason more men weren't going into the priesthood was the celibacy requirement: celibacy "emerges consistently as a major negative factor," it said. (The study's only recommendation was further research.)

In a private meeting after the Monte Casino ceremony, John Paul had again pressed Polish president Jablonski for unconditional freedom for the political prisoners still in jail.[4] By July 1984, Jaruzelski, recognizing the defeat of his plan to kill Solidarity and run the country under a deal with Glemp, granted amnesty to more than 630 prisoners; they were warned that they could be arrested again if they resumed political activity, but no promises were extracted from them. The pope publicly praised the amnesty, but reminded Jaruzelski that the 1980 accord still needed living up to.

A day later, the Polish government agreed to let the Church begin spending a fund it had started to finance private farming. Walesa had seeded the fund with the two hundred thousand dollars he received for winning the Nobel Peace Prize in 1983, but the communists had refused to let farmers use the money. Now, Jaruzelski recognized that the likeliest cure for persistent food shortages was to let private farmers raise foreign capital, as the government could not.

Because West German Catholics had promised money if the fund's independence was guaranteed, Jaruzelski agreed to let the Church operate the fund. In reality, it was a cover for encroaching private enterprise. Among the first practical results was new refrigeration equipment, which meant that Poland, a leading dairy country, would no longer lose so much milk to spoilage.

The communist government had begun its long backpedal to oblivion. The underground—now, really, the Polish people—exploited its new power prudently but firmly. Most priests seemed delighted that John Paul had won the struggle with Glemp. Churches helped coordinate demonstrations in August on the fourth anniversary of Solidarity's founding. Communist Deputy Prime Minister Mieczyslaw Rakowski was left to lament, "We are watching with concern the politicization of part of the clergy. One's hair stands on end when one hears what is being said in some pulpits."[5]

The next prize Jaruzelski got for his cooperation with John Paul was an end to the American economic sanctions. President Reagan invited Vatican Ambassador Laghi to fly across the United States for lunch at his California home, and said that after years of refusing the pope's importunities, Reagan now wanted to ease sanctions on Poland, including the ban on its membership in the International Monetary Fund. But he faced opposition from some Cold Warriors he had appointed.

Says a smiling Laghi, "He wanted to utilize the opinion of the Holy Father in order to convince those in his cabinet who opposed him. He asked, 'What is the mind of the Holy Father about this?' I said, 'I did not come here to tell you what the Holy Father thinks. But I tell you the people are suffering.'" And Laghi reminded Reagan that Cardinal Krol and other Polish bishops also wanted the sanctions removed. The sanctions were gradually loosened.[6]

42

Liberation Theology—the attempt to make Catholicism the focal point of Latin America's poor and powerless in their struggle for economic and political rights—reached a crisis in 1984.

Ratzinger gave a paper on it in March, then talked about it at a press conference. He praised that part of Liberation Theology that "put in a proper light the necessary responsibility of the Christian toward the poor and the oppressed." He said Jesus' Sermon on the Mount (which begins, "Blessed are the poor in spirit, for theirs is the kingdom of heaven . . .") "is in reality the choice on the part of God in favor of the poor." But the famous sermon wasn't a call to class struggle, Ratzinger said. And he added enigmatically that the Church's "special option for the poor . . . excludes no one."

In the Vatican's 1984 campaign against Liberation Theology, Ratzinger's zeal ran ahead of John Paul's. Friends like Bohdan Cywinski and Rocco Buttiglione recall tortured efforts by the pope to understand why Latin Americans wouldn't accept the middle ground he offered. Cywinski—who had been sent on learning trips to Latin America by Western labor unions—told John Paul that Liberation Theology was wrongly described in Europe as "Leftist-Rightist, ideologized." In Latin America, he said, "priests were active for social causes for the poor. When I asked about Liberation Theology, they used to say, 'It does not interest us. It's the concern of intellectuals.'" Buttiglione says that after voracious reading, the pope concluded that "there is not one Liberation Theology, there are many, few really Marxist."

Ratzinger showed no such reservations. His first targets were Fathers Clodovis and Leonardo Boff, Brazilian brothers (siblings) who worked in poor communities and had become nationally revered, like Archbishop Camara before them. As part of their Liberation Theology work, the Boffs had founded an organization that built plumbing systems and durable housing for the homeless of Petrópolis, Brazil's old royal capital. They had also converted a vast rubbish dump into a recycling center.

The Boffs had innovated "base ecclesial communities"—fifteen to twenty families that met "once or twice a week to hear the word of God, to share their problems . . . and to solve those problems through the inspiration of the Gospel."[1] An estimated seventy thousand such communities now met in Brazil, using the Boffs' books, which taught people to address practical problems themselves rather than depend on those with official power—much as Wojtyla had taught his flock in Krakow.

But unlike Wojtyla, the Boffs seemed to welcome antagonism with Rome. "The future of the institutional Church lies in this small seed that is the new Church, growing in the fields of the poor and powerless," said Father Leonardo Boff. "It is to be expected that the old Church will distrust the new Church. . . . The new Church . . . must not be drawn into the center's game of condemnation and suspicion. . . . It must have the courage to be disobedient to the demands of the center without anger or complaint."[2]

Just as Ratzinger wrote rebukes to the Boffs, the archbishop of Rio de Janeiro withdrew teaching licenses from Clodovis Boff and a colleague, Father Antonio Moser, saying they used Marxist analysis. The Brazilian Bishops' Conference formally objected, noting that Moser was on its doctrinal commission. The Boff brothers publicly acknowledged some mistakes but insisted that Liberation Theology was an application of the Gospel, not an alternative to it. They said Ratzinger wasn't paying sufficient attention to poverty.

The Nicaraguan front reopened when the Episcopate's Easter message called for peace negotiations with the Contras. This rankled the Sandinista administration, which argued that the Contras were mere puppets of the United States, and said it would negotiate only with Washington.

American Catholic industrialist Peter Grace, a Reagan favorite, sent a top aide to present John Paul with an ambitious plan to oppose the Nicaraguan government. The pope was told that under "Marxist-Leninist" Sandinistas, "the situation of the [Nicaraguan] Church was more dangerous than in Poland."[3] Ironically, Grace's plan to overthrow the Sandinistas resembled the "base ecclesial communities" that the Boffs had created to oppose aristocratic dictatorships elsewhere.

Under Grace's scheme, Nicaraguan Archbishop Miguel Obando y Bravo was to divide his archdiocese "into small groupings of Catholics" who would get "courses on leadership . . . along with religious instruction, plus instruction on hygiene, nutrition, and manual skills. The archbishop has given all of his resources and skills to developing leaders who can oppose the Sandinistas," the pope was told.

John Paul's reply to the proposal isn't recorded. But Archbishop Obando y Bravo arrived in Rome days later, and after seeing the pope, he seemed to back off from his Easter message, issuing an odd clarification that he hadn't intended it to be partisan.[4] And Cardinal O'Connor of New York—the admiral—said, on returning from Nicaragua, that "not a single bishop" had asked for support for the Contras. From all indications, Peter Grace's plan didn't get to first base. (Obando y Bravo didn't reply to my telefaxed requests for his recollections.)

Yet at just this time, the Sandinistas chose to rub salt in Rome's wound over priests in government by appointing Father Fernando Cardenal minister of education. Father Kolvenbach, the new head of the Jesuits, who himself was largely sympathetic with Liberation Theology, warned Cardenal that this new affront might force his expulsion from the order. The Vatican commanded all Nicaraguan priests to quit their government jobs.

∽

Another Liberation Theology battle front opened around Cardinal Arns of Brazil, who was compiling the history of terror, torture, and murder in his country under the generals. While taking great pains to keep that project secret, Arns was otherwise very public. In a speech about political repression by U.S. allies throughout Latin America, he sounded much like John Paul: "The real power of a revolution is moral," he said. "If it doesn't have that, the revolution doesn't exist. A true revolution has to unite a country; violence always divides it."[5]

As the Brazilian bishops vigorously promoted the redistribution of land, farm workers were killed in dozens of attacks. Before audiences in Europe and the United States, Cardinal Arns accused rich Brazilians of treating the poor like "miserable creatures who are in the way and disturbing their comfort." He blamed foreign-owned multinational corporations for some of the violence,[6] and said, "Things will not change for the better in Latin America unless U.S. foreign policy changes first." Aristocratic parties in Brazil called him a communist and published concocted documents smearing him.

In mid-1984, Ratzinger sent Cardinal Joseph Höffner of Cologne to Arns's archdiocese of São Paolo on a "visitation"—a polite word for an investigation. A complaint had been filed about Arns by the archbishop of Rio de Janeiro, who had already withdrawn teaching licenses from Clodovis Boff and another well-known theologian for their alleged Marxism. Höffner, Ratzinger's chosen investigator, was an outspoken foe of even democratic socialism.

That same summer, the Catholic Intelligentsia Club of Warsaw voted to support Liberation Theology, drawing the obvious parallel between Poland and Latin America. The club even called for a "Polish theology of liberation." Youthful protesters disrupted Ratzinger's speech to a hundred thousand worshipers at a German Church congress; a banner declared, "In spite of the Inquisition, Liberation Theology lives, Herr Ratzinger." A competing Mass by Hans Kung drew only four thousand people.

This was the atmosphere on August 6, 1984, when Ratzinger issued an "Instruction on Certain Aspects of the Theology of Liberation." It was said to have "almost the status of an encyclical," though for a reason that remains private between the two men, John Paul decided it wouldn't *be* an encyclical, or even come from him.

Ratzinger acknowledged that Christians should be "involved in the struggle for justice," and said his document "should not . . . serve as an excuse for those who maintain . . . indifference [to] . . . human misery." But he attacked Liberation Theology broadside, quoting John Paul II's neophyte speech on arriving in

Puebla in 1979, which told Latin American priests to stick to theology (a stance the Pope had soon departed from).

True to his brilliance, Ratzinger leapt to the heart of the argument: the notion that Marxist analysis could be separated from Marxist ideology. "No separation of the parts of [Marxism] is possible," he said. "If one tries to take only one part, say, the analysis, one ends up having to accept the entire ideology." Marxism in any dose inevitably "subordinates theology to the class struggle." This contradicted the asserted beliefs of the pope, but John Paul approved the document and it appeared to be the law of the Church.

What the public didn't know, however, was that the pope himself wasn't content with Ratzinger's "Instruction." As soon as it was issued, the pope put Cardinal Roger Etchegaray—his effervescent counselor on Justice and Peace— to work writing another document, refracting what Ratzinger had said into something socially positive.[7]

John Paul must have expected that Etchegaray would play the "liberal" to Ratzinger's "conservative." Etchegaray went at it with relish. He thought a better balance was needed to avoid both "politicization of the Church" on the one hand and inaction over social wrongs on the other, and their talks convinced him that the pope agreed. "To really understand the philosophy of this pope, you can't only look at what he says about Marxism," Etchegaray says. "He is just as severe about neo-liberalism"—unfettered capitalism.

As Etchegaray worked on balancing Ratzinger's "instruction," Ratzinger himself called in Father Leonardo Boff, September 7, 1984. To support him, Boff brought two fellow Brazilians, Lorscheider and Arns. Ratzinger's own staff acknowledged that having the firepower of two cardinals was "unusual" for an accused. Lorscheider and Arns weren't maverick radicals, like Kung; they were among the three bishops elected by their peers to represent the Western Hemisphere Church on the permanent council of the Rome synod (Bernardin being the third). Arns was one of five bishops chosen to write the synod's message. In a further show of support, the head of Boff's order, the Franciscans, announced that he was very proud of Boff, whom he called "a good theologian and a conscientious friar."

Just before the session, Boff published an article reaffirming his fealty to Church doctrine and denying that he looked to Marxism for anything more than a "better understanding [of] the reality of exploitation and . . . possible ways of overcoming the antipopular system that is capitalism." A priest who had worked twenty years with the poor in Brazil told the press, "Any condemnation of Leonardo Boff . . . would be . . . not just a theological judgment but a political pointer."[8]

After a four-hour session, in which Boff delivered a fifty-page reply to Ratzinger's six-page complaint, Boff said, "I was happy to explain my arguments. There was no talk of change or correction."

Suddenly an even more powerful defender stepped up. Casaroli, the secretary of state, exploded with eye-popping remarks to reporters to the effect that he should have been consulted about Ratzinger's Liberation Theology document but wasn't. Casaroli stressed that the document came from Ratzinger, not from the pope. It was "negative." A positive document would have been "preferable."

There followed rare public warfare within the Vatican. Ratzinger rebutted his critics—including Casaroli—in a magazine interview. He said the national bishops' conferences that disagreed with him were just "bureaucratic structures," lacking in "teaching authority."[9] He suggested to a daily newspaper in Madrid that he all but wanted to rewrite Vatican II. He said some of the Council's decisions had been "decidedly negative for the Catholic Church" and accused the Council of "an indiscriminate openness to ... an agnostic and atheist world." He said he was "searching for a new equilibrium," and that European theology was "old, sick with academic overindulgence ... more dangerous" than heresy because "it does not even react against Rome, which in its arrogance it already considers useless."[10]

A pope struggling to unify the Church could not have been happy with this. While not explicitly disclosing Etchegaray's follow-up assignment, John Paul hinted pointedly to reporters that a positive second shoe was still to fall on the Liberation Theology issue.[11]

Speaking in Latin America, Father Kolvenbach, the new Jesuit leader, pounded home a message that the question was not whether to "engage in politics, for in a certain sense we are constantly doing that." He said it was "absolutely necessary to use the terminology of Marxism" to describe real conditions: "Class struggle ... exists," he declared—just as Wojtyla had written thirty years earlier in his underground book in Poland.

A showdown occurred in the fall of 1984, when Ratzinger hauled in the Peruvian bishops as a body, aiming to extract a statement from them in accord with his August message. Although surviving participants now try to minimize the dramatic nature of the assembly, some bishops had just been in Rome for their every-five-year visits; their recall really *was* extraordinary.

How much of this was Ratzinger's idea, and how much the pope's, is known only to them. But Ratzinger had been prodding the Peruvians for a year to go on record rejecting the ideas of Father Gustavo Gutierrez, a Peruvian theologian who first popularized the term "Liberation Theology" in his 1971 book by that name. Ratzinger was upset that Gutierrez used Marxist analysis, overemphasized "social sin," and wasn't clear enough in condemning violence.

Prominent foreign Catholics pleaded on Gutierrez's behalf.[12] Peru's bishops were split. At a meeting in May, with Rome watching intently, they refused to condemn Gutierrez. When some Peruvian bishops came to Rome immediately afterward for their every-five-year visits, the pope seemed to take Ratzinger's side; in his formal statement, he didn't mention Liberation Theology by name, but stressed that the bishops must "be vigilant . . . attentive to any doctrinal or pastoral deviations . . . to prevent a believing people from suffering harm to their faith."[13]

Yet when John Paul brought up the subject at lunch, he revealed a different attitude. "There were disagreements," one attendee recalls.[14] "Some wanted the Church to condemn Liberation Theology. Someone said Gutierrez was a communist and ought to be disciplined." But John Paul responded with the same questions he had asked as a cardinal in 1968 when *Znak* wanted to publish an article about a controversial theologian.

"Does he say Mass? Does he have faith?" the pope asked.

Gutierrez's opponents conceded that, while wrong on many points, he was devoted to the Eucharist and prayer.

"Then we must give him time," John Paul responded. "We must not condemn him. We must say the true Christian doctrine, but in a way that avoids condemnation, that opens a dialogue."

During the extraordinary Peruvian assembly in Rome that fall, the *Tablet* reported a stunning rebellion in which the bishops refused to sign a statement Ratzinger wanted them to and persuaded the pope to let them off the hook, defeating Ratzinger. The *Tablet* now says the sources for its detailed articles were confidential, and I couldn't find participants who would admit to recalling it clearly. Cardinal Juan Landazuri Ricketts of Lima, who headed the delegation, says Ratzinger described criticisms of Gutierrez, and that the bishops were split in their views. But he says he doesn't recall being asked to sign a specific document. Ratzinger declines to discuss it, but surely he expected something more from the assembly than what he got—basically, nothing.

In the concluding public remarks, John Paul backed off the issue entirely. His message was mostly a ringing encouragement for the Peruvians to continue their work for social justice, recalling "the tragedy of people in your cities and countryside, daily threatened in their very subsistence, hounded by poverty, hunger, disease and unemployment." Some ideas, he said, must be rejected, but he worded them so generally that the Peruvians could easily agree ("ideologies foreign to the faith," for example).

He simply avoided the key question of whether Liberation Theology could at times use Marxist analysis without accepting Marxist solutions. This was a method that the pope had specifically approved of in his underground 1953 book *Catholic Social Ethics* but that Ratzinger now denied.[15] Undercutting Ratzinger's whole apparent purpose, John Paul's final statement didn't mention Marx or Gutierrez.[16] The Peruvians were delighted.

The philosophical distance between John Paul and Cardinal Ratzinger on this point persisted. When Cardinal Etchegaray's more positive thoughts on Liberation Theology appeared in April 1986, they came through Ratzinger's office, balanced by more caveats than Etchegaray now recalls. As much as John Paul had elevated the Council on Justice and Peace, it would never have the clout of the Congregation for the Doctrine of the Faith. Ratzinger salted the new statement with warnings about mistaken notions of freedom and the danger of class struggle.

The issue was marked by confusion for years, until John Paul finally weighed in with a nearly definitive encyclical in 1987, and the extremist political passions of the 1980s were cooled by settlements. In the interim, the pope seemed sometimes to endorse the gist of Liberation Theology, and sometimes to endorse Ratzinger's condemnation of it. Why would a pope so determined to offer certainty allow his opinion on a hotly contested issue to remain uncertain? The answer may lie in the deference to Ratzinger that Archbishop Weakland has observed on John Paul's part. On Liberation Theology, John Paul would not rein Ratzinger in, despite indications that the pope disagreed with him.

Another possibility is that—as sometimes in the past—the pope didn't see the same contradictions that others did. All along, he had envisioned consensus on this. The essence of what Ratzinger said about the faith, and what the Boffs said about justice, may have seemed perfectly compatible to him, even though it didn't to them.

43

While Ratzinger pondered what to do about Father Leonardo Boff, John Paul spelled out his own political priorities in a landmark speech in Edmonton, Alberta, Canada, September 17, 1984. He was on a twelve-day trip marked by massive security—five thousand detailed police—in the wake of bomb scares by a Quebec separatist group. He devoted extensive time to visiting the physically and mentally disabled, a message of caring that he clearly wanted to broadcast, but the big event was Edmonton.

His hands shaking the pages of his speech with emotion, John Paul told an audience of one hundred fifty thousand about the dilemma he saw confronting a post-communist world: a struggle between boundless capitalist individualism on the one hand, and, on the other, the need to balance the rights of individuals with the rights of communities. John Paul may even have sensed that with Solidarity now effectively sweeping aside communism, the next utopian threat to the human essence was capitalist. Quoting scripture for support as he went, he told his audience

> not to stop at an individualistic interpretation of Christian ethics. . . . The human person lives in a community. . . . And with the community, he shares hunger and thirst and sickness and malnutrition and misery. . . . In his or her own person, the human being is meant to experience the needs of others.

Community duty was not just national, but global, he said. He deplored the domination of the southern hemisphere by the northern, and the North's use of superior weaponry to achieve it. He accused the northern nations of

> amassing to themselves the imperialistic monopoly of economic and political supremacy at the expense of others. . . . In the light of Christ's words, the poor South will judge the rich North. The poor people and poor nations—not only lacking food, but also deprived of freedom and other human rights—will judge those people who take these goods away from them.[1]

If he was uncomfortable about the discipline of the Boffs, it may have been because he shared many of their views.

At his request, he visited several thousand Indians who were fighting the Canadian government over land they claimed was rightfully theirs. As usual, he avoided the specifics of the dispute, but his talk—his mere presence—clearly aimed to encourage the Indians to preserve their land and culture. He supported endangered fishermen on Canada's Atlantic Coast by bringing world news coverage to their fight against big commercial fishing companies that were depleting the harvest.

Besides championing the traditions of Indians and fishermen, he supported the Catholic clergy's own tradition of male domination, against a recent stance by the Canadian Episcopate in favor of gender equality. For the Church's first beatification in North America, he chose a woman who had founded an order of nuns to do domestic work for priests—just the sort of sexism the bishops had objected to.

He also summoned to Canada the president of the Nicaraguan Bishops' Conference and the regional heads of the Jesuit and Maryknoll orders, to discuss the Nicaraguan priests who remained in government office. "The pope wants this settled," he told them.

After a new anti-Mafia speaking tour of southern Italy, John Paul took on another rebellion within the Church, this time in Holland. Back in 1980, about the time of the Kung and Schillebeeckx hearings, he had brought the divided Dutch bishops to Rome for a special synod, and had persuaded them to declare unity on forty-six points.

But as Cardinal Willebrands acknowledges, "the conflicts reappeared" as soon as they went home. Now a lay council officially recognized by the Church had publicly accused the pope of "many big mistakes" in his recent bishop appointments. The Dutch bishops, including even John Paul's new appointments, had what they said were "legitimate" disagreements on issues on which he wanted unity—including how much power the pope should have.[2]

The pope was scheduled to visit Holland (as well as Peru) early in 1985 and did not want the parishes he visited to be war zones. The Dutch bishops were so afraid of protest demonstrations by Catholics that they were trying to limit him to one open-air Mass during his trip. Distraught at such defeatism, John Paul summoned veteran diplomat Edward Cassidy, an Australian (now a cardinal), from his post in South Africa, and made him nuncio in Holland.

Usually such transfers take months, Cassidy says, but "in this case I had to rush." People saw John Paul's new bishops "as a move by Rome to stop greater involvement in the running of the Church by lay people," he says.

Dutch priesthood candidates had been entering the university system as if it were any other course of study. John Paul wanted to restore the use of seminaries. "But bishops cannot simply reopen seminaries," Cassidy says. "First you have to persuade the students and the people who would run them." Polls showed most Catholics disagreed with the pope on seminaries, as well as on birth control, divorce, the ordination of women, cooperation with Protestants, and the involvement of priests in politics.

Dashing to Holland, Cassidy met priests and laymen in small groups. "I tried, first of all, to listen, but also to explain the position of the Holy See"—that the Dutch had gone beyond what Vatican II intended, and "that there was no future being outside the mainstream of Catholic thought. I was not always successful." The Dutch argued that under their former, popular bishops, Church attendance (20 percent weekly) was higher and abortion less frequent than in either Italy or France. One priest, a professor, publicly compared John Paul's imposition of new bishops to communist tyranny in Poland.[3]

American Catholics, too, besieged the pope in the fall of 1984. At Notre Dame, New York Governor Mario Cuomo gave an acclaimed speech defending his upholding of his state's law legalizing abortion, in spite of Cardinal O'Connor's having admonished him not to. Cuomo won widespread sympathy as a man sincerely trying to be both a good Catholic and a good citizen.

Representative Geraldine Ferraro of New York, the Democratic candidate for Vice President, pledged to support legal abortion (though saying she privately opposed it). Hundreds of prominent Catholics bought a page in the *New York Times* to declare their support for "diversity of opinion" on abortion; seventy-five priests and nuns then backed off, saying they had been threatened with loss of their jobs.

More than a hundred other priests and nuns who stuck by the *Times* declaration were told by Cardinal Jerome Hamer—John Paul's new appointment at the congregation supervising religious orders—to retract their support or be dismissed from their orders. A few did issue retractions. When one group of twenty-four nuns refused to do so, their superiors stood with them and said their views should be "respected." In a new advertisement, eight hundred prominent Catholics protested Hamer's action, saying, "Unanimity on any issue in the Church cannot be imposed. Over the centuries there have been changes in matters once affirmed as authentic, for example slavery, usury, ecumenism and matters of war and peace."[4]

Ratzinger had already shocked the American Catholic Church by ordering its imprimatur withdrawn from a common adult catechism, *Christ Among Us*. At 1.6 million copies in sixteen years of publication, *Christ Among Us* was the best-selling title in the catalog of the Paulist Press, the country's largest Catholic publisher, whose chief editor, a priest, called the book's withdrawal "amazing." The Vatican said passages on saints, divorce, masturbation, homosexuality, contraception, and Vatican II were all so far off the mark that even extensive revision wouldn't help. Another Paulist Press best-seller, *Sexual Morality*, lost its imprimatur after seven years. (Archbishop Peter Gerety of Newark, the Paulist Press's archdiocese, who had approved the books, was prematurely retired two years later.)

Then Ratzinger ordered Crossroad Press, another large Catholic publisher (which brought out Father Malinski's book about the pope), to withdraw *Challenge to Love: Gay and Lesbian Catholics in the Church*, an anthology with an introduction by Bishop Walter Sullivan of Richmond, Virginia. Sullivan withdrew his introduction, but Crossroad refused to stop printing, and soon was folded into Harper and Row, a commercial publishing firm (which also reissued *Christ Among Us* without a Church imprimatur).

John Paul's defenders asserted that he merely wanted the Church to speak with one voice, not to limit the speech of non-Catholics. But in August 1984,

Vatican pressure forced a small publishing house to withdraw a book, *God's Broker*, by an author[5] who claimed to have had long interviews with John Paul; a review had cast doubt on its accuracy.

Much worse, that October, Church pressure on the *New York Times* caused Times Books, which the newspaper company then owned, to force a serious journalist, John Cooney, to excise important portions of his biography of Cardinal Spellman. In order to get his book, *The American Pope*, published, Cooney, a former longtime *Wall Street Journal* reporter, had to delete pages of attributed statements that Spellman had been a practicing homosexual. After angry negotiations, he retained an allusion to homosexuality without the evidence, which led to unfair accusations that he was spreading unsupported rumors.[6]

John Paul put an enormous premium on unity. Unity was what had held the Church together in Poland during enemy occupations. He felt he owed unity, too, to Jesus, Mary, and God, for seeing him and his people through so many tribulations. But beyond that, he thought the Church needed unity to help mankind through a moral crisis.

People—the powerful and the unpowerful alike—seemed to have wandered away from a spiritual ethic and toward immediate self-gratification at the expense of others, and at the expense of what the pope saw as their human identity. If they were ever to find the way back, he thought, the Church had to be preserved as an uncompromised beacon of truth.

But the commitment to unity came at great cost. Overthrowing communism had never been an end in itself for John Paul; it was an opportunity to create his own ideal in its place—a universal Solidarity to work with the universal Church. Many people felt much as he did about society's direction, but they did not agree with him on every detail. When he refused to accommodate the fundamental human urge toward diversity—in the way we work, the way we love, and the way we think—he crippled his own capacity to realize his dream. He began drawing attention to what separated him from people instead of to those points on which his leadership might rally a majority to effective action, as it had against the totalitarian state.

On two trips to Latin America that fall and winter, 1984–85, John Paul leaned toward Ratzinger's rejection of Liberation Theology. In Venezuela, he denounced priests who "proclaim not the truth of Christ but their own theories . . . in search of an illusory earthly liberation." But he avoided confrontations, particularly in Peru. Even bishops and priests who support Liberation Theology recall his visit to Peru happily.[7]

Politically, the Peru trip was less successful. A priest reported "great efforts" by the government "to ensure that [the Pope] would not see the hovels occupied by the poor." Thousands of vagrants had been jailed for the visit, he said.[8] President Fernando Belaunde boasted in the press that he had received a list from Amnesty International of a thousand "disappeareds" and thrown it in the waste basket.

John Paul addressed the most visible opposition, the almost mindlessly violent "Shining Path" guerrilla movement, by playing off the word *path*, using such constructions as "Evil is never the path to good." As if in reply, the Shining Path attacked a power station and knocked out Lima's electricity. John Paul added a daring hourlong airplane stopover under tight security at Ayacucho, a city in the Andes where military attacks on the Shining Path had taken a heavy general death toll. He spoke in local dialect.

In Venezuela, Ecuador, and Trinidad, he warned audiences against alcohol, drugs, violence, idleness, prostitution, and easy sex. Crowds, though at times exceeding half a million, were reported listless during such talks, gaining spirit only when he scolded governments for not using their wealth to build housing and otherwise improve life for average people. While praising the CELAM bishops for their "preferential option for the poor," he repeated Ratzinger's puzzling admonition that the option somehow didn't distinguish the poor as a class and was open to anyone. He called on bishops to "remove from the flock the errors that threaten it, a delicate duty, which requires a special pastoral tact, both in order to win over those who err and to prevent the faith of the community from being damaged."[9]

In Rome, perhaps heeding these words, Ratzinger called back Father Leonardo Boff, who again brought Cardinals Lorscheider and Arns to support him. Said Father Boff later, "I invited Ratzinger to come to Brazil. He replied that he was too busy in Rome. It is too dangerous for Ratzinger to descend to the level of the poor because nobody could remain unmoved. He would have to say this is not the world God made. We have to change it. It is not the Church or the state or the ruling classes who can transform the world, but the poor themselves. That is the constant message of Liberation Theology."

Ratzinger cited statements by Boff that the Church was "feudal in style" and that "dogma . . . has value only for a determined time and in determined circumstances" (which Ratzinger took to mean that Boff thought the Catholic faith changed along with economic forces). In the end, Boff got a tempered sentence: no banishment, just a prohibition to speak publicly or publish books for one year.

Whether John Paul softened Ratzinger's punishment of Boff or merely approved it, one can only guess. Boff publicly accepted the sentence, saying, "I prefer to walk with the Church rather than walk alone. . . . The pope's speeches in Latin America have helped the cause of the poor, because he has criticized violations of human rights, and the abuse of wealth and capital. . . . The people know the pope is on our side and not on the oppressors' side."[10] But he again denied he was a Marxist, and noted the irony that the Vatican crackdown came just as his country, Brazil, was starting toward democracy.

More shockingly, retribution fell on Cardinal Arns, Father Boff's supporter, who was told his giant archdiocese, São Paolo, would be broken into five smaller archdioceses. Arns was left with the rich central city, but deprived of poor areas closer to his heart. He protested the division, and proposed plans to assure that each resulting diocese would include both rich and poor. He says the pope always treated him graciously—a friend says Arns was once denied an audience—but the territory was cut up against his wishes.

Arns and Boff remained heroes at home. In April 1985, Arns says, the Brazilian bishops received a message from John Paul, through Cardinal Gantin, that Liberation Theology was "legitimate, useful and necessary." In assembly, the bishops adopted that language, and voted suggestions for the positive statement on Liberation Theology that was being prepared by Cardinal Etchegaray.

The history of Brazil's repression that Arns had risked his life to compile was entitled *Brazil: Never Again.* He sneaked it to a foreign publisher, who released it in July 1985. It was the number-one best-seller in Brazil for twenty-five weeks, and stayed on the best-seller list through two years and twenty printings. It produced no prosecutions because the military rulers had been promised amnesty in return for ceding their power. Rather, the book's enduring impact was on the minds of younger Brazilians, who were inheriting a democracy.[11]

Vatican Radio announced that Father Fernando Cardenal, the Nicaraguan minister of education, had been dismissed from the Jesuit order in "an atmosphere of mutual esteem and respect," after "a painful affair" for all. Cardenal said that while he generally agreed with the Church canon against holding public office, Nicaragua was a legitimate exception because there the poor were under intense attack. "To abandon the revolution now would be a grave sin," he said. "The Holy See is a prisoner of political concepts reached because of the conflicts in Eastern Europe." Cardenal said he would "continue to live" as if he were a Jesuit: "With God's grace, I will try to keep my vow of celibacy. No one can take my priesthood away from me."

The head of the Maryknoll order, Father William Boteler, said that he, too, thought the U.S. attack on Nicaragua merited an exception to the priests-in-politics rule, but that the Vatican had forced him to remove Father Miguel d'Escoto, who refused to quit as foreign minister of Nicaragua. Father Boteler said two archbishops had told him, "This is a Marxist government. We've given these priests five years, and now we're going to act."

Father Ernesto Cardenal, the minister of culture, and Father Edgar Parrales, ambassador to the Organization of American States, were also defrocked. Ironically, Parrales had been petitioning on his own to get out of the priesthood for a year, and been stalled.

44

In September 1984, Jaruzelski was again called to meet in a railway car with top Soviet officials. For hours, he was castigated for allowing the Church too much freedom. "You can't imagine what I had to live through," he whined later.[1]

The first such meeting had been followed by a bomb attack on the outspoken priest Jerzy Popieluszko. This time—October 9, 1984—Father Popieluszko was motoring back to Warsaw at night after an appearance in Gdansk. At a treacherous spot, roadside assailants bombarded his car with large stones. But a professional driver from Solidarity sped his charge past a potentially fatal accident.[2]

At a memorial service for the son of an underground Solidarity worker who had been murdered by police, Popieluszko told the fifteen thousand mourners, "We do not want punishment of the guilty. We yearn for something that stirs the conscience, and generates courage to say, 'It was my fault,' and ask forgiveness."

The credo offered by Popieluszko illustrates just how close Solidarity really was to Liberation Theology—and how both, more often than not, were one with John Paul. Surely the pope, the Boffs of Brazil, Gutierrez of Peru, and the Cardenal brothers of Nicaragua all would have said, with Popieluszko, "To live in truth means to bear witness to it.... The truth ... cannot be destroyed by any decree or law. The source of our captivity lies in the fact that we allow lies to reign ... that we do not protest them every day of our lives ... that we do not confront lies with the truth but keep silent or pretend to believe the lies."

With the rosary from John Paul in his pocket, Popieluszko told an interviewer,[3] "Even if I am afraid, it makes no difference to what I must do and say. . . . How can I betray those who have begun to hope? If I must die violently, I'd be happier meeting death in a worthy cause than sitting back and letting injustice go unchallenged."

October 19, 1984, some students dropped by to tell Father Michael Czaj- kowski that his friend Father Popieluszko had decided to make an appearance in Bydgoszcz. The students said Popieluszko wanted Father Czajkowski to substitute for him at a student Bible meeting in Warsaw that night. Coming so soon after Popieluszko had been attacked on his way home from Gdansk, the wording of this new request struck Czajkowski as eerie: "Please tell Priest Czaj- kowski to conduct this reading even if I won't be back."

He did not come back. "There were days of uncertainty," Father Czaj- kowski recalls. Parishioners flocked to Popieluszko's church to pray for him. A steady crowd of twenty to thirty thousand kept a vigil. When Glemp went ahead with a scheduled trip to Germany, people resented it. October 21, Walesa appeared at the church, his voice shaking as he pleaded, "Dear coun- trymen: there is a great danger hanging over our Fatherland. I appeal to you, please, do not let anyone provoke you to bloodshed. I beg you to maintain peace and to pray constantly for Father Jerzy."[4]

John Paul called for those holding Popieluszko to release him.

No one was holding him. October 27, the government announced that it had arrested three members of the security forces in his presumed murder. Walesa returned to the church, still pleading for calm. The pope said more prayers. Riot police broke up a demonstration. October 30, Popieluszko's body was dragged from an icy reservoir, badly beaten. He had died from choking on his own blood and vomit while gagged. A rope had been thrown over his bat- tered head, tying him to a bag of stones.

A quarter of a million people mobbed the church for the funeral. Any attempt by authorities to stop them might have incited civil war. The two con- trasting funeral orations still ring in many minds. Glemp's was insulting in its tepidness: "Let Poles from whatever social level meet, not crying over the cof- fin of a priest, but around a table for dialogue to release initiatives for peace."

It was Walesa who delivered what the crowd came to hear. "Solidarity lives because you gave your life for it, Father Jerzy," he said. "A Poland that has such priests and such people—faithful and devoted to Solidarity—has not perished and will not perish. Over the coffin of our brother, we swear that we will never forget his death."

"We swear, we swear," chanted the crowd.

Afterward, Glemp told priests privately that if Popieluszko had followed orders and gone to Rome, he wouldn't have been killed. Father Antonin Lewek, who inherited the martyred priest's job, went to Glemp for permission to try to publish Popieluszko's sermons, but says Glemp turned him down, complaining that "he had received memos from the government that Father Lewek talks too little religion and too much about Popieluszko."[5]

But the revolution that had begun in the archdiocese of Cardinal Wojtyla had now grown too big for either the primate or the government to stop. With Father Lewek's secret help, booklets of Popieluszko's sermons arrived from underground printers, titled in the distinctive lettering of the Solidarity logo, and were handed out in churches. Soviet leader Chernenko wrote to Jaruzelski, "All the hostile elements are receiving support and protection from the Church.... The Church is now directly defying the socialist state.... It is preparing a counterrevolutionary army in the full sense of the word."[6]

Chernenko was absolutely right. But with the Soviet economy in tatters, his own army bogged down in Afghanistan, and his population disgusted, there was nothing he could do about it.

45

Two men other than the pope are often credited with bringing the Cold War to a peaceful and happy end. One, President Reagan, vigorously escalated armed combat by Third World guerrillas fighting to overthrow Soviet-assisted governments in 1984. But aside from his continuing the aid to Afghan rebels, begun by President Carter, the Soviets didn't seem much affected by this campaign.

The Soviets continued to propose broad arms-reduction talks and a ban on the "militarization of space." Reagan refused any deal that would obstruct his major weapons programs, even though the CIA told Congress that "the little evidence available" indicated that Soviet military spending had "not acceler-ated" but had been "leveling off... in recent years... accompanied by an increase in the share of machinery allotted to civilian uses."[1]

The other leader often credited with ending the era of totalitarianism and world war is Mikhail Gorbachev. As we shall see, Gorbachev's new policies had important consequences for Poland. But like Reagan, he never saw Poland as a critical issue. And at home in the USSR, he was largely ineffective. One cannot say the Cold War outcome was the result of Gorbachev's initiatives, any more than it was the result of Reagan's.

As the health of Chernenko, the third Soviet leader in two years, declined in 1984, the fifty-three-year-old Gorbachev stood out among the new generation in the Politburo. He had run the Party in the south-central rural outpost of

Stavropol until his agricultural successes won him the job of Soviet agriculture secretary in 1978. Intellectual yet practical, he then became a protégé of Secret Police Chief Andropov, just as Chernenko had been a protégé of Brezhnev.

Soon after Andropov became premier, he appointed a spate of commissions to study new approaches to problems. Gorbachev began as one of many officials assigned to this project, but he quickly formed alliances with other economists, all fresh faces from the hinterland. He was soon seen as the force behind a wave of influential articles they authored, calling for fundamental change.

On the same day that the Nicaraguan officeholder/priests lost their standing with Rome in 1984, Gorbachev delivered a speech to a Soviet Communist Party conference proposing the new ideas that he and his Siberian colleagues had developed in the 1970s. One he called *perestroika*, or "restructuring": plant managers, instead of taking direction from a national command center, would often decide what they produced, based on their direct dealings with customers. The law of supply and demand would thus play a much bigger part in the Soviet economy. A second idea was *glasnost*, or "openness": if supply-and-demand was to be added to the economy, people would have to feel freer to speak their minds, even though it might offend bureaucrats.

Just before Christmas 1984, Gorbachev took off for England—a trip plainly designed to make him better known in the West. In a speech before Parliament, he called for Eastern and Western Europe to regard their continent as "a common home ... and not a theater of military operations." Thus he expressed, in almost identical words, a main theme of John Paul II's. Gorbachev impressed Prime Minister Thatcher in private meetings that the West could "do business" with him. That is what she told Reagan days later on a visit to Washington.

Both in this conversation with her and in general, Reagan ignored what Thatcher said about Gorbachev. He went right on seeking support for new weapons systems, including "Star Wars."[2] Reagan had already succeeded in doubling the defense budget in four years rather than his original goal of five. At one point, the Pentagon acknowledged a $25 billion cost overrun for weapons projects in just three months[3]—enough money to transform life in the poor countries the pope visited so determinedly, or to fund the Solidarity underground at existing levels for fifty thousand years. It was instead treated like pennies that had slipped through the government's fingers and were hardly worth picking up.

In 1985, a previously cowed Congress finally wondered if maybe enough was enough. The Catholic bishops' letter against weapons no doubt added some impetus to a sudden sense of constraint.

The pope, in his New Year's message for 1985, specifically denounced "projects for global space systems"—obvious reference to Reagan's "Star Wars." He said it "escapes the understanding of the common person, whose soul is gripped by anguish at the threat of destruction." That same month, Cardinal Thomas Williams, John Paul's appointee as archbishop of Wellington, New Zealand, helped lead his country in refusing to let a U.S. warship dock because it might be carrying nuclear weapons. The Reagan administration, furious, vowed economic retribution against New Zealand.

From just before New Year's to February 7, 1985, Poles were gripped by the Popieluszko murder trial. The trial of government officers for killing an outspoken anti-communist was itself a novel event under communism, but beyond that, a flourishing, independent Polish press was reporting on the case, even though its newspapers were still technically illegal. The trial was another sign that communism was already losing its grip on Poland, as it inevitably then would on the rest of Eastern Europe and Russia—though the West, and particularly the United States, didn't perceive what was happening.

The communist trial prosecutor asserted that the officers who had killed Popieluszko were rogues acting on their own, and that Popieluszko shared the guilt in his own death. "In his sermons, he spoke of struggle against our system," the prosecutor said. "He called for unrest. He mocked our authorities. He fell victim to the defendants, who, just like him, felt they could act above the law."[4]

All four defendants were convicted, the lightest sentence being fourteen years. The government simultaneously said future Church sermons would be reviewed for sedition. Glemp again outraged Poles with a halfhearted defense of his priests, saying he could "understand" why some were "not liked very much." He refused to blame the government for Popieluszko's death, and at its request ordered his priests to steer clear of politics.

But Glemp, like the government he catered to, was increasingly ignored. A few days after the trial, half a dozen freed Solidarity leaders felt emboldened enough to meet Walesa in Gdansk to discuss new strikes. Police raided the meeting and rearrested Michnik, Bogdan Lis, and Wladyslaw Frasyniuk, but didn't dare hold Walesa (who in earlier days would probably have been shot by this point).

After his regime was toppled, in 1989, General Jaruzelski persuaded some Western reporters that Popieluszko had been murdered by rogues, as the communist prosecutor said at trial. Jaruzelski maintained his own innocence.[5] But the longest sentence—twenty-five years—was being served by General Adam Pietruszko, who gave the murder order.

Pietruszko was no rogue. Archbishop Dabrowski remembers him well: as a colonel, Pietruszko had been Jaruzelski's trusted personal liaison with the Church and the imprisoned Walesa under martial law, and had monitored Dabrowski's meeting with Walesa.[6] For this, he was promoted. In 1994, in democratic Poland, a court acquitted two other Jaruzelski colleagues in the Popieluszko case for lack of evidence, but declared they "were probably responsible for the murder."[7]

March 10, 1985, Chernenko died, the last Stalin official to lead the Soviet Union. That evening, the Politburo met to pick a replacement. With the outspoken support of some aging veterans, Gorbachev, the youngest and most reform-minded of the three major contenders, won. He was the best-educated Soviet leader since the 1920s. Soon he removed his two main rivals from power, replacing one with his own Siberian-born protégé, Boris N. Yeltsin.[8]

The new system proposed by Gorbachev and his allies wasn't capitalism. Labor wouldn't be hired. So remote was the concept of human employment that Gorbachev had a hard time selling the idea that people should be allowed to own horses (want of which to pull plows was restraining food production on private family plots at the edges of collective farms). In cities and towns, Gorbachev envisioned not corporations but mom-and-pop entrepreneurships, to make urban trades as efficient as private farm plots—which, even without horses, yielded 25 to 30 percent of the produce from only 3 to 5 percent of the land.

On taking office, Gorbachev tried to reassure the Politburo. "We do not need to change policy," he said. "It is correct and true Leninist policy. We need . . . to disclose shortcomings and overcome them and realize our shining future." As historian Raymond Garthoff has put it, "There is little question but that the Politburo that selected Gorbachev . . . expected him to be . . . a reformer in the limited sense of the term, not someone who soon would seek to transform the party and the country."[9]

Three days later, however, Gorbachev revealed a startling design: when Eastern European communist leaders came to pay their respects, he told them he aimed to cut Moscow's control and support of their governments. So unprepared was his audience for what he was saying that its dramatic importance sailed right over their heads.[10]

The only world leader who behaved as if Gorbachev's election created new circumstances was, suddenly, Ronald Reagan. For four years, he had treated Russians as thugs, to be triumphed over, not talked to. Yet from the first moments of Gorbachev's rule, his attitude changed. When Vice President Bush

went to Moscow for the combination Chernenko funeral/Gorbachev inaugural, he carried with him a Reagan proposal for a summit meeting.

Until the previous fall, Reagan hadn't even bothered to meet Soviet Foreign
Minister Gromyko on his occasional trips to the United States. And just two
months before Chernenko died, Reagan had said in a press conference that he
would go to a summit only if the Soviets did a fundamental turnabout. "To
have a meeting, as I said before, just to have a meeting, doesn't make any sense,"
he said.

So why did he suddenly propose a summit with Gorbachev? He later said
that his arms buildup had put the Soviets "in a different frame of mind," in
which they were "really going to try."[11] But there were no hints—even in transcripts of Politburo meetings now available—of a Soviet shift on those issues
that Reagan considered important. Secretary of State George Shultz's memoir
tosses off this monumental policy reversal, the decision for summit negotiations, in a line, without explanation.[12]

But Reagan, the consummate actor, now past halfway in his eight years of
office, may have realized that he had better move into the second act of his
drama if he was to vindicate his policy before the curtain fell. The first act, in
which he cured a missile gap that never really existed, had to be wound up if he
was to show that the result would be a just peace.

Something else, too, may have contributed to a sudden feeling that time was
short. Two days before Reagan proposed the summit meeting that he had just
said "doesn't make any sense," doctors at Bethesda Naval Hospital had found
a precancerous tumor in his lower intestine. One can only wonder how much
that may have motivated him to think of shifting the theme of his presidency
from war to peace.[13]

Publicly, Reagan and Gorbachev continued to carp at each other's interventions around the globe. CIA Chief Casey made wild public charges that
Nicaragua and Angola were "occupied territories" suffering a Nazi-like holocaust. (In both countries, the main killing of civilians was being done by
American-backed forces.)[14]

Reagan tried in vain to persuade Congress to vote $14 million in "humani-
tarian" aid to the Nicaraguan Contras after his request for lethal aid had been
turned down. In a last-ditch sales effort, he declared that the pope "has been
supportive of all our activities in Central America." Just as with Reagan's false
claim of papal backing on trade sanctions in Poland, the Vatican was forced to
issue embarrassing public denials.

Contrary to what Reagan said, John Paul went to the International Court of
Justice in Holland, May 13, 1985, to deliver what in papal terms was a stern
rebuke to the United States—a speech that went curiously unreported in the

U.S.[15] Nicaragua had complained to the court that the U.S. had violated international law by "supporting a mercenary army, . . . launching attacks on the territory of Nicaragua, and seeking to overthrow the government."

In its defense, the U.S. had argued—not that it wasn't true—but that the court didn't have jurisdiction. The court decided it *did* have jurisdiction. Reagan then declared that the U.S. not only wouldn't participate in a hearing on the merits of the case, but would withdraw its 1946 recognition of the court's authority altogether, an action that would significantly weaken the court.

The Nicaragua case was the most famous in the court's sixty-five-year history.[16] The fight over jurisdiction was at its height when the pope appeared in the court, before the judges and assembled diplomats. Typically, John Paul didn't name either the U.S. or Nicaragua, but he surely knew the weight of his words, as he called on countries to make "more intensive use of the International Court of Justice."

He complained that the court was coming "under pressure designed to prevent it from transcending ideologies and interests." He blamed this "pressure" on "power struggles and self-interest." And he called for "wider acceptance of the so-called compulsory jurisdiction of the court," whose work, he said, "I commend."[17]

The court found in favor of Nicaragua and against the United States, citing a long list of U.S. actions that it deemed "contrary to the general principles of humanitarian law." The U.S. rejected the judgment. (In 1989, after the Contra war was settled, the U.S. agreed once again to use the International Court of Justice in many matters.)

4 6

John Paul might have wished the international court could solve his problems with the Dutch Church. He had just appointed an outsider, Joannes ter Schure, as bishop of Holland's largest diocese, 's-Hertogenbosch. Ter Schure "received a great deal of opposition from the liberal side," according to Cardinal Cassidy, the new papal liaison to Holland. An editorial in the *Tablet* suggested that the appointment was "a humiliating gesture . . . on the eve of [the pope's] visit."

A poll showed that two thirds of the diocese opposed ter Schure, and that only 27 percent of Dutch Catholics were glad the pope was coming. Parishes were cutting back contributions and drafting protests. Books by the maverick Dutchman Father Schillebeeckx were flying off the shelves. (John Paul and

Ratzinger had closed the ongoing case against Schillebeeckx with an exchange of statements that left a door of ambiguity open—the very thing the pope didn't want, but apparently couldn't avoid. Essentially, Schillebeeckx would no longer say that laymen might give Mass in extraordinary circumstances, but he didn't deny thinking it.)

The visit to Holland, May 11 through 14, 1985, was the worst trip of John Paul's papacy. "It was not the kind of program the Holy Father has elsewhere," says Cardinal Cassidy, who arranged it. "On Sunday morning in Utrecht, we met for an hour with each of three groups. Quite a number of people had a great fight with the police [who were] keeping them away from where we were."

Protest banners complained that the pope had agreed to hear only moderate opponents whose statements were approved in advance. Says Cassidy, "It was impossible to agree to the pope's sitting in front of a group that would just harangue him about the way he was running the Church. We went as far as possible according to our view of what a papal visit was supposed to be. At one meeting, one lady went outside of her prepared text to criticize him. The Holy Father received her warmly. He hoped to show that he was not against the Dutch Church. I think that he succeeded to a degree."

Maybe a small degree. But he angered many—including the one man who had long sustained whatever unity existed in the Dutch Church. Cardinal Willebrands alone seemed to be respected by both the Vatican and the reformers; he had recently retired but wanted to help nonetheless. And he had been cut out. "I had no task in the preparation of that visit," he says. "I was not consulted by the Dutch bishops on how to organize it. The pope didn't consult me about the appointments of the bishops, [which] were not well received in Holland."

The pope had only one open-air Mass in which to strike his usual positive note. As he left Holland, he thanked Cassidy. "We had done as good a job as we could have," Cassidy says the pope told him. But he acknowledges that John Paul has barely mentioned the trip in the decade since, and that the tension in Holland has eased only gradually.[1]

The Dutch experience may have made John Paul all the more eager to prevent another such schism in the United States. He decided to do something about Archbishop Raymond Hunthausen in Seattle, who persisted in trying to minister acceptingly to homosexuals and divorced people.

When Hunthausen and twenty-two other American bishops had made their every-five-year visits to Rome in 1983, the pope had been alarmed by reports he read of Hunthausen's divided congregation: an antiabortion committee in Seattle had resigned, complaining that the archbishop wasn't supporting it, and a national convention of Dignity, a gay-rights organization, had been invited to hold Mass in the cathedral, provoking a demonstration by parishioners.

John Paul had lectured the American bishops at the time that homosexuality and premarital sex were "incompatible with God's plan for human love."* He further rebuked them for allowing their episcopal conference to talk to an organization of Catholic women who advocated women's ordination. The bishops were surprised that the pope's remarks were so "direct, absolute, and unconditional," in the words of Bishop Mark Hurley of Santa Rosa, California. Added Archbishop Weakland, "What the pope said will not be well accepted. Termination of discussion is a hard thing for [Americans] to accept."[2]

In fact, the U.S. bishops flouted John Paul's instruction a mere three months later, by welcoming a conference of 550 women, some of whom demanded not just ordaining women but throwing out the whole Church hierarchy in favor of something more democratic. Cardinal Laghi, the papal nuncio, scolded the bishops and told them to regard the pope's instructions "with utmost seriousness." Archbishop John Roach of Minneapolis, president of the U.S. Bishops' Conference, dismissed the matter as mere "growing pains in a maturing relationship."[3]

Commented the *Tablet*, "There is . . . tension between Rome and the United States right now. The pope sees the American Church as extremely vital, but also, like a plant that hasn't sunk its roots very deep, he believes it needs a lot of pruning." Ratzinger complained that many American Catholics "choose to dissent from the Church teaching authority rather than dissent from the secular values promoted by their wealthy nation."[4]

The pope appointed Archbishop James Hickey of Washington to "evaluate" Hunthausen's archdiocese and another in Virginia that had ministered to homosexuals. Hickey was not a neutral choice: he had campaigned against a "New Ways Ministry," which he said spread the notion that stable homosexual relationships were morally permissible, and he had a priest and nun expelled from their religious orders for running New Ways.[5]

---

* At about this time, the Vatican Congregation for Catholic Education issued guidelines for sex education that made the pope's 1960 book on the subject look daring by comparison. Graphic audiovisual materials were discouraged because they might "raise an unhealthy curiosity, which leads to evil." Masturbation was a "deviation"; teachers and parents should "identify the causes of the deviation" and help the masturbator "overcome the immaturity underlying this habit." Homosexuals "must be . . . supported in the hope of overcoming their . . . social maladaption." (As noted earlier, the possible genetic and chemical roots of homosexuality had not yet been discovered.)

But in the two years since 1983, Hickey hadn't changed anything in Seattle. Now, to make matters worse, pro-Reagan Catholics had launched a letter-writing campaign asking the pope to silence Hunthausen's antiwar sermons; Seattle's major employer was the Boeing Corporation, one of the two or three biggest beneficiaries of the Reagan military buildup.

A six-page letter went out over Ratzinger's signature, insisting on conformity in Church issues while taking pains to praise Hunthausen's compassion and reassure him of the pope's support against the political attacks being made on him. Hickey's report, Ratzinger said, "exhaustively documented" the need to correct the "rather widespread practice of admitting divorced persons to a subsequent church marriage"; "contraceptive sterilization . . . in local Catholic hospitals"; the use of general absolution in place of individual confession; continued debate on the role of women in the Church; and "the ill-advised welcome" of "pro-homosexual" groups that "make the Church's position appear to be ambiguous."

Ironically, John Paul's effort to distance himself from the political gang-up on Hunthausen may have misled Hunthausen and others about the severity with which he viewed the transgressions against Church doctrine: Ratzinger's letter went unheeded. So John Paul asked his most prestigious American bishop, Cardinal Bernardin, to bring Seattle back to the faith. The assignment would not bode well for Bernardin.

As plans for a November summit with Reagan took shape, Gorbachev made clear by his appointments and other actions that he was focusing his energy on economic reform and cutting back remaining Soviet foreign commitments, which were mostly in Cuba and Afghanistan. This was a policy the pope would later endorse as he tried to help Gorbachev.

Striking off in precisely the opposite direction, CIA Chief Casey held a secret lunch meeting in New York July 19, 1985, with chief executives of several dozen major American-based corporations that had operations in the USSR. Casey predicted that Gorbachev would try to increase commerce with the United States and warned the business leaders not to cooperate. Gorbachev himself might have been shocked at the degree to which U.S. businesses in his country saw themselves as active agents of U.S. Cold War policy, often providing cover for CIA spies and operatives. Casey predicted—accurately—that Gorbachev's reforms would fail. But he encouraged the corporate chiefs to view that failure positively, as a sign of Soviet weakness.[6]

Eight days later, Casey was called to a meeting of top national-security officials at the White House. Presiding was Reagan, in pajamas and bathrobe, having just returned from surgery to remove his tumor and a large part of his colon. He wanted to bring something to everyone's attention. While he was still in the hospital, groggy from anesthesia and his medical ordeal, National Security Adviser Robert McFarlane had come to see him with a major proposal. Some shadowy figures in and out of government had received overtures from Iranians.[7] Western hostages being held in the Middle East, they said, including a CIA station chief, might be released in exchange for high-tech weapons.

Of those present, only Secretary of State Shultz and Defense Secretary Weinberger seemed bothered by such a deal—to a greater or lesser degree, depending on whom you believe. Exactly what the President said is also in dispute. Astonishingly, he later declared he couldn't remember whether he authorized the arms shipments to Iran, which one month earlier (July 8) he had called "a new international version of Murder Incorporated." Reagan kept emphasizing that just because arms were sent to Iran in the expectation that Western hostages would then be released, it was not to be considered trading arms for hostages, or dealing with terrorists. These were propositions to which he remained outspokenly opposed.

But overtly, implicitly, or in some other way, the President—again starkly confronted by his own mortality—supported actions that (again, like the summit meeting) were the very antithesis of what he had been advocating in his popular speeches.[8]

John Paul flew to Paris to join Cardinal Lustiger and President Mitterrand for a Mass. Officially, it celebrated the anniversary of the end of World War II, but in many eyes it also marked an end to the rift between the Church and French civil leadership that the war had provoked.

Next came a seven-country African trip, with emphasis again on Moslem relations. In Morocco, King Hassan, who claimed direct descendance from the Moslem founding prophet Mohammed, joined John Paul for a Mass in the national sports stadium. But a visit to Senegal was canceled when Moslem leaders threatened to block the airport runway with their bodies.

In Cameroun, the pope achieved "a breakthrough" in relations with Moslems, according to his host, Cardinal Christian Tumi. "Christianity was not being treated with the same respect as Islam," Tumi says. But "there was a feast for baptism when he was there, and the Moslems gave us a cow for the feast. Relations changed. He treated Moslems as brothers." Less tactfully, John Paul inadvertently disturbed local bishops by lobbying the Camerounian president to provide state money for Catholic schools, and pushing the reluctant bishops to do likewise. "The state is bankrupt," and can't be blamed, Tumi says.[9]

The pope's other main agenda item in Africa was luring converts from among traditional animist spirit-worshipers. John Paul had decided that animists were the Church's great hope for growth in Africa: "I don't know of any Moslem who has become a Catholic," explains Cardinal Tumi, who spent twelve years in the Moslem-dominated north of Cameroun.

The pope incorporated traditional custom when ordaining priests in Togo, drinking a millet mixture from a ceremonial calabash and then pouring some on the ground. He made a show of meeting with an animist priest who worshiped tree spirits. At their public ceremony, John Paul declared, "Nature, exuberant and splendid in this place of forests and lakes, fills spirits and hearts full of its mystery and orients them toward . . . the Author of life."

Returning to Zaire, John Paul beatified a potential saint from modern Africa, a twenty-five-year-old nun murdered in 1964 when anarchists overran her mission. Further distinguishing the ceremony, the nun's killer was present, having been pardoned by Mobutu after claiming a religious conversion. John Paul declined to see the killer privately but said in his sermon that he forgave the man "with all my heart."[10]

In Ivory Coast, the pope praised the nation's one-party dictator of twenty-five years, Felix Houphouet-Boigny, for spending vast portions of his country's resources on Catholicism, in the form of a vanity cathedral in Houphouet-Boigny's hometown, population thirty thousand. On his 1980 trip, John Paul had dedicated the cornerstone of the basilica, which is taller and longer (at one third of a mile) than St. Peter's. Now he blessed the construction. "Those who are surprised that churches should be built, instead of dedicating all resources to improving material life, have lost the sense of spiritual realities," he said.[11]

But Houphouet-Boigny's spending habits were more regal than spiritual, and he was using the funds of Ivory Coast's ten million citizens to benefit its 1.5 million Catholics. The pope also toured the extravagant new capital Houphouet-Boigny was building, seeming to ignore the dignity that a papal visit bestowed on such spending. The cost—including the fee for fifteen hundred artisans to fit two acres of cathedral windows with hand-blown stained glass from France—was a major factor the next year when Ivory Coast defaulted on its $10 billion foreign debt, an economic collapse that sparked civil violence.[12]

Interviewers again asked John Paul how he could justify his friendship with black dictators when he boycotted the white South African dictatorship. He stuck to his line of 1980:

> Certain African situations cannot be judged by our criteria. This
> does not mean tolerating abuses. It means only that Africans find

themselves at a different moment of history. You have to visualize what European countries were like five, six, or seven centuries ago. The Africans are just beginning their independence.[13]

Back in Rome, the interfaith outreach continued when John Paul, already the first pope to pray in a Lutheran church and in an animist shrine, became the first since Peter (who was Jewish) to pray in a synagogue. He referred to Jews as "our respected elder brothers."

If there was one cardinal to whom John Paul owed a debt of personal friendship, it was Franz König of Vienna, the man most influential in pushing his candidacy for the papacy. König had befriended Wojtyla as a young bishop and had done much to help build the intellectual army he organized in Krakow, which was now ready to run the communists out of Poland.

But in September 1985, John Paul let his drive to control the Church drag him into an act of personal meanness totally at odds with his character. König's doctrinal inclination toward the Western "liberals" in the Church had been evident all along. He had brought the officially silenced Karl Rahner to Vatican II as his adviser. König's liberalism, like Willebrands's, had always been in the true sense of the word—an openness to dialogue with people of goodwill, never an insubordinate assault on Vatican doctrine. Now retiring at age eighty, he had earned a pyrotechnic of gratitude.

Instead, John Paul humiliated him. Not only was König not consulted about his replacement, but John Paul picked one of the few candidates König would have objected to, chosen by another Austrian cardinal whom everyone knew König didn't get along with. The rival cardinal was Alfonse Stickler, who had risen through the curia, not the Austrian pastorship; he ran the Vatican Library. König didn't socialize with Stickler on his visits to Rome and didn't host an Austrian celebration when Stickler became a cardinal.

"Stickler is a pedant, always with a book of canon law nearby to cite," says a prominent Vatican official who knows them both. "König is a man of dialogue."

König had been grooming as his replacement Bishop Helmut Kratzl, his former chief aide. But instead of Kratzl, John Paul elevated Stickler's choice, Father Hans Grör, a Benedictine monk who ran a shrine to Mary thirty miles outside Vienna. König wasn't entitled to name his successor, of course, but he wasn't even asked his opinion.

Even Stickler, Father Grör's patron, acknowledges that "Grör was not well known. Nobody imagined that he would be selected." Stickler also acknowledges that Kratzl was the popular choice of Vienna Catholics. But he says,

"These were people in the diocese who don't know what's going on." Stickler openly criticizes König's administration: "The faith was no longer practiced," he says. He says a poll showed that half of baptized Austrians did not believe in life after death. "If this fundamental truth is no more accepted, how could other truths be accepted that are less evident?"

So König, his contributions and ideas, were shunted off to a retirement residence. "It was a mystery for me," he says now. "I think he [John Paul] may have been influenced by some people around him that Vienna needed a radical change."

Lonny Glaser, König's former secretary who arranged the aid pipeline to Krakow in the 1960s, adds, "We would have been very glad to see Kratzl as archbishop. But people went to Rome and said untrue things—that he was too modern, he did not like the pope."

Were König's feelings hurt? "Yes," Glaser says. "But it was not in his character to talk about it. We were all very sad."

This was worse than what the pope had done in Holland to Willebrands (who had been in König's circle). After the experience with Glemp, perhaps John Paul was skeptical about chosen successors. But whatever he thought of Kratzl was no excuse for his treating König so cavalierly. The pressures of the job were draining John Paul of his own once-vibrant liberality.

47

Reagan and Gorbachev met in Geneva in November 1985, as John Paul prayed for them to end the arms race. To prepare, Gorbachev had actually watched Reagan's old movies.[1] On the eve of the summit, Reagan's top advisers fell out over whether to reinterpret an existing antiballistic-missile treaty to say that it allowed new weapons the Pentagon wanted, which the Soviets thought were prohibited. Reagan postponed a decision.

The President became so enthusiastic in Geneva that he accepted Gorbachev's proposal to declare that both sides "will not seek to achieve military superiority"—a surprising renunciation of the Republican Party platform that had pledged to regain military superiority. But Reagan wouldn't touch his "Star Wars" program, despite Gorbachev's efforts to negotiate it away. They did agree to visit each other's capitals, and settled on new cultural and air-safety arrangements. What the summit really did, historian Raymond Garthoff observes, was restore relations to where they had been before the Soviet invasion of Afghanistan.

Immediately after the summit, National Security Adviser McFarlane flew to Rome to brief John Paul. But he was interrupted—while in the Vatican, according to one government account—by a call from a general involved in the Iran arms shipments. Portugal wasn't letting an arms-delivery plane refuel because officials there refused to believe that a Boeing 747 carrying eighty Hawk missiles bound for Iran was on a "humanitarian mission." While John Paul waited unawares, McFarlane arranged new routings for the missile shipments.[2]

Reagan sent General Edward Rowny to Czechoslovakia, Poland, Hungary, and East Germany to brief government leaders. Rowny says he met quietly with Vaclav Havel in Prague and Walesa in Warsaw. Eastern Europe had finally caught the administration's attention. John Whitehead, the investment banker who thirty years earlier had arranged shipments of radios and speedboats to Hungarian rebels, had recently left the chairmanship of Goldman, Sachs to become Shultz's deputy, with specific instructions to focus on Eastern Europe.

Right off, Whitehead had stopped a large State Department policy meeting cold by saying to Shultz, "I know I'm still learning this business, but could you tell me why we can talk to Gorbachev but can't talk to Jaruzelski?" Shultz remembers a stark silence, during which he concluded that "a shift in policy was needed."

So Whitehead dropped the policy that had been in place since the 1940s, of treating the Eastern Bloc as a single, Soviet-run enemy. He began talking to the leaders of Eastern Europe the way Goldman, Sachs traders talked to bond-buyers: as individuals to be sold. He began visiting each country once or twice a year. "I tried to wean them away [from the Soviet Union] with friendship," he says.

Shultz has written that Whitehead's initiative "was actively opposed by many on the NSC [National Security Council] staff, in the CIA and in the Defense Department—people who believed that we should shun all 'evil empire' leaders." They even tried to block Whitehead's use of Air Force planes. Shultz persuaded Reagan to protect the new man.

By the time Whitehead arrived on the scene, however, the Polish government was already a declining force.

Catholicism was also affecting other Cold War crisis centers John Paul had visited. When Philippine dictator Marcos tried to stage an election, U.S. embassy officials met with Cardinal Sin, who then, using the embassy's name, persuaded the two opposition presidential candidates to unite. It was agreed that Corazón Aquino, widow of the slain opposition leader, would run for president. Marcos rigged the election (February 7, 1986), but he had been boxed into inviting prominent Americans as observers, and they exposed the fraud.

With U.S. support for Marcos wavering (Reagan, almost alone, still wanted to prop him up), Marcos's associates arranged a coup d'état and urged Cardinal Sin to join a five-member junta to run the country, pending new elections. When the coup began, Sin went on Radio Veritas—which the Church owned and the U.S. government secretly paid for—and called citizens into the streets to protect the coup forces. Tens of thousands came, blocking Marcos's troops and securing the victory. Marcos was flown out by the U.S. government.[3]

Sin was called to Rome and told he had been excessively political. But the rebuke appeared to be a formality and did not spoil his close relationship with John Paul.[4]

The day of the rigged Philippine election, Jean-Claude Duvalier, whom John Paul had embarrassed before his people, was overthrown as dictator of Haiti. His most popular opponent was a priest. Just as in the Philippines, a U.S. military plane carried the tyrant and his wife away—in Duvalier's case, to exile in France.

Princeton Russianologist Stephen F. Cohen has observed that the defining coming-of-age event for Gorbachev's generation of political leaders was the 1956 Party Congress at which Khrushchev blew away the Stalin legend. Although they couldn't demonstrate it openly, as American youth did, this generation of Soviets had learned that change was possible.

These were the very people Gorbachev hoped to move into control at the first opportunity: the every-five-year Party Congress, which conveniently came along eleven months into his administration, in February 1986. But Gorbachev faced a tougher task than Khrushchev, who merely stood on a podium and revealed Stalin's record. Gorbachev had to persuade Party cadres across his vast land not just to work differently, but to work harder, and take more risks. He couldn't do it, and the Party, even the 307-member Central Committee, stayed dominated by Brezhnev holdovers.

Gorbachev had an easier time changing international policy. He began promoting a concept John Paul had talked about for years: common security—the idea that neither superpower would be safe until *both* were. Saying he wanted to "act in such a way as to give nobody grounds for fears," he declared a unilateral moratorium on testing and deployment of intracontinental European missiles. He pledged to dismantle existing missiles if the United States did the same, and to permit the rigorous on-site inspections the U.S. demanded.

When a deadly leak occurred at a nuclear power plant at Chernobyl, near Kiev, April 26, 1986, the Soviet bureaucracy initially tried to cover it up. In the face of international fury, Gorbachev stepped in, broke with Soviet style, admitted the truth, and allowed access by Western experts. He pleaded that Chernobyl was "another grim warning that the nuclear era demands new policy."

Reagan's enthusiasm, however, had quickly cooled after the summit. He instructed top appointees to pressure the Soviets as before, in any available crisis center.[5] He interrupted Gorbachev's peace offensive by cutting back the Soviet UN mission, alleging that many Soviet diplomats were spies. This touched off several rounds of spy arrests by each side, roiling an area of contention that had recently been quiet.

March 13, the U.S. deliberately sailed warships equipped with nuclear missiles and sophisticated spy equipment into Soviet waters, provoking understandable Soviet outrage—all the more heated because Gorbachev was vacationing at the nearby seashore at the time, making it seem a personal gesture.[6] Then Reagan announced he would do as the Pentagon wanted, and reinterpret an existing treaty to allow new weapons that the Soviets thought had been banned years earlier.[7]

48

March 29, 1986, Sergei Antonov, the Bulgarian airline employee whom Mehmet Ali Agca had identified as his accomplice in the attempt to assassinate the pope, was acquitted, along with two other Bulgarians and six Turks whom Agca had also implicated. The trial lasted ten months; all went free.

Supporters of Reagan's foreign policy continued to assert that the prosecutors had shown that the Soviets (through the Bulgarians) were probably guilty in the attack, though the evidence fell just short of the certainty needed to convict. For their part, Reagan opponents said the acquittals vindicated their contention that the "Bulgarian connection" was a fiction planted with Agca in prison by Western intelligence agencies in a propaganda effort.

Former CIA Director Robert Gates, in now declassified congressional testimony, said, amazingly, that his former chief, Casey, "was persuaded by Claire Sterling's book ... that the Soviets had in fact" been guilty.[1] In his own 1996 memoir, Gates wrote that the question "remains unanswered, [a] great ... secret."[2]

Reagan himself appeared to doubt the truth, or at least the implications, of the charges; he met politely with Gorbachev, whose patron, former KGB boss Andropov, would surely have been implicated.

John Paul shared his views with Cardinal Deskur during the Bulgarians' trial, after Deskur remarked on the pope's seeming lack of interest in the proceedings.

He says the pope replied, "I know well that the responsible one is the devil. And whether he used the Bulgarian people or the Russian people or the Turkish people, it was diabolical."

Still curious, Deskur pursued the question concretely. He says the pope "was sure" the Bulgarians were not guilty of the crimes charged. But based on what evidence? Deskur says he doesn't know. Recent books have tended to accept Sterling's story, albeit hedgingly.

Eight years after the trial, I hoped to resolve lingering doubts. Commentators, including CIA Director Gates, kept talking about the case as if it were a political question. I wanted to focus on the evidence, as in any other crime.

After reading what I could, I visited Giuseppe Consolo, the Bulgarians' defense counsel. Half expecting the dumpy office of a Left-wing criminal lawyer, I instead found Consolo impeccably dressed in the elegantly furnished quarters of a major Rome law firm. When the Bulgarian ambassador was looking for a defense lawyer, Consolo was recommended by two clients of his, an American corporation that sold fertilizer to Bulgaria and an Italian concern that sold it computers. Consolo voted Christian Democrat; he also turned out to be known and respected by a devout Catholic friend of mine, a staunch defender of the pope's.

Consolo began by saying, "I am one of the few people who know the truth. Steps in court proved the 'Bulgarian connection' did not exist. Agca acted on his own. He was a killer. Gray Wolves [Agca's fascist-style youth organization] wasn't Right- or Left-wing. Terrorist groups don't necessarily have links with East or West. People want what is not there."

Consolo said Claire Sterling had told him, "You will see! Antonov will be convicted." He laughed. The truth, he said, was exactly contrary to the charges. "In Bulgaria, Agca tried to contact their secret service, but they wouldn't meet him. He said, 'I'm ready to kill the pope, will you help?' They said they wanted nothing to do with him."

This was an interesting story, but it came from the Bulgarian government. There was no way to verify that the Bulgarians had refused any such offer from Agca. Consolo correctly pointed out that the letter Agca wrote to the Turkish newspaper, declaring he would shoot the pope, was published before Solidarity existed; so Solidarity wasn't a motive. But the Soviets had been justly nervous about John Paul from the moment of his election. So far, Consolo was just one more defense lawyer who seemed to believe his clients.

Then he said something for which proof might exist: that while traveling in France, Agca had contacted the French secret service and offered to supply information about a plot to kill the pope. Alexandre de Marenches, the near-legendary French spy boss and a dedicated anti-communist, had informed the Vatican early in 1981 of such a plot, though de Marenches wouldn't say how he had learned of it. If Agca had gone to de Marenches's office, that would certainly cast doubt on the notion that he was working for the Soviets.

I asked Consolo about the detailed description Agca gave of Antonov and his daughter; didn't it prove he knew them? Consolo said Agca had described Antonov with a beard, the way he looked when he was arrested, eighteen months after the shooting. Before the shooting, when Agca claimed to have met him, Antonov was beardless. Furthermore, five credible witnesses testified in the Italian court that Antonov's daughter was in Bulgaria when Agca claimed to have met her in Rome. Agca then recanted his story of meeting her.

What about Agca's ability to describe Antonov's apartment as if he'd been there? This description had been cited as proof of Agca's veracity by Sterling and others. Consolo replied that Agca's description of the apartment proved just the opposite of what the "Bulgarian connection" crowd said: it proved he had been fed a lie.

Agca had described Antonov's apartment with a wooden partition dividing it. This was an accurate description of every apartment in the group—*except* Antonov's. Evidently preferring more open space, Antonov had removed the partition before the time Agca claimed he visited. Someone, it appeared, had showed Agca a neighboring apartment, or described it for him, thinking it was like Antonov's.

Who? Consolo didn't know. But before he came out with his Bulgarian story, Agca had frequent, unusual visitors to his cell, all approved by the Italian government—people with connections to Italian intelligence, to the burgeoning scandal around the secret Masonic lodge, to the Mafia, and even to the Church. These people had motives—some political, some involving their own legal problems—to persuade Agca to tell a politically convenient story.*

---

* Most of the information I went over with Consolo had been presented in greater detail in *The Rise and Fall of the Bulgarian Connection* by Edward S. Herman and Frank Brodhead (New York: Sheridan Square Publications, 1986). The same authors, writing in *Covert Action Information Bulletin* (now *Covert Action Quarterly*) for Winter 1986, speculated on how Agca might have obtained a description of the surrounding apartments, which had been like Antonov's until Antonov's wooden divider was removed. Directly below Antonov, they said, lived Father Felix Morlion, a longtime agent of American intelligence. Other sources say Morlion was put in the Vatican by U.S. intelligence, as an agent.[3] Through the reign of Pius XII and into that of Paul VI, Morlion—a member of the Knights of Malta—worked covertly against communism in Europe and Latin America. I have found no reference to Morlion in any Vatican capacity during the papacy of John Paul II, but he certainly still knew people in the intelligence agencies. There has been some controversy about exactly whom Agca saw or didn't see in his cell, and his own testimony on this score has changed, but there were clearly opportunities for him to be coached.

I asked Consolo about the widely reported presence of Antonov and another Bulgarian at the assassination scene. He assured me the only evidence of that was Agca's unreliable assertion, volunteered long after he was convicted. Seven court witnesses, some impartial, had placed Antonov in his office on the afternoon of the shooting. A famous photograph that Sterling said showed a Bulgarian-connected friend of Agca's fleeing St. Peter's Square with a gun actually showed a frightened tourist with a camera, Consolo said. Besides, he said, Agca and Antonov did not even speak the same languages.

What about Agca's stay in Sofia, and his travels around Europe for more than a year before the shooting? Sterling offered this as evidence that Agca was being cared for by plotters. Consolo said there was no indication that Agca had been doing any more than living by his wits, or in the homes of contacts from his Gray Wolf organization. He had admitted to some holdups to pay his expenses. When he stayed in hotels, they were cheap ones. He claimed to have stayed in a good hotel in Sofia, but that was undocumented and doubtful.

I told Consolo the point that impressed me most in Claire Sterling's front-page coverage of the case in the *New York Times*[4] was her story about a supply truck that she said left the Bulgarian embassy in Rome "just over an hour after the pope was shot." She said police had "evidence" that the truck was there to provide Agca's escape to Bulgaria, and that it was actually used for the escape of a fellow plotter.

Sterling said the truck was "sent to Bulgaria under a diplomatic procedure not used before or since by the Bulgarians," which allowed customs officials to seal the truck and waive inspection at the border. The *New York Times* kept re-iterating that it was "the first and last time" the Bulgarians availed themselves of this customs procedure. Wasn't "the exceptional nature of this operation" strongly suspicious, as the *Times* reported?

Consolo smiled. Agca "had no possibility to escape," he said. "He didn't try to run away, or Sister Lucia [the nun] couldn't have stopped him. He wanted to be arrested to satisfy his own ego." As for the truck, Consolo said, everything about it was routine, and reports to the contrary were just wrong. The embassy got customs-free truck deliveries every two weeks, like other embassies.

The customs men who had inspected the truck testified at the trial. Because the embassy's main gate wasn't big enough to accommodate it, the truck was parked on the street, not "on the embassy grounds," as Sterling had reported. Its movements were out in the open. On top of that, reports that the truck left after the shooting were also wrong; the supposedly suspicious truck actually left the Bulgarian compound *before* the shooting—the day before, he said. Some escape route![5]

Consolo and I went over other details of the story, as reported in the *New York Times* and in books that have been produced by the two sides. Consolo had an answer for every alleged piece of evidence for a "Bulgarian connection." "One thing I know," he concluded, "is he did not act in a plot. He acted on his own."

It was an impressive performance. But I knew it was also one lawyer's side of a contentious case. Before going to the prosecutors, I called Claire Sterling, who lives outside Rome, and who had stuck by her story. She agreed to meet, then canceled, saying she wouldn't talk to me. She realized, she said, that I had written a story she didn't like in the *Wall Street Journal*, mentioning sources for her book on international terrorism.

I proceeded to the office of the chief prosecutor, Rome Magistrate Antonio Marini, who was still gathering evidence hoping to reopen the case against the Bulgarians. I expected it would be the first of several visits, as I would shuttle between him and Consolo until I had refined each point in the argument as close as I could get to an agreed-on truth.

It turned out only one visit was necessary, though it ran on several hours, beginning in broad daylight in a busy court building and ending at night in corridors eerily empty except for Marini's armed bodyguards.

Prosecutor Marini began by acknowledging that in light of the acquittals, he could no longer be sure of a Bulgarian-Soviet plot. Using his hands like scales, he gestured to show that the facts were evenly balanced. But he still believed Agca's story about the Bulgarians, he said, because the USSR had an overwhelming motive to commit the crime. The USSR's collapse after the Solidarity revolution proved to Marini how desperate the Soviets felt in 1981.

He was quite impassioned about this, and angry at Agca for sabotaging the prosecution's case. He vividly described the high point of the trial, the day Agca suddenly declared he was Jesus Christ and rambled on from the witness stand like a madman. "The audience was packed, crammed full of journalists from all over the world," Marini said. "When Agca sat on that chair and said he was Jesus Christ, the next day the courtroom was empty. After this performance, his word was worthless. He simulated madness. The big question is why. Out of court, he acted normally."

Marini said he suspected that the reason for Agca's turnaround was the Geneva summit between Reagan and Gorbachev. By the time the trial began, May 27, 1985, the United States was on a summit track with the Soviets and had decided it no longer wanted to prove a plot in the papal shooting. Somehow, Agca had been told in prison to back off. "Agca put on an act because he had to," Marini said. To continue to accuse the Bulgarians in the face of American opposition "could be very dangerous for him."

That the U.S. had asked Agca to turn around a second time to follow its Cold War tactic of the moment seemed nearly preposterous, for many reasons—not the least being the idea that Washington would trust such stakes to a twenty-six-year-old fugitive Turkish murderer who had been lunatic enough to shoot the pope in St. Peter's Square to begin with. But Marini seemed sincerely distressed each time he referred to Agca's subversion of his case, which was often.

Eventually we began a point-by-point examination of the evidence. To my surprise, instead of disputing Consolo's defense case, or even quibbling with it, Marini basically confirmed, with a few twists and turns, the facts Consolo had provided. Yes, the French secret service had tipped off the Vatican about an assassination plot. But Marini had been unable to learn what Agca's role was in this warning. De Marenches, the French master spy, "would never say what was said to the Vatican. He has never wanted to tell what he knew."[6] More surprising, Marini said, was that the Vatican had also refused to tell him.

"The Vatican just says the pope has forgiven Agca," Marini sighed. "It's a way of saying, 'For us, this issue is closed.' The Vatican didn't help us try to look for the truth. Right from the start, they didn't want to get involved."

On a critical point, Marini agreed with defense attorney Consolo that the supply truck at the Bulgarian embassy left *before* the shooting and so couldn't have been intended, or used, as an escape vehicle. (Marini said it left earlier on the day of the shooting; Consolo had said the day before.) Nor did Marini dispute that such trucks were routine at the embassy, not unique, as Claire Sterling had reported—nor that it was out on the street, not in the embassy compound, as she claimed.

Marini said he now discounts the importance of the truck altogether. "I don't think Agca would have turned himself over to the Bulgarians," he said. "They might have shot him."

But, I persisted, the truck had been a major building block of the original accusations, particularly in the *New York Times*. If Marini succeeded in bringing a new trial—his current mission—what would he say about it? Barring some startling new disclosure, he replied, he would not introduce the truck at all in a new trial. Knowing what he knew now, he wouldn't have used it in the previous trial.

Could he trace any payments from communist hands to anyone in connection with the shooting? No, he said, adding that Agca's Sofia hotel bill had been paid by "the Turkish Mafia, with its own money." The "Turkish Mafia" is a common name for Turks who make their living running drugs or guns around the Mediterranean perimeter. Agca knew some. The money they gave him could still have been communist, Marini asserted, because the Bulgarian secret police sometimes did business with the Turkish Mafia. But this was con-jecture, Marini agreed, not the kind of evidence anyone could take to court.

What about the alibi witnesses who had placed Antonov in his office at the airline instead of at St. Peter's? Marini said the court had concluded that the witness evidence allowed Antonov time to make a quick round-trip to St. Peter's in the midst of his office appointments. Yet as Marini talked, his shoul-ders sank: this was hardly the picture Agca had drawn, of an afternoon spent with Antonov and another Bulgarian, picking up a gun and grenade (to create a diversion) and preparing for the crime.

And what about Agca's incorrect description of Antonov's apartment? "I challenge anybody to go into a house" and later describe it perfectly, Marini said. He said Antonov, too, had made a poor witness and got some details wrong (though Marini couldn't remember any when I asked). When I pressed him about the wooden room divider that accurately described neighboring apartments but conspicuously *not* Antonov's, Marini's shoulders sank still fur-ther. Then he began to laugh, as if at himself. "Yes, this is a strong point," he acknowledged. "That is why Antonov was acquitted."

Marini continued to bring up Agca's sabotage of the case. If Agca hadn't destroyed his credibility with the Jesus Christ act, I asked, would his story have stood up? Marini readily acknowledged that a serious cross-examination by defense attorney Consolo—which Consolo never got to make—might have broken Agca's story anyway.

Running out of specifics, I asked if there was any evidence at all to support the notion of a Bulgarian-Soviet plot.

"All you need to see is what happened later," Marini said. "The Berlin Wall comes down. Communism ends in Russia. And the knowledge that the pope was an important element. They had an interest. But today we don't have any proof."

He described the trip he and his team had made to post-communist Bulgaria to look for evidence. "What we always asked ourselves is how come a Turkish terrorist [Agca] could get into Bulgaria so easily. At the time it was very diffi-cult to get into Bulgaria." (On that point the prosecution differed with the defense, which argued that a million Turks a year crossed into Bulgaria, since it was the only overland route from Turkey to Europe except through hostile Greece. Agca had a well-made phony passport.)

So what did Prosecutor Marini learn from his team's investigation in Bulgaria?

"We couldn't find anything," he said.

Of course, it was hard to prove a negative, or to say there might not be some unknown evidence that still might implicate the Russians. The issue was whether the whole case until now had been built on a hoax. I repeated my question: Was there any evidence at all to support the notion of a Bulgarian-Soviet plot? Earlier he had said no *proof.* I emphasized: any *evidence,* at all? He looked me sadly in the eye and made the admission we both knew he had been making in so many words for the past three hours. "There isn't any evidence that the Soviets were trying to kill the pope," he said.

By this time, we were all fairly relaxed, neckties loose, the two of us and my interpreter in Marini's otherwise deserted office. I asked the prosecutor to repeat it to make sure I had it right. He did. I stressed how important this was. He said he still hoped something might turn up, because a plot seemed so logical. Then, for a third time, he said, slowly, "There isn't any evidence the Soviets were trying to kill the pope."

49

For the six-hundredth anniversary of Lithuanian Christianity, the Soviets agreed to open churches and ring bells as John Paul requested. Under the new Gorbachev design for openness, a message from the pope was even read over loudspeakers. But John Paul was denied permission to go to Lithuania for the anniversary.

He discussed it with Jan Novak, the former Radio Free Europe official (who was in Europe arranging a new pipeline for AFL-CIO aid to Poland, through a priest in France). The pope said he suspected his Lithuanian trip had been blocked less by Gorbachev than by Russian Orthodox churchmen, who feared he would encroach on their religious turf. As if joking, but with clear serious overtones, the pope said he could go to the USSR "only if they convert to Roman Catholicism. It's not the communists who hate me as much as [it is] the Orthodox."

John Paul already saw beyond the Cold War and into the ugly religious clash that loomed in the 1990s. His desperation to heal the rift with the Orthodox was well reasoned: at stake was not just the future of the faith in what was then the USSR but also countless lives in what was then Yugoslavia. In May 1986, the pope reached out to the Orthodox in an encyclical, *Dominum et Vivificantum* ("Lord and Giver of Life"), stressing the urgency of reuniting the churches before the end of the millennium in which the rift began.

Even before the Orthodox formally separated from Rome in 1054, the heart of their theological complaint was that Catholics made the Holy Spirit subsidiary in the trinity. So *Dominum et Vivificantum* stressed the importance of the Holy Spirit. It said ecumenical unity was needed to restore religion's force in life, so essential because of the rise of materialism.

After noting the "extreme practical consequences" of Marxist materialism, John Paul laid out a new idea: that capitalist materialism was linked with death. There was a striking similarity between the pope's new formulation and the unified philosophy of life that Cardinal Bernardin had described in his speech at Fordham eighteen months earlier:

> The signs and symptoms of death have become particularly present and frequent. One has only to think of the arms race and its inherent danger of nuclear self-destruction. Moreover, everyone has become more and more aware of the grave situation of vast areas on our planet, marked by death-dealing poverty and famine. It is a question of problems that are not only economic, but also and above all ethical. A custom has become widely established—in some places it threatens to become almost an institution—of taking the lives of human beings even before they are born, or before they reach the natural point of death.

The pope would cultivate these ideas until they became his characteristic topic of the 1990s.

Several figures in John Paul's orbit suffered blows in early 1986. Michele Sindona, who had first turned IOR crooked by showing Vatican officials how much money they could make, never telling them it was stolen, was sentenced to life in an Italian prison. A few days later, he took one swallow of his morning coffee and fell dead from a massive dose of poison; most believe it was self-inflicted.

William Wilson, the friend of President Reagan's who had become the first U.S. ambassador to the Vatican, was forced to resign. An irate Secretary of State Shultz had discovered that Wilson was secretly conducting talks with Libyan dictator Muammar Qaddafi.

And Kurt Waldheim, the secretary-general who had first brought John Paul to the UN, was identified as a Nazi war criminal. Files from the UN War Crimes Commission showed that as an Austrian officer in Hitler's army, young Waldheim had sent Jews and war prisoners to their deaths. Waldheim was running for president of Austria; the World Jewish Congress urged that he be tried for murder instead.

While there's no evidence that John Paul lost any sleep over the problems of Sindona or Wilson, his determination to stay loyal to Waldheim, a tub-thumping Catholic, would further tarnish his once-shiny public image.

The Polish government made one last effort to stall the onrushing tide of freedom. In May and June 1986, authorities arrested a slew of Solidarity leaders,
among them Konrad Bielinski (this time with Ewa Kulik) and—after four and
a half years—the underground's top dog, Zbigniew Bujak.[1]

Soon after these targets were imprisoned, however, government officials
began calling them in for surprisingly cordial "discussions," then releasing
them. By September, all remaining Solidarity prisoners had likewise been
released. Several thousand activists who were free were also called in for talks,
the contents of which appeared in the underground press.

Jaruzelski seemed to be offering a new deal to Polish society. The activists
had been given accounts of their underground work, to impress them that the
police were watching and "that their activities were futile." But then they were
told, "We are entering a new stage" of "stabilization" and "national accord."
It was time for everyone to work together for the good of the country.[2]

What had provoked this new policy? First, the economy was in dreadful
shape even for communism. The system's natural incompetence had been com-
pounded by Gierek's borrowings, by the siege mentality of martial law, and by
the effect—still lingering—of the U.S. embargo: the pope was right, it really
did hurt ordinary Poles. Jaruzelski knew he could not keep losing manpower to
civil strife. Another factor was also in play, however: word had spread that Gorbachev's new agenda was real. The Soviets wanted a bigger private sector and
fewer central controls. Polish communists, who had wanted to go that route for
forty years, no longer had to fear Soviet roadblocks.

September 29, 1986, Walesa brazenly announced the formation of a seven-
member provisional council of Solidarity—aboveground and including former
underground leaders. "We don't want to act clandestinely," he told a press conference.[3] Just holding a press conference proved his point: the freedom movement was now far too advanced to be stopped.

One last mistake by Jaruzelski hastened Solidarity's victory. To punish the
activists he released, he ordered them blacklisted from government jobs. Unable
to work in the communist economy, they had only one way to put food on their
tables: taking up private business, legal or illegal. They did—with a vengeance.

Back in May 1986, John Paul, having already cast lines to animists, Lutherans,
Jews, Anglicans, and Orthodox, had decided to become the first pope to hold
a broad, multifaith religious event. The long-range goal remained to bring all
humanity into the one true Church, which he was determined to keep pure; but

in the meantime, this pope was going to encourage other religious people of goodwill to work together in their own ways to cultivate human spirituality.

Summoning Cardinals Arinze of Interfaith Dialogue and Etchegaray of Justice and Peace to a papal lunch with senior aides, John Paul declared that he would invite some 150 religious leaders that fall to Assisi, home of Saint Francis—"for the first time in history, to come and fast and pray for peace," Arinze says. He would call rabbis, mullahs, sikhs, African animists, Buddhists (including the Dalai Lama), Protestant evangelicals, Shintoists, the archbishop of Canterbury—any leader he could find who was committed to the spiritual path.

With each point the pope brought up, excitement mounted. "We all saw it was something new," Arinze says, though "care was needed not to give the impression that religions were relative, one as good as another." Non-Catholic religions were to get auditoriums, not churches, for their prayer (though the Assisi diocese assigned the Buddhists a church anyway).

Despite the precautions, "it was very controversial in Italy," says one priest involved. "Many people thought it was demeaning to Catholicism, putting other religions on the same level." Some Protestants objected. An Orthodox group threatened not to come if another was invited, and vice versa. Some Moslem groups imposed difficult conditions.

John Paul willed the event to fruition, and talked about it with delight frequently afterward, though in the end it proved but one step on a long journey. The groups prayed independently at their assigned sites, then met for an open-air joint service. Thinking that a common prayer would become too diluted by the time everyone agreed on it, the Pope gave each religion five minutes to offer its own prayer. He told the group:

> I humbly repeat here my own conviction: peace bears the name of Jesus Christ. But at the same time . . . I am ready to acknowledge that Catholics have not always been faithful to this. . . . We have not always been peacemakers. . . .
>
> We hope that this pilgrimage to Assisi has taught us anew to be aware of the common origin and common destiny of humanity. Let us see in it . . . what God would like the developing history of humanity to be: a fraternal journey in which we accompany one another towards the transcendent goal he sets for us. . . .
>
> This day at Assisi has . . . also made the world, looking at us through the media, more aware of the responsibility of each religion. . . . In the great battle for peace, humanity, in its diversity, must draw from its deepest and most vivifying sources where its

conscience is formed and upon which is founded the moral action
of all people. . . .

There is no peace without a passionate love for peace. . . . Peace
awaits its prophets. . . . Peace awaits its builders. . . . Peace is a universal responsibility: it comes about through a thousand little acts
in daily life.

"Diversity is the nature of the human family," he told an interviewer later.[4]
"We must go beyond [Catholicism] to persons of goodwill who do not share
our faith."

50

All through 1986, as the Assisi meeting was being planned, General Secretary
Gorbachev struggled to change the Soviet economy. He complained to visitors
that "resistance is spreading through all the institutions." He said the State
Planning Committee acted as if "there is no general secretary, no Central Committee. Its officials do whatever they want."[1]

He had no better luck selling weapons reductions to Washington. Much as
Reagan said he wanted dialogue, he wouldn't sacrifice his arms buildup. Gorbachev feared that if he visited Washington as planned without an arms deal,
his adversaries would say he had caved in. So he proposed—and got—another
"interim summit" with Reagan, this time at Reykjavik, Iceland, October 11
and 12, 1986.

Gorbachev arrived with a full team of advisers and sweeping proposals for
cutbacks in weapons testing and all ranges of missiles—*so* sweeping, in fact,
that the CIA reported that Soviet generals had talked of assassinating Gorbachev.[2] Reagan came with few advisers and warmed-over concessions. Surprised by Gorbachev's offers, he at first threw up the usual rejoinders about
Soviet aggression and unwillingness to undergo inspections. Gorbachev kept to
the weapons issue and offered strict verification.

Reagan and Shultz were soon caught up in a dizzying contest of counter-
offers until they and Gorbachev had stunningly agreed to eliminate all their
nuclear weapons—*all*—within ten years. And this before any of them had
digested lunch the first day. The Soviets even agreed to recognize human rights
as a legitimate part of the agenda between the countries.

Could it be?

Well, no. A snag arose over space weapons during the ten years. Reagan still wanted his "Star Wars" missile shield, but Gorbachev said it violated the existing treaty against antiballistic missiles, which had been adopted in the first place because a country with a defensive shield might be tempted to launch an offensive first strike. Gorbachev wanted the old understanding, which limited research on such weapons to the laboratory. Reagan refused.

That was it.

News traveled the world of the sudden hope and its equally sudden deflation. In his memoir, Shultz said Gorbachev came to Reykjavik with "an elaborate chesslike performance" to get Reagan to drop "Star Wars," and that Gorbachev failed.[3]

On the heels of Reykjavik came the Assisi meeting. Reality proved a mirror image of John Paul's dream. When Shultz met Soviet Foreign Minister Eduard Shevardnadze in Vienna soon afterward to follow up Reykjavik, both sides withdrew their generous offers. In November, Reagan gave a speech condemning "three decades of Soviet adventurism around the world" and vowing to respond militarily. His White House effectively blocked the membership the Soviets sought in the World Bank and International Monetary Fund. The warming was over.

It is widely thought that at this point, the Soviets decided they had to build their own "Star Wars" defense system and otherwise match the United States stride for stride, and that they went broke doing so. In all the material released from Soviet archives since the fall of communism, however, scant evidence of this has appeared.

What seems to have happened instead is that Gorbachev resolved to go his own way, without Reagan. After clearing it with the Politburo, he summoned leaders of the Eastern Bloc countries November 10 and 11, a month after Reykjavik, and told them they were on their own—that, in the words of historian Raymond Garthoff, "they must take steps to restructure their own rule and gain legitimacy. . . . The Soviet Union could no longer be expected to keep them in power."[4]

It was an era-changing message. Gorbachev had hinted at the idea shortly after taking office, but no one had grasped his meaning. Even now, it was not publicly announced. But the effect in Poland was swift.

Jaruzelski immediately invited Catholic leaders to join communists on a new "social council" to advise the government. John Paul's longtime friends and colleagues Jerzy Turowicz, Tadeusz Mazowiecki, and Andrzej Wielowiejski were among those asked to participate. That Mazowiecki was a Solidarity leader seemed to pose no obstacle.

The "social council," if it worked, sounded much like Wojtyla's design for teamwork between government and lay Catholics. But after much debate, the Catholic Intelligentsia Clubs—Father Wojtyla's children—voted to decline the offer because the council's rulings wouldn't be binding. "We were against Jaruzelski," says Turowicz. "Giving [his council] this legitimacy would be a fiction." They would hold out for more.

General Rowny, Reagan's aide, briefed Jaruzelski, Walesa, and the pope about Reykjavik. Rowny, himself of Polish descent, says John Paul greeted him in good humor, asking, "How are you getting along with your bishops?"—a joking reference to the Reagan administration's struggles with the U.S. Episcopate over weapons and social programs. "He knew I had been fighting their policies," Rowny explains. "I said, 'I thought they were *your* bishops.' " John Paul laughed, patted Rowny, and proclaimed, "*Moledyetsk!*"—a Russian word they both knew meant "tough guy."

"As usual, there was no response, no evidence [the Vatican] did anything" as a consequence of their talk, Rowny says.

Gorbachev continued his unilateral peace plan. December 12, 1986, he brought the Afghan Politburo to Moscow and gave them the same shock he had just given the Eastern Europeans. Flanking himself with his top generals for emphasis, he said the Soviets would withdraw all forces from Afghanistan within two years. Until then, he would do what he could politically to help the communists control the country. But after that, they were on their own.

Next, Gorbachev relaxed controls on dissidents and rescinded the law prohibiting agitating and propagandizing against the government.[5] The anti-Stalinist novel *Dr. Zhivago* and many other banned works were legalized. Reaction within the Party was so negative that Gorbachev had to postpone the scheduled January 1987 Central Committee meeting several times, and then publicly threaten to resign in order to collect its endorsement. His next push was for secret voting and multiple candidates for Party office, including heads of local and district government and business enterprises.[6]

He went to Czechoslovakia to proclaim his new international policy openly. "The entire framework of political relations between the socialist countries must be strictly based on absolute independence," he said. "Every nation is entitled to choose its own way of development." Most people still read "within the communist system" into that sentence, as Gorbachev himself seemed to. In most Eastern Bloc countries, including the USSR, the Party remained the lone authority. But not in Poland.

Just as Gorbachev was dealing the cards of his own defeat, Reagan suffered a startling drain of *his* remarkable power. November 4, 1986, voters restored control of the Senate as well as the House of Representatives to the Democrats. Less than three weeks later, a Lebanese newspaper reported the secret, illegal arms sales to Iran, which led to a White House disclosure that money from the sales had been illegally used to fund the Contra war behind Congress's back. National Security Adviser John Poindexter and his assistant Colonel Oliver North were fired. Investigators lined up at Reagan's own door. Suddenly, the actor President whom Americans had indulged as a fond father became the butt of jokes, just as predecessors had been.

Turmoil also roiled the American Church. August 19, 1986, John Paul fired Father Charles Curran from his controversial professorship at Catholic University in Washington.

"We could not permit a Catholic theologian in a Catholic university to teach that which is contrary to what the Church teaches," the pope told a dinner guest, journalist Wilton Wynn, three days after the firing. When Wynn said some Catholics didn't regard the birth-control dictums as final because they weren't issued infallibly, John Paul replied,

> Infallible declarations...have been extremely rare.... If you believe only those declarations, you have very little left to believe. After all, no solemn declaration of infallibility ever was made regarding the Ten Commandments.... Does that mean you have the right to dissent on those teachings?... Moral questions are covered by the "ordinary" magisterium [teachings of the Church], and it is our duty to insist on their being obeyed....
>
> It is a mistake to apply American democratic procedures to the faith.... Truth is not determined by voting. It is something that must be accepted. This is not my teaching we are talking about. This is the teaching of the Church, and it is my responsibility to insist that it be obeyed. I cannot change that teaching. I have no *right* to change it.[7]

Father Curran thought he had a right to augment Catholic teaching with his own clearly labeled dissents, when he had them. The faculty committee at Catholic University agreed, voting to keep him a tenured professor. But a U.S. District Court judge said the Vatican was within its rights to fire him. Curran wound up teaching at Cornell, the University of Southern California, Auburn, and finally, of all places, Southern Methodist University.

As for Archbishop Hunthausen, after several trips to Seattle early in 1986, Cardinal Bernardin felt he "was within an inch" of resolving the crisis.[8] But Hunthausen backed off from the compromise Bernardin thought he had arranged. So, on a visit to Rome, Bernardin and some other American bishops recommended over lunch that Hunthausen get an unsought assistant, and the pope agreed.[9] But apparently Bernardin couldn't bring himself to tell Hunthausen.

In September, an irate Hunthausen announced that an assistant bishop from Pittsburgh, Donald Wuerl, had been sent by the Vatican to supersede his authority in five important areas, including marriage, preparation of priests, and liturgy. It looked like an unparalleled slap at a sitting archbishop. Worse, it didn't work—for which Vatican officials, off the record, blame Bernardin.

A prominent American Catholic who was involved in the turmoil that followed says Hunthausen didn't know when his new assistant arrived that he was being superseded: "At some point, Wuerl told him, or challenged him in some way. He woke up to reality. It was a disaster. You had two bishops who weren't speaking to each other."

Despite Hunthausen's detractors at Boeing, many people in the pews supported him for his patience with the divorced, and even with homosexuals. They saw Wuerl as a hit man from out of town. Passions spread from Seattle to Catholics across the nation. The annual meeting of U.S. bishops in November veered toward tumult. Hunthausen sought support. Many bishops, though on Hunthausen's side, didn't want to confront the Church in public. The *New York Times Magazine* ran a cover story on the divided U.S. Church, featuring the Hunthausen and Curran incidents.

If John Paul had put Tony Bevilacqua on track to be a cardinal for neatly quieting a potential scandal, one can imagine how he felt now about Cardinal Bernardin. Catholics across America were choosing up sides between two bishops—Hunthausen and Wuerl—who the newspapers said were fighting over everything down to which one was entitled to the better parking space.[10] The rift was especially embarrassing coming on the eve of John Paul's greatest ecumenical event, the Assisi conference.

Gathering in Washington for their convention, the nation's bishops were greeted by documents from Cardinal Laghi and Archbishop Hunthausen, giving mutually incompatible accounts of how Bishop Wuerl came to Seattle. Thousands of Seattle Catholics paraded with candles in support of Hunthausen. Bernardin still thought the joint administration would work if Hunthausen would just bend a bit more, but Hunthausen wouldn't. He denied he was a dissenter, and said his alleged transgressions either had been corrected long ago or, in the case of allowing homosexual groups to say Mass, were common practice in American archdioceses. He spoke at an emotional meeting that produced what, for bishops, was almost a revolt.

The bishops rejected a draft resolution saying that the pope's action in Seattle had been "just and reasonable," and voted instead to declare that it "deserves our respect and confidence." They also declared that it wasn't working, and offered their services resolving the problem. They rejected the bid of the pope's new appointee, Cardinal Law, to be a delegate at the next synod, voting instead for Bernardin and Weakland. Law then ran for another post and was defeated again, by two relative unknowns.[11]

In meetings at Laghi's house over the next few weeks, it was agreed that Bernardin, Cardinal O'Connor of New York, and another bishop would reinvestigate the Seattle affair for the Vatican. Through March and April 1987, a dozen bishops and archbishops flew in and out of meetings. Bernardin again announced a deal. Hunthausen again backed out, asking to see the pope. Finally, Tom Fox, publisher of the *National Catholic Reporter*, who had been sympathetic to Hunthausen, lured him toward a compromise.

Hunthausen approved the appointment of Thomas Murphy of Great Falls, Montana, as his new helper bishop. Wuerl became bishop of Pittsburgh. Hunthausen would meet quarterly with Bernardin's commission, and if there were no problems in a year, his powers would be gracefully restored before an early retirement. He could see the pope, but only to convey his obedience, not to reargue the case.

Hunthausen signed. The document was overnighted to Bernardin, who then flew with it to Rome, accompanied by Laghi and O'Connor. John Paul wanted another telegram from Hunthausen confirming the whole thing before he said yes; he got it.

Announcement of the deal made the front page of the *New York Times* and the network newscasts—not what John Paul would consider the Church's best use of such prominent exposure. Simultaneous with the Hunthausen circus, however, a similar case against Bishop Walter Sullivan of Richmond, Virginia, was handled quietly by another papal mediator, Archbishop John May of St. Louis. Only Catholics paying careful attention knew anything had happened in Richmond.

Perhaps Sullivan—who remains at his post—was just more cooperative than Hunthausen. But the perception stuck in Rome that Bernardin was too weak for hard jobs. Later, John Paul returned to Bernardin's side, when tragedy evoked papal compassion. But for now, compassion was a virtue that Bernardin was thought to have in excess. In 1991, Hunthausen, aged seventy, retired and Bishop Murphy took over. Any policy changes were so subtle that most people didn't notice them.[12]

A prominent Jesuit compares the Hunthausen case to John Paul's replacement of Father Arrupe in the Jesuits. "Many [people] were offended both times," he says. "Things didn't work out as planned."*

The Hunthausen episode further persuaded many American Catholics that John Paul wasn't the caring pastor they wanted. Says publisher Fox, the mediator: "The Vatican today looks at faith and [it] comes down to doctrine. Other people look at faith and they see in it trust. And out of that trust grows a sense of community. What gets difficult is when one set of Catholics essentially says to the other, 'There's no room for you.' None of this is really over creed or the essentials of faith. It's about philosophy, it's about values. They grow out of faith, but they're not the essence of faith. Ultimately, it seems that this pontiff curiously lacks faith—that the Holy Spirit is here among all of us. He doesn't trust the bishops, the religious, the laity. His sense is, 'They're all going to go wrong if I let them.' "

Even Archbishop May, who had just resolved the doctrinal problem in the Richmond archdiocese, told the pope in front of colleagues at a meeting at the Vatican, "Authoritarianism is suspect.... To assert that there is a Church teaching with authority binding ... for eternity is truly a sign of contradiction to many Americans who consider the divine right of bishops as outmoded as the divine right of kings."[13]

The pope and his American critics had settled on opposite sides of a very old two-sided coin: If you sacrifice fundamental principle in order to reach agreement, you debase the agreement; but if you sacrifice human agreement in order to keep a pristine principle, you debase the principle by rendering it bloodless and ineffective. A successful leader somehow emerges with both principle and agreement—which is exactly what John Paul did in the struggle with totalitarianism. In addressing the spiritual needs of post-communist society, however, the Hunthausen affair was just one of many signs of a tragically doomed course.

Some 163 theology teachers from German-speaking Catholic universities signed a declaration accusing John Paul of ignoring local feelings in appointing bishops, of "suffocating" Vatican II's call for local consultation, and of valuing ideology over ability in appointing teachers. When the Vatican dismissed

* There was also criticism of John Paul at around the same time for disciplining Father Bernard Haring, a veteran Roman theologian who had served with Archbishop Wojtyla on a Vatican II committee. But Haring had stridently contested many papal stands, particularly on birth control, even going so far as to compare John Paul to Hitler. No organization could long tolerate such insubordination, and Haring never attracted the same broad support as Hunthausen.

the protest as a "local matter," 130 French-speaking theologians endorsed the declaration—then twenty-five Spaniards, and fifty-two Belgians. Sixty Italian theologians denied their job was "simply to follow Church teaching."[14] If the professors signing these complaints were mere cranks, then the Church was overrun with cranks.

Back in 1971, Cardinal Wojtyla had said the theologian's task was "to guard, defend, and teach the sacred body of revelation in strict subordination to the pope and his bishops." Faced with dissent in the late 1980s, John Paul simply imposed an oath on all theology professors, to "adhere . . . to the teachings which either the Roman pontiff or the college of bishops declare when they exercise the authentic magisterium."[15]

As the communist threat receded, John Paul was becoming a lone dissenting voice in a clanging popular culture that promoted short-term material and sensual gratification above transcendent values. People were committing to a kind of zero-based moral budgeting and then not finding the happiness that they had expected would follow. The pope was championing a blend of individual responsibility and community responsibility, which together had produced the American nation's stunning success. But he wasn't reaching his audience, and no amount of "eternal truth" could erase the significance of that.

51

In January 1987, John Whitehead, the investment banker in charge of Eastern European policy at the State Department, went to Warsaw. He was the first high-level U.S. diplomat to visit there in decades. Whitehead was in the vanguard of forces subtly reorienting U.S. policy, taking the reins slipping from the hands of Reagan and his original, ideological, foreign-policy team.

This new breed held communism in no higher esteem than the old, but it wanted to switch games, from Space Invaders to Monopoly. The new breed was trained in business and expected to win by *doing* business.

Whitehead found a Poland that was itself much changed from preceding years. The underground, with a final boost from Mikhail Gorbachev, had quietly won. The days of fugitive life and smuggling conspiracies were fading. Billionaire American investor George Soros donated twenty thousand dollars to buy computers for *Tygodnik Mazowsze*, and the computers arrived without trouble. Konstanty Gebert shelved the tedious silk screens that had carried him through martial law and began printing his underground newspapers on efficient offset presses.

Ironically, a shipment of computers and printers smuggled in through the usual Swedish route—goods costing U.S. taxpayers $125,000, via the AFL-CIO—had just been seized because the truck driver's license had been revoked for drunkenness. It was the last major shipment sent that way, as the need for secrecy waned.

Whitehead dined with Walesa and his advisers Michnik and Geremek, but they discussed no action for fear of government eavesdropping. Whitehead was alienated within minutes of meeting Cardinal Glemp, who talked as if he were a government mediator, not a Solidarity partisan. Whitehead bluntly told the primate that he was surprised by the churchman's closeness to the communists. Recalls Whitehead, "He bristled, and said it was necessary to keep the Church alive, that he deserved more credit than the West was giving him."

Jaruzelski gave Whitehead the same line, complaining angrily about the honors "your friend Walesa" was getting in the United States, and saying it was he, Jaruzelski, who had saved Poland from the Soviets. A scheduled thirty-minute meeting lasted three hours and "was very confrontational," Whitehead says. Jaruzelski insisted that Whitehead not refer to Solidarity, as it no longer existed.

"He felt personally challenged by Solidarity. For his own selfish reasons, he wanted to stamp it out," Whitehead says. When Whitehead cited specific human-rights violations, Jaruzelski replied that the U.S. had "no right to interfere in [Poland's] internal affairs. I agreed with that, but [said] we have a right to pick our friends. And he wanted to be friends with the United States."

In many ways, luring countries with the benefits of capitalism and trade was much more effective and humane than the original Reagan policy of military punishment. The old policy focused mainly on poor countries and mostly ignored Eastern Europe, which shared a common industrial language with Americans. Now, a workable bridge was being built to a peaceful, post-communist future.

But the new policy comprehended the message of John Paul II scarcely better than the old one did.

The pope himself was concentrating on his upcoming third visit to Poland, and on writing a major encyclical on government, which would address the economic questions Washington raised, and offer a key to the Liberation Theology problem as well. He continued to talk about Solidarity not mainly as a means of toppling Soviet power, but as a universal plan for running civil society according to Catholic social ethics.

Dziwisz, by now John Paul's alter ego, also talked to visitors about the broad social mission of Solidarity. Zdzislaw Najder of Radio Free Europe came away from such discussions with a reinvigorated enthusiasm that got him fired when he expressed it on the air. He says he was told he couldn't be an adviser to Solidarity and a radio official at the same time. But he feels the real reason for his firing was that American officials, while exploiting the trappings of Solidarity, neither understood nor believed in what Solidarity really was.

The AFL-CIO's Lane Kirkland also scoffed at the new American policy: "That freedom and democracy would be advanced by allowing capital to flow! The contrary is true in history," says Kirkland. "American business loved [Chilean dictator] Pinochet. They were quite willing to embrace [dictators] Franco and Mussolini. Business doesn't give a tinker's damn about the evolution of a civil society outside of capital in pursuit of profit. I don't believe it was the administration's policy to stand by Solidarity; they sought commercial normalization with Poland. I was in deep disagreement."

The campaign to sell the ethic of unfettered capitalism in Poland and Eastern Europe was the new challenge to John Paul II. He saw capitalism much as he did science: each could produce great benefits for humanity but needed moral governing. Without that, they yielded hardship.

On February 20, 1987, two Milan judges signed arrest warrants for Archbishop Marcinkus and his two lay aides at the Vatican bank. The judges disputed the Vatican's assertions that it had cooperated in the Banco Ambrosiano investigation. An appeals court upheld the warrants, finding that Marcinkus and his men had shown a "common will to deceive." Officially, they became prisoners in the Vatican, subject to arrest if they ventured out into Rome— though Marcinkus's defenders say that Italian authorities knew he left the Vatican regularly to play golf, and let him do it.

Asked about the investigation in late March on a flight to South America, John Paul said he would make sure the case was "studied by the competent authorities." In fact, his lawyers were making sure it would *not* be. After a battle, they got the arrest warrants overturned by Italy's supreme court. Marcinkus acknowledged to a newspaper that he had helped Calvi, the crooked banker, but said his Vatican colleagues saw it as ingenuousness and didn't reproach him for it.[1]

John Paul preferred to think about his destination, Chile. It was his first trip there, but he was determined to make a political difference. His bishops were still at war with the Pinochet dictatorship, now in its fourteenth year since seizing power, with Nixon administration help, by killing the elected Socialist president, Salvador Allende, along with thousands of his supporters. Priests were telling the poor they had a right to escape poverty, and Pinochet wanted the priests silenced.

From the airplane, John Paul made clear that he was on the side of the priests. He offered Pinochet no sympathetic talk about the excesses of Liberation Theology. Addressing reporters, he bluntly said that in Chile,

> we will find a system that is dictatorial, but one that is transitory by definition. It is not only possible but necessary that the Church work in defense of human rights, [though] there are those who would separate us from that mission.

His statement that Pinochet was a dictator who had to go soon was in world headlines the day he arrived, as he must have known it would be. At the airport, Pinochet, in a white uniform with gold trim, defended his human-rights record. He attributed Allende's election to "foreign-based . . . aggression," and said that Chile was now a "stable society based on the values of freedom, justice, and progress." But the pope refused to say a private Mass for Pinochet at his palace, as the dictator requested.

On the twelve-mile motorcade route to town, demonstrators chanted, "Our brother, Pope, take the tyrant with you." The same chants followed John Paul throughout Chile. Crowds cheered him outside the Church human-rights office—dubbed the "Vicarate of Solidarity"—which tallied the jailings, instances of torture, and disappearances.

The next day, in poor districts, hundreds of thousands of people crowded around him, many holding signs saying, "Holy Father, help me find my son" (or some other missing relative). At a large public rally, John Paul brought to the microphone a slim woman, Luisa Rivera, who (the *New York Times* said) "passionately described low salaries, unemployment, no medical attention," and other ills. When she was finished, John Paul embraced her in both arms. Other speakers followed with similar stories and received the same embrace.

He said an evening Mass in the stadium that Pinochet had used as a slaughterhouse for Allende supporters. He declared what the packed throng was already thinking: that the stadium was "a place of competitions, but also of pain and suffering in times past." Every politically infused reference was cheered. The crowd interrupted occasionally with chants of "Freedom" or "End to dictatorship."

Stores in the neighborhood had closed early that day, their owners expecting violence. Demonstrators who assembled after the Mass were dispersed with tear gas and water canons. Some civilians and police were injured by rocks and stray gunfire.

The next day, John Paul met with a coalition of opposition leaders, who showed courage just by coming; after the pope went home, they would still have to live with Pinochet. At the meeting, even communists agreed to renounce violence and work with the Chilean bishops against the dictator. The pope then visited a teenager who had been badly burned in a police attack in which a friend had been killed; after she told her story, he replied, "I understand it all." His real message, of course, lay in his coming to her, and bringing reporters.

At the main event, an open-air Mass in a large park before hundreds of thousands of people, John Paul presented speaker after speaker who complained of censorship, torture, and political murder. Demonstrations erupted early. Crowds burned barricades, threw rocks, and taunted police, as John Paul, never missing a beat, gave what Press Secretary Navarro-Valls singles out as one of his great speeches, endorsing the work of Chilean priests for justice, condemning the terrorism, and assuring people that "suffering for the sake of love, truth and justice is the sign of fidelity to God." As he spoke, police lobbed tear gas canisters and fired buckshot and water cannons to drive back crowds, while the pope proclaimed loudly, "Love is stronger, love is stronger."

White-robed priests surrounding the pope on the platform held handkerchiefs to their faces. Some entered the crowd, urging youths to stop throwing rocks. "You're not hurting the police! Your rocks are hitting innocent people!" one said. The young man he was addressing replied, "Padre, it doesn't matter. They are killing us. Today they are getting the message." Another priest bled badly from the head after being struck with a rock.[2]

Afterward, John Paul was led away by Vatican security guards as tear gas wafted across the stage. The Red Cross treated six hundred people for gas inhalation and others for buckshot wounds. Three Chileans, including a female journalist and a thirteen-year-old, were hospitalized with bullet wounds. A homeless man was shot dead.

The government tried to keep television cameras from showing the violence, but viewers got the picture anyway when the pope appeared for a televised meeting, wiping his eyes and pointing to stricken adults and students at the pulpit. Asked later to assign blame, the pope, in his typical indirect fashion, declared that there had been "an extremely base, primitive, and violent provocation." Then he praised the dignity of the crowd—clearly leaving the police to take the blame.

In Chile's second-biggest city, Concepción, the Church had cut off contact with the government after three Pinochet opponents were shot dead (one while being driven to the hospital after he survived a first attack). When the Church protested, the government accused it of supporting terrorists. No government representatives were invited to John Paul's Mass in Concepción, though the military governor, a general, showed up anyway, in the front row.

By the time the pope left, Chilean Church leaders believed they had received strong papal support for their work. Said Monsignor Carlos Puentes, head of the human-rights group, "It's not the pope's job to say to Pinochet, 'You have twenty-four hours, or else.' What he did instead was say to the workers, 'I am with you.' Chileans saw the pope embracing the workers, the homeless, the torture victims. They saw themselves as a people again. They had an identity."

Eighteen months later, Pinochet offered a plebiscite, and Chileans rejected his rule. A year after that, they voted in a new president, a Christian Democrat. Vatican officials say John Paul was a major "catalyst for change," just as he had been in Korea, Haiti, the Philippines, and Argentina, where he stopped after leaving Chile.

52

When the pope arrived in Poland in June 1987, only a minority of astute Poles seemed to discern the subtle change in the usual war of words. The issue was no longer communism, whose fate had already been sealed. The maneuvering now was about what would replace communism.

To Jaruzelski and other communists, the approaching death of the Stalinist police state did not necessarily mean the end of Marxist-oriented government—or of their jobs. They hoped to stick around, adding democracy and economic pragmatism, ditching doctrinaire bossiness. That June, Mieczyslaw Rakowski, not realizing he would be the last communist prime minister of Poland, wrote to Jaruzelski to propose such a new leadership format.[1]

A strong minority of churchmen behind Cardinal Glemp seemed prepared to accept an easygoing communism, provided that the Church could be restored to its former role as the government's official arm for faith and morals, as in aristocratic times.

The pope thought otherwise. With probably most priests and lay Catholics behind him, he remained focused on his utopian notion of Solidarity as a movement binding society, working with a democratic government and the Church to realize Catholic social ethics.

But Solidarity, the movement of 1981, hardly existed anymore. The democratic roots of Walesa's organization lay in seven-year-old union elections from different times. Solidarity no longer negotiated on behalf of workers for pay and job conditions, the government having little left to yield in that realm anyway. Walesa's leadership council survived simply because it was the only identifiable opposition body the government and the Church could talk to.

A new force was rippling through society, however: private enterprise. And it was born from the Solidarity underground, which Walesa, Michnik, and their jailed colleagues, through no fault of their own, weren't part of. The fugitives and ex-convicts who had run the underground, though less well known in the West than Walesa and Michnik, were now operating in the open.

Bujak, Bielinski, Kulik, and some colleagues had organized themselves publicly as the Warsaw Regional Executive Committee of Solidarity, though, as such, they had little to do. Blacklisted from "legitimate" employment in government offices, they tried business. Under communist law, they could sell personal services, but the only way to bring in substantial money, and affect society, was to operate in the guise of a nonprofit foundation.

Bujak and Janas—the two "Zbigs" whom the pope had supported with hand-carried messages during martial law—took the lead in organizing these "foundations." For legal purposes, they declared that their goal was to distribute welfare money among out-of-work citizens and families. Actually, however, the foundations worked more like private banks, investing Solidarity funds to help former union members begin new businesses.

Bujak helped one Solidarity friend get started making chemicals at home; another, electronic parts; another, screws and other small construction parts with a metal extruding machine; another, orange juice from oranges they found a supply of. Janas started a health-care foundation, and friends began making bandages and producing hypodermics.

"Our goal was not to give out money, but to create a place where a father earning fifty thousand zlotys a month would be able to earn a hundred fifty thousand zlotys," Bujak says. New sources of capital were found. For years, Poles had been encouraged to work in the West—mostly Germany—for a year or two, save what they could from their wages, and bring it home. Now, former Solidarity underground members began coordinating this work abroad. Money brought home was pooled to fund additional entrepreneurships.

That spring, the new Democratic Congress in the United States appropriated a million dollars for the Brussels office of Solidarity—three times the former contribution. It was intended to answer complaints from past years that more money was needed for printing equipment and the like. But in the changed atmosphere, much of the new U.S. money wound up creating "foundations": one in Gdansk officially aimed at reducing heart disease, another in Lodz for sick children, yet another in Warsaw. All helped fund individual enterprise.

One former local Solidarity leader started a trucking company, another a taxi service. Such businesses operated in a nether world between the legal and the illegal. In some ways, they were against the law, especially when they

employed others. But they operated openly, and if the government raised questions, the owners claimed to be part of a foundation. When the pope came in
1987, these entrepreneurships affected only a narrow slice of society. Most
Poles still worked halfheartedly at dead-end jobs in government enterprises.
They were so used to communism that they didn't look up to see the light at
the end of the tunnel. A vanguard, however, was in business.

June 1, 1987, just days before the pope arrived, the government took the
landmark step of legalizing *Res Publica,* a major underground publication dating
back to the days when not just the publisher but his readers risked prison. Like
Wojtyla's Krakow magazines, *Res Republica* was intellectual rather than revolutionary in style, but it was clearly anti-communist. Its editor-publisher, Marcin
Krul, was a graduate of the weekend communications seminars Wojtyla had
secretly run in Krakow, designed to inspire just such potentially influential
Poles as Krul. In his first aboveground issue, Krul declared that Poland was "a
changed country, a different country."

Soon afterward, Jacek Kuron, writing in *Tygodnik Mazowsze*—which was now
widely sold and only nominally illegal—added his judgment that the country
had indeed turned the corner. "The opinion can still be heard," he wrote, "that
all the recent changes in the system are just words without much substance."
That was "a major misunderstanding." The Polish government was acting contrary to the fundamental precepts of communism, he said. In fact, "the official
vision of the world has practically ceased to exist."

On the surface, the pope's 1987 trip was much like his previous visits. First-
timers such as Anthony Bevilacqua were still impressed when thousands of
Krakow citizens sang with the pope at the window of the archbishop's palace.
At the port of Gdynia, every balcony and doorway was crammed with people,
some weeping, as John Paul, in the central square, used the word *solidarity* seven
times in three minutes.[2] He concluded:

> In the name of the future of mankind, this word *solidarity* must be
> pronounced. Today, it is spreading like a wave throughout the
> world, signaling that we cannot live according to the principle of
> "all against all," but only according to a different principle of "all
> with all," "all for all." This word has been pronounced here in a
> new way and in a new context. And the world cannot forget.

Generally, though, people's memories—so vivid about John Paul's earlier
trips home—are blank on this one. Most people didn't know where the coun-

try was headed. With the old enemy disintegrating, and no new heroes, there was no common spirit to galvanize everyone as before. "There was only the remnants of Solidarity. It was very weak," says early leader Bogdan Borucewicz.

The pope met with both Walesa and Jaruzelski. He prayed silently for forty minutes at Father Popieluszko's grave, then avoided a waiting microphone and left without speaking to the crowd. Glemp conspicuously omitted Michnik and other Solidarity members he disapproved of from the guest list for a meeting between the pope and prominent intellectuals. In response, John Paul sent a pro-Solidarity message by asking Michnik's friend and colleague Stefan Bratkowski to pass on his greetings.[3]

The site John Paul chose for his final Mass was wonderfully ironic: Warsaw's huge, garish, Stalin-built Palace of Culture, an object of local ridicule. The last thing Stalin had expected there was a religious rally. (Well, maybe not the *last*; after communism ended, a Las Vegas–style casino moved in.) But the pope wanted to remind everyone of the transcendent force of the Church—"the Church, which is in Rome and in Antioch and in Jerusalem and in Alexandria and in Constantinople. . . ."

What Bevilacqua remembered, however, was a moment at the farewell gathering at Glemp's residence. John Paul was saying good-byes and having his ear bent by someone. Bevilacqua—who was still puzzled at being invited—tried to slip past inconspicuously. "He looked tired, I didn't want to bother him," Bevilacqua says. Suddenly John Paul reached behind him, took Bevilacqua's hand, and squeezed it, never looking away from the man who was talking to him.

What was that for? Bevilacqua wondered. "I didn't even know he knew me that much." Barely back home again, he got a call from Laghi, the nuncio, saying that John Paul wanted Bevilacqua—now an auxiliary bishop in Pittsburgh—to represent the pope at the forthcoming bishops' synod in Rome, along with the elected representatives. Bevilacqua says he still didn't understand the reason for this sudden attention, or associate it with the fact that John Paul's friend Cardinal Krol, then seventy-seven, the archbishop of Philadelphia, had just undergone major liver surgery.

April 27, 1987, the U.S. government had placed Kurt Waldheim, now president of Austria, on its no-admittance list because of his bloody Nazi collaboration as a young officer. Defending the decision, Secretary of State Shultz and Attorney General Edwin Meese said that even that year, Waldheim had lied to the United States about his record and defended Hitler's wartime murder of prisoners.[4]

All this was a powerful slap in Waldheim's face—which the pope then did what he could to erase by welcoming Waldheim to the Vatican two months

later, and praising him for a lifetime's work for peace. The ceremony was boycotted by diplomatic envoys from the U.S., Italy, and many other countries.
Why John Paul was so eager to help Waldheim that he would invite worldwide
rebuke remains unclear. In 1994, he bestowed yet another honor on Waldheim,
a knighthood.

Waldheim did have a big supporter in his fellow Austrian, Cardinal Stickler,
the Vatican librarian who had engineered an unwelcome replacement for Cardinal König. Stickler and Waldheim had known each other since the 1930s,
when their fathers were friends in Vienna. When Waldheim visited the pope in
1987, "he came to the Library," Stickler beams. "He remembered me, his
father and my father."

I asked: Wasn't Waldheim a Nazi? No, "he was a victim," Stickler said, of
"manipulations" by political opponents. "He was a young officer. Certainly he
was imprudent because he didn't immediately say all he could of his past. But
in two terms as [United Nations] secretary-general, there were no problems."

BBC Correspondent David Willey says the Austrian bishops were upset by
the friendly treatment Waldheim received. Still smarting from the König affair,
they told Willey they weren't consulted by the pope about his invitation to
Waldheim, though many were in Rome for their every-five-year visits when the
invitation was announced.

In September 1987, John Paul returned to the United States, but this time
avoided Washington and stuck to the southern and western coasts. He focused on
America's immigrants, largely Hispanic, who often suffered discrimination in
their new home, just as immigrant Poles had suffered nearly a century before. Reagan met John Paul at the airport in Miami and spoke platitudes. The pope
responded with a sharp speech about America's obligation to share more of its
wealth with poorer countries and with its own poor, whose numbers had begun to
rise as a percentage of the U.S. population under Reagan after decades of decline.

With the dust of the Hunthausen case still settling, John Paul met the archbishops and was told that American lay Catholics wanted more power to decide
things on their own. But he was as unyielding with his bishops as he had been
with Reagan, telling them:

> It is sometimes claimed that dissent is totally compatible with
> being a good Catholic.... This is a grave error. Dissent from
> Church doctrine remains what it is, dissent; as such, it may not be
> proposed or received on an equal footing with the Church's authen-
> tic teaching.[5]

His most publicized stop was San Francisco, probably the most heavily homosexual city in the United States. Already staggered by losses from AIDS, gays were especially angry over John Paul's declarations about them—for example, that same-sex love is "an intrinsic moral evil," and that homosexually inclined people should remain celibate. At a church in the gay section, the pope visited sixty-four AIDS patients, including a priest, and said, "God loves you all without distinction, without limit."[6]

Any goodwill he created was undone, however, when he posed for a publicity photo hugging a four-year-old boy who was dying of the disease. Gays resented the disproportionate attention given to the relatively few child sufferers, who were often referred to as "innocent victims," as if gays were "guilty." They were also angry that U.S. priests had been ordered by Rome to omit any mention during AIDS counseling that condoms were a barrier to transmitting the virus.

Perhaps reflecting the tension of the San Francisco visit, soon after the pope left town, Archbishop Quinn checked himself into a private psychiatric retreat in Connecticut, for what an aide says was "stress." He stayed on leave until Easter 1988.

More happily, John Paul warmed up again to Archbishop Weakland during his 1987 visit. Although he was among the most respected intellects in the American clergy, Weakland had felt the pope's quiet wrath for years. The *New Yorker* magazine published two long articles in July, 1991, sympathizing with Weakland, whose rise in the Church had halted in Milwaukee, without a cardinal's hat, because he listened to the complaints of women who thought the Church treated them as second-class Catholics.

But Weakland says he now noticed the pope relax, look him in the eye instead of at the ceiling, and prolong their conversations—which Weakland had sought out since their Polish days because of John Paul's knowledge on so many subjects. Right after the U.S. visit, Weakland went to Rome for the synod as an elected representative of the U.S. bishops. He pulled no punches at the lectern: "Women ask to be treated in a way that is not condescending or paternalistic," he said, "in the way that Jesus treated women: with trust and respect." He says John Paul seemed no less friendly to him at the lunch table afterward.[7]

During the synod, however, Weakland decided that the Church itself had changed. "The great disappointment for me was that I found much less tolerance than at the 1974 synod, the last I attended," he said later. "We didn't get to know each other well enough. It was all too formal. We lived in different parts of Rome, and when the meetings were over, we rushed home."

A greater difference, he said, was "that the Church is no longer identified with Western culture. The dominant forces are the Africans and the Spanish-

speakers. Some of the hypersensitivity over dissent and the trend toward orthodoxy in the Church is an attempt to maintain a unity in the light of all that
diversity."[8]

The two factions of Solidarity—one, the Walesa leadership, which had lost its
grass roots, and the other, the former underground activists who had started
into business—seemed about to split openly in the fall of 1987. Twenty-two
members of the old Solidarity National Commission, as it had existed before
martial law in 1981, wrote to Walesa, accusing him of "a virtual lack of concern with social and standard-of-living problems." They asked him to restore
Solidarity to the union it had once been. He offered some cosmetic changes,
but what really closed Solidarity's ranks again was a move by Jaruzelski.

Still trying to keep power, the communist leader announced a popular referendum November 29 over whether there should be "radical economic reform"
and greater democracy. This posed a dilemma: a "yes" vote would be considered a vote of confidence in Jaruzelski, but who could vote "no" to Solidarity's
own proposals?

On instructions from Walesa's restructured leadership group, most voters
stayed home (though the word *boycott* was avoided as too provocative). It was a
smashing victory for Solidarity, and a true exercise of democracy in the heart
of the Soviet empire. The communists had sought a mandate to govern and
had been denied.[9] Still, no one in the West seemed to grasp that anything special had happened.

Gorbachev finally came to Washington for a summit December 7 to 10,
1987, despite not having obtained much of an arms deal. All year, he had tried
in vain to sell his concept (and John Paul's) of mutual rather than unilateral
security. A leaked transcript from a U.S. National Security Council meeting
showed just how contrary this approach was to American policy. Defense Secretary Weinberger argued that the United States should deploy an antiballistic-
missile system he wanted despite the long-standing treaty against it; Secretary
of State Shultz proposed talking first with the Soviets. Reagan interjected,
"Why don't we just go ahead on the assumption that this is what we're doing
and it's right. . . . Don't ask the Soviets. Tell them."[10]

Neither the administration nor the American press believed Gorbachev had
changed anything substantial. He had made the Soviet Union "less of a police
state but a more efficient police state," said a *Washington Post* editorial. The *Wall
Street Journal* declared that the nature of Soviet ideology "makes genuine reform
a practical impossibility." "There's nothing new at all going on over there,"
agreed Rupert Murdoch's *New York Post.* Henry Kissinger asserted that the

USSR "will be a totalitarian state even after the reforms are completed." And a *Miami Herald* columnist said of Gorbachev, "Dress a monkey in silk and he'll still be a monkey."[11]

The administration refused Gorbachev's proposal to immediately eliminate intermediate-range missiles in Europe. It refused to join his unilateral nuclear-testing moratorium, provoking the Soviets to resume their own testing after nineteen months. Reagan said Gorbachev's talk of arms reduction was just a reaction to "our new strength," and continued to allege "Soviet aggression" in the usual complement of Third World countries.

In the Kremlin, the pro-change and anti-change wings of the Central Committee almost came to blows in October 1987. Gorbachev had been paring away Brezhnev holdovers, hoping finally to forge a majority. But Yeltsin, fiercest of the reformers, lit into the old-timers so viciously that Gorbachev had to remove him in order to maintain propriety. The bureaucracy stayed entrenched.

At the summit, a compromise treaty on intermediate-range missiles was signed with great fanfare, though in reality it only showed how far the two sides really were from any meaningful reduction of the nuclear terror. The new treaty affected a mere 5 percent of the two huge arsenals. The main resistance to doing more was clearly on the U.S. side. So thorough was the change in Soviet policy that embarrassed American negotiators had to withdraw their persistent demands for on-site inspections; when the Soviets suddenly accepted, the Americans realized they didn't want the Soviets to have such a close look at American weapons.[12]

As the Soviets tried to beat an orderly retreat from Afghanistan under UN auspices, the U.S. reneged on its promise to wind down its own Afghan war aid commensurate with a Soviet withdrawal. Reagan kept the Afghans fighting, seemingly bent on humiliating Gorbachev. At the summit, he told anti-Soviet jokes to Gorbachev's face. Shultz, in his memoir, says he was "disturbed and disappointed" by Reagan's behavior.[13]

Gorbachev was irritated. But he left Washington after the summit with a 65 percent "favorable" rating among the American people—higher than Reagan's 61 percent, which itself had been boosted by his hosting of Gorbachev.

53

John Paul's government encyclical, *Sollicitudo Rei Socialis* ("On Social Concern"), finally provided the strong papal authority that Cardinal Etchegaray and the proponents of Liberation Theology wanted for their programs. *Sollicitudo Rei Socialis* mostly accorded with Pope Paul's encyclical *Populorum Progressio* ("The Development of Peoples") twenty years earlier on the same subject. But John Paul's was twice as long, more powerful—and more courageous.

Paul VI had also condemned "liberal capitalism," but that was in the heyday of Keynesianism and Lyndon Johnson's "Great Society," when the welfare state was widely accepted. John Paul II dared to swim against the tide, championing the welfare state just when free-market economics was ascending as a utopian ideal, promoted with all the zeal once accorded to utopian socialism.

In John Paul II's era, the leaders of the free nations of the West, from their positions of authority, taught the virtue of private gain above the virtue of generosity, and the virtue of individual will above the virtues of family and community. Social efforts to meet the needs of crumbling families, or community institutions, were increasingly lumped together with outmoded programs under the general category of "government waste." There was dwindling regard for what people might hold in common.

Making John Paul's document still more timely was a fundamental global economic shift. An entire class of corporations, expanding internationally, was gradually separating itself from the responsibilities of citizenship in the places the corporations had once called home. Without the wealth of these companies to draw on, communities once supported by them were being cut adrift. Work—which John Paul thought elevated human beings above animals—was an increasingly insecure proposition, even among executives.

There was a growing faith in the ability of capital—the unregulated marketplace—to dish out to people their just deserts, and thus to make good public policy. Unlike socialism in its ascendancy, the new faith in capital was, by its very nature, powerfully financed. Its advocates had almost limitless access to the mass media. But John Paul took them on.

Sollicitudo Rei Socialis also attacked communism as incompatible with human happiness, not only in practice but even as an ideal. The pope asserted that private property, entrepreneurial spirit, and the profit motive are necessary foundations of a successful economy—both a moral and a practical imperative:

> In . . . concern for the poor, one must not overlook that special form of poverty which consists in being deprived of . . . the right to freedom of economic initiative. . . . The denial . . . of . . . the right to share in the building of society, . . . to organize and to form unions, or to take initiatives in economic matters—do these not impoverish the human person as much as, if not more than, the deprivation of material goods?

But his encyclical spent its greatest energy assailing the current notion that private property, entrepreneurial spirit, and the profit motive should be free from restraint by other values. Betting everything on the profit motive, John Paul said, placed man's instincts for wealth and power above his instincts for love, community, and responsibility:

> We are . . . faced with a serious problem of unequal distribution of the means of subsistence originally meant for everybody. . . . And this happens not through the fault of the needy people, and even less through a sort of inevitability dependent on natural conditions. . . .
>
> Problems in industrial enterprises or in the workers' and union movements of a particular country or region are not to be considered as isolated cases. . . . The very concept of development changes . . . if considered in the perspective of universal interdependence. True development cannot consist in the simple accumulation of wealth and the greater availability of goods and services, if this is gained at the expense of the development of the masses, and without due consideration for the social, cultural, and spiritual dimensions of the human being. . . .
>
> Political leaders and citizens of rich countries . . . especially if they are Christians, have the moral obligation . . . to take into consideration in personal and government decisions . . . this interdependence that exists between their conduct and the poverty and underdevelopment of so many millions. . . .*
>
> The Church's social doctrine adopts a critical attitude toward . . . each of the two ideologies, . . . liberal capitalism and . . . Marxist collectivism. . . . The present division of the world is a direct obstacle to the real transformation of . . . the . . . less advanced countries. . . . We are confronted with a strange phenomenon: while economic aid and development plans meet with . . . insuperable ideological . . . and trade barriers, arms of whatever origin circulate with almost total freedom all over the world.

He compared the "passivity, dependence, and submission to the bureaucratic apparatus" of communism to "the traditional dependence of the

---

* On a recent visit to India, the pope had declared that those who reaped the profits should take responsibility for a leak at a Union Carbide chemical plant in Bhopal, in which two thousand Indian citizens died and several hundred thousand more were injured. A decade later, in 1996, corporate lawyers were still arguing over who would pay, while many victims remained uncompensated.

worker-proletarian in capitalism." This spirit, produced by both systems, he said, "provokes a sense of frustration or desperation, and predisposes people to opt out of national life."

He linked faith in material wealth to the Enlightenment notion that progress would arrive "as if it were automatic and limitless." But after two world wars, genocide, "and the looming atomic peril," fewer people now believed in the inevitability of progress. "A naive mechanistic optimism has been replaced by a well-founded anxiety for the fate of humanity," he wrote. He was also heartened by today's "more lively concern" for human rights and the environment. But the drive toward material wealth by the powerful needed further restraint. The gap between rich and poor people—and countries— could not be permitted to stand or to widen.

> Development either becomes shared . . . by every part of the world, or it undergoes . . . regression even in zones marked by constant progress. . . . In the countries of high economic development, the sources of work seem to be shrinking. . . . Opportunities for employment are decreasing rather than increasing. . . . Either all the nations of the world [must] participate or it will not be true development.

He addressed the system of Western bank loans whose repayment was guaranteed by the governments of poor countries, a system he had experienced in Poland. These loans were "counterproductive [because] the debtor nations, in order to service their debt, find themselves obliged to export the capital needed for improving or even maintaining their standard of living." This was all part of an

> international division of labor, whereby the low-cost products of certain countries that . . . are too weak to apply . . . effective labor laws . . . are sold in other parts of the world at considerable profit for the companies.

He denounced this trend but insisted that developing countries must also help themselves, by increasing food production and by replacing "corrupt, dictatorial, and authoritarian forms of government with democratic . . . ones." But the problem underlying all these ills, he said, was a misdirection of values. Destructive ideals promoted by the West were spreading around the globe:

> Side-by-side with the miseries of underdevelopment, themselves unacceptable, we find ourselves up against a form of superdevelop-

ment, equally inadmissible, [which] easily makes people slaves of possession and of immediate gratification, with no other horizon than the ... continual replacement of the things already owned with others still better.... An object ... is discarded, with no thought of its possible lasting value in itself, nor of some other human being who is poorer....

This then is the picture: there are some people—the few who possess much—who do not really succeed in "being" because, through a reversal of the hierarchy of values, they are hindered by the cult of "having"; and there are others—the many who have little or nothing—who do not succeed in realizing their basic human vocation because they are deprived of essential goods.

The evil does not consist in "having" as such, but in possessing without regard for the quality and the ordered hierarchy of the goods one has....

When individuals and communities do not see a rigorous respect for moral, cultural, and spiritual requirements, based on the dignity of the person, ... then all the rest—availability of goods, abundance of technical resources ... —will prove unsatisfying and in the end contemptible....

Nor can ... development exclude respect for the ... natural world.... One must take into account the nature of each being and its mutual connection in an ordered system.... Some ... natural resources are limited.... Using them as if they were inexhaustible ... seriously endangers their availability ... for generations to come.... The ... result of industrialization is ... often pollution of the environment with serious consequences for the health of the population....

Sin and structures of sin are categories seldom applied to [this] situation.... But one cannot gain a profound understanding of the reality that confronts us unless we give a name to the root of the evils which afflict us.

Then he aimed a verbal nuclear missile at the economic philosophy being preached in the Western nations:

The all-consuming desire for profit, and the thirst for power, with the intention of imposing one's will upon others, ... are ... opposed to the will of God ... and the good of neighbor.

Attitudes and structures of sin are conquered only ... by a diametrically opposed attitude: a commitment to the good of one's
neighbor.

There was, of course, a name for the attitude he wanted people to adopt:
"solidarity"—a word he used a dozen times within a few pages. He stressed
that his message was not just for religious believers. Rather,

I wish to appeal with simplicity and humility to ... all men and
women without exception. I wish to ask them to be convinced of the
seriousness of the present moment and of each one's individual
responsibility, and to implement—by the way they live ... by their use
of resources ... by their ... economic and political decisions ... —the
measures inspired by solidarity and love of preference for the poor.

The encyclical drew withering criticism from Reagan's Catholic supporters, of
whom there were many. One was the American "neoconservative" editor
Michael Novak, whom John Paul had invited to his conference on "The Common Christian Roots of Europe." Upon reading Novak's criticism of his economic views, says a longtime papal friend, the pope remarked, "He's Slavic, he
cannot be totally bad," and invited Novak to dinner.

The same friend heard John Paul comment that the neoconservatives' complaints paralleled those he heard from Liberation Theologians; both groups
thought the pope would change his mind if he would just read their work. "But
he read them all very seriously," says the friend. "Many people who think they
are not listened to really are."*

54

February 1988 brought an unusual sight to the Vatican: the Red Army Choir
performing Schubert's "Ave Maria"—the pope's choice—in full military dress,

* In line with the message expressed in *Sollicitudo Rei Socialis*, before issuing it, John Paul
signed an agreement with the Vatican employees' union after years of negotiation. Work
hours were cut from forty-two to thirty-six a week so that more time could be spent with
families. The pope gave in completely on a requested 43 percent raise for the lowest-paid,
but raises fell off sharply at higher levels. John Paul said seniority shouldn't bear on pay,
because a worker needed less after his children were reared.

a sure sign of thaw if there ever was one. At the end of the performance, the Soviets gave John Paul a wooden bear and he gave them blessings and rosaries.[1]

But when John Paul again tried to wangle an invitation to the USSR—for that year's thousandth anniversary of Russian Christianity—Gorbachev refused. He did, however, let the government-linked Orthodox Church invite ten cardinals. So the pope put his highest-ranking stand-in, Secretary of State Casaroli, atop the delegation. "It was a gesture that he was open to anything," says Press Secretary Navarro-Valls. "The second decision, more daring, was to write a letter to Gorbachev, and give it to Casaroli to carry."

In the Kremlin, Gorbachev and Foreign Minister Shevardnadze charmed Casaroli for ninety minutes. "Cardinal, you shouldn't be afraid," Gorbachev began. "Mr. Shevardnadze and I have both been baptized"—and he added that he had grown up with an icon of Mary in his home. Then Gorbachev opened and read the pope's letter. He said he would reply later.[2] As it turned out, he would wait too long.

Although the letter's exact contents are still secret, the Vatican says it listed Church grievances to be resolved.[3] Vatican and Soviet diplomats were at odds over what John Paul considered to be a major international treaty then being negotiated on religious freedom.[4] Given that, and given John Paul's passion to heal the breach with the Orthodox and with Russia—and given the extraordinary outpouring of support the pope would later show for Gorbachev and his program—the letter had enormous importance.

Either tacitly or explicitly, the letter offered what may have been Gorbachev's last hope for success. Gorbachev could have had the pope as a substantial ally in exchange for concessions on religious freedom, and on Poland, that he wound up making later anyway. From this might have come a real "Holy Alliance." But Gorbachev lacked either the wisdom or the courage to take the pope up on his offer.

Strikes broke out in Poland in the spring of 1988. "The same pictures of the same pope were hung on the same iron slats in the same shipyard," one observer wrote. "But whereas those were strikes of hope, these were strikes of despair,"[5] protesting higher prices and worsening conditions. Walesa came around to show his sympathy, but in fact, he supported the introduction of market pressure on the economy, which was causing the higher prices. For now, the strikes petered out.

John Paul took off for Latin America again, armed with his encyclical. Now he trumpeted the clear, positive message that had sometimes been filtered out in earlier documents on Liberation Theology. He spoke in Oruro, a hotbed of the movement, in Bolivia, South America's poorest country, and brought to the platform local people with faces full of suffering.

"We miners are hungry," one man told him, his voice choking. "They treat us like animals. Our children cry out for a loaf of bread. When we say these things, they say we are communists."

John Paul accepted the miner's hard hat that the man gently placed on his head as a crown. Then a woman gave the pope an empty cooking pot. A spokesman for the Liberation Theology communities said, "We thank you, Holy Father, for having accepted Liberation Theology, for having written the encyclical on workers' rights." The pope reminded his audiences that Polish miners were striking at that very time, and said Bolivians, too, had a right to unionize and strike.[6]

His next scheduled stop was Asunción, Paraguay. General Alfredo Stroessner, the Paraguayan dictator since 1954, grew so alarmed at the emotional outpourings at papal events in Uruguay and Peru that he tried to cancel a promised meeting with opposition leaders. John Paul asked his liaison to tell Stroessner that if the opposition meeting was canceled, the whole papal trip would be called off, which would look even worse. Stroessner backed down.

As the pope arrived in Asunción, hunger strikers occupied a nearby church, which was surrounded by police. At the welcoming ceremony, John Paul avoided any chummy-looking pictures with Stroessner such as Pinochet had arranged in Chile. He listened as Stroessner called himself "the most Christian ruler on earth" and declared that "Paraguay is a country without social or political problems."

John Paul replied, "The Church can and must remind men—and in particular those who govern—of their ethical duties for the good of all society. The Church cannot be isolated inside its temples, just as men's consciences cannot be isolated from God." The roomful of invited guests was stunned by this chiding. Stroessner broke a long hush with three hand claps, then rose to attention as the pope left.

It was a different scene at the opposition meeting Stroessner had tried to prevent. To great applause, the pope talked of "fundamental human rights" and said "peace is not compatible with the kind of social organization set up by only a few individuals for their own benefit." At a Mass, he decried the lack of "daily bread [for] *campesinos* [farm workers]" and admonished, "The authorities must feel obliged to ensure that more people have access to the ownership of land." A youth rally became a political protest, with hundreds of thousands of voices chanting, "Freedom! Freedom!"

In large part because of the attention and enthusiasm brought by John Paul, Stroessner's thirty-five-year reign of terror became untenable. Nine months after the Pope left, Stroessner was chased into exile by a coup. The *Tablet* compared it to Haiti, Chile, and the Philippines, noting a pattern: "Right-wing dic-

tators try to demonstrate how popular they are with the Holy Father by joining him on his cavalcades and taking Communion from him, but then six
months later are either toppled or suffer serious reverses." Elections, flawed but
genuine, occurred in Paraguay in 1993, and three years later a democratically
chosen government withstood another attempt by the military to take over.

In Bolivia, the pope had visited the town where the late Castro ally Che Gue-
vara had begun his quest to spread revolution. Pleading for an earnest attack on
the "inhuman" poverty he saw, the pope noted that he had entered the cathedral by an aisle that seemed to be on his right, and would exit by the same aisle,
which would now be on his left. He explained,

> As soon as the pope turns around, his left becomes his right. . . .
> The pope and the whole Church, all of us, have to create a meeting
> point between the so-called world of the Left and the so-called
> world of the Right. A point of reconciliation, because the world
> cannot live in continuing division. . . . The solution for overcoming
> the divisions of Left and Right must be found here in your human,
> Christian, and social reality.

As he had in Africa, he warned against communist or capitalist solutions
imported from abroad. "You know how to pray, how to weep, how to sing,
and how to dance," he said; the wealthy countries had much to learn from the
poorest.[7]

Returning to Rome, he maintained this tone during the scheduled visit of
Bishop Pedro Casaldaliga, an outspoken Liberation Theologian from the
Brazilian rain forest. Casaldaliga told the BBC's David Willey that he made
his case and expected the worst, whereupon the pope "asserted several times
that 'the Church must take on the social issues,' " then "opened his arms
and—half warning and half jesting—said to me, 'So, you see, I am no wild
beast!' "

On the other hand, when Archbishop Lefebvre, the French renegade whom
John Paul had coddled for ten years, consecrated four more anti-Vatican II
bishops against the pope's explicit orders, John Paul formally excommunicated
him. Lefebvre died of cancer three years later.

Another trip to Africa persuaded John Paul to address the world's growing
problem of political refugees. In 1988 he radically expanded a Church council
on migrants, which until then had merely provided priests for seafarers, airport
workers, and the like. John Paul put Archbishop Giovanni Cheli in charge, and

told him to push the world's bishops, not just to start caring for refugees but also to negotiate an end to the wars and economic discrimination that created refugees.

To this day, Cheli discusses world trouble spots regularly with the secretariat of state and the pope. He hustles funds from Catholic charities and UN agencies, which sometimes farm out refugee work to him. "We deal with poor people," Cheli says. "If we decide to hold a conference in Africa and want bishops to attend, we have to pay not only for room and board but also for transportation. If we cannot raise the money, we postpone the operation."

The council takes credit for helping to repatriate the swelling population of Mozambican refugees that threatened to overwhelm surrounding countries in 1993. Cheli sensed an opening when majority rule came to South Africa, whose white government had long provoked civil strife throughout the area. With peace now likely, his council organized volunteers to provide water and infrastructure for a mass repatriation. Soon the refugee camps were emptied.

John Paul remained so interested in refugees that when the UN said it was short of money to care for people fleeing from the Balkan war in the 1990s, Cheli's staff felt free to interrupt the pope's vacation in the mountains. By spending just a few hours on the phone, John Paul raised the needed cash from Church organizations in rich countries.

55

One of John Paul's favorite priests, Bronislaw Dembowski, who hosted the pivotal hunger strike at St. Martin's Church in Warsaw, and later made the church a depot for secret aid to Solidarity, became a hero again in 1988. Since spring, he had been working on a peace plan to bring the government and Walesa together. At first, Jaruzelski balked, but events soon made Dembowski's vision possible.

By late summer, local wildcat strikes over rising prices and scarcity once again crippled Poland. Jaruzelski had no place to turn but to Walesa—even though any control Walesa had over the strikers was symbolic, not organizational. Dembowski arranged for General Czeslaw Kiszczak, Jaruzelski's chief domestic-affairs minister, to meet secretly with Walesa at a villa near Warsaw. "General Kiszczak couldn't have talked with Walesa without an intermediary," Dembowski explains, because it would have been "too big a loss of face." Dembowski warned Primate Glemp that "this role was dangerous"—the Church would be a broker in talks that could blow up. Glemp let him go ahead with the plan, "for the good of Poland."

Bujak instantly recognized that the talks could be climactic. "Jaruzelski and the whole communist leadership knew it was the end of an era," he says. Identifiable Solidarity membership was down to just a few thousand, but "the communists remembered the problems they had with thirty-two members of KOR. They knew there was an organized underground power they could not fight off."

General Kiszczak brought Walesa a stunning government proposal for a "pact . . . a coalition form of government and"—here was the key word—"pluralism."[1] Obviously, Jaruzelski had approved the offer, though the general would not say that. After just four hours of negotiating, Walesa and Kiszczak announced a deal. The government would legalize free associations, obviously meaning Solidarity, though it wasn't named. Walesa endorsed the government's new, more market-oriented economic policy. With that, the two big demands from the early 1980s had been met. Solidarity became legal; the prisoners were already free.

But when Walesa announced his victory to workers at the Gdansk shipyards, they were furious. He had obtained no concessions—and apparently sought none—on price increases and pay levels, which is what the workers were striking over. On top of that, there was talk that the market-oriented reforms Walesa had endorsed could result in the shipyard's being closed altogether, throwing them out of work. The angry crowd accused Walesa of selling them out.

Debate arose within Solidarity over whether to keep him as leader. He had always been a political pragmatist, not a champion of ideas. Yet, says Bujak, "any attempt to change the leader would have accelerated war at the top"— split the opposition just as it stood on the threshold of victory. "We wanted to avoid that. We also needed his charisma. And I had the feeling, why not have Walesa as president? He could have been quite good. The quality would have been the competence of the people around him."

Besides, it was already clear to Bujak and other Solidarity veterans who might have challenged Walesa that the future of power in Poland lay in another direction: private enterprise.

I arrived in Poland in October 1988 to tape two television programs for my PBS series. The difference I saw from previous travels there, and to other communist countries, was fundamental: Despite continuing American perceptions, Poland was simply no longer a communist state.

By the Polish government's own figures, more than twenty thousand new, officially registered private business enterprises were operating. Each could hire fifty employees per eight-hour shift. True, there were encumbrances that seemed ridiculous by American standards—taxes sometimes as high as 80 percent, and a requirement that the entrepreneur couldn't take home, even in profit, more than three times the average worker's salary. But these laws were changing almost weekly and would inevitably fade. Already a lot of entrepreneurship was going on unregistered with the state.

"If you want to do something concrete, set up a business to support it," Bujak told me. He, Zbigniew Janas, and another former Solidarity underground leader were expanding their "foundation" enterprises. The cottage-industry firms they had helped start for out-of-work Solidarity members had produced "activists who are financially independent," Bujak said.

Grzegorz Lindenberg, who had spent a year in jail for his underground work, ran a computer resale firm. He wouldn't disclose his income or employee roster, both of which exceeded regulations. But the government encouraged enterprises like his because they allowed Poland to import capital and evade Western banking sanctions.

Under the sanctions, Poland, like other debtor countries, had to repay its loans from the proceeds of its exports to the West. As a result, the exports didn't bring in new money for growth and modernization (as John Paul had long complained). But firms like Lindenberg's got around all that by encouraging Poles who worked abroad to buy needed goods—such as computers—with the money they earned, and then import them one or two at a time. Lindenberg paid handsomely for the goods in Poland, but in zlotys. He added Polish software and resold the computers, mostly to the government, which couldn't buy such goods abroad directly because of its debts.

Thus, former Solidarity leaders like Lindenberg were now supplying the government they hated. But business seemed the surest way to topple the government eventually. Many factors propelled this focus on business: the lack of any charismatic on-the-scene champion for the original Solidarity ideal; the sapping of collective energy by the obdurateness of Jaruzelski and Glemp; the natural impulse to profit from the inevitable privatization of the Polish economy; the government's new emphasis on making the economy efficient; and the new American foreign-policy team, led by investment bankers instead of guerrilla-warfare specialists.

Entrepreneurship was an integral part of John Paul's program, too. But the concentration of energy on business threatened the spirit of the program. Those who suffered were the ones he most wanted to protect: the typical Polish family of four was still crowded into a one-bedroom apartment assigned to it by a state housing agency. It lived on income from jobs with state enterprises and had no idea how to exploit the new entrepreneurship rules. (One woman I met wanted to sell knitted handicraft, but state stores wouldn't buy from her because she was employed in another industry and so wasn't eligible for a knitting license.) For such people, the new economy just meant rising prices and stagnant wages.

Power would fall to others, who were both making money *and* addressing social problems. One blacklisted unionist had begun a business with former underground colleagues designing single-family houses, a way to get around the state housing bottleneck. A large state farm, unproductive and in danger of being shut down, had hired a former bureaucrat to manage it as if it were a private business; he installed equipment for on-site food processing and packaging, and made it viable. A sound engineer had started a private record label and was organizing a radio station that would broadcast openly; so far, the government hadn't interfered. And he was meeting with East Germans, Czechs, and Hungarians he knew, who were eager to start their own record companies and radio stations.

Clearly, what was left of communism in Poland was being dismantled with only minor government opposition. Vice Prime Minister Zdzislaw Sadowski frankly admitted to me that the game was over. "We need to get people at all layers of life used to a new mode of behavior," he said. Then he disclosed what Walesa and General Kiszczak had agreed to in their continuing secret talks: multiparty elections would be coming.

If Poland did this, then, given the technology that connected it to the region, communism was over—everywhere.[2]

Shortly after this, December 18, 1988, Walesa announced the formation of a Solidarity Citizens Committee composed of 128 prominent intellectuals. Leading it were John Paul's former editor Mazowiecki, the historian Geremek (whom John Paul had brought to the Vatican conference on Europe), and Henryk Wujec, another founder of KOR. The committee was divided into separate groups concerned with economics, housing, agriculture, and so on. The heads of these groups were referred to, not in jest, as a "shadow cabinet."

A replacement government was in formation. But there wasn't much evidence of the Solidarity ideal the pope had championed.

Reagan left office in January 1989, not appreciating what had happened. There had been a final summit with Gorbachev, May 29 to June 2, 1988, but no headway was made on reducing nuclear weapons. Reagan declined the openings Gorbachev offered for a five-hundred-thousand-man reduction of forces in Europe. When Gorbachev suggested a joint declaration endorsing the very ideals the United States had long claimed to champion—renouncing military solutions to disputes, "peaceful coexistence as a universal principle . . . equality of all states ... and freedom of sociopolitical choice"—Reagan turned him down.[3]

Even after Gorbachev unilaterally cut back his European troops, Reagan complained that the Soviets still had "a large conventional advantage." December 10, 1988, Reagan spoke with the same tone he had used entering office, of an Eastern Europe dreaming of freedom. Neither he nor his successor, George Bush, showed any sign of knowing the world had changed, or even of expecting change soon. Bush charged into office pledging to renew the war against the Soviets in Angola.

Gorbachev's fellow Soviet leaders continued to stall his program. At the same time, the Baltic states, including John Paul's beloved Lithuania, saw what was happening in neighboring Poland and inevitably wanted more independence themselves. So did Georgia and Armenia, where there were growing nationalist movements.

The sixty-eight-year-old pope skied Italy's Dolomite Mountains early in 1989. Striking terror into the rest of his party, he declared he would hike to a cross atop a nearby mountain, a round trip that took even hearty mountaineers— count the pope among them—twelve hours. Dziwisz and others fell by the wayside, according to Press Secretary Navarro-Valls, who says that, though exhausted, he kept pace. Near the top, he says, they passed some other hikers headed down and exchanged hellos. A few yards past the other group, Navarro-Valls recalls, he and John Paul heard a sudden shriek behind them, in German: "My God! It's the pope!"

Holding his ground philosophically as well as physically, John Paul won Soviet consent on the international religious-liberty treaty he sought. To visiting bishops from Sudan, where Christians and animists struggled for their rights against a Moslem majority, he spoke words on religious liberty that would have been astonishing from a pope even fifty years earlier:

> No individual or group, or the state, can claim authority in the sphere of religious convictions. Where the state grants a special status to one religion as representing the belief of a majority of its citizens, it cannot claim to impose that religion upon all its people or restrict the religious freedom of other citizens.[4]

January 18, 1989, General Jaruzelski told Party leaders that Solidarity was being recognized, and that he would meet Walesa for a series of "Round

Table" talks about the future of Poland. He offered to resign if anyone didn't like it, and got no takers. When Walesa appeared at a Solidarity rally in Gdansk, workers jeered him and called him a "traitor" to them.[5]

The Round Table negotiations began February 6. As they proceeded, Polish television viewers were treated almost nightly to the spectacle of veteran jail-birds Michnik and Kuron appearing on government television to comment on what was happening. At *Tygodnik Mazowsze*, Chojecki's heirs, Halina Luczywo and Joanna Szczesna, dropped all pretense and simply went public; an initial "overground" press run of five hundred thousand copies was sold at street stands alongside the government's propaganda sheets. Konstanty Gebert announced that his newspaper would voluntarily stay underground because paper was easier to get on the black market.

Zbigniew Janas began talks with Solidarity's Czech counterpart, Charter 77, to put the same wheels in motion in Czechoslovakia.

April 5, the accords were signed. Solidarity was relaunched with a hundred work-site locals and sixty thousand members.[6] Contested Parliamentary elections were set for June. Under a complex plan, a onetime majority of seats would be reserved for communists. Solidarity would be a loyal opposition for one year, after which new elections would put everything at stake.

A few days later, Tadeusz Konopka, Solidarity's longtime man in Rome, arranged for Walesa and some colleagues to come to the Vatican for another triumphal celebration with John Paul, with Communion and Liberation to pay for the trip. Communist official Jozef Czyrek visited the pope at about the same time and found him buoyant: "I described the concept: Solidarity would win, but the communists were guaranteed a certain number of seats," Czyrek says. Replied John Paul, "I thank God that He allows Poles to make such a decision."

John Paul again went to Africa, then became the first pope to visit Scandinavia since before Protestantism. From the time of Luther until the mid–nineteenth century, Scandinavian law had prohibited Catholic church services.[7] Now, John Paul praised Luther, promised "a reassessment" of the issues he had raised, and agreed to Vatican-Lutheran cooperation on a charitable project. Cardinal Cassidy, the diplomat, ranks the Scandinavian trip behind only the Dutch trip as the pope's most important religious visit.

Gorbachev had planned to liberalize the USSR politically in order to liberalize it economically. He may have put the cart before the horse. He scheduled genuinely contested elections in March 1989 (though the contests were all within the Communist Party). Yet he delayed ending central price controls and the government monopoly on farmland, hoping voters would first clear the government of the opponents who were blocking his reforms.

Without the economic improvement, however, the public was angrier than ever. Given the chance, it rejected many Party leaders with a simple "no" vote even where there was no opposing candidate. Yeltsin, the onetime protégé who had lately become a strident embarrassment to Gorbachev, won an overwhelming victory against opposition.

All three Soviet-occupied Baltic republics elected nationalist-inclined majorities for their legislatures. Seeing what had just happened in Poland, the legislature in Lithuania voted May 18 to give itself "sovereignty." The Latvian legislature followed its lead.

While Gorbachev walked a high wire into the future, Bush clung to the past, denouncing the Soviets for the war in Nicaragua. U.S. politicians and press generally retained their old outlook. Even after the Soviets completed their pullout from Afghanistan on schedule, February 15, Bush rejected Gorbachev's appeal to stop sending arms there.[8] The U.S.-supplied rebels then began fighting each other.

In the end, change surprised and overwhelmed both men.

56

The first truly free, multiparty elections in Soviet Eastern Europe occurred in Poland, June 4, 1989. They produced not a landslide but an avalanche that shocked both sides, routed the communists, and upended the intricate Round Table scenario: Solidarity won all 162 seats it was allowed to run for in the lower house—35 percent—and ninety-nine of a hundred seats in the newly created Senate. Only the communist-engineered guarantees kept Jaruzelski in the presidency, and by the thinnest of margins; almost nobody supported him by choice. Communists estimate that 80 percent of the party members themselves voted for Solidarity.[1]

Then an idea grew: if a few communist Parliamentarians saw the inevitable and switched sides, Solidarity would have enough votes to elect its own prime minister and take control of the government. Walesa hadn't run for Parliament, preferring to lead Solidarity from the outside, so he couldn't be prime minister. But someone else . . .

While that was being discussed, the new Parliament's first order of business was to establish normal state-to-state relations with the Vatican. Not even Jaruzelski would fight that. It passed July 18.

President Bush, by long-standing plan, arrived in Warsaw July 10, still mostly clueless. He praised Jaruzelski's "leadership, ... wisdom, and courage" in the effort to change what Bush continued to refer to as "a communist system." He urged Solidarity to work with the communist government. He passed out bats and balls to a newly formed Polish Little League. Addressing Parliament, he pledged $100 million in U.S. business investment. Aides said he was disappointed at the lackluster response he received from Polish crowds.[2]

Seeing the results of the Polish election, Hungarian officials opened their country's border with Austria. When Bush arrived in Hungary from Poland, he was presented with a piece of the barbed wire that had just come down. The Hungarian government was still nominally communist, but showed its true feelings by reburying, with honor, the hero of the 1956 revolt, Imre Nagy.

Massive independence demonstrations broke out in Lithuania, Estonia, and Latvia on the fiftieth anniversary of the Hitler-Stalin pact. No Red Army intervened. Half a million Soviet coal miners struck—unheard-of in the USSR. Gorbachev shook up the local party leadership and gave the strikers what they wanted: more pay and benefits and recognition of their bargaining rights.

August 7, Walesa declared he wouldn't accept a communist prime minister. August 19, with support from some switch-over communists, Solidarity elected its own man: John Paul's former editor at *Wiez*, Tadeusz Mazowiecki. Three days later, Gorbachev phoned a nervous Mieczyslaw Rakowski, who had succeeded Jaruzelski as Polish Party boss, and told him to accept the vote—as if he had a choice.[3]

Jacek Kuron became minister of labor. Adam Michnik, out of jail for good, took off for Moscow, where he spoke openly to reform-minded communist deputies. His remarks were printed in the official press, and the deputies voted to cooperate with Solidarity in Poland. Michnik then went to Kiev, where rebels, including Solidarity's longtime contacts, were meeting publicly to form the Ukrainian National Movement. "Long live a free Ukraine!" Michnik shouted in his address to them.[4]

Gorbachev, his world crumbling, finally replied in late August to John Paul's offer of the year before, and asked for a meeting. He told a Vatican envoy he had read the pope's speeches and encyclicals carefully and liked John Paul's "concept of the human being, not society, as the center of concern." John Paul, on hearing that remark, declared it was "Marxism turned upside down"—and it was![5]

More than fifty thousand East Germans and Hungarians fled to West Germany through the newly opened Hungarian-Austrian border. Protesters filled East German streets, chanting, "Gorby! Gorby!" The East German Politburo, feeling the spirit, began to rebel against seventy-seven-year-old Party boss Erich Honecker, the last Stalinist.

The secret of Soviet impotence was out: the emperor had no clothes. Poland was free, and others could be free, too. October 7, the Hungarian Communist Party voted overwhelmingly to transform itself into a Western-style socialist party. Free national elections would be held in the spring.

In East Berlin, Honecker abdicated. His successor tried briefly to stem the demonstrations, but could not. November 9, mobs tore down the Berlin Wall. The government scheduled free elections, renounced the "leading role" of the Party, and began talks to reunify Germany.

John Paul had just returned from an October 1989 trip to the Far East that would have been dramatic had European events not overshadowed it. He became the first world leader to visit the half-island of East Timor in the fifteen years since ruling Indonesia began repressing an independence movement there. Civilians were still being murdered in great numbers, and the pope's was among the few global voices raised. But while he couldn't free East Timor, events told him the time was ripe for Czechoslovakia.

He swiftly established a rallying point by canonizing the first Czechoslovakian saint in three hundred years, Agnes of Bohemia, who had abandoned her riches to live with the poor in the thirteenth century. November 12, the pope brought ten thousand leading Czechs to Rome for the ceremony, including many from the underground church he had molded, and many more from the Charter 77 freedom movement.

Five days later, back in Prague, many of his listeners acted. Students at a memorial for a Czech executed by the Nazis fifty years earlier began demanding freedom. Intellectuals and leaders of Charter 77 took over, and thousands poured into the streets. Police tried to break it up, clubbing their way into the crowds. Vaclav Havel, the Charter 77 leader, decided this was his moment. November 19, he assembled his leadership in a Prague theater. They demanded release of the prisoners taken during the demonstration, punishment of the police who beat them, and a purge of officials who had cooperated with the 1968 Soviet invasion.

The government then quietly approached ninety-year-old Primate Frantisek Tomasek and asked him to mediate. Cardinal Tomasek, whom John Paul had been prodding for fifteen years without much luck, finally stood up: boldly refusing the communists, he said he wouldn't mediate because he didn't want to divide the Church and the opposition.

Students went from factory to factory, rallying workers to the streets. To head off a scheduled general strike, the Party leadership sent the prime minister to Havel to surrender.

Tomasek's own statement was read at a rally of 250,000 Czechs in Prague's Wenceslaus Square, by his spokesman, Father Vaclav Mali, himself an often-arrested member of Charter 77. It said, "Citizens of Bohemia, Moravia, and Slovakia: I returned from Rome some hours ago [the ceremony for Saint Agnes]. I must not remain silent at the very moment when you have joined together in a mighty protest against the great injustice visited upon us over four decades. . . . The time has come. . . . We need a democratic government."[6]

Poor Archbishop Cassidy at the Vatican! "Within a month at the end of '89," he recalls, "we went from not being able to appoint bishops to suddenly having to appoint them all before Christmas."

Gorbachev himself, his doomed empire shrinking by the day, finally appeared at John Paul's door, hat in hand, December 1. He was still trying—too late—to deal his way out of the abominations of his predecessors, and to save what he could of the communist dream—that "kernel of truth" that he and John Paul both saw.

What caused the collapse of communism? Those who consistently advocated violent tactics against it, and then saw it fall nonviolently, now credit *economic* violence. They say the "Star Wars" program and other parts of the Reagan military buildup led to the economic ruin of the Soviet system (though such intentions were specifically denied at the time of the buildup; Reagan justified it only on the ground that U.S. defenses were inferior). Referring to the buildup, one former Soviet official, apparently trying to flatter the Americans, said in 1993, "You accelerated our catastrophe by about five years."[7]

Former National Security Adviser Robert McFarlane commented, "The American contribution to the collapse of Marxism was relatively small." Still, he contended, it was important. He said more money was saved by hastening communism's fall than was spent on "Star Wars."[8]

Yet in all the debates and discussions that went on among Soviet policy-makers—reflected in records that have become public of Politburo and Central Committee meetings—there is hardly mention of, let alone emphasis on, a race to catch up with Reagan's new weapons. A top general who proposed such an effort was fired for it in 1984.[9] The Soviets had a long-standing problem of overcommitting resources to the military, a problem that burdened the United States as well. The Afghan commitment was an enormous drain, preceding Reagan. The increased firepower Reagan introduced in Afghanistan certainly caused more bloodshed, but there's no good evidence it altered the result.

From available evidence, the communist economic crisis of the 1980s was about the way the entire economy, domestic and military, was to be run. Poland

and the other occupied states of Eastern Europe were in a similar economic bind, and *they* weren't trying to build a competitive "Star Wars" system.

Communist governments simply reached the rational conclusion that the only way to meet their needs was to reduce state command of their economies in favor of the marketplace law of supply and demand. Once cracks appeared in the communist facade, Solidarity and its spinoffs in other countries were ready to jump in and pry the cracks wider until the facade shattered.

To a very large degree, however, Solidarity made its own cracks in that facade. When mass resistance grew in Poland in the last few years of the 1970s, hardly anyone—in Washington, in Moscow, or anywhere else—thought communism was in a terminal economic crisis. It was understood that communism generated economic misery, but that had been true for decades, and there was no reason short of KOR and Solidarity to think it wouldn't continue for decades.

Even when Solidarity was wresting actual control of Poland from the communists in 1986, few people recognized it as the last stage of communism. The economic crisis of communism was the egg to Solidarity's chicken: without either one—economic failure or the mass movement—the revolution probably would have fizzled.

One could also say that communism was doomed by technology. The arrival of the information age meant the end of mass industrial labor—Marx's proletarian class—in modern economies. "No class in history has ever risen faster than the blue-collar worker," the economist Peter Drucker has written, "and no class in history has ever fallen faster. In 1883, the year of Marx's death, 'proletarians' were still a minority."[10] A century later, they had become a minority again, at least in the West.

Hand-held television cameras and satellite transmission also affected totalitarianism. It has been written that television ended the war in Vietnam by showing Americans the reality of combat; after that, its power only grew. An Auschwitz or a Gulag Archipelago couldn't be run effectively if television showed pictures of it every night. (Even in distant, fledgling Bosnia, pictures of killing eventually provoked Americans to action.)

One could say that if Solidarity had not come along to take advantage of these sweeping technological changes, something else would have. But Solidarity *did* come along—not anything else.

John Paul's longtime ally Bishop Bronislaw Dembowski says it is "unthinkable" that the pope would have accepted a military spending competition as a means to end communism.

Mieczyslaw Rakowski, the last communist prime minister of Poland, laughs out loud at the notion that Reagan's military strategy was decisive. "From the

1950s, the Soviet Union was under pressure to make our military force stronger because the Americans had new [weapons] systems," he says. "This competition was a mistake by the Soviet leaders. The reason the system failed was the flaw in the system. But the pope's influence was very important." He says Gorbachev talked constantly about the pope.

Father Avery Dulles, the theologian and son of the U.S. secretary of state who helped father the Cold War, says John Paul's role was "crucial. It wasn't the whole thing, but it was decisive. Poland was the key to the end. It influenced the other countries in Eastern Europe. Walesa was on TV saying he never would have had the courage to act without the pope. Gorbachev said it."

"The Poles influenced everyone," says Vatican diplomat Cassidy. "The Czechs and Romanians saw it, enough to make the point."

Mark Kramer, Director of the Harvard Project on Cold War Studies, says that based on declassified Soviet documents, Schweizer's and other books that credit U.S. policy for the collapse are "just plain wrong. The Reagan military policies were a background thing. Poland was of vastly greater importance. I've looked at hundreds of documents from the Politburo" showing debates about how to prevent civil unrest in the USSR "in response to the developments in Poland. In light of what was going on in Poland, they would send directives to local Party leaders to bring out consumer goods, improve working conditions, not have workers do unpaid Saturdays, to crack down very harshly on anyone who tried to start a protest organization. The threat posed by Poland was much more immediate and vivid."

Says Vatican spokesman Navarro-Valls, "The single fact of [John Paul's] election in 1978 changed everything. In Poland began everything. Not [in] East Germany or Czechoslovakia. Then the whole thing spread. Why in 1980 did they lead the way in Gdansk? Why did they decide, now or never? Only because they knew there was a Polish pope. He was in Chile and Pinochet was out. He was in Haiti and Duvalier was out. He was in the Philippines and Marcos was out. On many of those occasions, people would come here [to the Vatican] thanking the Holy Father for changing things."

Gorbachev himself (while not responding to my requests for an interview) wrote in 1992, "Everything that happened in Eastern Europe during these past few years would have been impossible without the pope, without the political role he was able to play. . . . *Perestroika* encompassed religion, a turnaround that culminated in the approval of the law on freedom of conscience. . . . This liberalization has a strong moral significance for all citizens, believers and nonbelievers. Today, even after the great change . . . Pope John Paul II will have a leading political role. We are in a very delicate state of transition, in which the human being, the person, can and should have a really decisive weight."[11]

Says Kazimierz Kakol, Poland's former communist minister for religious affairs, "The role of the Church was not [just] any role, it was the deciding role. The Church supported the illegal organization that became Solidarity. Without Wojtyla, there would have been no Solidarity and no defeat of communism. The [weakness of the] Soviet economy was not enough."

Christian Führer, a Lutheran pastor in Leipzig, East Germany, was inspired by events in Poland to organize demonstrations that helped bring down the Berlin Wall. He called it "unbelievable, that after fifty-seven years of . . . dictatorships the Christian spirit of nonviolence had come over the people, non-Christian as well as Christian. They turned to genuinely peaceful force and spilled no blood. In 1914, when all Germany was baptized . . . when the throne and the altar were one, the nation went to war. That, for me, was a blasphemy against God. And here, people who had never grown up as Christians behaved as if they had grown up on the Sermon on the Mount."[12]

John Paul II himself told visiting Poles in the summer of 1989, "It is not an exaggeration when we say that it was Poland that resolved the gigantic dilemma of the division of Europe."[13] He told a newspaper interviewer,

> I think that, if any role was decisive, it was that of Christianity, . . . of its content, its religious and moral message, its fundamental defense of the human person and his rights. I have done nothing other than call to mind, repeat and insist that this principle is to be observed.[14]

Later, in his 1991 encyclical *Centesimus Annus*, he wrote:

> The fall of this . . . empire was accomplished almost everywhere by means of peaceful protest, using only the weapons of truth and justice. While Marxism held that only by exacerbating social conflicts was it possible to resolve them through violent confrontation, the protests that led to the collapse of Marxism tenaciously insisted on trying every avenue of negotiation, dialogue, and witness to the truth, appealing to the conscience of the adversary and seeking to reawaken in him a sense of shared human dignity.
>
> It seemed that the European order resulting from the Second World War and sanctioned by the Yalta Agreements could be overturned only by another war. Instead, it has been overcome by the nonviolent commitment of people who, while always refusing to yield to the force of power, succeeded time after time in finding effective ways of bearing witness to the truth. This disarmed the

adversary, since violence always needs to justify itself through deceit and to appear, however falsely, to be ... responding to a threat posed by others.

To John Paul, the key to the victory was not the violent threat that had been marshaled but the violent threat that had been denied. His creed had won a great contest. Now came a greater one.

General Wojciech Jaruzelski

Tadeusz Mazowiecki

Cardinal Joseph Ratzinger

BOOK FIVE

JUDGMENTS

1

After the dazzling events of 1989, John Paul faced a reversal so profound as to recall the fate of Winston Churchill, considered by many the greatest man of his time. Midway through a final summit with Roosevelt and Stalin at Potsdam, Germany, in 1945, to plan the world to come, Churchill was voted out of office. People everywhere were astonished that Britons rejected such a leader at the hour of victory. But though the British welcomed Churchill home with love and gratitude, they preferred the Labour Party to direct the reconstruction ahead over Churchill's Conservative Party.

After 1989, Poles, at least, appreciated what John Paul II had accomplished. But people on both sides of the former Iron Curtain turned to the future. They could not, of course, vote the pope out of office. But they chose alternatives to his program.

How was such victory reduced so quickly to such defeat?

Harvard professor Jeffrey Sachs, just thirty-five, hardly seemed a match for the pope in a contest for the future of Eastern Europe. But the forces behind Sachs helped undo the Solidarity dream.

Sachs was a shooting star in a constellation of economic consultants who sold their services to countries having trouble paying their international debts. Before Poland, Sachs had helped Brazil, Ecuador, and Bolivia redesign their economies toward marketplace rule, as demanded by the International Monetary Fund (IMF) and the Western governments that controlled it. The IMF seemed pleased with his work.

By now, few doubted that prosperity required private markets. What the pope opposed was Western demands that countries surrender unconditionally to the marketplace by stopping social programs in order to pay debts *first.* In his encyclical *Sollicitudo Rei Socialis,* and in his speeches, John Paul criticized the IMF.[1] Professor Sachs, in contrast, worked closely with it.[2]

The Polish communists had approached Sachs for help in cutting their debt load, but he had refused to work with them.[3] When he learned of the success of the Round Table talks, however, he came to Poland. He found his connection to Solidarity at a Warsaw dinner party: Grzegorz Lindenberg, the former Solidarity officer who had started a computer business after his release from jail. Recently, Luidenberg had become business manager of *Gazeta Wyborcza,* a new Warsaw daily newspaper built from the underground paper *Tygodnik Mazowsze* and edited by Adam Michnik. Lindenberg, already driving a new Toyota, had ambitions "to make a lot of money" in the new Poland.[4]

Lindenberg introduced Sachs, his new acquaintance, to Michnik and other leaders. By the time Mazowiecki's Solidarity government took power, in August, Sachs knew the right people. It was the ideal time for a consultant with a cure: when communist controls ended, there was "crisis and hyperinflation. The shops were totally empty," recalls Jan Bielecki, a Solidarity leader in Parliament who would succeed Mazowiecki as prime minister. "There was a strong demand from the people for immediate progress. Everyone was scared."

Mazowiecki, the Catholic philosopher and editor, felt lost in statistics and sought a competent finance minister to solve the crisis. At least two economists turned the job down as hopeless before Leszek Balcerowicz, a generation younger than the others, agreed to try. Although he had taught socialist economics at a government institute right up to the end of communism, Balcerowicz had become enamored of the free-market philosophers in vogue in the West.

Amid the economic crisis, Solidarity leaders like Balcerowicz and Bielecki began talking to Sachs and IMF representatives. Mazowiecki sometimes joined them, but hated the blizzard of numbers. Walesa was back in Gdansk, mostly uninvolved.[5]

Each side now suggests that it was led by the others into the final plan. Sachs says he merely helped the Poles implement their own ideas. But the Westerners held the power. Finance Minister Balcerowicz immediately had to beg for $500 million in Western credits "to cover essential imports" and "avoid serious economic upheaval."[6] Instead of extending unconditional help to the new postcommunist Poland, the United States and other Western countries used their leverage to push for—even impose—their own policies.

Sachs wound up not only talking to Solidarity's confused politicians but addressing all Poland on prime-time television. Even people who don't like his economics say Sachs is a dynamic and inspirational salesman: his plan was adopted. Its language was of currency exchange, price and wage controls, and the like.*

But a main point of the plan was unspoken: without subsidies, life in government-sponsored jobs, where most Poles worked, became so miserable that people were pushed to seek income from the private sector. It was commonly referred to as "shock therapy." One by one, other post-communist countries adopted such programs.

Says Mazowiecki, "We faced the alternative of either [adopting] the Western system, or looking for some third way." In the inflationary crisis, "We decided to avoid [an] experiment."

The Solidarity group assumed, however, that the Soviet Union would continue buying the products of the big steel, chemical, and other plants it had built in Poland. "Factories built by communism were producing tanks, and we did not need them," says a Mazowiecki aide.[7] Although the Poles wanted Russia to be free, too, they "didn't expect it would have such serious implications for Poland." As the Soviet military faded, Polish factories became useless. "It was a personal tragedy for me," says Mazowiecki. "Those most endangered by the reforms were [workers] from the gigantic communist factories" who had been the backbone of Solidarity.

Today Sachs is proud that in the mid-1990s, Poland has among the highest growth rates in Europe, and conditions are normalizing. The issue is what it cost—and that the workers who won the revolution suffered most. "The crisis will be over in six months," Sachs declared in 1989.[8] The IMF said so, too.[9] It wasn't. The suffering went on for years.

A Solidarity delegation led by Mazowiecki paid a triumphant call on John Paul that fall. The pope repeatedly stressed that he wanted them to stay unified—as if he sensed what was coming.[10]

A dispute had already arisen over how to treat former communists. John Paul and Mazowiecki agreed there should be "no persecution of the [communist] leaders—that is the Christian ethic."[11] Many in the Glemp wing of the Church, and some in Solidarity, wanted to ban Party members from government jobs.[12]

---

* To halt inflation, foreign currency became freely exchangeable for the Polish zloty, driving down the zloty's value and wiping out family savings. Price controls were removed, but—at the IMF's insistence—wage controls remained. In return for this hardship, Poles were told that if they kept to the plan, the foreign debt would be reduced; it was, by about 42 percent after four and a half years.

John Paul moved swiftly to cut Glemp down to size. For his first nuncio to Poland under the new diplomatic agreement, he chose not an Italian, as previous popes had, but a Pole from the Roman curia, Archbishop Jozef Kowalczyk. "Glemp understood very well it was a rival authority," says a veteran priest. The primate tried in small ways to make life difficult for Kowalczyk.[13]

Gradually, the nuncio began siphoning power from Glemp. At seminaries, Polish priests were appointed as papal representatives and reported to the nuncio, not to Glemp. Dioceses were rearranged to dilute the primate's authority. After Wyszynski's long, mysterious rule as if he were an independent pope, it was, ironically, the Polish pope who made the Polish Church like any other. Glemp just seethed.

The pope also overruled Glemp on a convent established by Carmelite nuns in a building where Germans had stored extermination gas at Auschwitz. In 1985, when the nuns announced they were seeking "the conversion of strayed brothers," Jewish groups had begun to protest: it was bad enough that the special Jewish symbolism of Auschwitz was being challenged, worse still that the nuns seemed to imply that Judaism itself was misguided.

Jews differed from Christians in their basic perception of suffering. John Paul talks about suffering as redeeming and ennobling, and Church art often depicts it as such; Jews saw no consolation in Auschwitz, and wanted it kept ugly. Although the controversy had its origin in Poland, the whole Church came under attack in the world press.

"Glemp didn't understand why Jews were upset," says a spokesman for major Jewish groups.[14] "He saw pressure to remove the convent as part of an anti-Church movement." Learning of the furor from a newspaper,[15] John Paul likewise failed to understand it: in 1978, he had dedicated a similar Carmelite site at the death camp in Dachau, Germany, and no one had complained.

Cardinal Macharski of Krakow, in whose archdiocese Auschwitz lay, met with leaders of complaining Jewish groups and agreed to have the convent moved out of the camp to a nearby site by 1989. The dispute seemed over. But in 1989 the convent remained, with the support of many Polish bishops. Glemp spoke, in different forums, on both sides of the issue, but didn't move the nuns.[16] A radical American Jewish group staged a made-for-TV clash at the site, shouting demands for respect while nuns cried back that the demonstrators had been sent by the devil.

During his inauguration festivities, Mazowiecki told Jan Novak, the Polish-American former official of Radio Free Europe, that the convent affair was poisoning Catholic-Jewish relations. He asked Novak to talk to John Paul about it. So Novak "got myself invited for lunch at Castelgandolfo. I was saying, 'The whole thing has to be closed down right now. The Carmelites have to leave.' I sensed he [the pope] was absolutely on my side."

"Leave the problem to us," John Paul told Novak.

The Vatican ordered the convent moved. Even then, the nuns stayed put until the pope himself sent them a written command. "He waited as long as he could," says John Paul's friend Jacek Wozniakowski, with whom he also discussed the matter. "When he saw the Polish Episcopate was incapable of dealing with the situation, he acted."

John Paul later told his friend André Frossard, "The Jews wish Auschwitz to be a place of silence, and we fully understand. This silence signifies a reproach, a complaint, against God himself. We fully understand this need for silence because Jesus Christ himself, on the cross, said, 'My God, My God, why have you forsaken me?' Jews and Christians must understand each other on this."[17]

2

Just when Solidarity, for better or worse, got Jeffrey Sachs, John Paul brought his own money manager in from the United States.

Edmund Szoka was the Polish-American whom John Paul had picked to be cardinal/archbishop of Detroit in 1981, and who had then needed help with a nun involved in politics. Szoka and the pope had since developed an unusually close relationship, lunching whenever Szoka was in Rome and speaking in Polish except when financial technicalities forced them into Italian. Szoka had shepherded finances at the U.S. Bishops' Conference, Catholic University in Washington, and Catholic Relief Services. He realized that the pope saw him increasingly as someone who knew about money. And during their stops for prayer, he in turn decided that John Paul was "the holiest person I have met, in deep communion with Christ."

One Monday, Cardinal Laghi phoned Szoka to say that the prefect for economic affairs, Cardinal Giuseppe Caprio—who hadn't made a dent in the Vatican deficits—was retiring, and the pope was considering replacing him with Szoka. Szoka was in Rome and at the papal lunch table that Friday. The pope knew that Szoka had just solved a financial crisis in Detroit by closing thirty-five inner-city parishes where priests regularly said Mass for as few as fifty people, sending the priests instead to the suburbs to serve thousands of people. Szoka was being labeled anti-black and anti-poor. But the pope didn't mention that as he made his offer.

Says Szoka, "To give up a big archdiocese, where you could be a pastor and do good things, to come to another culture and work in an office, in a language you're not used to, without the contact with people you have as an archbishop—it's not something most Americans would look forward to. He left the door open for me to refuse. He said, 'Well, I told them to ask you to *consider* this job.' He offered to let me try doing both jobs."

Szoka asked for six months to arrange finances and personnel in Detroit as he wanted them. Then he would come to Rome full-time.

On December 1, 1989, Mikhail Gorbachev, still general secretary of the Communist Party in the world's leading communist country, came to the Vatican. He had told a lecture audience in Rome the night before, "We have changed our attitude toward religion. Now Church and State are separate, and no one should interfere in matters of the individual's conscience." Coming from a Russian leader—communist or tsarist—this was a leap as exhilarating as the one the Church had made with its Declaration on Religious Liberty.

Gorbachev, who once described himself as a nonpracticing atheist, was the first Russian leader to visit the Vatican since Tsar Nicholas I met with Pope Gregory XVI in 1845.[1] He should have come sooner. Afterward he gave gushing accounts of the "spiritual agreement" and "deep sense of trust" that he and John Paul had developed, and in fact, more substance really did pass between them than did in the ceremonial meetings the pope held with most heads of state.

They spoke alone in Russian for a few minutes, then requested interpreters. Persuaded that Gorbachev was sincere in trying to change the USSR fundamentally, the pope explicitly encouraged him, though he observed that the human dignity Gorbachev talked about would be "difficult to give in an atheistic philosophy."[2] The two men then announced the establishment of formal diplomatic relations—no small feat after seventy years.

André Frossard, waiting in the papal dining room, said the pope walked in immediately after leaving Gorbachev and declared, "This man has a problem: *comment changer le système sans changer le système*"—a French phrase meaning, loosely, "how to reform something without destroying it," or, in Frossard's words, "how to democratize it without losing his own job."[3] Still, Navarro-Valls says, John Paul sized up Gorbachev as "a man of principles more than a man of power," who ultimately lost power because he was "open to all the consequences of his principles."

Just before Christmas 1989, the United States—having beaten Grenada, lost to Vietnam and Angola, and tied several Central American countries—invaded

Panama, a nation of two and a half million souls. As with Marcos in the Philippines, the dictator the U.S. sought to remove in Panama was one it had helped create: Manuel Noriega. In the early 1980s, Washington had accepted Noriega's offer of assistance in its covert wars against Nicaragua and Cuba, even though it knew he was involved in the drug trade.[4]

By the end of the decade, the wars were winding down and Noriega had become an embarrassment. The Bush administration had him indicted for drug shipments to the U.S. and sent twenty-four thousand soldiers as a sort of posse to arrest him. As these troops secured Panama City, two dozen Americans, several hundred Panamanian soldiers, and about a thousand Panamanian civilian bystanders were killed.

The morning of the invasion, several of Noriega's powerful cronies sought asylum in the residence of the Vatican nuncio, Archbishop José Sebastian Laboa. Laboa was vacationing in Spain at the time, but when his aides called him, he caught the first plane to Miami. Expecting to have to scavenge his way back to Panama, he was startled when U.S. officials met him at the gate and flew him to Panama City on a military aircraft, all the while pressuring him to turn over Noriega's men.

Not only did Laboa refuse, but a few days later, when the fugitive Noriega himself called from a pay phone, Laboa agreed to admit *him*—the most-wanted man in the Western Hemisphere. Noriega later charged that Laboa and the Americans had conspired to trap him in the nuncio's home, as evidenced by the ease with which he entered; Laboa argues, persuasively, that the Americans were not guarding the house because they did not expect Noriega to show up there.

Laboa still expresses warm feelings for Noriega, though he disapproves of the dictator's drug deals. Based on their personal friendship, and not knowing of the drug deals, he told Noriega he would shield him from the Americans and try to help him find permanent asylum. They approached Spain, Libya, Nicaragua, and Cuba, but all turned Noriega down. Laboa says the U.S. hounded him to hand over the general. A personal emissary from President Bush annoyed Archbishop Laboa so much that "at one point, I lost my temper with him. I said, 'As long he [Noriega] is in here, we're not going to make him do anything. It's up to him.'"

Soon after New Year's, however, Laboa told Noriega, "The Americans are never going to let you leave here. And I can't guarantee that an assassin can't get in." Noriega feared not only angry Panamanian compatriots but also merciless Colombian drug lords who didn't want him in American hands. According to Laboa, it was Noriega's reasonableness—nothing else—that led to his surrender; he remains today in prison in the United States.

Laboa says that his phone lines to the Vatican were down and that he was able to exchange only a few messages during Noriega's stay; Cardinal Casaroli has said that he and the pope had to rely on CNN for news. But Laboa insists he was never criticized by the Vatican for his handling of the affair. One Noriega crony being sought by the U.S. stayed six months in the nunciature before sneaking out to safety at an undisclosed location.[5]

3

After 1989, John Paul's papacy changed direction. "Before, the biggest problem was the fear of communism," says Father Gianpaolo Salvini, editor of the semiofficial Vatican magazine *Civil Catholica.* "Now it is the problem of secularization, and the self-made world without God—that the Church will lose its missionary spirit and become an administration, as in many Western churches. In Germany, Switzerland, Italy, they are occupied with parishioners, and forget about the majority, who are not *in* the Church."

For John Paul, the end of the Cold War represented an opportunity to spread out. Years earlier, he had told Polish bishops that the Church worried too much about militant atheism and too little about the way most people lived. Now, in talks to Vatican departments and visiting bishops, he stressed evangelism, asserting, as Salvini recalls it, that "the world is pluralistic. The Christian mentality is not the mentality of the majority. The Church must address the modern world. The prayers in missals talk about rain and agriculture problems, but not about inflation and unemployment."

He urged still more contact with Protestants and non-Christians. In January 1990, he toured five more African countries, stressing the theme that excitement over the fall of communism shouldn't distract attention from development needs in poorer countries.

Nowhere did the Church have more aggressive evangelizing plans than in the Soviet Union and Eastern Europe. It had been dreaming of this day practically from the moment of the Russian Revolution. In 1920, the Vatican had quietly created a Russian College, known as the Russicum, to train priests to reclaim Orthodox Russia for Rome after communism fell. Few knew about it; for seventy years, the Russicum's constant flow of graduates had been sent back home, unable to pursue their mission. In the 1920s and again in the 1950s, small, secret hierarchies of priests and bishops were created in the USSR, only to be wiped out by the secret police.[1]

Right after meeting Gorbachev, John Paul decided to move again and appointed "apostolic administrators"—temporary archbishops—for Moscow and the Western USSR (Siberia and Kazakhstan). He put fresh blood atop the

Russicum: Father John Long, who, like the new Russian archbishops, got a vigorous papal mandate to evangelize.

They also got a surprise. "When communism finally fell, nothing worked out as planned," Long says. The priests the Russicum had produced in the past "were [now] either too old to move to Russia, or too involved in their home dioceses." Moreover, the Vatican had grossly misjudged the state of religion in the USSR.

"We had the vision of atheists, and making them all Catholic," Long says. Instead, the Church found strong Orthodox traditions throughout the former Soviet Union. And where there were Catholics—as in Lithuania—"the bulk of the community was unready for the results of Vatican II. We discovered real hostility about interrelations. Catholics insisted on preserving their own traditions." In other words, all the fractious Orthodox and Catholic groups that had existed before communism began to reemerge as communism fell.

In Byelorussia—soon to be independent, as Belorus—a handful of priests found themselves without buildings, books, bishops, or, most important, parishioners. The public was both Orthodox and hostile.[2]

In Ukraine, talks were begun to reestablish the Church, but in March 1990, the Catholic leader, Archbishop Volodymyr Sterniuk, walked out. He and some parishioners accused Rome of betraying their Church's five million members, some of whom had suffered for years in Soviet labor camps, in order to make peace with the Orthodox.[3] According to Father Long, John Paul was merely trying to get the Ukrainians "to share churches: Catholics would use them one day, Orthodox another. But there was a reaction. They were taught that even to put a foot in an Orthodox church was a mortal sin. Now, to let an Orthodox priest say a Mass 'on *my* altar' " was unacceptable. "There's been a tendency to say, 'My way of celebrating the faith is the only legitimate way.' "

The reunion of the Catholic and Orthodox Churches, which John Paul had thought imminent when he visited Patriarch Dimitrios in 1979, was now nowhere in sight. Was John Paul disappointed? "It's not so much disappointment, because of his understanding of Slavic history," Father Long says. "His reaction is to insist very much on the legitimacy of variety in celebrating [Mass]—that the Church is capable of accepting a large variety of cultures. But people aren't buying it. It's taking time. Religion and nationality are closely intertwined."

Refusing to yield to these initial ecumenical setbacks, John Paul made a glorious entry into Prague in April 1990. As soon as the pope had kissed the ground, Vaclav Havel—like John Paul, a head of state with a literary background—declared, "The Messenger of Love comes today into a country devastated by the ideology of hatred."

Alexander Dubcek, surviving hero of the doomed 1968 rebellion, was on hand with ninety-one-year-old Cardinal Tomasek to hear Havel call the pope "the Living Symbol of civilization," and then add, "Your Holiness, I do not know what a miracle is. Nevertheless, I dare to say at this moment that I am party to a miracle. A man who only six months ago was taken prisoner as an enemy of his own state [Havel once served five years in prison] is welcoming today, as president, the first pope . . . to set foot in Czechoslovakia. For long decades the spirit has been chased out of our homeland. I have the honor to be a witness when its soil is kissed by the Apostle of spirituality."

John Paul said Mass before half a million people. He met with the students and teachers of the Czech version of the "flying university" he had helped launch in Poland, and countless other heroes of the Czech nonviolent revolution. Buoyant, he grasped again for his evangelistic dream and proclaimed a "Euro-synod" in Rome the next year, to bring together the churches of Eastern and Western Europe.

Meanwhile, along the Baltic, citizens of Lithuania, Latvia, and Estonia were campaigning for independence. While John Paul was in Prague, the president of Lithuania begged him to recognize that country's independence and tell the Soviet troops to leave. The pope declined to do so. Only now did the effect of Gorbachev's trip to the Vatican the previous December become manifest. As pressure mounted in coming months, John Paul held loyally to Gorbachev's reform plan and told the Baltic countries to wait. He said their demands for independence were "justified by the past" but must be achieved through "dialogue." *Perestroika*, he said, "takes into account the whole dimension of an immense country made up of many peoples."[4]

His own Lithuanian cardinal, Vincentas Sladkevicius, spoke out for independence. "We never trusted him [Gorbachev] as much as the West [does]," Sladkevicius told reporters. "Perhaps he is not the complete communist like Stalin, but he is a Russian who wants to dominate."[5]

It was in John Paul's own Poland, however, that things were to fall apart most painfully.

Through 1990, prices continued to soar, and Polish living standards plummeted. Walesa had retreated to Gdansk and separated himself from Mazowiecki's government. Aiming to take over the presidency from Jaruzelski when the job came up for election that fall, he started speaking out on behalf of striking workers and farmers, pitting himself against the Solidarity government.

It appeared to many Poles that Walesa was challenging the "shock therapy" plan of Finance Minister Balcerowicz and the Westerners. In retrospect, however, it is clear he wasn't. When he later took power, he retained Balcerowicz, the IMF group, and their plan. What Walesa was doing in 1990 was casting himself as a man of the people, against the intellectuals, who, he suggested, had hijacked Solidarity.

According to Zbigniew Bujak, the former underground leader and by this time a senator, Walesa "realized that during the Round Table talks he had badly assessed the political situation. After the talks, he stayed cautious [and] decided not to run for Parliament. Then it turned out that a man of Solidarity, Mazowiecki, became prime minister. The public-opinion polls gave him much more support than Walesa. Walesa got very envious, and angry. The debate was over political leadership, not the economy."

Many others agree that Walesa was running on ambition, not on principle. Walesa's old ally, Lane Kirkland of the U.S. AFL-CIO, recalls two frustrating lunches with him, one in Poland, one in the United States, in the year after the Solidarity government took power. Kirkland really did oppose the "shock therapy" plan; like John Paul, he had campaigned against IMF-style programs.

He says he pleaded with Walesa: "A revolution created by working people has been usurped by bankers, academics, and finance ministers at the expense of working people. What Poland needs is something like what the New Deal did here [in the U.S.]. The condition Central and Eastern Europe faces is much closer to the depression of the 1930s than [to] any other condition. It doesn't matter whether it was brought about by the excesses of a command economy or the excesses of a market economy. Either one can bring ruin."

He says Walesa replied, "I agree with you, but I have a pistol at my head: the IMF. Conditions have been imposed on Poland [in exchange] for a reduction of debts and new credits."

Kirkland denounced Balcerowicz for knuckling under before the IMF, and argued that Poland needed "social programs to provide full employment."

At that, he says, Walesa told him, "You'll have to discuss this with [Balcerowicz]. There was compulsion from the West."

Yet in public, Walesa launched a political campaign appealing to hard-hit workers. For them, the word *shock* was no exaggeration. Hundreds of thousands of Poles streamed into Italy in 1990 seeking low-paying jobs. "Changing the politicians did not prepare them for competition," says Bishop Wesoly, who had been living in Rome since 1968 to pastor to Polish visitors. "They had a welfare state [under communism,] and they didn't have it now. I said to people, 'If you want money, you have to start some business.'"

Balcerowicz himself has written, "At the congress of Solidarity in April [1990], many delegates were very critical of the economic program. In June, farmers blocked important roads, demanding . . . higher milk prices. The government ordered the police to unblock the roads, provoking furious attacks in Parliament from the . . . peasant parties."[6]

That summer, Walesa visited Castelgandolfo, seeking John Paul's blessing for his campaign. Ostensibly, he was running against Jaruzelski, though everyone could see it was Mazowiecki he attacked. He and the pope shared Mass, breakfasted, and talked alone for hours. Sadly, the pope asked why Solidarity had split. Walesa's answer is not recorded. To the press, John Paul made noncommittal statements, asserting only that Walesa was "still an active figure and full of dynamism" and that his charisma was "not exhausted."[7]

What John Paul really thought came out on a trip to Mexico that summer, as he made perhaps the most politically focused series of speeches of his papacy. Few of the usual religious pieties diluted his constant message that in celebrating the victories of 1989, people and nations must not make the mistake of replacing collectivism with "liberal capitalism."

John Paul didn't specifically mention the economic trauma that was splitting Solidarity, but he repeatedly denounced Western pressure on countries struggling to establish their own economic systems. He cited Mexico for his examples, but it took little imagination to see that the shoe fit Poland. He constantly quoted his encyclicals on social welfare, *Laborem Exorcens* and *Sollicitudo Rei Socialis.* According to press accounts, he sometimes went beyond the already vigorous texts he brought with him (quoted here from *Osservatore Romano*).[8]

The overthrow of communism, he said, had

> been interpreted, at times superficially, as the triumph . . . of one system over another—specifically, the triumph of the liberal capitalist system. Certain interest groups want to . . . present the system that they consider the winner as the only path for our world, . . . avoiding an essential critical judgment of the effects that liberal capitalism has produced, at least up until now, in the so-called Third World countries. . . .
>
> It is always the weakest who endure the worst consequences and find themselves hemmed in by a circle of growing poverty; how can we not repeat the words of the Bible, that the misery of the weakest cries out to the Most High? It is undeniable that the foreign debt has aggravated the situation even further.

John Paul took pains to show that he had read the recent writings of American Catholics who claimed he did not really mean to attack capitalism along with Marxism. He *did* mean to. To cultural leaders in Mexico City, he said:

The system based on Marxist materialism has been a disappointment.... Yet ... cultural models ... in industrialized countries do not assure a civilization worthy of man, either.... Immediate and transitory values are incapable of sustaining the effort it takes to construct a promising civilization such as yours.... Mexico is the cradle of civilizations that ... reached a high level of development and left behind a priceless legacy of culture and knowledge.... Latin America has to reaffirm her identity ... from within herself, from within her most authentic roots.

"Do not forget," he told a group of businessmen,

that the only legitimate title to the ownership of the means of production is that they should serve labor. One of your chief responsibilities has to be the creation of jobs....

Surely, many of you present are motivated in your work by a sincere desire to serve. But ... a serious danger stalks you: submission to earthly possessions, *the desire for mere gain*—which is usually linked to *the thirst for power*—at any cost. Yielding to this temptation [produces] a crass materialism ... and the fundamental dissatisfaction that a person feels trying to extinguish the thirst for the Infinite Good through material creations. [Italics John Paul's]

In Monterrey, he specifically endorsed a mixed economy, praising "the good results achieved by the joint efforts of the public and private sectors in countries where freedom rules."

In late summer, Mazowiecki declared that he would challenge Walesa for the presidency of Poland. "Mazowiecki didn't want to run. It took a long effort for others to convince him to run," says John Paul's friend and former editor Stefan Wilkanowicz. The old intellectual inner circle of Solidarity had decided at last to repudiate Walesa's ego and criticism.

Despite often-repeated rumors to the contrary, Mazowiecki insists there was "no attempt [by] the pope or anyone close to him to make me withdraw or not enter." He says Turowicz and others who saw the Pope that year conveyed John Paul's "best regards," and nothing more.[9] (Turowicz confirms this.) Still, as Archbishop Dabrowski, then secretary of the Polish Episcopate, says, "The Holy Father didn't want that split, that's obvious. All of us were very sorry."

Mazowiecki bluntly accuses Walesa of hypocrisy in attacking the Balcerowicz-IMF-Sachs program to get votes, then retaining the program once he took office. It is Mazowiecki who now seems uncomfortable with what his finance minister, Balcerowicz, did. He acknowledges being bothered by the suffering he saw, and says he knew John Paul wanted the economic encyclicals to be put into effect by Solidarity.

During the presidential campaign, Mazowiecki began talking about a "social market economy" and saying that his program was really aimed at a welfare state after all. He maintains today that "the reforms I initiated in 1989 are in agreement with the encyclicals. The difference is [that] you cannot do both things simultaneously—to reform and to build things up, and to provide welfare. We had to make decisions. Believe me, it was a dramatic situation whether to put more money into retirement, or into health services. Everything was below minimum standard. Therefore the philosophy was, We must make a breakthrough first to switch the economy," to make it "competitive."

Mazowiecki notes that Poland still has a larger public sector than the United States, and that his free-market model was closer to Sweden's than to America's. Still, his administration was associated with the shock-therapy policies of Balcerowicz, the longtime communist, who went from one extreme to its opposite. During the 1990 election campaign, Balcerowicz ridiculed Mazowiecki's "social market economy" idea on television, advocating strictly free markets.[10]

"There were very few economic specialists in opposition circles" when communism fell, says John Paul's friend and former editor Wilkanowicz. "They were not very practical people. The pope's concept was and still is on levels of theory, not very close to reality. When they started to reform, people had to act very fast. They found that one new regulation required a change of four hundred others. The whole economy was like that. They had to grab what was ready. And it was Jeffrey Sachs [saying,] 'Do this, this and this.' There was no time to experiment. They were under pressure from the IMF. 'What has worked in the West, you do the same.' "

Now, Wilkanowicz says, "We pay a price for that. Much should be changed in the West, too." He recalls that on his trips to the West, friends warned, "Don't do the same as we do."

The campaign is widely considered to have been a tragedy for all concerned. "Geremek, Michnik, and Turowicz thought they could destroy Walesa," says Zdzislaw Najder. "But the backlash carried against Mazowiecki and all politicians."

Lacking a counterpolicy, Walesa instead appealed to nationalism. He constantly said or implied that the Mazowiecki group was too liberal, intellectual, and influenced by the West.[11] The Polish Church was as deeply split as Solidarity. One prominent bishop, Tadeusz Goclowski of Gdansk, held political meetings at his church aimed at setting up a Christian party to back Walesa. Many rural priests openly endorsed him.

"Today's bishops are of Wyszynski's popular Church—different from the nobility bishops before," says Catholic historian Zygmunt Kubiak. "Communism could not be overthrown by intellectuals. It could only be overthrown by a real popular force. And now we have to drink a bitter drink because of this. The election was a conflict between the intelligentsia and these popular forces."

By the end, both sides had turned nasty. Michnik wrote editorials in *Gazeta Wyborcza* attacking even Walesa's grammar—"hideous propaganda, saying Walesa was a simple man," Kubiak says. Many Poles still recall a moment during a televised debate when Turowicz stood to ask a question, and Walesa berated and taunted him, even as Turowicz himself tried to retreat from the confrontation. Mazowiecki, Walesa, and Turowicz were all fervent Catholics. Yet the much younger Walesa, champion of the working man, caustically turned on the white-haired intellectual, Turowicz, on television.

Many voters were disappointed when Walesa, right after his election, had Balcerowicz reappointed and endorsed his program. The president of the Solidarity unit at the Polish Academy of Sciences—Maria Wosiek, cofounder of KOR and a pillar of the underground relief effort at Laski—quit the union after the 1990 election, along with most of her membership.

"The tragedy we see now is that Solidarity has become anti-intellectual," Professor Wosiek says. "Within Solidarity there are only workers. They feel they have been betrayed by all the professionals who went into government. Intellectuals got convinced that only capitalism could heal the economy. But privatization entails unemployment. Solidarity today has a program that supports big state enterprises, a program mostly of socialism. If the budget has no money, they say it was just stolen by officials. It's a tragedy. But democracy is not Solidarity. Solidarity was possible only when human freedom was threatened. Where there was one enemy."

Solidarity, as John Paul dreamed of it, was gone in one year.

4

The 1990 synod in Rome addressed the priesthood. Since 1979, the world had 19 percent more Catholics and 4 percent fewer priests.

John Paul was less alarmed about the decline in priests than were many of his bishops. He had already decided not only that quality was more important than quantity, but also that quality would, in time, *produce* quantity. He was persuaded that other young men liked a challenge just as he had, and that lowering standards not only would produce inferior priests but in the long run would deter many potentially good priests from answering the calling. Moreover, the worst decline had come in the 1970s, after the revolution in sexual and other living customs. The *rate* of decline was now being stemmed.

And the decline (or as the Vatican called it, the "laborious renewal") was limited to Europe (down 8.1 percent) and North America (down 5.7 percent). Third World ordinations were increasing, despite the celibacy vow that many claimed was a deterrent.

The decline was also disproportionately among religious orders—those priests who taught, ran do-good agencies, or contemplated. The pastors in the parishes were replenishing themselves. In Africa, for example, the 67 percent increase in diocesan priests during the 1980s outstripped the 50 percent increase in Catholics. Asian figures were similar. In Latin America, the increase in diocesan priests (17 percent) trailed the increase in Catholics (24 percent) only slightly.[1]

All this led John Paul to dismiss suggestions at the synod for any relaxation of rules, though he was told that more and more parishes worldwide (some said more than half) lacked a full-time priest to say Mass or take confession. In the United States, seminary attendance had peaked in 1966 at 8,325, falling fairly steadily to 3,324 in 1994, a drop of 60 percent over eighteen years. At thirty-two, the average seminarian was now seven years older. In 1966, 20,139 American boys were in special high school programs to become priests; in 1994, there were just 1,229. The Church replaced only six of every ten priests it lost.[2]

The Chicago archdiocese spent $4.5 million a year to maintain seminaries that had been built for hundreds of students but that now turned out only a dozen priests. (At that rate, declared one study, "The cost of educating seminarians may be second only to turning out astronauts.")[3] Seminary facilities elsewhere were visibly underused. An American who had examined the problem complained, "You can throw all the studies you want at Rome, but it won't change. They work off a long historical timeline, and in their view this present shortage is just a glitch."[4]

That wasn't necessarily the view of "Rome," but it was the view of John Paul II. Knowing he would oppose dramatic change, some bishops suggested that the synod consider ordaining *viri probati,* or older men "of tested faith," even if married. John Paul merely reprimanded them: "Calling upon the *viri probati,*" he said, was "systematic propaganda hostile to priestly celibacy."

In the end, the bishops voted overwhelmingly to confirm the *value* of priestly celibacy, though they were clearly less resolute than the pope about the *necessity* of it. When Cardinal Bernardin observed that celibacy "often appears unattractive and unattainable," John Paul's relator, Cardinal Moreira Neves of

Brazil, replied that the issue had been resolved "in a definitive way" and shut off debate.[5] Yet during the synod, a new code of canon law was proclaimed, still allowing marriage for Eastern Rite Catholic priests (whose Orthodox ancestors had been promised this when they reunified with Rome in 1596). If some priests could marry, why not all?

Because the pope thought celibacy was a meaningful demonstration of a life committed wholly to God. He felt people needed such examples.

November 5, 1990, Cardinal Etchegaray's Justice and Peace Council hosted a daylong conference of sixteen economists, highlighted by lunch with John Paul. Professor Hendryk Houthakker (Anna-Teresa Tymieniecka's husband) says he proposed the conference to the pope as a preparation for his inevitable 1991 economics encyclical in the tradition of *Rerum Novarum* of 1891. Still trying to make a capitalist sympathizer of John Paul, Houthakker urged him to invite Houthakker's Harvard economics colleague, Jeffrey Sachs. The pope did.

Despite what many Western officials have said, however, John Paul did *not* embrace the "shock therapy" plan for Poland during Sachs's day at the Vatican.[6] Sachs himself, whose only meeting ever with the pope was at a lunch also attended by fifteen other economists, says John Paul "listened, raised questions, expressed worries, concerns. He did not enunciate a doctrine."

A senior Vatican official involved in the event[7] says John Paul's skepticism about the Western system emerged at one point during lunch when the glories of capitalism were being explained to him. "It is not every day I have economists here," he remarked wryly. "But every day there are bishops here, and they give me a much more pessimistic view than you do. They see people suffering."

Cardinal Casaroli, at seventy-six, retired as secretary of state in December 1990. Planning for his replacement, John Paul had two years earlier brought Bishop (now Cardinal) Cassidy, his diligent, much-traveled diplomat, to the secretary of state's office as *sostituto*, or chief of the Vatican staff, in line for the top job. But when the job finally opened up, Cassidy, an Australian, was moved elsewhere (to run the Council on Christian Unity).

John Paul had previously chosen Italians for the top offices in the secretariat of state because he thought they could best steer the agenda of a Polish pope through the largely Italian curia. After eighteen months of Cassidy, he saw that conditions had not changed. Much as John Paul valued Cassidy, in the words of journalist and papal friend Wilton Wynn, the Australian had been "eaten alive by the Italians."

The other man considered in line for secretary of state *was* Italian: Archbishop (now Cardinal) Achille Silvestrini, Casaroli's ally and deputy for foreign relations. But as Cassidy struggled, John Paul moved Silvestrini aside as well (to run the Congregation for Eastern Churches). Surprising many, the pope then brought in a dark horse, Archbishop (now Cardinal) Angelo Sodano, a longtime diplomat in South America, who had been in Chile at the end of the Pinochet era. Sodano replaced Silvestrini, and when Casaroli retired, he became secretary of state.*

As the new *sostituto,* or deputy secretary of state for Vatican administration, the pope appointed Archbishop Giovanni Battista Re, a striking Italian with a toothy grin and booming, carefully enunciated voice loud enough to be heard and understood by the lowest clerk in the Vatican. Sodano and Re still hold these jobs.

Cardinal Alfonso Lopez Trujillo of Medellin, Colombia, was brought to Rome to fill a vacancy running the Council for the Family. After John Paul named him archbishop of Medellin in 1979, Lopez Trujillo had tried to tip the Latin American Bishops' Conference away from Liberation Theology, which he opposed. Instead, he had become a carping minority voice against a persistent majority of bishops—including many appointed by John Paul— who wanted the Church active against injustice.

While some at the Vatican thought Lopez Trujillo's appointment in Rome was a promotion—and thus a new blow against Liberation Theology—others, probably more astute, say just the opposite, that John Paul transferred the outspoken Lopez Trujillo in order to remove him as a problem for the other Latin American bishops.

Either way, Lopez Trujillo's exceptional energy was applied to the pope's pro-family agenda. He began pushing bishops to promote political policies to keep families together, including regulated working hours, housing assistance, and tax incentives. At John Paul's direction, Lopez Trujillo pushed for more vigorous campaigns against birth control and abortion in Europe and North America and against child prostitution in Asia. He authorized scientific studies of devices to make the rhythm method more effective, including temperature-measuring wrist straps and tests of urine, saliva, and even armpit sweat to enable women to determine their fertile periods more precisely.[8]

---

* Silvestrini is still mentioned as a candidate to succeed John Paul. In reply to my request for an interview, he asked for, and I supplied, a letter outlining the information I was after. He then wrote to invite me in. It was a mysterious visit. I arrived at the assigned time and after waiting for an hour and ten minutes was welcomed into his office. Then, in response to every question, he politely said he never answered questions for journalists because "our task is confidential." After half a dozen tries, I gave up and left.

In the same round of late 1990 staff changes, Archbishop Marcinkus left the Vatican bank and retired to Phoenix. He told the Catholic News Service in an interview, "There is no way I can get away from it [the IOR scandal]. It is like the scarlet letter you carry around with you all the time. I sometimes felt I was a pariah, a leper."

The 1990s also brought signs that Ratzinger wasn't the papal alter ego some assumed he was. He took several stands that the pope didn't back him up on— as when he publicly suggested reconsidering the Vatican II decision that priests should face their congregations during Mass.[9] Ratzinger's attempt to quietly deny Archbishop Weakland of Milwaukee an honorary degree from Fribourg University in Switzerland backfired. Weakland hadn't been accused of any doctrinal error, and Fribourg's faculty raised a public outcry, prompting an embarrassing Vatican apology to Weakland. "Friends tell me the pope was upset at the way this was handled," Weakland says, though he says neither he nor the pope ever mentioned it in their conversations afterward.[10]

Ratzinger even questioned the use of the sainthood process by John Paul, who in his first ten years beatified more than half again as many potential saints as all previous twentieth-century popes combined (123 to 79, by the most authoritative account).[11] John Paul had raced past Paul VI in canonizing actual saints and was closing in on the previous leader, Pius XII, who had been in office twice as long.

Although never called on to explain this, John Paul clearly wanted to recognize local heroes during his many travels, so people everywhere would feel they were part of the Church. Also, as noted elsewhere, he made political statements by his selection of whom to honor.

For example, when Spain's new Socialist government removed religious classes from public schools and legalized abortion in extreme cases, the pope tried but failed to persuade the Spanish prime minister to back down. Two days after their meeting, John Paul retaliated by resuming the sainthood process for Catholics who had died fighting on the side of the Fascist General Franco in the Spanish Civil War of the 1930s. (Paul VI had halted the sainthood process for these Catholics because it seemed to him to glorify fascism.)[12] Many Spaniards were insulted by John Paul's action.

A more general problem was that since every saint is given a day, the Church calendar was becoming crowded. With about four hundred canonized saints (121 just from 1900 to 1989), there was already overlapping.

Ratzinger first challenged this trend in April 1989, responding to a question after a speech near Milan. He said John Paul had advanced some candidates "who perhaps mean something to a certain group of people, but do not mean a great deal to the multitude of believers." Later, he told an interviewer that the increase in sainthoods was "a problem that now gradually must be confronted," adding, "It seems legitimate to me to ask whether the standards generally in effect until now" should be tightened.[13]

Far from accepting Ratzinger's advice, John Paul only stepped up his pace: by 1996 he had canonized 276 saints—about two thirds as many as all his predecessors combined—and beatified 760.[14] But Ratzinger never seemed to fall out of favor as the pope's favorite companion among the cardinals.

5

Iraq, a Soviet-armed military dictatorship, and Kuwait, a monarchical dictatorship allied with the United States, both claimed rights to a major oil field along their shared border. After months of tension, on August 2, 1990, Iraqi troops surprised and overran Kuwait. In the crisis that followed, John Paul took another step toward formalizing his new doctrine, drastically restricting, if not ending, Augustine's notion of a "just war."

As the $28-billion-a-year CIA had failed to prepare the American President for the end of communism, it also failed to prepare him for a military crisis in the Persian Gulf. Bush didn't react strongly at first to Iraq's invasion. But he happened to meet soon afterward with Prime Minister Thatcher of Britain, who gave him what an aide of hers called "a backbone transplant."

Bush then startled his own military staff by announcing that the invasion "will not stand." He began a huge deployment of allied forces in neighboring Saudi Arabia to roll the invasion back—three quarters of a million troops. Whatever his mission against Iraq, Bush also clearly aimed to display the force America could deliver, and the uses to which it might be put, in the post-communist world. He began talking about the "new world order" he wanted to establish.

From the first sign of troops, the Vatican tried to discourage an American attack on Iraq. Its statements were worded so strongly against the United States that some observers thought the pope was siding with Saddam Hussein, the Iraqi dictator, even though Saddam's seizure of Kuwait was also condemned in the Vatican statements. The Arab League later thanked the pope for his efforts to forestall a U.S. attack.[1]

Some on the American side accused the pope of toadying to the Moslems, in whose countries he wanted permission to evangelize. Iraq itself had been one third Catholic a century before; all but six hundred thousand Catholics had left under hardening Islamic rule. The Vatican's Council for Interreligious Dialogue acknowledges that it is preoccupied with Islam. Bishop Michael M. Fitzgerald, Cardinal Arinze's deputy there, says visiting bishops often "complain we pay too much attention to Islam when there are Hindu, Taoists, Buddhists, and so forth. The most attention is paid to Islam because it is a world presence, and others are largely confined."

John Paul challenged the American claim that an attack on Iraq would be a just war. Innocent people and the environment would suffer greatly, he said.

> The needs of humanity today require us to proceed resolutely toward the absolute banning of war and the cultivation of peace as a supreme good to which all programs and strategies must be subordinated.

Nevertheless, after a month of heavy bombing and missile attacks, the United States and its allies launched a scorched-earth ground invasion of Iraq February 24, 1991. In a four-day, overwhelming U.S./allied victory, an estimated hundred thousand soldiers in the conscript Iraqi army were slain. Unprecedented television coverage largely controlled by the Pentagon alerted the world to the breathtaking accuracy of America's missiles and the devastation of its firepower (though it later appeared that the Pentagon had exaggerated the success of its technology). Reliable casualty figures weren't released, a fact that the Vatican still stressed years later. "Perhaps the governments are silent because the war was a tremendous, pointless slaughter," commented the semiofficial Jesuit magazine *Civil Catholica.*

The Vatican's strongest statements about the war came in articles that continued to run for nearly a year in *Civil Catholica.* Its editor, Father Gianpaolo Salvini, says "every page" was combed in advance by the secretary of state's office to ensure that it was what the pope wanted to be said. U.S. officials protested the articles loudly at the Vatican, but to no avail.[2] Some quotes:

> With violence, everyone knows how it begins but not how it ends.... The liberation of Kuwait was purchased at the price of destroying a country and killing hundreds of thousands of people. At this point can we talk about a "just war"? Shouldn't we say instead that "just wars" can't exist because even when just causes come into play, the harm wars do by their very nature is so grave and horrendous that they can never be justified in the forum of conscience? This is all the more true ... because there are always peaceful mechanisms for settling conflicts so long as one has the will and patience to make use of them....

The declaration that war is the extreme [recourse] is often really an attempt to justify one's own wish to make war.... Most of the time the "just cause" serves as a legal and moral pretext for a war meant to be waged for reasons far different from the official ones.

The Vatican officials who published this were well aware that the United States government referred to its recent invasion of Panama as "Operation Just Cause."

Except in self-defense, the *Civil Catholica* articles said, "there are no just wars" and no "right to wage war." When the harm of war outweighs the injustice provoking it, "one can be obliged to suffer the injustice." Although written in the pope's usual style of not quite naming names, the articles strongly implied that the U.S. attack on Iraq was a matter not of

> defense, but [of] the annihilation pure and simple of all human life within the war zone. This is not permitted for any reason whatsoever.
>
> Apart from being immoral, war today is useless and harmful. Not only does war not resolve—except momentarily and speciously—the problems that triggered it ... it aggravates them, making solution impossible.... Thus the seed of World War II was the "peace" of Versailles, which ended World War I. In reality, war almost never ends with a true peace. It always leaves behind it a trail of hatred and the longing to get even—feelings that will explode the moment a suitable opportunity arises.[3]

The pope had long argued that cost of weaponry was indirectly borne by the world's poor, and *Civil Catholica* even printed a cost list of U.S. weapons in the war, from $8.3 million tanks to $108 million Stealth bombers. After the war, Bush visited John Paul, saying he wanted to offer "homage to the highest moral authority." His statements implied an alliance with the pope such as Reagan had claimed. But the Vatican says the pope held his ground on Iraq.[4]

In 1993, John Paul sent Cardinal Silvestrini to Baghdad to try to improve relations. But when Silvestrini suggested that Iraq make peace with Israel, he was brusquely sent home and ridiculed in the government-controlled press. Still, John Paul continued to pray publicly for the U.S. to end its economic sanctions against Iraq and America's other main Moslem enemy, Muammar Qaddafi of Libya.

The pope himself in 1993 visited Sudan, whose militant Islamic dictatorship, representing the north of the country, was feeling growing international pressure to stop its bloody repression of Christians and animists in the south.

Civil war had raged on and off for decades. The government apparently hoped a papal trip would relieve the international pressure without requiring any substantive concessions. After the visit, it continued to make life difficult for Church schools, clergy, and aid agencies.

But Christians began to assert themselves, and later credited John Paul with raising their visibility and legitimacy. At first, fighting persisted. But early in 1994, a Sudanese Islamic leader, Hassan Turabi, met with John Paul at the Vatican.[5] Peace talks and a ceasefire followed.

The pope's 1991 encyclical *Redemptoris Missio* ("The Mission of the Redeemer") had tried to define the Church's relationship with Islam and other religions, suggesting that "interreligious dialogue is part of the Church evangelizing mission." But the pope encountered negative reactions on all sides. Other religions feared the Church wanted to steal their members, while many Catholics felt that evenhanded dialogue contradicted the obligation to promote the one true faith.

6

In his scheduled 1991 economics encyclical, *Centesimus Annus* ("On the Hundredth Anniversary," referring to Pope Leo XIII's *Rerum Novarum* in 1891), John Paul, without changing his position, indulged some American Catholics who advocated uninhibited free markets. These commentators had complained that his earlier encyclicals ignored the benefits of capitalism.

His generosity backfired. As soon as *Centesimus Annus* was published, some free-market advocates began quoting the pro-capitalist passages out of context, making it appear that the pope had turned in their direction when he hadn't. The single most quoted line was, "On the level of individual nations and of international relations, the free market is the most efficient instrument for utilizing resources and effectively responding to needs." Usually *not* quoted was the very next sentence, and what followed it:

> But this is true only for those needs which are "solvent," insofar as they are endowed with purchasing power, and for those resources that are "marketable," insofar as they are capable of obtaining a satisfactory price. But there are many human needs that find no place on the market. It is a strict duty of justice and truth not to allow fundamental human needs to remain unsatisfied.

From there, John Paul began an argument that resulted, two paragraphs later, in exactly what the free-marketers did not want to hear, or quote:

> It is right to speak of a struggle against an economic system, if the latter is understood as a method of upholding the absolute predominance of capital.... In the struggle against such a system, what is being proposed as an alternative is not the socialist system, which in fact turns out to be state capitalism, but rather a society of free work, of enterprise, and of participation. Such a society is not directed against the market, but demands that the market be appropriately controlled by the forces of society and by the state, so as to guarantee that the basic needs of the whole of society are satisfied.
>
> The Church acknowledges the legitimate role of profit as an indication that a business is functioning well. When a firm makes a profit, this means that productive factors have been properly employed.... But profitability is not the only indicator of a firm's condition. It is possible for the financial accounts to be in order, and yet for the people—who make up the firm's most valuable asset—to be humiliated and their dignity offended.... In fact, the purpose of a business firm is not simply to make a profit, but is to be found in its very existence as a community of persons who in various ways are endeavoring to satisfy their basic needs, and who form a particular group at the service of the whole of society. Profit is a regulator of the life of a business, but it is not the only one; other human and moral factors ... are at least equally important for the life of a business....
>
> It is unacceptable to say that the defeat of so-called "Real Socialism" leaves capitalism as the only model of economic organization.

Some free-market advocates who have quoted the encyclical out of context have also suggested in public that they were responsible for changing John Paul's mind—and even that they helped him draft the encyclical. According to a senior Vatican aide intimately involved in editing and publishing the encyclical, who didn't want to be quoted by name, it was drafted in John Paul's own handwriting and was not intended to contradict or change anything he had said in the past. Rather, the pope meant to apply his continuing message to the new situation created by the fall of communism. And he expressly wished to depict the defeat of communism as a victory for the human spirit, not as a victory of one group or philosophy over another.

A second passage from *Centesimus Annus* that is frequently quoted out of context in the West is:

> By intervening directly and depriving society of its responsibility, the social-assistance state leads to a loss of human energies and an inordinate increase in public agencies, which are dominated more by bureaucratic ways of thinking than by concern for serving their clients, and which are accompanied by an enormous increase in spending.

Alone, this sentence could be mistaken for part of a Republican Party platform. What usually is *not* quoted is what precedes it:

> Society and the state must ensure wage levels adequate for the maintenance of the worker and his family, including a certain amount for savings. . . .
>
> The state must contribute to the achievement of these goals . . . indirectly . . . by creating favorable conditions for the free exercise of economic activity [and] directly, according to the principle of solidarity, by defending the weakest, by placing certain limits on . . . working conditions, and by ensuring in every case the necessary minimum support for the unemployed worker. . . .
>
> The fact is that many people, perhaps the majority today, do not have the means that would enable them to take their place effectively . . . within a productive system. . . . Thus, if not actually exploited, they are to a great extent marginalized; economic development takes place over their heads. . . .
>
> The activity of a market economy cannot be conducted in a . . . political vacuum.

The state, John Paul wrote, must guarantee individual freedom, private property, a stable currency, and efficient public services. It must also oversee "the exercise of human rights in the economic sector." The next sentence is another that is sometimes quoted out of context: "Primary responsibility in this area belongs not to the state, but to individuals and to the various groups and associations that make up society." But John Paul immediately added,

> This does not mean, however, that the state has no competence in this domain, as is claimed by those who oppose any laws in the eco-

nomic sphere. Rather, the state has a duty to sustain business activities by creating conditions that will ensure job opportunities, by stimulating those activities where they are lacking or by supporting them in moments of crisis.

The state has the further right to intervene when monopolies create delays or obstacles to development.... In exceptional circumstances, the state can ... substitute [for private enterprise] when ... businesses ... are too weak, or just starting, and are not equal to the task at hand....

Economic freedom is only one element of human freedom. When economic freedom becomes autonomous ... it loses its necessary relationship to the human person and ends up alienating and oppressing him.

It is the task of the state to provide for the defense and preservation of common goods, such as the natural and human environments, which cannot be safeguarded simply by market forces....

Here we find a new limit on the market: there are ... important ... collective ... human needs that escape its logic. There are goods that by their very nature cannot and must not be bought or sold. Certainly the mechanisms of the market offer secure advantages.... Nevertheless, these mechanisms carry the risk of an idolatry of the market.

John Paul's warning about the excesses of the welfare state did not mean he thought the welfare state itself should be abolished. Rather, he advocated an enhanced role for the family and for private, nonprofit organizations encouraged by the state. "The first and fundamental structure for human ecology is the family," he wrote.

Here we mean the family founded on marriage, in which the mutual gift of self by husband and wife creates an environment in which children can be born and develop....

It is necessary to go back to seeing the family as the sanctuary of life. The family is indeed sacred: it is the place in which life—the gift of God—can properly be welcomed and protected against the many attacks to which it is exposed.

In this context, John Paul warned, as he had in the past, against overreliance on the state. State interventions must be as brief as possible, to avoid removing permanently from society and business the functions that are properly theirs. . . .

The principle of subsidiarity must be respected: a community of a higher order should not interfere in the internal life of a community of a lower order, depriving the latter of its functions, but rather should support it in case of need and help to coordinate its activity with the activities of the rest of society.

It is in these words that John Paul's friend Rocco Buttiglione finds what is really new in *Centesimus Annus:* the idea of "subsidiarity," a layer of private institutions between the state and the marketplace, comprising families, charities, and other associations that ought to be supported by the state and that should act instead of the state whenever they are up to it. "It is dangerous for the state to try to satisfy all the needs that are not met in the market," paraphrases Buttiglione, who has discussed these ideas with the pope. But "the state should allocate resources to intermediary institutions that can answer" the needs of society.

"Beware!" Buttiglione sums up. "*Centesimus Annus* is not the position of an apologist for capitalism."

Rather, the pope seemed to be the one world leader proclaiming both economic lessons of the twentieth century: on the one hand, that obstructing free markets reduces economic efficiency, and on the other, that any society that makes economic efficiency its primary value becomes miserable.

Archbishop Weakland says that when he saw John Paul after the encyclical came out, the Pope was irritated over distortions in the press, and even departed from his usual calm demeanor to complain about suggestions that he had become purely pro-capitalist.

To his old friends in Poland, however, the encyclical was a sad reminder of the widening gap between the pope and the rest of society. "He hasn't succeeded in making his own people live by this principle," says Halina Bortnowska, his former student and aide. "Walesa said we cannot afford experiments. We must adopt what worked in the West, which is capitalism. But the brutal capitalist approach is not compatible with the Gospel. Jesus didn't tell us to get rich."

"I think the pope couldn't foresee that liberalism [capitalism] would appear that fast in Poland," says his friend Bohdan Cywinski. In perhaps a metaphor for the national experience, Cywinski himself bought a small grain mill in northeast Poland, then promptly lost several fingers trying to operate it.

"Most of the Polish clergy is fascinated with the practical possibilities of liberalism," he says. "Priests want access to radio and the mass media. To own good cars. And they know that their parishioners also want to have them. Priests are not prepared to talk of difficult things. They would find great passages in John Paul's encyclicals."

Returning to Fatima, Portugal, May 13, 1991, to pray on the tenth anniversary of his escape from a would-be assassin, John Paul warned that Europe was being "tempted by a vast, theoretical and practical atheistic movement that appears to seek a new materialistic civilization." Communism was dead. He clearly meant rule of the market.

7

June 1, 1991, John Paul returned to Poland. It was a different place. The population remained in economic pain, but the Church itself had now become the main issue dividing President Walesa and his new political party from the original Solidarity group under Mazowiecki. Mazowiecki's party, the Democratic Union, still controlled Parliament; it wanted pluralistic democracy with Church-state separation. But Walesa and Glemp had made a pact to restore the Church as an effective arm of government, subsidized with tax money. They sought to ban abortion, require public-school students to take Catholic religious classes,[1] and let the Church censor television. Parliament opposed all this.

These weren't the issues Walesa had campaigned on. If he had, he probably would not have won the election. Opinion polls showed that overwhelmingly, the public wanted the Church to be *less* involved in politics. Even Father Jozef Tischner, John Paul's longtime philosophy colleague (and some say his preference for primate over Wyszynski's choice, Glemp), spoke out that Poland was in danger of becoming "a republic of parish priests."[2]

The country was almost as depressed and confused as it had been before John Paul's papacy. It was not, however, united as it was then. On previous trips home, the pope had captured Poland's mood and hopes in his hand; this time, he grasped only air.

Walesa went all out to welcome him, spending $23.8 million in scarce state funds. Traffic was shut down, normal television programming preempted, and 130 train trips diverted to haul visitors from neighboring countries. Yet crowds still fell far below expectations. Chartered buses arrived at Mass sites half empty and returned home spiritless.

The encouragement that had been John Paul's trademark seemed to have curdled into negativism. He berated the crowds for accepting consumerism ("a freedom that enslaves"), and scolded Parliament for not outlawing abortion. What applause he got came mainly from priests.[3] Most telling, however, are the recollections of his former disciples—people who had been uplifted by his visits in 1979, 1983, and 1987, and sustained by his secret exhortations during martial law.

"It was like he had lost touch with the country," says Ewa Kulik, who had carried the pope's messages to the Solidarity underground. "We had so many problems. Instead of even talking about them, he talked about these things we were sick and tired of—abortion. Instead of trying to understand us and teach us, he was wagging his finger: 'Everything that comes from the West is corrupt—liberalism, capitalism, pornography.'"

Adds her husband, former underground Solidarity leader Konrad Bielinski, "Before, when we met friends from abroad, they said, 'He's reactionary.' And we said it's not true, he's very open. But after the last visit, we have come to agree with them; he is a reactionary—or at least very conservative."

"He showed no understanding of the economic suffering of the people under the reforms," says Bohdan Cywinski. Jacek Kuron, Zbigniew Bujak, and even John Paul's old seminary mate Father Malinski felt much the same way. Maria Tarnowska, who as a teenager was counseled through her parents' divorce by John Paul and practically adopted by him, was so distressed by his 1991 visit that she wrote him "a long, long, long letter." She focused on contraception, saying "that some artificial methods, I can't understand why they are so wrong." Her husband, Karol Tarnowski, the pope's student and philosophy disciple, nods in agreement.

Several months later, they met with John Paul in Rome, and "his reaction seemed to be sadness. He said, 'You know, I spent all my life on a concept of the person, and these problems.' I think he believed that he had told everything clearly, and people like us should understand. That if people like us don't believe . . ." Her voice trails off.

Even Halina Kwiatkowska, John Paul's close friend since youth, talks of the 1991 trip with disappointment. Former classmates were invited to Mass in Wadowice, but there was confusion as John Paul hopped among three simultaneous dinners for different groups.

Marcin Przeciszewski, president of the Catholic Press Agency of Poland, says John Paul was distraught that his old circle in Krakow—particularly Mazowiecki, Turowicz, and Wilkanowicz—were at the center of the Democratic Union, a party that aimed to keep the Church from the role it wanted.

"Until 1989, the pope was a symbol of freedom," Przeciszewski says. "After '89, it turned out he was in favor of a very specific vision of a democracy."

His old friend Jacek Wozniakowski says the pope was so saddened by the economic and social program his former Krakow team had adopted "that he felt an urgent need of Church intervention into the moral stamina of the people. And this ran against the feelings of a great many."

John Paul even turned down Turowicz and other *Tygodnik Powszechny* and *Znak* editors when they asked to meet with him during the trip.[4] Turowicz says his group represents the spirit of Vatican II, and accuses the Polish bishops of wanting to "replace Marxist ideology with Christianity. They are against Europe." Turowicz even defends abortion as "a lesser evil" in some circumstances.

When Silesian miners struck in 1992, government pollsters were sent to see what it would take to lure them back to work. Krzysztof Novak, the sociologist in charge, says the results amazed him: "My expectation was that they would say the work is quite dangerous, there is no money, the danger of unemployment. Instead, they talked about the abortion law. That it is our business and our women's business. Uniformly, their first reaction was abortion. That's why the last visit of the pope was not as warm as before."

Katarzyna Mroczkowska-Brand, who bounced on Father Wojtyla's knee as a child and wept with joy at his return to Krakow as pope in 1979, says, "What has made him much more conservative and rigid is that he sees that in the West there is such a decadence of moral standards that if he doesn't hold the rigid line, then everything will fall apart. He's almost going against his own nature because he thinks he should. I think he's going too far, but I think it comes from [his] feeling he has to. He was always open to new ideas. But some people tend to lose that as they age."

8

From the moment Poland led other communist countries into democracy in 1989, the Soviet empire's days were numbered. Gorbachev's ally Eduard Shevardnadze resigned as foreign minister in December 1990, warning that a new dictatorship was coming. Other Gorbachev allies also departed, while forces of reaction to his changes gathered strength. In mid-August 1991, Gorbachev took a seashore vacation pending the signing August 20 of a treaty shifting authority from Moscow to regional centers. His enemies were determined that he wouldn't sign it.

John Paul had returned to Poland August 14 to attend the 1991 World Youth Day in Czetochowa. He urged more than a million young people to build a "common house" for the former Eastern and Western Europe, a house that would respect a "diversity of cultures." He was no doubt thinking of the coming Euro-synod he had announced in Prague in 1990, a pet project designed to build that common house.

From Czestochowa, he went on to Hungary, where he repeated the messages from his Polish trip about abortion, divorce, and Catholic education in public schools. He was woken from sleep in Budapest August 18 with the news that a coup was under way in the USSR, and that Gorbachev was being held at his seaside resort. As the world, and the Soviet people, waited to see whether the coup would succeed, John Paul began working vigorously to support Gorbachev.

He ordered his nuncio back to Moscow from vacation. In a unique public endorsement of a politician, the pope spoke out about Gorbachev's "sincere desire ... and ... lofty inspiration ... in the promotion of human rights and dignity, as well as his commitment to the well-being of his country."

Gorbachev was rescued—but by Boris Yeltsin, the onetime ally whom he had deposed from office after Yeltsin accused him of reforming too slowly. Now Yeltsin took command, aiming to outlaw communism. His life on the line, he stood atop a tank and defied the coup. Hundreds of thousands of citizens filled the streets to support him, putting their bodies in the path of the coup forces.

The army was split, and the coup folded. Statues of Lenin tumbled down. Gorbachev was restored as head of the Soviet Union, but by December, there was no Soviet Union, and Yeltsin led Russia. Gorbachev was literally locked out of his former Kremlin office.

Throughout the 1980s, John Paul had seemed unable to fail. Even such ventures as the multifaith meeting at Assisi, while they didn't bring instant peace, were public-relations triumphs and gave the world something good to think about. Against this backdrop, the collapse of the Euro-synod was an unprecedented fall flat on his face. The synod was to open November 28, 1991, and—John Paul hoped—finally heal the breach between East and West. But that summer, word trickled in that some Orthodox wouldn't attend. Then other churches. When large churches canceled, smaller churches backed out as well.

"Most of the argument was [over] what they considered new missionary activity by Catholics," says Father John Long, head of the Vatican's Russicum school and a major organizer of the affair. The pope's appointment of a

Catholic hierarchy in Russia earlier in the year had especially angered the Russian Orthodox, who had been involved in talks with Cardinal Cassidy at the time and yet weren't warned of the appointments. "The Orthodox thought it was poaching," Father Long says. "It was a major problem."

Cardinal Martini and even the eighty-six-year-old Cardinal König, with their long history of Eastern contacts, were dispatched to Russia to try to save the Euro-synod. In September, Long himself visited Patriarch Alexis in Moscow to encourage him to bring his problems to Rome and talk them out. Nothing worked.

The Euro-synod was widely boycotted. Alexis even went so far as to torment the pope by inviting the archbishop of Canterbury to Moscow while refusing to issue the invitation John Paul had wanted for so long. The Anglicans, too, felt Rome had been high-handed in unity discussions. On his visit to Moscow, their leader seemed to be forging a Christian alliance with the Orthodox, against the pope. The ecumenical initiative was moving in reverse.

Even when his dream of a Euro-synod was destroyed, however, John Paul told Father Long, "We're not going to break off relations with these people. It's something we have to get over." He instructed Long to invite Easterners to Rome to study Catholicism free at the Russicum. Long did, but few accepted the offer. He started preparatory programs inside the Eastern countries instead.

When the Euro-synod was finally staged, Catholics wound up talking mostly to each other. Even then, divisions came to the fore. The Polish objections were long familiar, but now Lithuanians and Hungarians, too, complained that the Church was spending its energy on issues like pornography instead of addressing people's real problems.[1]

Longing, perhaps, for some bit of progress amid the disasters, John Paul chose that month—November 1991—to move quickly and secretly to establish relations with Israel. When the new Israeli ambassador to Italy arrived, he got a surprise lunch invitation from the Italian ambassador to the Vatican. A senior Vatican diplomat also turned up and proposed formal talks to settle differences and exchange diplomats.[2]

But here, again, mere wishes couldn't topple old stumbling blocks. The Vatican wouldn't recognize countries with unsettled borders. Only after Israel and the Palestine Liberation Organization made peace at the White House September 13, 1993, did Israel and the Vatican, three months later, at last recognize each other.

John Paul's eagerness to speed the Catholic evangelization of Russia had wrecked his Euro-synod. Suddenly, the master maneuverer seemed to be a bull in a china shop. The next glass to shatter was post-communist Yugoslavia, several of whose regions had declared independence and sought international recognition. Civil wars raged as the central government fought to keep the country together. The United States also tried to keep Yugoslavia in one piece—for peace.

January 13, 1992, the pope recognized Croatia and Slovenia, two predominantly Catholic regions, as having seceded from Yugoslavia, which was dominated by Orthodox Serbs. Although the Vatican says other European states had indicated that they, too, would recognize Croatia and Slovenia, only Germany had actually done so. The Vatican sent a note to the Yugoslav government denying that the recognition of the breakaway states was "a hostile act," but it could hardly have been perceived otherwise. Yugoslavia called it "a flagrant violation of the principles and provisions of international law."

Bosnia and Herzegovina was in the middle of Yugoslavia both geographically and politically—a mix of Moslems, Catholics, and Orthodox. When Croatia and Slovenia split off, it declared its own independence. Irate Serbs, both from what remained of Yugoslavia and from within Bosnia and Herzegovina itself, then began slaughtering other ethnic groups in a grisly crusade that became known as "ethnic cleansing."

To be sure, the local hatreds, and the use of violence in pursuing them, had long preceded John Paul's papacy and his decision to recognize the independence of Catholic parts of the country. But the Serbian Orthodox patriarch, Pavel, declared that "the origin of the conflict in Yugoslavia and the Balkans . . . is the insistence with which the Church of Rome considers the Balkans, which are inhabited mainly by people of Orthodox religion, as missionary territory." He dusted off old complaints that Catholics had persecuted Serbs in World War II, and predicted it would happen again in an independent Croatia.

Distorted and self-serving as Pavel's statement no doubt was, the pope had inadvertently given him cause. The Vatican justified its recognition of Croatia partly on the ground that Catholics had been attacked there. But each retaliation only led to another. War spread. Orthodox Serbs attacked Catholic churches. Croatian Catholics helped kill Moslems in Bosnia. Everywhere, innocent civilians predominated among the dead.

John Paul soon begged for European countries and the United Nations to "intervene" to "stop the hand of the aggressor" and "disarm those who would kill." The statements evoked inquiries about war doctrine, to which Ratzinger replied that the issue needed further study. The Vatican now says the pope has never condoned military force, but by what other means the Serbs could be disarmed is hard to imagine.[3]

Another doctrinal problem was presented by the Serbs' decision to make rape a conscious strategy of war. Their aim was not just to create terror but to populate the territory with Serbian-fathered children. The pope begged rape victims not to have abortions, and offered maternity care. At the same time, he issued a dispensation for nuns and other women in the war areas to use contraceptives, on the ground that the evil being prohibited was not contraception itself, but rather sexual intent without openness to children. (Pope Paul's birth-control encyclical allowed contraceptive pills for noncontraceptive medical reasons.)

It was hard to argue with the Orthodox archbishop of Zagreb, Croatia, when he asserted that the pope had lost all the ecumenical ground gained under Popes John XXIII and Paul VI. The Holy Synod of the Greek Orthodox Church accused John Paul of "deceit." The University of Athens theology faculty charged him with "treachery." The Russian Parliament forbade non-Russians—clearly meaning Catholics—to engage in "missionary, publishing, or propaganda activities." The government of Belorus claimed the Vatican had wildly exaggerated the number of Catholics there—in other words, the country was Orthodox and didn't want clergy from Rome.

As if all of this were not trouble enough, the Dutch problem flared up again. John Paul's unpopular bishop, Joannes Gijsen, made sweeping changes in the schools of his diocese, thus implying that other bishops' schools were inadequately Catholic. Dozens of Gijsen's own schools rebelled against his new rules. His intention, like the pope's, had been to establish uniformity; the result was chaos.

Next was Switzerland, where John Paul had decided to phase out the ancient tradition that allowed dioceses to approve their own bishops. A firestorm erupted when the chief bishop of Chur suddenly resigned and the Vatican appointed his new and unpopular auxiliary bishop, Wolfgang Haas, to take over. The president of the Swiss Bishops' Conference, Joseph Candolfi, met with John Paul and later said he told the pope that Bishop Haas couldn't stay if he wasn't liked. The pope's reply was not related, but Chur got downright churlish.

Local priests voted 133 to 4 that "confidence in the bishop...has been completely destroyed," and that Bishop Haas was "in our opinion, not the...rightful bishop of Chur." Haas plunged ahead anyway, canceling a popular program that permitted lay men and women to study in the seminary without becoming priests, and vetoing the faculty's choice of a new rector. Three Swiss bishops now visited John Paul, begging him to remove Bishop Haas. In 1993, John Paul finally gave in and appointed two other, popular bishops to assist Haas. The new men got ovations at their installation ceremony.

Across the ocean, Colombia, 95 percent Catholic, voided its hundred-year-old treaty with the Vatican. Civil law was given authority where Church law had broken down. Nearly half of all marriages split up, and unmarried couples were cohabiting because they couldn't get divorces. Abortion was already legal.

All these insults and defeats hurt. When *Tygodnik Powszechny* ran an open debate on allowing exceptions to the abortion ban, John Paul blew up and had Turowicz thrown off the board of the John Paul II Foundation, which distributes research grants.[4] Turowicz, who in 1978 had been called John Paul's best friend, was so angry at him by 1994 that he disclaimed any memory of the pope's support for him under communism.[5]

The pope's inclination to put Church discipline ahead of other concerns also got him on the wrong side of a political tragedy in Haiti. As noted earlier, he had helped push out the father and son dictators named Duvalier, who had ruled Haiti from 1957 to 1986. The popular leader who then emerged under democracy was a charismatic priest, Jean-Bertrand Aristide, who had founded what was called the "Parish of the Poor."

The Haitian Church hierarchy had never liked Aristide, and when his supporters turned violent in the 1980s, he was repudiated and thrown out of his religious order. In 1990, his victory in the first post-Duvalier presidential election split the government from the bishops. After a year, he was overthrown by a coup with ties to the old regime. Aristide fled to the U.S., which continued to recognize him as president, as did the Organization of American States. John Paul's Holy See, alone among governments, recognized the military dictatorship.

Even as murders and human-rights violations mounted, and the UN voted to impose economic sanctions, the pope wouldn't bend on Haiti. He ignored the pleas of thousands of Haitian Catholics, including a substantial minority of bishops. In public, at least, Aristide appeared humble. He said he still respected and loved the pope and the Church, because it was wrong to "love only those who love you."

Westerners increasingly regarded John Paul as a curmudgeon who had outlived his usefulness. He refused to pay them mind. Skiing at age seventy-two in February 1992, he said the slopes chosen for him were too easy, and spent four hours on "moderate" slopes instead. He visited several Moslem countries in Africa.

In Angola, he talked about the shared values of Catholicism and animism, the dominant religions. The U.S. ambassador described the atmosphere as "carnival-like"[6] when the pope warmly greeted Angolan President José Eduardo dos Santos, who would soon be reelected after withstanding fifteen years of American-backed war against his government.[7] Flying home, John Paul told reporters,

> Sometimes the question is asked, "Why does the pope always go back to Africa?" Sometimes, perhaps, we Westerners, whose lives are based so much on scientific and technological process, distance ourselves from values [that are] primitive, yes, but fundamental. Try to reflect a little on this.

Back in Rome, John Paul tried to reward Opus Dei, which had stuck with him through his trials, with a festive ceremony in St. Peter's Square May 17, 1992, to beatify Monsignor Escrivá, the Opus Dei founder. But the pope just sparked another controversy: only seventeen years had passed since Escrivá's death. "Indecent haste—it was vulgar," says Monsignor George Higgins, a prominent Catholic University professor, echoing the thoughts of many around the world. Kenneth Woodward, *Newsweek*'s veteran religion editor and author of a 1990 book on sainthood, said, "It seemed as if the whole thing was rigged. They [Opus Dei] were given priority, and the whole thing was rushed through."[8]

Archbishop Re, the *sostituto*, insists "the process was completely ordinary." Apparently, though, John Paul himself had some qualms: Re says the Pope took time to double-check with the Congregation for Saints, which "assured him" it could act fast "because of the reform of procedures." Archbishop Re acknowledges that "some were against it."

America, a prominent Jesuit magazine, ran a long article quoting disenchanted former Opus Dei members, who described a secrecy so paranoid that lecture notes had to be taken in code in case outsiders found them. Recruitment was described as a hustle. "They tell you it's a decision you have to make now, that if you don't take it, you're not going to have God's grace for the remainder of your life," said one former member. Negative publicity about Opus Dei accelerated.

Then, on top of the pope's other problems, came abdominal pain and indigestion.

9

July 12, 1992, John Paul concluded his Sunday public prayer by announcing that he was going into the hospital that night. Three days later, surgeons at the Polyclinic—Gemelli—the hospital where he had recovered from the assassination attempt in 1981—removed a tumor the size of an orange from his lower intestine. Rumors swept the world that he was dying of cancer. At first it was announced that the tumor was benign, later that it was in the process of turning cancerous but had not spread. He left Gemelli after sixteen days to recuperate at Castelgandolfo.

In the ensuing years, he suffered recurrent digestive illnesses, each time triggering cancer rumors, each time denied. American churchmen complained, as they had in 1981, that he wasn't getting the best care, and that the tumor should have been caught earlier.[1] Dr. Crucitti, who tended to him in both crises, insists the care was "at a very high level. It's very difficult to take care of him because the pope won't tell you of his disturbances if he's feeling ill. He refused certain checkups. I know that [John Paul's regular physician] has wanted certain tests done that the pope refused."

John Paul still balanced science and faith in his own life as he did in Church policy: faith came first. Even his admission of Church error in the Galileo case—finally released in October 1992, after thirteen years' study—seemed reluctant. Galileo, knowing his findings needed to be integrated into "the culture of the time," could have presented them with less assuredness, as a mere hypothesis, the pope said. In the end, though, he declared that "Galileo, a sincere believer, showed himself to be more perceptive . . . than the theologians who opposed him." John Paul even said the Church might have been wrong in totally rejecting "modernism" at the turn of the century.

The worst part of the Galileo error, he wrote, was that it

> helped to anchor a number of scientists of good faith in the idea that there was an incompatibility between the spirit of science and its rules of research on the one hand, and the Christian faith on the other . . . a tragic mutual incomprehension. . . .
>
> The Bible does not concern itself with the details of the physical world, the understanding of which is the competence of human experience and reasoning. There exist two realms of knowledge, one that has its source in Revelation and one that reason can discover by its own power. . . . The distinction between the two . . . ought not to be understood as opposition. The methodologies proper to each make it possible to bring out different aspects of reality.

For their third big conference, the Latin American bishops chose October 1992 and the Dominican Republic to commemorate Columbus's landing there five hundred years earlier. John Paul blocked proposals for a critical re-examination of the Spanish and Portuguese colonization of the continent. Opening the conference, he made clear that he wanted a celebration, not a re-appraisal. Yes, he said, colonization had entailed injustice, but with Christianity, the European conquerers had brought "more light than shadows."

Compared to the contentious air at the earlier meetings in Medellin and Puebla, the atmosphere at Santo Domingo was subdued. New rules discouraged any challenges to Rome. Invitations were no longer proportional to population, which reduced the influence of the fiery Brazilian Episcopate. Representation from religious orders was restricted, keeping away the best-known advocates of Liberation Theology.

Father Gustavo Gutierrez, who coined the term Liberation Theology, and who still packed lecture halls in Europe, was kept away from Santo Domingo. Leonardo Boff even resigned from the Franciscan order, saying he wanted "to continue work in which I was being severely hampered.... Doctrinal power is cruel and merciless.... Before I become bitter, before I see the human bases of Christian faith and hope destroyed in me . . . I prefer to change course."[2]

Ignoring these efforts to control them, the bishops voted down the draft statements the Vatican had prepared, complaining that the drafts were bland, and the system authoritarian. The statement the Vatican ultimately released was unmemorable.[3]

John Paul seemed to grow less compromising as he became more embattled. When cancer forced Archbishop May of St. Louis to retire, the pope rejected multiple replacements proposed by the St. Louis and American hierarchies. After more than a year, he finally filled the job with an outsider, Archbishop Justin Rigali. Although born in Los Angeles, the fifty-seven-year-old Rigali had spent his career at the Vatican, five years of it as Cardinal Gantin's deputy at the Congregation for Bishops.

Many U.S. bishops objected to Rigali's appointment in St. Louis on the ground that he lacked sufficient pastoral experience.[4] James Hitchcock, a history professor at St. Louis University, a Catholic school, saw it as a sign that the pope was toughening up (which Hitchcock applauds). Previously, he says, John Paul had appointed "people who are personally conservative" but "very leery of causing controversy." Not so Rigali.[5]

When the Anglican Church synod voted to allow the ordination of women in November 1992, the Vatican declared, "This decision of the Church of England constitutes a new and grave obstacle to the entire process of reconciliation." Some Anglican vicars also objected and vowed to become Catholic, but the Vatican quickly discouraged any one-issue conversions.

Three weeks later, American bishops, after nine years of disagreement, voted to discontinue work on a pastoral letter on the role of women in society and the Church. The reasons for their failure were illustrated by an unusual back-and-forth between Archbishop Weakland and Cardinal O'Connor in their respective diocesan newsletters. Weakland had wanted the door on ordination of women left open a crack for "further study, debate and reflection." In escalating responses, Cardinal O'Connor favored the ban, though he expected "years and years of confrontation."

The German Bishops' Conference released a poll showing that German Catholic women rejected Church teachings on contraception, divorce, and celibacy. Two thirds wanted exceptions to the abortion ban, and half thought abortion should be legal. Only 25 percent felt "close" to the Church, down from 40 percent in 1982.[6]

A *Time* magazine/CNN poll in the United States said that only 14 percent of U.S. Catholics felt bound to the Vatican's moral teachings; most thought such matters were their own business.[7] Ninety percent of young Catholics surveyed in a Gallup poll felt the same way. The poll showed two thirds of all American Catholics thought women should be in the priesthood.

John Paul read it all, and did not waver. Cardinal Bernardin, visiting Rome, complimented the pope on how well he looked so soon after major surgery. "You seem to have made a full recovery!" Bernardin beamed.

"Some people wish I hadn't," the pope replied wryly.

He took heart visiting Albania, then a blessedly peaceful and Serb-free corner of the Balkans that seemed to be putting its communist past behind it. Crowds of more than half a million jammed his Masses. "I never saw him smiling more spontaneously," says an American monsignor who accompanied him.[8]

He also released the new Catholic catechism, twelve years after ordering it. It reaffirmed all the traditional rules; Ratzinger praised it as "a unified and organized vision of faith." Cardinal Oddi—whom the pope had originally assigned the task of compiling the catechism, but who had long since retired—thought it was too complicated and, at 1,350 pages, too long. "I wanted something you could give to boys in school," he complains.

The catechism identified some new sins: tax evasion, drunk driving, drug abuse, paying unfair salaries, cornering the market on commodities, and genetic engineering. It also exempted poor people from being charged with theft "when the only way of meeting immediate and essential needs is to use goods belonging to others."

10

One result of maintaining celibacy for priests amid the sexual revolution in the West was that the priesthood attracted some men with sexual adjustment problems. Some were latent homosexuals raised in a religion that condemned homosexual behavior. Although a small minority, more than a few were so deviate as to crave sex with children or young teenagers.

Until recently, the hierarchy had hidden this problem. But the United States was now a hotbed for lawyers, social workers, and psychotherapists bent on finding someone to blame for their clients' problems. Accusations of sexual abuse of minors abounded, many accurate, many not, but all tragic. The Church became a common target for lawsuits, particularly by young men recalling events from their school days. Declaring that the priesthood had become "a haven for homosexuals," Father Richard McBrien, a theology professor at Notre Dame, observed, "Bishops are caught in the middle and running scared. Instead of discussing holy days . . . bishops should raise hell about this on the floor of their conferences."

In 1992, a young Catholic journalist, Jason Berry, published *Lead Us Not into Temptation: Catholic Priests and the Sexual Abuse of Children.*[1] His book detailed case after case, not just of priests who admitted to abusing children, but also of bishops' reassigning such priests to other dioceses, even after criminal convictions, allowing the crimes to be repeated.

Although the evidence piled up, statistics were hard to come by. For years, Berry learned, the Vatican embassy in Washington had received reports almost every week of another priest who had molested children, often altar boys. When a priest was guilty, he usually had preyed on multiple victims. The Church had paid about $400 million in legal settlements in such cases. Many culprits were allowed to stay in the priesthood, provided that they agreed to take a drug called Depo-Provera—a female contraceptive that suppresses the male sex urge—and avoid being alone with minors.

Berry's book named priests who had seduced grade-school boys, videotaped their sex acts, and even submitted the tapes for commercial reproduction and sale. The photos were proof of the acts. But on their discovery, these cases had been covered up by bishops, and even prosecutors, disinclined to take on the Church. On the other hand, Berry's book also showed how dangerous it was to accept unproven accusations. He described cases in which such high Church figures as Papal Nuncio Laghi in Washington and Cardinal Bernardin in Chicago had been criticized by the parents of self-described victims for permitting priests to remain in their parishes while complaints were being investigated. In each case, independent authorities determined that the allegations were unfounded, and that the accusers themselves were suspect.

Rome had remained silent on the problem, as had most American clergy. But in 1993, events escaped control. In March, the popular TV show *Sixty Minutes* revealed accusations by five women that Archbishop Robert F. Sanchez of Santa Fe, New Mexico—until recently the secretary of the U.S. Bishops' Conference—had seduced them repeatedly, several from the time they were teenagers. Sanchez resigned.

Instinctively, as in the bank scandals, John Paul saw the publicity as more damaging than the crime. He urged prayers for "our brother from Santa Fe" and "for the persons affected by his actions." He warned that

> a person's fall, which in itself is a painful experience, should not become a matter for sensationalism. Unfortunately, however, sensationalism has become the particular style of our age. In contrast, the spirit of the Gospel is one of compassion, with Christ's saying, "Go and sin no more."[2]

True to his fears, the case opened the floodgates for reports of current and past allegations all over the country. Most involved sexual abuse of boys, with twelve lawsuits in Santa Fe alone being brought against seven of Archbishop Sanchez's priests. It turned out that priests with a history of abuse elsewhere had been sent to a treatment center in Sante Fe. In thirty years, forty priests had abused an estimated two hundred boys. Eleven religious brothers at a Santa Fe seminary had seduced thirty-four boys aged seven to sixteen. Before the year was out, the archdiocese faced bankruptcy over the resultant lawsuits.

Father Thomas Doyle, a canon lawyer studying sex abuse by clergy, estimated that three thousand of the fifty thousand U.S. priests had seduced minors. Other estimates roughly concurred.[3] If these figures were exaggerated, as the Vatican suspected, the problem was no less real.[4] The U.S. hierarchy went from covering up to taking cover. Cardinal O'Connor observed in a speech, "It's getting increasingly difficult for some priests and some bishops to hold their heads up. Everyone is under suspicion."[5]

A delegation of U.S. bishops headed by Cardinal Bevilacqua went to Rome seeking the right to make "summary judgments" to remove priests accused of pedophilia. John Paul turned them down, saying, "My dear bishops, I lived all those years under communism. I am not about to have that come into the Church." The bishops protested that the rash of damage suits threatened financial disaster. He told them to keep priests on their payrolls even if they were suspended from duty. "You'll get no quick fixes out of me," he added.[6]

The pope wrote a public letter to the U.S. bishops. It acknowledged pain for "the little . . . victims" but stressed the need for compassion to help the guilty priests "be reconciled and find peace of conscience." It asserted that the penalties in canon law for such transgressions were "fully justified," but didn't refer to criminal penalties. Instead—as in the case of every scandal John Paul had encountered—his emphasis was on shielding the faithful from information that might throw doubt on the Church.

Many parents and victims had praised the press for prodding the Church to stop the abuses. Not John Paul:

> While acknowledging the right to due freedom of information, one cannot acquiesce in treating moral evil as an occasion for sensationalism. . . . The mass media play a particular role. Sensationalism leads to the loss of something essential to the morality of society. Harm is done to the fundamental right of individuals not to be easily exposed to the ridicule of public opinion. Even more, a distorted image of human life is created.

He told the bishops to worry not just about justice in particular cases, but about "the whole of society systematically threatened by scandal."

Neither he nor his bishops, however, could keep the lid on. Church lawyers even argued that the First Amendment's protection of religious freedom shielded the Church from having to disclose how it treated sex offenders. Such obstinacy just made the public angrier. (The case involved a priest with a history of sex abuse, who was sent to Poughkeepsie, New York, put in charge of a youth group, and pleaded guilty to molesting a boy of sixteen.) The New York Times said the U.S. Church had paid a billion dollars in damages and still faced two thousand lawsuits; the Church called these figures exaggerations, but agreed the numbers were very large.[7]

The wave of litigation soon engulfed Cardinal Bernardin himself. A thirty-four-year-old drug counselor sought $10 million in damages, saying Bernardin and another priest had sexually abused him during a high school program for potential priests. Bernardin maintained his innocence. After eighteen months of torture by lawyers and headline writers, the charges were discredited and withdrawn. Bernardin then forgave and prayed with his emotionally unbalanced former accuser.

In his case, the tragedy produced a dividend: a reknitting of Bernardin's frayed brotherhood with the pope. John Paul welcomed Bernardin privately in Rome and stood by him throughout the ordeal.

Elsewhere, however, the charges—true or false—rarely had such happy endings. And the scandal spread. In Ireland, a TV documentary shined the spotlight on a priest with a forty-year history of abusing minors. Superiors who had learned of his crimes had simply transferred him to new assignments and fought all attempts to bring him to justice. Also in Ireland, a monsignor pleaded guilty to raping an eighteen-year-old; a monk pleaded guilty to having sex with three eleven-year-old girls; and a priest was convicted of raping six boys, all under the age of twelve.[8] A bishop resigned after admitting he'd fathered a child.

Most embarrassing was Austria, where John Paul had angered both the faithful and his own bishops—and insulted his old friend Cardinal König—by promoting the unpopular Hermann Grör to be cardinal/archbishop of Vienna. It was now learned that Cardinal Grör's strict adherence to doctrine ended in the bedroom, where he had frolicked with seminary students. He did not deny the accusations, though he did try to hold on to his office by saying that the allegations were twenty years old. A few weeks later, he resigned.

Amid the controversy, John Paul flew to Denver for World Youth Day in August 1993. The huge gatherings Father Danzi had pioneered were now among the high points of the pope's life. His friend André Frossard said John Paul sought live crowds because he perceived "a bias against him by the media and intellectuals. He never talks of why the American media resists him. He just accepts it. He can't rely on press coverage."

The hundreds of thousands of young people who gathered in Denver obviously loved him. A twenty-year-old German girl told a reporter she relished the positive surroundings because "most people back home don't like the pope. They only see the Church as something bad." To be near these crowds, John Paul tolerated the commercialism, the vendors hawking Styrofoam pope hats for a dollar, the local bar selling "Ale Mary," and companies suing over rights to papal logos.[9]

At one point in Denver, John Paul attacked "the media" for promoting violence, then ad-libbed, "So the pope is speaking against the television that presents him!" The audience cheered his attacks on commercialism and popular culture—a "culture of death," he said, where "objective goodness and evil no longer . . . matter. Good comes to mean what is pleasing or useful at a particular moment. Evil means what contradicts our subjective wishes."

He stood out all the more starkly during a nationally televised exchange with the new President, Bill Clinton. Knowing that Clinton had run on a right-to-abortion platform, the pope challenged him to "defend life" if he really wanted to promote "justice for all and true freedom." He wondered aloud on camera—as he must have wondered to himself many times—whether the Americans who applauded him really wanted to hear his message.

In Clinton, he had found a good foil. Clinton's support for legal abortion was popular, and even his admitted history of adulterous affairs needn't have been scandalous in the right frame; his administration's integrity in administering public funds, if imperfect, was still far more fastidious than that of the Reagan and Bush administrations that preceded it. But Clinton and his wife, a corporate lawyer, projected precisely the concern for efficiency and quick gratification, against a background of profound moral indirection, that John Paul was casting himself against.[10]

Back in Rome, reinvigorated, the pope took his stand.

11

Champions of Catholic theology have called John Paul's 1993 encyclical *Veritatis Splendor* ("The Splendor of Truth") his masterpiece.

The best introduction to it may be his answer to my question about it, passed through Press Secretary Navarro-Valls. The response begins as a quote from the pope, then fades into Navarro-Valls's paraphrase:

> The idea of human dignity is not new. What is new is the way of approaching it. The most important reason for respecting another person is that he is a creature of God. I think that the cornerstone of my pontificate is to explain the transcendental value of the human person. If you believe in God, you cannot behave in the same way as a person who doesn't believe in God.
>
> This is a moment of history in which the identity of the Christian tends to be diluted. The trend of modern society is to make all equal. One example is the temptation of priests in the United States, Europe, and Africa to become social workers—members of humanistic organizations doing nice things for the poor. There is the expression, "You cannot preach God to somebody who is hungry."
>
> To the pope, this is absurd. The key point of religion is salvation, and that is not preached at all. In our age, we are accustomed

to hearing about human rights, but you have the impression sometimes that the United Nations or the United States thinks human
rights is something they graciously gave to the world. This is outside Christianity. A person has rights because that person has something God gave that nobody can take from him, including the
communists. But certainly communism is not the only lie on
humanity. Wild capitalism is another lie, and infidelity between
man and woman is another lie. And that you are in this life just to
be happy is another lie.

Much more than John Paul's overtly political encyclicals, *Veritatis Splendor* is a
religious work. Its main contention is in its opening sentence: truth shines from
God. But in *Veritatis Splendor*, the pope also tried to explain to those who rejected
his ideas why a strong moral code is so important:

Certain currents of modern thought have ... exalted freedom to
such an extent that it becomes an absolute. ... The individual conscience is accorded the status of a supreme tribunal of moral judgment that hands down ... infallible decisions about good and
evil. ... Claims of truth disappear, yielding their place to a criterion
of sincerity, authenticity, and "being at peace with oneself." ...

Such an outlook is quite congenial to an ... ethic wherein each
individual faces his own truth, different from the truth of others.
Taken to its extreme consequences, this individualism leads to a
denial of the very idea of human nature. ...

A new situation has come about within the Christian community, ... the spread of numerous doubts and objections ... with
regard to the Church's moral teachings. It is no longer a matter of
limited and occasional dissent, but of an overall and systematic
calling into question of traditional doctrine on the basis
of ... anthropological and ethical suppositions. At the root of
these suppositions [are] currents of thought that end by detaching
human freedom from its essential ... relationship to truth.

Thus the traditional doctrine regarding ... universal and permanent ... natural law ... is rejected; certain of the Church's moral
teachings are found simply unacceptable. ... The [Church] is considered capable of intervening in matters of morality only ... to
"exhort consciences" and to "propose values," in the light of which
each individual will independently make his or her decisions. ...

The question is asked: Do the commandments of God, which are written on the human heart and are part of the Covenant, really have the capacity to clarify the daily decisions of individuals and entire societies?...

Those who live by the flesh experience God's law as a burden,... a denial or... restriction of their own freedom. On the other hand, those who are impelled by love... and who desire to serve others... feel an interior urge—a genuine necessity and no longer a form of coercion—not to stop at the minimum demands of the Law, but to live them in their fullness....

This vocation to perfect love is not restricted to a small group of individuals. The [Gospel's] invitation to "Go, sell your possessions and give the money to the poor" and the promise "You will have treasure in Heaven" are meant for everyone.

To John Paul, opinion polls, like psychotherapy, were devices frequently used to escape responsibility for doing the right thing. People were "tempted to take as the standard for their discipline... the results of a statistical study" showing what other people did. Others said that biological urges entitled them to satisfy immediate desires; he compared this to "treating the human body as a raw datum, devoid of any meaning."

An entire section under the heading "Conscience and Truth" seemed to be aimed at Western theologians who favored "so-called 'pastoral' solutions contrary to the teaching of the Magisterium." These theologians

stress the complexity [of] the whole sphere of psychology and the emotions, and... the individual's social and cultural environment.... The Church's teaching... prohibiting intrinsically evil acts is... seen as... an intolerable intransigence.... [Against] the enormously complex... situations... in the moral life of individuals... today, this intransigence is said to contrast with the Church's motherhood. The Church, one hears, is lacking in understanding and compassion.

But it was absurd to say that "an individual could... remain faithful to God independent of whether... his... acts are in conformity with specific moral... rules." Referring by title to his own book *The Acting Person*, John Paul said a person's actions define what he stands for.

Answering the many critics who accused him of reversing Vatican II, John Paul quoted the words of the Council:

> The task of authentically interpreting the word of God, whether in its written form or in that of Tradition, has been entrusted only to those charged with the Church's living Magisterium.

While ostensibly speaking up for freedom, *Veritatis Splendor* also displayed the pope's long-standing ambivalence about it:

> Reason and experience not only confirm the weakness of human freedom, they also confirm its tragic aspects. Man comes to realize that his freedom is in some mysterious way inclined to betray [his] openness to the True and the Good. All too often he actually prefers to choose finite, limited, and ephemeral goods.

"Freedom itself needs to be set free," John Paul declared in italics. As in the past, however, he resolved this enigma only by relying less on logic and more on faith in divine revelation:

> Christ reveals, first and foremost, that . . . there can be no freedom apart from or in opposition to the truth. The categorical— unyielding and uncompromising—defense of the absolutely essential demands of man's personal dignity must be considered the way and the condition for the very existence of freedom.

There lay the heart of John Paul's problem. To many, it was a beautiful summation. To others, it was an oxymoron: freedom came with "the condition" of accepting one Church's sometimes changing definition of "the truth." (Beyond the well-worn reminders that the Church once threatened to kill people for teaching that the earth was in orbit, this was also the same pope who endorsed a Vatican statement denying that IOR received money from Roberto Calvi, and who declared he wanted all the facts out about the IOR case even when he was paying lawyers to keep the facts secret.)

Veritatis Splendor comes close to being a modern preface for Thomas Aquinas. Yet like John Paul's other attempts to forge unity, the new encyclical stirred as much dissent as it quelled. Nicholas Lash, a Catholic professor of divinity at Cambridge University, noted that many bishops were among those whom the pope accused of dissent. Yet since Vatican II said the bishops ruled "with and under the pope," those who were scolded "might well have thought that it was *they* who were the magisterium."[1]

The pastor of Wadowice, John Paul's old seminary mate Kazimierz Suder, says he often tries to discuss *Veritatis Splendor* with students, who "question everything, just as in the 1950s. The pope's encyclical is a sort of key for them now, just as his [secretly copied] catechism was for us against the communists back then." But Suder observes a difference: "In the 1950s, the students were always friendly, looking for answers. Now, youth are more aggressive. It's very difficult to make a dialogue."

12

In September 1993, John Paul visited the one part of the former Soviet Union that would have him, the Baltic states: heavily Protestant Estonia, Catholic Lithuania (still 8 percent Polish), and Latvia, a mixture. Economic times in all three were worse even than in Poland, where recovery had finally started. In the Baltics, prices of staples like bread had quadrupled. Without the accustomed Soviet oil subsidy, people lacked heat and hot water. Still, they turned out—in Lithuania, 10 percent of the population—to see the pope.[1]

Western press coverage of John Paul was still misinformed by the story of a "Holy Alliance" between him and Reagan, and by the claim that *Centesimus Annus* had endorsed capitalist rule. Political reporters unfamiliar with his real thoughts were startled by his speech in Riga, Latvia, which produced headlines around the world.

Since Pope Leo XIII, the Church "has always [held] capitalistic ideology . . . responsible for grave social injustices," he said. He denounced "the international imperialism of money,"[2] and said it was the duty of post-communist countries to prevent community and family values from being destroyed by commercial forces.

More sharply than in *Centesimus Annus*, he pointed out that while market-based economies made common sense, it was quite another thing to have "a system in which freedom in the economic sector is not circumscribed" by laws "that place it at the service of" other human needs. He spoke of "Marxism's kernel of truth" and invoked some Marxist terminology—shocking many, although he had been speaking so for forty years:

> The needs from which that system [Marxism] arose were real and
> serious—the . . . exploitation to which an inhumane capitalism had
> subjected the proletariat since the beginning of industrialized society.

He set forth six "essential . . . requirements":

—The universal destination of goods [meaning universal access to them];

—The legitimacy of private property . . . an indispensable condition for the autonomy of the person and the family;

—The recognition of the importance of work, beginning with the dignity of the human subject who performs it . . . ;

—The promotion of a human ecology, implying respect for every human person . . . ;

—A balanced concept of the state that emphasizes its value and necessity while protecting it from totalitarianism; a state conceived . . . as a service . . . for civil society . . . that guarantees everyone an orderly existence and assures the most vulnerable the support they need in order not to succumb to the arrogance and indifference of the powerful;

—Democracy, understood as participative management of the state . . . in the service of the common good.

Throughout his trip, he continued to stress these themes. In two important speeches in Lithuania, he warned that "the long-standing democratic societies" suffered "the dangers of an ambiguous peace," because of "an economic liberalism that scorns every limitation and is unconcerned about the demands of solidarity."

Days later, John Paul's fears and warnings were vindicated, as new Polish elections swept the remnants of Solidarity out of power in favor of a coalition of "Left" forces, many of them former communists. By late 1993, the onetime stooge unions created by the old communist government had more members than Solidarity. The trend intensified two years later, when Walesa himself came up for reelection and was roundly defeated by a former communist.

In part, these votes protested the radical economic changes that left workers and farmers unprotected. But they also protested the intrusion of the Church into what people regarded as their private lives—as illustrated by the Polish miners who were angrier over abortion laws than they were over pay. Just before the 1993 vote, Walesa and his supporters in Parliament rammed through a concordat with the Vatican that gave the Church tax subsidies and government influence. People resented it, and Parliament balked at enforcing it.

Throughout the post-communist world, former communists were returning to power in democratic settings. In Estonia, where the pope had just visited, voters elected the former editor of the communist newspaper and other former communist officials to office.

The election results amazed many in the West whose understanding of Eastern European politics had been clouded by Cold War propaganda. Neither the voters nor the candidates in these countries would have dreamed of returning to Soviet communism. The candidates being elected were mostly social-welfare democrats who had accepted a pragmatic alliance with communist parties back when the Soviet system seemed a permanent fixture. Although they might have been spineless or foolish before 1989, they still seemed preferable to law-of-the-jungle capitalists or Catholic theocrats, the two other apparent choices in the power struggle.

In the Czech Republic, Vaclav Havel continued as president, but voters elected a prime minister from a secular party running against two "Christian" parties. The Christian parties wanted to give the Church back the vast farm and forest lands it had owned before the war. Polls showed Czechs overwhelmingly opposed that.

"People were tired of all government," says Jan Blonski, a literature professor and papal friend.[3] "They thought some actions of the Church were the same as communism."

In the midst of all these setbacks, John Paul was visited in October 1993 by the Russian writer and traditionalist Alexander Solzhenitsyn. A decade earlier, John Paul had been so attracted to the spirituality of Solzhenitsyn's anti-communist books that he had asked his friend André Frossard to arrange a meeting. Solzhenitsyn had refused. Several other meetings were proposed over the years, but, Frossard said, Solzhenitsyn was always "too busy."

Now, returning home from years of self-exile in the United States, Solzhenitsyn himself suggested it was time. John Paul had reason to expect a happy occasion: besides everything else, Solzhenitsyn had recently expressed the same objection to radical capitalism that John Paul had. The Western press reported a joyful meeting between the two men—but based only on the word of press agents.

Solzhenitsyn's interpreter later revealed that the Russian had come not in admiration at all, but rather to complain about Catholic expansion into Russia. Echoing the Orthodox Church and Russian Parliament, Solzhenitsyn politely but firmly accused the Vatican of arrogance. The interpreter—herself the editor of a Russian magazine in Paris—said that John Paul repeatedly tried to warm up the conversation by lavishing praise on Russians in general and on

Solzhenitsyn in particular. But Solzhenitsyn pressed on, even interrupting the pope once to say that Catholics were offending the Orthodox.

The conversation finally turned to economics, but there was still no respite. John Paul was surprised to find that Solzhenitsyn believed the misleading Western reports that the Pope had been won over by free-market "reformers." Solzhenitsyn evidently didn't realize that *Centesimus Annus* was in line with much of his own argument.[4]

Days after the Solzhenitsyn visit, John Paul took the unprecedented step of inviting a journalist to dinner for a lengthy interview, to try to get across his message using language of rare bluntness for any pope. He chose a writer he could trust, Jas Gawronski of the Italian daily *La Stampa*—a Pole living in Italy (whose sister Wanda had delivered aid to Solidarity).

John Paul began by releasing his anger at the West's failure to intervene to stop the killing in Bosnia:

> The European Community, turned in on itself, is too indifferent and of little use in resolving the problem. It leaves the innocent to suffer. The heartfelt appeals of the pope and the Holy See for peace become almost like a voice crying in the wilderness.

Answering critics who said the Vatican had encouraged the war by recognizing the Catholic breakaway states, he asserted that the states "had every right" to independence, and that a confederation still could have been negotiated, but "unfortunately, things moved very quickly in another direction."

Most of the interview, however, concerned Poland and the collapse of Solidarity. At first, the pope seemed to deny the problem, instead blaming "the mass media of a certain ideological orientation" for trying "to present the ... pope in a rather negative light. . . . This Polish media strategy does not in any way reflect the deepest sentiments of the Catholic population."

Then he said the "root" of the breakdown was

> a mistaken concept of what joining Europe means. I faced this problem during my last visit to Poland. . . . I am not against Poland's membership in Europe, but I am against the attempt to make this initiative into a kind of idol, a false idol, . . . that whole ultra-liberal, consumerist system that is devoid of values, and introducing it with the power of propaganda. . . .

Poland has no need to join Europe, because it is already in Europe, at its center. Poland should become a member with its own values, without adapting itself uncritically and blindly to Western customs.

He said "the ordinary people" agreed with him that the

grains of truth...in the socialist program...should not be destroyed or lost.... The extreme champions of capitalism...tend to disregard the good things achieved by communism: the struggle against unemployment, the concern for the poor.... In my opinion, at the root of many serious social and human problems troubling Europe and the world today are the degenerate aspects of capitalism.

He advocated what he called "modern capitalism," which

has changed, and in large part due to socialist thinking.... It has introduced some social safety net.... It is checked by the state and by trade unions. In some countries in the world, however, it has remained in its unbridled state, almost as it was in the last century.

Continuing in this vein—too blunt for an encyclical—he presented an eye-opening critique of communism, not based on economic policy:

In each country, a real struggle developed between proletarian internationalism and the national identity, which was to be suppressed at all costs. It was said the worker had no homeland because his homeland was the working class. In the end, it was clear that this class ideology, this class conflict and dictatorship, did not succeed in overcoming national awareness, nor did it succeed in overcoming the religious conscience.

He seemed on the verge of stating the capitalist parallel that was emerging—that today it was the capitalist class that preached an internationalist utopia and wanted to separate itself from nations, cultures, and religions—but in the end, he left it unsaid. The recent Eastern European elections were in part a backlash. John Paul stressed that the vote didn't signify

a return to communism, but a reaction to the ineffectiveness of the new governments, which is not surprising. The only political class in existence for fifty years was communist. The others . . . were not ready to govern.

It was now the pope's challenge, he said, to show that the East had the power to save the West.

> Eastern Europe, through all its experiences imposed by totalitarianism, has matured. . . . Another human dimension has been preserved. Perhaps this was also a reason why fifteen years ago a pope from Poland was elected. If one lives under a system that is systematically atheistic, one realizes more clearly what religion means.
> In the West, man does not see this so clearly. . . . Everything is reduced to the economic dimension, or almost. . . . A huge task and a great challenge face the Church, the pope, and the bishops: defending and promoting . . . other values that are often forgotten. It is a demanding message to which not everyone listens. Not all of those who do listen really take it seriously.

November 3, 1993, the day after the interview appeared, John Paul opened his apartment to fifteen visiting Polish churchmen, including his old friend Mieczyslaw Malinski. One after another, they told him that the election results were not as bad as they appeared, and that Walesa's program had lost support because it hadn't deserved any. That was essentially what John Paul had told Gawronski. He asserted again that the United States, France, and the West had the greater problem.

At an opportune moment, Malinski pulled out three magazines from Polish newsstands—*Popcorn, Bravo,* and *The Girl*—and handed them to the pope. "Everybody was struck dumb," Malinski smiles. Anything given to the pope was supposed to be cleared. "Father Dziwisz looked like he wanted to grab the magazines. But I wanted to show the pope what the young people are interested in, what they read. He thumbed through them twice as we were talking."

What John Paul saw were mostly articles on rock music and how to attract the opposite sex. The illustrations were vivid but not lewd.[5] Finally, he said, "There are a lot of wrong materials in it, but taken all together it's not so bad." By the time the evening ended, Dziwisz had even proposed starting a magazine on the same themes but with a Christian context.

At a private dinner with Malinski a few days later, John Paul delivered a monologue on the need for a strong state presence in marketplace economics. Ordinary people needed protection, he said. He had just been visited by a free-market advocate who argued that if people wanted protection against misfortune, they could buy private insurance. That was impractical, the pope went on emotionally: "To get really full insurance, you need quite a lot of money. A poor person can't afford to do it."

November 11, 1993, John Paul shared his fears about the West with visiting bishops from Pennsylvania and New Jersey. Their challenge, he said, was "a spreading 'practical atheism'—an indifference to God's loving plan." That afternoon, he told a convention of UN Food and Agricultural Organization workers to push for more equitable sharing of foodstuffs by wealthier countries. There was plenty for the world population to eat if it was distributed fairly, he said.

Then, as he headed off the podium to shake hands in the crowd, his foot caught his robe, and suddenly he was tumbling down the several steps. In pain but unaware that his shoulder was broken, he greeted his audience with his left hand, then went to the hospital. After one night there, he returned to work, complaining only that he couldn't write. He finally gave in to long-standing suggestions that he use a dictating machine. Days later, he confessed to Archbishop Re, the *sostituto*, that his staff had been right all along: he *could* work faster with dictation than in longhand. Even after the cast came off, early in 1994, he stuck to the dictating machine.[6]

In February, he sneaked out for what was to be his last ski trip.[7] He canceled a scheduled journey to Lebanon after a church was bombed there, not wanting to be responsible if innocent people were hurt in any further violent protest against his coming.

April 10, 1994, he took time to write—not dictate—a letter to Maria Kydrynska Michalowska, who still lived in the same sunny Krakow apartment where he had performed with the Rhapsody Theater during World War II. She was about to go into the hospital and was worried because her son was moving from Canada to Hong Kong. "Even though we are getting older, we should remain young in spirit," the pope penned. "Hong Kong can be as good as Canada."[8]

April 28, within a month of his seventy-fourth birthday, he slipped in the bathtub and broke his hip. An artificial hip was installed during another stay at Gemelli, but he never seemed to recover his ability to walk painlessly. After this second accident, people started joking that the pope might be infallible, but he wasn't un-fallable. John Paul himself, though, became uncharacteristically melancholic. At his first Sunday public prayer after the accident, he dwelt as never before on his own distress:

> I have to lead Christ's Church into this third millennium by prayer, by
> various programs, but I saw that this is not enough. She must be led

by suffering, by the attack thirteen years ago and by this new sacrifice.... The pope has to be attacked, the pope has to suffer, so that
every family and the world may see that here is ... a higher Gospel,
the Gospel of suffering by which the future is prepared.... I am
indebted to the Blessed Virgin for this gift of suffering and I thank
her for it. I have to meet the powerful of this world, and I must speak.
With what arguments? I am left with the subject of suffering.[9]

Later, he would try to make the best of it, sometimes waving his cane in jest
at crowds. He asked an audience in Sicily, "Are you pro-cane or anti-cane?
Some people say it makes me look older." But in 1995, for the first time, he let
cardinals preside during Masses that he attended at St. Peter's.

Speculation grew about his possible death, though Navarro-Valls and others
insisted he was constitutionally sound and there had been no recurrence of the
abdominal tumor. The increasing tremor in his left hand suggested Parkinson's
disease, which was not precisely denied. Considering the step John Paul himself
had taken toward the papacy by leading Pope Paul's Lenten retreat in 1976, the
curia took exceptional notice in 1994 when he asked Cardinal Giovanni Sal-
darini of Turin to lead another retreat.

John Paul continued to be a celebrity pope. St. Peter's on holidays was filled
with as many tourists as worshipers—people interested mainly in him, as if he
were a rock star. They applauded his appearance, called out his name, and
dashed about to get a better snapshot of him as he seemed bent on prayer. He
was a rock star who wished more people would heed his music, not his persona.

13

By the mid-1990s, Cardinal Szoka finally seemed to have eliminated the perpetual budget crisis. Whether he had truly wrestled the shortfall to the turf or
merely got a rope around it was uncertain because of the vagueness of the available figures.

Perhaps a touchstone of John Paul's papacy is that while he spent several
hours every Friday with Cardinal Ratzinger discussing doctrine, and several
more hours every Saturday with Cardinal Gantin discussing bishops (plus more
conferences when needed), he saw Szoka, who paid for everything, twice a year.
Corporate executives with operations far smaller than the Vatican often complain that they have to spend so many hours writing and adjusting budgets that
they can't tend to their products. Not John Paul.

"When the budget's finished in November we go over it for about an hour," Szoka says. "He can't look at all these details. I keep him aware of what's going on and how we're doing." When I asked Szoka how he likes taking a backseat to, say, Gantin, he replied that the pope feels "personally responsible for appointing bishops. Here [at Economic Affairs], we've got an ongoing system and he depends on me to operate it."

Shortly after taking over, in 1991, Szoka called to Rome more than a hundred presidents of episcopal conferences around the world. He sat them in red velvet chairs with matching red desk sets around dark boardroom tables—befittingly, Szoka's prefecture has some of the Vatican's most elegant accommodations—and said the deficit had reached a record $87 million. A way had to be found to raise money.

A motion was passed that national conferences would contribute according to their means. Szoka insists he was "not assigning quotas," but merely "asked them to explain the situation to their bishops and decide how to get the money." The next year, about $8 million in new funds arrived. In succeeding years, that figure mushroomed as groups like the Papal Foundation, the Knights of Columbus, and various religious orders were tapped.

A downturn in the Italian economy gave the Vatican a big boost. As the lira's value plunged, the dollars and marks the Vatican took in could be exchanged for more lira, which is what the Vatican mostly paid out. It was the easiest way to balance any budget. Pressure was also brought on Vatican agencies to cut expenses. "If they cut us any more, I don't know what we're going to do," Joan Parenti of the Council on the Family moaned to me in 1994. Translation and printing was bought "on a shoestring," she said.

Like many Vatican agencies, the Council on the Family had to go outside the Vatican budget to raise independent money for projects like its Third World conferences on child exploitation. West German foundations had once donated generously for such events, but after the Berlin Wall fell in 1989, German funds were diverted to reunification costs.[1] Money for many Vatican activities therefore remained tight, even as the central budget figures improved.

In 1994, Szoka announced a surplus of half a million dollars, after twenty years of deficits. But the budget's exclusion of major income and expense items made it hard to assess how the Vatican was really doing. At the time of Szoka's announcement, the magazine 30 Days—published by seven-time Italian Prime Minister Giulio Andreotti, a Vatican insider—said it had obtained a "strictly top-secret letter" signed by cardinals, declaring that the Vatican really had a $26.3 million deficit on indicated expenses of $180 million in 1994.

To try to square the conflicting figures, Szoka sent me to his deputy, Monsignor Luigi Sposito, who showed me some healthy-looking cash-flow sheets the Vatican hadn't previously released. The problem continued to be that something always seemed to be left out that could change the picture. For example, international mission work was often funded separately from the figures I was seeing; since Cardinal Gantin had just told me that global evangelism was the main function of the Church, I asked for those figures.

Sposito showed me a two-year combined statement for mission work (the Congregation for the Evangelization of Peoples), indicating $132 million in expenditures and $36 million in income. How could they spend nearly four times what they took in? Sposito said he didn't know, and to call the congregation. But Cardinal Tomko, head of the congregation, told me he can't explain the discrepancy, suggesting possible confusion with still other accounts of other Church organizations.

The political paradigm of Italy—the country the Vatican most depended on—was changing as surely as that of Eastern Europe. The Christian Democrats were falling apart over continuing scandals. A third of the party's elected Parliamentarians were reported talking to judges about payoffs, and the Vatican bank had again laundered much of the money; bonds paid for by corporations and held in IOR had wound up with politicians. The brother of Cardinal Sodano, the Vatican secretary of state, was among those arrested. Former Prime Minister Andreotti, meanwhile, stood accused of doing paid favors for the Mafia.

At first, the Church seemed split over how to react. Some, notably Cardinal Martini of Milan, said the abuses were so bad that a new alignment was called for. The pope weighed in predictably: stolen money interested him no more than the honest kind. He didn't endorse the Christian Democrats by name, but he did say that a party that had helped stabilize Western Europe after World War II shouldn't be discarded just because many of its leaders were crooks. "The guilty must be judged," he said, "but . . . a well-constituted society cannot hand over decisions concerning its future to the judicial authorities."

Again, the voters thought otherwise, and in 1994 elected a new party headed by a publishing tycoon, Silvio Berlusconi, who himself was forced to resign after less than a year in office because of corruption charges. The defeated Christian Democrats reorganized and elected John Paul's old friend Rocco Buttiglione as their leader. The pope drew widespread criticism by welcoming Andreotti, Waldheim-like, to the Vatican, even as he awaited trial for crimes of the very sort the pope had denounced on trips to Sicily. True fans of Italian politics could not have been surprised.

✑

Old Liberation Theology divisions were reawakened on New Year's Day 1994, when rebels in southern Mexico seized municipal offices and radio outlets to protest low pay by American-based employers. They killed two dozen Mexican soldiers and lost about as many men themselves. The affair threw a spotlight on the local bishop of thirty-five years, Samuel Ruiz García, who unequivocally condemned the violence but nonetheless sympathized with many rebel demands. He had been outspoken in opposing a pending "free trade" treaty with the United States that promised to promote new business at the risk of lowering wages.

The Mexican government accused Ruiz and his seminary of helping the rebels, and found an ally in the papal nuncio, Archbishop Girolamo Prigione, who had already talked to the Congregation for Bishops about what he called "serious doctrinal" problems concerning Ruiz. The nuncio told government officials that the Vatican would remove Ruiz. But many Mexican bishops supported Ruiz, including his new archbishop (in Guadalajara) and the cardinal from Mexico City, Ernesto Corripio Ahumada.

For eighteen months, Ruiz mediated peace between the rebels and the government, while he and the nuncio flew in and out of Rome. People could only speculate as to which one the pope supported. Those who still thought John Paul was inflexibly against Liberation Theology were surprised by the compromise that evolved in 1995: a much younger bishop from another diocese, whom the seventy-one-year-old Ruiz had publicly commended, was named with his blessing to assist and eventually succeed him.[2] More important, there was no war.

Former President (now elder statesman) Jimmy Carter rescued John Paul from further embarrassment in Haiti. In September 1994, U.S. troops prepared to invade the island to restore Father Aristide as president, against Vatican opposition. But Carter instead persuaded the dictators to step aside to allow the peaceful return of Aristide, who agreed to resign his priesthood. With time, and new elections—in which Aristide didn't run—the Vatican's role in the crisis quietly faded.

An uneasy truce had settled over war-weary Central America. A plan mediated by Costa Rica let the big powers and the UN literally buy peace in El Salvador, by creating a $2.4 billion fund to acquire land for former rebels and to train a civilian police force. Change proceeded slowly, but without bloodshed. Relieving the pressure at home, hundreds of thousands of Salvadorans fled to jobs in the United States, helping spark a wave of anti-immigrant sentiment among some Americans that angered John Paul, for whom open immigration for work was a major cause. Guatemala also edged tenuously toward democracy.

Nicaragua seemed largely reconciled when John Paul visited in 1996. Land (the plantations of the old Somoza dictators) had been permanently redistributed, and power was effectively democratized. A truly middle-ground president had been elected: Violetta Chamorro, from a newspaper family that had displayed principled resistance to both the Somoza and the Sandinista dictatorships. Still, landless former soldiers from both sides continued to terrorize rural areas.

The former Sandinista priests mostly broke with the party after it became the opposition. Several ran literacy and antipoverty programs funded by overseas Catholic charities. One, former Foreign Minister Miguel D'Escoto, asked the Vatican to restore his priestly functions, but was told he was insufficiently repentant.

The pope sent a public message of "solidarity" to thirteen Colombian union leaders who were jailed for opposing a government plan to "privatize" the state telephone system, effectively transferring much of it to U.S. ownership.[3] His political interventions were such that the prominent Jesuit Giuseppe Pittau says, "Many of John Paul's statements now are like those of Romero. There has been great progress in the Church."

The pope gingerly offered his services to ease the inevitable transition from Fidel Castro's rule in Cuba. Without Soviet aid—previously several thousand dollars a year for each Cuban family—Castro had little to offer his people. Formerly empty Cuban church pews began filling up. John Paul made a cardinal of his Havana archbishop and found other ways to give his Cuban hierarchy more visibility and thus more strength.

Yet the pope steered clear of Castro's vocal opponents in Washington and Florida, positioning the Church as a mediator. He publicly denounced the long-standing U.S. embargo on goods to Cuba (as he consistently opposed all such embargoes). Sometimes Castro seemed ready to take the bait and enter into negotiations; but in the end he would make anti-Church statements and clutch his dictatorship, oblivious to changing times and the economic plight of his people.*

In a similar vein, John Paul offered a benign presence to another communist holdout when he sent Cardinal Etchegaray of Justice and Peace to Beijing. But in China, unlike Cuba, Catholicism had never been more than a fringe movement, and little came of the initiative.

---

* In late 1996, Castro finally committed himself to bringing the pope to Cuba, visiting him first in the Vatican. As this book went to press in 1997, John Paul was preparing a trip to Cuba that both Castro and U.S. President Clinton plainly hoped would help both of them escape the trap of economically self-destructive and often bloody warfare their countries had blundered into after Castro's takeover in 1959.

By early 1994, Christians were fighting Moslems in post-communist Azerbaijan, Armenia, and Chechnya. The pope begged both sides to stop fighting, but his call for Western intervention to disarm the Orthodox Serbs in Bosnia had wholly alienated the Russian Patriarch, Alexis II, who supported his fellow Orthodox. Alexis and Serbian President Slobodan Milosevic talked about John Paul as if he were the head of a hostile country. Milosevic's invitations for a papal visit sometimes read like veiled threats. John Paul tried to arrange a peace meeting with Alexis and Moslem leaders in Sarajevo, but negotiations broke down. A scheduled papal trip to Sarajevo in 1994 was canceled for fear of violence.

In September, John Paul went instead to Catholic Croatia, where he blessed the "martyred city" of Sarajevo from across the border. While there, he suffered extreme pain moving about on his new hip. His recovery had been going so well that he had accelerated his itinerary and dealt himself a setback. He had to be lifted into the popemobile, wincing.[4] He postponed another scheduled visit to the U.S.—including a UN speech—knowing it would entail a lot of climbing into and out of helicopters. Rumors again circulated that he was dying.

He tried to keep attention focused on Bosnia. "How can we not listen to the heartrending cry for help [of] the martyred people?" he pleaded. Back at St. Peter's, fists flailing the air, he cried "Stop, stop, stop!" In 1995, when Western forces bombed Serbs who had beseiged Sarajevo and other cities, the Vatican excused it. *Osservatore Romano* said the raids "cannot and should not be considered an act of war," but were instead intended to "restore hope to . . . martyred people."

As if to emphasize that the Bosnian exception didn't signal any change in his general views on war, John Paul began a new antiweapons campaign. With the threat of nuclear holocaust diminished and conventional conflicts spreading, land mines had become a particularly heinous weapon, planted, in the pope's words, "on roads and in fields with the intention of indiscriminately harming as many people as possible." Moreover, they kept killing and maiming civilians long after a war ended. As with nuclear weapons, John Paul called for an absolute ban on the production of land mines.

Still seeking to stem his ecumenical debacle, John Paul went all out to welcome the other main Orthodox leader, Bartholomew I, patriarch of Constantinople, to the Vatican. The pope hoped to renew the harmony achieved during his visit to Bartholomew's predecessor, Dimitrios, in 1979. Instead, scarcely believable feuding broke out. John Paul underestimated the Orthodox resentment against Eastern Rite Catholics, who had defected with the Orthodox in 1054 but later came back to Catholicism.

The pope planned to invest an Eastern Rite archbishop during a Mass at St. Peter's, at which Bartholomew was to assist. When Bartholomew found out about this the day before, he was enraged at the prospect of honoring an Eastern Rite Catholic and threatened to boycott the ceremony. John Paul invested the archbishop that night instead, and he and Bartholomew made it through the Mass at St. Peter's without a public break. But they were a long way from ecumenism.

Trouble arose in Czechoslovakia over priests and bishops who had been secretly ordained during communism. When the secret clergy surfaced, many were married. Some claimed to have been ordained as priests or bishops by others who had since died, leaving doubts and no proof of their status. Primate Miloslav Vlk of Prague angered many former underground clergy in 1991 by declaring that the legitimacy of their ordinations would have to be studied before they were recognized.

Years passed while men who had risked their lives to keep the Church going under communism were left hanging. John Paul never intervened. Cardinal König met with Primate Vlk and came away saying that only guesswork could identify the underground priests, in an atmosphere that reeked of suspicion. "People look at each other and say, 'He was never in prison. I was five years in prison. Why?'" König says. "It's not good. An Iron Curtain is still buried in the ground."[5]

When John Paul went to Prague in May 1995, the "miracle" that President Havel had described during his joyful 1990 visit was gone. Protestants boycotted meetings with the pope, complaining that a seventeenth-century priest he canonized during the trip had really been a Polish spy, and that the Czechs had been right to kill him. Most Czechs now told pollsters they had no religion at all. Fewer than a hundred thousand people showed up for a papal Mass designed for half a million. Havel told the pope that the enthusiasm of 1990 "has given way to a more sober thinking about everyday life."[6]

With so many others angry at him, the last thing John Paul needed (or would have intended) was to insult the world's 339 million Buddhists. But now that his luck had turned bad, there seemed to be no stopping it. In his 1994 bestseller, *Crossing the Threshold of Hope*, the pope expressed concern that many Western Catholics thought they could also follow Buddhism, as if it were a mental exercise and not an alternative religion. To discourage this, John Paul talked about the different approaches that Buddhism and Catholicism took to salvation. Buddhism's approach, he said, was

> almost exclusively negative. . . . The "enlightenment" experienced by Buddha comes down to the conviction that the world is bad. . . . To liberate oneself from evil, one must . . . break with . . . external reality. . . . Buddhism is in large measure an "atheistic" system. . . . The fullness of . . . detachment from the world . . . is not union with God, but what is called nirvana, a state of perfect indifference with regard to the world.

Many Buddhists took one look at the words *negative* and *atheist* and screamed that the pope was a bigot with a colonialist mind-set. The Vatican issued clarifications: John Paul had been making a theological point, not implying that Buddhism was negative in its purpose or effect. He had "esteem for Buddha as a historical figure and for followers of Buddhism." Still, the attacks continued,[7] spoiling his previously scheduled January 1995 trip to Sri Lanka, where Buddhists—69 percent of the country's population—boycotted events they were expected to participate in.

Lithuania, Ukraine, Azerbaijan, Hungary, and even Russia itself joined Poland in freely turning their governments back over to former communists. Ex-communists had become the leading advocates of social-welfare democracy in countries where unemployment regularly exceeded 10 percent and inflation 20 percent. Free-market interest rates of up to 40 percent made local borrowing impractical and invited foreign domination of economies, which people resented.

In 1994, John Paul moved to reestablish relations with his old Polish intellectual friends, in hopes of re-creating a middle ground between the ex-communists and the free-marketers. A *Tygodnik Powszechny* delegation under editor Turowicz came to dinner at the Vatican, and the Episcopate in Warsaw reached out to the Democratic Union political party of the old KOR crowd. Glemp even endorsed sainthood for Father Popieluszko.

But it proved to be too little, too late. *Tygodnik Powszechny* itself had already sold a 40 percent stake to a French publishing consortium.[8] The pope's old ally Father Tischner complained publicly that the Polish Church had fumbled away the pope's ideals through its political blunders. "In my lifetime as a priest, I never met anyone who lost his faith after reading Marx, Lenin, or Nietzsche, but we can count in large numbers those who lost it after meeting their own parish priest," Tischner said. The Episcopate rebuked him, but he was voted the most popular contributor to *Tygodnik Powszechny*.[9] The Episcopate may even have cost Walesa the 1995 election: as soon as it endorsed him, his ex-communist opponent jumped 20 percent in the polls.

14

African bishops had long sought to break from European ritual and introduce more African tradition into Catholic practice, a process they called "inculturation." Their parishioners wanted it, and inculturation would also help the Church compete against animism and Islam. In 1988, John Paul agreed to let the African bishops meet to discuss the problem, just as the Latin American bishops regularly met. Despite the pope's emphasis on Africa, however, it was six years before a meeting finally occurred, and then it was in Rome.

"At the beginning, all of us including the pope envisioned the synod in Africa," with John Paul there to preside, recalls Cardinal Christian Tumi of Cameroun. "Then almost every country we proposed [as a site] suffered political turmoil." Cardinal Arinze says the pope moved the synod to Rome for fear that selecting one African country would slight the others, and also to avoid an expensive-looking extravaganza amid African poverty. But as the bishops assembled, many complained to Arinze's office that the real reason Rome had been chosen was that the pope feared a truly African synod might escape his control.[1] Both Arinze and Tumi deny this.

The agenda had also been a problem. African bishops were focused on animism, the main source of converts, while Europeans in the curia worried about Islam. Although the Catholic population of Africa had nearly doubled during John Paul's reign, to 14 percent, Islam had grown even faster, to 41 percent (another 17 percent was Protestant).[2] Old-timers like Cardinal Oddi considered Moslem growth "the biggest danger to the Catholic Church. Morocco, Turkey, Syria—all those countries were Christian. Now they're all Moslem."

The African inculturation agenda called for increased emphasis on Jesus' timelessness, to satisfy African desires to involve ancestors in religion; an overhaul of the marriage ceremony to appeal to the African view that two families were marrying, not just two people; and even the expansion of the Eucharist into more of a community meal in the African tradition, including an animal sacrifice.

Many bishops also wanted to address political problems. With its abundant resources, moderate population size, and stable traditions, Africa had seemed destined for a rosy future after colonialism. Yet it was developing much more slowly than either Asia or Latin America. Many of the continent's best-trained professionals had taken off for Western countries, seeing no future for themselves in the corrupt dictatorships of their homelands. Africa needed a spiritual rebirth, says Cardinal Tumi: "What is lacking is a respect for the common good. You cannot look at evangelizing without looking at this."

Much of the problem could be traced back to ethnic hatreds, which were as strong in Africa as in the Balkans. Although priests were supposed to be universal, members of one tribe serving in an area dominated by another were often rejected by the Catholic community.

These differences erupted to cast a pall over the synod. Just as the assembly opened in St. Peter's, April 10, 1994, amid rhythmic drums, xylophones, and chanting voices, confirmation came that eight priests and nine others had been massacred at a Catholic center in the Rwandan capital of Kigali; all had been members of the Tutsi tribe, which had been struggling with the Hutu tribe for control of Rwanda and neighboring Burundi since just before those countries won independence from Belgium, in 1962. Recently, Rwandans had been squeezed by the same IMF pressures as Poland; the devalued currency, cutoff of imports, and spiraling inflation no doubt contributed to the violence.

The massacre of Tutsi Catholics was but a droplet in the bloodbath to follow: over the next few months, as the African synod met, an estimated eight hundred thousand Rwandans were murdered. The radical Hutu army killed every Tutsi it could find, as well as Hutus it considered too moderate, or who had befriended or married Tutsis. The killing spared neither women nor children. People crowded into churches in the mostly Catholic country, only to be massacred there. More than a million refugees poured into neighboring Zaire, where dictator Mobutu had just executed three priests on charges of opposing his policies in their sermons.

John Paul's pleas for peace weren't answered. Father Bernard Ardura of the Council on Culture compares the pope's anguish over Rwanda and the former Yugoslavia to the suffering of Jesus. "This is his way of the cross," Ardura says. "In the life of the pope, the present moment is very important. After the decolonization of Africa, many had hope of liberty and development. And after the liberation of Europe, many hoped for the same thing. It was a dream. A united Europe, a united Africa. This is for the pope an experience of the cross."

John Paul closed the African bishops' synod with an address from his hospital bed, after hip surgery. Pending his final report, the synod spoke out on its own. Of the fourteen cardinals and 122 bishops who participated, more than a hundred signed an open letter asking American and European bishops to work together to cancel foreign debt and end IMF pressure. The synod also requested a ban on all arms sales to Africa. It said priests should live in their home villages during training, instead of in the seminary, so they could retain close ties to their families and culture. And it advocated the establishment of "small Christian communities"—like the ones in Liberation Theology—where Africans could both pray and address the real problems of life.

When John Paul delivered his final statement—in Africa, as promised, in September 1995—he backed up his bishops politically, telling the IMF and international banks (without his usual polite indirectness) to erase the debt and stop squeezing money out of Africa. But he blamed Africans themselves for undermining their own countries with tribalism, dictatorship, and the embezzlement of needed aid money by leaders. He made good on his pledge to visit South Africa when it was finally free of apartheid, and was welcomed by President Nelson Mandela, who praised him for his support.

But the pope refused most African bishops' proposals for adapting Catholic liturgy to local culture. He attended a Mass in South Africa that incorporated plenty of traditional clothing, music, and dance, but skipped a more radical service in an "alternative cathedral" that had been founded in the former all-black area of Soweto. Back in Rome, Ratzinger spoke out against the very idea of "inculturation."

15

If a sex scandal was the price John Paul paid for mandating priestly celibacy, the price for opposing contraception was to be isolated and distracted at three major UN conferences where he might have advanced other parts of his agenda.

In June 1992, an "Earth Summit" was held in Rio de Janeiro to encourage international agreement on environmental protection. This was just the sort of action John Paul supported enthusiastically in his encyclicals and speeches. But when the summit came, instead of seeking to preserve rain forests and other threatened life systems, the pope felt obliged primarily to defend his position on birth control by working to defuse the issue of population growth.

Dozens of scientists with impressive credentials and data had lined up on both sides of the population question. Some said the earth's expanding billions were exhausting its limited resources, while others said that with better management and use of technology, the earth could support many more people. A good writer could make a persuasive case either way. The Vatican put its writers to work marshaling arguments that growth was good.

They built a strong case that the main threat to the environment came from industrial countries with small populations, not from developing countries where population growth was said to be running amok. "A just ecological balance ... cannot be obtained" without a fairer distribution of wealth, the Vatican said. The problem wasn't Third World population but rather "rich societies" that had to "seriously reconsider their hedonistic, consumerist life-styles." Cardinal Sodano, the Vatican secretary of state, accused the rich countries of asserting a "devastating dictatorship" over the developing world by trying "to limit the freedom of couples in deciding the size of the family." Sodano demanded that development aid "not be made conditional on acceptance of programs of contraception, sterilization, or abortion."

Luckily for the Vatican, President Bush, then running for reelection, also adopted a stance of environmental concern and moral conservatism. With the United States and the Vatican on parallel tracks, the population issue was successfully sidestepped.

The situation changed two years later, however, at a UN conference in Cairo on population and development. The new U.S. President, Clinton, was determined to assert that "access to safe, legal, and voluntary abortion is a fundamental right of all women." March 16, 1994—six months before the conference—the U.S. demanded "stronger language" on abortion and birth control than the draft documents provided. The U.S. was forcing the issue to a head.

Three days later, John Paul issued his own open letter saying the conference text already went too far. The traditional family was disintegrating because of divorce and single-parenthood across the West, with all sorts of tragic consequences. The trend had to be stopped. The pope had designated 1994 as the Vatican's "Year of the Family," yet the text for the Cairo conference, instead of emphasizing the importance of families, seemed mainly concerned with protecting sex and even reproduction *outside* the family. The conference draft called for teaching adolescents about sex "with no mention of the rights and duties of parents," John Paul complained.

> The idea of sexuality underlying this text is totally individualistic to such an extent that marriage now appears ... outmoded. ... [It] leaves the troubling impression of something being imposed: a lifestyle typical of certain fringes within developed societies that are materially rich and secularized. ...
>
> Are countries that are more sensitive to the values of nature, morality, and religion going to accept such a vision of man and society without protest? ... The very complex issue of the relationship between population and development, which ought to be at

the center of the discussion, is almost completely overlooked....
What threatens the family in fact threatens mankind.[1]

He wrote to Clinton in early April, then phoned him, trying to change the President's mind and avoid a shoot-out in Cairo. But the pope wanted no reference at all to permissible abortion. June 2, Clinton visited John Paul at the Vatican, and for forty-five minutes the two talked mainly about Cairo. It got them nowhere.

Unable to bend the U.S. President, the pope instead sought alliances with Moslem states that shared his views on abortion. Archbishop Tauran, the Vatican's foreign-affairs minister, even visited Libya and Iran. Pressure was intense; Opus Dei asked companies to withdraw advertising from a Guatemalan newspaper that supported population control.[2] But the battle was all uphill. Professionals and volunteers affiliated with organizations dedicated to contraception and legal abortion were important members of the delegations from more than sixty countries. The president of the International Planned Parenthood Federation chaired the committee that negotiated the draft language.

For the conference in September, John Paul made a rare pragmatic choice: the Vatican would merely register its objection on contraception, and apply all its resources to the abortion fight. The tactic worked. After a battle royal, and with the help of Moslem delegations, the pope succeeded. The final document stressed that abortion shouldn't be used as a means of family planning, and that "all attempts should be made to eliminate the need for abortion." At the Vatican's urging, a statement was added that all recommendations were to be considered in light of religious and ethical values. And a section on the rights, duties, and responsibilities of parents was added to the sex-education material.

But the Vatican paid a high public-relations price to achieve these victories. Delegates who thought the world was overpopulated blamed it on the Church, and their views permeated many news reports—although the accusation was largely untrue: Catholics paid no more attention to John Paul's position on sex than they did to his position on war. Population growth among Catholics worldwide is average at most.*

---

* Births per thousand are 43 in Nigeria, 39 in Pakistan, 36 in Iran and Bangladesh—all mostly Moslem; corresponding figures in Catholic countries are 27 in Mexico, 25 in Brazil, 22 in Chile, 14 in Ireland, 12 in Poland, and 9 in Italy, whose population is actually shrinking. For comparison, it is 16 in the U.S. and 13 in Norway. Moreover, these 1993–94 figures show a slight but uniform downtrend from 1990, suggesting that growth rates may be receding, regardless of religion. China has brought its rate down to 18 per thousand,[3] but only by resorting to infanticide. Facts link birth rates more to underdevelopment than to Catholicism. In rapidly developing Colombia, for example, average births dropped from 7 children per woman in 1965 to 2.9 in 1990, though the country stayed Catholic.[4]

Many delegates at the Cairo conference became angry at the Vatican because the abortion dispute shunted aside a pressing debate they wanted to have with the rich nations about money. This was ironic indeed because John Paul shared their agenda. If Third World countries had been able at Cairo to win a new economic deal such as John Paul had outlined in *Sollicitudo Rei Socialis,* and if it had worked, then population growth might have been curbed by increased wealth, as often happens when economies are modernized.[5]

Whether or not President Clinton planned it that way, shoving the development issue aside to fight over abortion certainly saved money for U.S. taxpayers. In the little time left at Cairo after the abortion debate, the Vatican urged Western nations to multiply their Third World development aid. The Vatican also supported Third World requests that workers emigrating to richer countries be allowed to take their families, so husbands wouldn't be separated from wives and children. When these pleas were rejected, *Osservatore Romano* editorialized that "rich countries revealed their greed" and that their "attitude is simply neocolonialist."

Much the same scenario was repeated at a UN Conference on Women, September 1995 in Beijing. Just as John Paul had focused his thoughts on families for a year before the Cairo conference, he seemed to concentrate on women in the year leading up to Beijing. Late in 1994, angry nuns demonstrated at St. Peter's to protest a bishops' synod about their profession, to which only a token handful of nuns had been invited, without voting rights.

The Vatican banned an American revision of the Bible that catered to feminist protests against male-root words (like *mankind*) that are used in standard English to refer to both sexes. Ratzinger expressed particular concern that neutering pronouns like *he* and *him* in the psalms would change the Christian interpretation that these were prophecies of Jesus. The rejection shocked the book's supporters—and its hard-hit publisher—because another Vatican congregation (Divine Worship and Sacraments) had long ago given its approval.

The pope also tried to quell once and for all the continuing debate over the ordination of women, with a letter sent to all bishops:

> In order that all doubt may be removed regarding a matter of great importance ... I declare that the Church has no authority whatsoever to confer priestly ordination on women and that this judgment is to be definitively held by all the Church's faithful.

The letter caused an uproar. Among those who had apparently considered the matter still open to debate was John Paul's own Cardinal Martini of Milan, thought to be a conservative and a possible successor to the papacy, who had recently told an interviewer, "We should come to it little by little. . . . I foresee decades of struggle ahead."[6] American Catholic reaction was loud and generally hostile. Margaret O'Brien Steinfels, editor of the prominent Catholic magazine *Commonweal*, said, "If one purpose of this letter is to end the discussion, as is often the case the appearance of the letter will only increase discussion."

The pope's annual Holy Thursday message to priests in 1995 also concerned women, providing advice on how to relate to them without being tempted away from celibacy, and admonishing that their ineligibility for the priesthood was no cause to look down on or discriminate against them. The priesthood, said John Paul, was "an expression not of domination but of service." Jesus' decision to appoint only male apostles meant that only men should be priests, but a woman, Mary Magdalene (who the Gospels say announced Jesus' resurrection), was "almost on a par with the Apostles."

Specifically to shape the atmosphere for the Beijing conference, John Paul released a sixteen-page letter trying every appeal he could think of to the militant feminists who would be represented there in disproportionate numbers. He said that

> women have contributed to . . . the history of humanity . . . as much as men and, more often than not, they did so in much more difficult conditions . . . excluded from equal educational opportunities, underestimated, ignored, and not given credit for their intellectual contributions.

He shared their unhappiness that "so many parts of the world still keep women from being fully integrated into social, political, and economic life." He called for stricter laws to protect women from "sexual violence." He lavished praise on feminists themselves,

> those women . . . who have devoted their lives to defending the dignity of womanhood by fighting for their basic social, economic, and political rights, demonstrating courageous initiative at a time when this was considered extremely inappropriate, the sign of a lack of feminity, a manifestation of exhibitionism, and even a sin.

But there seemed to be little John Paul could say that would mollify his adversaries—the many women who saw abortion, contraception, and the priesthood as "rights" they were entitled to. They continued to view him as one who relegated women to the kitchen and nursery.

The most telling evidence that this was untrue lay in the pope's own relationships with women, which were little known. In a life unusually devoid of close friendships and deprived of much family, three women stood out. Few men had been closer to him than were Halina Kwiatkowska early in life and Wanda Poltawska later in life. He had also displayed a unique, time-consuming fascination with Anna-Teresa Tymieniecka.

All three women to whom he was drawn were powerfully consumed by demanding intellectual careers at which they were driven to succeed: Kwiatkowska in classical literary theater, Poltawska in psychiatry, and Tymieniecka in philosophical scholarship.

To head his delegation to the Beijing conference, John Paul selected—not a homemaker and mother of nine children—but Mary Ann Glendon, a Harvard law professor and author of nine books. Glendon endorsed Church teaching on abortion and population control, but her view of Catholic social justice had also led her to an outspoken defense of women's economic equality in divorce. She had annulled her own failed marriage to a colleague in the civil rights movement in the 1960s—she insists it wasn't a divorce because it was only "an attempted marriage"—and married another man, who is Jewish. She even says she understands why others oppose the Church's ban on contraception, though she supports it.

In Beijing, though, Joan of Arc couldn't have saved the pope's agenda. Professor Glendon's mere appearance at the podium was greeted with what one reporter described as "a groan, hiss, and faint booing." As at Cairo, the Vatican challenged proposed text references to "reproductive rights," "safe sex," and "safe abortion." It blamed the Clinton administration for such language. As at Cairo, it objected that the final statement disrespected the family and was more concerned with preventing parenthood than with assisting it.

In the end, the Vatican's main consolation was how little effect the conferences had. The best assessment of all three may have been the one Professor Glendon gave to a reporter on the last night in Beijing: the decisions reached, she said, were "paper promises unless backed up by real commitment on the part of wealthier nations. I don't see that happening. There would have to be a change of heart."[7]

As predicted, the debate over women in the priesthood continued. So John Paul reached for a bigger gun. The ban, he now declared, was

> founded on the written Word of God, and . . . has been set forth
> infallibly by the . . . universal magisterium . . . to be held always,
> everywhere, and by all, as belonging to the deposit of the faith.

Was the ultimate tool of infallibility being used here—for perhaps only the second time in Church history? Maybe not. As Father Avery Dulles sees it, "The pope did not engage his own infallible magisterium in the declaration. . . . Rather, by his ordinary and noninfallible teaching authority, he vouched for the infallibility of the teaching." In other words, the pope made a fallible declaration that the teaching had already been stated infallibly.

And lest women feel they were the only ones being excluded, Ratzinger announced that men who were allergic to wheat or recovering from alcoholism also couldn't be ordained, because consuming the wafer and wine was too important a part of the job to omit.

16

Try as John Paul might to impose order on his Church, its behavior continued to reflect the diversity of its membership.

In January 1995, the pope removed French Bishop Jacques Gaillot, whom he had appointed in 1982. Despite warnings from Gantin and Lustiger, Gaillot had continued to speak out for homosexual relationships, a married priesthood, and condoms for persons at risk of contracting AIDS. (He was best known for his support for immigrant workers and their families.) When he was symbolically reassigned to a nonexistent diocese in Mauritania, the protest surprised the pope: four other bishops and twenty thousand worshipers came to Gaillot's farewell Mass to show their support.

The president of the German Bishops' Conference and two other German bishops spoke out in favor of readmitting divorced and remarried people to the sacraments. Ratzinger called them in several times, but they wouldn't bend, and they couldn't all be sent to Mauritania. The German bishops as a body refused a Vatican request to formally endorse John Paul's stance against the ordination of women. Talk soon spread of a schism within the German Church.

When John Paul forced out the editor of the leading English-language Catholic magazine in Africa for publishing articles critical of the Vatican's handling of the African synod, African Catholic press officials backed the editor.[1] The eight superiors in his religious order, which covered all of Africa, asked that he be allowed to stay on. (The pope refused.)

A Swiss bishop John Paul had appointed, Hansjoerg Vogel of Basel, announced in June 1995 that he had just become an out-of-wedlock father. Instead of grieving that their bishop had fallen from his life's vow, Swiss Catholics seemed to consider him the victim of an unreasonable chastity rule.

He resigned, but many lay leaders pleaded with him to stay on. Women congratulated him for taking responsibility for his child, and the president of a Catholic women's union said her group "would like to see you as bishop and father of a family."

This reaction must have stung John Paul even more than the sexual act that gave rise to it: How was he to teach the world that freedom didn't release a person from ethical accountability, if his own bishops were not to be held accountable for their vows? Father Hans Kung, the dissident Swiss theologian whom John Paul had disciplined, not only joined the support for Bishop Vogel but was accorded a high honor by the German government for fostering ecumenism.[2]

Only two years earlier, John Paul thought he had pacified the Swiss Church by appointing popular new bishops in Chur. Now Bishop Vogel's fatherhood, plus the coincidence of several illnesses, confronted the pope with more openings to be filled, amid polls showing that 90 percent of Swiss Catholics favored a married priesthood.

In Austria, where Catholics were still simmering at the replacement of the revered Cardinal König by the unchaste (and homosexual to boot) Cardinal Grör, a new rebellion broke out. John Paul had appointed yet another unpopular bishop, Andreas Laun, this time in Salzburg. The priests and bishops of the Salzburg Cathedral Chapter were irate at not being consulted (though Church law didn't require them to be).

By the summer of 1995, half a million Austrian Catholics (of 6.3 million, including children) had signed a petition calling for an end to the celibacy rule; the ordination of women; exceptions to the birth-control ban; and local involvement in bishops' appointments. Opinion polls showed that 40 percent of Austrian Catholics sympathized with the initiative, and perhaps more striking, 34 percent did not care one way or the other; just one in four opposed it. Cardinal König wrote an article demonstrating that except for women priests, there was precedent in Church history for everything the petition called for.

The Swedish Bishops' Conference openly discussed admitting divorced and remarried worshipers to communion; some said it was already done in practice.[3] Doctrinal dissent was blamed for a plunge in Belgian church attendance, to 18 percent of Catholics. John Paul's appearance for a beatification there in 1995 drew only twenty thousand (thirty thousand chairs were set out) in a spot where a hundred thousand had seen him ten years before.[4]

Catholic University in Washington, having struggled to rid itself of Father Curran, appointed a new dean of religious studies, Father Raymond Collins, who had signed the same dissent from the Vatican's birth-control ban that Curran had. He acknowledges he also signed a 1987 protest against John Paul's use of power, and is "not a person to be looking over my shoulder," even now.[5]

While some said the Church was split because John Paul was too strict in his discipline, others said it was because he wasn't strict enough. "It is extraordinary that bishops and professors speak against the pope," Cardinal Stickler says. "They know he does not discipline. He avoids anything that would hurt people."

⁂

John Paul appointed a bumper crop of thirty new cardinals in November 1994. He had now appointed a hundred of the 120 cardinals who were under eighty and eligible to vote in the next conclave. Proving he held no grudges, he chose to honor Yves Congar, now ninety, who had been condemned as a "new theologian" during John Paul's student days. Congar had also signed at least three statements protesting John Paul's own decisions (the discipline of Father Schillebeeckx, the requirement that priests leave government jobs in Nicaragua, and the muzzling of theologians).

Eight of the new cardinals had been in prison—one for just a few hours, but another, Mikel Koliqi of Albania, for thirty-eight years. Congar had been jailed by the Nazis in World War II, and Vinko Puljik very recently in his native Sarajevo. At forty-nine, Puljik became the youngest cardinal.

Geographically, the voting college of cardinals was almost the same as in 1978, when John Paul was elected: 48 percent European, 17 percent Latin American, 12 percent African, 10 percent each Asian and North American, and 3 percent Australasian. Africa had gained 3 percent, and Europe, North America, and Australasia had each lost 1 percent.

Coming as it did on the heels of his canceled visit to the United States and the UN, the naming of new cardinals brought more speculation that the pope was near death. Just before a Mass for the cardinals at St. Peter's, as John Paul got out of the Mercedes that had driven him from his quarters to the basilica, the door slammed on his finger. Despite what must have been excruciating pain, he did not cry out. He started the ceremony only five minutes late, a bandage on the finger. Many of the cardinal's rings he handed out that day came with the pope's blood on them. At one point in the prayers, he reached his injured right hand behind the altar, and an attendant changed the dressing.[6]

Despite the talk of death, the pope was preparing a mammoth celebration for the year 2000 and clearly planned to lead it himself. Among the profuse global activities John Paul discussed with cardinals, several stood out. One was a confession of Church wrongdoing throughout history. The Church, he said,

> cannot cross the threshold of the new millennium without encouraging her children to purify themselves through repentance, of past

> errors and ... infidelity.... [Religious unity] has been painfully
> wounded ... for which at times ... both sides were to blame....
> These sins of the past ... still burden us.... It is necessary to make
> amends for them.

He had hinted at such ambitions years before, in reevaluating the Galileo
case. Then, too, in 1983, at the three-hundredth anniversary of the Turkish
defeat by Poland and other Christian forces in the Battle of Vienna, he had
broken with precedent by apologizing for Christian war crimes, including the
burning alive of wounded Moslem soldiers after the battle:

> Acts of outrageous cruelty were committed not only by Ottoman
> soldiers but by the Imperial army and its allies.... The disciples of
> Mohammed now live in your midst, and many of them may serve
> as a model for us in their devout worship of the one God.

And in Jamaica, in 1993, he had apologized for Church assistance to the slave
trade, and for slavery's dissolution of families: "The tragic fruits of this evil
system are still present in attitudes of sexual irresponsibility," he said.

His 1995 message on wrongs done to women said, "If objective blame
... belonged to not just a few members of the Church, for this I am truly sorry."
And in the former Czechoslovakia, that same year, he talked about the "wrongs
inflicted on non-Catholics" during the repression of Protestantism, specifically
citing Jan Hus, a Czech hero who had been burned at the stake in 1415 for challenging papal authority. John Paul has also referred to the Inquisition and "wars
of religion"—the Crusades?—as appropriate matters for apology.

Critics, particularly in the British Church, said John Paul wanted to atone
for long-ago mistakes merely to draw attention away from current controver-
sies.[7] On the other hand, acknowledging major errors committed by past popes
might suggest to almost anyone that this pope, in trying to impose his own
vision of God's will, might also be wrong.

John Paul also planned extraordinary travel for 2000, including

> to visit the places on the road taken by the people of God of the
> Old Covenant, starting from the places associated with Abraham
> and Moses, through Egypt and Mount Sinai, as far as Damascus,
> the city that witnessed the conversion of Saint Paul.

Besides these published thoughts, he told his friend Stefan Wilkanowicz
that he wanted "to convene on Mount Sinai [the leaders of] Christianity,

Judaism and Islam to work together to give our world a more metaphysical dimension." He aimed to further the interfaith work begun at Assisi in 1986, which he had quietly continued. In January 1993, he had met, again in Assisi, with representatives of American and European bishops' conferences and Protestant, Moslem, and Jewish officials. (Many Orthodox rejected his invitation.) The agenda was prayer and fasting to end the proliferating civil wars, and to replace "a society based on selfishness and greed" with "the civilization of love."

In November 1994, he officiated in Rome at the sixth World Conference on Religion and Peace, an organization founded by Japanese Buddhists and American Christians in 1968, which now included other religions. Cardinal Cassidy hosted a similar interfaith gathering in Florence in 1995. The pope obviously sought to change the world through spiritual thought, regardless of denomination.

In 1995, he issued two encyclicals: *Evangelium Vitae* ("The Gospel of Life"), which further pursued Cardinal Bernardin's idea of a unified philosophy championing life, and *Ut Unum Sint* ("That All May Be One"), which tried to breathe new life into John Paul's unshakable desire to unify Christianity by the year 2000. He recalled by name leaders of other churches he had met with happily, half a dozen times mentioning the Orthodox Dimitrios—though never Dimitrios's successor Bartholomew, with whom he would clash at the Vatican a month later.

Ut Unum Sint contained some tantalizing ecumenical language, perhaps for the first time offering an olive branch long enough for something to perch on. John Paul called ecumenism "a dialogue of conversion," but said that meant a "conversion to the will of the Father." Did he mean to omit a conversion to Catholicism? He talked about "the primacy of the bishop of Rome." But then he said,

> I have a particular responsibility . . . above all in acknowledging the ecumenical aspirations of the majority of the Christian communities and in heeding the request made of me to find a way of exercising the primacy, which, while in no way renouncing what is essential to its mission, is nonetheless open to a new situation.

A "new situation"? He didn't elaborate. Was it truly a sign that papal power might be shared in a merger, even though he believed the power descended from Jesus, through Peter? Or was the encyclical one more wishful but futile thought—one more desire to clear the ecumenical hurdle while refusing to jump? Time would tell.

∽

As John Paul left for trips to the United States and Latin America in late 1995 and early 1996, he had reigned longer than all but eighteen of the 263 previous popes. He had made sixty-eight foreign trips, and 120 within Italy. He had written twelve encyclicals and several dozen other major documents known as letters, or exhortations. He had written one year's biggest best-seller, and his recorded recital of prayers had recently hit number 53 on the charts of British pop albums—ahead of the latest work by pop singer Sinead O'Connor, who had offended many people by tearing up the pope's picture on the *Saturday Night Live* TV show several years before. He had met 510 heads of state and 150 prime ministers, and had created 137 cardinals.[8]

He had also led the peaceful overthrow of communism, and maybe ended the threat of one-world totalitarianism altogether. He had shown how to win nonviolently a war that other leaders considered a competition of violence. But his main work, in his eyes, was undone.

In the United States, illegitimacy had risen from 5 percent of all births in 1960 to 18 percent in 1980 to 31 percent now—a figure that would have astounded earlier generations. In some cities, most children were now born out of wedlock. Political leaders carried on as if they were unconcerned that these children might produce a radically less stable and productive society. Many talked as if the problem were racial, though only 36 percent of the illegitimate babies were black. From 1960 to 1990, white illegitimacy increased tenfold, from 2.3 percent to 21.8 percent, while black illegitimacy tripled, from 23 percent to 67.9 percent.[9] How could the necessary reconciliation of races occur if two of three black children entered the world without the basic benefit of married parents?

Families were fragmenting. Increasingly, household units consisted of only one or two people. Only 35 percent of living units included children, down from 56 percent in 1970. One might theorize that affluence allowed more independent living—except that one in four white families with children and a whopping 63 percent of black families with children now had only one parent at home.[10] The birth rate among teenagers had more than doubled since 1970 and was now higher than that among women in their thirties.[11]

Half of all American marriages ended in divorce, up from 21 percent in the first half of the century. Children of divorced parents are much more likely—and children of twice-divorced parents many times more likely—to get divorced themselves, or to suffer anxiety and depression and have marital problems.[12]

On any given day, one black man in three was either in jail or on probation or parole. Although about the same percentage of whites as blacks used illegal drugs, black users were many times more likely to be arrested for it.[13]

The United States had become the most economically unequal of the industrial nations. Its child poverty rate was four times that of the others. The share of private wealth owned by the richest 1 percent of Americans had fallen from 45 percent in 1929 down to 20 percent in 1980, the end of the New Deal era. By 1990 it was back up to 35 percent.[14] Whereas in 1975, the chief executive of General Electric Company was paid the equivalent of thirty-six average family incomes, in 1995 he was paid the equivalent of 133 average family incomes.[15] Meanwhile, the middle class—once America's unique pride—shrank: 90 percent of the nation's population now lived on less than one third of its wealth.[16]

If the elite were creating a prosperity in which everyone participated, they might claim to have earned their larger share. But while the official unemployment rate remained low, at around 6 percent (double that for blacks), a sharply increasing and not well measured percentage of employed workers faced declining security, wages, and benefits. "Many contingent workers face daunting child-care and family problems without any of the usual safety nets such as paid sick or personal days, flextime or even a controllable work schedule," reported the *Wall Street Journal*.[17]

Eighty-one percent of Americans said they were dissatisfied with the international situation (more than during the Cold War), and 73 percent didn't like how things were going at home (more than in a long time). They worried increasingly about losing their jobs.[18] It was often said that insecurity was the necessary price of society's advancement from an industrial to an informational economy—as if the purpose of an economy was to satisfy some abstract academic goal rather than to satisfy the people in it.

Seventy percent of black teenagers and 31 percent of white knew someone who had been shot within the past five years. Fifty-seven percent of teens said they had cheated on a test, and almost all thought cheating was all right because jobs and college admissions depended on it.[19]

A growing number of American voters and presidential candidates wanted to eliminate Social Security, the basic safety net added to the American economy in the 1930s. Younger taxpayers in particular argued that they could more profitably invest in private retirement plans—which was often true, but it lost sight of the social concern over millions of uncared-for elderly people that had inspired Social Security in the first place. There was increasing support for taxing capital gains at a lower rate than wages gained from labor—the ultimate profanation of John Paul's fundamental creed about the superior value of work (as well as a cash transfer from poorer people to richer ones). Like the neutron bomb, the capital-gains preference valued the product over the man who made it.

A general rebellion against paying taxes at all to support common activity was sweeping the U.S., propelled partly by self-centeredness and partly by dissatisfaction over poor government management. A new Congress was pledged to deflate government across a broad front. It was commonly asserted that religious and other voluntary private organizations could provide the social safety net. Like many such organizations, Catholic charities said they would be overwhelmed and unable to fill the gap in a government abdication.[20]

As John Paul flew to the U.S., Paul Bauman, associate editor of the Catholic magazine *Commonweal*, wrote that it was unfair of the pope to label U.S. society a "culture of death." Bauman said that "Americans rightly detected a note of very European petulance" in the pope's reaction to their country. Consumerism was not "the simple manifestation of greed that the pope implies it to be. It is much more the inevitable result of a culture of very competitive individualists. It is, for better and worse, the signature of mass democracy."

On one point, Bauman was surely right: John Paul did not, truly, understand and embrace democracy—especially the idea of a pendulum that constantly swings back and forth in the competition of interest groups. He did not grasp the notion that some kinds of conflict were perpetual and beneficial within a community committed to maintaining a common system. In democracy, there was no one correct place for the pendulum of power to be, except always in motion.

Not understanding this would continue to cost John Paul a vital audience in countries—particularly the United States—with long records of success. And it would also cost his audience the chance to see that the pendulum might have swung out of balance. In a vacuum of political leadership, the pope was one of the few voices, and perhaps the strongest voice, pulling the pendulum back toward values that many people considered basic to humanity, which were being trampled.

The underlying economic and political problem of the world John Paul was flying into continued to be the rise of the multinational corporation as a power replacing the nation-state. Whether the rise of corporate power was the cause or the result of moral decay could be debated—probably it was a little of both, chicken and egg.

Historian Arthur Schlesinger, Jr., wrote, "The assault on the national government is represented as a disinterested movement to 'return' power to the people. But the withdrawal of the national government does not transfer power to the people. It transfers power to the historical rival of the national government and the prime cause of its enlargement—the great corporate interests."[21]

Marx and Engels had theorized that when working people took charge, the state would "wither away." Ironically, as commentator Anthony Giddens wrote, "Marx and Engels are almost forgotten.... But perhaps the very global triumph of capitalism, perversely, is bringing about the disappearance of government they believed only communism could achieve.... Contracting out much of their work, the multinationals have created a stateless web of corporate alliances."[22] The biggest international corporations owned more assets than all but a handful of the world's countries.

It was a problem that reduced many people to the same feeling of helplessness Poles had felt under communism until 1978.

More than 80 percent of Americans considered themselves religious, and more than 40 percent said they attended services at least weekly—about 25 percent more than in Spain, with other European countries trailing far behind. American church attendance was rising, particularly among adults in their forties.[23] But barely one in three Catholics went to Mass weekly, only about half as many as a generation before. Since 1965, thirteen thousand Catholic schools had dwindled to nine thousand. Increasingly, small parishes were led by nuns or laymen for lack of priests. The number of nuns had shrunk by nearly half since 1965—from 181,000 to 94,000—and half of them were over sixty-five years old.[24]

More than 90 percent of American Catholics thought they could be good Catholics even if they divorced and remarried, or used contraceptives. Two thirds thought that the Eucharist was symbolic, not the actual body and blood of Jesus, as the Church teaches, and believed that priests should be allowed to marry. Fifty-nine percent said that the Church was out of touch with the needs of its members, and that women should be accepted as priests. Half felt they could be good Catholics and still doubt the authority of the pope.[25]

American women aborted about 1.6 million fetuses a year, an average of two abortions for every five live births. (By comparison, Moscow registered 137,000 abortions in 1994, more than double its 64,000 live births; the average Russian woman had five abortions in her lifetime.)

A shift in ethics and morality was occurring throughout Western culture. As Vaclav Havel put it, "We live in the postmodern world, where everything is possible and almost nothing is certain.... Experts can explain anything in the objective world, yet we understand our own lives less and less."[26] In *Evangelium Vitae*, John Paul wrote of a diminishing reverence for the human spirit:

> A culture has emerged that denies solidarity.... This culture is actively fostered by powerful cultural, economic, and political currents that encourage a ... society excessively concerned with efficiency.... A person who, because of illness, handicap, or, more simply, just by existing, compromises the well-being or life-style of

those who are more favored, tends to be looked upon as an enemy to be resisted or eliminated.

John Paul would lecture Americans on the shame of their turning their backs on their brethren with falling fortunes and on immigrants—and thus on their own history. They would remember mainly his opposition to abortion, birth control, and women priests. Once more, they would applaud him, praise him—and not change. And he would struggle back onto the plane, looking frailer, praying that the year 2000 would bring a second miracle.

NOTES

Before I rely on a book or publication for information that is especially significant or subject to dispute, my practice is to try to talk with the author involved, to go over what he or she has written, assess the evidence, and sometimes to talk with original sources. Interviews with an author can determine what I write as much as what appears on the printed page. I have spent many hours, often over many days, talking with the authors whose books are most referenced below.

BOOK I: REVELATIONS

Chapter I

I. My observation at a spellbinding University of Chicago lecture. **2.** (Kansas City: Andrews and McMeel, 1979.) **3.** My description comes from viewing videotape but is confirmed by eyewitnesses.

Chapter 2

I. The Center for European Meetings and Studies. Gawronska says it never asked for, nor to her knowledge received, any U.S. government funds. **2.** One was Jerzy Turowicz. **3.** Wilton Wynn of *Time* magazine. **4.** Two colorful stories were published about the inauguration by reputable authors who say their sources can't be identified. I couldn't confirm them. George Weigel, in *The Final*

Revolution (New York: Oxford University Press, 1992), pages 93–94, wrote that John Paul prolonged the ceremony to thwart the communists. He said John Paul learned that Polish TV had allotted four hours for the Mass so that government commentators could put their own spin on it afterward, exploiting the visual backdrop of the Vatican. Weigel said the pope ordered the ceremony stretched out to four hours to preclude any commentary. That, he says, inspired the tiresome procession of cardinals.

Andrew Greeley, in *The Making of the Popes 1978*, page 229, said John Paul moved the ceremony from afternoon to morning so that he and other Europeans could watch a big soccer match on television later in the day; the morning schedule disrupted the intentions of U.S. networks to carry the inauguration live. **5.** William Brand, an American linguist who had married into a Krakow intellectual family close to Wojtyla and the Church. 6. Quoted in Weigel, *Final Revolution*, page 175. 7. Father Mieczyslaw Malinski. 8. Interview with Kakol.

BOOK 2: GENESIS

Chapter I

1. Norman Davies, *God's Playground* (New York: Columbia University Press, 1984), page 212. 2. In Isaac Deutscher's *Stalin: A Political Biography* (New York: Vintage, 1960), page 116, Stalin quotes Lenin saying, "The Poles hate Russia, and not without reason. We cannot ignore the strength of their nationalist feeling. Our revolution will have to treat them very gently and even allow them to break away from Russia if need be." 3. Isaac Deutscher, *Stalin*, chapter 6. 4. See William L. Shirer's landmark history *The Rise and Fall of the Third Reich* (New York: Simon and Schuster, 1960), chapters 1–3. 5. Many Poles I talked to wondered wryly if a communist victory at the Vistula might have aborted the rise of Hitler, forced the moderation of Soviet communism by Western ideas—thus possibly averting Stalin's rise to power—and led to the demise of communism through its own inefficiency and unpopularity, without decades of bloodshed. But most Poles nonetheless remain glad of the victory.

Chapter 2

1. Except where other sources are cited, the family history comes mostly from *Kalendarium*, which was published in Rome in 1983 under the imprint of Znak, the Krakow publishing house with which Wojtyla was associated for many years. The chief chronicler was Father Adam Boniecki. The book is available only in Polish and was translated for me on commission by Barbara Mezei. I also used the biographies of Longford, Nemec, Szczypka, and Williams, cited individually below. 2. Neither his friends nor his letters mention her. 3. I have been unable to find a specific date for the baby girl's birth. In his interview with André Frossard, published as *"Be Not Afraid!"* by André Frossard and Pope John Paul II (New York: Image Books, 1985), the pope gives the date as "six years before my birth," which was in 1920. 4. Janina Kaczor, quoted in *Sercu Najblizsze* by R. A. Gajczak (Krakow: 1987), translated for me by Jerzy Kopacz without page numbers. 5. André Frossard and Pope John Paul II, *"Be Not Afraid!"* page 13. 6. Jerzy Kluger, Lolek's classmate and friend from the first grade on, says, "She was always being treated by doctors." Another close friend, Zbigniew Silkowski, has written that Lolek later remembered his mother "as a person of poor health, suffering, seeking help from doctors often outside Wadowice [and] as a person who required silence" (quoted in *Mlodziencze lata Karola Wojtyly*, ed. Julius Kydrynski, an anthology of remembrances published by Oficyna Cracovia in Krakow in 1990 and translated for me by Jerzy Kopacz without page numbers). 7. Interview with André Frossard, reported in *"Be Not Afraid!"* I have interviewed Frossard at length and am confident of his diligence and accuracy about his extensive conversations with the pope, much of whose content was not published in their book. 8. See particularly the account of Janina Kaczor. 9. One disease speculated on is tuberculosis, which was rife in Poland then and was often kept secret because of a misguided association with shame. Doctors say TB could have produced her other symptoms. I have checked every source available, but there is simply no good record of her illness. 10. Thomas Bokenkotter, *A Concise History of the Catholic Church* (New York: Doubleday, 1979), page 345. 11. See Bokenkotter, above, chapter 32.

Chapter 3

1. I couldn't locate Banas; the Wadowice parish priest thinks he is dead. But he was interviewed by Mieczyslaw Malinski, a priest from Krakow and friend of Wojtyla's, for a brief biography, *Pope John Paul II*, published in 1979, right after the pope's election (New York: The Seabury Press). I spent extensive time with Malinski and others who knew Banas. 2. From my own interviews with surviving family friends, including Kluger and the Kotlarczyk family survivors, as well as recollections gathered by other biographers. 3. Kluger has produced a memoir, *Letter to His Jewish Friend*, about his times with the pope, with the help of writer Gianfranco Svidercoschi. An English-language edition was to be published in London by Hodder and Stoughton. Kluger graciously gave me a handbound copy of the translation, and I interviewed him at length. 4. Particularly the account of Janina Kaczor. The heart-kidney ailment is medically referred to as myocarditis nephritis. 5. Janina Mrozowa, a friend of Lolek's, says she died at home, while a biography recommended and sold by the nuns who maintain his former home says she died away and entirely alone (*Jan Pawel II, Rodowod*, by Jozef Szczypka [Warsaw: Instytut Wydawniczy Pax 1991]). 6. One is a biography by Monsignor Ludvik Nemec, a Polish priest; his book, *Pope John Paul II: A Festive Profile* (New York: Catholic Book Publishing Co., 1979), was handed to me with a high recommendation by Polish-American Cardinal John Krol of Philadelphia, a close friend of the pope's (who, like other papal friends, says the pope has never told him how his mother died). Even more impressive is a 1982 biography authorized by the Vatican and written by Lord Longford of England, with an enthusiastic endorsement by Cardinal Basil Hume of England in the foreword (published by Papal Visit [Scotland] Ltd.;

U.S. edition, New York: Morrow, 1982). Other sources that say Emilia died in childbirth include a 1988 British Broadcasting Corporation documentary series on the pope, recommended to me by the Vatican, and a 1994 A&E network *Biography* program featuring interviews with people who purportedly knew the pope well. I heard the story that Emilia died in childbirth from many people. 7. From Helena Szczepanska, a teacher and neighbor, quoted in Szczypka, *Jan Pawel II, Rodowod*, page 18. 8. Maria Kydrynska Michalowska, a close friend of Wojtyla's during his school years, says Mrs. Bernhardt, now dead, told her this long ago. She also remarked on Lolek's perhaps overly mature reaction, though she says he finally broke down in private, after the burial. 9. They were in crumbling ill repair by the time I saw them, in 1994, but that only rendered them more a natural part of the foliage and landscape.

Chapter 4

1. Boguslaw Banas, cited in Ludvik Nemec, *John Paul II: A Festive Profile*, early chapters. 2. Wojtyla's later recollections to Archbishop Deskur. 3. Josef Szczypka, *Jan Pawel II, Rodowod*, unnumbered chapter entitled "Smutki i chwile lepsze." 4. Interview for a 1988 BBC documentary, "Papa Wojtyla." 5. Mrs. Janina Kotlarczyk, now dead, quoted in *Pope John Paul II* by Father Mieczyslaw Malinski, page 267. I have interviewed both Malinski and Mrs. Kotlarczyk's daughter. 6. He told this to Father Kazimierz Suder, his seminary classmate in Krakow and now pastor of the Wadowice church, who relayed it to me. 7. From his book with André Frossard, "*Be Not Afraid!*" page 14. 8. Mrs. Szczepanska is quoted in Szczypka's *Jan Pawel II, Rodowod*, page 18. 9. Frossard, "*Be Not Afraid!*," page 14. 10. In both Nemec, *Festive Profile*, and Jerzy Kluger, *Letter to His Jewish Friend*, page 16.

11. Janina Kotlarczyk Mrozowa, interviewed by me, and Janina Opidowicz Kotlarczyk, interviewed by Father Malinski, quoted in Malinski, *Pope John Paul II*, pages 266–267. 12. Bohdanowicz in *Kalendarium*.

Chapter 5

1. Kluger's book *Letter to His Jewish Friend* and an interview and correspondence with him provided much of the information about school conditions in this section. He satisfied me that he had friendly access to the pope even after his book was published, suggesting that the pope accepted it. 2. Much of the theatrical history obviously comes from Lolek's friends who are quoted. But I also owe a huge debt to Jan Ciechowicz, who received his doctorate from the University of Gdansk in 1992 with a thesis on Mieczyslaw Kotlarczyk. He was kind enough to send me not just a copy of it, but also an English-language translation of an article, "Wojtyla and the Theater," adapted from his research. Thanks to Ciechowicz's work, it has been possible for me to go beyond the imprecise memories expressed in interviews and to cite specific dates and events with confidence. 3. From a participant quoted by Ciechowicz (see note 2 above). 4. This story is related in both Jozef Szczypka, *Jan Pawel II, Rodowod*, unnumbered chapter entitled "Smutki i chwile lepsze," and Mieczyslaw Malinski, *Pope John Paul II*, chapter 24. 5. Szczypka, *Jan Pawel II, Rodowod*, unnumbered chapter "Smutki i chwile lepsze." 6. If my judgment is unfairly harsh, I apologize. But I once had to tell my two young daughters of their mother's death, and later, as a widower, show up for various performances and occasions at school. I struggle to imagine a father's abdicating such support.

Chapter 6

1. Hlond accused Jews of pimping, usury, anti-Church plots, and other depravities. See

quotes in Tad Szulc, *Pope John Paul II* (New York: Scribner's, 1995), page 41. 2. Entitled *Zmory*, or "Nightmares," the novel was summed up by George Hunston Williams, a Harvard theology professor with an expertise in Polish culture, in a book he wrote on the pope's philosophical development, *The Mind of John Paul II* (New York: The Seabury Press, 1981), pages 54–55. Unfortunately, like many books cited here, it is now out of print, and its publisher is out of business. Professor Williams also graciously provided many hours of interview time. 3. After World War II, Zegadlowicz's reputation was revived by the communists, who admired his opposition to the Pilsudski government of the 1930s. The Wadowice high school was renamed in his honor. He had died in 1941, at age fifty-three, and was no longer around to object to the communist dictatorship, as—to judge from his work—he likely would have. 4. Wojciech Zukrowski. 5. Kasia Zak moved out of Wadowice with her family soon after graduation. I couldn't trace her.

Chapter 7

1. Interview with Jerzy Kluger. 2. Recollection to reporters while in Rome visiting Pope John Paul II. 3. The play was *The Un-Divine Comedy*, a twist on Dante by Zygmunt Krasinski (1812–1859), whose father had been a friend and defender of Russian Tsar Nicholas I, even after the tsar repressed a Polish rebellion in 1830. The play is described in detail in George Hunston Williams, *The Mind of John Paul II* (New York: The Seabury Press, 1981), pages 58–60. 4. Pius XI's defenders point out that he later expressed second thoughts about the wisdom of aiding Mussolini and signing the Lateran Treaty, and that he declared himself (though not at maximum volume, it must be said) against Germany's anti-Semitic policy after Hitler took over. He died before the extermination program began. 5. William L.

Shirer, *The Rise and Fall of the Third Reich* (New York: Simon and Schuster, 1960), page 234. **6.** From Monsignor Angelo Rancalli's letters, published by Giustino Farnedy, abbot of San Giacomo of Pontida, 1993, quoted in the *National Catholic Reporter,* July and December, 1993. **7.** Many versions of this story exist. Jerzy Kluger's book, *Letter to His Jewish Friend,* has Lolek himself responding to Sapieha's question. I have presented a consensus version, weighted toward accounts drawn from my interviews with contemporaries, particularly Halina Krolikiewicz. **8.** Quoted in André Frossard and Pope John Paul II, *"Be Not Afraid!,"* page 15.

Chapter 8

1. Lord Longford's authorized biography, *Pope John Paul II,* page 42. **2.** The Bober sequence, except where otherwise noted, is from remembrances in *Mlodziencze lata Karola Wojtyly,* ed. Juliusz Kydrynski, translated for me by Jerzy Kopacz. **3.** Danuta Michalowska, in an interview with me in Krakow. **4.** *Kalendarium* is the source of all information in this paragraph. **5.** Halina. **6.** I saw some of Sapieha's correspondence courtesy of Church historian Robert Graham in Rome. **7.** *Kalendarium.*

Chapter 9

1. From Mieczyslaw Malinski. **2.** William Shirer, *The Rise and Fall of the Third Reich,* page 625. **3.** Quoted in *Kalendarium.* **4.** Lolek's later recollection to Jerzy Kluger. **5.** To papal biographer David Willey, in *God's Politician: John Paul at the Vatican* (New York: St. Martin's, 1992). I spoke with Kydrynski by phone in Poland in November 1993; he was traveling and unable to meet me, but was most cordial and promised to see me when I returned. The day I arrived in Poland the next spring, four days before I was to interview him, he died. I did speak with his sister, Maria

Kydrynska Michalowicz, and with Willey, who is the British Broadcasting Corporation's correspondent in Rome. **6.** From Jerzy Kluger, who exchanged stories with the pope at a reunion to be described later. **7.** Letter from Lolek to Mieczyslaw Kotlarczyk, reprinted in *Kalendarium.* **8.** Interview with Roszkowski. **9.** Quoted in William L. Shirer, *The Rise and Fall of the Third Reich,* pages 634–635. **10.** Shirer, *The Rise and Fall of the Third Reich,* page 662. **11.** Maryjane Osa, "Resistance, Persistence and Change: The Transformation of the Catholic Church in Poland," *Eastern European Politics and Societies,* vol. 3, no. 2 (1989), pp. 267–298. I also interviewed Osa by telephone. **12.** Pope John Paul II with André Frossard, *"Be Not Afraid!,"* page 14. **13.** From Vatican Press Secretary Joaquin Navarro-Valls. **14.** Here, as in many cases, I am combining translations. If reputable translators differ, I have chosen what seems to me the most readable language. In this case, I have blended the work of Jerzy Kopacz, my Krakow interpreter, with that of Boleslaw Taborski, who published parts of this letter in his edition of Pope John Paul II's *Collected Plays and Writings on Theater* (Berkeley: University of California Press, 1987).

Throughout this section, I have used information from nearly a dozen letters written by Wojtyla to Kotlarczyk, which I was allowed to read in Krakow by Kotlarczyk's daughter Anna Kotlarczyk Pakosiewicz. I could not locate Kotlarczyk's alternating letters back to Wojtyla.

Mrs. Pakosiewicz, who says she has been taken advantage of in the past, imposed complex conditions on my quoting from the letters, which may have produced some awkward syntax. Some of this material has been published elsewhere, as in the Taborski book, but much else has not been. **15.** The *Tablet* (London), Aug. 11, 1984. **16.** Reported by Jan Novak, himself a courier for the Polish resistance and later head of the Polish desk of Radio Free

Europe, now a resident of Washington, D.C.
17. This according to Cardinal Andrzej
Deskur, a Pole whom John Paul II made head
of social communications at the Vatican.

Chapter 10

1. George Hunston Williams gives a good
account in his chapter on Tyranowski in *The
Mind of John Paul II,* though the account here
comes also from Malinski and others who
knew him, and from what Wojtyla himself
wrote about Tyranowski in *Tygodnik Powszechny*
and said in the Frossard interviews. I saw the
photograph at the Znak office in Krakow.
2. He credited this thought to the apostle
Paul in the Gospels. 3. From *John of the
Cross: Selected Writings,* ed. Kieran Kavanaugh,
(New York: The Paulist Press, 1987), pages
45, 67, 69, and 71. 4. Pope John Paul II
and André Frossard, *"Be Not Afraid!,"* page 18.
5. Although I spent countless hours with
Malinski and have used what he said in those
interviews, I have also woven in here some
language from his book, *Pope John Paul II* (New
York: The Seabury Press, 1979), and an
interview he gave to the British Broadcasting
Corporation. Everything that is in quotation
marks here was clearly in quotation marks in
the Malinski original.

Chapter 11

1. Some accounts, including Ciechowicz's,
describe this as their first meeting. Maria
Kydrynska Michalowska was quite certain in
our interview that the boys had met Osterwa
the previous summer in connection with his
attendance at the performance of *Moon Cavalier* at the university. She seemed clear and
detailed enough that I have stuck with her
version. 2. From Zukrowski. Others say
Mrs. Kydrynska found them the jobs; Maria
Kydrynska Michalowska, who detests
Zukrowski, insists it was not he but Mrs.
Lewaj, the French teacher, who got them

work. On this point I believe Zukrowski.
Mrs. Lewaj found Lolek a later job at a factory where she had a personal connection;
Zukrowski's connection was at the quarry,
where the whole group originally worked.
Since the Kydrynskis disliked Zukrowski, they
would not likely have procured a job at the
quarry for him. 3. This comes not only
from Zukrowski but from Franciszek Labus, a
shot-firer, who wrote about it in a book of
recollections put together for Cardinal
Wojtyla in 1966 by Sister Jadwiga of the
Krakow curia. 4. Quoted in the *National
Catholic Register,* Dec. 1993. 5. Margaret Stan-
islawska, who accompanied Ms. Michalowska
to the interview I arranged, and contributed
many of her own insights. 6. Letter to
Kotlarczyk. 7. Kydrynski, in the BBC documentary series on the pope. 8. As published in the *Tablet* (London), April 14, 1979.

Chapter 12

1. Now Mrs. Maria Kydrynska Michalowska, no relation to Danuta Michalowska.
2. Juliusz Kydrynski, interview with *Polityka*
magazine, Warsaw, reprinted in *Philadelphia Sunday Bulletin,* Nov. 5, 1978. 3. As noted earlier, Kydrynski died four days before my
scheduled interview with him. 4. To André
Frossard, published in Pope John Paul II and
Frossard, *"Be Not Afraid!,"* page 13. 5. In
response to written questions I was allowed to
submit through Press Secretary Navarro-Valls,
who returned with answers after a discussion
with the pope. 6. Maria Kydrynska
Michalowska. 7. *The Soul-King* by Juliusz
Slowacki. 8. Danuta Michalowska. 9. By
Sister Jadwiga of the Krakow curia. Malinski
found the album and quoted some of it in his
own book, *Pope John Paul II.* Some of these
accounts are also cited in *Kalendarium.* I have
omitted, as did Malinski, the story told by one
worker cited in *Kalendarium* because it sounded
so melodramatic as to rouse skepticism, and
none of the other accounts supported it: Jozef

Dudek, a lab technician, said Lolek had come to work freezing and coatless in winter because he gave his fur-lined jacket to an old man he met on the road, who he feared might freeze to death. Dudek also said that Lolek once intervened to prevent his colleagues from lynching a German at the plant. The reader is free to decide whether, in the absence of any other mention of these remarkable incidents, they are true.   **10.** This comes both from Professor George Hunston Williams and Father Mieczyslaw Malinski.   **11.** Untitled work, as published in the *Tablet* (London), Jan. 20, 1979, translated by Noel Clark.

Chapter 13

1. In the 1988 British Broadcasting Corporation documentary. He was speaking in English, with unsteady syntax, but his meaning seems clear enough as bracketed here. **2.** Pope John Paul II and André Frossard, *"Be Not Afraid!,"* page 15.   **3.** *Kalendarium.* **4.** This information relayed to me by Joaquin Navarro-Valls, the Vatican press officer, in response to my written questions to the pope. **5.** I have combined in this quote descriptions that the pope gave of his experience with the Wais book in interviews with Mieczyslaw Malinski and André Frossard. Every word is his own.   **6.** His last part was the title role in *Samuel Zborowski,* about a sixteenth-century revolutionary who was beheaded in Krakow. Kotlarczyk himself played the devil. **7.** Kudlinski died long ago.

Chapter 14

1. John Paul acknowledged as much on a visit to Germany in June 1996, declining to read prepared texts that praised the Church and instead charging that it should have done more during the war.   **2.** The *Tablet* (London), March 2, 1985, quoting a new study by the German Bishops' Conference.   **3.** The Polish figures are taken from Polish Mon-

signor Ludvik Nemec, *Pope John Paul II: A Festive Profile.* One might be skeptical of such exact figures in times of uncontrolled turmoil, but they accord roughly with calculations found elsewhere.   **4.** Archbishop Cesare Orsenigo. **5.** In 1943, Pius finally appointed a British archbishop as his representative to the exile government, without the rank of nuncio, but it was very little, very late.   **6.** From various reports I found at the U.S. National Archive. **7.** Reports cited in this section came from the OSS, or Office of Strategic Services; I found them at the U.S. National Archive in Washington.   **8.** Recounted in Wilton Wynn, *Keepers of the Keys* (New York: Random House, 1988). Verified by Church historians at Jesuit headquarters in Rome.   **9.** The earliest painting I found on personal inspection. **10.** Fathers Mieczyslaw Malinski and Kazimierz Suder, in interviews, both recalled such remarks. Widespread Polish folklore holds that on May 5, 1944, Sapieha invited Governor General Frank for dinner, then served him only dry bread. Most accounts depict Sapieha as having been defiant. Harvard's Professor George Hunston Williams reports that some old Nazi records he found—which he says have since been stolen from his office— describe the meeting and claim Sapieha made a cowardly plea for help on behalf of the Church, denouncing Jews and partisans; such a record, of course, could have been concocted for purposes of propaganda. A relative of Sapieha's, Andrzej Potocki, who as a youth was involved in the archbishop's dealings with the Germans, made a strong case to me that the fabled Frank-Sapieha meeting never occurred; Potocki has also served Pope John Paul II, as will be related later.   **11.** From Boleslaw Taborski in his edition of Wojtyla's *Collected Plays and Writings on Theater,* pages 147–159.   **12.** Marek Skwarnicki, poetry editor of *Tygodnik Powszechny.*   **13.** I have used Taborski's translation in his book *Collected Plays and Writings on Theater.* Here as elsewhere in this book, I have made occasional minor changes to a published translation to improve slight awkwardnesses in English style, but never in such a way as might alter the original meaning. **14.** Documents seen by me at the National Archive. **15.** Published reports that Wojtyla entered the priesthood immediately after Halina's marriage, as if his decision were a reaction to this event, are simply untrue. **16.** Information given on Wyszynski before and after this anecdote comes mostly from Andrzej Micewski, *Cardinal Wyszynski: A Biography* (San Diego: Harcourt Brace, 1984), marvelously translated into English by William R. Brand and Katarzyna Mroczkowska-Brand, both of whom were very helpful to me in Poland, as was Micewski. The anecdote is from John Krol, the retired cardinal/archbishop of Philadelphia, who also supplied material about Wyszynski. **17.** Andrzej Micewski. **18.** Andrzej Micewski, *Cardinal Wyszynski,* pages 15–16.

Chapter 15

1. From the story he later told Jerzy Kluger. **2.** This particular quote from the BBC documentary. **3.** This paragraph from *Kalendarium.* **4.** This information from declassified reports I read at the National Archive. The public actions of what was called the Lublin Committee are detailed in many histories. **5.** Wojtyla described this conversation in a lecture he gave during a spiritual retreat at the Vatican in 1976, published as *Sign of Contradiction* (New York: The Seabury Press, 1979). **6.** Mieczyslaw Malinski, papal biography and interviews. **7.** Wycislo is now retired and living in Wisconsin. **8.** *Triumph and Tragedy* (Boston: Houghton Mifflin, 1953), page 368. **9.** Feb. 13, 1945.

Chapter 16

1. A fellow seminarian, Andrzej Bazinski, witnessed the incident and was quoted in

Kalendarium. **2.** From a U.S. intelligence report I saw at the National Archive. The Uniates had appealed to Pius to intervene with the Polish bishops on their behalf; he replied with an insultingly small cash contribution, and offered no help with the Poles. **3.** As reported and translated by Professor George Hunston Williams, *The Mind of John Paul II,* page 92. **4.** U.S. intelligence reports, National Archive. **5.** Accounts of this era can be found in many histories, but I most like Maryjane Osa's article "Resistance, Persistence and Change: The Transformation of the Catholic Church in Poland," *Eastern European Politics and Societies,* vol. 3, no. 2 (1989), pp. 267–298. Christopher Simpson's book *Blowback* (New York: Weidenfeld and Nicolson, 1988) gives a good account of the so-called "rat-line" by which some churchmen and Western government officials secretly helped thousands of German Nazis escape justice for the mass murder of civilians. Insight into Pius XII's Vatican management comes from Wilton Wynn, *Keepers of the Keys* (New York: Random House, 1988). **6.** The information in this section comes from *Kalendarium* and from Professor Williams. **7.** From Mieczyslaw Malinski. **8.** From Konstanty Gebert, a Jewish journalist and Solidarity hero and now a featured writer for *Tygodnik Mazowsze,* Poland's leading post-communist newspaper. His accounts are supported by a collection of books and articles he showed me, including *From a Ruined Garden* by Jonathan Boyarin and Jack Kugelmass (New York: Schocken Books, 1983), and by various 1940s reports by S. L. Shneidermann in the *Jewish Chronicle* (London), which include the Hlond quote. Hlond's anti-Semitic attitude in general has been widely cited, for example in Tad Szulc, *Pope John Paul II* (New York: Scribner's, 1995), pages 40, 41, and 68. **9.** This idea comes from Konstanty Gebert, who has collected impressive documentation of

Polish anti-Semitism. 10. Interview with Mazowiecki. 11. Jude Dougherty, dean of philosophy at Catholic University in Washington. 12. Technically, November 1 is All Saints' Day and November 2 All Souls' Day. But in practice, November 1 is when Polish Catholics visit the graves of their relatives and loved ones. 13. Discussed in a letter he wrote from Rome to Mrs. Lewaj, shown to me by the family of Mrs. Szkocka.

Chapter 17

1. Jan Bosco, who founded a minor religious order. 2. Jozef Szczypka, *Jan Pawel II, Rodowod*, page 120. 3. Father Konrad Hejmo says Sapieha liked to say, "If you want to have a good understanding of Catholicism, I am not in favor of the Gregorian." 4. From George Hunston Williams. Interviews with him elaborating on chapter 4 of his *The Mind of John Paul II* were one important source for this section. 5. Williams, see note 4. 6. *Wisdom of the West* (London: Crescent Books, 1959), pages 82, 87. 7. Paul Kahn, Yale law professor. 8. From his conversation with Wilton Wynn, Aug. 22, 1986, to be further described in the portion of this book describing that day. 9. Garrigou-Lagrange was a friend of Maritain's, and specialized in reconciling Thomism with mysticism. He wrote admiringly of Saint John of the Cross, which probably helped draw Wojtyla to him. 10. Quoted in Thomas Bokenkotter, *A Concise History of the Catholic Church*, page 375. 11. *Kalendarium* says four teachers gave him a perfect score of 40, but Ciappi insisted to me it was only three.

Chapter 18

1. Sources for information on Pio include C. Bernard Ruffin, *Padre Pio: The True Story* (Huntington, Ind.: Our Sunday Visitor, Inc., 1991). Ruffin, obviously a devout Catholic, is convinced that Pio was everything he

claimed to be. Other sources include D. Scott Rogo, *Miracles* (New York: HarperCollins, 1982), a 1956 *New York Times Magazine* profile by Herbert L. Matthews, and other *New York Times* articles over the years, plus quoted interviews. 2. Ruffin quotes firsthand accounts by a doctor who prescribed a mind-altering drug for Pio and by a priest/colleague of Pio's who helped administer various such drugs and said he weaned Pio from them (*Padre Pio*, page 370). 3. That this was the purpose of the trip is reiterated in *Kalendarium* and Wojtyla's own letters. 4. Fathers Bill Conrad, Bill Weinheimer, and Robert Schiefen, all of Florida. The impression in Poland was that Sapieha paid for the trip, but Bishop W. Thomas Larkin and Monsignor Joseph Dawson have assured me that he did not. 5. *Kalendarium.* 6. Joseph Cardijn. 7. When my first translator complained that the Polish in his letters was so awkward that she couldn't produce good English from it, I tried several other translators; each had the same complaint. 8. I have seen the title variously translated as "The Problem of Faith" and "The Virtue of Faith." 9. I have relied on the translation and summary of Harvard professor and papal biographer George Hunston Williams, *The Mind of John Paul II*, pages 107–109. 10. Father Hieronymous Noldin. 11. For further details on these operations, beginning with the Italian scheme, see my book *Endless Enemies* (New York: Congdon and Weed, 1984; reprint, New York: Viking Penguin, 1987). The covert operations will reappear later in the pope's story.

BOOK 3: LAMENTATIONS

Chapter 1

1. This date from *Kalendarium* (Rome: Znak, 1983). Lord Longford, *Pope John Paul II* (New

York: Morrow, 1982), page 58, dates his arrival to July 18.   **2.** Quoted in Longford, *Pope John Paul II*, page 58.   **3.** Again, the date given for Hlond's death varies depending on which source you consult, though the matter should be beyond dispute. I have accepted the account of Andrzej Micewski, who did, after all, write the biography of Wyszynski, who replaced Hlond.   **4.** Literature about this kind of thing is ubiquitous. For one source, see Wilton Wynn, *Keepers of the Keys* (New York: Random House, 1988).   **5.** Document dated February 28, 1950, from the National Archive.   **6.** Cardinal Krol, who granted me several long interviews and lent me some valuable books to help with this project, died in 1996.

Chapter 2

1. From Lord Longford, *Pope John Paul II*, page 59. The material about Malinski's visit came from my interviews with him and from his book, *Pope John Paul II* (New York: The Seabury Press, 1979), chapter 10.   **2.** From Longford, *Pope John Paul II*, page 60, confirmed by interviews with parishioners who were young then.   **3.** Father Michael Zembrzuski, whom I interviewed.   **4.** From U.S. embassy documents seen at the National Archive. The meetings were infiltrated by CIA sources. They were also infused with Polish government shills who encouraged members to go along.   **5.** The group, the Union of Catholic Intellectuals and Leaders, is described in U.S. embassy documents at the National Archive. Turowicz acknowledges supporting peace movements in his youth, but in his written reply to me dodged the issue of the specific group, merely asserting that his positions were consistent with those of the bishops.   **6.** Most material in this section comes from records of cable traffic from the U.S. embassy in Warsaw in 1950, seen by me at the National Archive.   **7.** The U.S. embassy, in secret, now declassi-

fied reports at the National Archive, also reported that its contacts with bishops—probably through the CIA—were "fleeting, irregular and surreptitious." Whatever may have been going on with Pius and Mindszenty, cooperation between the CIA and the Polish Church was less substantial than propaganda for either side in the Cold War suggested.   **8.** U.S. intelligence report, National Archive. Interviews with former communist officials suggest that such "guidance" was almost always imposed by the Soviets, not requested.   **9.** From various cables seen at the National Archive. April 30, 1950, U.S. embassy official Cecil B. Lyon cabled the State Department, "While the Church has . . . gained little, if anything, the [government] has won almost all the points it has been pressing."   **10.** From my interviews with Zembrzuski.   **11.** State Department cables identify the source only as a "Polish underground leader" from London.   **12.** From State Department cables seen by me at the National Archive. The American spies were presumably from the CIA, though the documents don't spell that out. The cables refer to input from British and French spies as well as American. In notes to each other, the spies lamented their inability to approach Sapieha directly for fear that the communists would find out and accuse him of spying for the West. Unlike American records, European diplomatic and intelligence documents are generally not publicly available.   **13.** A State Department document spells the name "Vijciech," but I have used the more usual Polish spelling. The documents supporting this section were seen by me at the National Archive.   **14.** Wojtyla probably knew Turowski: due to a communications breakdown, the Belgian College was not ready to receive Wojtyla when he arrived in Rome in 1946, so he stayed for a month at the Pallantine residence.   **15.** A report was compiled by Garret G. Ackerson, Jr., a diplomat, and dated August 29, 1950. National Archive.

Chapter 3

1. An unidentified U.S. informer infiltrated a vacation home for Polish priests near Krakow and reported what the guests said. 2. Interview with Kazimierz Suder. 3. Others say Sapieha ordered Wojtyla to use a pseudonym for writing published outside the Church. 4. Peter Levi, writing in the *Tablet* (London), April 7, 1979. Samples of the poems are included in his article. 5. From Zdzislaw Najder. 6. Truman was pressured to use the A-bomb to help win in Korea, and said once at a press conference that he was considering it. 7. His friends in Poland told American agents that he spoke of it frequently, as reported in State Department cables seen by me at the National Archive. 8. This last quote from historian Peter Raina, now of the Free University of Berlin, who gained Wyszynski's confidence and has written many books about the Polish Church in this period. Raina was gracious with interview time and access to files. 9. Interviews with König. 10. Other sources include Grzegorz Pollak of the Catholic Information Agency in Warsaw. 11. See Wilton Wynn, *Keepers of the Keys,* chapter 4. The other cardinal in faver of a council was Ernesto Ruffini. Ironically, Ruffini and Ottaviani would both oppose the central work of the Second Vatican Council when it finally was convened, 1962–65. 12. George Hunston Williams, *The Mind of John Paul II* (New York: The Seabury Press, 1981), chapter 5, and Mieczyslaw Malinski, *Pope John Paul II,* pages 109–110. 13. Interviews with Bardecki (who was Baziak's former aide), Turowicz, and others. 14. Malinski, *Pope John Paul II,* pages 109–110, and interviews with him and others who knew Wojtyla at this time. *Kalendarium* covers some of this material. 15. Wyszynski's homilies were often reported by American agents in attendance, whose accounts are now filed in the National Archive. When he wanted to advocate "bringing up your children in the spirit of God," for example, he would add that doing so rendered "an important service to the community, to the Nation, and to the State, for you introduce into public life citizens who are well disciplined, prepared for social life, and respectful of authority." Communists would have a hard time faulting that. Another illustration: he solicited contributions of books for religious classes by lecturing on the virtue of charity and citing books as an example.

Chapter 4

1. Pope John Paul II, *Crossing the Threshold of Hope* (New York: Knopf, 1994), page 38. 2. Father Edward Vacek, a Scheler scholar at Weston School of Theology in Cambridge, Mass., says it's not clear how much Scheler got from Kierkegaard and how much he did on his own, but in any event, the ideas set down by Kierkegaard reappear—importantly—in Scheler. 3. He was not much studied at Wojtyla's schools, and his books weren't on Wojtyla's scholastic library list. 4. Although some say Kierkegaard didn't call his ideas existentialism, he often referred to the "existential." 5. Interview with Lustiger. 6. Professor George Hunston Williams has noted this as well. 7. This is Monsignor Richard Malone's theory. 8. George Hunston Williams, *The Mind of John Paul II,* chapter 5. One major point of contention was whether an ethic should be based on duty, as Kant believed, or on value—what one could derive from it—which Scheler (as might be expected from his life) preferred. As described in the text, Wojtyla based his conclusions mostly on other issues. Kant called his duplication of the Golden Rule the categorical imperative.

Chapter 5

1. Interview with Stanislawa Grabska, a former student and later a colleague of Wojtyla's, in addition to comments from Danuta, Malinski, and others who will be quoted later. The material from Danuta is taken from Mieczyslaw Malinski, *Pope John Paul II*, pages 247–248. **2.** Zygmunt Kubiak of the Laski intellectual group. **3.** Quoted in Andrzej Micewski, *Cardinal Wyszynski: A Biography* (San Diego: Harcourt Brace, 1984) pages 92–93. **4.** Interview with Father Andrzej Bardecki. **5.** Bardecki, who covered the trial, agrees with Kozlowski that confiscation of the documents now appears to have been the main impetus for the raid on the archbishop's palace, though rumors at the time blamed the raid on police efforts to embarrass a priest who was having an affair with a woman. In either case, evidence of foreign plotting is said to have been discovered accidentally. **6.** Andrzej Micewski, *Cardinal Wyszynski*, page 99. **7.** Interviews with Jan Novak, director of the radio's Polish branch, and others at Radio Free Europe (to be cited later), as well as with Archbishop Bronislaw Dabrowski, whose role will be explained at a later point in the text. **8.** I saw Wyszynski's texts—and the embassy's reports—at the National Archive. **9.** This missive became known by its most popular phrase, the Latin *non possumus*, referring to those points that Wyszynski said it was "not possible" for the Church to concede on. From U.S. embassy records at the National Archive. (A still-undisclosed source continuously provided the embassy with advance inside details on Wyszynski's battles with the Polish government. The U.S. government has rejected my requests to see files that might disclose how that information was obtained.) **10.** *Kalendarium*.

Chapter 6

1. *Kalendarium* says two books of Wojtyla's were published in 1951 and suggests that their content was mostly religious. I could not find these volumes, but through Professor Nina Gladziuk I did manage to locate Kukolowicz, who showed me copies of the work discussed here, published in 1953 (158 pages) and 1954 (135 pages) as two volumes of the same title. They do not seem to be the books that are described in *Kalendarium*. Nor do they contain the philosophy lectures that Wojtyla delivered later in the decade, which are now being published as *The Lublin Lectures*, and which are of much less general interest. The volumes Kukolowicz printed, *Catholic Social Ethics*, are, in contrast, a fresh and highly revealing find. **2.** From Pieronek's description, this seems to have been the book Kukolowicz printed. The printing network was secret, of course; Pieronek had always assumed that each copy had been individually typed by hand by student volunteers. Other former Wojtyla students also remember such a manual. **3.** A section he wrote on "racism" is among those I was unable to obtain. **4.** I submitted this passage for multiple, careful translations, all of which produced the statement as definitively as I have quoted it. **5.** In the book, he attributed the thought in part to Pope Pius XI. **6.** The original text includes the words "and wars" here, which seems to contradict Wojtyla's earlier reference to war as an unacceptable choice. I have had both passages rechecked by translators, and the contradiction remains. The earlier passage on war, however, is a precise assertion, while in this case *wars* is one word that seems an afterthought in a sentence about something else. An interview with the pope might have clarified this point, but he declined to grant me one.

Chapter 7

1. From historian Peter Raina. 2. Aristo-crats actually began rejecting him. According to Andrzej Micewski, his biographer, Wyszynski sought support from the former head of the Conservative Party, Prince Janusz Radziwill, and was told that Radziwill and his friends needed the government's friendship to survive economically. The aristocrats, who had opposed communism before it came to Poland, now seemed to be abandoning their principles to make what deals they could. 3. These accounts from Micewski, George Weigel, Bishop Tadeusz Pieronek (secretary of the Polish Bishops' Conference), Cardinal John Krol, and U.S. embassy files. 4. Cables seen by me at the National Archive. 5. All from documents seen by me at the National Archive. 6. One priest suggested to me that these group trips supervising young people may have been "not much of a vacation" for Wojtyla, but rather a sacrifice. Those who participated, however, uniformly assert that Wojtyla seemed to love the outings. He cer-tainly did not *have* to organize them; his colleagues didn't. 7. Maria Tarnowska, in an interview. 8. This paragraph from Mieczyslaw Malinski, *Pope John Paul II,* page 249. 9. Jerzy Janik, interviewed in the BBC documentary. 10. Krzysztof Rybicki, in the BBC documentary. 11. M. Tarnowska interview. 12. Malinski, *Pope John Paul II,* pages 111–113.

Chapter 8

1. His biographer, John Cooney, provides a long list of these in *The American Pope* (New York: Times Books, 1984), chapter 9. 2. This is a fair consensus of historians now, though it contradicts U.S. propaganda during the war. See the *Columbia Encyclopedia,* among other reference works. An elaboration may be found in my book *Endless Enemies* (New York:

Congdon and Weed, 1984; reprint, New York: Viking-Penguin, 1987). The out-standing history remains *Fire in the Lake* (Boston: Atlantic Monthly Press, 1972) by Frances FitzGerald, whose father was a major CIA official at the time. 3. Father Andrzej Bardecki, of *Tygodnik Powszechny,* attended a meeting at which Wyszynski, after gaining his freedom, outlined the plan for other senior churchmen. "The whole thing was political," Bardecki now acknowl-edges. 4. From *Kalendarium.* I added the skiing speculation based on what others have told me of his usual practices on such visits. 5. Figures from the *New York Times* and other press reports. The Polish govern-ment maintained that only fifty-three peo-ple died. 6. Micewski, *Cardinal Wyszynski,* page 159. See also Lord Longford's account in *Pope John Paul II* (New York: The Seabury Press, 1979), page 58. 7. From the excel-lent compilation of documents in *Cold War International History Project Bulletin,* no. 5 (Spring 1995), published by the Woodrow Wilson International Center for Scholars, Washington. 8. The ambassador was Joseph Jacobs. Cables seen by me at the National Archive.

Chapter 9

1. Wyszynski's sermon is reproduced here verbatim from a State Department document at the U.S. National Archive. 2. In a fair comparison with dozens of other Polish apartments I saw of similarly situated people. 3. Here is the bibliography of Dr. Wanda Poltawska, exactly as typed by her husband:

Anthropological and Social implications of contraception. [In:] Capella A. (ed.) For a Responsible Transmission of Life. Twenty Years from "Humanae Vitae". IV Interna-tional Congress for the Family of Africa and Europe. Rome. March 12–15, 1988. Roma 1990 [1991], p. 209–221.

Abortion's Devastation. Effects on the Psychical Health of Women. Sorrow's Reward. Gaithersburg, Maryland USA vol. 1:1989 nr 2 p. 1–2, 4.

The Role of the Family in the Development of Personality. Proceedings of the Fifth International Conference "The Human Mind", November 15–16–17, 1990, Vatican City. Dolentium Hominum, Vatican, Year 6 n. 16 p. 84–86.

The Maryland article contained such statements as: "A woman who is denied an abortion by her obstetrician and who is urged to bear her child, is always grateful to the man who has saved her child." This was based on one anecdote about one woman, reported by another doctor. **4.** Among these methods are intrauterine devices and some oral contraceptives that work by inducing menstruation, as opposed to those that work by discouraging ovulation. Poltawski said these accounted for "most" artificial means of contraception. **5.** From Jan Turnau, later an editor at *Wiez.* **6.** From diary entries by Jerzy Zawieyski, a member of the council of state, and by Wyszynski—both as seen and relayed by Micewski. **7.** Interview with Lonny Glaser, the secretary.

Chapter 10

1. Andrzej Micewski, who quit Pax with Mazowiecki, explains that the two of them were "used" because of their "inexperience." Eventually, he says, "We got convinced that Mr. Piasecki [Boleslaw Piasecki, the Pax leader] was supporting the conservative forces in the Party. We were associated with the liberal forces." Mazowiecki obviously preferred not to discuss his affiliation with Pax, instead simply telling me to see Micewski, who he said had a much better memory. As late as 1953, according to documents in the U.S. National Archive, Mazowiecki signed a resolution accusing Primate Wyszynski of having "an improper attitude . . . toward . . . a State

progressing towards socialism," and urging Wyszynski to "support the new economic program." **2.** From multiple interviews with Wozniakowski. Andrzej Micewski also mentions Wyszynski's meeting with the editors in *Cardinal Wyszynski* page 183. **3.** Mieczyslaw Malinski, *Pope John Paul II*, page 124. **4.** Malinski—from Chapter 14 of his book and interviews. **5.** Confirmed by Stanislawa Grabska. **6.** From Andrzej Wielowiejski. **7.** The same story is told by many sources, with slight variations. This precise version is from Andrzej Potocki, president of the Krakow Catholic Intelligentsia Club and a personal translator for Wojtyla's writings. **8.** From Monsignor John Quinn of Chicago, who says Primeau, now dead, told him the story when John Paul II was elected. **9.** From documents seen by me at Dom Polski, the Polish House of Studies, in Rome. There is no evidence that Wojtyla acted as anything more than a messenger in this incident.

Chapter 11

1. The charts are missing from the U.S. edition, published after Wojtyla became pope. **2.** See Saint Augustine, *The Enchiridion on Faith, Hope and Love* (Chicago: Regnery, 1961), page 93, and the concluding essay by Adolph von Harnack. Some Catholic theologians, apparently determined to avoid confrontations among the venerable, assert that there really is no disagreement among Augustine, Aquinas, and Wojtyla, but only various levels of understanding. Saint Augustine, however, explicitly rejects "carnal pleasure" ("Who, then, can deny that it is a sin . . . ?") and admits only "the procreation of children" as a fit motive for marital sex. He ponders the argument that nonprocreative marital sex may prevent the partners from committing the deadlier sins of adultery or fornication, but finally rejects that as a motive along with "carnal pleasure." His discussion omits any association of sex with love and understanding, which is Wojtyla's fundamental thrust. Augustine based his remarks on the writings of Saint Paul, who seems to lament the desire for sex beyond procreation but not to reject it: "It is good for a man not to touch a woman. Nevertheless, to avoid fornication, let every man have his own wife and let every woman have her own husband.... If they cannot contain, let them marry: for it is better to marry than to burn." **3.** Pope John Paul II, *Love and Responsibility* (New York: Farrar Straus & Giroux, 1981). **4.** Wojtyla's canoeing companion and later philosophy colleague Karol Tarnowski emphasizes Poltawska's importance. **5.** Wojtyla also said Malthus had been accepted only by people already prejudiced by "sensualist empiricism and the utilitarianism that goes with it." **6.** For example, Bohdan Cywinski, and Krzysztof Kozlowski, already quoted.

Chapter 12

1. Father Matthew Bednarz of Chicago, who also organized aid to the Rome and Paris institutions, tells similar stories. **2.** Father Michael J. Zembrzuski says he found U.S. officials similarly uninterested in the trips he regularly took to Poland with scores of Polish-Americans. **3.** These were his words to Cardinal Franz König, but they accord with what else is known of his stance. **4.** Sadly, Cardinal Krol, who gave me three enormously helpful, long interviews and a fine lunch, died in 1996, after this book was written but before it was published. **5.** The communists had imprisoned Cardinal Alojzije Stepinac in 1946 on charges that he was a Nazi collaborator, a matter of legitimate dispute. **6.** Information in this paragraph comes from Andrzej Micewski, who touches on it in chapter 4 of *Cardinal Wyszynski.* **7.** Her name was Marketa Fialkova; her parents were Mr. and Mrs. Jiri Nemec. **8.** As far as I know, the lecture was never translated into English; I have relied

here on George Hunston Williams and Wilkanowicz, who read it in Polish. Quoted phrases are from Williams, *The Mind of John Paul II,* pages 147–151. **9.** Interview with Cardinal Andrzej Maria Deskur. Cardinal Deskur says it was the first time he had seen his countryman since 1946. Deskur had gone to work for the Roman curia and had not returned to Poland.

Chapter 13

1. I was shown this report in the archives of Radio Free Europe, Munich, by officials there. Although labeled "State Department," it was heavily classified and almost surely the work of the CIA. **2.** Motyka remembers this incident as happening instead during the winter of 1958–59. But the incident, or one just like it, is reported in *Kalendarium* as having taken place on September 18, 1962, and I have stuck with that time frame. Such an initiative seems a bit brash for Wojtyla to have undertaken right after he became a bishop, and in any case he would not then have been issuing orders to priests about volunteer work details. By 1962, however, he was acting archbishop. **3.** This direct quote is taken from *Karol Wojtyla: Jako, Biskup Krakowski,* a compilation of items about Wojtyla seen by me at Polish House in Rome. **4.** A direct quote from Motyka's interview with me. **5.** This story seems to be ubiquitous, but I first heard it from Thomas Melady, former U.S. ambassador to the Vatican, in an interview. **6.** Fathers Malinski and Bardecki, both of whom had regular, intimate conversations with Wojtyla throughout this period, say they are sure of this. **7.** Among these friends were Catholic Intelligentsia Club members Andrzej Wielowiejski and Andrzej Potocki and *Znak* editor Jacek Wozniakowski. **8.** Motyka says a formal list was not submitted this soon, but that the names were offered in informal talks. **9.** Barcikowski also served on a commission running Church-state affairs. **10.** According to Kazimierz Kakol, minister of religious affairs after Kliszko. 11. Kliszko is now dead, and Czeslaw Domagala, the Party boss in Krakow between Motyka and Barcikowski, declines to answer questions.

Chapter 14

1. Gerald P. Fogarty, *The Vatican and the American Hierarchy* (Stuttgart: Anton Hiersemann, 1982), pages 382–385. 2. Bernard C. Pawley, ed., *The Second Vatican Council* (London: Oxford University Press, 1967). 3. Michael Novak, *Crisis,* May 1993. 4. From historian Peter Raina of the Free University of Berlin, who was allowed wide access to Wyszynski's files. Raina has published half a dozen books on Poland under communism with various European presses, quoting at times from Wyszynski's diaries. He retains a strong reputation among Polish churchmen and appears to have had access to materials unavailable to Andrzej Micewski, who basically got what he was given in order to prepare an authorized biography. Micewski does not mention the pamphlets and devotes only a few paragraphs to the 1962 Council session. Micewski began working on his biography after Raina was expelled from Poland by the communist government for publishing a 1978 book about political opposition. 5. Raina found records of the meetings of the Polish delegation, which were held at two P.M. each Thursday. I spent many hours looking through his impressive documentation at his apartment in Berlin. 6. The direct quotes are from Renzo Allegri, *Padre Pio, Man of Hope,* as quoted in the *Tablet* (London), Oct. 13, 1984. The incident is also recounted in *Padre Pio* by C. Bernard Ruffin (Huntington, Ind: Our Sunday Visitor, 1991), pages 360–361. 7. Cardinals Paul Léger of Canada and Achille Lienart of France. 8. Bishop Aloysius J. Wycislo of Green Bay, Wisc., who attended the Council and wrote a book about it (*Vatican II Revisited* [New York: Alba House, 1987]), was only one of many

sources for this (pages 45–46), though perhaps the most detailed. Bishop Wycislo was kind enough to augment his thoughts in a telephone interview. 9. Father Karl Becker, professor at the Gregorian University in Rome, to whom Ratzinger directed me as a stand-in for an interview he declined to give personally. 10. Wycislo says 2,908 attended over the four years; presumably this figure includes some newcomers in later years. 11. Early in the Kennedy administration, the actual figure was 200 (U.S.) to 4 (USSR). The Pentagon wanted this ratio secret to keep its budget high, and Kennedy wanted it secret because he had won office in the first place by falsely accusing his Republican predecessor of letting the U.S. fall behind in a "missile gap." 12. Raina found a record of the note. 13. Reprinted in the Italian newspaper *Il Giorno.* The gist of this conversation has been published widely. The emissary was the American editor and author Norman Cousins; the archbishop was Josyf Slipyi. 14. In the original conversation, Khrushchev promised only to reopen Archbishop Slipyi's case. A month later, he agreed to release him. 15. A detailed account appeared in the *Tablet,* London, Sept. 18, 1971. For an inside look at the mood in the White House, see also chapters 33 and 34 of *A Thousand Days* by Arthur M. Schlesinger, Jr. (Boston: Houghton Mifflin, 1965), and chapter 25 of *Kennedy* by Theodore C. Sorensen (New York: Harper and Row, 1965). The main issue in the nuclear test treaty was on-site inspections. Khrushchev was the first Soviet leader to offer any inspections. Purely for domestic political reasons, Kennedy insisted on more than his own scientists thought necessary.

Chapter 15

1. From *The Human Way of the Church,* a collection of speeches and papers by Karol Wojtyla (Rome: John Paul II Foundation, 1992). 2. Wojtyla did write a paper at

about the same time citing documentable anti-Church actions by Polish communists. But that was a far cry from alleging that the reform-minded bishops at Vatican II were communist dupes. Wyszynski's paper is at Polish House in Rome. **3.** Recounted in the *Tablet* (London), Aug. 16, 1969. **4.** See particularly Wilton Wynn, *Keepers of the Keys* (New York: Random House, 1988).

Chapter 16

1. Widely published reports have claimed that a cardinal, presumably Spellman, wore a hidden microphone into the conclave on behalf of the CIA. The reports apparently all trace back to a single Italian journalist, who supplied no documentation. It is highly unlikely that it ever happened. **2.** Interview with Siri's good friend Cardinal Alfonse Stickler of Austria—including the "smoke of the devil" remark. Stickler is among several sources who say that Siri would have won the papacy instead of Paul had he not withdrawn his name because he feared the responsibility. Others—whom I am inclined to believe— think this is self-serving, and that Siri would not really have declined the job. **3.** This information is from Andrzej Bardecki. Stomma was in the hospital during my repeated trips to Poland and said he was too ill to answer any questions. Over more than a year, I spent at least fifteen hours with Bardecki, exhausting him and two interpreters. I never found him to be anything less than gracious, cooperative without trying to sell me on anything, and reliable. **4.** Quoted in Mieczyslaw Malinski, *Pope John Paul II*, page 42. **5.** Malinski set down his words, reprinted in chapter 8 of Malinski's book. **6.** The document was *Lumen Gentium*, or "Light of the Nations." **7.** From his encyclical *Vehementer Nos* ("They Are Conveyed unto Us"). **8.** Paul Blanshard, in *Paul Blanshard on Vatican II* (Boston: Beacon Press, 1966), page 62, says the constitutional chapter on collegiality cited

papal primacy at least twenty times. And in *A Concise History of the Catholic Church* (New York: Doubleday, 1979), page 370, Thomas Bokenkotter writes, "The Second Vatican Council took pains to safeguard [the pope's] absolute authority; its concept of collegiality merely gave the bishops a consultative position, leaving the Pope free to use them or not in his governing of the Church. **9.** Account of the meeting from Stanislawa Grabska. **10.** Historian Peter Raina found Wyszynski's diary entry for this date when I visited him. **11.** Records seen at the home of Peter Raina (his translation). Wyszynski's diary stated only what he did, not why he did it, but considering the history of the affair, the motivation seems obvious. **12.** Andrzej Micewski, *Cardinal Wyszynski*, chapters 4 and 5. **13.** As shown by the repeated entries in *Kalendarium*. **14.** Father Melchior Cichy, quoted in the *Tablet* (London), Dec. 9, 1978. **15.** Archbishop Rembert Weakland, then head of the Benedictine order, tells similar stories. **16.** A Catholic explanation: modern transportation accords with the goal natural to the feet, whereas contraception contradicts the goal natural to sex. **17.** See Wilton Wynn, *Keepers of the Keys*, page 110.

Chapter 17

1. Quotes are from George Hunston Williams, *The Mind of John Paul II*, pages 169–170. **2.** Participants disagree about what Wojtyla said, even in private. Cardinal Deskur recalls Wojtyla angrily comparing the working draft of the religious-liberty declaration with "communist propaganda" because "it gives the impression there is no difference between truth and error." But Deskur says he doesn't remember what changes allowed Wojtyla to support the declaration in the end. Cardinal Willebrands says he chaired a meeting on the subject that was attended by Wojtyla, and that Wojtyla didn't seem to have a strong opinion. **3.** Based on interviews with Bishop W. Thomas Larkin of Florida and Bishop Wycislo, among others. **4.** In dozens of interviews about the Council, I asked if anyone specifically knew whether Wojtyla had signed this petition; no one did. But I was assured that he would not have signed. **5.** See my book *Endless Enemies* (New York: Congdon and Weed, 1984; reprint, New York: Viking Penguin, 1987). I interviewed some participants. **6.** An account of the 1964 overthrow appears in my book *Endless Enemies*. See also Irving Louis Horowitz, *Revolution in Brazil* (New York: E. P. Dutton, 1964); William Blum, *The CIA: A Forgotten History* (London: Zed Books, 1986); and John Gerassi, *The Great Fear in Latin America* (New York: Collier Books, 1966). Many details still aren't known. **7.** Interviews with Cardinals Gantin and Christian Wiygham Tumi of Cameroun. **8.** Catholic News Service. **9.** The quotations from this speech are woven together from several translations I found, which agree in sense but often not in language. I have tried to use those passages from each which seem to me the most natural and compelling in English. The translations came from Williams, *The Mind of John Paul II*, the contemporaneous reporting of the Catholic News Service, material that Bishop Wycislo sent me from the U.S. Bishops' Conference, an article in the *Tablet* (London), Nov. 11, 1978, and Andrew Greeley, *The Making of the Popes 1978* (Kansas City: Andrews and McMeel, 1979). **10.** From the minutes found by historian Peter Raina. **11.** Different sources offer slightly different versions of the makeup of the subcommissions, but certainly included were future cardinals Henri de Lubac, Yves Congar, and Jan Danielou. **12.** *Kalendarium.*

Chapter 18

1. *Commentary on the Documents of Vatican II,* vol. V (Herder and Herder, 1969), page 50. My thanks to Bishop Wycislo for sending it to me.

2. The bishop was Basil Welychowski. **3.** Andrzej Micewski, *Cardinal Wyszynski*, page 248, corroborated in gist by Kazimierz Kakol and others. **4.** Interview with Andrzej Potocki. **5.** According to Cardinal Krol, the notion that Paul was indecisive "is ridiculous." **6.** Wilton Wynn, *Keepers of the Keys*, page 111. **7.** Quoted in Bernard C. Pawley, ed., *The Second Vatican Council* (London: Oxford University Press, 1967). **8.** Micewski: his book, *Cardinal Wyszynski*, my interviews with him, and his documents. **9.** The one in Ecuador said, "The Catholic...religion shall...be the single religion of the Republic of Ecuador and...no other dissident cult and no society condemned by the Church can ever be permitted." **10.** The *Tablet* (London), Feb. 16, 1980, and Wynn, *Keepers of the Keys*, pages 235–241. **11.** Writing in the *Tablet* (London), Oct. 23, 1982. **12.** From Hansjakob Stehle, *Eastern Politics of the Vatican 1917–1979* (Ohio University Press, 1981), quoted in Peter Hebblethwaite, *Paul VI: The First Modern Pope* (Mahwah, N.J.: The Paulist Press, 1993), page 446. **13.** That Wojtyla was appointed to the commission has been widely reported. My account has been fleshed out by an interview with Andrzej Poltawski. **14.** These are Micewski's words, but Raina, the other historian who had access to Wyszynski and his papers, agrees. Somehow, legend has proclaimed the letter a success; the accounts I found suggest otherwise. **15.** Adam Krzeminski. **16.** Micewski says he had "no role," while Archbishop Dabrowski says his "role was decisive" in sending the peacemaking letter after Wyszynski had claimed the territories.

Chapter 19

1. Interview with Kryzstof Kozlowski. **2.** Interview transcript seen at historian Peter Raina's house. **3.** Andrzej Micewski, *Cardinal Wyszynski*, chapter 5, augmented by interview to clarify Wyszynski's response.

4. From *The Human Way of the Church*, a collection of speeches and papers by Karol Wojtyla (Rome: John Paul II Foundation, 1992). 5. Diary quotes from Micewski, *Cardinal Wyszynski*, chapter 5. 6. Wojtyla's poems translated by Jerzy Peterkiewicz, published in the *Tablet* (London), April 14, 1979. 7. Micewski, interview. 8. Even Pope Paul, during the public beatification of Father Kolbe, on Oct. 17, 1971, said that the Poles' "Marian piety arouses a certain mistrust." He then went on to praise Mary's "subordinate" role. Just before the beatification, Paul had declined Wyszynski's request that he bestow new honors on Mary. 9. Professor Williams told me that one prominent theologian, Professor Wladyslaw Wicher, was excluded from the committee for his suspect views on contraception. 10. John Cooney, *American Pope*, page 306. 11. From Wilton Wynn, whose Vatican sources are extraordinary. Talked about on page 196 of *Keepers of the Keys*. 12. This story mostly from Micewski, Wyszynski's authorized biographer with access to him and his records. In his book, pages 278–279, Micewski, as usual, uses the most polite language; he wrote under not just a communist dictatorship but martial law, and also subject to his own advisory relationship with Wyszynski's successor. Instead of referring bluntly to a disagreement, for example, Micewski writes, "The news [of a papal visit] was completely unexpected. . . . One can imagine the Primate's surprise." One certainly can, given that it meant the pope had overridden Wyszynski's policies behind his back with the communists. But Micewski just leaves the inference open. In my interview with him, he was much more blunt, saying that Gomulka was "seeking an accord without Wyszynski," and that "Wyszynski thought he was the only cardinal who understood what communism was" and thought "the Vatican was under an illusion." Regarding Paul's decision on the trip, Micewski

reports that Wyszynski "tried to obtain an explicit answer by sending the Pope a telegraph," but apparently didn't get a reply. Just how sharp the conflict was, Micewski told me, is "one of the Church mysteries that laymen don't have access to."

Chapter 20

1. Quoted in *Time* magazine, via Andrew Greeley, *The Making of the Popes 1978* (Kansas City: Andrews and McMeel, 1979), 206. 2. From Father Bednarz. 3. The 1968 report cited book 3, chapter 13, note 1, seen at Radio Free Europe. 4. From Bishop Pieronek. 5. My own tour was conducted by Sister Franceska of the Krakow archdiocese, who graciously supplied many recollections. I have also relied on Mieczyslaw Malinski, both his personal remarks and his book, *Pope John Paul*. He says much of his information about Wojtyla's routine came years ago from Sister Jadwiga, a longtime servant who was aged, bedridden, and unable to see me when I arrived. 6. *Kalendarium*. 7. This episode from Anna Kotlarczyk Pakosiewicz, in an interview. A name day—the day honoring the saint one is named for—is as gaily celebrated in Poland as a birthday.

Chapter 21

1. These vote totals are from Father Francis X. Murphy, who wrote both under his own name and for the *New Yorker* as Xavier Rynne. Other sources are less specific, but the Vatican itself acknowledges the votes followed the patterns Murphy described. 2. Shown me by the Warsaw journalist Konstanty Gebert, who keeps a collection of such evidence. 3. Motyka told me about the Soviet pressure. Otherwise, the incident is widely known. 4. David Ost, *Solidarity and the Politics of Anti-Politics* (Philadelphia: Temple University Press, 1990), chapters 1 and 3. The author teaches at Hobart College. 5. Quoted in

Andrzej Micewski, *Cardinal Wyszynski*, page 289. **6.** Interview with Seweryn Blumsztajn. **7.** Micewski, *Cardinal Wyszynski*, page 301. **8.** Ratzinger interview, the *New York Times*, Dec. 27, 1992. **9.** Quoted by Wilton Wynn, *Keepers of the Keys*, page 106. **10.** Both Andrew Greeley and Father Francis X. Murphy have written that Cardinal Albino Luciani of Venice, who later became Pope John Paul I, was among those advising Pope Paul not to issue the encyclical. When I pressed both men for their sources, Greeley said he couldn't remember who had told him—"someone in Rome," he said—and Murphy said he had heard it from a student in his seminary class who lived in Venice. I could not find documentation I considered satisfactory for so weighty a charge. More generally, however, Murphy notes that Luciani was an important voice among the Italian bishops, who issued a written interpretation of the encyclical in less ironclad terms than those used by either Paul VI or Wojtyla. **11.** This quote from Father Vincent O'Keefe, a senior official of the Jesuit order. Others told me much the same thing. **12.** From Wojtyla's report to the Episcopate on his meetings.

Chapter 22

1. In addition to other sources already cited, Stanislaw Grygiel, Wojtyla's student and later assistant, was helpful with this material. **2.** Since no one involved knew what was happening at the other end of the operation, neither Modzelewski, Zajac, or any others could connect any one printing run with any particular smuggling job. Modzelewski emphasizes that many books he printed entered Poland legally during the brief periods when the communists were on their best behavior to try to obtain Church or Western cooperation on some matter or other. **3.** Father John Long, rector of the Vatican's Russian College, confirms that most Polish Catholic bishops would not ordain Ukrainians because of "ethnic hos-

tility." **4.** Wilkanowicz and Bardecki also told stories that supported this. **5.** I found Father Zajac on the recommendation of Wojtyla's Krakow intellectual friends, and have much reason to trust him. **6.** Wilkanowicz still has records from those days, confirming the numbers given here. **7.** This incident is recounted by many sources. Wyszynski's words come from Andrzej Micewski (*Cardinal Wyszynski*, page 297), who worked with the cardinal's own records.

Chapter 23

1. Quoted in the *Tablet* (London), July 7, 1969. **2.** Figures from the *Tablet* (London), May 29, 1976. **3.** Quoted in Mieczyslaw Malinski, *Pope John Paul II*, page 204. I also interviewed Wesoly about the trip. **4.** Bishop (now Cardinal) Franciszek Macharski, who traveled with Wojtyla from Poland, is quoted in Malinski, *Pope John Paul II*, page 234. Macharski declined to be interviewed. **5.** The refusal of Cardinal Macharski to allow me access to the diary and other records of the Krakow curia forced me to rely on the work Malinski did in preparing his own book. Malinski received Macharski's full cooperation—he was granted interviews and a look at the diary—and was kind enough to give me gracious amounts of his time. **6.** Based on interviews with those he talked to at the time of each trip. **7.** His remarks on both sex and authority came in speeches outside the proceedings of the synod, but they were clearly intended for the ears of the assembled bishops. **8.** Malinski, *Pope John Paul II*, page 116.

Chapter 24

1. From George Hunston Williams, who attended. Williams discusses it on pages 189–197 of *The Mind of John Paul II*. **2.** From several priests. **3.** Wojtyla, *The Acting Person* (Dordrecht and Boston: D. Reidel, 1979), pages vii–viii. **4.** Kissinger's aide Roger Morris, quoted by journalist Seymour Hersh in his book *The Price of Power* (New York: Simon and Schuster, 1983), page 416. **5.** Ironically, Wyszynski was in somewhat the same position as Gomulka: the settlement he had long claimed to want would open the way for a Polish government concordat with the Vatican and threaten the independence of the Polish Church, which he headed. Against Wojtyla's advice, Wyszynski went to Pope Paul urging last-minute changes in the dioceses that might have angered Germany and blocked the treaty, but Paul waved him off with minor concessions. The Western press, not suspecting Wyszynski's real stance, credited him with helping to bring about the treaty. **6.** Words by Eugene Pottier, 1871, set to music by Pierre Degeyter, 1888. **7.** Anna-Teresa Tymieniecka, of whom more later. Professor Williams is another source for this, as were several members of the Znak group whom I interviewed in Krakow. **8.** From Professor Williams, *The Mind of John Paul II*, page 196. **9.** On page 233 of the U.S. edition, Wojtyla says, "Emotionalists—such as, for instance, M. Scheler—go so far as to maintain that feelings are the only source of man's cognitive relations to values and that apart from them there are no other authentic means of knowing values." He then says this "is not in itself sufficient; in view of the person's transcendence in the action still another integration is necessary—namely, the integration through 'truthfulness.'" He goes on to say that sensitivity must be fused with "truthfulness" as a "necessary condition" for "authentic choices and decisions.... The fulfillment of freedom...depends on the certainty of truth." **10.** Professor Kenneth L. Schmitz of the University of Toronto.

Chapter 25

1. David Ost, *Solidarity and the Politics of Anti-Politics* (Philadelphia: Temple University Press, 1990), chapters 3 and 4, and various issues of the *Tablet* (London) throughout this period. **2.** This quote of Tischner's is from the BBC documentary on the pope. I telephoned the professor to try to schedule an interview, but he consistently begged off, saying he was too busy, even when I followed him to an academic conference in Germany. **3.** A former staff member of *Weiz*, Turnau now writes for *Gazeta Wyborcza*, the leading Warsaw daily. **4.** As we have seen, Wyszynski spoke of human rights, importantly and courageously. But Turnau and others associate such talk with Wojtyla because Wojtyla made it the visible theme of a movement. **5.** Interview with Wojciech Arkuszewski. **6.** Professor Ossowska (first name unknown). From Andrzej Wielowiejski. **7.** Quote from Father Bednarz, but Cardinal Krol and others told me the same thing; apparently they believed it. **8.** Interview with Weakland. Jesuits reported similar problems. **9.** From Wielowiejski, president of the Krakow branch.

Chapter 26

1. A theologian advises me that the practice is technically optional in Western countries at the discretion of resident bishops, but it is generally banned. **2.** The *Tablet* (London), Oct. 17, 1971. **3.** Defenders noted there was no evidence that Kolbe himself had ever espoused anti-Semitism, though they generally acknowledged that he should have policed his group more closely. **4.** Stanislaw Krajewski of Warsaw, an official of several international groups concerned with Christian-Jewish relations, told me about these protests, in which he took part. **5.** The murdered predecessor was Patrice Lumumba; the story is told in detail in my book *Endless Enemies* (New York: Congdon and Weed, 1984; reprint, New York: Viking Penguin, 1987). **6.** Translation by Joanna Tyrpa; the Polish original may be found in *Kalendarium* for Nov. 18, 1971.

7. Walter Isaacson, *Kissinger: A Biography* (New York: Simon and Schuster, 1992), pages 436–437.   8. The *Tablet* (London), Jan. 5, 1974.   9. Judging from the space it is given in *Kalendarium*, where this story comes from.   10. Andrzej Micewski, *Cardinal Wyszynski*, chapter 6.   11. Micewski, chapter 6. See note 12 for chapter 19 of this section for an explanation of how Micewski gingerly strove, writing under difficult conditions, to downplay conflicts that clearly existed based on the facts he revealed, and which he largely acknowledges in an interview.   12. From Wilton Wynn, *Keepers of the Keys*, page 199.   13. Quoted by Cardinal Jozef Glemp, Jan. 6, 1982.

Chapter 27

1. For documentation on all this material, including the Gulf of Tonkin incident, see my book *Endless Enemies.*   2. See *Endless Enemies*, chapter 9, for a chronology.   3. As judged by the World Bank in the late 1970s.   4. Detailed in my documentary on the dictator Jonas Savimbi, part of the Public Broadcasting Service series *The Kwitny Report.*   5. Occasional prisoners were freed, but their cells were quickly filled by others.   6. From Vatican Press Secretary Joaquin Navarro-Valls.   7. Cardinal König told me, "Mindszenty said 'No dialogue'—the Pius XII line. Communism was the enemy. Opposition was the only way. And Wojtyla continued the main line of Wyszynski—[that] if you go and talk to people, you get a better idea of what's going on. John XXIII, and Casaroli, they believed in talking and looking for a compromise. Neither John XXIII nor Paul VI fully approved of Wyszynski's way of doing things."

Chapter 28

1. Tymieniecka and Houthakker gave me the account that follows during a long interview; it accords with her written record of events, which she also graciously provided me a copy of, in *Phenomenology Information Bulletin*, vol. 3, (Oct. 1979).   2. Williams dwelled on this in a long interview with me in his home.   3. The professor was Stefan Swiezawski.   4. Interview with Jan Novak.   5. Jude Dougherty, dean of philosophy at Catholic University of America, mentioned this in an interview with me. Other, similar comments are recounted in John Cornwell, *A Thief in the Night* (New York: Simon and Schuster, 1989), page 225.   6. This account is derived mostly from continuous coverage in the *Tablet* (London), and Mieczyslaw Malinski, *Pope John Paul II* (New York: The Seabury Press, 1979), pages 246–247. I also discussed the matter with various bishops, particularly Abramowicz.   7. From Sherwood's award-winning articles in the *Camden Courier-Post*, Sept. 9, 1979, and over subsequent weeks, confirmed in interviews with him and his editor, Father Salvatore Adamo. Guilfoyle is now dead, and Boyle says he does not have a copy of his reports and remembers "very little" of the episode.   8. Andrzej Micewski, *Cardinal Wyszynski*, pages 355–357, and various issues of the *Tablet* (London), 1975, particularly March 25 and May 24.   9. This account comes mainly from Zdzislaw Najder, who later took over the Radio Free Europe job, and Jan de Weydenthal, a senior staff member all along. I also interviewed Novak.   10. Wojtyla's secret meetings were recounted by Radio Free Europe's research director, Jan de Weydenthal.

Chapter 29

1. Throughout his biography *Paul VI*, particularly on pages 3 and 618, Peter Hebblethwaite blames all of Paul's dealings with Sindona on Papal Secretary Monsignor Pasquale Macchi, who he says was a friend of Sindona's. This is both implausible and contrary to other accounts, both cited and

uncited here.   2. From my interviews with
Ed Marciniak, who was Marcinkus's roommate in the Chicago seminary, and Chicago
Monsignor John Quinn. Another monsignor,
who does not want his name used, says he lived
in the same building as Marcinkus for eight
years, and that Marcinkus's apartment was no
larger than that of many colleagues.   3.
Quoted in John Cornwell, *A Thief in the Night*
(New York: Simon and Schuster, 1989), pages
82–84. As will be explained in more detail
later, Marcinkus wouldn't answer questions for
me.   4. David M. Kennedy, chairman of the
bank and later secretary of the U.S. Treasury,
who did much to grease Sindona's entry into
the United States.   5. Quoted in Cornwell,
A Thief in the Night, page 132.   6. Marcinkus
told author John Cornwell that he met Sindona "about twelve times, sometimes for a
minute, sometimes at a baptism, once or twice
at lunch, at a reception, a ceremony" (from *A
Thief in the Night*, page 131). Cornwell, the only
journalist I could find who was able to talk to
Marcinkus at much length, admits to a dis-
like for financial details. Although his printed
comments imply that he doubted what
Marcinkus said, he didn't cross-examine the
archbishop over many particulars.   7. Once
I even scheduled an airport stopover in
Phoenix, thinking that if he knew I was in
town, Marcinkus might agree to give me his
account. But when I called from the airport
to get his address, he told me it still wasn't the
right time.   8. Interview with Vagnozzi by
Paul Horne, published in *Institutional Investor*
magazine for January 1971 and quoted in
Charles Raw, *The Money Changers* (London:
HarperCollins, 1992), page 65.   9. I covered the case for the *Wall Street Journal*. My
memory has been helped by Raw, *The Money
Changers*.   10. I wrote about this case as well
for the *Wall Street Journal*. The head of the
New York City police investigation into the
crime, Joseph Coffey, remains angry to this
day that he could not obtain Vatican records
that might have proved whether or not it

received or paid for the counterfeit bonds, as
the counterfeiters themselves alleged. I talked
with him both at the time and in 1995, for
this book. The case was the subject of *The
Vatican Connection* by Richard Hammer (New
York: Holt, Rinehart and Winston, 1982).
11. Antinucci has since died. A letter I sent to
the last address I could obtain for his widow
was returned undelivered.   12. There are
many other sources besides those specifically
identified in the notes for the IOR story told
in this book. As a reporter for the *Wall Street
Journal* from 1971 to 1988, I several times
covered Vatican financial scandals, each time
conducting numerous interviews. In addition
to the two best works on the subject, Raw,
The Money Changers, and Larry Gurwin, *The
Calvi Affair* (London: Macmillan, 1983), the
following were of help to me: Rupert Cornwell, *God's Banker* (New York: Dodd, Mead,
1983); Nick Tosches, *Power on Earth* (New
York: Arbor House, 1986); and, to a lesser
extent, Nino Lo Bello, *The Vatican Empire* (New
York: Trident Press, 1968). I am also grateful for the cordial help of Carlo Calvi
(Roberto's son) and his investigators at Julius
Kroll and Associates in New York, Steve
Rucker and Nancy Baumwald.   13. Interview with Halina Bortnowska.

Chapter 30

1. *Kalendarium.*   2. The book is *Sign of Contradiction* (New York: The Seabury Press,
1979). In his introduction, Cardinal Basil
Hume of England promises that the book is
worth the work required to read it.

Chapter 31

1. Additional information from interview
with Adam Krzeminski of *Polytyka* magazine.
2. From Andrzej Bardecki.   3. The *Tablet*
(London), Jan. 28, 1984.   4. M. Kamil
Dziewanowski, a professor at Boston University.   5. As summarized by Professor

Dziewanowski, who by then had heard it many times. I couldn't locate a copy of the speech. **6.** From Mieczyslaw Malinski, *Pope John Paul II,* page 257. **7.** From Tymieniecka's article in *Phenomenology Information Bulletin,* vol. 3 (Oct. 1979). A Catholic theologian explains that "mirroring" is an important concept in the argument over whether Descartes was right that consciousness is more important than action or objective reality. **8.** Interview quoted in Tad Szulc, *Pope John Paul II* (New York: Scribner's, 1995), page 260. **9.** From Father Francis X. Murphy and Carlton Sherwood's coverage in the *Camden Courier-Post,* beginning Sept. 9, 1979, and throughout the fall. **10.** My sources for the Doylestown story include the Pulitzer Prize–winning *Camden Courier-Post* series by Carlton Sherwood, William F. Schmick, and John Hanchette; other documentation supplied by Monsignor Salvatore Adamo, the Camden diocesan newspaper editor; and interviews with Adamo, Sherwood, Zembrzuski, Krol, Boyle, and Father Francis X. Murphy, who followed the case and wrote about it. Bishop Guilfoyle was dead by the time I came onto the story. When I first approached Boyle with questions, he faxed me a response challenging the accuracy of the *Courier-Post* articles, which had been carried nationally by the Gannett News Service. Although he vehemently denounced several findings, he avoided most of my queries, pleading a poor memory. When I checked out his complaints with other sources, it became apparent that they were largely semantic—for example, when he objected that Paul had not issued a directive, it turned out that someone else had issued it on Paul's authority. In a subsequent exchange of faxes and e-mail, Boyle, adopting a very different tone, confirmed the gist of the *Courier-Post* story, though he still pleaded poor memory on many of the details. I asked if he could cite any remaining inaccuracies; he said he did "not now recall" any.

11. Slightly differing accounts of this incident come from George Weigel in *The Final Revolution* (New York: Oxford University Press, 1992), pages 172–173; Cardinal Korec; and Father John Bukovsky, the Vatican envoy who delivered Paul's directive. Bukovsky insists there was no deal with the Czech government and no shutdown of underground activity in general, but that Paul halted ordinations in Czechoslovakia because it was discovered that another bishop had ordained married priests; he says that six months later Paul approved resumed ordinations for religious orders, although not for diocesan priests. Weigel and Korec talk of a broader, *Ostpolitik*-motivated shutdown, though Korec says he still thinks the initiative came from "diplomats" acting behind Paul's back. "The diplomats were to search [for] a possible agreement with the government—and they worked on their own," Korec says. "I indeed let Bukovsky know they wouldn't gain anything that way—and I was right. About one and a half years later I was given new instructions from Rome saying that I could continue my underground work." Korec says he was in regular contact with Wojtyla, who supported his underground activities fully.

Chapter 32

1. Wilton Wynn, *Keepers of the Keys,* page 247. **2.** Wynn, *Keepers of the Keys,* page 246. **3.** Interview with Stanislaw Grygiel, the former student Wojtyla selected to edit the Polish edition. George Hunston Williams, in *The Mind of John Paul II* (New York: The Seabury Press, 1981), also talks about the *Communio* idea, in chapter 9. Some participants in *Communio* tried to play down its opposition to *Concilium,* and the staffs even cooperated on a symposium. But the two magazines were widely perceived as representing conflicting strains of thought. A Polish edition of *Communio* finally did come out in the 1980s.

Chapter 33

1. The incident was recalled by several witnesses. I could find no written record of it; there may not be one. Nor could I find the exact quotation in my edition of the New Testament, though I found many phrases that convey the same idea. 2. Quoted in *Osservatore Romano*, June 23, 1977. 3. Quoted in the *Tablet* (London), Sept. 24, 1977. Michnik declined to be interviewed by me. 4. *Kalendarium*.

Chapter 34

1. Gleaned from others; Kuron declined to answer my questions. 2. Walesa's autobiography, *Lech Walesa: A Way of Hope* (New York: Henry Holt, 1987), is vague on the exact date, but Borucewicz looked it up for me in his diary. 3. Police records of these conversations were found by Walesa's colleagues in the post-communist government and caused a scandal when published. 4. Quoted in Malinski, *Pope John Paul II*, page 250.

Chapter 35

1. Among my sources, besides those cardinals I have already listed, was Beni Lai, a journalist who was Cardinal Siri's authorized biographer and obtained his information directly from his subject. Cardinal Alfons Maria Stickler, a close ally of Siri's until Siri's death, confirmed for me that Lai enjoyed Siri's confidence and candor. 2. Father Francesco Farusi, to author John Cornwell for *A Thief in the Night* (New York: Simon and Schuster, 1989), page 205. 3. There are many colorful stories, some contradictory, about how the quarantining practice began, but the version of Wilton Wynn in *Keepers of the Keys*, chapter 1, is backed up by Father Thomas Bokenkotter, author of *A Concise History of the Catholic Church* (New York: Doubleday, 1979), in an interview. 4. That he

did get some votes was officially confirmed to me by Vatican Press Secretary Joaquin Navarro-Valls in 1994. The "other journalist" was Indro Montanelli, according to his colleague Beni Lai. 5. I have also seen his words translated as both "done to me" and "done in my regard." 6. Several high American churchmen remarked to me on the inferior health care accorded their European colleagues. One, Cardinal Krol, later sent his own physician to Rome to check up on John Paul II's care because of this. 7. Cornwell, *A Thief in the Night*. Father Pattaro had since died; Cornwell got the story from Father Giovanni Gennari, a friend of both Pattaro's and John Paul I's.

Chapter 36

1. Unlike almost every other former KOR and Solidarity leader I interviewed, Romaszewski was shifty and unforthcoming, which leads me to suspect he is still concealing something. At first he denied knowing of an embassy furniture auction, or mimeo machines. He "maybe" remembered it only after two former KOR leaders—Chojecki and Wojciech Arkuszewski—insisted the machines had come from the embassy through a friend of Romaszewski's, whom he wouldn't identify to them. Romaszewski then gave me a name for the political officer, but I haven't been able to locate such a man through the State Department. The title "political officer" is a common cover for CIA officers. If this was CIA aid to what became Solidarity, it's worth noting that it happened during the Carter administration. 2. This firsthand account comes from Malinski, who described it for the BBC documentary on John Paul II. A French documentary, by Television Française One, quoted Wojtyla's driver, who claimed he broke the news to Wojtyla later that day during a visit to a small parish. Malinski's version makes more sense than the driver's: John Paul I's death was big

news everywhere, and Wojtyla's diary shows him not arriving at the parish until six P.M. **3.** (New York: Bantam Books, 1984.) **4.** (New York: Simon and Schuster, 1989.) **5.** From Beni Lai. **6.** This version comes from König. The story is told slightly differently by Zbigniew Brzezinski and others, but König was the one there. Andrzej Micewski is adamant that Wyszynski wanted an Italian pope. **7.** Oddi was eighty-four when we talked, and still clear as a bell. He spoke fluid English, and over several hours, expounding on many subjects, seemed as candid as any cardinal I met. **8.** This was first reported in Andrew Greeley, *The Making of the Popes 1978*, but Wynn says Wojtyla himself confirmed it to him over dinner. **9.** From biographer and confidant Beni Lai.

BOOK 4: ARMAGEDDON

Chapter 1

1. Quoted in George Hunston Williams, *The Mind of John Paul II* (New York: The Seabury Press, 1981), page 290. **2.** Quoted in the *Camden [N.J.] Courier-News*, Sept. 9, 1979. **3.** I have spoken to many people and read many articles about Opus Dei. I found James Martin's article "Opus Dei in the United States," *America* magazine (published by the Jesuits), vol. 172, no. 6 (Feb. 25, 1995), particularly helpful. **4.** Of eighteen Spanish cabinet ministers, three were Opus Dei members and another twelve were sympathizers. **5.** The *Tablet* (London), Nov. 24, 1979, when the facts began to leak out. In the quote, I have added semicolons in place of some commas for clarity. **6.** Much of the material in this section was gathered from numerous issues of the *Tablet* (London), from Michael Walsh's book *Opus Dei* (San Francisco: Harper and Row, 1992) and from Kenneth Woodward, *Making Saints* (New York: Simon and Schuster, 1990).

Chapter 2

1. The *Tablet* (London), Oct. 10, 1982, and *Osservatore Romano*, January 22, 1979. **2.** The story here comes from Wilton Wynn, who spoke in depth with Casaroli over a planned coauthored autobiography that was never completed. John Paul himself referred to his desire to go to Bethlehem in his talk at Christmas midnight Mass; he said he didn't go because "circumstances do not allow me to do that." **3.** *Osservatore Romano*, January 15, 1979. **4.** Andrei Gromyko, *Memoirs* (New York: Doubleday, 1989), pages 212–213. Gromyko reported a similar meeting with John Paul in 1985. **5.** Wilton Wynn, *Keepers of the Keys*, (New York: Random House, 1988), page 66. **6.** Men of Sakharov's prominence were no longer routinely jailed, but rather publicly denounced, blacklisted from work, and forced to live in "internal exile." They were, of course, threatened with imprisonment should they step further out of line. **7.** The English-language paperback edition was published by Image Books, New York, in 1985. **8.** This entire paragraph, and other quotes from Potocki, came from an interview with him in Krakow.

Chapter 3

1. Particularly Cardinal Sebastiano Baggio. **2.** I have sewn together translations of speeches as seems to me to make the best English, taking from Francis X. Murphy, *The Papacy Today* (London: Weidenfeld and Nicolson, 1984), Chapter 8; George Hunston Williams, *The Mind of John Paul II* (New York: The Seabury Press, 1981), chapter 10; the *Tablet* (London), and *Osservatore Romano*. **3.** Murphy, *The Papacy Today*, chapter 8. The responsibility of the secret police (DINA) was established in later investigations. **4.** Dominic Milroy, a monk, writing in the *Tablet* (London), Oct. 7, 1978. Another source on the political diversity of Liberation Theology was Father Gianpaolo Salvini, editor of the Vatican magazine *Civil Catholica*.

Chapter 4

1. One account was published by Father Francis X. Murphy, who used the pseudonym Xavier Rynne. Dutch Cardinal Willebrands acknowledges there was a disagreement; he says he doesn't remember a formal statement but may have forgotten it.   2. To this logical defense of priestly celibacy, John Paul regularly adds a scriptural defense, the Gospel of Saint Matthew, chapter 19, in which Jesus says, "He that is able to receive [celibacy], let him receive it." John Paul reads this as a command to priestly celibacy, though the passage is obviously open to less stringent interpretation. Other Catholic theologians cite several other Gospel passages as requiring priestly celibacy, though Protestants disagree. Those who think priestly celibacy should be optional note that Jesus appointed married apostles; supporters of a celibacy requirement say the apostles left their families to follow Jesus.   3. April 8, 1984, quoted in the *Tablet* (London), April 21–28, 1984.   4. Oct. 20, 1979, quoted in *Osservatore Romano*, Nov. 19, 1979.

Chapter 5

1. Quotes from the *Tablet* (London), April 5–12, 1980.   2. Father Gianpaolo Salvini, editor of the Vatican-supervised magazine *Civil Catholica* in Rome.   3. For translations of the Romero diary, I have relied on David Willey, *God's Politician: John Paul at the Vatican* (New York: St. Martin's, 1992), and Tad Szulc, *Pope John Paul II* (New York: Scribner's, 1995).   4. Gierek was interviewed for a biography by Janusz Rolicki, *Edward Gierek: Przerwana Dekada* (Warsaw: Wydawnictwo Fakt, 1990), quoted in Szulc, *Pope John Paul II*, page 299.   5. Statement from Vance. I stressed to Vance's spokeswoman my initial

difficulty in believing there was no connection between his visit and the pope's Polish trip; she stressed to me that she had checked with Vance, and he said it was just a coincidence. She said no record was kept of the meeting.   6. From Wilton Wynn, who interviewed Vagnozzi, now dead.

Chapter 6

1. The *Tablet* (London), June 9 and 16, 1979.   2. A cardinal who for his own reasons didn't want to be identified as the source of this section.   3. To André Frossard, in a private conversation.   4. Christopher Bobinski, writing in the *Tablet* (London), June 9, 1979.   5. Interview with William Brand.   6. Interview with Anna Kotlarczyk Pakosiewicz.   7. For most of the quotes from this trip, I have used the English text printed in *Osservatore Romano*. Where other versions of what was obviously the same text were available, for example in the *Tablet* (London), they were usually better, and I wove them in. For the last speech in Krakow, I have used the translation by Katarzyna Mroczkowski-Brand provided in Andrzej Micewski, *Cardinal Wyszynski: A Biography* (San Diego: Harcourt Brace, 1984), pages 422–423, compared with which the *Osservatore Romano* version seemed dull and stilted.

Chapter 7

1. I wrote about the Knights of Malta for the *Wall Street Journal*. For this book, I visited the Knights' headquarters in Rome—they claim their building is the equivalent of an independent country—and talked to the highest officials there who would see me. There are two well-researched magazine articles about them: one in *Covert Action Information Bulletin*, winter 1986, written under a pseudonym, and the other by Martin A. Lee in *Mother Jones* magazine, July 1983.   2. Tymieniecka and Houthakker say they did not discuss the book with John Paul on

the 1979 Castelgandolfo visit because they considered it finished.   **3.** Quoted in the *Tablet* (London), March 29, 1980.

Chapter 8

1. Message to the UN Conference on Trade and Development, April 26, 1979. In this and the next paragraph, I have used quotes from April and November speeches because they seem concisely and effectively to sum up ideas he was also expounding in the October U.N. speech.   **2.** This quote from a speech Nov. 24, 1979, to two thousand members of the Christian Union of Entrepreneurs and Managers, meeting in Rome, reprinted in *Osservatore Romano,* Dec. 24, 1979.   **3.** Message to the UN Conference on Trade and Development, April 26, 1979.   **4.** Speech given Oct. 2, 1979, reprinted in *Osservatore Romano,* Oct. 22, 1979.   **5.** From a transcript in the archives of Radio Free Europe in Munich, and another that Sister Kane herself supplied.   **6.** Speech at Catholic Institute of Paris, June 1, 1980.   **7.** Interview with Father Francis X. Murphy.   **8.** Quotes taken from weekly addresses Sept. 5, 1979, through March 12, 1980, as reprinted in *Osservatore Romano.*   **9.** Quoted in *Osservatore Romano,* Nov. 19, 1979.   **10.** I left many messages for Lewandowski, both at his office in Rome (which said he was now back in Poland), and with colleagues in Poland (who said that no, he was still in Rome). He never called. I have no reason to disbelieve Father Hejmo's account.   **11.** Father Alojzy Orszulik, who rebuffed my attempts to interview him, as described later.

Chapter 9

1. Wilton Wynn, *Keepers of the Keys,* page 164.   **2.** Interview with Lustiger.   **3.** Nov. 15, 1980, in Cologne, Germany.   **4.** Cardinal Paul Poupard, who was on the Galileo commission and later became its

chairman, told me that the pope took up the case not to right a wrong but because "Leftist or Enlightenment thought used [Galileo's case] to accuse the Church of being oppressive." He described it as a public-relations problem. Poupard also denied there was any controversy surrounding Lustiger's Jewishness. But Poupard's word seems not nearly as good as the pope's or Lustiger's own on these two points.   **5.** On the mission of papal representative Monsignor Annibal Bugnini, Francis X. Murphy, *The Papacy Today* (London: Weidenfeld and Nicolson, 1984), page 213.

Chapter 10

1. Cardinal Willebrands, Schillebeeckx's fellow Dutchman, confirms the airing of the interview and says he complained to John Paul about it. Wilton Wynn, in *Keepers of the Keys,* page 252, describes an "angry . . . dressing-down" by the pope of radio chief Roberto Tucci. Tucci says Wynn's detailed account "is not true," but won't say what parts of it he disputes, or whether the pope ever talked to him about the matter. Perhaps more perplexing, he urged me to print the story regardless of its truth because it would "show the liberal side of the pope."   **2.** Janik quote from the 1988 BBC documentary on the pope.   **3.** From the BBC documentary.   **4.** I covered the invasion of Afghanistan for the *Wall Street Journal.* A history appears in my book *Endless Enemies* (New York: Congdon and Weed, 1984; reprint, New York: Viking Penguin, 1987).   **5.** From the *Tablet* (London), other newspaper accounts, and Francis X Murphy, *The Papacy Today* (London: Weidenfeld and Nicolson, 1984), page 219. When I called Drinan, he seemed still bitter about it and brusquely declined to talk to me. Almanacs disagree over his time of service in Congress, but six years is a minimum.   **6.** Interview with University of Chicago sociologist Maryjane Osa.

Chapter 11

1. I have found no reference anywhere, other than my interview with Cardinal Oddi, that this meeting occurred or that such a decision had been contemplated. After Oddi stunned me by volunteering this story an hour into our conversation, I went over the matter thoroughly with him; his memory was clear and precise. Both Seper and Baggio are now dead. 2. Until late 1979, d'Aubuisson had been deputy security chief of the Salvadoran government. He left his official post, taking the files with him, to become unofficial director of the death squads. He expressed admiration of the Nazis for killing the "communist" Jews. See Martin A. Lee and Norman Solomon, *Unreliable Sources* (New York: Lyle Stuart, 1990), and Raymond Bonner, *Weakness and Deceit* (New York: Times Books, 1984). D'Aubuisson founded his own political party, ARENA, with a private army like the Nazis'. ARENA took power in El Salvador in March 1989 after a stacked election held under the aegis of the U.S. government. 3. I have the toll printed by the *Tablet* (London), April 5–12, 1980. The *New York Times* report of the shooting said "at least" twenty-six had died. 4. *Osservatore Romano*, June 30, 1980. Carter wouldn't be interviewed.

Chapter 12

1. Observations from my own travels and reporting in Kenya. 2. Sources for this story are Lotstra's article in the *Tablet* (London), Jan. 26, 1985, letters that appeared in succeeding weeks, and my correspondence with the nuncio, Archbishop Agostino Cacciavillan, who is now nuncio in Washington; I was unable to locate Father Lotstra. Cacciavillan stresses that in his talk about the different approaches in the pulpit and the confessional, he never condoned violations of Church law, though that is what Lotstra said he understood. 3. Interview with Francis

X. Murphy. 4. With the BBC's David Willey. 5. With Jas Gawronski, a Polish-Italian journalist in Rome.

Chapter 13

1. Figure from Francis X. Murphy, *The Papacy Today*, pages 227–231. 2. Nov. 15, 1980, quoted in *Osservatore Romano*, Nov. 24, 1980. 3. Feb. 25, 1981, quoted in *Osservatore Romano*, March 9, 1981. 4. This quote combines excerpts that appeared in the *New Republic*, Dec. 26, 1994, and Tad Szulc, *Pope John Paul II*, page 442. 5. Quoted in Wilton Wynn, *Keepers of the Keys*, page 230. 6. Wynn, *The Keepers of the Keys*, page 231.

Chapter 14

1. The death threats were anonymous public notices, but everyone knew they came from government-sanctioned death squads. 2. *Osservatore Romano*, March 24, 1980. 3. Report quoted in Francis X. Murphy, *The Papacy Today*, page 233. 4. The speeches, and most of the Brazil trip, from continuing contemporaneous coverage in *Osservatore Romano* and the *Tablet*.

Chapter 15

1. There had been a cost-of-living increase, but it was less than the actual increase in living costs. 2. Interviews with Cerullo's assistant, Alessandro Candi, augmented the clippings I found. Cerullo repeatedly pleaded that he was seriously ill and unable to talk to me. 3. Alina Pienkowska, who would become Mrs. Borucewicz. I interviewed Borucewicz; Walesa declined to meet with me. The remarks of Mrs. Borucewicz are from Lech Walesa, *A Way of Hope* (New York: Henry Holt, 1987), the autobiography to which he had her and others contribute. 4. Janusz Rolicki, *Edward Gierek: Przerwana Dekada* (Warsaw: Wydawnictwo Fakt, 1990),

quoted in Tad Szulc, *Pope John Paul II*, page 341.   **5.** Quoted in David Ost, *Solidarity and the Politics of Anti-Politics* (Philadelphia: Temple University Press, 1990), page 77.   **6.** Interview with Father Michael Czajkowski of Warsaw.   **7.** Rolicki, *Edward Gierek*, quoted in Szulc, *Pope John Paul II*, page 345.   **8.** Walesa, *A Way of Hope*, pages 122–123.   **9.** When Wyszynski saw later how wrong he was, he tried to backpedal and claim that the communists had edited his taped statement and taken his words out of context. But while they may have left things out (as he asserted), they didn't invent what people watched him say.   **10.** Political scientist David Ost attributes Solidarity's disavowal of politics to its links with young Western radicals of the New Left who "did not want to possess power so much as to abolish it." The notion is interesting and may have a bit of truth. But everyone in Solidarity knew the pope's ideas, and important Solidarity advisers had discussed them with him personally. There really is no need to import an answer from the West.

Chapter 16

1. In a letter he wrote in response to my questions, Quinn added that after the synod, John Paul "entrusted me with the very important responsibility of being his personal representative for the National Pastoral Service of the Bishops on Religious Life," which he said showed the pope's continued confidence in him.   **2.** I tend to trust Kukolowicz on this, for reasons to be explained later.   **3.** Peter Schweizer, *Victory* (New York: Atlantic Monthly Press, 1994), page 57. The book is largely a compilation of self-serving leaks by former Reagan administration officials.   **4.** Admiral Bobby Ray Inman, then director of the National Security Agency, says "The Soviets were right on the edge of invading."   **5.** Part of what appears here comes from an interview with Brzezinski, who also published

his thoughts and diary excerpts regarding the 1980 Polish crisis in *Orbis* magazine, Winter 1988 issue. Brzezinski says the Soviets didn't invade because the United States used its advance warning to deprive them of surprise.   **6.** *Osservatore Romano* translations, no doubt done in a hurry, are sometimes ungrammatical. In quoting remarks the pope made in other languages, I have regularly cleaned up official translations, but never in such a way as to change their meaning.   **7.** See my book *Endless Enemies*, chapter 20.   **8.** The assistant was Adrian Karatnycki, whom I interviewed.

Chapter 17

1. Arkuscewski was also a source for this.   **2.** Peter Schweizer, *Victory*, pages 6 and 7. Defense Secretary Caspar Weinberger, who was at the meeting, was a primary, exclusive source for Schweizer.   **3.** Details are in *Endless Enemies*, Chapter 10.   **4.** Raymond Garthoff, *The Great Transition* (Washington: The Brookings Institution, 1994), page 558. Garthoff includes the caveat "except for concern about possible Soviet intervention in Poland," and adds, "Not until twenty months into the Administration's first term was a policy toward Eastern Europe adopted."   **5.** Eugene Kennedy, a former priest and now a professor of psychology at Loyola University in Chicago, in his biography *Cardinal Bernardin* (Chicago: Bonus Books, 1989), page 199.   **6.** In *Archbishop: Inside the Power Structure of the American Catholic Church* (New York: Harper and Row, 1989), chapter 1, author Thomas J. Reese says John Paul never again asked Jadot's advice on bishops' appointments in the U.S..   **7.** Father Thomas J. Reese, *Archbishop* (San Francisco: Harper and Row, 1989), chapter 1. I also interviewed Reese, probably the most thorough current chronicler of the U.S. Catholic hierarchy.   **8.** The *Tablet* (London), Nov. 17, 1984. Laghi said he had been visiting a bishop friend near the camp. Newspapers at the time quoted a speech they said he had given to soldiers, urging them to repel an invasion of alien political ideas.   9. Don Grammont, abbot of Bec-et-Hellouin monastery. Information about other candidates comes from Steven Englund, an American Catholic scholar who was close to Marty and is still close to Lustiger.   10. Quoted in Raymond Bonner, *Waltzing with a Dictator* (New York: Times Books, 1987), page 303.   11. Bonner, *Waltzing with a Dictator*, page 304.   12. Father John Navone of the Gregorian University assures me he was first.   13. Schweizer, *Victory*, page 35.   14. Inman's comments from my interviews with him.

Chapter 18

1. Statement of the Polish News Agency, quoted in Peter Schweizer, *Victory*, page 33. 2. The *New York Times*, March 15, 1981; the *Tablet* (London), Jan. 30, 1982.   3. One was Romuald Kukolowicz, who had helped Father Wojtyla publish his 1953 book *Catholic Social Ethics* and who worked closely with Wyszynski and the Episcopate. See Bogdan Czajkowski, *Next to God . . . Poland* (New York: Saint Martin's, 1983).   4. David Ost, *Solidarity*, page 125.   5. A detailed account appeared in the *Tablet* (London), Oct. 15, 1994. Some corroboration appears in former CIA official Robert M. Gates's *From the Shadows* (New York: Simon and Schuster, 1996), chapter 13. 6. Quotes from Wyszynski in this section are from Andrzej Micewski, *Cardinal Wyszynski*, chapter 6, and the *Tablet* (London), Feb. 20, 1982. Other quotes are from my interviews. Gates, *From the Shadows*, says (chapter 13) John Paul met three more times with the Soviet ambassador between April 19 and 25 to discuss the Polish situation. The April 17 date comes from Micewski. The May legalization of rural Solidarity was a public event; Walesa says in his autobiography, *A Way of Hope* (New York: Henry Holt, 1987), page 11, that he negotiated it. 7. This information comes from historian

Peter Raina, to whom Wyszynski and his circle granted extensive access, resulting in a series of books. Raina says Wyszynski conveyed his choice several times, once in a letter hand-delivered by Dziwisz. Dziwisz declined to talk to me.   8. André Frossard said the pope told him that problems with a first ambulance required a change to a second, but no one else has related this information, and Dr. Crucitti denies it. These two are the only ones I could find (besides Dziwisz, who wouldn't talk to me) who say they received firsthand accounts from John Paul. 9. Medical details from interview with Crucitti.   10. Interview with Crucitti. 11. Wilton Wynn, *Keepers of the Keys*, pages 205–206.   12. Archbishop Dabrowski denies published accounts that an inadequate extension cord had fouled up a previous attempt at a papal phone call.   13. Read to me, quite dramatically, by Dabrowski from his original notes, during an interview.

Chapter 19

1. The semiofficial Jesuit journal *Civil Catholica*, which is vetted by the Vatican before publication.   2. The story told here is pieced together from accounts that diverge in places. It begins with Margherita Guarducci's book *La Tomba di San Pietro: Una Straordinaria Vicenda* (Milan: Rusconi, 1992), as explained and partly translated for me by Christopher Ciccarino, an American seminary student and official tour guide at the Vatican. Ciccarino's own studies have also given him independent knowledge of these events, and I am in his debt. My associate Silvia Sansoni interviewed Professor Guarducci to verify the material, and found her, in her eighties, apparently confused about certain verifiable historical dates.   3. The hedge was that he had "no information" because he had not been there. Other questions on the same list, however, had obviously been researched and received full answers.   4. Zdzislaw Najder, a writer

and Solidarity adviser, of whom more later. 5. Wilton Wynn and André Frossard are also sources for these events.

Chapter 20

1. Charles Raw, *The Money Changers* (London: HarperCollins, 1992), page 27.   2. Raw, *The Money Changers*, page 355.   3. As elsewhere, my discussion of the IOR-Calvi affair is based not just on Raw's splendid book, but on my own research for articles for the *Wall Street Journal*, my interviews for this book with Calvi's son and his private investigators, and the several other books already cited. 4. Peter Schweizer, *Victory*, page 55. 5. Monsignor George Higgins, whom I interviewed.   6. Figures from the *Tablet* (London). An article Oct. 10, 1981, discusses most of the cases, and others are discussed in continuing coverage.   7. An editor for *Notre Dame* magazine who was working on a profile of Greeley.   8. I owe a large debt to Church scholar and former priest Eugene Kennedy, author of *Cardinal Bernardin* (Chicago: Bonus Books, 1989), for his account of these matters.

Chapter 21

1. Monsignor George Higgins of Catholic University was particularly emphatic on this point.   2. The quotes in this section have been cobbled together from whole or partial translations published in the *New York Times*, the *Tablet* (London), and *Osservatore Romano*, which did not always agree. The first two sentences of the last paragraph quoted come from John Paul's general audience a few days later, when he was asked the implication of the surrounding material on women in the workplace.

Chapter 22

1. Interview with Father O'Keefe. 2. O'Keefe says Wilson told him at a social

affair that he had pushed Casaroli to change the Jesuits. Wilson declines to talk about it now.   3. Some Jesuits say the action was unprecedented, but a Church historian points out that Pius XII annulled an election of the Dominicans and imposed his own father general. Certainly such intervention is rare. 4. Because I have had to rely on anonymous quotes—though from sources definitely in position to know—I should make clear that Father O'Keefe was *not* a source for this paragraph and spoke to me entirely on the record. 5. The *Tablet* (London), Jan. 2, 1982. 6. Elden F. Curtiss and Thomas J. Murphy. 7. Speech delivered May 9, 1982, to Catholic Action, reported in the *Tablet* (London), May 22, 1982.   8. The plans were included in a defense policy that Reagan approved in March 1982.   9. A point made by the *Tablet* (London) in reporting many of these statements.   10. To summarize and extend earlier notes: Walesa and Dziwisz wouldn't see me. Kukolowicz behaved strangely when I and my Polish associate tried to obtain a photocopy he had promised us of Wojtyla's 1953 book. But every test I could apply to the information Kukolowicz gave me affirmed his truthfulness about historical events. Sources already named corroborated the authenticity of the Wojtyla manuscript he showed me. Among others, Micewski and Turowicz confirmed Kukolowicz's importance as a secret liaison between the Episcopate and Walesa, and Walesa mentions it in his autobiography. Kukolowicz's wife, a former nun whom Wyszynski dispensed from her vows so she could marry him, is a respected professor at Catholic University in Lublin.

Chapter 23

1. This account comes from Andrzej Micewski, who sat in on the meeting. He had continued to work at the Episcopate on Wyszynski's biography and especially im-

pressed Glemp by having informal access to old colleagues in the Party from his Pax days. Glemp made him an adviser. **2.** General Anatoly Gribkov, then chief of staff of the Warsaw Pact, describing the recommendation made jointly by him, Defense Minister Dmitri Ustinov, and others, in an interview by Walter Russell Mead in *Worth* magazine, Feb. 1996. **3.** Raymond Garthoff, *The Great Transition* (Washington: The Brookings Institution, 1994), page 547, quoting from documents, formally "Top Secret" but made public after the fall of communism. Garthoff concludes that the record isn't definitive on whether Jaruzelski believed the Soviets would intervene if he didn't act. **4.** Interviews with Chojecki and Richard Pipes, the Soviet–East European specialist for the National Security Council. **5.** Interview with Father Hejmo. Orszulik's office scheduled an interview for me, but he stood up my interpreter and me after we rode two hours by train to Lowicz, where he is now bishop. His nun and priest assistants were apologetic but gave contradictory excuses for his always being unavailable when we tried to rearrange our schedule to see him after that. I concluded that he was evading an interview. **6.** The *Tablet* (London), Jan. 23, 1982. **7.** Lech Walesa, *A Way of Hope* (New York: Henry Holt, 1987), pages 221–222. He uses the word *shouted.* **8.** Interviews with Mrs. Anna Krzysztowicz, a professor at Jagiellonian University who was asked to head a committee, and Bishop Bronislaw Fidelus, Macharski's deputy.

Mrs. Wosiek. **6.** Schweizer, *Victory,* pages 68–69. Besides gaining exclusive access to top officials and their papers, Schweizer wrote the book with the support of the Hoover Institution, a think tank at Stanford University that serves as a sort of halfway house for Republican officials pondering retirement. Clark confirmed his relationship with Schweizer to me. Weinberger didn't return several phone messages, but has since coauthored a book with Schweizer on the continuing need for a strong military. In an interview, Schweizer told me, "As you can probably tell by the account [in *Victory*], there are some parts that are detailed and other parts that are a little bit more fuzzy. I just didn't have time to investigate the Polish side of this drama as much as I would have wanted." **7.** National Catholic News Service. I am indebted to Father Ken Doyle for making many of his old news stories available to me. Schweizer says he doesn't recall hearing Chojecki's name, and didn't know Casaroli was at the White House. **8.** My only identifiable source for this is Najder. But several Polish clergymen who proved reliable on other matters told me this on condition that I not attribute it to them. This is understandable since Glemp is still their boss. Glemp wouldn't speak to me. **9.** Among my sources are Polish churchmen who deal with both men, and who for that reason do not want to be quoted on this point. **10.** Quoted in the *Tablet* (London), Jan. 16, 1982. **11.** Kozlowski will not quote John Paul's exact reply.

Chapter 24

1. Archbishop Dabrowski acknowledges this. Some anonymous complaints from bishops aired on Radio Free Europe. **2.** The *Tablet* (London), Jan. 23, 1982. **3.** Peter Schweizer, *Victory,* page 68, and interview with Richard Pipes. **4.** See Pipes's account in footnote, page 420. **5.** Interview with

Chapter 25

1. CIA support for the International Confederation of Free Trade Unions has since been publicly exposed. **2.** See Peter Schweizer, *Victory,* page 70. **3.** From Wilton Wynn, who reported on it for *Time* magazine, referred to on page 202 of *Keepers of the Keys,* augmented in an interview. **4.** Explaining

Vatican policy in an interview, Cardinal Poggi said, "Sanctions always harm the people. An arms embargo is understandable. But when there are sanctions against importing [other goods], it is only the poor people who are without. The elite always has food."

Chapter 26

1. This quote from the *Tablet* (London), Nov. 10, 1984. Other material in this section is drawn from interviews with persons named and, in one case, unnamed. 2. Incident originally told to me by a priest who knew Popieluszko well but who needs to remain anonymous; confirmed by Bishop Kraszewski in an interview with my associate, Joanna Tomaszewska in Warsaw.

Chapter 27

1. From a cardinal involved in the situation who didn't want to be quoted. 2. Fokcinski was also Przydatek's direct superior in the Jesuits. 3. My articles describing Pazienza's relationship with the administration, and particularly with Reagan aide Michael Ledeen, appeared in the *Wall Street Journal*, August 7–8, 1985. 4. Marina De Laurentiis. 5. Obviously, there will be more to come on this later in the text, but sources for the Carboni-Pazienza-Przydatek activity so far described include my interviews with Fokcinski, Przydatek, Pazienza, Hejmo, Konopka, and others, plus Italian news clippings and interviews with Italian journalists who covered the matter, including particularly Antonio Carlucci, now of *L'Espresso*, then of *Panorama*. I did not know about Przydatek when I interviewed Pazienza in an American prison in 1985, and so could not ask him specifically about their relationship. Pazienza is now in an Italian prison and thus harder to get to. 6. Quoted earlier in this book to describe Wyszynski's imprisonment. 7. From

interviews with Modzelewski, Dabrowski, and Radio Free Europe officials.

Chapter 28

1. The quotes above, and many similar remarks, may be found in Raymond Garthoff, *The Great Transition* (Washington: The Brookings Institution, 1994), and Andy Pasztor, *When the Pentagon Was for Sale* (New York: Scribner's, 1995). In March 1980, Reagan told the Chicago Council on Foreign Relations, "In military strength, we are already second to one: namely, the Soviet Union. And that is a very dangerous position in which to be." He spoke to the *Washington Post* in June 1980 about a Soviet advantage and a "window of vulnerability" in which new Soviet rockets could surprise and destroy U.S. missile sites. His Pentagon advisers conveyed the same message. Once, on being criticized for lax cost controls, Defense Secretary Weinberger replied, "I was obsessed with the idea that we might not have much time." He cited "an absolutely vital catch-up situation."

Chapter 29

1. (Washington: The Brookings Institution, 1994.) 2. Brzezinski says he learned from persons in Reagan's entourage that Reagan dozed off during one slow moment. 3. Bernstein did add one sentence in parentheses acknowledging the pope's frequent appeals for peace in Central America and his implicit criticism of U.S. policy there. But buried in an article covering eight pages of *Time*, the sentence didn't soften the message. 4. I could not draw an absolute conclusion from looking at the Polish passports, but Dabrowski seemed earnest and intent on proving his point. I have no reason to doubt him. 5. The newspaper was *Corriere della Serra*. Archbishop Dabrowski says that a young assistant on his staff, Jerzy

Dabrowski—no relation—did accompany Glemp to the United States as an English-speaking aide. But he says Jerzy Dabrowski would not have had the high-level meetings or discussions Bernstein describes, and besides, he reported everything back to his boss, Bronislaw Dabrowski. Jerzy Dabrowski died in an airplane crash in 1991.

Chapter 30

1. From Wilton Wynn, who has worked closely with Franco on a writing project. Investigators found an April 18, 1982, letter from Calvi to Franco thanking him for his "valued intervention with Vatican authorities." Franco didn't respond to my faxed inquiries.   2. Again, Przydatek would not answer my questions about this.   3. Charles Raw, *The Money Changers*, pages 325–326. 4. Precise figures from Raw, *The Money Changers*, chapters 31 through 35 and page 7. 5. Interviews with Calvi and Pazienza. 6. The *Tablet* (London), covered the Argentine crisis, including the pope's visit, weekly as it happened and published a retrospective April 20, 1985.   7. Macharski himself declined to talk to me.

Chapter 31

1. A fuller account may be found in my book *Endless Enemies.*   2. The National Catholic News Service, a Church agency, used the phrase "approaching a scream."   3. The quotes are from Maciej Koslowski, then a staff writer at *Tygodnik Powszechny,* now a Polish diplomat in Washington, and at all times a close cousin of the newspaper's deputy editor, Krzysztof Kozlowski. Others conveyed the same general impression.   4. Quoted by Konstanty Gebert in his underground newspaper.   5. Many people I interviewed in Poland brought up this situation. 6. Glemp declined to answer my questions.

7. Since then, Los Angeles has become the largest.

Chapter 32

1. *Il Sabato*, Oct. 23–29, 1982. I am relying on Raw's translation, as published in his book *The Money Changers,* page 11.   2. Starr was identified in the *Tablet* (London), July 14, 1984. According to a UPI story in the *New York Times* July 11, 1984, the White House acknowledged that Wilson tried to intervene in the case and was scolded for doing so by a Justice Department official, but said he retained President Reagan's full confidence. 3. The *Tablet* (London), July 14, 1984. Lorna Richardson of Wilson's office told me that at eighty, he was now too old to answer questions. Smith has died, and Starr—who in 1996 was under fire for conflicts of interest as an independent counsel investigating President Clinton's finances—didn't return my several detailed phone messages.   4. Besides Swiss and Italian financiers, the panel included Joseph Brennan, former president of Emigrant Savings Bank in New York. Krol acknowledged to me that he hadn't been shown the report.   5. The information doesn't appear in his book on Agca (*The Plot to Kill the Pope* [New York: Scribner's, 1985]), or on its covers. Edward S. Herman and Frank Brodhead, in *The Rise and Fall of the Bulgarian Connection* (New York: Sheridan Square Publications, 1986), on page 147 cite evidence that Henze insisted on nondisclosure of his CIA work as a condition for appearing on television.   6. Just before the Ambrosiano scandal exploded, John Paul had appointed Marcinkus to the additional job of temporary president of the commission that ran the Vatican—street and building maintenance, sewage, and so forth. The holder of this job, sometimes known informally as the Vatican mayor, normally gets the honor of being made a cardinal.

Chapter 33

1. From personal interviews in Nicaragua, as well as my experience in neighboring countries. 2. Father Cardenal released the letter in early 1985, after the Jesuits dismissed him. 3. The quote comes from Wilton Wynn, *Keepers of the Keys*, page 70. 4. Interview with Father Gianpaolo Salvini, director of the semiofficial Vatican publication *Civil Catholica*. 5. Gates's 1996 memoir, *From the Shadows* (New York: Simon & Schuster), said the CIA had helped fund the Church in Nicaragua but included no details. This provoked a denial by Obando y Bravo, backed up by the Vatican. In an interview, Gates told me that the money was funneled through a South American so the Church wouldn't know where it came from, and that it wasn't much—"maybe $50,000 at most, in the low hundreds of thousands." He reiterated that in regard to neither Nicaragua nor Poland did the CIA ask for or obtain any Church action. 6. This was Roberto Alejos, a tycoon and Knights of Malta ambassador to Honduras, whose land had been used to train the Bay of Pigs invaders in 1960. See John Prados, *Presidents' Secret Wars* (New York: William Morrow, 1986); Scott Anderson and Jon Lee Anderson, *Inside the League* (New York: Dodd, Mead, 1986); Penny Lernoux, *People of God*, (New York: Viking, 1989), excerpted in the *National Catholic Reporter*, May 5, 1989. 7. The audience was arranged by Mercedes Wilson, a Catholic charity official who knew both the pope and Macauley. 8. Much information in this section is drawn from what Macauley told author George Getschow for an as-yet-unpublished biography of Peter Grace. Getschow, a former colleague of mine at the *Wall Street Journal* and one of its best reporters and bureau chiefs, was kind enough to share his Americares file with me. The New York Archdiocese eventually saved the youth shelter, Covenant House, minus Father Ritter. Although these matters received wide expo-

sure, I found *National Catholic Reporter* particularly helpful in compiling this account. Archbishop Theodore McKerrick of Newark, N.J., a friend of Grace's, says, "It was Peter who got Knights of Malta involved with Latin America. Before Peter came, [membership in the Knights] was an honor, period." 9. Mansour and her provincial superior, Helen Marie Burns, point to a statement from Szoka that appeared in Detroit newspapers two days after Mansour's appointment, applauding her selection as a chance to "give a powerful witness to the Christian dimension of the Department of Social Services." He points to a portion of the same statement that said he expected Mansour would use her post to bring new attention to the evil of abortion. He says he expected her to oppose public funding, though that is not clear in his statement—and therein may lie the ambiguity she says she felt. Szoka also stresses that he dealt not with Kane, but with the order's regional head. The incident is described in a book, *Authority, Community and Conflict*, edited by Madonna Kolbenschlag (Kansas City: Sheed and Ward, 1986), containing many original documents.

Chapter 34

1. Raymond Garthoff, *The Great Transition*, pages 36–39. 2. Amply documented in Garthoff, *The Great Transition*. 3. See speeches by Andropov and Defense Minister Ustinov, November 22, 1982. Garthoff, *The Great Transition*, contains many frightening examples of how the USSR and U.S. misread each other's behavior. 4. Lech Walesa, *A Way of Hope*, page 258. 5. Boniecki organized the publication of *Kalendarium*, among other things. On each of my trips to Europe, I tried to talk to him, but he was never able to find an opening in his schedule. 6. Interview with Mazowiecki. 7. I interviewed Sister Ruth Woziek, who witnessed the beatings, and her birth sister, a lay relief worker at the church,

as well as Bishop Dembowski and Archbishop Dabrowski. **8.** The reporting here on Glemp and Popieluszko is based on several sources at various levels of the Polish Church who knew Popieluszko well. All still work for Glemp, and their wish not to be quoted on these matters is understandable. One quotable secondhand source who heard these same stories is Adrian Karatnycky, who worked in Poland for the AFL-CIO and now runs Freedom House in New York City.

Chapter 35

1. For this quote, I have combined part of my conversations with Doyle with a sentence from his news dispatch. **2.** Tad Szulc, in *Pope John Paul II*, page 392, says Jaruzelski (for whom Szulc's book is in many ways an apology) had agreed to a Walesa meeting before John Paul arrived, as a condition of the trip, and because "the Holy See ... presented it as a matter of principle." All accounts I have found say the meeting with Walesa was denied until the confrontation at Belvedere Palace. Urban says he stayed calm while making the announcement. **3.** As noted above, Jaruzelski's spokesman told me that Szulc had paid him about a thousand dollars for the interview. Szulc—whom I consider the more credible source—denies having paid it. Jaruzelski wouldn't answer any questions for me without payment. **4.** This account is confirmed by high-placed Church sources who do not wish to be named. **5.** Zbigniew Brzezinski contributed to my understanding of this story before I talked to Lustiger about it. Lustiger's assistant Jean Duschene also filled in some parts. **6.** Jaruzelski would tell author Szulc another self-serving story, claiming that the pope said to him, "General, please do not feel insulted, but I have nothing against socialism. I just want socialism to have a human face." **7.** The gist of this account was also confirmed for me by sources in the Polish hierarchy who have heard about it.

Although I generally eschew sources who don't want to be identified with their opinions, in the case of clashes between John Paul and Cardinals Casaroli and Glemp, the motive for other churchmen to want anonymity is understandable. **8.** This from Wilton Wynn, who knew Casaroli well enough to undertake ghost-writing his memoirs. Bishop Dembowski, in an interview, and the *Tablet* (London), in its coverage of June and July 1983, provided similar versions of events. Levi wouldn't answer my questions, but Cywinski says papal assistant Boniecki told him the editorial resulted from a misunderstood conversation Levi had in an elevator with Boniecki (who also wouldn't see me). **9.** Interview with Father Hejmo. **10.** Wilson's office told me he was too elderly to answer questions.

Chapter 36

1. The *Tablet* (London), July 8, 1982, quoting a letter from the pope's pro-nuncio to Milingo. Other material in this section comes from an interview with Willey and from his book *God's Politician*. **2.** Quoted in the *Tablet* (London), Oct. 8, 1983. **3.** Interview with Cardinal Oddi. **4.** Rosemary Reuther, who writes a column for the *National Catholic Reporter*. **5.** The *Tablet* (London), March 24, 1984. **6.** Although I did not see Father Kolvenbach, I interviewed Pittau, Salvini, and other prominent leaders. Since two of these did not want to be quoted on certain matters, I have lumped them together. **7.** The quotes from Father Sainz de Baranda and Casaroli are taken from the *Tablet* (London), March 23, April 6, May 4, 1985.

Chapter 37

1. Figures from the *Tablet* (London), Sept. 22, 1984. **2.** The *Tablet* (London), Nov. 5, 1983. Worlock declined my request for an interview. **3.** The U.S. said the Soviets had killed civilians on purpose, though the White House had radio intercepts showing otherwise. The Soviets countered that the plane had been on a military mission, though repeated investigations have found no evidence of that. But the U.S. did have a program that called for military planes to fly regularly in and out of Soviet air space to "destabilize" Soviet defenders, and a military plane had flown along the border shortly before the airliner went off course. **4.** Two weeks before the U.S. invasion, the island had been taken over by Maoist crazies. For the whole story, including the pretext of rescuing U.S. medical students, see the postscript of my book *Endless Enemies*. **5.** Jaruzelski disclosed the letter to author Tad Szulc, who quoted from it in *Pope John Paul II*, page 396. **6.** From the *Tablet* (London), Dec. 6, 1983. **7.** From Father Lewek (see note following). **8.** The story and diary passages come from Popieluszko's friend Father Antonin Lewek, pastor of his former church. The diary was translated for me by my associate Professor Nina Gladziuk. Jaruzelski assured Szulc that he disobeyed Andropov and pursued friendship with the Church. Szulc apparently took him at his word and didn't report the Glemp and Popieluszko matters. Again, Glemp wouldn't see me. **9.** Interview with Vatican Press Secretary Joaquin Navarro-Valls. **10.** Eugene Kennedy, *Cardinal Bernardin* (Chicago: Bonus Books, 1989), page 249. **11.** Kennedy, *Cardinal Bernardin*, pages 258–259. Cardinal Law didn't respond to my requests for a self-characterization. **12.** In 1986, O'Connor called his Vietnam book "a very poor book that I . . . would like to rewrite today, or hide." **13.** When I sought to interview O'Connor, his press secretary, Father Joseph Zwilling, asked for and got a detailed telefax about this book; then he stopped returning my calls. But Nat Hentoff wrote a biography, *John Cardinal O'Connor* (New York: Scribner's, 1988), which is brimming with long direct quotes from his sub-

ject. **14.** From Wilton Wynn, and the *Tablet* (London) Jan. 7, 1984.

Chapter 38

1. At John Paul's request, Marcinkus had prepared a twenty-two-page memo the previous summer, which Charles Raw, in *The Money Changers*, sums up as "seriously misleading" (page 45). **2.** The concordat was signed Feb. 18, 1984. The Ambrosiano deal wasn't announced to the public until May, when it was legally formalized. **3.** Statistics in this paragraph from the *Tablet* (London), Oct. 13, 1984. **4.** See Peter Schweizer, *Victory*. Then National Security Adviser William Clark is said by Schweizer to have authorized the attacks as well. Clark confirmed to me that he had reviewed Schweizer's manuscript as it pertained to him and that it was accurate, but he said he wouldn't discuss specifics because he had "to protect intelligence sources and methods." **5.** Schweizer, *Victory*, pages 181–183. **6.** Poggi told this to my associate Silvia Sansoni. I interviewed him at length before hearing of Casey's alleged trip; on learning of it, I asked Sansoni to go see the cardinal again. His remarks to her entirely accorded with what he had already told me, in different contexts. **7.** At the time, John Paul knew that independence would bring to power a group called SWAPO, which the Reagan administration accused of being communist. Since then SWAPO has won elections that the United States has recognized as fair. **8.** This particular quote comes from a speech delivered May 22, 1984. The speech to the diplomatic corps in January did call for an immediate reduction of nuclear weapons, contrary to American policy. **9.** The Cato Institute in Washington published a laundry list compiled by Barbara Conry. **10.** Interview with Bujak. **11.** Interviews with Milewski and his assistant Joanna Pilarska. **12.** The *Tablet*

(London), Feb. 11, 1984. **13.** Speech January 26, 1984, as reprinted in *Osservatore Romano* Feb. 13, 1984. **14.** Caroline's childless brother Albert was evidently seen as too precarious a bloodline and her sister Stephanie also had marital problems. **15.** See Peter Steinfels in the *New York Times*, Jan. 28, 1995, among many accounts.

Chapter 39

1. Interview with Wilton Wynn. **2.** Interviews with curial staff who see the pope's papers. **3.** Interview with Father Becker. **4.** Interview with Jerzy Kluger. **5.** Information in this section comes mainly from personal interviews, but a fine article about papal routine was written by William D. Montalbano for the *Los Angeles Times*, June 2, 1992. **6.** Other staff members made the same observations but asked not to be quoted by name. **7.** Laurenti, a native of Malta, accompanied the president of Malta on such a visit in 1991 but also saw many others close up. **8.** Interview with Archbishop Re. **9.** This figure from Father Thomas Reese, who has gained exceptional access for a book he is writing. **10.** Interviews with Poupard and his staff. **11.** Interview with Dr. Cristina Carlo-Stella, the art historian who directs the commission's staff.

Chapter 40

1. From Macierewicz, who says he himself favored Glemp's compromise at the time. But he was in hiding, not in the Solidarity leadership, and had little say in the matter. I also discussed this with Andrzej Micewski, whom Glemp had asked to advise him on the plan. **2.** The *Tablet* (London), Feb. 11, 1984, and interview with Father Antonin Lewek. **3.** I interviewed him in Paris. Other Glemp material comes from news accounts and interviews with Joanna Szczesna. **4.** Interview with Milewski. **5.** Confirmed for me by a Roman cardinal close to John Paul both then and now. **6.** Interview with Father Hejmo, who was sympathetic to Glemp. **7.** Jaruzelski is quoted by Tad Szulc in *Pope John Paul II*, page 397. In ways, the Jaruzelski-Glemp interaction parallels the strange bond twenty years earlier between Wyszynski and Gomulka, who, in order to preserve a livable status quo, had jointly resisted a German settlement they both claimed to want. **8.** Konstanty Gebert, who published the second-largest underground Solidarity newspaper, showed me some of these pamphlets in his home. He pointed out telltale typographical irregularities and other signs clearly indicating that they all came from the same press turning out Church material. **9.** Walesa's emissary Jaroslaw Kaczynski, whom I interviewed, says many Solidarity leaders supported the deal. Archbishop Dabrowski claims that only Michnik blocked it (singling out a Jew). Mazowiecki, Bujak, Macierewicz, and the other Catholic Solidarity leaders I talked to confirm the story as I have related it here. Walesa declined to comment.

Chapter 41

1. The *Tablet* (London), May 12, 1984. **2.** As noted earlier, Przydatek fled our meeting rather than comment on these matters. **3.** Sam Nujoma, now Namibia's elected president. **4.** Interview with Jerzy Kuberski, the Polish communist ambassador to Rome, who accompanied Jablonski. **5.** Quoted in the *Tablet* (London), Sept. 8, 1984. **6.** Carl Bernstein's "Holy Alliance" story in *Time* says that Laghi requested the meeting, and that Reagan, as a Vatican ally, gave in to him because sanctions had suddenly started to affect ordinary people. Laghi flatly contradicts Bernstein's version, as do other facts already cited.

Chapter 42

1. Article by Nicholas Lash, Catholic professor of divinity at the University of Cambridge, in the *Tablet* (London), March 30, 1985. **2.** Quoted in the Lash article. **3.** This according to a memo from Grace's aide, dated May 5, 1984, and uncovered by my former *Wall Street Journal* colleague George Getschow in doing research for a prospective biography of Grace. The aide, John Meehan, is now dead. **4.** The *Tablet* (London), April 22, 1984. **5.** Quoted in the *Tablet* (London), March 13, 1982. **6.** Arns's speech was reported in the *Tablet* (London), Oct. 9, 1982. Over the years, I have reported on numerous murders of labor leaders at Latin American plants owned by U.S.-based multinational corporations, particularly on *The Kwitny Report* on PBS in February 1989. **7.** Etchegaray's previously undisclosed role comes from my interview with him, corroborated in part by remarks of John Paul to be quoted later. Ratzinger's "Instruction" specifically promised "a subsequent document that will detail in a positive fashion the great richness of . . . the vast theme of Christian freedom and liberation in its own right," but this suggested something more theological than social. In his interview with the magazine *Jesus*, to be quoted later, Ratzinger called the whole notion of class struggle an "illusory myth," again directly contradicting the ideas of John Paul, as stated in *Catholic Social Ethics* and speeches to be quoted later, after the fall of communism. **8.** Quoted in the *Tablet* (London), Sept. 8, 1984. **9.** The Italian monthly *Jesus*, quoted in the *Tablet* (London), Dec. 8, 1984. **10.** *El Pais*, quoted in the *Tablet* (London), Nov. 17, 1984. Ratzinger declined to confirm or deny the quotes, but, rather, referred me to texts he approved whose sentiments were similar though more politely worded. **11.** Various stories appeared that more was to come on liberation theology and social justice, particularly after John Paul spoke to reporters accompanying him on a plane trip to Canada in early fall. There was speculation he would issue an encyclical. See the *Tablet* (London),

through October 1984. **12.** Particularly poignant was a letter written on his deathbed by Father Karl Rahner, the German theologian whose leadership had been singled out for praise by Wojtyla during Vatican II. **13.** Attitude of the bishops from an interview with Cardinal Juan Landazuri Ricketts, then head of the Peruvian bishops' conference. John Paul quote from *Osservatore Romano*, June 18, 1994. **14.** A prominent official who asked to remain anonymous in this instance. **15.** *Catholic Social Ethics* said, "The economic factor . . . explains, rather substantially, the different facts of human history" (which is the essence of Marxist analysis) and "Criticism of capitalism—the protest against the system of exploitation of human beings and human work—is the unquestionable 'part of the truth' embodied in Marxism." **16.** I interviewed Landazuri by phone. When I faxed Ratzinger for his recollection, he had his secretary reply that the office couldn't undertake to research it, and that Ratzinger's thoughts on the matter were in a book, *The Ratzinger Report* (San Francisco: Ignatius Press, 1986); but the book doesn't mention the Peruvian meetings. The quotes from John Paul are blended from the translations in *Osservatore Romano* and the *Tablet*. The key concluding speech, in *Osservatore Romano*, Nov. 19, 1984, gave a nod of praise to Ratzinger's recent "instruction," but quoted only a platitude on which everyone agreed.

Chapter 43

1. Reprinted in *Osservatore Romano*, Oct. 8, 1984. **2.** A pastoral letter read in all Dutch churches said the dispute was over "the way in which the pope's ministry should be embodied in practice" (quoted in the *Tablet* [London], Oct. 20, 1984). **3.** Father Walter Goddijn of Tilburg University, in the *Tablet* (London), Jan. 28, 1984. **4.** These matters were covered continuously in *The Tablet* and *National Catholic Reporter*, among other publications, from the fall of 1984 through the spring of 1985. **5.** Antoni Gronowicz, *God's Broker* (New York: Richardson and Snyder, 1984). **6.** I was a colleague and friend of Cooney's at the *Journal* and discussed this with him during the negotiations over his book in 1984 (when I saw the offending passages), and again more recently. **7.** Interviews with Cardinal Juan Landazuri and Father Gustavo Gutierrez. **8.** Father Geoffrey Pye, writing in the *Tablet* (London), March 2, 1985. **9.** Information on the South American trip is drawn largely from accounts in the *Tablet* (London), *Osservatore Romano*, and David Willey, *God's Politician*. **10.** From the 1988 BBC documentary on the pope. **11.** See Lawrence Weschler, *A Miracle, A Universe* (New York: Penguin, 1990).

Chapter 44

1. Interview with Tad Szulc for *Pope John Paul II*, page 397. **2.** Interview with Father Antonin Lewek. **3.** Mary Craig, for the *Tablet* (London), Nov. 10, 1984. **4.** Quoted in George Weigel, *The Final Revolution* (New York: Oxford University Press, 1992), pages 149–150. **5.** Sources in a position to know confirm that Glemp, as one priest put it, "began treating Lewek as he had Popieluszko." Again, Glemp would not talk to me. **6.** Quoted in Szulc, *Pope John Paul II*, page 398.

Chapter 45

1. Quote from hearings before the Subcommittee on International Trade, Finance and Security Economics of the Joint Economic Committee, Sept. 20, 1983; there is no evidence that the situation changed over the next year. **2.** There are many published accounts of the Thatcher-Reagan meeting. Reagan's attitude is illustrated by his first press conference afterward. **3.** See Andy Pasztor, *When the Pentagon Was for Sale* (New York: Scribner's,

1995), page 29. **4.** Quoted in the *Tablet* (London), Feb. 2, 1985. **5.** Tad Szulc, on page 397 of *Pope John Paul II*, is among those who have depicted the murder as the work of renegade officers. **6.** See Archbishop Dabrowski's earlier account of Pietruszko's taking him and another bishop to see Walesa right after martial law was imposed. **7.** The *New York Times*, Aug. 21, 1994. **8.** David Remnick, *Lenin's Tomb* (New York: Random House, 1993), chapter 12 and part 5, and Raymond Garthoff, *The Great Transition*, pages 203–205. **9.** Garthoff, *The Great Transition*, page 205. **10.** Garthoff, *The Great Transition*, page 571. Garthoff writes about the meeting with Eastern European leaders based on his interviews with participants. **11.** From a speech Reagan gave to magazine publishers on March 14, 1985, quoted in Garthoff, *The Great Transition*, page 207. **12.** George P. Shultz, *Turmoil and Triumph* (New York: Scribner's, 1993), page 527. **13.** To show another way of looking at this, Condoleeza Rice, a former Reagan-Bush aide on Soviet affairs, now provost at Stanford University, says it was the Soviets, not Reagan, who reversed abruptly; she credits the "rather aggressive" Reagan foreign policy. She says the Soviets changed attitude when Gromyko met Reagan in September 1984, by proposing resumption of the Geneva arms negotiations. Reagan's summit proposal was a response to this Soviet turnaround, she says. But in their memoirs, Reagan and Shultz don't portray the Gromyko meetings so dramatically. They attribute the resumption of the arms talks to proposals made by Reagan himself. Reagan still rejected the idea of a summit months after the arms talks had resumed, and changed his mind without their having achieved perceptible progress. **14.** The Contras in Nicaragua and the Unita forces of rebel dictator Jonas Savimbi in Angola, both operating with U.S. arms, routinely attacked civilians in a conscious effort to spread terror and distrust of government.   **15.** It is not even in the index of the *New York Times.* I am indebted to Howard N. Meyer of New York City, who brought the speech to my attention as a result of a notice I placed in the *Times Book Review* seeking information on the pope.   **16.** The opinion of Howard N. Meyer, a Manhattan lawyer who has written an unpublished history of the court. The only two cases that come close, he says, are a 1928 dispute over the German-Austrian border and a more recent one involving the independence of Namibia from South Africa.   **17.** When I showed a transcript of the speech and explained its context to Cardinal Edward Cassidy, a Vatican diplomat who had accompanied the pope to Holland, he told me, "I can honestly say it never entered my head he was taking a position on Nicaragua. The Americans never mentioned it might have had implications." Given the headlines at the time concerning the U.S. renunciation of the court's jurisdiction, it seems scarcely believable that the pope didn't know the import of his words.

Chapter 46

1. My interviews were augmented by continuing coverage of the Dutch crisis in the *Tablet* (London) and the account in David Willey, *God's Politician,* chapters 4 and 8.   **2.** Both quoted in the *Tablet* (London), Sept. 17, 1983.   **3.** The reporting of the bishops' trip and the conference on the ordination of women is drawn entirely from accounts in the *Tablet* (London), in continuing coverage, particularly Sept. 17 and Nov. 26, 1983.   **4.** Ratzinger interview with *Jesus,* an Italian monthly, quoted in Eugene Kennedy, *Cardinal Bernardin* (Chicago: Bonus Books, 1989), page 277.   **5.** The *Tablet* (London), March 24, 1984, and continuing coverage.   **6.** The meeting is described in Peter Schweizer, *Victory,* pages 234–235. Corporations identified include Seagram's, Gulf and Western/Paramount

(later Viacom), Pepsico, the Chase Manhattan Bank, Mobil Oil, and Archer-Daniels-Midland, the grain company.   **7.** One of the go-betweens, Michael Ledeen, had also been Reagan's primary contact with Francisco Pazienza, the businessman-spy in the Ambrosiano-IOR case.   **8.** On the Iran-Contra affair, I have used details from a variety of sources, particularly *The Report of the Congressional Committees Investigating the Iran-Contra Affair,* the report of Reagan's own investigatory commission headed by Texas Senator John Tower, and Theodore Draper's excellent book *A Very Thin Line* (New York: Hill and Wang, 1991), which synthesizes the official reports and other available sources. I also consulted various newspaper clippings and notes from reporting I did on my own at the time, while working for the *Wall Street Journal.* Other helpful accounts I have used, which differ by a day or two on dates and other details, include Shultz's memoirs, *Turmoil and Triumph,* and Bob Woodward's *Veil* (New York: Simon and Schuster, 1987). As to Reagan's memory, one might speculate that the Alzheimer's Disease with which he would be diagnosed eight years later might have affected him. That seems unlikely, given the momentousness of the events involved, but medical science is still learning about Alzheimer's.   **9.** I talked to Tumi in Rome in 1994.   **10.** Quoted in Willey, *God's Politician,* page 151.   **11.** Quote from his 1981 trip; he said much the same on his revisit.   **12.** Frequent coverage in the *New York Times,* the *Washington Post,* and *Africa News.* I am indebted to Tami Hultman of *Africa News* for sharing her file on the subject.   **13.** Recorded by BBC correspondent David Willey in his book *God's Politician,* page 155.

Chapter 47

1. Raymond Garthoff, on page 236 of *The Great Transition,* reports interviewing "a senior Soviet official" who accompanied Gorbachev and said Gorbachev impressed Reagan by discussing the plot of Reagan's 1942 film *King's Row*. **2.** This information comes from a national-security document (number 1825) produced at the congressional hearings and seen by me at the National Security Archive in Washington. The missiles were to be shipped indirectly, through Israel, so it would look as if it were Israel that was sending the missiles to Iran. **3.** See Raymond Bonner, *Waltzing with a Dictator* (New York: Times Books, 1987). **4.** Sin's trip was reported in the Catholic press; I got an account from Father Vincent O'Keefe. Sin's continuing good relations with John Paul are evidenced by their many meetings since. In response to detailed inquiries, Sin sent me a published account confirming his role in the coup but not commenting on the other matters, and said he didn't wish to add to it. **5.** See his 1986 State of the Union address. **6.** Raymond Garthoff says this was confirmed for him by Gorbachev himself, in an interview. Gorbachev's presence was not publicly disclosed at the time, to keep the world from knowing just how weak Soviet defenses really were, but the U.S. surely knew of it. **7.** This was the so-called SALT II treaty, replacing the expired SALT I. Both nations had kept to the SALT II deal until now, even though it had never been formally ratified. Throughout this section on Soviet-American relations, I have drawn on translations and a chronological compendium of facts provided in Raymond Garthoff's *The Great Transition*.

Chapter 48

1. Oct. 2, 1991, before the Senate Intelligence Committee. **2.** Robert M. Gates, *From the Shadows*, page 323. In his biography *Pope John Paul II* Tad Szulc attaches much importance to a document he obtained, secretly approved by the secretariat of the Communist Party of the Soviet Union, dated Nov. 13, 1979. As Szulc reproduces it, however, the document seems to be an innocuous call for "propaganda against the policies of the Vatican," and contains nothing about a violent plot. **3.** Anthony Cave Brown, *The Last Hero* (New York: Times Books, 1982). Brown describes a personal relationship between Father Morlion and Major General William J. Donovan, head of the Office of Strategic Services, precursor of the CIA. **4.** Sunday, June 10, 1984. The story occupied the upper-left-hand corner of the front page and two full pages inside. While it began with the caveat that it was based on a secret prosecution report that had fallen into Sterling's hands, it was presented without a trace of skepticism or any countercomment on the elaborate details it contained. The clear implication was that Sterling and the *Times* accepted the accuracy of the report unreservedly. The story referred to the contents of the report as "the judge's findings." It further asserted that the truth of the story was "borne out by independent witnesses and verifiable evidence." **5.** A note found in Agca's pocket when he was arrested mentioned plans for a train trip to Naples. This contradicts the Bulgarian truck-escape theory, but it also casts doubt on Consolo's contention that Agca had resigned himself to being caught. Consolo discounts the significance of the note, and other curious scraps left here and there by Agca, as discrete pieces in the life of a lunatic, which don't necessarily fit neatly together. As we shall see, the question of a trip to Naples loses importance in light of what I learned from the prosecutor. **6.** Marini speculated that the French might have learned of the plot from a communist spy who defected, rather than from Agca (as Consolo had assumed). Marini said he specifically raised this point with de Marenches, who wouldn't tell him.

Chapter 49

1. Political scientist David Ost suggests that the government's success in arresting Bujak in this sweep shows it could have arrested him earlier but wanted him free so that the underground leadership wouldn't fall to more radical elements. He mentions this on page 191 of *Solidarity* and elaborated on it when we talked. Bujak and other former underground leaders say they doubt this theory, and the former communist officials I talked to all denied it. The ease of the 1986 arrests could also be explained by the group's relaxed sense of security in the new atmosphere.   **2.** This comes both from my own interviews and from David Ost, *Solidarity*, which includes a version of the events provided by General Kiszczak in an officially published interview.   **3.** Quoted in Ost, *Solidarity*, page 160.   **4.** In the 1988 BBC documentary on John Paul II.

Chapter 50

1. June 19, 1986, quoted in *La Republica*, cited by Stephen F. Cohen in *The Nation*, Nov. 15, 1986.   **2.** Shultz says in his memoir *Turmoil and Triumph*, page 757, that he received the report Oct. 11. The rest of my account comes from assorted news reports and sources already mentioned, particularly Shultz and Raymond Garthoff, *The Great Transition*.   **3.** Shultz, in chapter 36 of *Turmoil and Triumph*, noted another important potential snag: the Soviet draft talked about eliminating "strategic offensive arms," and the U.S. draft about eliminating "offensive ballistic missiles." The USSR relied more on missiles, while the United States had more bombers.   **4.** Garthoff, *The Great Transition*, page 297.   **5.** Garthoff, *The Great Transition*, pages 301–302. **6.** Katrina Vanden Heuvel, quoting the *Moscow News* in *The Nation*, March 7, 1987. **7.** Quoted in Wilton Wynn, *Keepers of the Keys* (New York: Random House, 1988), pages 257–259.   **8.** Eugene Kennedy, *Cardinal Bernardin*, page 276.   **9.** Interview with Bernardin.   **10.** According to the

National Catholic Reporter. Neither Hunthausen nor Wuerl would talk to me about the affair. **11.** Kennedy, *Bernardin*, pages 290–291, mostly confirmed in the *Tablet* (London), Nov. 22, 1986. Law didn't respond to my requests for comment.   **12.** The Hunthausen story was told with the help of half a dozen sources who wished not to be quoted. That makes it difficult to allocate responsibility. Cardinal Bernardin also gave a valuable interview. Eugene Kennedy, both in his book *Bernardin* and in our conversations, was a big help, as were Wilton Wynn, Church historian Gerald Fogarty, and Bishop Sullivan in interviews. Hunthausen, Murphy, and Wuerl all declined to discuss it.   **13.** March 1989, Rome, quoted in David Willey, *God's Politician*, page 87. **14.** Exact numbers from Willey, *God's Politician*, chapter 4, and the *Tablet* (London) throughout the affair.   **15.** The Vatican says this oath was merely a modification of an earlier one instituted by Pope Pius X, but enough changes were made that priests remember it as being new.

Chapter 51

1. Interview in the Spanish daily *Ya*, quoted in Willey, *God's Politician*, page 219.   **2.** This and other crowd scenes are taken from the vivid descriptions of Peter Eisner of *Newsday*, who was kind enough to talk about it in an interview and send me his articles of April 1 through 6, 1987. Some material also comes from other newspapers and from Willey, *God's Politician*.

Chapter 52

1. Interview with Rakowski.   **2.** The Gdynia scene and the following quote are from David Willey, *God's Politician*, page 43.   **3.** Interview with Bratkowski.   **4.** The *New York Times*, March 13, 1994, on the opening of the previously classified files.   **5.** Quoted in Willey, *God's Politician*, page 86. **6.** Willey, *God's Politician*, page 180. **7.** I have woven together contemporary news accounts with my own interview with Weakland. **8.** The quotes in these two paragraphs come from an interview Weakland gave to David Willey of the BBC. **9.** A detailed account may be found in David Ost, *Solidarity*, pages 170–172. **10.** Quoted in Raymond Garthoff, *The Great Transition*, page 309. **11.** Quotes collected by Stephen F. Cohen in *The Nation*, June 13, 1987. **12.** Garthoff, *The Great Transition*, page 327. **13.** Shultz, *Turmoil and Triumph*, page 1011.

Chapter 54

1. Willey, *God's Politician*, page 14. **2.** This incident from an interview with Vatican Press Secretary Navarro-Valls, who was in the room with Casaroli and Gorbachev. **3.** Navarro-Valls. **4.** The deputy secretary of state for foreign affairs, Archbishop Jean-Louis Tauran, told me in an interview that the treaty was the most important achievement of his stay in office (which continues), and that the pope was deeply concerned about it. **5.** Ost, *Solidarity*, page 182. **6.** These two paragraphs from the 1988 BBC documentary on the pope and from Willey, *God's Politician*, pages 131–132. The sources differ slightly in their translations; I have blended them. **7.** Mostly from Willey, *God's Politician*, page 131.

Chapter 55

1. The direct quotations in this paragraph are from Ost, *Solidarity*, page 183. He attributes the words to Foreign Minister and Politburo member Jozef Czyrek, who Ost says had been propounding these ideas for months, though a majority of the Politburo wouldn't go along until the August 1988 strikes. I didn't have these quotes to check with Czyrek when I interviewed him in Warsaw, but the thoughts are all in accord with what he and Dembowski told me, and

Ost's accuracy has proved excellent in other instances. The other quotes in this section, from Dembowski and Bujak, come from my interviews with them. **2.** My documentaries opened with the news that this "could be the death knell of the Marxist state," a proposition that still struck many viewers— including my colleagues—as far-fetched. **3.** Garthoff, *The Great Transition*, page 355. **4.** Willey, *God's Politician*, pages 147–148. **5.** Ost, *Solidarity*, page 210. **6.** Ost, *Solidarity*, page 213. **7.** Interview with Cardinal Cassidy. **8.** Garthoff, *The Great Transition*, page 378.

Chapter 56

1. This figure in particular from Lucjan Motyka, John Paul's old counterpart in Krakow. **2.** My account of Bush's trip is drawn mostly from reports in the *New York Times*, July 10–13, 1989. **3.** Interview with Rakowski. **4.** Ost, *Solidarity*, page 218. **5.** Interview with Vatican Press Secretary Joaquin Navarro-Valls. **6.** Where material is not attributed to persons whom I have interviewed, I constructed my description of the fall of communism largely from reports in the *New York Times*, various almanacs, and the work of five particularly helpful authors whose books are cited elsewhere in these pages: Theodore Draper, Raymond Garthoff, David Ost, George Weigel, and David Willey. **7.** Vladimir Lukin, former chairman of the foreign-relations committee of the Supreme Soviet, quoted in the *New York Times*, Aug. 24, 1993. **8.** The *New York Times*, Aug. 24, 1993. **9.** Marshal Nikolai Ogarkov. **10.** *The Atlantic Monthly*, Nov. 1994. **11.** In the Italian publication *Stampa*, March 1992. **12.** Quoted by Melanie McDonagh in the *Tablet* (London), July 13, 1991. **13.** Quoted in Willey, *God's Politician*, page 2. **14.** Interview with Jas Gawronski of *La Stampa*, widely published throughout Europe, Nov. 1, 1993.

BOOK 5: JUDGMENTS

Chapter 1

1. The "counterproductive mechanism" for debtor countries that he talked about in the encyclical clearly referred to the IMF. 2. The IMF team in Poland worked with Sachs "quite closely," according to Jan Bielecki, who was later prime minister. 3. Sachs says the Polish government approached him in January 1989; his associate David Lipton says it was in the fall of 1988. 4. He told this to my associate, anthropologist Janine Wedel. I also interviewed him for *The Kwitny Report*. 5. Bielecki and others say so. Sachs says Walesa was involved before Mazowiecki took office in August, but not, to his recollection, afterward, which is when the major decisions were made. 6. Balcerowicz, *Socialism, Capitalism, Transformation* (Budapest: Central European University Press, 1995), page 360. Balcerowicz referred me to his book when I tried to interview him. 7. Wojciech Wieczorek, who succeeded Mazowiecki as editor of *Wiez*. 8. From Janine Wedel. 9. Interview with Bielecki. 10. From Andrzej Bardecki, who met with them in Rome. 11. Interview with Vatican Press Secretary Joaquin Navarro-Valls. 12. Father Hejmo says, "Mazowiecki made the greatest mistake since World War II—he left the communists with their jobs." 13. Denying public recognition and not having quarters prepared when Kowalczyk arrived were two examples cited. Kowalczyk, like Glemp, declined to answer my questions. The priest quoted is in a position to know and has understandable reasons for wanting anonymity; I heard corroborating accounts, also unattributable. 14. Stanislaw Krajewski, who represents the groups in Poland. 15. Interview with André Frossard. 16. For example, he gave an interview to *Tygodnik Powszechny* in which he sounded conciliatory, then a speech at Lublin

arguing for the nuns' right to keep the convent. 17. This incident happened after Frossard's book with John Paul, *"Be Not Afraid!,"* was published, and was related to me by Frossard in an interview at his house in Versailles.

Chapter 2

1. David Willey, *God's Politician: John Paul at the Vatican* (New York: St. Martin's, 1992), page 16. 2. The quote comes from Rocco Buttiglione, who heard about it from John Paul. 3. I interviewed Frossard Nov. 22, 1993, a year before his death. 4. Evidence had been supplied in various congressional narcotics hearings for years, but the news made the front page of the *New York Times* under Seymour Hersh's byline June 12 and 13, 1986. At least four months later, as documents from the Iran-Contra investigations show, White House aide Oliver North was still meeting with Noriega to discuss his offers of help in the Contra war. See also Theodore Draper, *A Very Thin Line* (New York: Hill and Wang, 1991). 5. Laboa was interviewed in Spanish by my associate Donna De Cesare. The Departments of State and Defense declined comment but referred me to Arthur Davis, the U.S. ambassador to Panama at the time. Davis did not reply to my letters.

Chapter 3

1. For the 1920s episode, see George Weigel, *The Final Revolution* (New York: Oxford University Press, 1992). The 1950s episode, involving Cardinal Slipyi, is described earlier in this book. 2. The *Tablet* (London), Dec. 1, 1990. 3. David Willey, *God's Politician*, page 20. 4. From an airborne press conference reported in the *Tablet* (London), May 12, 1990. 5. Quoted in the *Tablet* (London), April 7, 1990. 6. When I phoned Balcerowicz with questions, he referred me to his

book *Socialism, Capitalism, Transformation* (Budapest: Central European University Press, 1995), which is largely an economics text but contains some autobiographical material; I am quoting from it here, page 298. 7. Quoted in the *Tablet* (London). David Willey also describes this incident in *God's Politician*, page 21, though he misidentifies the year as 1989. 8. May 14 and 21, 1990. 9. I interviewed Mazowiecki in his office June 20, 1994. 10. Balcerowicz's book *Socialism, Capitalism, Transformation*, without citing Mazowiecki by name, lists "social market economy" among "Common Fallacies" and "Logical Mistakes." 11. Fairly summing up what I heard from Poles, Peter Hebblethwaite wrote in the *Tablet*, Nov. 24, 1990, that the Mazowiecki group was accused of being "liberal, cosmopolitan, excessively pro-Western, insufficiently vigorous in getting rid of former communists ... pro-Jewish and anti-clerical."

Chapter 4

1. Most statistics in this section were presented to the synod by Cardinal Laghi and reported in *Osservatore Romano*, Oct. 29, 1990. 2. Most figures given here are from the Center for Applied Research in the Apostolate, a Church-recognized body. The average ages were provided by Tim Unsworth, an author and columnist specializing in the priesthood, reporting on a lengthy study in the *National Catholic Reporter*, May 6, 1994. 3. Reported in the *National Catholic Reporter*, May 13, 1994. 4. Eugene Hemick, quoted in the same article. 5. David Willey, *God's Politician*, page 130. 6. Sachs's former consulting associate in Poland, David Lipton, an assistant U.S. treasury secretary in the Clinton administration, was among those who assert that the pope agreed with the program. 7. Speaking on condition that he not be quoted directly. 8. Information in this paragraph comes from an interview with Dr. Joan Parenti, an Ameri-

can living in Rome and serving as a senior staffer for Lopez Trujillo. She was assigned to field my request for an interview with him. 9. In an interview with *Il Sabato*, an Italian weekly. 10. Technically, the award was blocked and the apology issued by Cardinal Laghi, who had been brought from Washington to run the Congregation for Catholic Education. Laghi said he acted because Ratzinger had withheld approval of a report Weakland had written on abortion hearings. Weakland says it was Ratzinger's decision to deny him the award. (Fribourg should not be confused with the University of Freiburg in Germany, where Husserl and Heidegger taught.) 11. The leading book on saints is *Making Saints* (New York: Simon and Schuster, 1990), by Kenneth L. Woodward, religion editor of *Newsweek*. The Church has issued inconsistent figures. 12. The *Tablet* (London), Oct. 29, 1983. The prime minister was Felipe Gonzalez. 13. Quoted in Kenneth Woodward, *Making Saints*, pages 374–376. 14. Figures supplied to me by Vatican Press Secretary Joaquin Navarro-Valls.

Chapter 5

1. Interview with Joaquin Navarro-Valls. 2. Salvini and Archbishop Tauran both confirmed this in interviews with me. 3. These excerpts appear here as extracts, as if they were John Paul's words, because he approved them. The articles appeared in *Civil Catholica* from November 1990 through July 1991. English-language copies were given me by the magazine. 4. Interview with Navarro-Valls. 5. *National Catholic Reporter*, Jan. 19, 1994.

Chapter 7

1. A few loopholes enabled the Church to claim its program was not "compulsory," but people generally thought—and the president of the Catholic Press Agency now concedes—that the lessons were, in effect,

mandatory. **2.** Tischner was quoted by Ana Husarska in the *New Leader,* July 15–29, 1991. I earlier recounted my fruitless efforts to talk to him. **3.** Facts presented in this and the preceding paragraph come from Ana Husarska, writing in the *New Leader* and speaking in an interview with me. The gist of her observations is backed up by other interviews. **4.** From Marcin Przeciszewski of the Catholic Press Agency. Turowicz laughs the incident off but does not deny it.

Chapter 8

1. The Lithuanian was Kestutis Gerinius, the Hungarian was Beata Farkas, and their remarks came at a lay symposium in conjunction with the synod, which was officially for bishops. Their remarks were quoted in the *Tablet* (London), Nov. 9, 1991. **2.** Tad Szulc, *Pope John Paul II* (New York: Scribner's, 1995), pages 449–454. Szulc presents John Paul's 1991 gambit to Israel as successful, even though nothing happened until after the Israeli deal with the PLO—as had been the condition all along. **3.** Vatican Press Secretary Joaquin Navarro-Valls, in response to my question, 1996. He did not offer suggestions as to how else the Serbs could be disarmed. **4.** Turowicz told me that he was merely rotated off the board, and that it had "nothing to do with" his articles on abortion. I heard the story as reported here from Maciej Kozlowski, a Polish diplomat who is closely related to Turowicz's deputy at *Tygodnik Powszechny,* a former cabinet minister. It was confirmed by others in Krakow, and by the timing of the move. **5.** Turowicz was hostile and biting about John Paul when I interviewed him. He said people—obviously those close to the pope—were spreading rumors about him. **6.** From a State Department document released on my request. **7.** The pope met American-backed rebel Jonas Savimbi in the same receiving line; Savimbi had briefly made peace with the government, but

rejected it again after his electoral defeat. **8.** Quoted in *America* magazine, Feb. 25, 1995. When I interviewed Woodward, he reiterated his belief that Escrivá's case got special help and speed. His book is *Making Saints.*

Chapter 9

1. Among those who complained to me were Cardinal Krol and Dean Jude Dougherty of Catholic University. **2.** Quoted in the *Tablet* (London), July 11, 1992. **3.** From coverage in the *Tablet* (London), the *National Catholic Reporter,* and *Osservatore Romano.* **4.** Father Gerald Fogarty, church historian at the University of Virginia, was a source for details on this. **5.** When I asked to interview Rigali, his secretary requested, and got, letters of recommendation and other materials from me, then stopped returning my calls. This happened in Rome, before he moved to the United States. **6.** *Churchwatch,* March 1993. **7.** Reported in the *New York Times,* December 27, 1992. **8.** George Sarauskas of the U.S. Bishops' Conference staff. I also interviewed Archbishop McKerrick, whom John Paul had invited along.

Chapter 10

1. (New York: Doubleday, 1992.) **2.** Statement to visiting U.S. bishops on March 18, 1993. **3.** One estimate was by Father Andrew Greeley, a sociologist as well as a writer. **4.** Cardinal Jose Sanchez, head of the Congregation for the Clergy, says he thought they were exaggerated, but that because he had no figures of his own he was quoted out of context in the press as if he had confirmed the studies. **5.** The *National Catholic Reporter,* March 19, 1993, reporting on a speech given March 10 in Rome. As noted earlier, O'Connor did not respond to my several requests, made through his press assistant, for an interview. **6.** From a monsignor close to one of the bishops, who relayed the story. Bevilacqua declines to comment on its accuracy. **7.** Interview with William Ryan, deputy director for communications of the U.S. Bishops' Conference. **8.** Data collected by Richard Sipe, chairman of the Interfaith Sexual Trauma Institute, Collegeville, Minn. **9.** This material is drawn from coverage in the *National Catholic Reporter* and the *Denver Post*, and from my own interviews at the event. Regarding the lawsuit, Famous Artists Merchandising Exchange Inc. sued World Youth Day Inc. in Federal Court in Denver (reported by Religious News Service in the *National Catholic Reporter*, Aug. 26, 1994). **10.** As this goes to press, Clinton is being exposed for tawdry tactics to raise campaign funds. There has been no evidence of wrongful expenditure of public money, aside from the trivial cost of inviting donors to visit the White House, against the drain of tens or hundreds of billions of tax dollars to Reagan-Bush allies in scandals involving the defense and savings-and-loan industries during prior administrations. But, again, Clinton had put immediate gratification over an example of ethical propriety.

Chapter 11

1. Writing in the *Tablet* (London), Nov. 13, 1993.

Chapter 12

1. Robin Wright in *The Atlantic Monthly*, July 1994. **2.** A phrase borrowed from Pope Pius XI, and repeated by Paul VI. **3.** Blonski, on the faculty of the Jagiellonian, was twice brought to Rome at John Paul's invitation. **4.** The interpreter was Irina Alberti; her account was published by the Italian Catholic daily *Avvenire* and reprinted in both the *Tablet* (London), Oct. 30, 1993, and the *National Catholic Reporter*, Nov. 19, 1993. **5.** I saw the magazines. **6.** Interviews with Archbishop Re and Vatican Press Secretary

Navarro-Valls. **7.** Tad Szulc, *Pope John Paul II*, page 421. **8.** She shared the letter with me. **9.** *Osservatore Romano*, June 1, 1994.

Chapter 13

1. Dr. Parenti detailed this for me in an interview, but I heard similar complaints at other agencies, such as the Council on Migrants and Refugees. **2.** After reading continuing coverage of this long affair in the press, I did fax "interviews" with Prigione and Ruiz to refine my presentation. Prigione says the solution was not proposed by Ruiz, but came out of Prigione's own negotiations with the Mexican bishops; he says his relationship with the cardinal is excellent. Ruiz credits "Providence" with the solution, and says the affair was blown out of proportion by Mexican politicians and journalists with an anti-Church attitude. **3.** The *National Catholic Reporter*, July 30, 1993. The unionists had briefly shut down the phone system using talcum powder, thus delaying the privatization plan. **4.** This description is from my interview with Archbishop Theodore McKerrick of Newark, who was along on the Zagreb trip. **5.** Interview with König. **6.** A good account by Celestine Bohlen appears in the *New York Times*, May 20, 1995. **7.** See, for example, *Tricycle: The Buddhist Review*, Fall 1995. **8.** The *Tablet* (London), May 8, 1993. **9.** The *Tablet* (London), May 8, 1993. These attitudes were confirmed for me in many interviews. My unsuccessful attempts to meet with Tischner have been noted elsewhere.

Chapter 14

1. Interviews with Bishop Michael M. Fitzgerald, secretary of Arinze's council (who denies the charge), and Arinze. **2.** The precise figures have been taken from *National Catholic Reporter*, April 29, 1994. Similar but inexact figures were provided by many other sources.

Chapter 15

1. The last sentence of this excerpt is taken not from the letter but from John Paul's Sunday public appearance at St. Peter's the same week. **2.** The *Tablet* (London), Sept. 17, 1994. **3.** These figures are from the 1996 *Information Please Almanac.* Rival almanacs and the CIA's *World Factbook* from earlier in the 1990s show slight differences in numbers but not in the proportion among countries, which is the point here. **4.** The *New York Times,* Sept. 6, 1992. **5.** A relevant article by scientist Gerard Piel appeared in *The Nation* before the Cairo conference, March 21, 1994, arguing that Third World countries had outgrown not their land and resources but their technology. **6.** Quoted in the *National Catholic Reporter,* June 17, 1994. Martini's office declined my request to see him. **7.** To Annabel Miller, writing in the *Tablet* (London), Sept. 23, 1995.

Chapter 16

1. Father Renato Kazito Sesana. **2.** The award was the Federal Cross of Merit; reported in the *National Catholic Reporter,* April 1, 1994. **3.** Facts in this section to this point are from various issues of the *Tablet* (London), from November 1994 through July 1995. **4.** The *Newark Star-Ledger,* June 3, 1995. **5.** Interview with Collins. **6.** From an interview with Archbishop Theodore McKerrick of Newark, who saw it happen. **7.** Peter Hebblethwaite, writing in the *National Catholic Reporter,* July 1, 1994. **8.** Figures originally from the *Tablet* (London), checked by me with the Vatican press office. **9.** The *Indianapolis Star,* Sept. 28, 1995. **10.** Associated Press. **11.** The *New York Times,* Feb. 11, 1996, using statistics from the U.S. Census Bureau. **12.** The *New York Times,* March 19, 1995. **13.** Knight-Ridder Newspapers, from a study by the Sentencing Project, a Washington-based organization; the Justice Department did not dispute the figures. **14.** The *New York Times,* April 22, 1995. **15.** Donald L. Barlett and James B. Steele, reporting in the *Philadelphia Inquirer,* Sept. 22, 1996. The families referred to earned median incomes. **16.** The *New York Times,* March 13, 1996. **17.** The *Wall Street Journal,* Feb. 1, 1995. **18.** Poll by the Times Mirror Center for the People and the Press. **19.** The *New York Times,* July 10, 1994. **20.** I faxed these several pages of American social problems to Rosemary Winder Strange, long-time Director of Social Services for Catholic Charities USA, for her comment—afraid perhaps that I had painted too bleak a picture of what was the world's leading economy and still quite a wonderful country. She replied that I had not, and encouraged me to include that the prison population was growing rapidly across demographic lines. She also said that the statistics gathered here from a variety of sources generally accorded with her knowledge of conditions. Strange recently left Catholic Charities USA to take a similar post at Catholic Charities of Venice, Florida. **21.** The *Wall Street Journal,* June 7, 1995. **22.** The *Observer* (London), reprinted in the *National Times,* Oct.–Nov. 1995 **23.** The *Economist* (London), reprinted in the *National Times,* Oct.–Nov. 1995. **24.** Religious editor Peter Steinfels, writing in the *New York Times,* May 29, 1994. **25.** New York Times/CBS News poll, published in the *New York Times,* June 1, 1994. **26.** Vaclav Havel, op-ed page article, the *New York Times,* July 8, 1994.

A NOTE ON PRONUNCIATION

W is pronounced as if it were a *v* in English.

J is pronounced as *y*.

Many *l*'s are pronounced as *w*. (They are distinguished in Polish text by a diagonal "slash" through the *l*.)

Thus, Wojtyla is pronounced "Voy-tih-wa." And Jaruzelski is pronounced "Yar-u-zel-ski." (His *l* in Polish doesn't have a slash through it; Wojtyla's does.) The common name-ending "-slaw" has a slashed *l*; hence, Miroslaw is "Miroswahv," Stanislaw is "Staniswahv," and Boleslaw is "Boleswahv" (the first *l* isn't crossed).

Sometimes *e* and *a* before a consonant carry a hook under them that adds an *n* sound, though it is a bit more nasal and not quite as hard as a normal *n* in Polish or English. Thus, Walesa becomes "Vah-wen-sa," with the *n* a little bit soft and through the nose.

A *c* except before an *i*, *h*, or *z* is usually pronounced as *ts*. Thus, Bardecki is "Bar-det-ski." And Wroclaw is "Vrohts-wahv."

Ch is pronounced as *h*. Thus, Chojecki is pronounced "Hoy-et-ski."

Cz (and to some degree *ci*) is pronounced as *ch*. Thus, Czestochowa is pronounced "Chesto-hova," though with a barely perceptible nasal *n* after the *e*. And Czajkowski is pronounced like the composer, "Chai-kov-ski."

Sz is pronounced as *sh*. Thus, Wyszynski is pronounced "Vih-shin-ski."

Dz is pronounced as a hard *j*. Thus, Dziwisz is pronounced "Jee-vish."

Rz is pronounced as a soft *j*, or *zh*, as in "azure" or *Dr. Zhivago*. The *p* often in front of *rz* is pronounced voicelessly. Thus, Przydatek is pronounced "Zhi-datek," with a hurried *p* sound in front.

ACKNOWLEDGMENTS

Many people were indispensable in producing this book. Janine Wedel encouraged me to undertake reporting in Poland in 1988 and introduced me to many Solidarity sources, whom she had gotten to know during her years of academic research. That provided the premise for this book years later.

During my research in Poland for the book, Nina Gladziuk in Warsaw and Jerzy Kopacz in Krakow devoted countless hours to arranging interviews, interpreting questions and answers (surely the hardest job in the world), and translating documents. Wedel, Gladziuk, and Kopacz, all Ph.D.s, also contributed vital advice. Others providing research assistance in Poland were Anna Kubiak (herself now a Ph.D.) and Joanna Tomaszewska.

In Rome, Wilton Wynn was a human Baedeker of the Church and its people, and a font of good sense. Silvia Sansoni was a cheerful, resourceful, and indefatigable interpreter and translator, ably relieved at times by Dorothy Berbec. Dr. Joaquin Navarro-Valls was immensely patient and helpful despite the hectic demands on his time; if anyone ever needed more paid assistants, it is he.

Wendy Wood Kwitny was as good an editor as I've ever had on a book, and the daunting hours she spent reading and rereading the same material in different versions, refining and rerefining, throughout such a long book, never seemed to faze her. She was also a vital facilitator of interviews with many sources in Rome and Poland, above and beyond her personal support through these four years. Others who cheerfully read and gave important advice (even when I didn't take it) were Nancy Malone, Stephanie Trudeau, and Tony Scaduto.

A prominent theologian who has asked to remain anonymous donated enormous time toward this effort, and toward my education in Catholicism. I earnestly hope this volume will satisfy him.

Jack Macrae made this book possible. Without his stubborn demands, the book would have been much easier to write and quite less readable. Michael Naumann was a calm voice of reason in a couple of crises. Albert LaFarge and Rachel Klauber-Speiden of Henry Holt also had to put up with a lot.

Ellen Levine, my agent, continues to combine the talents of Mother Teresa and Field Marshal Rommel, depending on my need. And Diana Finch sold foreign rights like a true Ellen protégée. Alice Wood of Little, Brown and Company (U.K.) contributed valuable ideas.

Father Ken Doyle, formerly of the National Catholic News Service and now a parish priest near Albany, was greatly helpful in getting me started with the U.S. Church.

Barbara Mazei translated the *Kalendarium* for me, an arduous task. Joanna Tyrpa, my main U.S. translator, worked arduously on that and other matters. Donna De Cesare did some Spanish-language interviews and translating for me. Charles R. Eisenhart, our local Latin teacher, helped with the Latin, as did Elizete Savino with the Portuguese, Mindy Ellis with the French, and Jan Kubek with Polish grammar.

It was Sharon Churcher who planted the idea of a papal biography, something she wanted to attempt herself but could not.

Jim O'Halloran and the staff of the Maryknoll Library were extremely generous, as was the staff at the Seton Hall University library and Father Theodore Hesburgh, who invited me to use the Notre Dame University Library. My local librarian Phylis Vail worked overtime tracking down books and arranging interlibrary loans.

Father Edward Vacek of the Weston School of Theology and Professor Paul Kahn of Yale kindly donated some free philosophy lessons.

Inevitably, in such a long work, some errors will have slipped in past all my defenses. They are not the fault of any of the above-named people. I hope anyone who finds an error will very calmly inform me of it so I can seek its correction in any later editions.

Two major sources died as this book was being edited: Cardinal John Krol, who could not have been more kind, even opening his personal library to me despite my habitually arriving in Philadelphia late during recurrent bad weather, and Jerzy Milewski, a hero of the Polish revolution. Perhaps I should have gone through the book putting every reference to them in the past tense, but I didn't have the heart. They are missed.

INDEX